WITHDRAWN

CHINA IN TRANSITION: 1517–1911

己酉仲夏

西風東漸錄

廣德李敦仁譯著

CHINA IN TRANSITION: 1517–1911

EDITED BY **DUN J. LI**
PATERSON STATE COLLEGE

VAN NOSTRAND REINHOLD COMPANY
NEW YORK • CINCINNATI • TORONTO • LONDON • MELBOURNE

Van Nostrand Reinhold Company Regional Offices:
Cincinnati, New York, Chicago, Millbrae, Dallas

Van Nostrand Reinhold Company Foreign Offices:
London, Toronto, Melbourne

Copyright © 1969 by Litton Educational Publishing, Inc.

Library of Congress Catalog Card Number 70-94763

All rights reserved. No part of this work covered by the copyright hereon may be reproduced or used in any form or by any means—graphic, electronic, or mechanical, including photocopying, recording, taping, or information storage and retrieval systems—without written permission of the publisher. Manufactured in the United States of America.

Published by Van Nostrand Reinhold Company
450 West 33rd Street, New York, N.Y. 10001

Published simultaneously in Canada by
D. Van Nostrand Company (Canada), Ltd.

10 9 8 7 6 5 4 3 2 1

Preface

This is the second book of a three-book series. The first book, *The Essence of Chinese Civilization* (Van Nostrand Reinhold Company, 1967), deals with "traditional China as it really was." The third book, *The Road to Communism: China Since 1912* (Van Nostrand Reinhold Company, 1970) traces factors and developments that led to China's embrace of communism as a state ideology and a way of life. The purpose of this book is to summarize for the reader, through the use of pertinent documents, the main events and ideas that marked China in the period of transition, from the time when the first Portuguese ships arrived at Canton to the establishment of the Chinese Republic on January 1, 1912.

Periodization, in Chinese as well as in Western history, has always been a controversial matter, and the selection of 1517 as the beginning of this book is no exception. The rationale for this selection is that the arrival of the Portuguese around 1517 materially changed not only the traditional relationship between Chinese and non-Chinese but also, in the long run, the internal structure of Chinese society, even though at that time neither the Chinese nor the Westerners, whom the Portuguese only served as vanguards insofar as Western expansionism was concerned, recognized the implications. The Westerners had a civilization sophisticated and advanced enough to challenge the cultural supremacy which the Chinese had always taken for granted and martial enough to demand the Chinese to meet it on its own terms. This, indeed, had never happened before! Though it is far from clear whether, at this early stage, Western civilization was really more "sophisticated" or "advanced" than its Chinese counterpart, there is no question, however, that technologically the Westerners were definitely more inventive and dynamic.

Subsequent decades and centuries widened this important gap, first in technology and then in practically every sphere of human endeavor, until eventually Westernization or "modernization" became the accepted norm for practically all the civilized peoples on earth. The failure or refusal on the part of the Chinese to recognize this challenge made little difference; if anything, it merely prolonged the agony of adjustment. It took a long time before the Western impact was fully felt; but, if one chooses to trace the beginning of this impact, it was as early as the 1510's. The fact that the year 1517 also marked the beginning of the Protestant Reformation is all the more interesting, since one may argue that it was the same burst of inner energy that prompted Martin Luther to post the ninety-five theses on the church door at Wittenberg, besides sending thousands of Western Europeans to the far corners of the earth to discover or conquer new territories, to trade, and to serve as missionaries.

To begin China's modern period with the year 1517 of course has disadvantages. These disadvantages result because of the slowness with which the Western impact was felt, aside from the fact that a periodization of this nature fails to take into consideration domestic developments. The impact was barely noticeable at the beginning and had little or no effect at all on the domestic structure of the ageless Chinese society. In fact, it was not until the middle of the nineteenth century that it began to accelerate, culminating, for the time being, in the establishment of the Chinese Republic in 1912. Taking into full consideration the slow, gradual, but eventually accelerated, nature of the Western impact, I, accordingly, have apportioned only one chapter to the sixteenth and seventeenth centuries and another chapter to the eighteenth and the first half of the nineteenth centuries, while the rest of this book, nine chapters in all, is devoted to developments during and after the Opium War (1839–1842). In short, more than four-fifths of this book deals with a later and comparatively short period (1834–1911), even though nominally it begins with the year 1517.

While few historians can deny that the Western impact was the single most important event in the course of China's modern history, emphasis on this event tends to lead one to de-emphasize internal developments that are also important. The answer to this criticism is that these internal developments, insofar as they are not related to the Western impact, are essentially an integral part of the ebb and flow of traditional Chinese society that has been covered adequately in *The Essence of Chinese Civilization*; while those that are related to the Western impact properly belong to China's response with which this book is also concerned. As for China's response to the Western impact, it may be more correctly characterized as "resistance" than as "response" for most of the period under discussion. It was not until the aftermath of the Opium War that China began to respond technologically to the Western challenge and not until the end of the nineteenth century that she began to respond politically in a fashion, though this political response played a decisive role in the establishment of the Chinese Republic in 1912. In fact, social and cultural response in a broad sense did not occur until the 1920's and is covered in the third book of the series, *The Road to Communism: China Since 1912*. Because of this, there are in this book more materials on "impact" than on "response."

Documentary materials are by definition partisan or even biased in nature. They reflect the views of those who write them, views that may not be shared by a dispassionate scholar. As primary and in most cases original materials, they reflect history-making in its most intimate stage, even though the views their authors express may, from hindsight, be highly controversial. This indeed marks the difference between a textbook and a book of documents: the former attempts to achieve a judicial balance on each issue discussed, while the latter is a reflection of the time and circumstances under which these documents were written. In the discussion of the unequal treaties, for instance, I include a short essay written by Chiang Kai-shek which reflects, in my judgment, the thinking of many millions of his fellow countrymen, even though this thinking may not be shared by a China expert in Europe or America. The essential point to remember is that the thinking of these millions of Chinese does influence or even dictate the course of Chinese history, while the views of a China expert in Europe or America do not. This is one of the reasons why I have scrupulously excluded any contemporary interpretation, however judicious or dispassionate, of the events involved. Moreover, as a teacher, I have found that primary or original sources are much more useful as readings than contemporary interpretations. The former stimulates discussion and debate, while the latter encourages agreement and acceptance. Needless to say, a classroom is less than lively when everybody agrees.

PREFACE

There are 89 selections in this book; all except those that are public properties are my own translations. Specifically, these exceptions are Selections 25, 27, 28, 29, 30, 31, 32, 33, 60, 65, 70, 84, and 85. In translating these documents, I try to be faithful to their authors while making sure that they are still readable.

The introduction at the beginning of each chapter is intended to introduce the documents rather than the subject matter which, in my judgment, properly belongs to a textbook. It is written in such a way as to link the selections together; it is not intended to be the final word on the subject discussed. As such, it is bound to be full of omissions; the matter is not helped by my decision to keep it short and concise so as to provide more room for the documentary material. Needless to say, a book of documents is never meant to be a substitute for a good textbook.

I wish to thank Professor Sung-Hwan Chang of Rutgers University and Professor Sung P. Choi of Paterson State College for helping me with the transliteration of many Japanese and Korean names.

Dun J. Li

Maps

1. The Canton Estuary — 4
2. Treaties of Nanking and Tientsin — 80
3. Origin of the Taiping Rebellion (Eastern Kwangsi) — 118
4. The Taiping Regime — 127
5. Sino-Russian Borderlands in the East (19th Century) — 171
6. Russian Expansion and Sino-Russian Borderlands in the West — 183
7. The Battle of Concessions, 1895–1905 — 222
8. The Allied Invasion and the Boxer Protocol — 285
9. The Revolutionaries' Uprisings Against the Manchu Regime — 299

Contents

PREFACE	v
MAPS	ix

CHAPTER I • THE COMING OF THE WEST

1. KU YIN-HSIANG: *The Arrival of the Portuguese*	3
2. CHANG T'ING-YÜ et al.: *The Portuguese Problem*	5
3. HUO JU-HSIA: *The Portuguese Problem*	6
4. P'AN SSU-CH'U: *The Macao Problem*	7
5. CHANG T'ING-YÜ et al.: *The Dutch and Their Activities*	9
6. CHANG T'ING-YÜ et al.: *The Jesuits*	14
7. LU JO-HAN (JOANNES B. RODRIGUES): *A Letter to Li Yung-hou*	17
8. LI MA-TOU (MATTEO RICCI): *The Earth Is a Sphere*	19
9. ANONYMOUS: *The Rites Controversy*	20
10. CLEMENT XI: *The Papal Bull of 1715*	22
11. INABA KIMIYAMA: *Jesuit Success and Failure in China*	55

CHAPTER II • THE CANTON TRADE

12. LI SHIH-YAO: *Five Rules to Regulate Foreigners*	29
13. CH'ANG-LIN: *A Reply to Henry Browne's Request*	34
14. CH'IEN-LUNG: *On the Payment of Debts to Foreign Traders*	37
15. JE-WO-ERH-JIH TI-SAN (GEORGE III): *A Letter to the Emperor of China*	39
16. CH'IEN-LUNG: *A Reply to George III, King of England*	41
17. TEH-CH'ING: *Co-hong Responsibilities*	43
18. SU LENG-EH AND KUANG-HUI: *The Kowtow Controversy*	46
19. CHIA-CH'ING: *The Kowtow Controversy*	47
20. HU HSIA-MI (HUGH HAMILTON LINDSAY): *A Brief Account of the British Nation and Character*	49

CHAPTER III • THE OPIUM WAR

21. HUANG CHÜEH-TZ'U: *The Evil of Opium*	54
22. ANONYMOUS: *Letters to Hu Hsia-mi*	60
23. LIN TSE-HSÜ: *A Message to Foreign Traders*	61
24. LIN TSE-HSÜ: *A Letter to Queen Victoria*	64
25. LORD PALMERSTON: *British Grievances and Demands for Redress*	67
26. TAO-KUANG: *Declaration of War on Great Britain*	72
27. LORD ABERDEEN: *The Advisability of Legalizing the Opium Trade*	74

Chapter IV • THE TREATY SYSTEM

28. The Treaty of Nanking	79
29. The Treaty of Wanghia	82
30. Lord Clarendon: *The Necessity of Treaty Revisions*	84
31. Treaty of Tientsin Between Great Britain and China	88
32. The Peking Convention	94
33. Anson Burlingame: *Political Relations of Foreigners with the Chinese*	97
34. Chiang Kai-shek: *The Unequal Treaties*	101

Chapter V • THE TAIPING REBELLION

35. Tseng Kuo-fan: *The Plight of the Chinese People*	111
36. Li Hsiu-ch'eng: *The Beginning of the Rebellion*	117
37. Chang Ju-nan: *The Days When the Taipings Arrived at Nanking*	121
38. T'ai-p'ing T'ien-kuo: *A Law of the Regime*	126
39. Lo Tun-yung: *Internecine Strife Among the Taiping Leaders*	132
40. Tseng Kuo-ch'üan: *The Capture of Nanking*	136

Chapter VI • THE IMITATION OF THE WEST: THE TECHNOLOGICAL PHASE

41. Li Hung-chang: *The Neccessity of Learning about Western Technology*	141
42. Li Hung-chang: *A Proposal to Establish a Language School in Shanghai*	142
43. Chang Chih-tung: *A Proposed Reform for the Examination System*	146
44. Tseng Kuo-fan and Li Hung-chang: *The Selection of Intelligent Boys to Study in Foreign Countries*	150
45. Yen Fu: *The Three Essentials in Making a New Nation*	153
46. Wo-jen: *No Need for Western Learning*	161
47. Yü Yüeh: *My Three Fears*	163

Chapter VII • SINO-RUSSIAN RELATIONS, 1689–1896

48. K'ang-hsi: *On the Repulsion of the Russians*	168
49. Treaty of Nerchinsk (1689): *A Summary*	170
50. K'ang-hsi: *Instruction to a Chinese Envoy*	172
51. Yen-feng et al.: *Russian Ships at Canton*	174
52. Ching-ch'un: *Russian Ships on the Amur*	175
53. Yi-shan: *Negotiation with Muraviev*	177
54. Treaty of Aigun (1858): *A Summary*	181
55. Treaty of Peking (1860): *A Summary*	181
56. Prince Kung: *Russian Occupation of Ili*	182
57. Tseng Chi-ts'e: *The Ili Issue*	184
58. Treaty of Ili (1881): *A Summary*	188
59. The Sino-Russian Secret Treaty of 1896	189

CHAPTER VIII • SINO-JAPANESE RELATIONS, 1871–1895

60. THE OKUBO-KUNG UNDERSTANDING (1874)	193
61. HO JU-CHANG: *The Annexation of Liu-ch'iu by Japan*	194
62. HSIANG TEH-HUNG: *A Refutation of Japanese Claims*	197
63. LI HUNG-CHANG: *The Opening of Korea to the Trade of All Countries*	200
64. YÜAN SHIH-K'AI: *Suppression of a Pro-Japanese Rebellion*	203
65. THE LI-ITO AGREEMENT (1885)	210
66. LI HUNG-CHANG: *The Eastern Learning Society*	210
67. ANONYMOUS: *A Conversation between Komura Jutaro and a Chinese Diplomat*	211
68. KUANG-HSÜ: *A Declaration of War against Japan*	213
69. ANONYMOUS: *Minutes: The Fifth Conference between Li Hung-chang and Ito Hirobumi*	215
70. THE TREATY OF SHIMONOSEKI (1895)	223

CHAPTER IX • CHINA'S RESPONSE TO THE WEST: THE REFORM MOVEMENT

71. K'ANG YU-WEI: *The Nation Is in Danger*	229
72. K'ANG YU-WEI: *The Need for Reform*	236
73. YÜN YÜ-TING: *The Hundred Days' Reform*	244
74. LO TUN-YUNG: *Kuang-hsü's Three Secret Decrees*	246
75. YÜAN SHIH-K'AI: *The Day When I Was Invited to Commit Treason*	247
76. YÜN YÜ-TING: *The Emperor and the Empress Dowager*	254

CHAPTER X • MISSIONARIES, BOXERS, AND THE OPEN DOOR

77. CHANG TEH-CHIEN: *Christianity and the Taiping Rebels*	265
78. PRINCE KUNG: *On the Treatment of Christian Converts*	270
79. ANONYMOUS: *Public Denunciation of Christian Missionaries*	272
80. CH'UNG-HOU: *The Tientsin Incident*	273
81. TSENG KUO-FAN AND CH'UNG-HOU: *The Background of the Tientsin Incident*	275
82. YÜN YÜ-TING: *The Empress Dowager Goes to War*	280
83. ALFRED VON WALDERSEE: *The Pillage of Peking*	284
84. THE BOXER PROTOCOL	288
85. JOHN HAY: *The Open Door Notes*	292

CHAPTER XI • THE DOWNFALL OF THE MANCHU REGIME

86. SUN YAT-SEN: *My Role in the Chinese Revolution*	297
87. SUN YAT-SEN: *The Purpose of Our Revolution*	317
88. WANG CHING-WEI: *We Want a Republic, Not a Constitutional Monarchy*	319
89. SUN YAT-SEN: *A Public Proclamation upon Assumption of Office as the Provisional President of the Chinese Republic*	325

CHRONOLOGY	329
INDEX	337

CHAPTER ONE

The Coming of the West

When the first Portuguese traders arrived at Canton in the 1510's, the Chinese did not know where they came from or exactly what they came for (Selection 1). They thought that the Portuguese had come to China to pay tribute so as to "partake of a superior civilization," only to learn with a rude shock that these foreigners were interested in trade or piracy, whichever happened to be more convenient at the moment. With their long and weakly defended coastline, the Chinese simply did not know how to cope with these "undesirable barbarians" (Selection 2).

Despite Chinese obstruction on the official level, trade between Portugal and China continued to prosper throughout the sixteenth century, for local Chinese merchants were just as anxious for the continuance and even enlargement of this trade as their Portuguese counterparts. In 1557 the Portuguese received permission from the Chinese government to reside "permanently" in a strip of land along the Kwangtung coast known as Macao, but counsel remained divided among Chinese officials over the so-called Portuguese problem. The problem was how to maintain profitable trade without jeopardizing China's coastal defense, a key consideration in the mind of every Chinese who chose to voice opinion on this matter. Not surprisingly, many believed that the only solution to the problem was to Sinicize or assimilate the intruders (Selection 3) and bring all the Portuguese in China under direct Chinese jurisdiction (Selection 4).

The profitable trade conducted by the Portuguese soon attracted other Europeans. The Dutch arrived early in the seventeenth century, and their presence was resented as much by the Portuguese merchants as by the Chinese government. While the Portuguese resented them as competitors, the Chinese regarded them as merely another group of undesirable foreigners who insisted on trade in defiance of what the Chinese considered vital principles. In the events that followed, one may trace the conflict between two interest groups within China: the coastal Chinese, who were more than willing to trade with the "red-haired barbarians" as long as there were profits to be realized, and the government officials, who were mainly concerned with coastal defense and the security of the nation. The Dutch occupied some Chinese islands and raided the coastal areas—moves that threatened China's national defense and thus gave them a bargaining point in negotiations over the privilege of trade. The Chinese, in response to the actions of the Dutch, became even more adamant in their refusal to grant this privilege. Such moves and countermoves went on throughout the latter part of the Ming Dynasty (Selection 5). It was not until 1683 that the Ch'ing government, rewarding the Dutch for their assistance in the conquest of Taiwan, granted them the right to trade officially in China.

Not all the Europeans who came to China had materialistic motives, however. Besides traders, there were also missionaries. The Protestant Reformation in Europe caused the Roman Catholic Church to lose many adherents, and the Church, after the Council of Trent (1545–1563), was anxious to win followers in new territories in the pagan world so as to make up its losses in Europe. In the Society of Jesus the Church found one of its greatest proselytizing agencies. The Jesuit Matteo Ricci came to Macao in 1582 and received official permission to preach in 1601. Other Jesuits followed, and soon a small but viable Catholic community, consisting mostly of scholars and officials, was created in Peking (Selection 6).

The Jesuits in China were among the most effective cultural ambassadors of modern times. They informed Europe on China and enlightened China on Europe (Selection 7). To the Chinese, however, the most impressive thing about the Jesuits was their knowledge of science and technology, for China had by then fallen behind Europe in these fields. While commonplace today, many of the ideas transmitted by the Jesuits (Selection 8) were eye-openers to the Chinese then. Throughout the seventeenth century the Jesuits served the Chinese government in a variety of capacities: as astronomers, cartographers, translators of scientific and technological works, and casters of cannon. Some of them rose high in the Chinese bureaucracy and held important, responsible positions with the imperial government.

The friendly relationship between the missionaries and the Chinese government did not last indefinitely, however. The Jesuits, being familiar with Chinese customs and traditions, realized that if the Church was to make any headway in its missionary activities in China, it would have to make compromise with some of China's basic beliefs, for example, the worship of Confucius and ancestor worship. This position was challenged by missionaries of other religious orders, notably the Dominicans, who had come to China in the wake of the Jesuit success. The so-called rites controversy split the Catholic missionaries into two camps, and the sectarian rivalries so familiar in Europe now reappeared in China. Pressed by the Dominicans, the papacy repeatedly ruled in their favor, only to be ignored by the Jesuits. In 1715 Pope Clement XI issued the famous bull *Ex illa die* (Selection 10), intending to settle the dispute once and for all. Since it was inconceivable that K'ang-hsi (r. 1662–1722), who prided himself on being a model Confucian monarch, would abide by a papal instruction which forbade his subjects to worship Confucius and their ancestors, the result was predictable. The missionaries were ordered to leave China (Selection 9), though this order was not strictly enforced until 1742. In that year Pope Benedict XIV issued the bull *Ex quo singulari* and cleared up whatever doubts the Jesuits might still have or pretended to have. The rites controversy came to an end, and one generation later (1773) the Society of Jesus was dissolved.

Despite this unhappy ending, China's experience with the Jesuits was one of the most fruitful in the course of Sino-European relations. Few Europeans have since acquired so much respect and inspired so much confidence among the Chinese as the Jesuits did. A basic reason for the Jesuits' success was that they knew as much about China as they knew about Europe (Selection 11), a happy combination which few people have been able to achieve since.

1 ● KU YIN-HSIANG: *The Arrival of the Portuguese*[1]

Fu-lang-chi was the name of a country [Portugal], not that of a cannon as generally assumed. In the Ting-ch'ou year of the Cheng-teh period [1517] I served as a senior assistant in the provincial government of Kwangtung and simultaneously as superintendent of maritime affairs. One day there suddenly arrived two oceangoing vessels sailing straight towards Huaiyüan Yi outside of Canton. Their owner was a man named Chia-pi-tan [sic, captain][2] who announced that he had come to China to bring tribute from Fu-lang-chi. He and his men all had high noses and deep-set eyes. They wore white turbans and dressed like Muslims. I immediately reported their presence to His Excellency Ch'en Hsi-hsien, then the governor-general, who subsequently came to Canton to take a look for himself.[3] As these foreigners knew nothing about proper manners, they were ordered to rehearse them at the Kuanghsiao Temple for three days before they could be granted an audience.[4] Since Fu-lang-chi had never been a tribute-bearing country according to the *Istitutions of the Great Ming Dynasty*,[5] the decision whether its representatives should be received was referred to the imperial government. The imperial government consented to receive them, and they were escorted to Peking. At the time the emperor was making an inspection tour in the south,[6] and so foreigners were quartered in the Huit'ung Inn[7] for almost a year. When the present emperor[8] came to the throne, he was greatly annoyed by their lack of respect towards him. He ordered the interpreter to be punished according to law and the men to be escorted back to Canton and expelled from the country. Thus the matter came to a conclusion.

NOTES

[1] The Chinese original appears in Hu Tsung-hsien (*chin-shih* degree, 1538), *A Book on Coastal Defense* (*Ch'ou-hui t'u-p'ien*), roll 13. Ku, the author of this selection, was in charge of maritime affairs at Canton when the Portuguese arrived; he later rose to become the minister of justice in the imperial government.

[2] He was actually Fernao Perez de Andrade, sent by Affonso de Albuquerque, then the Portuguese governor of Malacca. Malacca had been conquered by Albuquerque in 1511.

[3] The governor-general's office was then located in Wuchou, modern Kwangsi province.

[4] One ceremony required to express so-called proper manners was the kowtow. For the kowtow, see pp. 46–49.

[5] *Ta Ming hui-tien.*

[6] In 1520 Cheng-teh, the lively emperor of the Ming Dynasty, was touring the Yangtze Valley.

[7] Hui-t'ung kuan, a temporary residence for tribute-bearing envoys during the Ming Dynasty.

[8] Ming Shih-tsung or Ming Chia-ching (r.1522–1567).

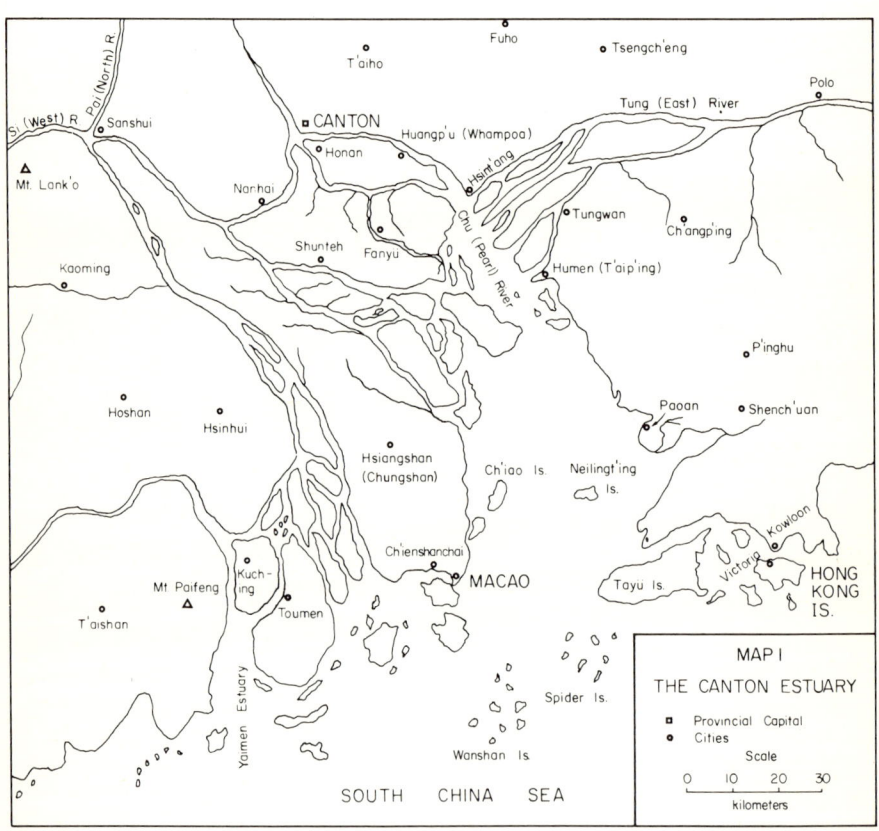

2 • CHANG T'ING-YÜ et al.: *The Portuguese Problem*[1]

Fu-lang-chi was geographically near Malacca.[2] During the Cheng-teh period [1506–1521] it occupied Malacca and expelled their king.[3] In the thirteenth year of Cheng-teh [1518] it sent its minister Chia-pi-tan Mo [Captain Moor] and others to bring tribute to China and requested an investiture from the Chinese emperor. This was the first that China had heard of such a country as Fu-lang-chi. The emperor decreed that the tribute bearers should be given gifts in accordance with the value of their tribute and then sent home. These men, however, refused to leave. They robbed travelers and went so far as to kidnap small children for food. Later, by intrigue and bribery, they ingratiated themselves with some influential officials and were consequently granted permission to proceed to the capital [Peking]. When Emperor Wu-tsung[4] traveled in the south, one of their representatives, Huo-che-ya-san, became an imperial retainer through the influence of Chiang Pin. The emperor often mimicked his language for fun. Meanwhile the Fu-lang-chi who were left behind in Huaiyüan Yi[5] continued and in fact extended their practice of kidnaping people of good family. They built houses and erected fortifications. They intended to stay for a long time.

In the fifteenth year of Cheng-teh [1520], censor Ch'iu Tao-lung presented to the emperor a memorial which read as follows: "Malacca is a country which has received our investiture, and yet Fu-lang-chi was impudent enough to conquer it. Trying to mislead us with the prospect of profits, Fu-lang-chi now requests a Chinese investiture and the privilege of sending tribute missions to China. By no means should this request be granted! Her envoy should be dismissed outright so as to impress upon her the difference between obeisance and open defiance. Let it be decreed that only after Fu-lang-chi has returned Malacca to its rightful rulers can she be allowed to send us tribute missions. If she insists upon her evil ways, we should make her behavior known to all heads of foreign states and send a military expedition against her on account of her crimes."

Censor Ho Ao also presented a memorial in connection with the Fu-lang-chi problem. "The people of Fu-lang-chi are as brutal as they are treacherous, and their military equipment is far superior to that of other foreigners," said the memorialist. "Sometimes, borne on large ships, they suddenly burst into the capital of Kwangtung [Canton]: the sound of their cannons could be heard far and wide. The Fu-lang-chi who remained at Huaiyüan Yi violated the law by communicating with the Chinese, and those who went to the capital [Peking] were arrogant enough to show off their so-called talents. If we allow them to travel freely and trade, strife is bound to break out, and the mischief they can start among the people in the south will never come to an end. The ancestors of our dynasty specified the years when tribute missions were allowed and provided us with guides to keep our national defense strong. As a result, the visits of tribute missions from foreign countries have been infrequent. Lately, owing to the acceptance of governor Wu T'ing-chü's contention that there is an inadequate supply of fragrant materials[6] in the capital, we have allowed these Fu-lang-chi people to come and trade in any year they choose. The result is that foreign ships keep sailing into our rivers and seas, and foreigners themselves live side by side with the Chinese in our towns and cities. As we continue to relax our defense measures, foreigners have become more and more familiar with our waterways. This is the reason why Fu-lang-chi was able to make intrusions into our territory without our advance knowledge. I accordingly suggest that all foreign ships currently anchored in our bays and harbors should be expelled at once and that all foreigners who live in China without permission should be deported immediately. Clandestine communication with foreigners should be prohibited, and our defense should be further strengthened. Only in this way can our coastal areas again enjoy peace and security."

After the two memorials had been handed down for discussion, the Ministry of Rites reported as follows: "Tao-lung once served as a magistrate of Shunteh, [7] from which Ao, the second petitioner, hails. Both, consequently, know thoroughly the serious problem faced by people in that area. It is hereby suggested that when the envoy of Malacca arrives at the court, he should be questioned about the crime which Fu-lang-chi has committed in annexing a neighboring country and in creating disturbances in that part of the world. Then the Ministry of Rites will propose measures to be taken in this matter. As for the other points in these two memorials, they should be carried out as the petitioners have requested."

The emperor replied: "Let this be done."

NOTES

[1] The authors were famous scholar-officials of the seventeenth and eighteenth centuries. This selection is taken from "Foreign Countries VI" (*wai-kuo liu*); *History of the Ming* (*Ming shih*), roll 325.
[2] This shows how little the Chinese knew about the Western countries during this period.
[3] This occurred in 1511.
[4] Ming Wu-tsung or Ming Cheng-teh (r.1506–1521).
[5] Located in the suburb of Canton.
[6] This may refer to such items as spices which the Portuguese had regularly shipped to China from the East Indies.
[7] A subprefecture south of Canton.

3 • Huo Ju-hsia: *The Portuguese Problem*[1]

There is a vast difference between peaceful trade and piratical raids. To be unable to pacify the barbarians who have come from afar to partake of our civilization is a reflection on our own goodness. To criticize them for their shortcomings while only too gladly collecting taxes from them is not what a righteous man should do. Without making any effort to observe their conduct or to differentiate the law-abiding from the evildoers, we indiscriminately call all of them bandits. Once we have branded them as bandits, we are obligated to exterminate them—only to see more of them come. Is this policy really wise?

What then should we do?

There are three measures we can take, each exclusive of the others. The best measure would be to govern them in the same manner as we govern our own people: to convert the territory they have occupied into a subprefecture and to place them under the jurisdictional control of duly appointed government officials. The next best measure would be to expel them and make sure that they never come back again. The worst measure would be to cut off their food supply, which would force them to revolt, and then use armed forces to exterminate them.

Ironical though it may seem, the best way to carry out the first measure is to threaten them with the adoption of the second. The government should issue an order addressed to them as follows: "It is reported by military authorities that you have gathered hooligans around yourselves and equipped yourselves with horses and cannons. We are afraid that some unprincipled, avaricious Chinese may incite you to illegal activities which will do harm to local communities. Therefore we have ordered the armed forces to demolish your dwellings and send you back to where you came from, to avoid trouble for all parties." While proclaiming this order, we should alert our troops for action. If the barbarians obey the order, they will leave China for other countries, where they are welcome to do whatever damage they choose. If on the other hand they beg us to let them stay and declare that they have no objection to being subject to Chinese administration, we should petition the imperial government to build cities for them and to govern them with Chinese officials. From then on they will be subject to Chinese law. This is the way barbarians have been transformed into Chinese; it is by far the best course to follow.

Some people may say that once these barbarians are expelled from China, there will be no further disturbances on our frontier and our people will be much better off. How, they may ask, can expulsion be regarded as the second best course? I reply that to have confidence in the barbarians' natural goodness for our own defense is reflective of the greatness of the Son of Heaven, that to welcome all barbarians to partake of our civilization is indicative of the benign nature of the Celestial King, and that to provide food for our enemy so as to pacify the frontier betokens the farsightedness of a powerful nation. Besides, there are also practical considerations: (1) For the past hundred years the yearly revenue derived from overseas trade has been as large as the total revenue of a first-rate subprefecture, and this revenue has been used to support the armed forces in the Liangkwang region [Kwangtung and Kwangsi]. If this trade is cut off, where can we find funds to meet the military demand? (2) Macao has proved to be an effective buffer for Hsiangshan.[2] Because it is there, pirates like Lao-wan, Tseng Yi-pen, and Ho Ya-pa have not dared to launch attacks, and the whole area has remained peaceful as a result. If the barbarians in Macao are expelled, Hsiangshan will have to defend itself. In short, to construct cities for them and to govern them with Chinese officials in accordance with the Chinese law will be the best policy to follow. It is best because it is a policy of kindness by which peace can be secured without great effort.

NOTES

[1] The author was a scholar-official who lived during the first half of the seventeenth century. Source: Lu K'un, *A Broad View of the Coastal Defense of Kwangtung (Kuang-tung hai-fang hui-lan)*, roll 3.

[2] Hsiangshan has since been renamed Chungshan in honor of Dr. Sun Yat-sen (better known to the Chinese as Sun Chung-shan), founder of the Chinese Republic, who was born there in 1866.

4 • P'AN SSU-CH'Ü: *The Macao Problem*[1]

Within the subprefecture of Hsiangshan is a district called Macao which stretches for a distance of more than 10 *li*. On three sides it is surrounded by sea which extends all the way to the ocean. To reach it there is only one land route via

Ch'ienshanchai, which links the district with the capital city of Hsiangshan. It is a strategic site for coastal defense as well as an important port for oceangoing ships.

When the Westerners came to Kwangtung to trade during the Ming Dynasty, they were allowed to take up temporary residence on the offshore islands. The shacks they built were to be demolished, however, once the traders had completed their business and sailed for home. Later, by order of the imperial government, these Western traders were allowed to pay annual rent for the land they occupied, [2] and it was then that they began to build storied houses in Macao and brought their families to live with them. Often they rented the lower floors to others and collected rent. As usual, they constructed ships and made their livelihood by trade. When the present dynasty [3] was established, it followed the same policy of friendship towards foreigners and continued to allow them to reside in Macao. Today there are about 3,500 foreigners in this district, plus approximately 2,000 Chinese who live there as either laborers or artisans. The fact that they can all live harmoniously together is an indication of Your Majesty's boundless benevolence.

The reason why these foreigners have come to reside in China is to practice trade and make a profit, and it does not serve any useful purpose to cancel their residential rights. Censor P'ang Shang-p'eng of the Ming Dynasty considered them illegal squatters who served as spies for a foreign power and once suggested in a memorial that their dwellings be demolished and they be ordered to reside in boats only. To me this seems too extreme a measure. If it were adopted today, it would entail a loss of homes for all foreigners who now reside in the coastal areas.

It should be borne in mind, however, that these foreigners are as tricky as they are avaricious and the black slaves they employ are especially brutal and violent. The situation is not helped when many evil elements from the Chinese community go to their settlements secretly and incite the residents to break the law. Arrogant and untamable, these foreigners bully local people and view lightly the sanctity of the law. They also entice ignorant people to join their church and peddle men and women as slaves. Sometimes they even ship contraband abroad. Though the governor has proclaimed the unlawful nature of these activities and I, your humble servant, have done my very best to enforce the law, Macao is so far away in the corner of the sea that without a special official in charge we cannot carry out all our intentions.

Ignorant though your servant is, he believes that there should be specific rules to govern these foreigners, though he realizes that the law governing our own people is too complicated and strict for them. At one time during the Ming Dynasty an official post was established to govern Macao, and later Macao was put under the jurisdiction of the subprefecture of Hsiangshan. In the eighth year of Yung-cheng [1730] magistrate Ho Yü-lin, realizing that he was too busy with subprefectural business to be able also to take care of affairs in Macao, petitioned for the establishment of a deputy magistrate's office for the Hsiangshan subprefecture to be stationed at Ch'ienshanchai. There the deputy magistrate would be geographically close enough to Macao to supervise affairs in that district effectively. But the position of a deputy magistrate was too low to command respect for the law, and it did not help the Macao situation materially.

It is the opinion of your humble servant that in governing the foreigners at Macao we should follow the example of governing such minority groups as Yao and Li [4] by establishing the post of an official-in-residence who would be made responsible not only for strengthening coastal defenses and suppressing piracy but also for demonstrating to the foreigners the concern and goodwill which the imperial government has always felt for them. He should make it clear to all residents in Macao, Chinese as well as foreigners, that they must abide by the law of the land. He should make timely inspection of all foreign ships that sail into or from the Macao port. He should investigate and then report on all lawless activities such as the concealment of bandits and other evil elements, acts of violence, theft and robbery, buying and selling of slaves, and finally, secret shipment of contraband. Only when petty crimes are checked at the beginning will the foreigners in Macao be prevented from committing more serious crimes. It is hoped that these foreigners can continue to enjoy the good fortune of living within the jurisdiction of the Celestial Empire without posing a threat to the peace and security of our sea frontier.

NOTES

[1] This memorial was presented to the imperial government c. 1743. The author was then the inspector-general (*an-ch'a shih*) of Kwangtung province. A copy of the Chinese original can be found in Kuo T'ing-yi, *A History of Modern China* (*Chin-tai Chung-kuo shih*) (Taipei: The Commercial Press, 1952), pp. 132–133.
[2] The permission was given in 1557.
[3] The Ch'ing or Manchu government.
[4] These minorities lived in Yunnan, Kweichow, and Kwangsi provinces.

5 • CHANG T'ING-YÜ et al.: *The Dutch and Their Activities*[1]

Holland, also known as the Land of Red-Haired Barbarians,[2] is located not far from Fu-lang-chi [Portugal]. During the reigns of Yung-lo and Hsüan-teh [1403–1435], Cheng Ho made seven voyages to the "Western Ocean" and traveled in dozens of countries, but in all of his travels he never heard of such a country as Holland. The Hollanders have deep-set eyes and long noses, and their hair, eyebrows, and beards are all red in color. They are twice as big as average people, and their feet are as long as one [Chinese] foot and two inches.

During the Wan-li period [1573–1619] the Hollanders, guided and supported by Chinese merchants from Fukien, traded in such countries as Ta-ni [Pattani], Lü-sung [Luzon], and Chiao-liu-pa [Java], but had not yet dared to land in China. Later, when they learned that Fu-lang-chi had traded in Hsiangshan[3] and had also occupied Lü-sung, they became very envious. In the twenty-ninth year of Wan-li [1601] they brought with them large ships and big cannons and went straight to Lü-sung, which they intended to attack and then occupy. Meeting strong resistance from the defenders, they changed their course and sailed towards Macao instead. The people in Macao asked the purpose of their visit, and the Hollanders replied that they merely wished to trade with China and that they had no piratical intentions. Despite this assurance, the Chinese authorities were reluctant to comply with their request. Li Tao, the tax administrator, invited the Dutch chief to the city, where he stayed as a visitor for about a month. Since Li did not dare to forward the Dutchman's request to the imperial government, he eventually had to dismiss the man. The people in Macao were afraid that the foreigners might land without their permission, and accordingly they strengthened their defenses. This fear proved to be unfounded, since the Hollanders soon left of their own accord.

Li Ching of Haich'eng and two unscrupulous merchants named P'an Hsiu and Kuo Chen had lived in Ta-ni for a long time and had learned from the Hollanders their language. They taught these foreigners things about China. "There is no better place for trade with China than Changchou," [4] said Li Ching. "South of Changchou are the P'enghu Islands [the Pescadores], which lie far off the shore. If you seize and hold these islands, you will succeed in achieving your purpose of trade."

"What shall I do if the garrison commander refuses permission?" asked the Dutch captain Ma-wei-lang.[5]

"The tax administrator in that area is a man named Kao Ts'ai who is unusually greedy for gold and silver," Li Ching replied. "If you bribe him heavily, he will write a special memorial to be presented to the imperial government on your behalf. I can assure you that if Kao Ts'ai decides to assist you, His Majesty will grant your request to trade. The garrison commander will not dare to disobey the emperor's order."

"That is a good idea," said the Dutch captain.

Li Ching then wrote three letters on behalf of the king of Ta-ni, one addressed to Kao Ts'ai, one to the deputy commander of coastal defense, and one to the garrison commander. The letters were to be delivered in person by P'an Hsiu and Kuo Chen. Having read the letter addressed to him, garrison commander T'ao Kung-sheng was much alarmed. He threw P'an Hsiu into jail and immediately reported the incident to his superiors. Kuo Chen, seeing what had happened to P'an Hsiu, did not dare enter the city.

Previously P'an Hsiu had made an agreement with the Dutch captain: if he, P'an Hsiu, was successful in his mission, he would send a ship to report the good news. But the Dutchman was too impatient to wait. Before any news arrived, he sailed straight towards P'enghu with two large warships. This event occurred during the seventh month of the thirty-second year [of Wan-li, 1604], after the Chinese government had already taken the garrison troops off the islands. Accordingly, the Hollanders did not meet much resistance. Once on the islands, they began to fell trees to build houses; it seemed that they intended to stay for a long time.

Meanwhile Li Ching went secretly to Changchou to spy for the Dutch captain. He falsely stated that he had been captured by the Hollanders but had managed to escape. However, the authorities, forewarned of the true nature of his business, threw him into jail. Later they decided to send Li Ching and P'an Hsiu, together with Kuo Chen, who had also been captured, to request the Dutch captain to return to his own country. If these men succeeded in their mission, said the authorities, the crimes they had committed would be forgiven. The three men, since they had promised to acquire for the Dutchman permission to trade in China, chose not to reveal that they could not possibly succeed in their mission. When they saw the foreigner, they merely stated that the Chinese government had not yet made up its mind whether it would allow him to trade in China. Later, Army Lieutenant Chan Hsien-chung was sent to the islands, carrying with him the order for the intruders' expulsion. But the lieutenant also brought to the foreigners a large quantity of food, silk, and money, in the hope that they would reward him abundantly for the gifts he presented. Meanwhile the people in the coastal areas secretly shipped their own goods to the islands for purposes of trade. Because of these developments the Hollanders were all the more reluctant to go. Time and again the Chinese government sent messengers to the islands ordering the intruders to leave. But when they saw the Dutch captain, these messengers had little to say to impress him. As a result, the Dutchman became more and more contemptuous of them. Meanwhile Kao Ts'ai had decided to send his confidential agent Chou Chih-fan to the islands, saying that if the captain was willing to pay 30,000 taels of silver, he would be allowed to trade. The captain was pleased with this arrangement and handed over the money as requested. As far as he was concerned, a solemn agreement had been reached.

Shortly afterwards, military commander Shih Teh-cheng sent Colonel Shen Yu-yung at the head of a military contingent to order the foreigners to leave. Confident of his own courage and wisdom, Shen argued with the Dutch captain in a stern voice. The latter became submissive for the first time, saying: "I have never heard this kind of talk before." His followers unsheathed their swords and questioned Shen in a hostile manner. But Shen was fearless and continued to argue with them in great anger. Finally enlightened, the Dutch captain showed remorse for the first time. He stated that he only wanted Chou Chih-fan to return his money. This, of course, was promptly done. Then he proposed to present Kao Ts'ai with a gift of woolens, glassware, foreign swords, and wine, in the hope that Kao would be good enough to petition the imperial government to allow him to trade. Kao, however, did not dare to accept this gift. Meanwhile the governor issued a strict order to forbid unscrupulous people to sail towards the sea; those who were caught making the trip, said the governor, would be put to death without mercy. Since their supply of food was cut off, the Hollanders were forced to leave the islands towards the end of the tenth month. Governor Hsü Hsüeh-chü brought P'an Hsiu, Li Ching, and others to trial, and they were punished by either death or exile.

At this time Fu-lang-chi was the most powerful country on the high seas; nevertheless Holland chose to challenge her. The Hollanders returned to the east with warships and conquered the kingdom of the Moluccas. They divided the kingdom between themselves and Fu-lang-chi.

Later, the Dutch invaded and occupied Taiwan.[6] They built houses and began to cultivate the land, with every intention of remaining. Knowing that there were profits to be realized, great numbers of unscrupulous people of the coastal areas proceeded to the island. Using Taiwan as a base, the Hollanders also occupied P'enghu, where they constructed fortifications for defense and sent out repeated requests for trade with the mainlanders. Fearful that disaster would overtake them, the officials responsible for coastal defense told the intruders that they would be allowed to trade if they demolished their fortifications and left the islands. The Hollanders agreed. In the third year of T'ien-ch'i [1623] they demolished their fortifications and sailed away as they had promised. Governor Shang Chou-tso reported to the imperial government that the Hollanders had obeyed the emperor's edict by leaving the islands. However, they continued to occupy Taiwan.

The Hollanders were much displeased when they learned that their request for trade had again been rejected. Once more they built fortifications on the P'enghu Islands. To facilitate their construction, they pirated 600 Chinese fishing boats and forced their crews to help them in moving earth and stone. Shortly afterwards they invaded Hsiamen [Amoy]. Defeated by the regular army, which killed or captured almost a hundred of them, they pretended to sue for peace. They were told to demolish their fortifications and to remove to a distance, but they continued to build their fortifications as before. Subsequently they became extremely active among the numerous islands off the Fukien coast, and time and again they presented a request to trade. To make the situation worse, the pirate Li Tan also helped them in their activities. The authorities were so alarmed that they put all the coastal cities on the alert.

It was in the same year [1623] that Nan Chü-yi came to this area as governor. Deciding to send troops against the foreigners, he petitioned the imperial government as follows: "Upon my arrival, I learned that five foreign ships have been standing at anchor in this area. This force has been augmented by six ships from Fengkueitzu, bringing the total to eleven ships. Previously Lieutenant Ch'en Shih-ying was assigned to deliver to the king of Chiao-liu-pa an edict from Your Majesty the Emperor. On his way he encountered Dutch ships at the island of San-chüeh, and their crews informed him that the king of Chiao-liu-pa had already gone to the kingdom of A-nan. The Dutch ships took him to Ta-ni. The ruler there told him that the king of Chiao-liu-pa had mobilized a large number of warships to sail towards P'enghu in search of trade and that war was inevitable if the Chinese government refused to grant permission for it. A-nan, incidentally, is the same as the Land of Red-Haired Barbarians. Since Chiao-liu-pa and Ta-ni have formed an alliance to carry out their joint plot, it is obvious that we can no longer reason with them. War seems to be the only course for us to follow."

In his petition the governor also elaborated on his plan of mobilizing troops, securing the supply of provisions, and overall strategy. After deliberation, the Ministry of War reported favorably on his petition.

In the first month of the fourth year [of Chia-ch'ing, 1624] the governor first sent his troops to seize and fortify Chenhaikang. The troops fought while continuing to build their fortifications. After the Dutch had retreated to Fengkueicheng, the governor dispatched more troops as reinforcements. The attack persisted for several months, but the enemy refused to withdraw. Finally the governor mobilized all of his armed forces and attacked from all sides. Hard pressed, the enemy sent an envoy to plead for a truce, saying that they would withdraw immediately if they were allowed to provision their ships with rice. Believing that one should never engage in hot pursuit against a defeated enemy, the Chinese generals decided to grant the request. After their ships were supplied with rice, the enemy sailed away.

One enemy leader named Kao Wen-lü, supported by eleven of his followers, held a tall building and refused to leave. The generals attacked, captured all of them, and sent them to the imperial government as prisoners-of-war. At last peace was restored in the P'enghu area.

Meanwhile the Hollanders continued to occupy Taiwan. During the Ch'ung-chen period [1628–1644] they were defeated by Cheng Chih-lung,[7] and for several years after this defeat they did not dare to invade the mainland. However, they continued to cooperate with the Fu-lang-chi of Hsiangshan in trade on the distant seas.

In the tenth year of T'ien-ch'i [1630] the Hollanders sailed with four of their ships from Hut'iaomen to Canton, announcing that they wished to trade with China. Their captain swaggered through the street, and the unscrupulous elements in the city looked on him as a gold mine. Fortunately the man in charge of the city was a responsible member of the gentry who, in viewing what had happened to Macao, suggested expelling these intruders from the city. Though others raised objections, Governor-General Chang Ching-hsin, who had only recently arrived at his post, insisted that the privilege of trade should not be granted to these people. The intruders finally fled.

Later, enticed by an unscrupulous man named Li Yeh-yung, the Hollanders contacted Ch'en Ch'ien, superintendent of transportation, in the hope that the latter would use his influence to enable them to stay at Canton and to come and go as they pleased. The conspiracy was discovered; Li Yeh-yung was arrested, and Ch'en Ch'ien requested transfer to another post to avoid any calamities that might fall upon him. Later Ch'en Ch'ien was impeached by Ling Yi-ch'ü and others in the Military Office and was arrested and brought to trial. Only then did the unscrupulous elements in China realize that they would not succeed in their efforts to gain permission for the Hollanders to trade in China; in fact, they never thereafter repeated the attempt. Meanwhile the Dutch continued to occupy Taiwan.

The home of these Hollanders is located in the Western Ocean, far away from China. In fact, no Chinese has ever visited that country. There are two things the Hollanders are most dependent upon and proud of, namely, large ships and big cannons. Each ship has a length of 30 *chang* and a width of 6 *chang* and is more than 2 *ch'ih* in thickness.[8] It is equipped with five masts. On its stern is a five-storied structure around which are small windows where bronze cannons are placed. Underneath the mainmast can be found two large cannons made of cast iron, each about 2 *chang* in length. When fired, they could tear a huge hole in a stone wall, and their noise could be heard tens of *li* away. The so-called "red-barbarian cannons" in fact originated with these people. Their ships are equally large, so large that it is difficult to maneuver them. Once grounded in shallow water, they become immobile. Despite their equipment, the Hollanders are not particularly proficient in warfare; that is why they often suffer defeat. Among the people they employ are a group called "black devils"[9] who, unsinkable in water, can walk on the surface of the sea as if it were solid ground. Behind the rudder of each ship they place a searchlight which is several *ch'ih* in diameter and can be seen from a distance of several hundred *li*.

All the people in Holland believe in a religion called Christianity. Their country produces gold, silver, amber, agate, glass, velvet, and woolens. Since their country is so rich, they do not mind paying a high price for any Chinese product they happen to like. That is why the Chinese love to trade with them.

NOTES

[1] Source: "Foreign Countries VI" (*wai-kuo liu*); *Ming shih*, roll 325.
[2] *Hung-mao fan-ti*.
[3] Macao was a district under the jurisdiction of the Hsiangshan subprefecture.
[4] Also known as Lunghsi, Fukien province.
[5] Believed to be Wijbrand van Waerwijk.
[6] This occurred in 1623.
[7] The father of Cheng Ch'eng-kung or Koxinga who defeated the Dutch and chased them out of Taiwan in 1661.
[8] One *ch'ih* is one-tenth of a *chang* and equal to approximately 14.1 inches.
[9] *Wu kuei*.

6 • Chang T'ing-yü et al.: *The Jesuits*[1]

Italy is located in the Great Western Ocean and had no relationship with China in ancient times. During the Wan-li period [1573-1619] an Italian named Li Ma-tou [Matteo Ricci] came to the capital [Peking] and presented an atlas of the world. "There are five continents in the world," he said. "The first continent is Asia, consisting of more than one hundred countries, including China. The second continent is Europe, consisting of more than seventy countries, including Italy. The third continent, Africa, also has more than one hundred countries. The fourth continent, America, is even larger and has two constituent parts, North and South America. The last or fifth continent is Australia. These five continents are all the land in this world." His words were so vague and incoherent that they could not be verified in any of the books then in existence. But the fact that people from these remote lands did roam about in China seemed to indicate that there was some truth in his remarks.

All these people came from European countries and believed in a religion called Roman Catholicism. Jesus, the man whom they worshipped, was born in the second year of Yüan-shou during the reign of Han Ai-ti [6-1 B.C.] in a country called Judea. Fifteen hundred eighty-one years later, in the ninth year of Wan-li [1581], Li Ma-tou sailed 90,000 *li* across the ocean and arrived at Macao off Canton. With his arrival in China came his religion.

In the twenty-ninth year of Wan-li [1601] Li Ma-tou arrived at Peking. He called himself a man of the Great Western Ocean,[2] and, through the intermediation of a eunuch named Ma T'ang, presented his native products to the emperor as tribute. Responding to his presence, the Ministry of Rites memorialized the emperor as follows: "In the *Institutions*[3] only a country called So-li of the Western Ocean is listed. Since there is no mention of the so-called Great Western Ocean, we do not know whether this man has stated the truth. Moreover, he stayed in China for twenty years before he paid his tribute. This procedure is totally different from that normally followed by other foreigners who, admiring China and her moral superiority, come here to present their treasures. The tribute this man has presented consists of the images of a Heavenly Lord and His Mother,[4] a tribute that is highly irregular. He has also brought with him 'bones of the immortals.'[5] The term 'bones of the immortals' is self-contradictory since a true immortal can fly by himself without any bones. These things, to quote Han Yü,[6] are 'unclean, inauspicious items that should not be allowed to enter the imperial palace.' Moreover, these things were presented to Your Majesty without being examined in advance by us in the Ministry of Rites. In this respect both the ministers of the Inner Court [eunuchs], who did not follow the normal procedure when bringing tribute to the palace, and we, who have failed to perform our assigned duties, are equally guilty. Having been ordered by Your Majesty to report to this ministry, this man Li Ma-tou, instead of proceeding to the ministry's foreign quarters as he was supposed to do, chose to live in a Buddhist temple without being authorized to do so. He is, in fact, a puzzle to us. However, according to the precedents governing tribute-bearing envoys, a foreigner who pays tribute to China should be given gifts and granted dinners in return. It is hereby suggested that this Li Ma-tou be granted hats and belts and be sent back to his own country. He should not be allowed to live in the two capitals [Peking and Nanking] or to associate with Chinese. Only in this way can unpleasant incidents be prevented." The emperor did not reply.

In the eighth month the Ministry of Rites presented the emperor with another memorial which read as follows: "Some time ago your humble servants suggested sending Li Ma-tou back to his own country. Though five months have elapsed since then, we have not received any instruction from Your Majesty on this matter. It is no wonder that he is homesick and wishes to return home. From what we can observe, his words are honest and sincere; he does not wish to be rewarded and titled in a worldly manner, and he merely hopes to repair to deep mountains and live as a hermit. Like a fowl or a deer, the longer he is detained in a worldly atmosphere, the more longing he has for deep forests and rich meadows. What he wants is clearly understandable. It is hereby suggested that he should be sent to a place like Kiangsi [7] with Your Majesty's blessing as soon as possible so that he can wander about in the remotest mountains and valleys and enjoy life in the way he chooses for his declining years." The emperor did not reply to this memorial either.

Later the emperor, pleased that this man had come such a long way to visit China, granted him living quarters and a food allowance, plus numerous gifts. All the ministers at court thought highly of the man and associated with him. Li Ma-tou was so happy with his new home that he decided to stay until the end of his life. He died in the fourth month of the thirty-eighth year of Wan-li [1610] and was buried in the western suburb of Peking.

On the first day of the eleventh month of the same year [1610] there was an eclipse of the sun. The court astronomers had made so many errors in forecasting heavenly phenomena that suggestions were made that the old calendar be examined and corrected. In the following year [1611] an official named Chou Tzu-yü remarked that many Sinicized Westerners such as P'ang Ti-o [Didacus de Pantoya] and Hsiung San-pa [Sebastianus de Ursis] were versed in the making of calendars and that their calendar books were superior to those in China. These Westerners, he continued, should be ordered to translate these books into Chinese and present them to the government for reference purposes. Meanwhile Weng Cheng-ch'un, vice-president of the Ministry of Rites, petitioned the emperor to follow the precedent of adopting the Muslim calendar early in the Hung-wu period [1368-1398] by inviting Ti-o and others to help prepare a new calendar. The emperor agreed.

After Li Ma-tou reached China, many others followed. One of them, Wang Feng-su,[8] took up residence in Nanking and used his Roman Catholicism to confuse and deceive the masses. He enticed and led astray many intellectuals as well as ordinary citizens. His activities aroused the resentment of Hsü Ju-k'o, a secretary in the Ministry of Rites. Hsü was particularly resentful when foreigners boasted of the achievements of their respective countries, which, they said, were far superior to those of China. Hsü gave two of them paper and pen and asked them to write down what they could remember about their home countries. When their writings were compared, it was found that the contents were not only erroneous but also contradicted each other. It was then that he decided to advocate their expulsion.

In the forty-fourth year of Wan-li [1616] Hsü Ju-k'o, together with two other officials, Shen Huai and Yen Wen-hui, presented a memorial to the emperor that criticized the foreigners' unorthodox ideas, which, they said, had confused and led astray many people in China. They intimated that the foreigners were really the agents of Fu-lang-chi and should therefore be expelled from China as soon as possible. Meanwhile Yü Mo-tzu, another official, also memorialized the emperor with the same recommendation. "Since Li Ma-tou's arrival in the east," said Yü, "China again has a religion called Roman Catholicism.[9] Foreigners like Wang Feng-su and Yang Ma-no [Emmanuel Diaz] take advantage of their residence in the capital to spread deceptive ideas, and those who have fallen under their unhealthy influence number no fewer than ten thousand. On the first and fifteenth days of each month, frequently more than a thousand persons are assembled for worship.[10] Our country has specific orders to prohibit the spread of foreign and heretical doctrines. Yet these people openly gather in the evening and choose not to disperse until early in the morning, just as the White Lotus Society[11] and other Taoist sects used to do. Furthermore, these foreigners travel regularly between the capital and Macao, where they maintain close contact with foreigners residing in that city and conspire with them. What will happen to the law of the land if the government does not choose to expel them?"

The emperor assented to Yü's request and, in the twelfth month of the same year [1616], ordered Wang Feng-su, Ti-o, and others to proceed to Kwangtung and from there sail for home. Despite this order, the foreigners kept on delaying their journey, and the officials in charge, for reasons of their own, did not choose to enforce it. In the fourth month of the forty-sixth year [1618] Wang Feng-su and Ti-o presented the emperor with the following petition: "We—the late Li Ma-tou, the petitioners, and many others—sailed 90,000 *li* across the ocean to visit a superior country and have served in China as officials for the past seventeen years. Lately many officials have criticized us and have suggested deporting us from this country. Your humble servants, worshiping the Heavenly Lord and guarding our conduct, are far from wishing to engage in any conspiratorial activities which, if conceived, would certainly bring condemnation. We are pleading for Your Majesty's sympathy to let us stay a little longer, and we shall return home when the winds on the high seas are of the right direction. We are also making the same request for all of our compatriots who presently reside in southern China." The emperor did not reply, and sorrowfully these foreigners had to leave the capital. Later Wang Feng-su changed his name and reappeared in Nanking, preaching and proselytizing as usual. The officials in the capital did not know anything about his activities.

The country that these foreigners came from was skilled in making cannons. The cannons it made were even larger than those of the "Western Ocean." Some of these cannons wound up in China, but the Chinese were unable to operate them. During the T'ien-ch'i and Ch'ung-chen periods [1621–1644] the government was waging war in the Northeast,[12] and foreigners at Macao were often invited to the capital to teach the soldiers how to use foreign cannons. These foreigners were generally very enthusiastic with their assistance.

During the Ch'ung-chen period [1628–1644] the calendar then in use became even more inaccurate. Hsü Kuang-ch'i, President of the Ministry of Rites, requested the emperor's approval to establish an institute to revise the old calendar and to order such men as Lo Ya-hu [Jacobus Rho] and T'ang Jo-wang [Johannes Adam Schall von Bell] to use their country's calendar as reference for the proposed revision. The emperor granted this request, but it took a long time for the new calendar to be completed. The new calendar was called the Ch'ung-chen Calendar, after the emperor's reigning title. It was much more accurate than the Ta-t'ung Calendar and was praised highly by those who were in a position to know.

The people who came from the Great Western Ocean were mostly intelligent and highly knowledgeable. They were only interested in spreading their religion and did not care for fame or wealth. The books they wrote dealt with topics which the Chinese rarely mentioned, and those who loved different and strange things were anxious to learn from them. Chinese intellectuals like Hsü Kuang-ch'i and Li Chih-tsao[13] were the first to show such interest and helped them to publish their Chinese writings. As a result, this religion, called Roman Catholicism, suddenly flourished in China.

Besides those mentioned above, the foreigners who had earned fame in China included Lung Hua-min [Nicolaus Longobardi], Pi Fang-chi [Franciscus Sambiasi], Ai Ju-lioh [Julius Aleni], and Teng Yü-han [Johann Terrenz]. Lung Hua-min, Pi Fang-chi, Ai Ju-lioh, and Hsiung Sun-pa were Italians; Teng Yü-han was a German; P'ang Ti-o was a Spaniard; and Yang Ma-no was a Portuguese. All of them were Europeans. When mentioning the customs, traditions, and products of their respective countries, they often spoke in exaggerated terms. Books like *Foreign Countries*[14] describe these countries in detail, and there is no need to repeat their contents.

NOTES

[1] Source: "Foreign Countries VII" (*wai kuo ch'i*); *Ming shih,* roll 326.
[2] *Ta-hsi-yang jen.*
[3] *Ming Institutions* (*Ming hui-tien*). The first edition, completed in 1497, was published in 1502. A revised edition was completed in 1576 and published in 1587. The authors were Ming officials.
[4] Christ and the Virgin Mary.
[5] *Shen-hsien ku*; relics.
[6] Han Yü was a famous essayist of the T'ang Dynasty.
[7] A province in South China.
[8] His Western name cannot be easily identified.
[9] The first group of Catholic missionaries came to China as early as the thirteenth century.
[10] This may refer to Sunday worship.
[11] A Taoist secret society.
[12] This refers to the military campaign against the Manchus in Manchuria.
[13] Both were converted to Roman Catholicism at a later date.
[14] *Chih-fang wai-chi,* written by Matteo Ricci and subsequently revised by Didacus de Pantoja and Julius Aleni, was published early in the seventeenth century.

7 • Lu Jo-han (Joannes B. Rodrigues): *A Letter to Li Yung-hou*[1]

People of my country love to travel abroad. Since our arrival in China, we have been well received by your government. As a token of our gratitude, we have been offering firearms[2] for whatever use your government chooses to make of them.

Upon arriving at Tungmou,[3] I congratulated myself for having the privilege of meeting you. I presented you with some of the Western books I have translated into Chinese, and I was flattered to learn that you liked them so much.

The world atlas[4] places China in the center of the world so as to be easy for the Chinese to read. Since the earth is a sphere, any country can in fact claim that it is located in the center of the world. After a Chinese sees this map or a Westerner in person, he may appreciate how large the world really is and how numerous are the countries in it. Great sages exist everywhere, East or West, since all men belong to the same species, and a man in one group has much the same endowment of mental faculties and reasoning power as a man in any other. Wherever he is, a man can achieve a great deal if he devotes himself to learning.

Through my own studies, I have come to know a little about the works of Fu-hsi, Yao, Shun, King Wen, Duke Chou, and Confucius, in addition to Buddhist and Taoist scriptures.[5] According to Chinese teaching, the Absolute[6] generates the Two Elements,[7] which in turn produce the Four Figures.[8] The Four Figures split to become the Eight Diagrams, which in turn produce Heaven, Earth, and man, and everything else in the universe. As a Westerner sees it, the nature of the Absolute seems to indicate that the Absolute itself is nonsensical and mindless. Unless the Creator is all-powerful and all-wise, how can he possibly create all the things in the universe?

As for the Three Duties,[9] the Five Constant Values,[10] the Five Cardinal Relationships,[11] and other principles that govern a country, they are secular doctrines and are similar to those we abide by in our own country. In ancient China there was a field of learning called astronomy. Owing perhaps to Ch'in Shih-huang's book-burning campaign,[12] this branch of learning is not so advanced as it should be. The Chinese rely too heavily on ancient writings; they cling fast to ancient findings even if these are sometimes erroneous. We in the West are different in the sense that from very early times we have repeatedly appraised and reappraised what we know until we reach the very root of each of the problems we try to resolve. If we apply logic to our reasoning process, it would not be difficult for us to see the absurdity of such religions as Buddhism and Taoism, which in fact can be easily refuted. Why should any man place faith in them?

We human beings come and go. There is a beginning, and there is also an end. Where did we come from? Where shall we go? These are important questions, and we have to know their answers. Yet none of the Three Religions[13] even discuss these questions. It is my hope that you, who are so wise, will pay attention to them.

The universe waxes and wanes; that is why all the years cannot be of the same length. Since the Han-T'ang times, the Chinese calendar has had to be revised many times. Even a man like Governor Kuo Shou-ching of the Yüan Dynasty[14] did not understand the underlying reason for these revisions. It is no wonder that the Chinese calendar continues to err.

His Majesty the Emperor[15] has ordered us to revise the calendar. Once the related materials are translated, a good calendar can be devised which will not err for an infinite time to come. The finer points of astronomy cannot be expressed in a few words, and we have to wait for a leisurely time when we can discuss them in detail. To understand the process of calendar-making, we must first master the fundamentals. I am looking forward to seeing you. . . .

NOTES

[1] This letter was written in 1631 or thereabouts; the addressee was a Chinese translator then serving the imperial government. A copy of the Chinese original can be found in Fang Hao, *A History of Intercourse Between China and the Non-Chinese World* (*Chung hsi chiao-t'ung shih*) (Taipei: The China Publishing Society, 1959), vol. 4, pp. 101–102.

[2] Mostly cannons.

[3] Located in modern Shantung province.

⁴ This refers to *An Atlas of the World* by Matteo Ricci.
⁵ Fu-hsi was a legendary culture hero. Yao and Shun were two saintly rulers reported to have lived in the twenty-fourth and twenty-third centuries respectively. King Wen and Duke Chou were founders of the Chou dynasty (1122?–249 B.C.).
⁶ *T'ai-chi.*
⁷ *Yin* and *yang.*
⁸ *Ssu hsiang.*
⁹ *San kang*; the duties of a prince, father, and husband.
¹⁰ *Wu ch'ang*; they are: *jen* (love or benevolence), *yi*, (righteousness), *li* (propriety), *chih* (knowledge or wisdom), and *hsin* (sincerity or faith).
¹¹ *Wu lun*; relationships between king and subjects, father and son, elder and younger brothers, and among friends.
¹² Ch'in Shih-huang (d. 210 B.C.) was the first emperor of the Ch'in dynasty; the book-burning campaign was conducted in 213 B.C.
¹³ Confucianism, Buddhism, and Taoism.
¹⁴ Kuo Shou-ching was a famous astronomer and irrigation expert of the thirteenth century.
¹⁵ Ming Ch'ung-chen (r.1628–1644).

8 • Li Ma-tou (Matteo Ricci): *The Earth Is a Sphere*[1]

The people of the T'ang Dynasty [618–906] maintained that the earth is a square, but I say that the earth is really a sphere. Which one of these two opinions is more correct?

Suppose a man is sailing on the high seas on a clear day, and there is a huge mountain 100 *li* away on the horizon. The man cannot see the peak of the mountain even though there are no clouds surrounding it. Why? Because the surface of the water is spherical, and the mountain falls below his line of vision. As the boat comes closer and closer to the mountain, the peak of the mountain will first appear, and eventually the rest of the mountain will also come into view. Had the earth been a square, the man would have been able to see the mountain a thousand *li* away, and there would not have been the slow, gradual appearance of the mountain, first the peak and then the rest. Take another example. Suppose two boats are sailing towards each other. At a distance of 40 *li*, each can see only the other's mast. Only when the distance is reduced to 5 *li* can each see the hull as well as the mast of the other boat. This phenomenon would not occur if the earth were a square. . . .

Now let us use the revolution of the sun and the moon to prove our point. The sun is so strong and bright that nothing in the space can prevent its rays from reaching the earth. The moon, on the other hand, has no light or heat of its own. It merely reflects the light of the sun, and consequently its light is dim. As our earth casts its shadow upon the moon, we have such phenomena as the half-moon and the first and last quarters of the moon. In each case, the shadowed section forms an arc, indicating the fact that the earth is a sphere. Moreover, during the eclipse of the moon, the shadow cast upon it by the earth also forms an arc. Since we know from experience that the shape of an object's shadow is the same as the shape of the object itself, we have to conclude from the above evidence that the earth is a sphere, not a square. . . .

NOTES

[1] The Chinese original appears in Li Ma-tou (Matteo Ricci), *A True Record of the Infinite Roman Catholicism* (*Wu-chi t'ien-chu cheng-chiao chen-ch'üan shih-lu*), published in China in 1592, one of the earliest Jesuit publications in China. A copy can also be found in *Chung hsi chiao-t'ung shih*, vol. 4, pp. 144–145.

9 • ANONYMOUS: *The Rites Controversy*[1]

On the thirteenth day of the twelfth month in the fifty-ninth year of K'ang-hsi [January 10, 1721] the emperor issued the following edict: "On the third day of the twelfth month [December 31, 1720] Chia-yüeh [Patriarch Mezzabarba], an envoy sent by the Italian Pope [Clement XI], came to pay me his respects and to thank me for the love and care which I have extended to the Westerners in China during past years. Considering the fact that the West is 90,000 li away and has never sent tribute missions to China since history began, I cannot but be pleased that the Pope should choose to send you to express his deep sincerity towards me. Since you, Chia-yüeh, are the Pope's duly authorized envoy, I have bestowed upon you great honors and unusual favors. Now that you are about to send a man back to the West, I would like him to take the Pope a few curios as presents. I am doing this in order to show my intention to treat all foreigners with kindness."

On the seventeenth day of the twelfth month [January 14, 1721] the emperor summoned the Western envoy Chia-yüeh, together with the Westerners whom he had brought to Peking and all other Westerners who then resided in the capital, to the Yüan-chien Study for an audience. He addressed the papal legate as follows: "Since you are the duly authorized envoy from the papacy, I would like you to speak out whatever opinions or arguments you may have in front of me. Unlike you Westerners, who relish deceptive, evasive remarks, we in China believe in speaking out frankly what we have in our minds. I cannot possibly overemphasize this point. Moreover, if you wish to speak on Chinese matters, you must read all of the Chinese classics and be thoroughly familiar with Chinese literature. Only then can you argue with me in a convincing manner. I cannot read any Western language; that is why I have always refrained from discussing anything Western. I, for one, cannot understand your insistence that all the missionaries since the time of Li Ma-tou have erred on religious doctrines while preaching your religion in China. If they did violate your religious teachings as you have said they did, you should bring them back to your own country and punish them according to your own law. Am I wrong about this? Now answer my question."

Chia-yüeh replied that Li Ma-tou had violated many of the Catholic teachings while preaching in China and that the worship of ancestral tablets and the identification of *T'ien* [Heaven] as God were examples of such violations.

In refutation the emperor said: "The worship of ancestors did not begin with Confucius; it came about as a result of people's desire to show reverence for their forebears. How can it be described as a heresy?[2] As for addressing *T'ien* as God, it is the same as people addressing me as "Ten Thousand Years"[3] or "Emperor." Though they address me differently, they are nevertheless motivated by the same reverence towards their monarch. If you take everything literally, how can I possibly be called "Ten Thousand Years" in view of the fact that the universe itself has existed only for some seven thousand six hundred years? Moreover, the questions you have raised are of such minor importance that they should more properly have been discussed with local officials. You should not have raised them in front of me in the first place."

Upon hearing this Chia-yüeh prostrated before the emperor and kowtowed, saying that he had been sent by the Pope only to pay his respects and express his gratitude; that the Pope had never authorized him to argue about Chinese customs and he, Chia-yüeh, certainly did not wish to argue about them; that he had instructed all the Westerners in China to be friendly and harmonious towards one another and to devote all their hearts and minds to the service of His Majesty the Emperor so as to repay the kindness which His Majesty had chosen to bestow upon them; and that he and his fellow Westerners would pray to Almighty God that His Majesty and Emperor would live a long, long life.

"You have said the right words," the emperor replied. "Should you wish to renew the arguments, I will argue with you to the very end. But I am glad that you have acquired a better understanding of things in general. The fault lies with those small, irrational men like Yen Tang [Maigrot, a Dominican missionary] who have brought absurd, erroneous messages to the Pope, falsely accusing such men as Li Ma-tou, Nan Huai-jen [Ferdinandus Verbiest], T'ang Jo-wang [Joannes Adam Schall von Bell], Li Lei-ssu [Ludovicus Buglio], An Wen-ssu [Gabriel de Magalhaens], Lo Li-shan[4] and Hsü Jih-sheng [Thomas Pereira] as violators of your religion. This kind of falsehood should not be allowed to continue, and my deepest sympathy goes to all of you who have become its victims."

"Listening to Your Majesty's words," said Chia-yüeh, "I feel deeply grateful for the kindness with which you speak of the old missionaries. I request Your Majesty's forgiveness for all of those who have brought absurd, erroneous messages to the Pope." Then he led all the Westerners, old and new,[5] in expressing thanks to the emperor.

On the same day [January 14, 1721] the emperor ordered a decision to be made with regard to Chia-yüeh's return to the West....

On the twentieth day of the twelfth month [January 17, 1721] the emperor ordered Yi Tu-li and Chao Ch'ang to deliver to Chia-yüeh the following edict: "The other day when you were in my presence, you must have seen for yourself the lack of discipline on the part of the Westerners and the bizarre manner in which they contradicted one another. The translator also failed in the performance of his duties: not only did he fail to transmit fully my ideas to you, but he also added his private opinions when interpreting your words to me. As long as we speak different languages and cannot comprehend each other, how can we possibly solve any problems? Report to me if you have any suggestion to make for improving this situation."

This edict was delivered to Chia-yüeh on the same day, and Chia-yüeh replied as follows: "Your humble servant is very much distressed by the fact that the Western translators have not been able to transmit clearly and fully Your Majesty's ideas to me or my replies to you. It should be stated, however, that your humble servant has no other intention in all matters except to follow Your Majesty's wishes. I have brought with me a papal proclamation,[6] and I hope that Your Majesty will order the Westerners to translate it into Chinese and present it to you for examination. Moreover, I request Your Majesty to indicate those parts in the document that are compatible with Chinese customs and traditions and can therefore be approved for implementation in China. As for other parts that are contradictory to Chinese customs and traditions, I further request that they also be pointed out so that I can transmit Your Majesty's wishes to the Pope."

On the same day [January 17, 1721] the emperor issued the following edict to his ministers: "You gentlemen are hereby instructed to bring the Westerners to Chia-yüeh's residence where the papal proclamation will be translated into Chinese. Then present the translated document to me for examination."

The next day the Westerners were brought to Chia-yüeh's residence as the emperor had ordered. The papal proclamation was translated into Chinese and was then presented to the emperor on the twenty-first day of the twelfth month [January 18, 1721].

Having read the papal proclamation, the emperor wrote the following comment: "Reading this proclamation, I have concluded that the Westerners are petty indeed. It is impossible to reason with them because they do not understand larger issues as we understand them in China. There is not a single Westerner versed in Chinese works, and their remarks are often incredible and ridiculous. To judge from this proclamation, their religion is no different from other small, bigoted sects of Buddhism or Taoism. I have never seen a document which contains so much nonsense. From now on, Westerners should not be allowed to preach in China, to avoid further trouble." . . .

NOTES

[1] Translated from a photographed copy of the Chinese original issued by the Palace Museum of Peking (*Ku-kung po-wu yüan*). The author who recorded this event cannot be identified.

[2] *Yi-tuan*.

[3] *Wan sui*.

[4] He could be either Christianus Henriques or Philippus Grinaldi; this translator has not been able to identify him.

[5] Missionaries who had resided in Peking on a more or less permanent basis and missionaries who had only recently arrived in Peking with the papal legate.

[6] This refers to the papal bull *Ex illa die* which appears as Selection 10 in this book. Instead of "bull," the word *t'iao-yüeh* is used in the Chinese original. *T'iao-yüeh* literally means agreement or treaty.

10 • CLEMENT XI: *The Papal Bull of 1715*[1]

Pope Clement XI wishes to make the following facts permanently known to all the people in the world.

Though numerous cares confronted me on the day I ascended the papal throne, I considered the sectarian controversy between the Westerners in China one of the most important. The controversy involved certain Chinese words and rituals. Some maintained that these words and rituals were heathen in nature and should therefore be prohibited, while others maintained that they were not heathen and should not be prohibited. They debated with one another but were unable to agree among themselves. Unable to resolve their differences, they appealed to me for a decision. In reply I asked them to cooperate fully and work harmoniously together. This controversy began during the reign of Pope Innocent XII; I inherited it after he died. Having carefully studied the presentations of both sides, I have, on the twentieth day of November in the year of Our Lord seventeen hundred and four, reached the following decisions:

I. The West calls *Deus* [2] the creator of Heaven, Earth, and everything in the universe. Since the word *Deus* does not sound right in the Chinese language, the Westerners in China and Chinese converts to Catholicism have used the term "Heavenly Lord" [3] for many years. From now on such terms as "Heaven" and "Shang-ti" should not be used; *Deus* should be addressed as the Lord of Heaven, Earth, and everything in the universe. The tablet that bears the Chinese words "Reverence for Heaven" [4] should not be allowed to hang inside a Catholic church and should be immediately taken down if already there.

II. The spring and autumn worship of Confucius, together with the worship of ancestors, is not allowed among Catholic converts. It is not allowed even though the converts appear in the ritual as bystanders, because to be a bystander in this ritual is as pagan as to participate in it actively.

III. Chinese officials and successful candidates in the metropolitan, provincial, or prefectural examinations, if they have been converted to Roman Catholicism, are not allowed to worship in Confucian temples on the first and fifteenth days of each month. [5] The same prohibition is applicable to all the Chinese Catholics who, as officials, have recently arrived at their posts or who, as students, have recently passed the metropolitan, provincial, or prefectural examinations. [6]

IV. No Chinese Catholics are allowed to worship ancestors in their familial temples.

V. Whether at home, in the cemetery, or during the time of a funeral, a Chinese Catholic is not allowed to perform the ritual of ancestor worship. He is not allowed to do so even if he is in company with non-Christians. Such a ritual is heathen in nature regardless of the circumstances. A Chinese convert might say: "I have not been engaged in any heathen activities; I merely wish to express my feeling of gratitude towards my ancestors. Before them I pray neither for good fortune nor for protection from disasters." The prohibition is applicable despite this argument.

VI. To avoid difficulties with non-Christians, a Catholic convert may be allowed to stand by while the non-Christians are performing the ritual of ancestor worship. [7]

VII. A Chinese convert to Roman Catholicism should not be allowed to place ancestral tablets inside his house in accordance with the Chinese custom. This is because these tablets have on them such words as "spiritual residence" [8] and "divine lord" [9] which seem to indicate that the spirits of the dead are actually residing in them. If on the other hand these tablets have on them only the names of the deceased and if, meanwhile, the making of these tablets does not in any way reflect a heathen orientation, they may be allowed to be kept at home. In any event, on both sides of each of these tablets the following words should be added: "The Heavenly Lord teaches everyone to be filial and reverent towards his parents."

Despite the above decisions, I have made it clear that other Chinese customs and traditions that can in no way be interpreted as heathen in nature should be allowed to continue among Chinese converts. The way the Chinese manage their households or govern their country should by no means be interfered with. As to exactly what customs should or should not be allowed to continue, the papal legate in China will make the necessary decisions. In the absence of the papal legate, the responsibility of making such decisions should rest with the head of the China mission and the Bishop of China. In short, customs and traditions that are not contradictory to Roman Catholicism will be allowed, while those that are clearly contradictory to it will not be tolerated under any circumstances.

The prohibitions just described were reaffirmed on the twenty-fifth day of September in the year of Our Lord seventeen hundred ten after repeated investigations of the issues involved. On the twenty-fifth day of January in the year of Our Lord seventeen hundred seven, Tournon, the papal legate to China, reiterated these prohibitions. "The prohibitions are clear and definite," said the papal legate; "The Holy Father will not tolerate any infringements." Again they were made undisputably binding in the bull issued on the twenty-fifth day of September in the year of Our Lord seventeen hundred ten. But some people continued to be disobedient. I hear that some Westerners in China said that I myself had revoked these prohibitions. Other Westerners refused to obey them on the ground that the prohibitions were not at all clear and they would not enforce them pending further clarification. Some went so far as to say that on the twenty-third day of March in the year of Our Lord sixteen hundred fifty-six Pope Alexander VII issued a bull specially allowing Chinese Catholics to practice the rituals now forbidden. I was much distressed with remarks of this kind and consequently, on the nineteenth day of March in the year of Our Lord seventeen hundred fifteen, I issue this bull ordering all Westerners in China to be thoroughly familiar with these prohibitions and to enforce them strictly the moment they receive it. Those who choose to ignore it will be punished in accordance with the law of the Catholic Church.

It is hereby decreed that all the Western missionaries now working in China and all the Westerners about to do missionary work in China are henceforth required without exception to take an oath before the Holy Altar that they will faithfully abide by the prohibitions described above and that they will not violate them under any circumstances. Once the oath is taken, it should be immediately forwarded to Rome.

NOTES

[1] This is the famous bull *Ex illa die* issued by Pope Clement XI in 1715 regarding the rites controversy. This selection is a translation of the Chinese version of the original that was written in Latin. As for Emperor K'ang-hsi's reactions to this document, see Selection 9.

[2] *Tou-ssu.*

[3] *T'ien-chu.*

[4] *Ching t'ien.*

[5] According to an imperial edict issued by Emperor K'ang-hsi in 1652, all officials, scholars, and students were required by law to assemble twice a month in the temple of Confucius to recite aloud the emperor's *Sixteen Sacred Injunctions,* once on the first and again on the fifteenth of each lunar month. As for the *Sixteen Sacred Injunctions,* see Dun J. Li, *The Ageless Chinese: A History* (New York: Scribners, 1965), p. 323.

[6] According to the Chinese custom, a newly appointed official should worship in the temple of Confucius before he assumed his post; a successful candidate in the civil service examination had to do likewise once the result of the examination was known.

[7] This seems to be contradictory to Rule II. A possible explanation is that Chinese Catholics are not allowed to witness the ritual of ancestor worship under normal circumstances, but may be allowed to do so if circumstances make it compelling.

[8] *Ling-wei.*

[9] *Shen-chu.*

11 • Inaba Kimiyama: *Jesuit Success and Failure in China*[1]

The missionaries who came to China during the seventeenth century not only possessed a martyr's spirit and devotion but were also familiar with China's customs and traditions. Knowing that the Chinese would make fun of the Western or "barbarian" garb they wore, they changed to the costume of Chinese intellectuals. They ate Chinese food and conducted their lives in the Chinese manner. In fact, they called themselves Chinese whenever they spoke with a Chinese. To make themselves more competent to defend their religion and thwart Chinese attacks on it, they studied the Chinese language and familiarized themselves with Chinese literature; in short, they passed through the same educational process as the well-educated Chinese. When preaching the gospel to the lower strata of the population, they used simple, vernacular Chinese. When mingling with the intellectuals, however, they switched to literary Chinese of the most elegant style. They impressed people first with their knowledge of science, and then only gradually and slowly did they speak of the spirit of Christianity. The purpose was to make conversion to Catholicism spontaneous and to enable the proselyte to accept the new faith of his own accord. They paid great attention to this voluntary, spontaneous method.

Except in matters that involved direct violation of Christian teachings and papal injunctions, the missionaries did their best not to infringe upon beliefs and customs that were part of the Chinese tradition. For instance, they allowed their converts to worship Confucius and ancestors. Before this decision was taken, however, they had debated among themselves and with Chinese intellectuals; it was only after long hesitation that they finally reached this decision. The reasoning was that the Chinese worshiped Confucius not because they wished to obtain wisdom or good fortune, but because they respected him as a great, virtuous man. Similarly, the worship of ancestors was motivated by the love of the deceased and the desire to express one's filial memory rather than the seeking of good fortune. The honoring of ancestral tablets did not mean that the Chinese believed that their ancestors' spirits were residing in the tablets; it only showed that the descendants, being so grateful for their entry into this world, could draw comfort from the thought that their beloved ones were still with them even though they were not. In this matter of Heaven worship, the Chinese did not regard Heaven as the blue sky in a sensible form; rather, they worshiped Heaven and Earth as the origin of the universe. This was exactly what Confucius meant when he said that the worship of Heaven and Earth was to serve God.[2] By interpretations like this, the missionaries avoided denouncing ancestor worship, whatever form it took, as a superstition. Consequently the converts were allowed to worship their ancestors. . . .

Towards the end of the seventeenth century the number of converts in the provinces where the missionaries had been active greatly increased. During its prime, Christianity could claim seven churches in Kwangtung and more than a hundred in the Kiangnan provinces [modern Kiangsu and Anhwei]. In 1663 there were 120,000 converts in the twelve provinces where statistics were available; there were no statistics in the other six provinces, but the number of converts is believed to have been large.[3] In 1696, 630 persons were baptized in Peking alone. . . .

In 1704 Pope Clement XI sent Cardinal [Charles Mailland de] Tournon as the papal legate to Peking. The papal bull which the legate had brought with him stated explicitly that the Chinese *T'ien* [Heaven] should not be mistaken for the Christian God and that all Christian converts in China were absolutely forbidden to worship ancestors. In reply Emperor K'ang-hsi explained in detail to the papal legate the meaning of ancestor worship as practiced by the Chinese. Tournon did not make public the papal bull; he summarized its most important points and issued the summary in his own name. In this summary he repudiated the emperor's theological ideas and said that those who did not obey the pope's order would be expelled from the church. The emperor ordered his arrest and sent him to Macao, where he took refuge with the Portuguese. In 1710 Tournon died while still in confinement.

In 1742 Pope Benedict XIV issued another bull, saying that those missionaries who disobeyed papal bulls would be excommunicated. As a result of this order, the Christians in China could no longer worship ancestors. This decision on the part of the pope had the greatest impact on missionary activities since the arrival of the first missionaries. Previously, regarding the pope as having interfered with China's domestic affairs and infringed upon China's independence when he insisted that his orders must be obeyed within China's territorial jurisdiction, the Ch'ing government had issued an order in 1707 which said in effect that those missionaries who had not received a permit from the Ministry of Interior to preach in China would have to repair to Macao; this amounted to saying that unless specially authorized, the activities of the Roman Catholic Church in China would be forbidden from then on. In 1717, acting upon the recommendation of Ch'en Ang, a garrison commander then stationed at Kwangtung, the imperial government prohibited any foreigner to reside within the borders of China, and those who violated this prohibition would be forever barred from returning to their own countries. Though the government's attitude towards the missionaries varied from time to time for the next hundred and thirty years, it did not lift this ban on foreign residence.[4]

NOTES

[1] Translated from Inaba Kimiyama, *A Complete History of the Ch'ing Dynasty* (*Ch'ing-ch'ao ch'üan-shih*).

[2] *Shang-ti*.

[3] At this time China proper was divided into eighteen provinces.

[4] The situation completely changed after the Opium War and the Treaty of Nanking (1842). See Chapter Ten.

CHAPTER TWO

The Canton Trade

Though British traders are reported to have arrived in China as early as 1596, it was not until 1700 or thereabouts that England began to play a major role in the China trade. As the power of Great Britain continued to grow on a world-wide scale throughout the eighteenth century, she also became by far the most important country trading in Canton, which by then had overshadowed Macao as the largest port of entry. In 1763 England defeated France in India in the Seven Years' War; with India fully secured as a British possession, she pushed forward vigorously with her commercial interests in the eastern seas, including those in Canton. Though all the major commercial powers, including the United States, participated in the profitable Canton trade, it was to Great Britain that they looked for leadership in their dealings with the Celestial Empire.

From the very beginning of Sino-European trade, China had been intent upon the attainment of two important and, for her, conflicting goals: the continuance of foreign trade, which was as profitable to the Chinese as it was to the Europeans, and her own coastal defense. The dilemma, already manifest in China's relations with Portugal and Holland (Chapter 1) became even sharper during the eighteenth century, since England was a stronger power than either Portugal or Holland. With no better guidance than her own historical experience, China tended to view European traders of the modern period in the same way as she had always viewed the nomadic caravans who passed across mountains and deserts to reach her northern frontiers for the same purpose. But a Western country like England was hardly another Turkish or Mongolian tribe: this unrecognized difference lay at the root of most of the Chinese difficulties with Western traders. However, as long as Western traders were willing to go along with the Chinese rules (Selection 12), the Chinese, out of habit if not conviction, merely followed the ancient routine of "managing barbarian affairs," which, after all, had proved effective in the past.

However satisfactory these strict rules may have been to the Chinese government, they were not only obviously inconvenient but also downright degrading from the point of view of European traders, who were prevented by them from trading on a wider basis and realizing a larger profit. Time and again the Westerners sought redress; their demands were met in some cases, but insofar as they involved a broadening of contact between Chinese and Europeans, either for groups or for individuals, they were almost without exception rejected (Selection 13). In hindsight this policy of isolating Europeans in China seems to be as naive and senseless as it was futile; it could at best succeed for a short time only. However, as long as it succeeded, it prevented "unfortunate incidents" (*shih-tuan*) and possible clashes between two groups of people entirely different in their cultural orientation. In numerous cases the Chinese were willing to go a long way to avoid the much-feared "unfortunate incidents" (Selection 14).

The Chinese may have had good reasons for regulating trade as strictly as they did, but these reasons were obviously not good enough from the British point of view. On the contrary, Great Britain wanted not only to broaden the existing trade but also to place it on an official basis and let it be conducted in the manner familiar in the West. In 1792 she sent to China a diplomatic mission headed by Lord George Macartney, who brought with him a letter from King George III requesting British representation in Peking and the opening of more Chinese ports for trade (Selection 15). Ostensibly the request was rejected on the ground that it was inconsistent with Chinese custom (Selection 16), but the real reason seems to have been security considerations: the proposal, if accepted, would not only increase contact between Englishmen and Chinese but also enhance England's knowledge about China, a knowledge which the Chinese believed would be detrimental to their interests. In 1816 when Lord Amherst arrived on a similar mission, the Chinese insisted that he should perform the humiliating ritual of "three kneelings and nine knockings of the head" (*san kuei chiu k'ou-shou*) in front of the Manchu emperor; when he refused, he was ordered to leave China immediately (Selections 18 and 19). This incident could have been dismissed as a tragicomedy of the first order in the history of international relations but for what it truly revealed: the total and almost unbelievable ignorance on the part of the Chinese about the world they lived in and the great difficulties that beset the meeting of two entirely different cultures. In any event, it is safe to assume that even if Lord Amherst had complied with the Chinese demand and had performed the kowtow, the Chinese government would not have granted his request either for the enlargement of Anglo-Chinese trade or for British representation in China. In fact, three years before Amherst's arrival, the Chinese had already devised even more stringent rules to regulate the relationship between foreign and Chinese traders, all on good grounds of preventing friction and "unfortunate incidents" (Selection 17).

The reasons for Chinese isolationism, whether fear of foreigners or unmitigated arrogance, will be debated for a long time. But no matter how long China insisted on isolating herself from outside contact, expansionist Europe would keep knocking at her door. Throughout the first half of the nineteenth century English traders, on their own initiative, attempted to open the Chinese door a little wider after their government had failed to do so. The most enterprising of them was a man named Hugh Hamilton Lindsay, known to the Chinese by his Sinicized name Hu Hsia-mi, who in the spring of 1832 sailed from Canton northward and tried to make contact with each of the prospective ports of trade along the way, including Amoy, Ningpo, Shanghai, and Weihaiwei. Having sensed that the self-imposed Chinese isolation was caused as much by fear as by ignorance, he took upon himself the task of enlightening the Chinese. Along his journey he distributed pamphlets among any group of Chinese who happened to be interested, proposing to tell them the kind of country Great Britain was and her true intention with regard to China. The most interesting of these pamphlets contained an essay entitled *A Brief Account of the British Nation and Character* (*Ying-chi-li kuo jen-p'in kuo-shih lioh-shuo,* Selection 20). The Chinese would have been better off had they listened to him, but they did not. Thus shortly before the Opium War (1839–1842), the first major clash between Europe and China, China remained as ignorant of Europe as she had been a hundred years earlier, while Europe, despite Chinese efforts, knew a great deal more about China than the Chinese would have preferred.

12 • LI SHIH-YAO: *Five Rules to Regulate Foreigners*[1]

Foreigners who live in the distant seas do not normally understand the Chinese language. Formerly, when they came to Canton to trade, they relied upon Chinese translators to conduct their business. Lately foreign merchants like Hung Jen-hui [James Flint] have proved to be not only familiar with Cantonese as well as Mandarin but also able to read Chinese words and understand their meanings. There are several who have achieved this proficiency. How could they possibly have achieved it, had not some traitorous Chinese secretly taught them? For instance, there was this treacherous man named Liu Ya-pien who taught foreigners how to read in order to swindle them. Later he served them as an adviser, incited them to start lawsuits, and even wrote petitions for them. Lacking any sense of principle, people like him have consistently conspired with foreigners to the detriment of national welfare....

Since foreigners are outside the sphere of civilization, there is no need for them to have any contact with our people other than business transactions, whenever they come to China for trade purposes. It is always better to forestall an unhappy event before it occurs than to punish the wrongdoers after it has taken place. Reviewing the file of documents, your humble servant judges that the old rules governing foreigners, drawn up by former superintendents of customs, governors, and governors-general, are not bad in the sense that they lack details. However, being proclamations intended for public circulation, they do not have behind them the force of compulsion as a legal statute. In an uncultivated, vulgar person the desire for material gain is always stronger than fear of the law; this is especially true of merchants, who often view law as a mere formality which can be violated at will. Local officials, in their desire not to create issues, often adopt an attitude of salutary neglect; no sooner has a regulation been adopted than they relax its enforcement. Only when a regulation becomes a permanent statute sanctioned by the imperial government and reinforced by strict rules of enforcement can it become prohibitive enough to achieve its purpose. The following rules, in the judgment of your humble servant, are both simple and practical enough to be adopted. They are presented here for Your Majesty's consideration.

(1) Foreigners should never be allowed to stay at Canton through the winter.

Normally foreign ships arrive at Canton in the fifth or sixth month and sail for home in the ninth or tenth month. Even if foreigners have to stay through the winter on account of business, they move from Canton to Macao after their ships have sailed for home. Lately many foreign traders, under the pretext that some of their merchandise has not been sold or that their debtors have failed to discharge their obligations in full, entrust their ships and cargoes to the care of other merchants who proceed home, while they themselves stay on in Canton. During their stay, they devote themselves to the study of the prices of various goods in different provinces, having in mind the profits they can make if somehow these goods can be purchased. Whenever there is a product they like, they provide capital and send a Chinese to buy it, hoping to realize the largest profit possible. This is precisely why England wishes to trade in Chekiang, in addition to Kwangtung Province.

Canton, being the capital of a province, is too important a place to allow foreigners to stay there on a permanent basis, since permanent residence will enable them to spy on our activities. From now on, when a foreign trader arrives at Canton, the Co-hong merchants should sell all of his goods as quickly as possible, pay him immediately, and instruct him to purchase Chinese merchandise at the earliest possible moment, so that he can return home in the ship that he came in. In case some of his merchandise cannot be sold in time and consequently the debt owed him cannot be fully paid, even though he thus has no choice but to stay in Kwangtung Province, he should nevertheless be sent to live in Macao. Meanwhile his unsold goods should be handed over to the Co-hong merchants, who will sell them for him and pay him immediately once they are sold. In the following year he will be ordered to go home in the ship of any of his countrymen who have also come to trade. After a foreign ship's departure, if it is discovered that a Chinese has secretly allowed a foreign trader to continue to stay in Canton or the foreigner is forced to wait in Canton because of the failure of some Chinese merchant to pay him for goods, the Chinese in question, whether he be a Co-hong merchant or a translator, should not only be ordered to pay his debt, if any, to his foreign creditor but also be severely punished. If local officials fail to observe this regulation or do not do their very best to force the indebted Chinese to make good his obligations to his foreign creditor, they shall be impeached and punished in accordance with their offense.

(2) While in Canton, foreigners should be ordered to reside in Co-hong headquarters so that their conduct can be carefully observed and strictly regulated.

Formerly, when foreigners came to Canton to trade, they resided in Co-hong headquarters, and the Co-hong merchants were held responsible for the visitors' conduct. Lately, many profit-minded Chinese renovate either their own houses or closed trading concerns for the purpose of renting them to foreigners to realize the largest profit possible. They close their eyes when unscrupulous Chinese, visiting these foreign residences, teach and incite the occupants to break the law. Sometimes they ordered their own servants to serve as guides to these foreigners, who wander about in the city looking for a good time. As a result, these foreigners often become drunk and commit breaches of the peace; sometimes they also visit houses of prostitution. Their behavior in this regard is of course extremely improper.

Even when engaging in trade, foreign traders often bypass Co-hong translators. Unregistered businessmen go to foreign residences in secret and conduct business with them in a clandestine manner. Together they bring about all kinds of abuse, including the evasion of tax payments. The Co-hong merchants, unable to enter private residences to carry out the rules of trade, consequently shift the blame. Among the foreigners the British are the most violent and are prone to create incidents.

From now on, the firms that have not been officially open for business should not be allowed to serve as residence for foreign traders. All foreigners, once they arrive in Canton, should be quartered instead in the officially recognized Co-hongs. They, of course, have the right to choose any of the Co-hongs with which they wish to stay. If a Co-hong does not have enough housing to accommodate them, it should rent additional housing by itself and dispatch a man or men to see to it that everything is in order. Only in this way can there be no shifting of responsibility. The number of foreign servants that a trader can bring with him should not exceed five, and under no circumstances should he be allowed to bring firearms and other military equipment to Canton. The Co-hong translators are held responsible for making a list of all foreign traders and their attendants and presenting it to local officials, including your humble servant, and other supervisory organs for examination. They should be diligent in regulating foreign personnel and should not allow any unauthorized, unscrupulous Chinese to enter foreign quarters for either social contact or business reasons. The only legal transactions are those conducted through the medium of the Co-hongs. However, the Co-hongs should neither artificially depress the prices of foreign goods nor deliberately raise the markups of native merchandise. To do so amounts to a deliberate harassment of foreign traders who have come far; such a practice is strictly forbidden.

In each of the Co-hongs where foreigners reside, honest and incorruptible guards should be placed in both the front and the rear entrances. The doors should be locked soon after sundown, and from then on no foreign servants are to be allowed to leave the premises to wander around. If a foreign trader has to go out to purchase goods, the Co-hong translator should accompany him in person. If the Co-hong translator allows him to go out without good reason and unfortunate incidents occur as a result, or if he conspires with the latter in violation of the law, he will be either reprimanded or dismissed in accordance with his offense. Local officials who do not enforce this rule vigorously will be punished, side by side with the offenders.

(3) Chinese merchants are not allowed to borrow from foreign traders, nor are foreign traders allowed to hire Chinese servants.

Formerly, whenever foreign traders sailed for other areas to trade, their purpose was merely to sell what they had brought with them; they returned to Canton to purchase native goods before they sailed for home. Nowadays these traders have become more cunning and shrewd. With idle capital in hand which amounts to hundreds of thousands of taels [of silver], some of them, in the hope of realizing even larger profits, negotiate and conclude contracts with native businessmen of great knowledge, under which the latter, with the money provided by these traders, proceed to the interior provinces to purchase goods for them. Sometimes even local shopowners borrow money from them so as to lend it to others and earn interest. Since these native businessmen and shopowners rely on foreign traders for the supply of capital so as to make a profit for themselves, they cannot but do everything in their power to please them, including adulation and flattery.

Wang Sheng-yi, for instance, had to be friendly with Hung Jen-hui after he had borrowed money from the latter to engage in business. Liu Ya-pien, wishing to obtain credit from the same foreign trader, went so far as to volunteer to write petitions for the latter to start lawsuits. As long as foreign traders have debtors in the Chinese community, naturally they will not wish to leave Canton for home; yet as long as they remain in Canton and continue illicit relationships with local businessmen, they are bound to create unpleasant incidents. It is hereby suggested that with the exception of Wang Sheng-yi and his son, who have been brought to trial in observance of Your Majesty's order, all other Chinese merchants who are indebted to foreign traders but who nevertheless have not violated any other law should be exempt from prosecution, because, had they been arrested and tried, there would doubtless be other complications. It is your humble servant's request that Your Majesty will be generous enough not to concern yourself with these offenders, provided that they make a detailed confession of their crimes and pay all the debts they owe to their foreign creditors within a set period of time. From now on, let it be known that Chinese merchants are not allowed to use foreigners' money to engage in business; in fact, they should be forbidden to borrow money from foreign traders for any purpose. If a Chinese is found to have willfully violated this rule, he should be prosecuted in the same way as if he had secretly communicated with a foreign country in the hope of obtaining material gain by immoral or unethical methods. The money he has borrowed from foreigners will be confiscated by the government, and his foreign creditors will be notified of this fact so that they will not lend any money to a Chinese again.

The servants brought by foreign traders to China are at present more than enough to render essential services; moreover, there are the Chinese translators and compradors who run errands for these traders. Despite this, there are still many unprincipled Chinese who, greedy for the money they hope to receive, willingly serve foreigners as servants. This is of course extremely improper. All the Co-hong merchants and translators should thoroughly examine and then prohibit this practice. If they are found to have condoned it, they will be prosecuted to the same extent as the Chinese servants involved.

(4) The accumulated abuse of allowing foreigners to hire messengers to transmit communications should be forever eliminated.

The postal system in Kwangtung does not hire mounted messengers. Whenever there is an official message of great urgency, it employs fast runners, nicknamed "fleet horses," who are given food as an incentive in addition to the payment of regular wages. Though their names do not appear in the official roster as governmental employees, rarely are the "fleet horses" hired by civilians. Lately foreign traders have sent their Chinese agents as far as Kiangsu and Chekiang to purchase merchandise, and they often hire and dispatch "fleet horses" in advance to find about the price of the merchandise which they wish to purchase. In the case of Wang Sheng-yi, for instance, long before the arrival of an order for his arrest, he had already heard about the order and fled. Since then your humble servant has arrested the informer as well as the messenger for further investigation. Here is another example. In the tenth month of last year and again in the ninth month of this year, the Westerner Liu Sung-ling [Augustinus von Hallerstein], who served on the Board of Astronomy in Peking, petitioned the imperial government to hire two expert astronomers, An Kuo-ning [Andreas Rodriguez] and Fang Shou-yi [J.F.M.D. d'Ollieres] of Macao, who, the petitioner said, were willing to proceed to Peking to help; he quoted letters from these two astronomers as proof of their willingness to serve. Had there been no Chinese messengers to bring these letters to him, how could Liu Sung-ling possibly have received them? Ignorant though your humble servant is, he proposes that only local officials at Canton should be in charge of all matters governing foreigners and that private transmission of messages by Chinese on behalf of their foreign employers should be forever forbidden. An order should be issued to all Co-hong merchants, "fleet horses," and other foot messengers that from now on they will not be allowed to transmit messages for foreigners. If they are impudent enough to violate this rule, they should be put under arrest and punished in accordance with their offense, regardless of whether they are messengers or merely go-betweens who have hired messengers on behalf of foreign traders. If the Westerners in Macao have any message of a business nature to be presented to the Board of Astronomy, they should be ordered to present it to the Office of Coastal Defense, which in turn presents it to your humble servant's office with detailed comments. Your humble servant, after weighing the importance of their request, will then transmit it to the imperial government for possible action.

(5) To strengthen inspectional work and to prevent possible disturbances, additional police forces should be introduced in the area where foreign ships are anchored.

Once a foreign ship enters the harbor, it is usually anchored in the Huangp'u [Whampoa] area. Each ship contains anywhere from one hundred to two hundred persons. There are all kinds of people among them, and most of them are headstrong and violent in temperament. It is very difficult to restrain them and they often create incidents by breaches of the peace. Meanwhile unscrupulous people in the vicinity, including those in the brothels, are only too happy to persuade them to get drunk or engage in illicit sexual relations. These foreigners buy and sell in total disregard of the official channel, with a resulting loss of tariff revenues. All these malpractices should be strictly forbidden.

The closest water-police station is located about 3 *li* away from the ship anchorage, and the area where foreign ships are normally anchored is too sandy and shaky to build another police headquarters. The usual procedure is this. Whenever a foreign ship arrives, the garrison headquarters at Canton dispatches a police sergeant, together with twenty soldiers, to the beach area, where they erect a temporary shed to live in and patrol day and night. But the rank of a sergeant is too low to command respect, and he cannot work effectively in suppressing disturbances. It is hereby suggested that as of the day that a foreign ship enters the port, a reserve officer shall be designated by your humble servant to be in full charge of the ship in question; he, assisted by the soldiers in the temporary shed, will be able to prevent any irregularities that might take place. Since a reserve officer does not receive any salaries, it is further suggested that whoever has been assigned to the task should be given a monthly allowance of eight taels of silver to be spent on food and other daily necessities, and that the said allowance should be appropriated from the surplus funds of the Maritime Customs. Meanwhile a patrol boat from the nearby Hsint'ang police headquarters will be specifically assigned to join the boat from the Left Wing Garrison that normally patrols this area. The two boats will cooperate in the performance of their duties and will not withdraw until the foreign ship that they are assigned to guard leaves the port. If the men in charge of these boats are found to have defaulted in the performance of their duties, and unfortunate incidents occur as a result, they shall be brought to account and punished accordingly.

Having studied the situation of foreign trade at Canton, your humble servant believes that the five rules described above are what we need to strengthen our preventive and inspectional work. . . . If adopted, they will not only endear foreign traders to us in view of our expressed regard for their welfare; they will also prevent unfortunate incidents. Meanwhile the relative position between China and foreign countries will become clearer and more exact. . . .[2]

NOTES

[1] This memorial, dated 1759, was written by the governor-general of Liangkwang Provinces. A copy of the Chinese original can be found in Kuo T'ing-yi, *A History of Modern China (Chin-tai Chung-kuo shih)* (Taipei: Commercial Press, 1952), pp. 380–385.

[2] This petition and the measures contained in it were approved by the imperial government on December 14, 1759.

13 • CH'ANG-LIN: *A Reply to Henry Browne's Request*[1]

With regard to the petition submitted by manager P'o-lang [Henry Browne] of England, His Excellency Ch'ang-lin, governor-general of Liangkwang, on the first day of the fourth month [April 29, 1794], replies as follows:

ITEM NO. 1: "We request a list of tariff rates for all goods imported into or exported from China in British bottoms. Once we know the tariff rates, we will pay accordingly."

REPLY: Since items of merchandise vary in quality and are priced differently, tariff rates cannot be decided in advance. In the fifty-eighth year of Ch'ien-lung [1793] a similar request was made by the British tribute-bearing envoy [Lord George Macartney] in the capital; it was then rejected. To grant this request now is out of the question.

ITEM NO. 2: "Whenever traveling on the water route between Canton and Macao, Englishmen are required to pay taxes not only on the goods they transport but also on their persons. If these impositions are legal, we wish to obtain a receipt for the taxes we have paid. If not, we wish to be exempt from such impositions."

REPLY: These impositions on the transportation of goods and personnel were in accordance with an old statute which has been abolished since the eleventh month of the fifty-eighth year [1793]. The soldiers who continued to enforce the defunct law have been dismissed from their posts and punished accordingly. They were locked up in the cage and paraded along the river as a warning to others. We shall again make the prohibition widely known through public proclamation. If the exaction continues, foreigners can petition for redress and the offenders will be punished in accordance with their offense. All goods on which taxes have been paid at the port of entry are exempt from further taxation, whether they are transported from or into Macao. Clothes, personal luggage, daily necessities, food items, and a ceremonial sword when carried by its rightful owner are all exempt from taxation. However, goods that are purchased in China will be subject to taxation as usual, whenever foreigners travel with them. This rule is necessary because many unscrupulous Chinese have transported goods in foreign ships for the purpose of evading tax payments.

ITEM NO. 3: "After we have paid taxes at Canton, we are again required to pay them at Macao. We request Your Excellency to look into this matter. If this double taxation is legal, we will of course pay it. If it is not, we hope to be exempt from it."

REPLY: All foreign ships that arrive at Macao via Takuan will pay taxes when the cargo is unloaded. Empty bottoms that arrive at Macao are not subject to taxation; taxes will be levied, however, when cargo is loaded in them. Whether leaving or sailing into Macao, all ships that pass through Tsunghsingk'ou, Hsi-p'aot'ao, Fushank'o, Tzunik'ou, and Aomenk'o should pay a transit tax for the goods that have been purchased in China. Foreign goods upon which tariff duties have already been levied, plus clothing and food for personal uses, are not subject to this kind of taxation.

ITEM NO. 4: "We foreigners love to take a stroll, being fearful that if we do not, we might incur illness. We are not allowed either to enter the city of Canton or to engage in outdoor activities in the countryside. We request Your Excellency to look into this matter and allow us to enter the city. If this cannot be done, please assign an area in the suburb where we can ride horses or take a walk. If this request is granted, we can assure Your Excellency that we will not become sick."

REPLY: The city of Canton is heavily populated. There are houses everywhere, and not a single spot of empty space can be found. If we allow you to amuse yourselves in the countryside, unfortunate incidents are bound to occur, due to the fact that you and the Chinese cannot communicate with each other. I understand, however, that being confined to the foreign quarters, you may become ill as a result of weariness. From now on, if foreigners wish outdoor recreation and have made a request to that effect, their request will be granted twice a month, on the third and again on the eighteenth day, and a man will be dispatched to escort them to the Hait'ung Temple or Ch'enchia Park where they can relax in whatever manner they please. This measure is taken so as to show our concern for their welfare. However, they should return to their quarters before sundown, since they are not allowed to stay overnight. The Co-hongs are hereby instructed to strictly regulate their conduct, and under no circumstances should sailors, who tend to be the cause of unfortunate incidents, be allowed to go with them.

ITEM NO. 5: "We have many sailors in our ships. Once they become ill, we tend to become ill too. We request Your Excellency to grant us permission to build thatched houses along the river or on some of the islands, so that whenever a sailor is ill, he can be moved to these houses. In this way not only will he recover faster, but we will not also incur his illness."

REPLY: Once a ship arrives at Huangp'u, foreigners are allowed to build temporary sheds on the nearby shore, which will be demolished once the ship leaves the port. We granted this privilege in order to show our special consideration for the welfare of the visiting foreigners. If thatched houses of a more permanent nature are to be built, who will take care of them after the visitors have left and when they are no longer occupied? To allow foreigners to take care of these houses themselves would mean that some of them would reside there on a permanent basis. Since we do not have administrative personnel to stay with them, we cannot prevent Chinese from going there to cause disturbances or exact illegal payments. What can we do should there be fire, flood, banditry, or theft? Because of these considerations, we cannot grant this request.

ITEM NO. 6: "After a cargo ship has left Canton, some foreigners have to stay behind to take care of unfinished business. But the regulation says that once a ship leaves the port, all of her former occupants have to proceed to Macao immediately. We request Your Excellency to let them stay in Canton for a few more days or proceed to Macao at any time that is convenient to them in view of the important business they have to take care of after the ship's departure."

REPLY: From now on, whenever foreigners have important business to take care of after their ship's departure, they are allowed to stay in Canton for as long as twenty days. Intentional delay beyond this time limit is a violation of the regulation and is therefore strictly forbidden.

ITEM NO. 7: "Our trade with China is controlled by the Co-hongs. If we are allowed to deal with anyone we choose, the Co-hongs would not be able to control us."

REPLY: A foreign ship that arrives at Canton can trade with any of the Co-hongs it chooses. There has never been a single case wherein trade is controlled by one man. If there is, foreign traders are allowed to start lawsuits against the offender who will be prosecuted to the full extent of the law.

ITEM NO. 8: "The custom has been that whenever an English ship arrives at Canton, only Chinese are permitted to repair to the customs office to pay tariff duties. We request Your Excellency's permission to pay these duties directly to the customs office ourselves."

REPLY: In paying tariff duties, all foreign currencies have to be converted into pure silver before they can be accepted by the customs office. Furthermore, the rules governing the payment of tariff duties are so numerous and complicated that it is unlikely that foreigners are able to comprehend them fully so as to pay the duties themselves. That is why the Co-hongs are entrusted with the responsibility of paying the duties for them. In fact, the former governor-general Li Shih-yao once wrote a memorial elaborating on this problem. Moreover, there are bad as well as good officials in the customs office; if foreigners are allowed to pay tariff duties directly to the customs office, some of these officials might cheat or even bully them, or, worse still, exact bribes by deliberately creating difficulties. For these reasons, this request will not work well if granted; it is therefore rejected.

ITEM NO. 9: "We Englishmen love to learn to speak Chinese. If Your Excellency allows the Cantonese to teach us, we would be thoroughly familiar with the Chinese law."

REPLY: Foreigners who trade in Canton are not allowed to hire too many Chinese as servants other than translators and compradors whose service is essential to the transaction of their business. This is a regulation that has been submitted to and subsequently approved by the imperial government. If they wish to learn to speak Chinese, foreigners can learn it from their Chinese translators and compradors. They should not be allowed to hire other Chinese for this purpose. To do so is a violation of our regulations.

ITEM NO. 10: "Each British ship has its own captain. If a member of the crew has violated the Chinese law, he alone is responsible for his offense. Innocent people in other ships should not be implicated for his wrongdoings."

REPLY: If a foreigner commits a crime, the representative of his firm is responsible for handing him over to the proper authorities for prosecution. Only the offender will be punished upon conviction; innocent persons should of course not be implicated. This request is granted.

ITEM NO. 11: "We Englishmen have our own flags. Though the Americans speak the same language and wear the same kind of clothing as we do, they have their own flags. We hope that we will not be mistaken for them."

REPLY: This request has been filed for reference. Whenever an unfortunate incident occurs, we shall of course identify the flag before starting legal proceedings against the offender. Rest assured that no mistake will be made on this score.

NOTES

[1] This document was written by the governor-general of Liangkwang and was addressed to the representative of the British East India Company at Canton. A copy of the Chinese original can be found in *Chin-tai Chung-kuo shih*, pp. 390–393.

14 • CH'IEN-LUNG: *On the Payment of Debts to Foreign Traders*[1]

In a memorial presented by the Ministry of Justice in connection with Ni Hung-wen's indebtedness to a British merchant named Francis Wood, Li Chih-ying, governor of Kwangtung, having failed to exact payment from Ni Hung-wen by means of flogging, suggested that further flogging should be administered before the convicted is punished by exile, while in the meantime continuous efforts were made to assure that the debtor will fulfill his obligations towards his foreign creditor. The suggested measure was approved by the Ministry, which further recommended that Li Shih-yao, governor-general of Liangkwang, should be reprimanded, that the Ministry should be authorized to interrogate Li Chih-ying for possible indictment, and that both officials should be ordered to confiscate and then auction off Ni Hung-wen's property, the proceeds of which would be used to meet obligations to his foreign creditor. The payment is to be made within a one-year period, at the end of which the two aforesaid officials are required to make a report. If the convicted man cannot pay at the end of this one-year period, the governor-general, governor, and their subordinates, together with the heads of the prefecture and the subprefecture who have handled this case, should contribute part of their salaries and allowances to meet the debt obligations which the convicted man is unable to fulfill.[2] A decree will be issued in my name when the debt is paid in full to the aforesaid foreign merchant. All this is done in order to show our kindness and sympathy towards all the foreigners who have come from afar to trade in China.

These foreign traders who take great risks in passing across the high seas to reach China are motivated by the realization of profits. Only when we trade with them in an honest manner so as to enable them to achieve their goal can we maintain our dignity as a nation. If there is one single unscrupulous Chinese who deliberately deceives them and causes them to lose goods or capital, he should be immediately brought to trial and punished accordingly. Yet, in the case of Ni Hung-wen, Li Chih-ying imposed upon the convicted man only light penalties, while ordering the parties involved to settle their disputes outside of the court. This is what I would call "the imposition of a sentence without being followed by enforcement," and the result has been to close avenues of redress for this lonely, stranded foreigner. Is this the proper way for a frontier minister to punish the guilty and treat kindly foreigners who come from afar?

Impartiality and fairness are the principles with which China governs all the foreigners who have come to live under her jurisdiction. The purpose to achieve is to induce in them a feeling of gratitude as well as of fear. If we view them as insignificant and allow local bullies to cheat or push them around, if we are only interested in protecting our own people and show no desire to redress their grievances which they have brought to the attention of our government officials, how can you blame them for harboring resentment at heart, since under the law they are not allowed to proceed to Peking to appeal? When they return home and spread the word of their unredressed grievances among their own people, will these foreigners not detest and despise our governor-general and governor and regard them as unworthy of the positions they hold?

Moreover, the decision I have made in this matter has a deeper meaning than appears on the surface. In the latter part of the Han, T'ang, Sung, or Ming Dynasty, the rulers were completely ignorant of the principle of treating foreigners with kindness. They viewed lightly or even insulted foreign countries when the latter were weak and impotent, only to become frightened appeasers after they became powerful and aggressive. This blind complacency and aimless drift eventually resulted in disasters of catastrophic proportions, from which they could not retrieve themselves. This is the reason why the Sung and Ming regimes passed into oblivion, a lesson which we can study with profit.

Now that the nation is at its peak of power and prosperity and all of our tributary states are fearful of our military might, it is unlikely that they will harbor rebellious thoughts at heart and venture to challenge our authority. However, thinking of the difficulties that might arise in the future, we cannot but take preventive measures. As far as this case involving a British trader is concerned, you, the governor-general and the governor, may consider it in financial terms alone and dismiss it as insignificant. But its ramifications could be very great. When continued, a small stream can emerge to become a roaring river. . . .

You generals, governors, and governors-general are appointed by and responsible to me, and you should try to understand my intentions without fail. Your security depends solely on this understanding. The same thing can be said about my descendants, who can preserve their regime for an infinite time to come if they continue, respectfully and unfailingly, to abide by my instructions. Let this decree be not only transmitted to all incumbent generals, governors, and governors-general but also listed as a transferable order to be observed by all of their successors. To ignore or violate it is not to be tolerated. A copy of this decree should be kept in the Upper study,[3] to be observed by all without fail.

NOTES

[1] This decree was issued to the governor-general and governor at Canton on January 5, 1777. The Chinese original appears in *Tung-hua Records* (*Tung-hua lu*), roll 84.

[2] The total debt amounted to 11,000 taels of silver. One year later, Ni Hung-wen, being totally bankrupt, was found to have been unable to pay. His brother and nephew contributed 6,000 taels and government officials, from the governor-general to the head of the subprefecture, contributed the remaining 5,000 taels. Thus the debt was finally paid in full. Ni Hung-wen was exiled to Ili (Central Asia) as his share of the punishment.

[3] *Shang shu-fang*, the emperor's personal library.

15 • JE-WO-ERH-JIH TI-SAN (GEORGE III): *A Letter to the Emperor of China*[1]

We in Great Britain know the great size of China and the numerousness of her people. We also know that you, the Grand Emperor, regard the affairs of the whole world as your own and supervise the peoples in other parts of the world from time to time. You protect not only Chinese territories but also foreign countries; foreign countries are only too happy to accept your overlordship because it provides them with peace at home as well as a harmonious relationship with their neighbors. Whatever knowledge or skill foreign countries may have, you the Grand Emperor only wish them to do their best to develop it further, so it can become as perfect as it is variable. For you, in your usual generosity, are concerned with the welfare of all of mankind.

My country has long wished to send an envoy to China; but owing to the repeated occurrence of warfare around our territory, we have delayed in taking such a step until the present time. Now that we have defeated all the enemies around us and secured peace at home, we are building large ships and sending our wise men to all parts of the world. We are doing this not because we wish to acquire new territories, of which we have already an ample number, nor to realize large profits through trade, but because we want to learn about the various countries of the world, the things they produce and the customs they cherish, in the hope that by maintaining a mutually beneficial relationship we can learn from them as they can learn from us. Our knowledge about different countries in the world is incomplete in some cases and all but nonexistent in others. Though we have always wanted to learn about them, it is not until recent years that, by the grace of God, we are able to pursue this goal. We want to know the fauna and flora of all countries and also their native products, so that we can exchange what we have for what we lack, to the benefit of all parties concerned. Because of this consideration, we want to be thoroughly familiar with the customs, traditions, and laws of each of the countries with which we wish to be engaged in trade.

Now I have heard that of all the countries in the world China is by far the most superior in the matter of customs, traditions, and laws. It is so superior that it inspires admiration and respect from all other countries in the world. The more I think of this, the more earnestly I wish to submit myself so as to partake of your great civilization.[2] Recently not only have we pacified the Atlantic Ocean; we have also defeated Holland and other countries in the Indian Ocean, none of whom, from now on, will have any reason to wage war against us. Since we have established peace with all the countries in the world, we wish to take this opportunity to present a petition to the Emperor of China and to pay our tribute,[3] in the hope that we may receive some benefit in return. My countrymen have in the past gone to Chinese ports for trade which brings benefit to China as well as England. Each of our two countries has its own laws governing such an intercourse, which naturally should be obeyed by the nationals of both sides. It is my sincere hope that wherever my countrymen go, they will conduct themselves in a proper manner and will not cause disturbances. However, there are bad as well as good elements in every group, and unfortunate incidents are bound to occur in the absence of a person who is in a position to strictly regulate them. In the hope of securing eternal peace and friendship with China, I believe that I should send a man with my authority to reside in China. His duty is to govern my countrymen in your country, punishing them when they are wrong and protecting them when they have genuine grievances. Only in this way can peace and harmony be maintained between our two countries.

For this reason, I am sending an envoy to China in full charge of these matters. Knowing that he must be a man with great understanding, knowledge, and authority and should be also able to converse with you, I have specifically designated Viscount George Macartney, Baron of Lissanoure, for this purpose. Lord Macartney, a kinsman of mine, is a sincere, honest, and loyal minister who has participated in deliberations on our national policy. He brings two documents from me to indicate his credentials. He was selected from among the most learned men in our country; he has had considerable experience in the administration of state affairs. He was once an envoy to Russia and an administrative official in Bengal, a British possession in India, besides serving capably in a variety of other capacities. I am sending him as my chief tribute-bearing envoy[4] to you, the Grand Emperor of China. In this petition you will find the seal of Great Britain which authorizes him to speak on my behalf after the petition has been duly presented. I am requesting you the Grand Emperor to grant him an audience and to treat him in your usual generous manner. When you see and speak to him, it is as if you were seeing and speaking to me.

Fearful that the chief tribute-bearing envoy might not be able to perform all his duties owing to circumstances beyond his control, I am also sending as his deputy Sir George Leonard Staunton, who is as learned and esteemed as his distinguished superior. Sir George has had administrative experience in the West Indies and once served as a negotiator for peace with King Tippo Suetamn of Hindustan in India. Because of these experiences and the ability he has clearly demonstrated, he is to accompany the chief tribute-bearing envoy in this trip and to assist the latter in every way he can. It is my earnest hope that you the Grand Emperor will treat him in the same generous manner as you would doubtless accord to Lord Macartney.

Since I know that you the Grand Emperor are of a saintly merit, authoritatively virtuous, and lovingly impartial, I request your indulgence to allow my envoys to visit Peking so that they may steep themselves in the great civilization of China and when they return to England, can also impart virtue to their fellow countrymen. Should you the Grand Emperor decide to utilize their knowledge and skill and to assign to them tasks of a technical nature, by all means do so. If for any reason they cannot perform the assigned tasks within China, they will send a letter to us, and we will see to it that your request will be honored and the purchase will be made in the Atlantic region. As for my countrymen who either reside in China or come to China for trading purposes, they should of course conduct themselves in the most proper manner. As long as they do this, it is my sincere hope that you, the Grand Emperor, will continue to extend to them your usual generosity and patronage. If they commit crimes, they should of course be punished. If on the other hand they are not at fault, I should hope that they will not lose the benefits which you, the Grand Emperor, have chosen to bestow upon them.

Before the tribute-bearing envoys leave England, I have instructed them in great detail that they should be reverent and respectful when meeting with you, the Grand Emperor, so as to show our utmost sincerity in this matter. If they please you, they please me too.

May the Almighty God bless the Grand Emperor of China with everlasting peace! May He also bless England with the same!

The year of Our Lord seventeen hundred ninety-second and the thirty-second year of the reign of George the Third, King of England.

NOTES

¹ The Chinese original (or translation), which Emperor Ch'ien-lung read, was not only couched in servile terms but also written in unidiomatic, spoken Chinese. Imagine King George referring to himself as *Ta Hung Mao*—the Great Red Hair! Source: *A Collection of Old Documents* (*Chang-ku ts'ung-pien*), vol. 8.
² The Chinese original is *hsiang-hua shu-ch'eng,* a phrase traditionally used by China's tributary states when addressing the Chinese emperor.
³ The Chinese original is *chin-hsien piao kung,* "to present a petition (or memorial) and pay a tribute."
⁴ *Cheng kung-shih.*

16 • CH'IEN-LUNG: *A Reply to George III, King of England*¹

Entrusted by Heaven to govern all men, the Emperor wishes to make the following decree known to the King of England:

Despite the fact that your country is located in the distant seas, you, as its ruler, have expressed your sincere desire to partake of the great civilization of China. You have sent your envoys to my court across the high seas: on your behalf they have presented a memorial, kowtowed on the occasion of my birthday,² and presented to me native products as tribute. How earnest and sincere a king you must be! As I read your memorial, I am particularly impressed with the sincerity with which you express yourself, indicating the fact that you, as the king of your country, are truly respectful and obedient. How much I am really pleased!

Taking into consideration the fact that the two tribute-bearing envoys have journeyed a long distance to carry out their mission, I have decided to be specially generous with them. I ordered my ministers to bring them to me for an audience, honored them with banquets, and repeatedly showered them with presents. This was done in order to show how kindly we view people of distant countries. As for the 600 men (officials, sailors, and servants) who have already returned to Chushan³ without proceeding to Peking, they shall also be given generous gifts, so that sharing the favor that I have chosen to bestow upon them, they will have no reason to feel that they have been discriminated against.

In your memorial you request my permission to allow a representative of yours to reside in the Celestial Empire so as to supervise the British trade. Since the granting of this permission is inconsistent with Chinese customs, I am afraid I must say that this request simply cannot be entertained. In the past we have occasionally allowed foreign representatives to reside in Peking after they had arrived here of their own accord. Once in China, they changed to Chinese dress and observed Chinese customs; they were granted houses to reside in and were not allowed to return to their home countries.⁴ This is the established law of the Celestial Empire, and you, as the king of your country, must have heard about it. Now you have expressed your wish to send an Englishman to reside in Peking. Since he will not follow the example of early Westerners who, after arriving at Peking, never returned home and since we, on our part, will not allow him to travel back and forth to transmit information, I cannot see how this representation you have requested can be successfully arranged.

Moreoever, the territories under the jurisdiction of the Celestial Empire are numerous and large. Whenever a foreign envoy comes to Peking, his conduct and movement, together with the provision and maintenance of his living quarters, are regulated in accordance with an established rule. There has never been a case in which we would allow him to do whatever he pleases. Since your representative cannot communicate with the Chinese because of the language difference and since he does dress differently from the rest of us, I do not know where I can place him if he is allowed to stay in Peking. Nor do I wish to compel him to follow the example of early Westerners who changed to Chinese dress upon their arrival at China—the Celestial Empire never relishes the thought of forcing foreigners to do things against their will. Would you entertain the thought of having a representative of the Celestial Empire reside permanently in your country? Of course not. Moreover, there are many Western countries, and yours is only one of them. If I grant your request to have an Englishman residing in Peking, how can I refuse a similar request from others? This simply cannot be done. How can you expect me to change the established rule of more than one hundred years simply to satisfy the wish of one king?

Now we come to the matter of supervising British trade. Your countrymen have been trading in Macao for a long time, and all of them have always been favorably received. Formerly when Portugal, Italy, and other countries sent their envoys to China, they also requested sympathetic consideration of their trade in China. Convinced of their earnestness and sincerity in this matter, the Celestial Empire treated traders of these countries in the most helpful and generous manner. For instance, when the Kwangtung merchant Wu Chao-p'ing defaulted in paying his debts to his foreign creditors, the imperial government ordered the governor-general at Canton to use official funds to pay off the debts in advance; in the meantime it brought the defaulter to justice and punished him severely in accordance with his offense. I presume that people of your country have heard about this incident. Since we are extremely generous with foreign traders, what purpose does it serve for a foreign country to have a representative at Peking? Why do you have to make this impossible request which is clearly a violation of our rule? Moreover, how can a foreign representative at Peking take care of his country's trade at Macao, which is tens of thousands of *li* away?

Now we come to the matter of admiring the Celestial Empire and wishing to observe and learn about its great civilization. The Celestial Empire has its own laws and customs, which are different from yours. Even if your representative can learn about them, you cannot transplant them to your own country, since you have your own laws and customs. In other words, no useful purpose will be served even if your representative learns about them.

The Celestial Empire comforts and cherishes all the people in the world. Meanwhile it also does its utmost to bring about the best administration within its jurisdiction. It does not value strange objects and foreign items, however valuable they are. Thinking that the tribute you sent me was sincerely inspired and came from afar, I have ordered responsible officials to accept it. Because the virtue of the Celestial Empire has spread far and wide, hundreds of countries have come here to pay their tribute, by land or by sea. Their tribute consists of all kinds of products which your chief envoy has seen for himself. We in China do not attach great importance to strange or clever objects, and we have no need of your manufactured products.

In short, the representation of your country at Peking is neither consistent with our customs nor beneficial to your own country. I take this opportunity to make my view clear, as I have already ordered your envoy to proceed safely home. I hope that you will understand my good intentions, to be doubly sincere in your submisiveness and to pledge unconditionally your loyalty and obeisance. I also hope that you will continue to bring happiness to your country and to enjoy with all of your countrymen the blessing of peace.

In addition to the primary and secondary gifts that have been given to the chief and deputy envoys and all their subordinates, including translators and soldiers, I am issuing you this decree to be presented to you when your envoys return home. As far as you are concerned, you will receive gifts in addition to the treasures normally presented to a foreign sovereign, including variegated satin, gauzed silk, paintings and other art objects, utensils, and many other valuable items, all of which are listed in a separate sheet. Accepting these gifts, you should understand how lovingly I feel towards you.

NOTES

[1] This is the first of the so-called "three decrees" (*ch'ih-yü*) issued by Emperor Ch'ien-lung in reply to King George's letter that appears as Selection 15. It is dated the 29th day of the eighth month (October 3) 1793. A copy of the Chinese original can be found in *Chang-ku t'sung-pien*, vol. 3.
[2] The emperor was then celebrating his eightieth birthday.
[3] Known as Chusan Islands today, located off the coast of modern Chekiang Province.
[4] The emperor had in mind the early Jesuits.

17 • TEH-CH'ING: *Co-hong Responsibilities*[1]

Once a foreign trader arrives at Canton from the distant seas, he depends upon the Co-hong merchants to transact his business. Through the assistance of these merchants, not only does he reap the profits which he has come to seek, he also becomes more cultured as a result of exposing himself to a superior civilization. Our Celestial Empire pursues this dual goal in order to show our generosity and kindness towards all the foreigners in the world.

Since your slave's[2] assumption of his present office,[3] he has followed the regulations of the past and has not, fortunately, encountered any dispute that requires his immediate attention. As he examines the old files, he has noticed that all lawsuits involving the failure of Chinese merchants to fulfill their debt obligations were, as a normal procedure, referred to the office of the governor or governor-general for appropriate action. The assets of the indebted merchants were first frozen and then auctioned off to satisfy the demands of their creditors. If the amount was insufficient to meet the demands, their successors, i.e., the merchants who had taken over their business, were required to make good the difference. If they had no successors after they themselves had gone bankrupt, all other Chinese merchants were required to contribute funds to pay off their debts. If indebtedness to foreigners continued to exist after the above measures had been taken, the superintendent of the customs office would consult the offices of the governor and the governor-general to make a special report to the imperial government, and those who were responsible for failing to pay off their debts would be severely punished. This has been the procedure followed in the past without any exception.

In the fifteenth year of Chia-ch'ing [1801], for instance, Teng Chao-hsiang of the Fu-lung Co-hong fled from Canton, having failed to make good his financial obligations towards his foreign creditors. After consulting with Governor-general Pai-ling, Ch'ang-hsien, then the superintendent of the customs office, issued an order to all local officials for his arrest. Meanwhile all his property was confiscated, and the confiscated property was employed to offset his debt obligations. Later, when it was found that Kuan Hsiang and his son Kuan Ch'eng-fa had been employees for this firm for many years, the younger Kuan was recommended by merchant Li Yen-yü to take over Fu-lung's business. Kuan was ordered by the government to pay with his own money the debts that his predecessor had owed; he would be compensated, however, when Teng's familial property, which was then under investigation, became available. Though the financial aspect of this case has been successfully settled, Teng Chao-hsiang, being still at large, has not been arraigned and punished. We have ordered local officials to double their effort for his arraignment, to make sure that he will be brought to trial and be punished in accordance with his offense.

As your slave sees it, the responsibility of the Co-hong merchants is extremely important, since they handle foreign merchandise valued at hundreds of thousands of taels and are required to pay tariff duties that amount to tens or sometimes hundreds of thousands of taels. Unless a man is as wealthy as he is honest, he will not be able to shoulder this responsibility. From the very beginning a man only needs the recommendation of one or two merchants before he is allowed to establish a firm to trade with foreigners, and in each case no report has been made to the imperial government to secure its approval. This to me is a very careless procedure. Whenever a merchant defaults, often all in the group of the Co-hongs are implicated and have to make good his debt obligations. Moreover, there are unscrupulous, financially unsound merchants who, when a foreign ship comes into port, approach foreign traders on an unauthorized, individual basis, offering high prices for the foreign goods they want to buy and asking low prices for the native goods they wish to sell. At the moment they are interested only in acquiring as much foreign merchandise as possible, giving little thought that they may lose money in the process. When the time arrives to fulfill their debt obligations towards the government, they may find themselves in such a bad situation that they are no longer able to do so.

Having studied this situation carefully, your slave is convinced that the basic cause for these difficulties is the absence of a head merchant to supervise or coordinate the activities of all the merchants. Nowadays all the merchants compete to acquire more business for themselves; one follows the example of another until this competition has become an accepted custom. Since your slave's arrival at his post, he, learning about this practice, has taken strict measures to prohibit it. Meanwhile, with the assistance of one or two honest, financially sound merchants, he has made periodical inspections and has done his very best to rectify the existing situation. He is happy to report that during the past two years the merchants have not made any errors in this respect.

However, not all merchants can reach complete solvency in a short time. Cases of default still exist whenever merchants are required to fulfill their obligations towards the government. If we dismiss all the financially unsound merchants, we have to find new merchants to replace them, which is very difficult at this moment. After consulting several times with Chiang Yu-hsien,[4] we decided that instead of making replacements which will not achieve any purpose, we should strive to correct the existing abuses. Though the merchants' tricks are numerous, they cannot hide them from their own colleagues. The difficulty, as your slave sees it, lies in the absence of a leader responsible for their conduct. As a result, wealthy merchants stay in the background to avoid blame, while the less affluent ones compete with one another to obtain more business for themselves. As this situation continues, it becomes increasingly difficult to reverse the trend, and the revenue of the Customs Office suffers as a result.

To rectify and regenerate the business of the Customs Office, we should first examine the situation of the merchants. To eliminate abuse, we have to locate responsibilities. The first step in this direction is the selection of a wealthy, impartial merchant to supervise all the activities of the Co-hongs that trade with foreigners. Whenever trade is conducted, he should take the leadership in negotiating with foreigners. The prices of goods should be determined in accordance with market demand and in conformity with the principle of equity: they should not be raised or lowered at will. Under no circumstances are individual merchants allowed to conduct business with foreign traders secretly or on an unauthorized basis. If a merchant is found to have violated this regulation in fact while observing it in appearance, the head of the merchants should report this violation to the responsible officials, and the offender will be prosecuted accordingly. Meanwhile your slave will from time to time instruct all the Co-hong merchants to shun luxury and to practice thrift and remind them that they should be concerned with the interest of the merchant group as a whole. The ultimate purpose is to eliminate all the accumulated abuses that now exist and to increase gradually the financial strength of the whole group.

Whenever a new merchant is needed as a replacement, the head of the merchants should notify all the Co-hong merchants of this fact. Upon receiving this notification, the latter will examine all the candidates with great care and then choose a wealthy, honest man whom they are willing to back up with guarantees. The name of the nominee, together with pertinent information about him, will be sent to the imperial government for approval. If information about him turns out to be false or if he later defaults in his financial obligations, all the merchants who originally recommended his appointment will be held responsible for making good any debt he owes. Whenever a merchant is dismissed from the conduct of his business, the fact should be reported to the imperial government so that his name will be deleted from the Co-hong roster. Once each year a list of Co-hong merchants, together with pertinent files, should be presented to the imperial government for reference purposes.

It is hereby suggested that a regulation incorporating the above recommendations be formulated so that all merchants will benefit therefrom and so that no irresponsible man can ever join the ranks of the Co-hong merchants. Meanwhile the Customs Office will also reap good results.[5]

NOTES

[1] This memorial was presented on March 23, 1813. The author was then the Superintendent of the Customs Office in Canton. Source: Palace Museum of Peking,

Historical Materials of Ch'ing Diplomacy (*Ch'ing-tai wai-chiao shih-liao*), the reign of Chia-ch'ing, roll 4, pp. 4–5.

[2] A Manchu official customarily referred to himself as "your slave" (*nu-ts'ai*) in front of his emperor, while a Chinese only called himself "your minister" or "your servant" on similar occasions.

[3] Superintendency of customs at Canton.

[4] Then the governor-general.

[5] Measures proposed in this petition were later adopted.

18 • Su Leng-eh and Kuang-hui: *The Kowtow Controversy*[1]

On the 20th day [August 13, 1816] and inside the governor's office in the city of Tientsin, your slaves respectfully set up an altar oriented in the direction where Your Majesty is located and burned incense. Then we abided by Your Majesty's order in granting a dinner and providing theatrical entertainment for the tribute-bearing envoy from England [Lord Amherst]. When the envoy arrived at the governor's office, we informed him that before we were seated, he should follow us in performing the ritual of three kneelings and nine knockings of the head[2] in front of the altar so as to show our profound gratitude for the meal Your Majesty had chosen to bestow upon us.

"The tribute-bearing envoy is sincere and reverent when he comes to China to pay his homage," said the translator Ma Li-sun [Robert Morrison]. "However, whenever meeting with another person, the ritual practiced in England is altogether different from that in the Celestial Empire. In our country, whenever a person meets a man of superior rank or title, he takes off his hat, stands erect, and then bows. When brought before a king, he takes off his hat, bends one knee, and then bows. If the seat of the king is vacant, he takes off his hat, salutes, and bows. This is the most reverent ritual practiced in our country."

Your slaves then informed the translator that if the envoy knew the true meaning of reverence, he should follow us in performing the same ritual; it was only then, we said, that he could be properly regarded as having assumed an inferior status. They looked as if they might have difficulty in complying with this demand, though we used every means of persuasion we could find to convince them of the necessity of performing this ritual. "Though outwardly the ritual of England is different from that practiced in the Celestial Empire," they explained, "the internal reverence we wish to express is nevertheless the same. There is no intention on our part to be disobedient."

"If taking off the hat followed by salutation is the ritual which you have to perform before a king's vacant throne," said we, "the Chinese ritual does not seem to be too complicated. Since His Majesty the Emperor has bestowed upon you a great favor, how can you not feel gratitude? When and if you are granted an audience, how can your ritual—taking off your hat, bending one knee, and bowing—be possibly regarded as being adequate to express your sincere desire to become Sinicized?[3] Would it fully express your king's true intentions?"

"Though the tribute-bearing envoy is sincere and reverent at heart," the foreigners explained again, "he does not dare to change the ritual of his own country, being fearful that if he does, he will displease his own sovereign upon his return to England. However, he is willing to repeat the same English ritual for as many times as you desire when granted an audience with His Majesty the

Emperor. This is the way he wishes to show his gratitude, and he thinks that His Majesty the Emperor will be pleased when he comes to think of this foreigner's basic loyalty."

Time and again your slaves tried to console and comfort the tribute-bearing envoy from England, who did not refute or contradict what we said to him. In fact, judging from the way he spoke, he seemed to be reverent, sincere, and obedient. There was no indication of any falsehood or pretensions. While we performed the ritual of three kneelings and nine knockings of the head before the altar, they took off their hats three times, made nine salutations, and bowed nine times. They said that whenever they were granted an audience with Your Majesty, they were willing to appear without a hat, bend one knee nine times, and bow nine times. As your slaves looked at their ritual, it did not seem to conform well with ours. Your slaves will continue to persuade them during our journey to make sure that they will obey; we hope that Your Majesty will not have to be overconcerned with this matter.

Following the performance of the required ritual before the altar, we led them to their respective seats. They were given as gifts several items of silk and velvet after the completion of the meal and the theatrical entertainment. The tribute-bearing envoy and his retainers all expressed gratitude to Your Majesty the Emperor.[4]

NOTES

[1] This selection is a memorial submitted by its authors to the imperial government on August 13, 1816. Su Leng-eh was then the Minister of Public Works, and Kuang-hui the Superintendent of Salt Administration at Ch'anglu. Both were responsible for entertaining and escorting Lord Amherst. Source: *Ch'ing-tai wai-chiao shih-liao*, the reign of Chia-ch'ing, roll 5, p. 29.

[2] Knocking the forehead gently against the ground.

[3] The Chinese original is *hsiang-hua shu-ch'eng* which means "looking forward to be assimilated and expressing one's sincere desire to be loyal (to the Chinese emperor)," a cliché often found in documents of this type. It is doubtful whether the authors of this selection really believed that Lord Amherst wished to be Sinicized.

[4] For Emperor Chia-ch'ing's reaction to this petition, see Selection 19.

19 • CHIA-CH'ING: *The Kowtow Controversy*[1]

In their memorial to the throne, Su Leng-eh and Kuang-hui reported that the tribute-bearing envoy from England took off his hat three times, made nine salutations, and bowed nine times when he expressed his gratitude to the emperor for the dinner that was given to him. They added that since they knew this foreign ritual did not conform well with ours, they intended to continue to persuade the aforesaid envoy during his journey to Peking, to make sure that he would abide by our rules. They further stated that they would escort the envoy to the capital beginning on the 21st day [August 14, 1816].

When Su Leng-eh was originally dispatched to Tientsin to arrange the visit of England's tribute-bearing envoy, he was instructed in person that the envoy must be thoroughly familiar with the proper rituals before he was allowed to pay his homage to the emperor, and that if he showed even the slightest irreverence, he should be instructed to wait at Tientsin and should not be brought to the capital. Now that the tribute-bearing envoy has made it clear that he will not perform the

Chinese ritual, Su Leng-eh and Kuang-hui should have reported this refusal to the imperial government and should wait for further instructions. That they took the liberty of escorting him on his way to Peking on the 21st amounts to rude, rash conduct. A decree should accordingly be issued to reprimand them.

Since Su Leng-eh and his company have already boarded a ship on their way to the capital, the only thing to do is to present Ssu Tang-tung[2] with the following instructions:

"In the fifty-eighth year of Ch'ien-lung (1793) you accompanied the then tribute-bearing envoy to China;[3] you must have seen for yourself the rituals that accompanied the performance of the act of homage, the bequest of gifts, and the granting of dinners. The former Grand Emperor [Ch'ien-lung] did not allow the English envoy to follow the English custom while in China, and only when he performed the ritual of three kneelings and nine knockings of the head was he properly rewarded and then sent home. The present Emperor follows closely the precedent established during the reign of his predecessor. If you are unwilling to observe Chinese customs, under no circumstances will you be allowed to pay homage to His Majesty; nor dare we present your request to him. According to the law of the Celestial Empire, all ministers, high or low, and all representatives from the one hundred buffer states, whether they be Korea, Vietnam, Liu-ch'iu, Siam, Nanchang [Laos], Burma, or Muslim tribes, have to perform the ritual of three kneelings and nine knockings of the head when they come to our capital to pay their homage. None of them has dared to violate this regulation. As for taking off the hat, the Celestial Empire considers it superfluous and does not require its performance, when a man is granted an audience with the Emperor. You should describe this matter in detail to the chief envoy Lo-erh A-mei-shih-te [Lord Amherst] and ask him to be reverently obedient. He should practice the ritual of three kneelings and nine knockings of the head and become proficient in it before we dare to bring him to the capital. If he continues to be stubborn, we will not dare to make any further request on his behalf, his tribute will not be accepted, and all the honors that accompany the conferring of dinners and the bequest of gifts will be automatically canceled. Furthermore, you will be sent home at this very moment in the ship that you came in. In such a case, would you have not wasted a long, tiresome journey in view of the fact that you came from the distant seas? Since you have lived in Macao, Kwangtung Province, for many years, you must be thoroughly familiar with Chinese laws. If His Majesty decides not to accept your tribute, your chief envoy would have to be ordered home. It is also possible that in a moment of anger His Majesty might decide to detain and then punish you. Would you not be regretful by then?"

The above instruction should be made clear to the English envoy. If he shows a willingness to comply, he should be immediately ordered to perform the ritual of three kneelings and nine knockings of the head towards the direction where the emperor is. If he makes no mistake in performing this ritual, he should be allowed to proceed to the capital according to schedule. If, knowing that the English envoy will not agree to our demand, Su Leng-eh nevertheless decides to make the best of the situation by allowing him to proceed to the capital, the said envoy would be immediately expelled from the palace when, facing the emperor and presenting his credentials, he is found to be woefully inadequate in performing the prescribed ritual. He would be then put under the custody of a high-ranking official and be sent to Tientsin, whence he would sail for home. Meanwhile Su Leng-eh and Kuang-hui would be dismissed from their respective governmental posts and be put under the custody of the Ministry of Justice. They would be punished according to their offense as a warning to all of those who have not performed well their assigned tasks. In short, they should be extremely careful in this matter!

NOTES

[1] This decree was issued by Emperor Chia-ch'ing on August 15, 1816. Source: *Ch'ing-tai wai-chiao shih-liao*, the reign of Chia-ch'ing, roll 5, pp. 34–35.
[2] Sir George T. Staunton, who then served as a deputy envoy.
[3] This refers to the Macartney mission of 1793.

20 • Hu Hsia-mi (Hugh Hamilton Lindsay): *A Brief Account of the British Nation and Character*[1]

The land where the British live is about 70,000 *li* from China. Before arriving at Canton, a British ship has to sail southward first and then around the huge continent of Africa before it proceeds northeastward. This is how far the British have to travel before they reach China! Though British ships are as fast as they are safe, the fact that the British dare to sail across large oceans indicates clearly how able and courageous they really are. Sometimes they encounter storms on the high seas. But they do not have to worry about such things as shipwreck since their captains are masterly in planning and their crews are courageous in carrying out the captains' command. No pirates on the high seas dare to attack them.

England exports to China native products of distant countries as well as manufactured products of her own. She takes from China such goods as tea. Because Chinese and English merchants are busy enriching themselves as well as their respective countries, the poor people in both countries can acquire employment to earn a livelihood and live happily like any other person. England has traded with China for 200 years, and nowadays from sixty to eighty of her ships enter Canton each year. Is it not true that this trade has created jobs for hundreds of thousands of people who otherwise would have to be unemployed?

England's true intention is often misunderstood by the people in the Orient. They say that England is avaricious and wishes to occupy more and more territories. Nothing, in fact, can be further from the truth. England already has large territories within her jurisdiction; she prefers to reduce rather than increase them. Besides the mother country, she has valuable land in Europe, large territories in North America, numerous islands in the West Indies, the Strait of Good Hope [2] in the southern tip of Africa, and an uncountable number of underdeveloped areas in the South Pacific. In addition, she possesses many islands in Asia, plus the ancient kingdom of Hindustan which is also part of the British Empire. Her possessions that are located closest to China include Colombo, Martaban, Malacca, and Singapore. Since she already has so many territories, why should she wish to have more? On the contrary, the thing she values most is that all her people enjoy peace and acquire good fortune. Since this is the purpose she wishes to achieve, she resents greatly those who push her around; in fact, she is determined to seek revenge against all those who have violated the principle of righteousness.

The Emperor of the Great Ch'ing Empire has the honest intention of treating foreigners with kindness. In recent years, however, many officials have time and again misinterpreted His Majesty's true wishes, and consequently the royal favor has not been extended to us foreigners. Because of these officials' exactions, foreign trade at Canton has encountered numerous difficulties. Chinese merchants who have contacts with Englishmen are often branded as traitors; they are fined, beaten, jailed, and sometimes die in prison. We Englishmen only wish to conduct legitimate trade in accordance with the established rules and we pay taxes whenever they are due. Where on earth is this so-called conspiracy? Besides the statutory tariff, we are often asked to pay extra fees, and even the lowest-ranking officials attempt to exact bribes in violation of the law. Needless to say, malpractices like this are oppressive and harmful to both foreign and Chinese merchants. We believe that His Majesty the Emperor has not heard about them in view of the great distance between Canton and Peking and in view of the fact that they are conducted in the most secret manner. It is inconceivable that His Majesty the Emperor, being truly great as he certainly is, would tolerate the wrongdoings of these low-ranking officials if he knew about them.

Sometimes we see posters on the wall that denounce and insult us foreigners, telling the lie that we are wicked and violent and thus provoking petty people to be hostile towards us. Because of this provocation, such unfortunate incidents as bloody fights do occasionally occur which result in serious injuries and sometimes deaths. Once these incidents occur, trade is ordered to be stopped, and business is adversely affected as a result. Is it not true that these sad incidents could have been prevented if the responsible officials knew how to handle them properly? Though they look crude in appearance, English sailors are really kind and tender at heart. The only thing they cannot stand is to be insulted. Unfortunate incidents occur when Chinese become impolite in words or deeds, and it is sad for all parties concerned that these incidents sometimes result in deaths. Each British ship that trades at Canton has its own regulations that govern its crew. It will definitely punish any sailor who has brought physical harm to others, regardless of whether the injured person is a Chinese or a foreigner. However, if local officials allow mean people to insult a sailor deliberately, unfortunate incidents will occur, however strict the British ship is in the enforcement of its rules.

According to the English law, a person who causes physical harm to an Englishman or a foreigner will be prosecuted and punished to the same extent; in other words, the nationality of the injured person is not a consideration insofar as law enforcement is concerned. However, the accused is allowed to present his own case in the court, and the court often assigns a lawyer to assist him in his defense. From our experience we know that the customs of different countries are similar on important points and dissimilar only on minor details. Whenever differences do exist, they can be resolved with mutual concessions by men of goodwill and understanding on both sides. We see no reason why the Chinese and the British people cannot be engaged in friendly and mutually beneficial trade. The English ruler repeatedly decrees that her subjects, wherever they go, should always maintain friendly relations with people of other countries and that they should at all times uphold the good name of Great Britain. If a Chinese ever decides to visit a British territory, we can assure you that he will be allowed to enjoy peaceful residence like the British people, and nobody will ever dare to oppress or harm him. If he is oppressed or harmed, British officials will see to it that redress will be made.

Such being the case, why should we two countries be hostile towards each other?

Why should we not encourage and compete with each other in the performance of good deeds? Whenever Chinese sailors are stranded in desolate islands on the high seas as a result of shipwreck, British sailors compete among themselves to rescue them and bring them back to China so they can rejoin their parents, wives, and children. Without the British help, these Chinese sailors would have no hope whatever of survival and would die of starvation on those remote islands. In fact, British sailors consider these loving deeds more honorable than the killing of enemies on the battlefield. It is truly detestable that some bad elements in this world still regard them as an insolent, contemptible group.

The Chinese people are intelligent, industrious, and consequently prosperous. But there are other peoples in the world who possess the same good qualities. Only an ignorant man can say that all good things exist in China only and that all other countries are despicable and worthless by definition. He considers himself a man, but his view is really that of a child. If he has the opportunity to visit foreign countries, he will know that Heaven is impartial in the dispensation of its favors and that many countries outside of China also produce an abundant supply of useful products. Take England as an example. Her people live in peace; their properties are protected by law; and no country dares to bring harm to them. The British believe in the teachings of Jesus Christ who, because of His love for all men, has bestowed peace on earth. Not only have they made great progress in science, technology, literature, and fine arts, they are also reared in the spirit of propriety, righteousness, sanctity, and goodness. They are feared when encountered on the battlefield and respected during the time of peace. No country in the world desires friendship with the Great Ch'ing Empire more than England, because, first, England attaches great importance to the China trade, and second, the territories of our two countries are geographically contiguous. [3] For instance, one of the rivers that originates in the Chinese Yunnan province passes through a British possession before it pours into the sea.

The overwhelming majority of the Chinese merchants are fair and businesslike; some of them even go out of their way to show their kindness and generosity to foreign traders. What we English value most is trade on an equitable, profitable basis. The representative of the British East India Company, having been in Canton for a long time, is widely known for his integrity. Once he promises to pay, he will pay all that is due, and he has never broken a promise in business matters.

The Chinese people are requested to think carefully about the important ideas presented above, so that they will not look down upon a group of people who are as able and virtuous as they are. Chinese officials should respectfully keep in mind their Emperor's wishes to receive foreigners with courtesy and to treat them with kindness. If this is done, the relationship between Chinese and British residents in China will become friendly and harmonious. All of them will be content with their respective occupations and will continue to enjoy their good fortune.

China and England are friends! May all of mankind be blessed with happiness!

NOTES

[1] This document did not have the impact its author intended. The original was written in unidiomatic, spoken Chinese, which caused many Chinese officials to dismiss it as "illiterate" and "incomprehensible" besides being "ridiculous." A copy of the Chinese original can be found in *Chin-tai Chung-kuo shih,* pp. 618–622.

[2] *Hao-wang chih chia.*

[3] By England the author, in this particular case, means the British Empire.

CHAPTER THREE

The Opium War

Though the opium poppy is mentioned in the medical works of ancient China, the use of opium as a habit-forming narcotic is of comparatively recent origin. The Spaniards introduced the smoking of tobacco to China early in the seventeenth century, and soon opium mixed with tobacco also appeared there. Previously the Dutch had used this mixture in Java and in Taiwan, which they then occupied, and from Taiwan it spread to nearby Fukien Province. Once in China, the opium was separated from the tobacco and taken independently. At the beginning it was regarded more as a medicine than as a habit-forming narcotic. Unfortunately, the dividing line was extremely fine, even for the most discriminating users. A person might use opium to relieve some physical pain, but he soon found that he would be forever in pain without taking it on a regular basis. In short, once he began to take it, it was extremely unlikely that he could ever free himself from addiction. As opium addiction spread, it eventually reached all the strata of the Chinese population in all the provinces, including those who could least afford it. When the gravity of the danger was finally recognized, opium smoking had become too widespread to be stopped.

The first shipment of opium to China in quantity was made by the Portuguese from Goa. From then on the importation of opium from foreign sources continued to increase as the number of smokers multiplied inside China. In 1790 the import from India alone reached 4,054 chests (each chest weighed approximately 133 pounds), and shortly before the Opium War (1839–1842) the annual import from all sources exceeded 30,000 chests, constituting more than 90 percent in value of the total import of all merchandise. England had by then become by far the largest shipper, though other countries such as France and the United States also participated. Before the increase of the opium traffic, Europe had consistently bought more from China than it sold to her, and consequently there had been a steady flow of bullion from Europe to China. Now, with the increase of the opium traffic, the flow of bullion was reversed. Before 1823 the yearly outflow of silver from China amounted to 1 million taels; it increased to 20 million taels from 1831 to 1834 and reached 30 million taels shortly before the Opium War.

It is ironic and perhaps typical of a degenerate Chinese bureaucracy that it was this outflow of silver rather than the inherent evil of opium that alarmed officialdom and prompted it to act (Selection 21). The outflow of silver caused its price to keep rising in terms of copper coins and farm

52

produce, and this rise in the price of silver, in the judgment of many Chinese officials, had caused great harm to government and people alike (Selection 35). To be sure, there had been a ban against the importation of opium ever since 1729, but the avarice of foreign traders and the corruption of Chinese officials combined to defeat whatever measures the government chose to take. Moreover, the long coastline of China made smuggling extremely difficult to stop (Selection 22). In the latter part of the 1830's when the opium problem had become too pressing for the government to delay further its solution, two schools of thought emerged in proposals of how to cope with it. One school emphasized the strict prohibition of opium smoking among the Chinese, while the other stressed the importance of an absolute ban on the importation of opium into China, though the two schools agreed that each measure had to be fully coordinated with the other if it were to be effective. The second school of thought eventually won the argument, largely because opium smokers were so numerous and so scattered over the large territory of China that the first measure—the strict prohibition of opium smoking among the Chinese—would be extremely difficult to carry out. The reasoning was that if the importation of opium was completely stopped, opium addiction would go out of existence by itself, simply because there would not be any opium available in China, no matter how much the smokers yearned for it. Following this reasoning, Emperor Tao-kuang (r. 1821–1851) sent one of his ablest servants, Lin Tse-hsü (1785–1850), to Canton in 1838, with the special mission to end the importation of opium, "once and for all."

After Lin's arrival at Canton in the spring of 1839, he ordered all foreign traders to surrender the opium they possessed (Selection 23). They complied, and more than 20,000 chests of British-controlled opium were burned in public. However, the British refused to make a pledge that thereafter they would refrain from shipping more opium to China, doubtless hoping, perhaps with justification, that Lin's stern measures could not be anything but a temporary phenomenon, since other Chinese officials, heavily bribed, had always been very cooperative in this matter in the past. Angered by their refusal, Lin appealed to Queen Victoria, saying that the gods would bring her good fortune and would reward her with "a multitude of children and grandchildren" if she were good enough to "plow under all of the opium plants and grow food crops instead," while punishing severely anyone who dared to plant opium poppies again (Selection 24).

We do not know what the reaction of Queen Victoria was to Lin's appeal, but her Secretary of State for Foreign Affairs, Lord Palmerston, was definitely not amused. In his eyes the Chinese had not only unjustifiably confiscated British property but also outrageously put under house arrest those British subjects who had not complied with the Chinese demand to refrain from shipping more opium to China. He demanded, first, compensation by the Chinese government for the confiscated opium; second, British representation in China to "watch over the commercial interests of Her Britannic Majesty's subjects;" third, the cession to Great Britain by China of "one or more sufficiently large and properly situated islands on the coast of China";

and finally, the payment by the Chinese government of the debts that insolvent Chinese merchants owed their British creditors. "In order to convince the Imperial Government [of China] that the British Government attaches the utmost importance to this matter and that the affair is one which will not admit of delay," he announced, "the British government . . . has determined at once to send out a naval and military force to the coast of China to act in support of these demands" (Selection 25).

After the British expeditionary forces arrived in China, they quickly captured some islands off the Chinese coast and destroyed some "indestructible" Chinese fortresses. The Chinese government accused the British of treachery, declared war, and ordered its army and militiamen to annihilate "all the invaders and their Chinese collaborators" (Selection 26). But the war, once begun, went from bad to worse as far as the Chinese were concerned. When the British threatened to attack Nanking and cut China in half, the Chinese sued for peace.

The Treaty of Nanking that concluded the Opium War was the first of the so-called unequal treaties that China signed (Selection 28). (For more detailed discussion of the unequal treaties, see Chapter IV.) It incorporated all of the British demands just described, plus some more. Ironically, the primary issue that prompted the war was barely mentioned. Theoretically the importation of opium was still illegal, but the Chinese government assured the British that "whether the merchant ships of the various countries bring opium or not, China will not need to inquire or to take any proceedings with regard thereto" (Selection 27). Believing that the withdrawal of the prohibition against the use of opium might have "a tendency to diminish the chances of its being used to excess," the British government continued to press for the legalization of the opium trade throughout the 1840's and the 1850's (Selections 27 and 30). However, the Chinese continued to dodge the issue and did not accept the British point of view until 1858, when once again China was defeated by Great Britain, this time allied with France. From then on opium continued to plague China for ninety more years. It was not until 1949 when the Communists conquered China that the opium trade, which had poisoned China for more than two hundred years, finally came to an end.

21 • HUANG CHÜEH-TZ'U: *The Evil of Opium*[1]

Your Majesty's selfless and tireless devotion to the affairs of the state is motivated by your sincere desire to safeguard the welfare not only of all the people in China today but also of generations to come. Despite such diligence and earnestness on your part, the treasury does not have enough funds to meet expenses, and the livelihood of our people remains poor and unsatisfactory. Recently this situation has gone from bad to worse, and each year is worse than the year before. During the Ch'ien-lung period [1736–1795] incomes of both the government and the people were more than adequate despite such large expenditures as those on national defense, imperial inspection tours, and public projects. In fact, this period is regarded as the most prosperous of our dynasty. As late as the Chia-ch'ing period [1796–1820] the nation was still economically sound, so sound that members of the gentry and wealthy merchants continued to live a life of luxury. What a different situation there is today! Is it true that the more a nation spends, the more wealthy it will become, or the more frugal a person becomes, the less he will have to spend? Your humble servant has had occasion to notice that lately there has been a steady increase in the price of silver in terms of standard coins, so great that one tael of silver is now worth more than 1,600 standard coins. The rise of the price of silver has nothing to do with the consumption of silver inside China; it results primarily from the outflow of silver to foreign countries.

Knowing that the inflow of opium would inevitably cause great harm to China, Emperor Chia-ch'ing specifically decreed its prohibition at one time. But his ministers had no idea then that opium poison would become so great and widespread a curse. Had they known the grave consequences, they would have enacted stringent laws to be enforced with severe punishments to prevent its spread. According to a well-established precedent, a foreign ship had to secure a clearance with the Co-hong merchants attesting that it carried no opium before it was allowed to enter the port of Canton. But the clearance, unfortunately, was no more than a formality, and foreign ships continued to bring opium to China in spite of it. By the third year of Tao-kuang [1823] the annual outflow of silver had increased to several million taels as a result of the increasing inflow of opium. At the beginning, opium smoking was confined to the fops of wealthy families who took up the habit as a form of conspicuous consumption; even they knew that they should not indulge in it to the greatest extreme. Later, people of all social strata—from government officials and members of the gentry to craftsmen, merchants, entertainers, and servants, and even women, Buddhist monks and nuns, and Taoist priests—took up the habit and openly bought and equipped themselves with smoking instruments. Even in the political center of our dynasty—the nation's capital and its surrounding areas—some of the inhabitants have also been contaminated by this dreadful poison.

The inflow of opium from foreign countries has steadily increased in recent years. The imported opium is usually loaded in barges which, being too large and clumsy to enter the Humen estuary, are anchored in places like Laowanshan and Tayüshan. Conspiring with sea patrol and coast guards, unscrupulous merchants at Canton use such small boats as "sneaking dragons" and "fast crabs" to ship silver out and bring opium in. From the third to the eleventh year of Tao-kuang [1823–1831] the annual outflow of silver amounted to more than 17 million taels. From the eleventh to the fourteenth year [1831–1834] it reached more than 20 million taels, and since the fourteenth year [1834] it has been more than 30 million taels. Large as they are, these figures do not cover the import of opium in other ports such as those in Fukien, Chekiang, Shantung, and Tientsin, which amounts to tens of thousands of taels per year.

Thus we are using the financial resources of China to fill up the bottomless hole in foreign countries. Besides, by taking up this evil product, we make the nation weak and ill. If this situation continues day after day and year after year, your humble servant does not know where the end will be. Besides, there is another matter to be considered. Today taxes in all parts of China are paid in copper coins. When tax revenue is transported to the central government, however, it has to be converted to silver before it can be accepted. Owing to the shortage of silver and consequently its increasingly higher price in terms of copper coins, the local governments which made a profit from this exchange in the past are now, without exception, taking a loss. Salt merchants in the provinces receive copper coins for the salt they sell, but they have to pay dues to the government in silver. Because of the high price of silver in terms of copper coins, the salt trade, which has hitherto attracted a large number of competitors in view of the size of the expected profit, is now regarded as a risky adventure. If the price of silver continues to go up in the next few years, how can the obligations to the imperial government be fulfilled by local communities and how can tax payments ever be delivered in full? If there are unexpected expenditures, where will the funds come from? When your humble servant thinks about this, he is often sleepless at night.

Now everyone knows that the outflow of silver is caused by the inflow of opium. Many people have studied the problem and suggested various ways to block this channel of exchange. Some people say that we should strictly enforce the regulations at the port of entry so as to make sure that opium cannot come in and silver cannot go out. At first glance, this looks like a sound measure. The problem is that not all the inspectors who enforce the law are immune from partiality or corruption. Since the total trade amounts to tens of millions of taels per year, a fractional cut will reach several millions. When there is so much profit to be realized, who among the inspectors can be really serious in enforcing the law? The number of wrongdoers who can be brought to justice will remain small. Moreover, our coastline zigzags for more than 10,000 *li* and smuggling can occur at any point of this long line. For these reasons, it is extremely difficult, if not impossible, to stop this opium and silver exchange.

Some people say that we should stop foreign trade altogether so as to eradicate the very cause of the opium peril. This argument sounds plausible enough. However, these people tend to forget that the legitimate section of the trade, consisting of the import of woolens and timepieces and the export of tea, rhubarb, and silk, amounts to less than 10 million taels, and that the profit foreigners can realize from this trade is only 2 or 3 million taels. In other words, the profit that can be realized from barter trade is only 1 or 2 percent of the profit now obtained from the trading of opium. In view of this vast difference, it is no wonder that foreigners are not interested in any other trade than that in opium. Suppose we decide to dispense with the tariff revenue collected at Canton and prohibit foreign trade altogether. The opium ships cannot enter our ports, of course; they will be anchored on the high seas instead. While they are holding their opium as if it were a great treasure, Chinese smokers are impatient to procure it. Such being the case, there are bound to be unscrupulous people happy and willing to transport this opium from foreign ships to the Chinese shore. The difficulty of preventing smuggling among unscrupulous Chinese is the second reason why we cannot stop effectively the outflow of silver from China.

Some people say that we should arrest all opium traffickers and strictly enforce the law that governs the operation of opium dens. By this method, they say, we would be able to control opium at the point of its consumption even though we cannot eradicate its source. They do not realize that since the promulgation of the opium control law, opium traffickers are indeed punishable by banishment to the frontier and the operators of opium dens are liable to punishment as provided in the *Act of Heretical Seduction Involving the Young and the Innocent*,[2] i.e., to death by hanging. Yet there are in China today countless opium traffickers and den operators, few of whom have been brought to justice. The people who handle opium at Kwangtung have established opium stations all over the country; moreover, they have made valuable contacts with all check points from Kwangtung to other provinces. If a wealthy merchant has bought opium in large quantities, these people will guarantee safe shipping all the way to wherever he wishes it to be delivered. Customs officials, on land or by water, close their eyes when the drug passes by, while they harass law-abiding merchants and demand bribes from them under the pretext of searching for opium. Wherever he happens to be located, the operator of an opium den is usually an unscrupulous ex-clerk or former soldier who makes a habit of enticing the degenerate members of the wealthy class as his customers. Once addicted to opium, these wealthy degenerates often practice their indulgence in groups within their family premises. As opium addiction continues to spread, sometimes half of a local official's staff and servants become its victims. Since so many people are addicted to this habit, they naturally protect one another insofar as the enforcement of the opium law is concerned. This is the third reason why silver outflow cannot be effectively stopped.

Some people say that we should lift the ban on the planting of opium poppies in China and allow people to manufacture opium with domestic material so as to counteract the importation of foreign opium. As domestically manufactured opium continues to increase with the passage of time, they say, the outflow of silver will be stopped. These people do not realize that domestically manufactured opium cannot quench the craving so well as foreign opium, and opium merchants often mix it with foreign opium in order to realize the largest profit possible. In short, the lifting of the ban on the planting of opium poppies cannot end the inflow of foreign opium and effectively stop the outflow of silver.

However, is it really true that harmful as opium is, we can never prohibit it? Your humble servant believes that we can if we use the right method to combat it. The outflow of silver is caused by the large volume of opium traffic, which in turn results from the great number of opium smokers. Without opium smokers, there would not be opium traffic; and without opium traffic, the import of foreign opium would stop by itself. Therefore, if the enforcement of strict laws is the right approach to the opium problem, the most severe penalty has to be imposed on the smokers. It is hereby suggested that a decree be issued in the name of Your Majesty, stating clearly that within a year's period, from a certain day of a certain month of this year to a certain day of a certain month of the next year, all opium smokers must get rid of their abominable habit. However addicted a person may be to opium smoking, there is no such thing as absolute inability to free himself from his addiction. If at the end of the one-year period he still smokes, it is fair to assume that he wishes to become a legal outcast of his own accord and should therefore be punished accordingly.

According to an old statute, an opium smoker, once convicted, will be put in a cage and given a beating. If he refuses to identify the merchant who has sold him opium, he will receive one hundred blows with a wooden stick and then be banished for a period of three years. In any case, there is no death penalty. Since the pain caused by the discontinuance of opium smoking is much more severe than that resulting from beating or banishment, an opium smoker prefers the latter to the former. If the penalty is increased to capital punishment, he would feel that the mental agony of waiting for execution is much worse than the sufferings he would have as a result of discontinuing opium smoking. Your humble servant is certain that he will prefer dying a natural death at home by shaking off his addiction rather than ending his life at the hands of an executioner in the market place. As your humble servant sees it, the reason behind Your Majesty's extreme caution in imposing severe punishment is the fear that if the law is made more strict, informers will multiply and many innocent people will inevitably be implicated. But this fear is unfounded as far as the enforcement of the opium law is concerned. Once an accused person is brought before the judge. the latter can immediately tell whether he is guilty or innocent. If a man does not smoke, no bitter enemy of his can implicate him. If he does smoke, no artful device can cover his addiction. Such being the case, the imposition of a severe penalty will not have harmful side effects.

In the *Taiwan Gazette,* Yü Wen-yi says that the Batavians were strong in body and proficient in warfare before the Dutch succeeded in enticing them to take up the smoking of opium. As they became weak and feeble, the Dutch took over their country and subjected them to Dutch rule. Whenever a Dutchman is convicted of opium smoking, the Dutch law requires him to be tied to the upper end of a tall pole and, surrounded and watched by other Dutchmen, to be shot by a cannon ball which sends him to the bottom of the sea. Because of the severity of this punishment, no Dutchman dares to take up opium smoking. The opium that comes to China today originates from such countries as England. The law in these countries says explicitly that the penalty for opium smoking is death. That is why the countries that manufacture opium do not have a single person who smokes it. Your humble servant has heard that on their way from Bombay to Canton, many foreign traders pass by Annam, where at one time they also tried to entice the Annamese to take up the opium-smoking habit. Realizing the devilish plot of these foreigners, the Annamese imposed severe punishment on the smokers to show their determination. All smokers were automatically sentenced to death.

If foreigners can prohibit the use of opium through the issuance of an order, we certainly can do so too. If like a thunderbolt Your Majesty makes your anger clearly known and your authority felt, even the most addicted, however ignorant and stubborn they are, will open their eyes to see and incline their ears to hear. This is an extraordinary decision to make, but Your Majesty, possessed of such saintly wisdom, alone has the power to make it. Besides, there is no need to reach a consensus on this matter. There are people too fearful of criticism to take the burden of the nation upon their own shoulders. They know only too well that without severe penalties the use of opium cannot be stopped; yet they continue to argue that, in view of the great number of opium smokers in the nation, a sudden tightening of the regulations will bring about a cleavage between the government and the people, a cleavage which they say should be avoided. Taking into consideration their reservations in this matter, your humble servant suggests a relatively long period of one year for the opium smokers to free themselves from their addiction. He does insist, however, that when the imperial decree is issued, it should be couched in the most urgent and uncompromising terms. Only when the imperial decree is strict enough will the officials become serious about implementing the provisions of the law; only when the officials are truly serious will the people be fearful enough not to violate the law. When and if the law is enacted, 80 or 90 percent of the smokers will end their addiction before any penalty can be imposed upon them at the end of the one-year period. In other words, because of the existence of this law, not only will smokers be enabled to live out the rest of their lives in peace by putting an end to their addiction, but nonsmokers will also thus be warned not to take up the habit and can thus live normal, healthy lives. In this particular case, the exercise of Your Majesty's omnipotent power corresponds well with the expression of the most saintly virtues.

It is further suggested that Your Majesty should make your wishes clearly known to all governors-general and governors, instructing them to circulate widely medical prescriptions that can be used to break the opium habit and to warn all smokers that under no circumstances will they be allowed to continue their addiction after the one-year period. Meanwhile all prefectures, districts, and subprefectures should be instructed to examine and make more effective the *pao-chia* organizations[3] within their respective jurisdictions and to warn all the inhabitants of the impending edict that is to be strictly enforced in order to root out the opium poison. Every five households should form a compact to guarantee one another's conduct, and at the end of the one-year period they are required to inform the government on any opium smoker found within their group. Upon conviction of the accused, the informer would be rewarded accordingly. If on the other hand they conspire to conceal an opium smoker within their group and this conspiracy is duly proved, all the five households within the compact unit would be punished in accordance with the law, in addition to the death sentence that is to be imposed upon the smoker. In large cities where there is a transient population and where merchants come and go, it is of course very difficult for one household to know what goes on in the next. Such being the case, the responsibility of locating opium smokers should be placed upon shopowners and hotel operators who are not allowed to take into their premises opium addicts. If they are found to have violated this regulation, they will be punished just as if they had deliberately concealed bandits within their premises.

As for civil or military officials who continue to indulge in their addiction at the end of the one-year period, they should be punished more severely than ordinary citizens, in view of the fact that they will have violated the very law which they have the responsibility to enforce. Not only would they be punished in accordance with the law, but all their descendants, from then on, would be excluded from taking the civil service examinations. If at the end of the one-year period an official is found to have been diligent in enforcing the law and to have brought to justice many opium addicts, he should be considered for promotion as a reward, in accordance with the law that governs the capture of bandits. On the other hand, if a member of his staff, a relative, or a servant who resides with him in his official residence, is found to have failed in shaking off his addiction, not only would the addict be punished in accordance with the law, but the official in question would be also examined for possible prosecution. Every squad of soldiers, Manchu or Chinese, should form a compact and guarantee one another's conduct in the same manner as the civilian population within the *pao-chia* organizations. The military official who has failed to discover opium smokers within his command and has thus defaulted in the performance of his supervisory duties would be punished in the same manner as civilian officials. The purpose is to eliminate the opium poison wherever it is found, in military as well as civilian circles and among government officials as well as ordinary citizens. The meaning of this new law should be made crystal clear to even the most isolated or remote region of the nation, so that all the people will know how much Your Majesty is concerned with the security of their lives as well as their financial well-being. Feeling grateful for Your Majesty's concern and fearing the impending punishment if they violate the law, the smokers will make a firm determination to change their evil ways and to live a new life.

If the above measures are carried out, not only will the outflow of silver be effectively stopped, its price will also be stabilized. Then we can proceed to devise the best means to administer the nation's finances so as to bring happiness to people of all generations, the future as well as the present.

NOTES

[1] The Chinese original, dated June 2, 1838, appears in *China's Management of Barbarian Affairs* (*Ch'ou-pan yi-wu shih-mo*), the reign of Tao-kuang, roll 2, pp. 4–9.
[2] *Tso-tao huo-jen yin-yu tzu-ti li.*
[3] During the Ch'ing Dynasty every ten households were organized as a *p'ai,* ten *p'ai* formed a *chia,* and ten *chia* became a *pao.*

22 • ANONYMOUS: *Letters to Hu Hsia-mi*[1]

Nowadays the soldiers are guarding all roads, and anyone who trades with your honorable country will be beheaded together with all members of his family. It is unfortunate that you have not been able to receive the letter which I sent you day before yesterday. Since I have a new plan now, I am dispatching this bearer to your honorable ship to discuss it with you. I have now in my possession dozens of piculs of tea and should be able to deliver them to your ship about ten o'clock in the evening. The tea will be loaded in small boats; when these boats come close to your honorable ship, one of my men will throw three pieces of earthen tile into the water, one at a time, to indicate their arrival. Since my men do not know much about foreigners, it is hoped that the moment you hear the sound made by the earthen tile, you will lower your boats to transport the cargo to your ship. The transportation will continue until all the merchandise is safe in your hand. Meanwhile you should sit tight in your commanding post in midcurrent of the river and should under no circumstances step in and out of your own cabin.

Words are inadequate to express what I wish to say. Please read carefully the two letters I sent you previously. . . . Under no circumstances should you reveal our dealings to others. I appreciate very much your cooperation in this matter.

Together with this letter is a bag of tea, serving as a sample of the kind of merchandise we have. One picul of tea is priced at three units of opium or forty silver dollars.

The fifth day of the fourth month (*May* 4, 1832), 2 P.M.

*   *   *

I am glad that you treated me as a friend when I visited your honorable ship shortly after 10 A.M., on the 26th day of this month [April 26, 1832]. I want to thank you for your gifts: twelve pieces of "seven stars" [rubies], a pamphlet entitled *A Brief Account of the British Nation and Character,*[2] and a financial report. I am convinced that you are a gentleman of kindness. . . .

To all areas along the coast our government has issued an order which prohibits us from sending food and water to your honorable ship; nor are we allowed to bring your goods into China. We will be severely punished if we are discovered to have had any dealings with you. All roads are carefully guarded by the soldiers, and people are afraid to come out to trade with you. . . .

However, as I said to you the other day, I shall use small boats to transport tea and other merchandise to the place where your ship is presently anchored, and you, on your part, should do exactly what I have told you in person. Everything should be done in secret, of course. When you come here next year, please notify me in advance. Not only can I deliver to you tens of thousands of catties of tea as I am doing this time, but I shall have no difficulty of purchasing for you millions of piculs if you so desire. Now you should sail away as quickly as you can; return for further discussion after our government's ships have withdrawn to the rivers in the interior. If you do not leave at once as I have suggested, my country will definitely take such strange measures as declaring you an enemy....

I have heard that the honorable merchants of your country often rescue shipwrecked Chinese merchants on the high seas. Since the English people are so gentle and kind, how can I sit with folded arms when I see clearly what our officials and soldiers intend to do to you? This is the reason I am sending a man to deliver this letter to you. [undated.]

NOTES

[1] These two letters were written by a Chinese merchant to Hu Hsia-mi (Hugh Hamilton Lindsay) in the spring of 1832 when the latter arrived at Foochow (Fukien Province) requesting the opening of that port for trade. The request was refused. As for Lindsay, see pp. 28–29. A Chinese copy of these two letters can be found in Kuo T'ing'yi, *Chin-tai Chung-kuo shih*, vol. 1, pp. 596–597.

[2] See Selection 20.

23 • LIN TSE-HSÜ: *A Message to Foreign Traders*[1]

This is an instruction to foreigners of all nations:

Foreigners who trade in Canton have realized large profits. They can sell all the goods they have brought to China and purchase on short order any merchandise they wish to buy. Because of this fact, the number of ships that come to China to trade has increased from 50 or 60 in the old days to more than 150 in recent years. His Majesty the Emperor allows all of you to trade in China without discrimination, and his generosity has provided you with the opportunity to realize the profit you desire. If the trade is stopped, where will your profit come from? Moreover, tea and rhubarb are essential to foreigners' livelihood, and we have never begrudged the fact that year after year you have shipped these valuable products to your own countries. The favor we have bestowed upon you is very great indeed.

Feeling grateful for the favor you have received, you should at least observe our law and refrain from enriching yourselves by deliberately inflicting harm upon your benefactors. Why do you choose to ship to China opium which you yourselves do not consume in order not only to swindle people out of their money but also to endanger their very lives? You have used this evil thing to poison the Chinese people for dozens of years, and the amount of profit you have realized from this immoral trade must be very large indeed. This devilish conduct on your part not only stirs the indignation of mankind but is intolerable to Heaven as well.

The Celestial Empire has until now not strictly enforced the ban; that is why you have been able to commit the wanton crime of smuggling into China this accursed drug. Having heard about this smuggling, His Majesty is extremely angry; he is determined to eliminate opium poison, once and for all. Chinese who are engaged in opium traffic or operate opium dens are to be executed immediately; even the smokers are liable to the death sentence. As long as you remain in the territory of China, you should abide by Chinese law to the same extent as the Chinese.

I was brought up in the coastal area of Fukien, and so am thoroughly familiar with your tactics. As a man who has pacified frontiers and performed meritorious deeds, I have been specially authorized by His Majesty the Emperor to come to Canton to study the local situation and take the necessary remedial measures. The crime you foreigners have committed against the Chinese people in transporting and selling opium to China is truly unforgivable. But taking into consideration the fact that you are foreigners and that you may not have fully understood the meaning of our law, I have refrained from punishing you without warning you in advance. I therefore take this opportunity to make clear to you what the law is.

I know that the barges you have anchored at Lingting and other places contain large quantities of opium. I also know that you intend to sell this opium clandestinely to smugglers. Do you realize that since a strict order has been issued at the port of entry to arrest anyone who ships opium, there is no one who will transport your opium for you? Do you also realize that since a similar order has been issued to all the provinces, there is no man in China who will sell your opium? Since your opium can no longer be marketed as a result of the prohibition and since everyone has by now realized how poisonous it is, what is the sense of storing it in the barges that are anchored indefinitely on the ocean? Not only will you waste the wages which you have to pay but will also run the risk of storm or fire which can materialize unexpectedly.

I hereby instruct you that the moment this order arrives, you should hand over all the opium presently stored in your barges to the proper Chinese authorities. The Co-hong merchants will examine and count all the chests that have been handed in and make a checklist to be presented to the officials for inspection. All the opium thus handed in will be subsequently burned so as to prevent the harm it can bring. Furthermore, all you traders should sign a pledge, in both foreign and Chinese languages, to the effect that you will never from now on bring any more opium to China, and that if you do, the Chinese authorities, having found the opium in question, are entitled to sentence you to death, besides confiscating all of your merchandise.

I have heard that you foreigners attach great importance to the word "faithfulness." If you abide by my order and hand over all your opium and if in the meantime you make a firm promise that you will never bring opium to China again, I would assume that you are as fearful of the punishment under the Chinese law as you are truly regretful for your past crimes. In that case, I, on my part, will be willing to forgive and forget all that has occurred in the past; together with the governor-general and governor, I will petition His Majesty the Emperor to be specially lenient with you. Not only will all of your past wrongdoing be forgiven, but His Majesty may also be indulgent enough to grant you rewards as an incentive for your deference and repentance. From then on you will be regarded as good foreigners, and you can conduct normal and legitimate trade so as to enrich yourselves. Will you not be more respectable in this manner?

If on the other hand you are obstinately foolish and refuse to be enlightened; if you still think that you can sell your opium clandestinely while professing innocence; if you mean to shirk responsibility by maintaining the myth that the opium was brought here by the sailors and has nothing to do with you; if you intend to deceive us by stating that the opium will be dumped in the ocean on your way home, while in reality you only seek an opportunity to sell it in other provinces;[2] if you contrive to hand in only 10 or 20 percent of your opium holdings as a nominal gesture—if you do any of these things, you, being obdurate and irredeemable, will be regarded as having clearly defied the Chinese authority. In such a case, you will be immediately and severely punished in accordance with the new law, which we cannot let you trample on with impunity, however benevolent our policy towards foreigners is.

While in the capital, I was instructed by His Majesty the Emperor to enforce the law without compromise. He granted me this official seal so I could proceed to do whatever the circumstances would require. I can assure you that mine is not a routine inspection of an ordinary matter. As long as this opium poison is not eliminated, I shall stay here and will not return to the capital. I have vowed to live or die on this issue, and I certainly will not stop with halfway measures.

All Chinese have been greatly angered by your selling of opium to China. If you foreigners do not repent of the crimes you have committed and insist on making profit at the expense of principle, our army and navy will be able to deal effectively with you, and even our militiamen, when called upon to demonstrate their might, will be more than strong enough to deliver you a deadly blow. There are a number of measures we can take: we can either seal your ships on a temporary basis or close the port of entry forever. In short, there is no difficulty on our part in terminating all trade. China has a territory measured by many thousands of square *li* and produces a variety of items in abundance. If she chooses not to supply you foreigners with her products, your very livelihood will be endangered. Being traders who have traveled far and wide, why can you not understand the vast difference between peaceful trade and hostile encounter and between the powerful and the numerous on the one hand and the wealthy and the few on the other?[3]

I have in my possession the names of those treacherous foreigners who peddle opium in the foreign quarters. I realize that there are good foreigners who do not trade in opium and consequently should be differentiated from the bad ones. Traders who report on their colleagues' wrongdoings, who urge the latter to hand in their opium, and who are among the first to sign the pledge not to ship any more opium to China are to be regarded as good foreigners and will be rewarded accordingly. It is up to you to decide whether you prefer honor to shame, happiness to disaster.

I am ordering the Co-hong merchant Wu Shao-yung to proceed to the foreign quarters to persuade you on this matter, and I expect a reply from him in three days. You should in the meantime write your pledge to be handed in on a date that will be announced later, after I have had the opportunity to consult with the governor-general and the governor. There should not be any hesitation or delay on your part, so that you will not have sorrowful but futile regrets in the future.

NOTES

[1] This message to foreign traders was dated March 18, 1839. Source: *Complete Works of Lin Tse-hsü* (*Lin Wen-chung kung cheng-shu*), vol. 2, roll 1.
[2] Chinese provinces other than Kwangtung.
[3] Chinese on the one hand and foreigners on the other.

24 • Lin Tse-hsü: *A Letter to Queen Victoria*[1]

His Majesty the Emperor comforts and cherishes foreigners as well as Chinese; he loves all the people in the world without discrimination. Whenever profit is found, he wishes to share it with all men; whenever harm appears, he likewise will eliminate it on behalf of all of mankind. His heart is in fact the heart of the whole universe.

Generally speaking, the succeeding rulers of your honorable country have been respectful and obedient. Time and again they have sent petitions to China, saying: "We are grateful to His Majesty the Emperor for the impartial and favorable treatment he has granted to the citizens of my country who have come to China to trade," etc. I am pleased to learn that you, as the ruler of your honorable country, are thoroughly familiar with the principle of righteousness and are grateful for the favor that His Majesty the Emperor has bestowed upon your subjects. Because of this fact, the Celestial Empire, following its traditional policy of treating foreigners with kindness, has been doubly considerate towards the people from England. You have traded in China for almost 200 years, and as a result, your country has become wealthy and prosperous.

As this trade has lasted for a long time, there are bound to be unscrupulous as well as honest traders. Among the unscrupulous are those who bring opium to China to harm the Chinese; they succeed so well that this poison has spread far and wide in all the provinces. You, I hope, will certainly agree that people who pursue material gains to the great detriment of the welfare of others can be neither tolerated by Heaven nor endured by men. Having learned about this deadly poison, His Majesty the Emperor was furious with anger; he dispatched me to Kwangtung Province to examine the situation more thoroughly and, in consultation with the governor-general and the governor, to adopt necessary remedial measures. One of our decisions was that any Chinese peddling or smoking opium would be put to death. In view of the fact that foreigners have shipped and sold opium for many years and have indeed brought indescribable harm to the Chinese people in order to enrich themselves, these foreigners should be executed in accordance with the new law. However, they have expressed repentance and begged for forgiveness; their consul Elliot[2] has handed over their opium, totaling 20,283 chests, to the responsible Chinese authorities. Subsequently, all this opium was destroyed by burning, and I have reported this fact to the imperial government. Taking into consideration the fact that these foreigners have voluntarily surrendered their opium and therefore deserve compassion, His Majesty the Emperor has decided to grant them a special dispensation: to forgive them for the crimes they have committed in the past. If they commit the same crime in the future, they will be punished in accordance with the new law. It is hoped that you, admiring China and the Chinese civilization as the ruler of England, will instruct your subjects to be diligent in observing the Chinese law. Emphatically you should let them know how grave the consequences will be if they choose not to observe it. Under no circumstances will we allow foreigners in China to violate the Chinese law.

Your country is more than 60,000 *li* from China. The purpose of your ships in coming to China is to realize a large profit. Since this profit is realized in China and is in fact taken away from the Chinese people, how can foreigners return injury for the benefit they have received by sending this poison to harm their benefactors? They may not intend to harm others on purpose, but the fact remains that they are so obsessed with material gain that they have no concern whatever for the harm they can cause to others. Have they no conscience? I have heard that you strictly prohibit opium in your own country, indicating unmistakably that you know how harmful opium is. You do not wish opium to harm your own country, but you choose to bring that harm to other countries such as China. Why?

The products that originate from China are all useful items. They are good for food and other purposes and are easy to sell. Has China produced one item that is harmful to foreign countries? For instance, tea and rhubarb are so important to foreigners' livelihood that they have to consume them every day. Were China to concern herself only with her own advantage without showing any regard for other people's welfare, how could foreigners continue to live? Foreign products like woolen cloth and beiges rely on Chinese raw materials such as silk for their manufacturing. Had China sought only her own advantage, where would the foreigners' profit come from? The products that foreign countries need and have to import from China are too numerous to enumerate: from food products such as molasses, ginger, and cassia to useful necessities such as silk and porcelain. The imported goods from foreign countries, on the other hand, are merely playthings which can be easily dispensed with without causing any ill effect. Since we do not need these things really, what harm would come if we should decide to stop foreign trade altogether? The reason why we unhesitatingly allow foreigners to ship out such Chinese products as tea and silk is that we feel that wherever there is an advantage, it should be shared by all the people in the world. The Chinese products you buy are not only good for your own consumption but can also be resold to other countries at three times the price you have paid to the Chinese. In other words, even if you did not trade in opium, you could still triple your investment in one exchange. Your profit being so large, why do you have to be so heartless as to send this poison to harm us in the pursuance of a boundless greed? If people of other countries shipped opium to England and enticed the English people to buy and use it, I am sure that you, as a responsible ruler of your honorable country, would equally resent such imposition and would be as much determined as we are to put an end to it.

I have heard that you are a kind, compassionate monarch. I am sure that you will not do to others what you yourself do not desire. I have also heard that you have instructed every British ship that sails for Canton not to bring any prohibited goods to China. It seems that your policy is as enlightened as it is proper. The fact that British ships have continued to bring opium to China results perhaps from the impossibility of making a thorough inspection of all of them owing to their large numbers. I am sending you this letter to reiterate the seriousness with which we enforce the law of the Celestial Empire and to make sure that merchants from your honorable country will not attempt to violate it again.

I have heard that the areas under your direct jurisdiction such as London, Scotland, and Ireland do not produce opium; it is produced instead in your Indian possessions such as Bengal, Madras, Bombay, Patna, and Malwa. In these possessions the English people not only plant opium poppies that stretch from one mountain to another but also open factories to manufacture this terrible drug. As months accumulate and years pass by, the poison they have produced increases in its wicked intensity, and its repugnant odor reaches as high as the sky. Heaven is furious with anger, and all the gods are moaning with pain! It is hereby suggested that you destroy and plow under all of these opium plants and grow food crops instead, while issuing an order to punish severely anyone who dares to plant opium poppies again. If you adopt this policy of love so as to produce good and exterminate evil, Heaven will protect you, and gods will bring you good fortune. Moreover, you will enjoy a long life and be rewarded with a multitude of children and grandchildren! In short, by taking this one measure, you can bring great happiness to others as well as yourself. Why do you not do it?

The right of foreigners to reside in China is a special favor granted by the Celestial Empire, and the profits they have made are those realized in China. As time passes by, some of them stay in China for a longer period than they do in their own country. For every government, past or present, one of its primary functions is to educate all the people living within its jurisdiction, foreigners as well as its own citizens, about the law and to punish them if they choose to violate it. Since a foreigner who goes to England to trade has to obey the English law, how can an Englishman not obey the Chinese law when he is physically within China? The present law calls for the imposition of the death sentence on any Chinese who has peddled or smoked opium. Since a Chinese could not peddle or smoke opium if foreigners had not brought it to China, it is clear that the true culprits of a Chinese's death as a result of an opium conviction are the opium traders from foreign countries. Being the cause of other people's death, why should they themselves be spared from capital punishment? A murderer of one person is subject to the death sentence; just imagine how many people opium has killed! This is the rationale behind the new law which says that any foreigner who brings opium to China will be sentenced to death by hanging or beheading. Our purpose is to eliminate this poison once and for all and to the benefit of all mankind.

In his petition to us in the second month last, your consul Elliot requested a longer period before the opium prohibition law takes effect on the ground that the punishment provided in it is too severe for it to be enforced immediately. He suggested that the law might be effective at the end of a five-month period for merchants who come from India and at the end of a ten-month period for those who come from England. I have transmitted this request to His Majesty the Emperor who, going beyond his usual generosity and being doubly compassionate in this particular case, has agreed that foreigners who bring opium to China by mistake during the next eighteen-month period will not be subject to prosecution if, on arriving in China, they voluntarily surrender the opium they have brought with them. If they continue to bring opium to China after the eighteen-month period, their action can only be interpreted as malicious and willful, and they will be tried and sentenced to death without mercy. I believe that in handling this particular issue, we have shown benevolence and generosity to the greatest extent possible.

Our Celestial Empire towers over all other countries in virtue and possesses a power great and awesome enough to carry out its wishes. But we will not prosecute a person without warning him in advance; that is why we have made our law explicit and clear. If the merchants of your honorable country wish to enjoy trade with us on a permanent basis, they must fearfully observe our law by cutting off, once and for all, the supply of opium. Under no circumstance should they test our intention to enforce the law by deliberately violating it. You, as the ruler of your honorable country, should do your part to uncover the hidden and unmask the wicked. It is hoped that you will continue to enjoy your country and become more and more respectful and obeisant. How wonderful it is that we can all enjoy the blessing of peace!

It is further hoped that once you receive this letter, you will immediately convey the reasons behind the prohibition of opium to all who need to know them. Please do not delay.

NOTES

[1] This letter was dated August 27, 1839. Source: *Lin Wen-chung kung cheng-shu,* vol. 2, roll 3.
[2] Charles Elliot (1801–1875).

25 • LORD PALMERSTON: *British Grievances and Demands for Redress*[1]

THE UNDERSIGNED, Her Britannick Majesty's Principal Secretary of State for Foreign Affairs, has the honour to inform the Minister of The Emperor of China, that Her Majesty The Queen of Great Britain has sent a Naval and Military Force to the Coast of China, to demand from The Emperor satisfaction and redress for injuries inflicted by Chinese Authorities upon British Subjects resident in China, and for insults offered by those same Authorities to the British Crown.

For more than a hundred years, commercial intercourse has existed between China and Great Britain; and during that long period of time, British Subjects have been allowed by the Chinese Government to reside within the territory of China for the purpose of carrying out trade therein. Hence it has happened that British Subjects, trusting in the good faith of the Chinese Government, have fixed themselves in Canton as Merchants, and have brought into that city from time to time property to a large amount; while other British Subjects who wished to trade with China, but who could not for various reasons go thither themselves, have sent commodities to Canton, placing those commodities in the care of some of their fellow Countrymen resident in China, with directions that such commodities should be sold in China, and that the produce of the sale thereof should be sent to the Owners in the British Dominions.

Thus there has always been within the territory of The Emperor of China a certain number of British Subjects, and a large amount of British Property; and though no Treaty has existed between the Sovereign of England and the Emperor of China, yet British Subjects have continued to resort to China for purposes of trade, placing full confidence in the justice and good faith of The Emperor.

Moreover, of late years the Sovereign of Great Britain has stationed at Canton an officer of the British Crown, no wise connected with trade, and specially forbidden to trade, but ordered to place himself in direct communication with the local Authorities at Canton in order to afford protection to British Subjects, and to be the organ of communication between the British and the Chinese Governments.

But the British Government has learnt with much regret, and with extreme surprise, that during the last year certain officers, acting under the Authority of The Emperor of China, have committed violent outrages against the British Residents at Canton, who were living peacefully in that City, trusting to the good faith of the Chinese Government; and that those same Chinese officers, forgetting the respect which was due to the British Superintendent in his Character of Agent of the British Crown, have treated that Superintendent also with violence and indignity.

It seems that the course [sic] assigned for these proceedings was the contraband trade in Opium, carried on by some British Subjects.

It appears that the Laws of the Chinese Empire forbid the importation of Opium into China, and declare that all opium which may be brought into the Country is liable to confiscation.

The Queen of England desires that Her Subjects who may go into Foreign Countries should obey the Laws of those Countries; and Her Majesty does not wish to protect them from the just consequences of any offences which they may commit in foreign parts. But, on the other hand, Her Majesty cannot permit that Her Subjects residing abroad should be treated with violence, and be exposed to insult and injustice; and when wrong is done to them, Her Majesty will see that they obtain redress.

Now if a Government makes a Law which applies both to its own Subjects and to Foreigners, such Government ought to enforce that Law impartially or not at all. If it enforces that Law on Foreigners, it is bound to enforce it also upon its own Subjects; and it has no right to permit its own Subjects to violate the Law with impunity, and then to punish Foreigners for doing the very same thing.

Neither is it just that such a Law should for a great length of time be allowed to sleep as a dead letter, and that both Natives and Foreigners should be taught to consider it as of no effect, and that then suddenly, and without sufficient warning, it should be put in force with the utmost rigour and severity.

Now, although the Law of China declared that the importation of Opium should be forbidden, yet it is notorious that for many years past, that importation has been connived at and permitted by the Chinese Authorities at Canton; nay, more, that those Authorities, from the Governor downwards, have made an annual and considerable profit to import Opium; and of late the Chinese Authorities have gone so far in setting this Law at defiance, that Mandarin Boats were employed to bring opium to Canton from the Foreign Ships lying at Lintin.

Did the Imperial Government at Peking know these things?

If it did know these things, it virtually abolished its own Law, by permitting its own officers to act as if no such Law existed. If the Chinese Government says it did not know of these things, if it says that it knew indeed that the Law was violated by Foreigners who brought in opium, but did not know that the Law was violated by its own Officers who assisted in the importation, and received fixed Sums of money for permitting it, then may Foreign Governments ask, how it happened that a Government so watchful as that of China should have one eye open to see the transgressions of Foreigners, but should have the other eye shut, and unable to see the transgressions of its own officers.

If the Chinese Government had suddenly determined that the Law against the importation of Opium should be enforced, instead of remaining, as it long had been, a dead letter, that Government should have begun by punishing its own Officers who were the greatest delinquents in this matter, because it was their special duty to execute the Law of their own Sovereign. But the course pursued by the Chinese Government has been the very reverse; for they have left unpunished their own officers, who were most to blame, and they have used violence against Foreigners, who were led into transgression by the encouragement and protection afforded to them by the Governor of Canton and his inferior Officers.

Still, however, the British Government would not have complained, if the Government of China, after giving due notice of its altered intentions, had proceeded to excute the Law of the Empire, and had seized and confiscated all the opium which they could find within the Chinese territory, and which had been brought into that territory in violation of the Law. The Chinese Government had a right to do so, by means of its own officers, and within its own territory.

But for some reason or other known only to the Government of China, that Government did not think proper to do this. But it determined to seize peaceable British Merchants, instead of seizing the contraband opium; to punish the innocent for the guilty, and to make the sufferings of the former, the means of compulsion upon the latter; and it also resolved to force the British Superintendent, who is an officer of the British Crown, to become an instrument in the hands of the Chinese Authorities for carrying into execution the Laws of China, with which he had nothing to do.

Against such proceedings the British Government protests, and for such proceedings the British Government demands satisfaction.

A large number of British Merchants who were living peaceably at Canton, were suddenly imprisoned in their houses, deprived of the assistance of their Chinese servants, and cut off from all supplies of food, and were threatened with death by starvation, unless other persons, in other places, and over whom these Merchants so imprisoned had no authority or control, would surrender to the Chinese Government a quantity of Opium which the Chinese Authorities were unable themselves to discover or to take possession of, and a portion of which was at the time not within the territories and jurisdiction of China. Her Majesty's Superintendent, upon learning the violence which was done towards these British Merchants, and the danger to which their lives were exposed, repaired, though with some risk and difficulty, to Canton, in order to enquire into the matter, and to persuade the Chinese authorities to desist from these outrageous proceedings. But the Imperial Commissioner did not listen to Her Majesty's Officer; and in violation of the Law of Nations, and in utter disregard of the respect which was due by him to an officer of the British Crown, he imprisoned the Superintendent as well as the Merchants, and, continuing to deprive them all of the means of subsistence, he threatened to put them all to death by starvation, unless the Superintendent would give to other persons, not in Canton, orders which he had no power or authority to give, for delivering to the Chinese Authorities a fixed quantity of Opium.

The Superintendent, in order to save the lives of his imprisoned fellow Countrymen, gave at last the orders required of him, and the parties to whom these orders were addressed, although by no means bound to obey them, and although a great part of the property demanded, did not belong to them, but was only held by them in trust for others, yet complied with these orders, wishing no doubt to rescue the British Merchants in Canton from death, and trusting that the Queen of Great Britain would at a future time cause them to be indemnified for their loss.

The British Government cannot condemn the steps which were taken by Her Majesty's Superintendent, under the pressure of an over-ruling and irresistible force, to rescue from the barbarous fate which awaited them, so many of Her Majesty's Subjects for whose special protection the Superintendent had been appointed, and the British Government highly applauds the readiness with which the persons to whom the orders were directed surrendered the Property demanded, and showed themselves willing to submit to the destruction of their Property,[2] in order to prevent the destruction of the lives of so many of their fellow Countrymen. But the British Government demands full satisfaction from the Government of China for these things. In the first place it requires, that the Ransom which was exacted as the price for the lives of the Superintendent, and of the imprisoned British Merchants, shall be restored to the persons who paid it, and if, as the British Government is informed, the goods themselves, which were given up to the Chinese Authorities, have been so disposed of, that they cannot be restored to their owners, in the same state in which they were given up,[3] then the British Government demands and requires that the value of those goods shall be paid back by the Government of China to the British Government, in order that it may be paid over to the Parties entitled to receive it.

In the next place, the British Government demands satisfaction from the Government of China for the affront offered to the Crown of Great Britain, by the indignities to which Her Majesty's Superintendent has been subjected; and the British Government requires that in future the officer employed by Her Majesty to watch over the commercial interests of Her Subjects in China, and to be the organ of communication with the Government of China, shall be treated, and shall be communicated with by that Government, and by its officers, in a manner consistent with the usages of civilized Nations, and with the respect due to the Dignity of the British Crown.

Thirdly—The British Government demands security for the future, that British Subjects resorting to China for purposes of Trade, in conformity with the long-established understanding between the two Governments, shall not again be exposed to violence and injustice while engaged in their lawful pursuits of Commerce. For this purpose, and in order that British Merchants trading to China may not be subject to the arbitrary caprice either of the Government at Peking, or its local Authorities at the Sea-Ports of the Empire, the British Government demands that one or more sufficiently large and properly situated Islands on the Coast of China, to be fixed upon by the British Plenipotentiaries, shall be permanently given up to the British Government as a place of residence and of commerce for British Subjects; where their persons may be safe from molestation, and where their Property may be secure.

Moreover, it appears that the Chinese Government has hitherto compelled the British Merchants resident at Canton to sell their goods to certain Hong Merchants,[4] and to no other persons, and the Chinese Government, by thus restricting the dealings of the British Merchants, has become responsible for the Hong Merchants to whom those dealings were confined. But some of those Hong Merchants have lately become insolvent, and the British Merchants have thus incurred great pecuniary losses, which they would have avoided, if they had been allowed to trade with whomsoever they chose. The British Government therefore demands that the Government of China shall make good to the British Creditors the Sums due to them by the insolvent Hong Merchants.

The British Government moreover has recently heard of further acts of violence committed by the Chinese Authorities against British Subjects; and it may happen that before this Note reaches the Chinese Minister, other things may have been done in China, which may render necessary further demands on the part of the British Government. If this should be, the British Plenipotentiaries are authorised to make such further demands; and the Undersigned requests the Chinese Minister to consider any additional demands so made, as being as fully authorised by the British Government as if they had been specified in this note.

Now as the distance is great which separates England from China, and as the matter in question is of urgent importance, the British Government cannot wait to know the answer which the Chinese Government may give to these demands, and thus postpone till that answer shall have been received in England, the measures which may be necessary in order to vindicate the honour and dignity of the British Crown, in the event of that answer not being satisfactory.

The British Government therefore has determined at once to send out a Naval and Military Force to the Coast of China to act in support of these demands, and in order to convince the Imperial Government that the British Government attaches the utmost importance to this matter, and that the affair is one which will not admit of delay.

And further, for the purpose of impressing still more strongly upon the Government of Peking the importance which the British Government attaches to this matter, and the urgent necessity which exists for an immediate as well as a satisfactory settlement thereof, the Commander of the Expedition has received orders that, immediately upon his arrival upon the Chinese Coast, he shall proceed to blockade the principal Chinese ports, that he shall intercept and detain and hold in deposit all Chinese Vessels which he may meet with, and that he shall take possession of some convenient part of the Chinese territory, to be held and occupied by the British Forces until everything shall be concluded and executed to the satisfaction of the British Government.

These measures of hostility on the part of Great Britain against China are not only justified, but even rendered absolutely necessary, by the outrages which have been committed by the Chinese Authorities against British officers and Subjects, and these hostilities will not cease, until a satisfactory arrangement shall have been made by the Chinese Government.

The British Government in order to save time, and to afford to the Government of China every facility for coming to an early arrangement, have given to the Admiral and to the Superintendent, Full Powers and Instructions to treat upon these matters with the Imperial Government, and have ordered the said Admiral and Superintendent to go up to the Mouth of the Peiho River, in the Gulph of Pechelee,[5] that they may be within a short distance of the Imperial Cabinet. But after the indignity which was offered to Her Majesty's Superintendent at Canton, in the course of last year, it is impossible for Her Majesty's Government to permit any of Her Majesty's Officers to place themselves in the power of the Chinese Authorities, until some formal Treaty shall have been duly signed, securing to British Subjects safety and respect in China; and therefore the Undersigned must request that the Chinese Government will have the goodness to send on board the Admiral's Ship the Plenipotentiaries whom the Emperor may appoint to treat upon these matters with the Plenipotentiaries of The Queen of England. Those Chinese Plenipotentiaries shall be received on board the Admiral's Ship, with every honour which is due to the Envoys of The Emperor, and shall be treated with all possible courtesy and respect.

The Undersigned has further to state, that the necessity for sending this Expedition to the Coast of China having been occasioned by the violent and unjustifiable acts of the Chinese Authorities, the British Government expects and demands, that the expenses incurred thereby shall be repaid to Great Britain by the Government of China.

The Undersigned has now stated and explained to the Chinese Minister, without reserve, the causes of complaint on the part of Great Britain; the reparation which Great Britain demands, and the nature of the measures which the British officer commanding the Expedition has been instructed in the first instance to take. The British Government fervently hopes that the wisdom and spirit of Justice for which The Emperor is famed in all parts of the World, will lead the Chinese Government to see the equity of the foregoing demands; and it is the sincere wish of Her Majesty's Government that a prompt and full compliance with those demands may lead to a speedy re-establishment of that friendly intercourse which has for so great a period of time subsisted between the British and Chinese Nations, to the manifest advantage of both.

The Undersigned, in conclusion, has the honour to state to the Minister of The Emperor of China that he has directed Her Majesty's Plenipotentiaries to forward to His Excellency the present Note, of which he has transmitted to the Plenipotentiaries a copy, with instructions to cause a Translation of it to be made into the Chinese language, and to forward to the Chinese Minister the Translation at the same time with the original Note.

The Undersigned avails himself of this opportunity to offer to His Excellency the Minister of The Emperor of China the assurances of his most distinguished consideration.

NOTES

[1] This diplomatic note, officially entitled "Lord Palmerston to the Minister of The Emperor of China," was dated February 20, 1840. The style of capitalization, punctuation, and spelling in the original document is carefully preserved in this selection. Source: Hosea Ballou Morse, *The International Relations of the Chinese Empire*; Vol. 1, *The Period of Conflict*, 1834–1860. London: Longmans, Green, and Co., 1910. Appendix A, pp. 621 626.

[2] This refers to the confiscation and subsequent destruction of British-owned opium by Commissioner Lin Tse-hsü.

[3] By then the confiscated opium had indeed been burned and reduced to ashes.

[4] Co-hong merchants.

[5] The Gulf of Pohai.

26 • Tao-kuang: *Declaration of War on Great Britain*[1]

The policy of our dynasty towards foreigners has always been that of kindness and generosity. As long as they are respectful and obedient, they are, without an exception, treated with courtesy and consideration. We adopt this policy so that both Chinese and foreigners can live happily together and jointly reap the fruit of peace.

Some time ago, owing to the spread of the opium poison, we issued special orders to prohibit its importation into the territory of China from the Western countries, a measure that was taken as part of our overall effort to reverse the trend of a long period of degeneration. Among Westerners the English were the only group that refused to make a pledge not to export opium to China again; such was their arrogance and want of principle. We consequently had no choice but to bar them from trading in China. Instead of feeling repentant after we had barred them from trading in China, they became even more rapacious with the passage of time. In the sixth month of last year, suddenly and without a warning, dozens of their ships attacked and subsequently captured Tinghai.[2] Moreover, their other ships moved up and down our coastline, creating disturbances in such provinces as Fukien, Chekiang, Kiangsu, Shantung, Chihli,[3] and Fengtien,[4] with no intention of desisting from their activities whatsoever.

By doing the things described above, these treacherous Englishmen have proceeded to the utmost limits of rapacity and cruelty. They should be punished, of course; and we could easily have mobilized our troops to exterminate them if we had minded to do so. However, taking into consideration the fact that they had presented a letter voicing their grievances, we decided to postpone any action until a thorough investigation could be made so as to show to all foreigners our fairness and impartiality in this matter. Subsequently I ordered Ch'i-shan to speed to Canton to make the aforesaid investigation. If these Englishmen had anything called a conscience within themselves, they should have proceeded to that city waiting for our decisions. No, they did not: only half of them sailed southward, while the rest continued to entrench themselves at Tinghai. How could anyone not become furious in view of this treachery! It is further reported that during the past several months they have raped our women, stolen our properties, built fortifications, and dug canals. Moreover, they have forced local officials to issue illegal orders for the purpose of exacting tax payments. How unjust it is that our innocent people should suffer this kind of treatment! Whenever I think of this, I am so concerned that I cannot enjoy peace even for a brief moment.

Upon his arrival at Canton, Ch'i-shan did his best to enlighten the English in the most frank manner. But the English were as greedy as they were ruthless. They demanded payments not only for all the opium we had confiscated but also for the expenses occasioned by their military expedition against China. Knowing how dishonest and unreliable they were and realizing the fact that they would not listen to reason and be convinced by it, I, during the last year, had taken the precaution of ordering troops from Szechuan, Kweichow, Hunan, and Kiangsi to proceed to Kwangtung, in preparation for attack against the invaders. Meanwhile orders were also issued to Hupeh, Hunan, and Anhwei to rush troops to Chekiang for the same purpose.

According to a recent report submitted by Ch'i-shan, the English, with the collaboration of many Chinese traitors, sailed towards Humen[5] on the fifteenth day of the twelfth month [January 7, 1841], opened fire, and injured many of our men and officers. Subsequently they attacked and then captured Tachiao and Shachiao fortresses. Being beastly in nature, they acted in violation of Heavenly reason as well as the sound principle that governs the relationship among men. The gods in Heaven and people on earth cannot tolerate a situation like this. The only course open for us is to exterminate them, so that the gods may be comforted in Heaven and people can once more enjoy peace on earth.

The troops we have mobilized will arrive at their respective destinations shortly. Let Yi-li-pu lead his men to recover Tinghai from the enemy so as to relieve the sufferings of our people in that area. Let Ch'i-shan rally his men and move forward courageously so as to capture the enemy[6] and bring him in a cage to the capital [Peking], where he will be punished in the manner prescribed by our law. All the invaders and their Chinese collaborators should be annihilated forthwith.

As for the coastal areas, orders have been repeatedly issued to strengthen the defense. Let the generals, governors-general, and governors alert their men for intensified patrol and attack the invaders whenever and wherever they make their appearance. Let all the officials and all the people be united as one man: to defeat the enemy and win victory over him at the earliest moment. Generous rewards await their success: may they not fail in this undertaking!

This proclamation is to be made known all over China and throughout the world.

NOTES

[1] This declaration of war, in the form of public proclamation, was issued on January 27, 1841, after Great Britain had already captured some of the Chinese fortresses along the coast. Source: *Ch'ou-pan yi-wu shih-mo,* the Reign of Tao-kuang, roll 20, pp. 24–25.
[2] Tinghai is a city on the Chushan Islands, off the coast of Chekiang Province. The British captured it on July 5, 1840.
[3] Modern Hopeh Province.
[4] Modern Liaoning Province.
[5] Located southeast of Canton.
[6] Captain Charles Elliot (1801–1875), Superintendent of British Trade in China.

27 • LORD ABERDEEN: *The Advisability of Legalizing the Opium Trade*[1]

Her Majesty's Government entirely approve the judicious Manner in which you called the attention of the Chinese Commissioners to the Opium Trade, in the Memorandum which you delivered to them on the 27th of August; and although it could scarcely be expected that the Commissioners should be prepared to at once state the determination of the Emperor on a subject of such great importance, Her Majesty's Government have received with no little satisfaction the assurance given to you by the commissioners "that the Officers of China shall certainly be enjoined to confine their jurisdiction in that respect to the Soldiery and people of the Country, not allowing them to make use of it. Whether the Merchant Ships of the various Countries bring Opium or not, China will not need to enquire, or to take any proceedings with regard thereto."

If the principle involved in this assurance is steadily acted upon by the Chinese Authorities, there appears no reason to apprehend collision with them on account of Opium. But it cannot be denied that as long as the Trade in opium is a Smuggling Trade, there will be always more or less risk of serious misunderstanding between the two Governments; as the Chinese Government will with difficulty be made to comprehend that Her Majesty's Government, however well disposed they might be to put a stop to the traffic being carried on by the British Subjects, have not the means of doing so, and even if they had, would be unable to prevent the introduction of Opium into China by the Subjects or Citizens of other Powers. It would therefore be very desirable that you should press upon the Chinese Government the expediency of legalizing the sale of Opium. Admitting that we place full reliance on their assurance that the British Smuggler will not be interferred with, you might point out to them that collisions must arise between their own Soldiery and the Chinese Smugglers, and that loss of life must ensue from such collisions. You may call their attention to the state of disturbance which must prevail in all districts in which this unlawful practice is carried on, and to the consequent demoralization of the people engaged in it, which may be more fatal in its results than the demoralization supposed to attend the use of the drug.

It may also be suggested whether it is not probable that the withdrawal of the prohibition against the use of opium, might not have a tendency to diminish the chances of its being used, as it is now said to be in defiance of that prohibition, to excess. It could be considered as no little gain for a paternal Government like that of China that a cause of offence against the law, and the consequent necessity for punishment of offenders, should be removed, and on the other hand the Chinese Government would gain largely by the Revenue which would accrue to it from the admission of Opium at such a rate of duty as would at once put an end to the Smuggling Trade and all the Evils attendant upon it.

But whatever may be the result of your endeavours to prevail with the Chinese Government to legalize the sale of Opium, it will be right that Her Majesty's servants in China should hold themselves aloof from all connection with so discreditable a traffick. The British Opium Smuggler must receive no protection or support in the prosecution of his illegal speculation; and he must be made aware that he will have to take the consequences of his own conduct. Her Majesty's Government, as I have stated above, have not the power to put a stop to this trade on the part of the British Smuggler; but they may perhaps impede it in some degree by preventing the Island of Hong Kong or its neighbouring waters from being used as the point from whence British Smugglers shall depart on their illegal adventures. As the case stands at present with regard to Hong Kong, the Queen cannot prohibit the importation of Opium into Hong Kong; but as soon as you assume the Government of the Island on the completion of its cession to the Crown, you will have the power to prohibit the importation of Opium into Hong Kong for the purpose of exportation, or its deposit on board receiving Vessels in the waters of Hong Kong for the same purpose. You will also have the power to prevent Vessels with Cargoes of Opium from frequenting the Port of Hong Kong on their way to the Coasts of China. If the importation of Opium into Hong Kong in greater quantities than are required for consumption in the Island is prohibited, the undue resort of Vessels with Opium on board, as giving room for suspicion that the Opium is intended to be introduced into the Island contrary to the prohibition, may also reasonably be prohibited.

Her Majesty's Government, however, are sensible that this Measure, though it may relieve them from the imputation of encouraging the Opium Trade, will do but little to mitigate the evils which result from the present system. They wish therefore that you would consider whether it would be possible to place the trade, even as a Smuggling trade, on a less discreditable footing than that on which it is now carried on. The only effectual remedy indeed is in the power of the Chinese Government, and therefore it will be proper that you do your utmost to induce that Government to sanction the trade even if they should confine it to the single Port of Canton. Her Majesty's Government would in that case endeavor to assist the Chinese Government in carrying this limitation into effect, by withholding clearances for Vessels having opium on board, which should be destined for other Ports. But so long as the prohibition against the introduction of Opium into China is absolute, Her Majesty's Government can do no more for China in that respect than prevent the Island of Hong Kong from being a resort and Market for the British Smuggler.

ABERDEEN

NOTES

[1] This instruction, dated January 4, 1843, was addressed by Lord Aberdeen (George Hamilton-Gordon, 1784–1860) of the British Foreign Office to Sir Henry Pottinger, the British Plenipotentiary to China. Source: Hosea Ballou Morse: *The International Relations of the Chinese Empire,* vol. I, appendix P, pp. 668–669.

CHAPTER FOUR

The Treaty System

The Treaty of Nanking (Selection 28), the first of a long series of the so-called unequal treaties, was followed by the Treaty of The Bogue (1843), in which China agreed to grant to Great Britain extraterritoriality in criminal cases and also the most-favored-nation treatment. Seeing the great advantages implied in these concessions, other powers began to follow suit, and through persuasion combined with the threat of physical force, demanded and received the same or even larger concessions. The American treaty, the Treaty of Wanghia (July 1844), for instance, extended the principle of extraterritoriality to include civil as well as criminal cases (Selection 29). France was given the right to build Roman Catholic missions at the treaty ports and the freedom to proselytize without interference from the Chinese government, though such concessions did not form a part of the official treaty (Franco-Chinese Treaty, October 1844). Because of the operation of the most-favored-nation clause which ensured that new privileges were automatically extended to all countries which had or were going to have treaty relations with China, understandably all the treaty powers worked in concert on their policy towards China.

For Western traders, the conclusion of these treaties was a master stroke; they opened new markets and brought about large profits. Not surprisingly, the traders wanted to enlarge further their sphere of commercial activities. Observant of their wishes and acting on their behalf, their respective governments began to exercise pressure on China to obtain more concessions, commercial or otherwise (Selection 30). Since the Chinese were unhappy about the existing concessions, to say nothing of granting new ones, it seemed clear that force had to be applied if Western wishes were to be fulfilled. In the war that followed (1858) the British and the French easily defeated the poorly trained, inadequately armed Chinese. When they threatened to attack Tientsin, the Manchu government sued for peace. The new peace, called Treaties of Tientsin (1858), granted new concessions and enlarged some old ones (Selection 31). But the Chinese refused to ratify them even after they had been signed. Hostilities were renewed, and Tientsin and Peking were soon captured by the allies. Great Britain dictated to the Chinese another treaty, the Peking Convention (Selection 32), incorporating some of the demands (such as the lease of Kowloon) which, owing largely to oversight, she had neglected to write into the Treaty of Tientsin.

The treaties of 1858–1860, together with those of 1842–1844, were the first of a series that provided the basis of relationship between China and the

Western powers (and later Japan) until World War II. The Chinese called them "unequal treaties," because the benefits provided in these treaties went exclusively to the treaty powers at the expense of China. They reduced China to the status of a subcolony with many masters, said Dr. Sun Yat-sen (1866–1925), all of whom exploited her without rendering anything in return. The question may be asked: how could these treaties that may have looked innocent enough from a Westerner's point of view become so evil in the eyes of a Chinese? Though this question is by no means easy to answer, it should be kept in mind that when these treaties were concluded, neither China nor the Western powers foresaw their implications. In other words, the abuse of treaty rights was by and large a later development, resulting mostly from the broad interpretation of treaty provisions.

To illustrate this point, consider the much-denounced concessions. As late as 1864 Anson Burlingame, the American minister to China, could still state emphatically: "There are no such things as concessions in the sense generally understood by that term. . . . We have no right for municipal or other purposes, to take jurisdiction of Chinese, or of the subjects of non-treaty powers, even though requested to do so by the Chinese authorities" (Selection 33). But a fair-minded man like Anson Burlingame was more an exception than a rule, and the so-called concessions gradually came to mean certain quarters of the treaty ports over which the Chinese had no jurisdiction. Since the Chinese who lived in these concessions were many times more numerous than the foreigners who also lived there, the broad interpretation of foreigners' right to reside in the treaty ports (as provided in the treaties) resulted in the loss of jurisdictional right on the part of China over a large number of her own citizens within the territorial boundaries of China. No one could deny that a violation of the treaties as well as of a general principle of international law had taken place. But as long as China was too weak to demand her rights, she lost them by default.

The broad interpretation of treaty terms and China's inability to resist it accounted for much of the abuse in the treaty system. Whatever their political orientations, all Chinese leaders, from Li Hung-chang to Mao Tse-tung, denounced the unequal treaties whenever they had the opportunity. They attributed most of China's ills, including her inability to modernize, to the existence of this unequal-treaty system, which to them was a clever but immoral device for bleeding China white so as to enrich further the more wealthy Western powers and Japan. The Chinese case may often have been overstated; it is nevertheless true that we cannot understand the China of the past one hundred years without bearing in mind the unequal treaties and China's bitter reaction to them (Selection 34). It may not be an exaggeration to say that the agitation for the abolition of the unequal treaties provided the strongest driving force for Chinese nationalism.

28 • *The Treaty of Nanking*[1]

ARTICLE I

There shall henceforward be peace and friendship between Her Majesty the Queen of the United Kingdom of Great Britain and Ireland and His Majesty the Emperor of China, and between their respective subjects, who shall enjoy full security and protection for their persons and property within the dominions of the other.

ARTICLE II

His Majesty the Emperor of China agrees, that British subjects with their families and establishments, shall be allowed to reside, for the purpose of carrying on their mercantile pursuits, without molestation or restraint, at the cities and towns of Canton, Amoy, Foochowfoo,[2] Ningpo, and Shanghai.

And Her Majesty the Queen of Great Britain, &c., will appoint Superintendents, or Consular Officers, to reside at each of the above named cities or towns, to be the medium of communication between the Chinese authorities and the said merchants, and to see that the just duties and other dues of the Chinese Government, as hereafter provided for, are duly discharged by Her Britannic Majesty's subjects.

ARTICLE III

It being obviously necessary and desirable that British subjects should have some port whereat they may careen and refit their ships, when required, and keep stores for that purpose, His Majesty the Emperor of China cedes to Her Majesty the Queen of Great Britain, &c., the Island of Hong Kong, to be possessed in perpetuity by Her Britannic Majesty, her heirs and successors, and to be governed by such laws and regulations as Her Majesty the Queen of Great Britain, &c., shall see fit to direct.

ARTICLE IV

The Emperor of China agrees to pay the sum of 6,000,000 dollars, as the value of the Opium which was delivered up at Canton in the month of March, 1839, as a ransom for the lives of Her Britannic Majesty's Superintendent and subjects, who had been imprisoned and threatened with death by the Chinese High Officers.

ARTICLE V

The Government of China having compelled the British merchants trading at Canton to deal exclusively with certain Chinese merchants, called Hong merchants (or Co-Hong), who had been licensed by the Chinese Government for that purpose, the Emperor of China agrees to abolish that practice in future at all ports where British merchants may reside, and to permit them to carry on their mercantile transactions with whatever persons they please; and His Imperial Majesty further agrees to pay to the British Government the sum of 3,000,000 dollars, on account of debts due to British subjects by some of the Hong merchants or Co-Hong, who have become insolvent, and who owe very large sums of money to subjects of Her Britannic Majesty.

ARTICLE VI

The Government of Her Britannic Majesty having been obliged to send out an expedition to demand and obtain redress for the violent and unjust proceedings of

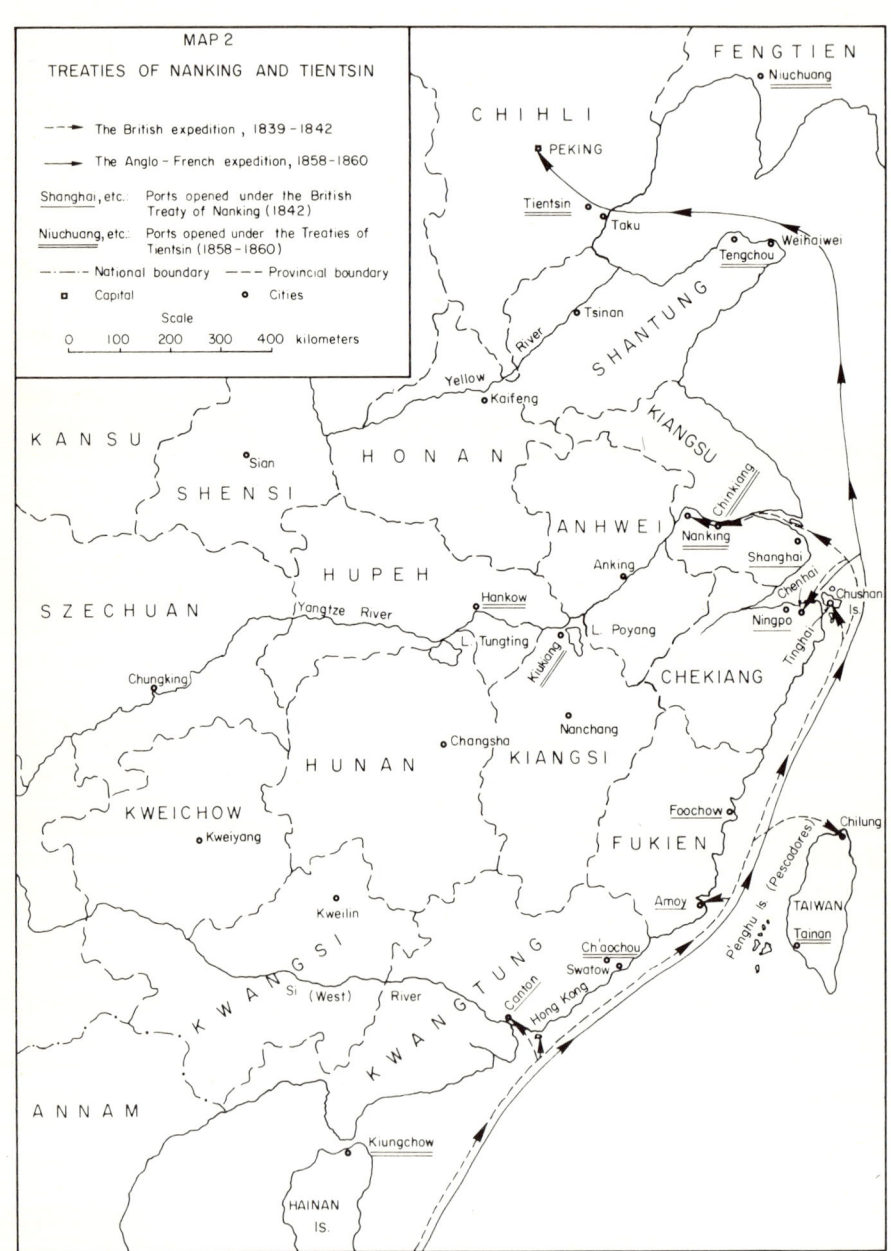

the Chinese High Authorities towards Her Britannic Majesty's Officers and subjects, the Emperor of China agrees to pay the sum of 12,000,000 dollars, on account of the expenses incurred; and Her Britannic Majesty's Plenipotentiary voluntarily agrees, on behalf of Her Majesty, to deduct from the said amount of 12,000,000 dollars, any sums which may have been received by Her Majesty's combined forces, as ransom for cities and towns in China, subsequent to the 1st day of August, 1841.

ARTICLE VII

It is agreed, that the total amount of 21,000,000 dollars, described in the 3 preceding Articles, shall be paid as follows: —

6,000,000 immediately.

6,000,000 in 1843; that is, 3,000,000 on or before the 30th of the month of June, and 3,000,000 on or before the 31st of December.

5,000,000 in 1844; that is, 2,500,000 on or before the 30th day of June, and 2,500,000 on or before the 31st of December.

4,000,000 in 1845; that is, 2,000,000 on or before the 30th of June, and 2,000,000 on or before the 31st of December.

And it is further stipulated, that interest, at the rate of 5 per cent. per annum, shall be paid by the Government of China on any portion of the above sums that are not punctually discharged at the periods fixed.

ARTICLE VIII

The Emperor of China agrees to release unconditionally all Subjects of Her Britannic Majesty (whether Natives of Europe or India) who may be in confinement at this moment, in any part of the Chinese Empire.

ARTICLE IX

The Emperor of China agrees to publish and promulgate, under His Imperial Sign Manual and Seal, a full and entire amnesty and act of indemnity, to all Subjects of China on account of their having resided under, or having had dealings and intercourse with, or having entered the Service of Her Britannic Majesty, or of Her Majesty's officers, and His Imperial Majesty futher engages to release all Chinese Subjects who may be at this moment in confinement for similar reasons.

ARTICLE X

His Majesty the Emperor of China agrees to establish at all the ports which are, by Article II of this Treaty, to be thrown open for the resort of British merchants, a fair and regular tariff of export and import customs and other dues, which tariff shall be publicly notified and promulgated for general introduction.

And the Emperor further engages, that when British merchandise shall have once paid at any of the said ports the regulated customs and dues, agreeable to the tariff to be hereafter fixed, such merchandise may be conveyed by Chinese merchants to any province or city in the interior of the Empire of China, on paying a further amount as transit duties, which shall not exceed [blank] per cent. on the tariff value of such goods.

ARTICLE XI

It is agreed that Her Britannic Majesty's Chief High Officer in China shall correspond with the Chinese High Officers, both at the capital and in the provinces, under the term "communication;"³ the subordinate British Officers and Chinese High Officers in the provinces, under the terms "statement"⁴ on the part of the former, and on the part of the latter, "declaration;"⁵ and the subordinates of both countries on a footing of perfect equality: merchants and others not holding official situations, and therefore not included in the above, on both sides, to use the term "representation"⁶ in all papers addressed to, or intended for the notice of, the respective Governments.

ARTICLE XII

On the assent of the Emperor of China to this Treaty being received, and the discharge of the first instalment of money, Her Britannic Majesty's forces will retire from Nanking and the Grand Canal, and will no longer molest or stop the trade of China. The military post at Chinhai will also be withdrawn; but the Islands of Koolangsoo, and that of Chusan, will continue to be held by Her Majesty's forces until the money payments, and the arrangements for opening the ports to British merchants, be completed.

ARTICLE XIII

The ratification of this Treaty by Her Majesty the Queen of Great Britain, &c., and His Majesty the Emperor of China, shall be exchanged as soon as the great distance which separates England from China will admit; but, in the meantime, counterpart copies of it, signed and sealed by the Plenipotentiaries, on behalf of their respective Sovereigns, shall be mutually delivered, and all its provisions and arrangements shall take effect.

Done at Nanking, and signed and sealed by the Plenipotentiaries on board Her Britannic Majesty's ship "Cornwallis," this 29th day of August, 1842; corresponding with the Chinese date, 24th of the 7th month, in the 22nd year of Taoukwang.⁷

NOTES

¹ This document is officially entitled "Treaty of Peace, Friendship, Commerce, Indemnity, &c.," between Great Britain and China," signed at Nanking, 29th August, 1842. Source: The Maritime Customs of China, *Treaties, Conventions, etc., between China and Foreign States* (2nd ed., Shanghai, 1917), vol. I, pp. 351–356.
² Foochow.
³ This is followed by the word *chao-hui* in Chinese characters.
⁴ This followed by the word *shen-ch'en* in Chinese characters.
⁵ This is followed by the word *cha-hsing* in Chinese characters.
⁶ This is followed by the word *pin-ming* in Chinese characters.
⁷ Tao-kuang.

29 • *The Treaty of Wanghia*¹

ARTICLE II

Citizens of the United States resorting to China for the purposes of commerce will pay the duties of import and export prescribed in the tariff, which is fixed by and made a part of this Treaty. They shall in no case be subject to other or higher duties than are or shall be required of the people of any other nation whatever.

Fees and charges of every sort are wholly abolished; and officers of the revenue, who may be guilty of exaction, shall be punished according to the laws of China. If the Chinese Government desire to modify in any respect the said tariff, such modifications shall be made only in consultation with the consuls or other functionaries thereto duly authorized in behalf of the United States, and with consent thereof. And if additional advantages or privileges, of whatever description, be conceded hereafter by China, to any other nation, the United States, and the citizens thereof, shall be entitled thereupon to a complete, equal and impartial participation in the same. . . .

ARTICLE XVIII

It shall be lawful for the officers or citizens of the United States to employ scholars and people of any part of China, without distinction of persons, to teach any of the languages of the empire, and to assist in literary labours; and the persons so employed shall not, for that cause, be subject to any injury on the part either of the Government or of individuals; and it shall in like manner be lawful for citizens of the United States to purchase all manner of books in China.

ARTICLE XIX

All citizens of the United States in China, peaceably attending to their affairs, being placed on a common footing of amity and good will with subjects of China, shall receive and enjoy, for themselves and every thing appertaining to them, the special protection of the local authorities of Government, who shall defend them from all insult or injury of any sort on the part of the Chinese. If their dwellings or property be threatened or attacked by mobs, incendiaries, or other violent or lawless persons, the local officers, on requisition of the Consul, will immediately despatch a military force to disperse the rioters, and will apprehend the guilty individuals, and punish them with the utmost rigour of the law.

ARTICLE XXI

Subjects of China, who may be guilty of any criminal act towards citizens of the United States, shall be arrested and punished by the Chinese authorities according to the laws of China; and citizens of the United States, who may commit any crime in China, shall be subject to be tried and punished only by the Consul, or other public functionary of the United States thereto authorized, according to the laws of the United States. And in order to the prevention of all controversy and disaffection, justice shall be equitably and impartially administered by both sides. . .

ARTICLE XXV

All questions in regard to rights, whether of property or person arising between citizens of the United States in China, shall be subject to the jurisdiction, and regulated by the authorities of their own Government; and all controversies occurring in China between citizens of the United States and the subjects of any other Government shall be regulated by the Treaties existing between the United States and such Governments respectively, without interference on the part of China. . . .

ARTICLE XXXIII

Citizens of the United States, who shall attempt to trade clandestinely with such of the ports of China as are not open to foreign commerce, or who shall trade in opium or any other contraband article of merchandize, shall be subject to be dealt with by the Chinese Government, without being entitled to any countenance or protection from that of the United States; and the United States will take measures to prevent their flag from being abused by the subjects of other nations, as a cover for the violation of the laws of the empire.

NOTES

[1] This document, officially entitled "Treaty of Peace, Amity, and Commerce Between the United States of America and the Ta Tsing Empire (China)," signed at Wanghia (or Wanghsia according to the Wade romanization), a small town near Macao, on July 3, 1844. Source: Edward Hertslet, *Treaties, &c., between Great Britain and China and between China and Foreign Powers* (London: Harrison & Sons, 1896), vol. I, pp. 385–397.

30 • LORD CLARENDON: *The Necessity of Treaty Revisions*[1]

The Queen having been pleased to appoint you to be Her Majesty's Plenipotentiary and Chief Superintendent of British Trade in China, it is my duty to furnish you with such information as to the views of Her Majesty's Government with regard to China, as may serve to guide you in the execution of the duties which you are called upon to discharge.

If you have not as yet reaped all the advantages which were anticipated at the conclusion of our Treaties with China, from the extended intercourse with that Country for which it was the object of those Treaties to provide, it is nevertheless unquestionable that the Commerce of Her Majesty's Subjects in that Quarter has made rapid progress under the protection of those Treaties, and there is therefore good reason to expect that by prudent management commerce may be still further developed, and our intercourse with the Chinese Authorities and People set free from those obstacles which have hitherto beset it. So far indeed from its being a matter of surprise that more has not been done, it is a subject for congratulation that such results have already been secured notwithstanding the difficulties of no ordinary character with which we have had to contend. It was not to be expected that the notions of superiority over other Governments, which the isolated position in which the Government of China had so long entrenched itself had served to foster, should at once give way to a conviction that its claims in that respect were unfounded; or that the arrogance of the Authorities and the prejudices of the people should be altogether exchanged for feelings of cordiality and goodwill towards those who by force of arms had acquired a right to be treated with consideration and respect.

Neither was it to be expected that Trade should immediately receive the full development of which, judging from the vast population of the Country and from the productiveness of the soil and industry of the inhabitants, it might be supposed susceptible. There were habits of long-standing to be overcome, prejudices deeply rooted to be softened down, new Marts for Trade to be established, new arrangements to be made for meeting the increased demands of the Foreign Merchants for the produce of the soil. And it cannot be doubted that much of the disappointment which had been felt at the limited expansion of our intercourse with China since the conclusion of the Treaties, has originated in a disregard of these considerations.

We have now however arrived at a stage in our intercourse with China in which we may hope to turn to account the experience which during the last few years we have acquired. On the 29th of August of this year the period will have arrived at which, in conformity with the stipulations contained in the French and American Treaties with China, admitted by Keying (in his note of the 13th of January 1845, inclosed in Sir John Davis's despatch No. 5 of the 7th of February of that year) to be applicable to ourselves in virtue of the eighth article of the Supplementary Treaty of Humanchai [The Bogue],[2] we are entitled to claim a revision of the British Treaties with China. It will accordingly be advisable at an early period after you enter upon the active exercise of your duties, to apprize the Chinese Authorities of your being instructed to require such a revision at the appointed time. I should observe however that there is a difference between the stipulations of the French and American Treaties on this point, the period of twelve years dating by the former from the exchange of ratifications, by the latter from the date of the Convention.

The Chinese Authorities may perhaps and with some degree of plausibility object that the circumstances of the time are unsuitable for the commencement of so important a work: that the Imperial Government, harassed by the insurrection which convulses so many of the provinces,[3] cannot be expected to give its immediate attention to the subject. You will best be able to judge of the validity of this excuse: but you will under any circumstances obtain a recognition of our right to claim the revision on the 29th of August next, and a formal admission that if out of consideration for the embarrassments of the Imperial Government we are willing not to insist immediately upon our right, we are not to be precluded by our forbearance from urging our claim at a later period.

Some advantage may indeed arise from the postponement of the revision for a moderate time. In the first place, we shall have better means of judging of the probable result of the insurrection and be enabled to shape our negotiations accordingly.

It is impossible moreover that the barriers which have hitherto opposed the extension of foreign intercourse can be maintained under the state of anarchy which now prevails in some of the provinces; and we cannot fail, as a consequence of the civil war, to obtain greater insight into the character of the Authorities and the people of China, and in regard to the points to which our commercial energies may be directed with greater prospect of success; while on the other hand, the Chinese Authorities themselves will be induced to take a more correct view of foreign nations by the conviction which has been forced upon them, and of which they have given proof in the anxiety shown at Shanghai to enlist them in the Imperial cause, that their own boasted superiority has no real existence.

A moderate delay in the revision of the British Treaties may not also be without advantage by causing that operation to be effected more closely in point of time with that of the French and American Treaties, for it may be expected that the combined endeavours of the British, French and American Negotiators will be more likely to carry weight with the Chinese Government, than any exertions which may be made by either of those Powers singly to effect an improvement in the present state of things. But whether acting singly or in conjunction with one or both of your colleagues, you will never fail to bear in mind that Her Majesty's Government have no exclusive or selfish views as regards China. They desire that all the nations of the civilized world should share equally with them in whatever benefits, commercial or political, circumstances may enable them to secure for the British Nation in the Chinese Empire. They have nothing to conceal as regards their policy, and therefore you will be at liberty to communicate to your colleagues with the most unreserved freedom all matters to which in the course of your negotiations with the Chinese Authorities your attention may be directed. And in the full assurance that the feelings of Her Majesty's Government in this respect are shared by the Governments of France and the United States, I shall not hesitate to direct Her Majesty's Representatives in those Countries to communicate in the respective Governments the Instructions contained in this dispatch.

In all your dealings with the Chinese Government you will always bear in mind that nothing is likely to be more fatal to our influence in China than the adoption of an authoritative tone in advancing points or urging concessions on which we are not prepared to insist. Such a course of proceeding would infallibly have the effect of encouraging resistance even to our best founded demands, and we might find ourselves on very inadequate grounds, and at a very inopportune moment reduced to the necessity of choosing between one of two alternatives, either of retracting our pretensions with loss of consideration and dignity, or of insisting on them at the risk of interruption of our commerce, and even of resort to force in support of our demands. There are unquestionably points which it would be desirable to secure, and to which we have even a right by Treaty; and among those I would mention free and unrestricted intercourse with the Chinese Authorities, and free admission into some of the cities of China, especially Canton. The treatment of these questions however requires much caution; for if we should press them in menacing language, and yet fail in carrying them, our national honour would require us to have recourse to force; and in order to obtain results the practical advantage of which is not clearly demonstrable, we might place in peril the vast commercial interests which have already grown up in China, and which with good and temperate management will daily acquire greater extension.

But whenever we negotiate for the revision of our Treaties we may make proposals and recede from them without dishonour, if found unpalatable to the Chinese Government; and I do not therefore feel any hesitation in pointing out to you several matters which Her Majesty's Government conceive may very properly be urged on the Chinese Government.

The points are stated at length in a despatch which I addressed to Sir George Bonham on the 7th of May last, and as you will have the means of referring to that desptach, it is unnecessary for me to do more than enumerate them. They are:

1. To obtain access generally to the whole interior of the Chinese Empire as well as to the cities on the Coast: or failing this,
2. To obtain free navigation of the Yangtze Kiang [River] and access to the cities on its banks up to Nanking inclusive, and also to the large and populous cities within the seaboard of the Chekiang Province.

But I must observe that in the improved prospects of the Port of Foochowfoo [Foochow], Her Majesty's Government would not be prepared, as they were in

May last, to barter without further consideration that Port for concessions in any other quarter.

3. To effect the legalization of the Opium Trade.

4. To provide against the imposition of internal or transit duties on goods imported from foreign Countries, or purchased for exportation to foreign Countries.

5. To provide for the effectual suppression of piracy on the coast of China.

6. To regulate, if possible, the emigration of Chinese Labourers.

7. To secure the permanent and honourable residence at the Court of Peking of a Representative of the British Crown: and if that cannot be obtained,

8. To provide for habitual correspondence between Her Majesty's Representative and the Chinese Chief Authority at the seat of Government, accompanied with sufficient security for the passage of the correspondence without interruption on the part of local authorities.

9. To provide for ready personal intercourse at the desire of either party, between Her Majesty's Representative and the Governor of the Province in which for the time being he may be residing.

10. To provide that, in the construction of the Treaty to be concluded, all doubts are to be solved by reference to the English version and that alone.

Your long experience of Chinese affairs may suggest to you other points for which it may be desirable to provide, and in regard to such, you may use your own discretion, taking care that whatever you urge be distinctly expressed, and in a manner not to admit of dispute or question hereafter, if the Chinese should agree to your proposals at the present time.

Much advantage would probably result from the negotiation for the revision of the Treaty being carried on at Peking, and you will accordingly propose to repair to that capital for the purpose. But as in the case of the permission given in 1850 to your predecessor to proceed to Peking for the purpose of having personal communication with the proper officers of the Imperial Government on matters of complaint which we had at that time against the Authorities at Canton, you will in the event of your going to the Chinese Capital for the negotiation of the new Treaty be careful not to give to your visit the character of a Mission to the Emperor involving questions of etiquette.

I need scarcely caution you against taking any part in the Civil contest which now rages in China. Justice and good policy equally prescribe to us the observance of the strictest neutrality between the contending parties. But you will at the same time take care that no injury is done to British Subjects by either party, as long as they keep aloof from the contest. If any ill-judging Individuals should be tempted by prospects of gain to favour the cause of either party, notwithstanding the declared determination of their Government to remain neutral, they will forfeit all claim to your protection, whatever prejudice they may suffer either in their persons or in their property from their wanton disregard of their obvious duty.

But as regards the rest of Her Majesty's subjects it will be your duty in communication with Her Majesty's Naval Authorities to afford them the most ample protection on all occasions and at all places where they stand in need of it.

I have only to add in conclusion that, in cultivating the most friendly relations with the Representatives of other Powers in China, you will act in the manner most consistent with the wishes of Her Majesty's Government.

CLARENDON

NOTES

[1] This dispatch, dated February 13, 1854, was addressed by Lord Clarendon (George William Frederick Villiers, 1800–1870) of the British Foreign Office to Sir John Bowring (1792–1872), Chief Superintendent of British Trade in China. Source: Hosea Ballou Morse, *The International Relations of the Chinese Empire*, vol. I, appendix Q, pp. 670–673.

[2] Major provisions in the Treaty of The Bogue were later incorporated into the Treaty of Tientsin. See Selection 31.

[3] This refers to the Taiping Rebellion.

31 • *Treaty of Tientsin Between Great Britain and China*[1]

ARTICLE I

The Treaty of Peace and Amity between the two nations, signed at Nanking on the 29th day of August, in the year 1842 (No. 1), is hereby renewed and confirmed.[2]

The Supplementary Treaty and General Regulations of Trade having been amended and improved, and the substance of their provisions having been incorporated in this Treaty, the said Supplementary Treaty and General Regulations of Trade are hereby abrogated.

ARTICLE II

For the better preservation of harmony in future, Her Majesty the Queen of Great Britain and His Majesty the Emperor of China mutually agree that, in accordance with the universal practice of great and friendly nations, Her Majesty the Queen may, if she see fit, appoint Ambassadors, Ministers, or other Diplomatic Agents to the Court of Peking; and His Majesty the Emperor of China may, in like manner, if he see fit, appoint Ambassadors, Ministers, or other Diplomatic Agents to the Court of St. James.

ARTICLE III

His Majesty the Emperor of China hereby agrees, that the Ambassador, Minister, or other Diplomatic Agent, so appointed by Her Majesty the Queen of Great Britain, may reside, with his family and establishment, permanently at the capital, or may visit it occasionally, at the option of the British Government.

He shall not be called upon to perform any ceremony derogatory to him as representing the Sovereign of an independent nation, on a footing of equality with that of China. On the other hand, he shall use the same forms of ceremony and respect to His Majesty the Emperor as are employed by the Ambassadors, Ministers, or Diplomatic Agents of Her Majesty towards the Sovereigns of independent and equal European nations.

It is further agreed, that Her Majesty's Government may acquire at Peking a site for building, or may hire houses for the accommodation of Her Majesty's mission, and that the Chinese Government will assist it in so doing.

Her Majesty's Representative shall be at liberty to choose his own servants and attendants, who shall not be subjected to any kind of molestation whatever.

Any person guilty of disrespect or violence to Her Majesty's Representative, or to any member of his family or establishment, in deed or word, shall be severely punished.

ARTICLE IV

It is further agreed that no obstacle or difficulty shall be made to the free movements of Her Majesty's Representative, and that he, and the persons of his suite, may come and go, and travel at their pleasure. He shall, moreover, have full liberty to send and receive his correspondence, to and from any point on the seacoast that he may select; and his letters and effects shall be held sacred and inviolable. He may employ, for their transmission, special couriers, who shall meet with the same protection and facilities for travelling as the persons employed in carrying despatches for the Imperial Government; and, generally, he shall enjoy the same privileges as are accorded to officers of the same rank by the usage and consent of Western nations.

All expenses attending the Diplomatic Mission of Great Britain in China shall be borne by the British Government.

ARTICLE V

His Majesty the Emperor of China agrees to nominate one of the Secretaries of State, or a President of one of the Boards, as the high officer with whom the Ambassador, Minister, or other Diplomatic Agent of Her Majesty the Queen, shall transact business, either personally or in writing, on a footing of perfect equality.

ARTICLE VI

Her Majesty the Queen of Great Britain agrees that the privileges hereby secured shall be enjoyed in her dominions by the Ambassadors, Ministers, or Diplomatic Agents of the Emperor of China, accredited to the Court of Her Majesty.

ARTICLE VII

Her Majesty the Queen may appoint one or more Consuls in the dominions of the Emperor of China; and such Consul or Consuls shall be at liberty to reside in any of the open ports or cities of China as Her Majesty the Queen may consider most expedient for the interests of British commerce. They shall be treated with due respect by the Chinese authorities, and enjoy the same privileges and immunities as the Consular officers of the most favored nation.

Consuls and Vice-Consuls in charge, shall rank with Intendents of Circuits; Vice-Consuls, Acting Vice-Consuls, and Interpreters, with Prefects. They shall have access to the official residences of these officers, and communicate with them, either personally or in writing, on a footing of equality, as the interests of the public service may require.

ARTICLE VIII

The Christian religion, as professed by Protestants or Roman Catholics, inculcates the practice of virtue, and teaches man to do as he would be done by.

Persons teaching or professing it, therefore, shall alike be entitled to the protection of the Chinese authorities, nor shall any such, peaceably pursuing their calling, and not offending against the law, be persecuted or interfered with.

ARTICLE IX

British subjects are hereby authorised to travel, for their pleasure or for purposes of trade, to all parts of the interior, under passports which will be issued by their Consuls, and countersigned by the local authorities. These passports, if demanded, must be produced for examination in the localities passed through. If the passport be not irregular, the bearer will be allowed to proceed, and no opposition shall be offered to his hiring persons or hiring vessels for the carriage of his baggage or merchandise. If he be without a passport, or if he commit any offence against the law, he shall be handed over to the nearest Consul for punishment, but he must not be subjected to any ill-usage in excess of necessary restraint. No passport need be applied for by persons going on excursions from the ports open to trade to a distance not exceeding 100 *li,* and for a period not exceeding 5 days.

The Provisions of this Article do not apply to crews of ships, for the due restraint of whom regulations will be drawn up by the Consul and the local authorities.

To Nankin [Nanking], and other cities disturbed by persons in arms against the Government, no pass shall be given, until they shall have been recaptured.[3]

ARTICLE X

British merchant ships shall have authority to trade upon the Great River (Yang-tsu). The Upper and Lower Valley of the river being, however, disturbed by outlaws, no port shall be for the present open to trade, with the exception of Chin-kiang, which shall be opened in a year from the date of the signing of this Treaty.

So soon as peace shall have been restored, British vessels shall also be admitted to trade at such ports as far as Han-kow, not exceeding 3 in number, as the British Minister, after consultation with the Chinese Secretary of State, may determine shall be ports of entry and discharge.

ARTICLE XI

In addition to the cities and towns of Canton, Amoy, Fuchow, Ningpo, and Shanghai, opened by the Treaty of Nangking [29th, August, 1842 (No. 1], it is agreed that British subjects may frequent the cities and ports of New-Chwang,[4] Tang-Chow[5] (Chefoo), Tai-Wan (Formosa), Chau-Chow[6] (Swatow), and Kiung-Chow (Hainan). [See No. 11, Art., VI.]

They are permitted to carry on trade with whomsoever they please, and to proceed to and fro at pleasure with their vessels and merchandise.

They shall enjoy the same privileges, advantages, and immunities, at the said towns and ports, as they enjoy at the ports already opened to trade, including the right of residence, of buying or renting houses, of leasing land therein, and of building churches, hospitals, and cemeteries. . . .

ARTICLE XV

All questions in regard to rights, whether of property or person arising between British subjects, shall be subject to the jurisdiction of the British authorities.

ARTICLE XVI

Chinese subjects who may be guilty of any criminal act towards British subjects shall be arrested and punished by the Chinese authorities, according to the laws of China.

British subjects who may commit any crime in China shall be tried and punished by the Consul, or other public functionary authorised thereto, according to the laws of Great Britain.

Justice shall be equitably and impartially administered on both sides.

ARTICLE XVII

A British subject having reason to complain of a Chinese, must proceed to the Consulate, and state his grievance. The Consul will inquire into the merits of the case, and do his utmost to arrange it amicably. In like manner, if a Chinese has reason to complain of a British subject, the Consul shall no less listen to his complaint, and endeavour to settle it in a friendly manner. If disputes take place of such a nature that the Consul cannot arrange them amicably, then he shall request the assistance of the Chinese authorities, that they may together examine into the merits of the case, and decide it equitably.

ARTICLE XVIII

The Chinese authorities shall at all times afford the fullest protection to the persons and property of British subjects, whenever these shall have been subjected to insult or violence. In all cases of incendiarism or robbery, the local authorities shall at once take the necessary steps for the recovery of the stolen property, the suppression of disorder, and the arrest of the guilty parties, whom they will punish according to law. . . .

ARTICLE XXIV

It is agreed that British subjects shall pay, on all merchandise imported or exported by them, the duties prescribed by the Tariff, but in no case shall they be called upon to pay other or higher duties than are required of the subjects of any other foreign nation.

ARTICLE XXV

Import duties shall be considered payable on the landing of the goods, and duties of export on the shipment of the same.

ARTICLE XXVI

Whereas the Tariff fixed by Article X of the Treaty of Nanking, and which was estimated so as to impose on imports and exports a duty at about the rate of 5 per cent. *ad valorem,* has been found, by reason of the fall in value of various articles of merchandise, therein enumerated, to impose a duty upon these, considerably in excess of the rate originally assumed as above to be a fair rate, it is agreed that the said Tariff shall be revised, and that as soon as the Treaty shall have been signed, application shall be made to the Emperor of China to depute a high officer of the Board of Revenue to meet, at Shanghai, officers to be deputed on behalf of the British Government, to consider its revision together, so that the Tariff, as revised, may come into operation immediately after the ratification of this Treaty.

ARTICLE XXVII

It is agreed that either of the High Contracting Parties to this Treaty may demand a further revision of the Tariff, and of the Commercial Articles of this Treaty, at the end of 10 years; but if no demand be made on either side within 6 months after the end of the first 10 years, then the Tariff shall remain in force for 10 years; and so it shall be, at the end of each successive period of 10 years.

ARTICLE XXVIII

Whereas it was agreed in Article X of the Treaty of Nanking, that British imports, having paid the Tariff duties, should be conveyed into the interior free of all further charges, except a transit duty, the amount whereof was not to exceed a certain percentage on tariff value; and whereas no accurate information having been furnished of the amount of such duty, British merchants have constantly complained that charges are suddenly and arbitrarily imposed by the provincial authorities as transit duties upon produce on its way to the foreign market, and on imports on their way into the interior, to the detriment of trade; it is agreed that within 4 months from the signing of this Treaty, at all ports now open to British trade, and within a similar period to all ports that may hereafter be opened, the authority appointed to superintend the collection of duties shall be obliged, upon application of the Consul, to declare the amount of duties leviable on produce between the place of production and the port of shipment, and upon imports between the Consular port in question and the inland markets named by the Consul; and that a notification thereof shall be published in English and Chinese for general information.

But it shall be at the option of any British subject, desiring to convey produce purchased inland to a port, or to convey imports from a port to an inland market, to clear his goods for all transit duties, by payment of a single charge. The amount of this charge shall be leviable on exports at the first barrier they may have to pass, or, on imports, at the port at which they are landed; and on payment thereof, a certificate shall be issued, which shall exempt the goods from all further inland charges whatsoever.

It is further agreed that the amount of this charge shall be calculated, as nearly as possible, at the rate of two and a half per cent. *ad valorem,* and that it shall be fixed for each article at the Conference to be held at Shanghai for the revision of the Tariff.

It is distinctly understood, that the payment of transit dues, by commutation or otherwise, shall in no way affect the Tariff duties on imports or exports, which will continue to be levied separately and in full. . . .

Article XLVII

British merchant vessels are not entitled to resort to other than the ports of trade declared open by this Treaty. They are not unlawfully to enter other ports in China, or to carry on clandestine trade along the coasts thereof. Any vessel violating this provision, shall, with her cargo, be subject to confiscation by the Chinese Government.

Article XLVIII

If any British merchant vessel be concerned in Smuggling, the goods, whatever their value or nature, shall be subject to confiscation by the Chinese authorities, and the ship may be prohibited from trading further, and sent away as soon as her accounts shall have been adjusted and paid.

Article XLIX

All penalties enforced, or confiscations made, under this Treaty, shall belong and be appropriated to the public service of the Government of China.

Article L

All official communications, addressed by the Diplomatic and Consular Agents of Her Majesty the Queen to the Chinese authorities, shall, henceforth, be written in English. They will for the present be accompanied by a Chinese version, but it is understood that, in the event of there being any difference of meaning between the English and the Chinese text, the English Government will hold the sense as expressed in the English text to be the correct sense. This provision is to apply to the Treaty now negotiated, the Chinese text of which has been carefully corrected by the English original.

Article LI

It is agreed, that henceforth the character "I"[7] (barbarian) shall not be applied to the Government or subjects of Her Britannic Majesty in any Chinese official document issued by the Chinese authorities in the capital or in the provinces.

Article LII

British ships of war coming for no hostile purpose, or being engaged in the pursuit of Pirates, shall be at liberty to visit all ports within the dominions of the Emperor of China, and shall receive every facility for the purchase of provisions, procuring water, and, if occasion require, for the making of repairs. The Commanders of such ships shall hold intercourse with the Chinese authorities on terms of equality and courtesy.

Article LIII

In consideration of the injury sustained by native and foreign commerce from the prevalence of Piracy in the seas of China, the High Contracting Parties agree to concert measures for its suppression.

ARTICLE LIV

The British Government and its subjects are hereby confirmed in all privileges, immunities, and advantages conferred on them by previous Treaties: and it is hereby expressly stipulated, that the British Government and its subjects will be allowed free and equal participation in all privileges, immunities, and advantages that may have been, or may be hereafter, granted by His Majesty the Emperor of China to the Government or subjects of any other nation. (See No. 11, Art. I.)...

ARTICLE LVI

The ratifications of this Treaty, under the hand of Her Majesty the Queen of Great Britain and Ireland, and His Majesty the Emperor of China, respectively, shall be exchanged at Peking within a year from this day of signature.

In token whereof, the respective Plenipotentiaries have signed and sealed this Treaty.

Done at Tien-tsin, this 26th day of June, in the year of our Lord, 1858; corresponding with the Chinese date, the 16th day, 5th month, of the 8th year of Hien Fung.[8]

NOTES

[1] This treaty, signed at Tientsin, 26th June 1858, is officially entitled "Treaty of Peace, Friendship, and Commerce between Great Britain and China." Source: Edward Hertslet, *Treaties, &c., between Great Britain and China* (London: Harrison & Sons, 1896), vol. I, pp. 16–32.

[2] This refers to the Treaty of Nanking; see Selection 28.

[3] Nanking and many other cities were then controlled by the Taiping rebels.

[4] It should be romanized Niuchuang according to the Wade system. Niuchuang is located in Liaoning province.

[5] It should be romanized Tengchou according to the Wade system. Tengchou is located·in Shantung province.

[6] It should be romanized Ch'aochou according to the Wade system. Ch'aochou is located in Kwangtung province.

[7] This is followed by the word *yi* in Chinese character.

[8] Hsien-feng.

32 • *The Peking Convention*[1]

ARTICLE I

A breach of friendly relations having been occasioned by the act of the garrison of Taku, which obstructed Her Britannic Majesty's Representative when on his way to Peking for the purpose of exchanging the Ratifications of the Treaty of Peace concluded at Tien-tsin in the month of June, 1858 (No. 6), His Imperial Majesty the Emperor of China expresses his deep regret at the misunderstanding so occasioned.

ARTICLE II

It is further expressly declared, that the Arrangement entered into at Shanghai in the month of October, 1858, between Her Britannic Majesty's Ambassador, the

Earl of Elgin and Kincardine, and His Imperial Majesty's Commissioners, Kweiliang and Hwashana,[2] regarding the residence of Her Britannic Majesty's Representative in China, is hereby cancelled; and that, in accordance with Article III of the Treaty of 1858 (No. 6),[3] Her Britannic Majesty's Representative will henceforward reside permanently or occasionally at Peking, as Her Majesty shall be pleased to decide.

ARTICLE III

It is agreed that the Separate Article of the Treaty of 1858 (No. 6) is hereby annulled; and that, in lieu of the amount of indemnity therein specified, His Imperial Majesty the Emperor of China shall pay the sum of 8,000,000 taels, in the following proportions or instalments, namely: —At Tien-tsin, on or before the 30th day of November, the sum of 500,000 taels; at Canton, and on or before the 1st day of December, 1860, 333,333 taels, less the sum which shall have been advanced by the Canton authorities towards the completion of the British Factory site at Shameen; and the remainder at the ports open to foreign trade, in quarterly payments, which shall consist of one-fifth of the gross revenue from Customs there collected. The first of the said payments being due on the 31st day of December, 1863, for the quarter terminating on that day.

It is further agreed that these moneys shall be paid into the hands of an officer whom Her Britannic Majesty's Representative shall specially appoint to receive them, and that the accuracy of the amounts shall, before payment, be duly ascertained by British and Chinese officers appointed to discharge this duty.

In order to prevent further discussion, it is moreover declared that, of the 8,000,000 taels herein guaranteed, 2,000,000 will be appropriated to the indemnification of the British mercantile community at Canton, for losses sustained by them, and the remaining 6,000,000 to the liquidation of war expenses.

ARTICLE IV

It is agreed that on the day on which this Convention is signed, His Imperial Majesty the Emperor of China shall open the port of Tien-tsin to trade, and that it shall be thereafter competent to British subjects to reside and trade there under the same conditions as at any other port of China by Treaty open to trade.

ARTICLE V

As soon as the ratifications of the Treaty of 1858 shall have been exchanged, His Imperial Majesty the Emperor of China will, by Decree, command the high authorities of every province to proclaim throughout their jurisdictions, that Chinese choosing to take service in the British Colonies or other parts beyond sea, are at perfect liberty to enter into engagements with British subjects for that purpose, and to ship themselves and their families on board any British vessel at any of the open ports of China; also that the high authorities aforesaid shall, in concert with Her Britannic Majesty's Representative in China, frame such regulations for the protection of Chinese, emigrating as above, as the circumstances of the different open ports may demand.

ARTICLE VI

With a view to the maintenance of law and order in and about the harbour of Hong Kong, His Imperial Majesty the Emperor of China agrees to cede to Her

Majesty the Queen of Great Britain and Ireland, and to Her heirs and successors, to have and to hold, as a dependency of Her Britannic Majesty's colony of Hong Kong, that portion of the township of Cowloon [Kowloon] in the Province of Kwang-tung, of which a lease was granted in perpetuity to Harry Smith Parkes, Esquire, Companion of the Bath, a member of the Allied Commission at Canton, on behalf of Her Britannic Majesty's Government, by Lan Tsung Kwang,[4] Governor-General of the Two Kwang [Liangkwang].

It is further declared that the lease in question is hereby cancelled; that the claims of any Chinese to any property on the said portion of Cowloon shall be duly investigated by a Mixed Commission of British and Chinese officers; and that compensation shall be awarded by the British Government to any Chinese whose claims shall be by the said Commission established, should his removal be deemed necessary by the British Government.

ARTICLE VII

It is agreed that the provisions of the Treaty of 1858 (No. 6), except in so far as these are modified by the present Convention, shall without delay come into operation as soon as the ratifications of the Treaty aforesaid shall have been exchanged.

It is further agreed that no separate ratification of the present Convention shall be necessary, but that it shall take effect from the date of its signature, and be equally binding with the Treaty above mentioned on the High Contracting Parties.

ARTICLE VIII

It is agreed that as soon as the ratifications of the Treaty of the year 1858 (No. 6) shall have been exchanged, His Imperial Majesty the Emperor of China shall, by Decree, command the high authorities in the capital and in the provinces to print and publish the aforesaid Treaty and the present Convention, for general information.

ARTICLE IX

It is agreed that, as soon as this Convention shall have been signed, the ratifications of the Treaty of the year 1858 (No. 6) shall have been exchanged, and an Imperial decree respecting the publication of the said Convention and Treaty shall have been promulgated, as provided for by Article VIII of this Convention, Chusan[5] shall be evacuated by Her Britannic Majesty's troops there stationed, and Her Britannic Majesty's force now before Peking shall commence its march towards the city of Tien-tsin, the forts of Taku, the north coast of Shang-tung [Shantung], and the city of Canton, at each or all of which places it shall be at the option of Her Britannic Majesty the Queen of Great Britain and Ireland to retain a force until the indemnity of 8,000,000 taels, guaranteed in Article III, shall have been paid.

Done at Peking, in the Court of the Board of Ceremonies, on the 24th day of October, in the year of our Lord 1860.

NOTES

[1] This treaty, officially entitled "Convention between Her Majesty and the Emperor of China," was signed at Peking on October 24, 1860. Source: *Treaties, &c., between Great Britain and China,* vol. I, pp. 45–48.

² It should be romanized Huashana according to the Wade system.
³ Treaty of Tientsin.
⁴ It should be romanized Lao Ch'ung-kuang according to the Wade system.
⁵ A group of islands off the coast of Chekiang province.

33 • ANSON BURLINGAME: *Political Relations of Foreigners with the Chinese*[1]

From many letters received by me from the ports, it appears that a misunderstanding prevails as to the extent of the rights and duties of American citizens under the treaty, and the regulations made in pursuance thereof. I have felt, therefore, that it might facilitate the administration of our affairs, if I express my opinions in relation to those questions about which there has been controversy. I accordingly address you, and through you the other consuls and my countrymen, giving my construction of the treaty and regulations, upon several disputed points, as well as a few directions in relation to ships, passports, etc.; and some general suggestions in reference to the co-operative policy agreed upon by the representatives of the treaty powers at Peking.

I hold that the Chinese government has the right, as an incident of its unyielded sovereignty, to enforce its own revenue laws, and to make such regulations as may be necessary to that end. (*See Rules 6 and 10 of the Supplementary Treaty and my dispatches to the Department of State, approved by Government, Nos. 30 and 32.*)

That the foreign minister, when notified of regulations, if he find them to be in accordance with the treaty, is, after having in his diplomatic character done what he could do to perfect them, under obligation to notify them to his countrymen, upon whom they then become binding. (*See letter of E. Hammond for British government in reply to the Shanghai Chamber of Commerce, and dispatches of British and American ministers in relation to the Yangtsze regulations, approved by their governments.*)

That no authority inferior to that which made and approved the regulations can absolve persons from their observance.

That the Chinese government having by treaty yielded jurisdiction over the persons of our citizens so that it cannot punish them even by fine, it is obligatory upon us to punish them for infractions of the Treaty and regulations. (*See dispatch of Mr. Marshall to Mr. Marcy, Nov. 25th, 1853, and the same to Mr. Cunningham, vice-consul at Shanghai, Nov. 1st, 1853; Mr. Cushing to Mr. Marcy, Sept. 9th, 1855; Fitzroy Kelly and James Stephen, Temple, May 22nd, 1862.*)

The manner of doing this is pointed out in Sec. 7 of the act of Congress approved June 22nd, 1860. It is to be done through the consuls, the minister only having original jurisdiction in cases of felony, murder and rebellion, and where a consul is interested. (*See Secs. 13, 24 and 27 of the Act.*)

The Chinese government cannot withdraw a consul's *exequatur*, for it has yielded this right under the law of nations, in the grant of entire jurisdiction over our citizens. Besides, the consuls in China have a peculiar *status*; they are judicial officers, and exercise many powers under the treaty unknown to similar functionaries in the West. (*See my dispatch, (72) and discussion with the Chinese government, also letters of Mr. Cushing to Sec. Marcy, Nov. 7th, 1854, and Oct. 8th, 1855.*)

That, though the Chinese government may not sue in the consular court as a party to the record, still it may go there to make a complaint and to give information, which the consul is bound to entertain. This is political action. (*See Cushing, idem*; G. Wingrove Cooke and James Hannen, Temple, Jan. 13th, 1862, *Ms.*)

If the consul shall fail to do his duty in respect to punishment, then the question becomes one for reference to the "superior officers of the government, who shall see that full inquiry and strict justice shall be had in the premises." (*Art. x of the treaty.*)

The Chinese government cannot be compelled to plead in the consular court at the suit of any one; hence, controversies between the consulates and the customs, if they cannot be arranged, become diplomatic questions to be referred to Peking. (*See Cushing, idem; Sir Frederick Bruce in re Bowman vs. Fitzroy, Bluebook No. 3, approved by British government; also my dispatch to Mr. Mangum, consul at Ningpo, Dec. 9th, 1862, in case of barque "Agnes," approved by U.S. government.*)

A citizen of the United States in the Chinese customs' service, cannot, in that character, be held to answer in the consular court of his country for acts done in the line of his official duty under the orders of the Chinese government. In such case the remedy is against that government. (*Opinion of Sir William Atherton et al. Temple, March 6th, 1862.*)

The Chinese government may confiscate goods landed in breach of port regulations, but only those in respect to which the infringement of the regulation was committed—that is to say, those landed and not those still on board. (*Sir F. Bruce in case of the "Blackburn." Bluebook No. 3—Also my dispatches in case of the "Agnes," and that of Prince Kung admitting this doctrine.*)

In cases of fine, where the words "not exceeding" are attached to the penalty, the consul may fix a smaller sum; but where the sum is fixed there is no option, and the consul upon proof must inflict the fine, and all efforts to mitigate such fine must proceed upon equitable grounds, and not as matter of legal right. (*Sir F. Bruce in case of the "Blackburn."*)

Only three ports are now by treaty open to trade on the River Yangtze, viz., Chinkiang, Kiukiang, and Hankow; and trade at any other ports subjects ship and cargo to confiscation. There can be no trade, directly or indirectly, by tacit consent of local authorities,—by towing and permitting the Chinese to cut the line where they please, or in any manner whatsoever. (*See Art. xiv of U.S. treaty, and Arts. xxx and Arts. x, xi of British treaty in connection therewith; also Provisional arrangements for the navigation of the R. Yantsze, Dec. 5th, 1861; and those adopted Nov. 10th, 1862, and approved by British and American governments.*)

If the Chinese authorities confiscate without sufficient proof of breach of regulations, then the aggrieved party may, through the consul, appeal against such action to the minister at Peking, whose duty it will be to reclaim against the Chinese government; but in no case is the citizen, or the consul for him, to take the law into his own hands. This would relieve the Chinese government from that responsibility which should attach to it, and render all friendly relations impossible. (*Sir F. Bruce in case of the "Pearl;" also his correspondence with Consul Gingell at Hankow approved by the British government; and instructions to Admiral Kuper, Bluebook No. 3.*)

To secure an honest application of the confiscation power, I have, in conjunction with my colleagues, urged the establishment of a joint tribunal, or mixed commission, to sit in cases of confiscation. The Chinese authorities have yielded this in principle, leaving the details to be arranged by the consuls and local authorities— first at Shanghai provisionally, and afterwards at the other treaty ports if found to work well. This will satisfy both sides, and facilitate settlements at the ports; or, if the cases shall come to Peking, by classification and arrangement of the evidence, make decisions practicable. (*See dispatch of Prince Kung to me, June 13th, 1864.*)

The greatest care should be taken before extending the protection of the American flag to purchased vessels. The proof of citizenship and the bona fide character of the purchase should be required. The flag should not be lent or sold to dishonor, or "be abused by the subjects of other nations as a cover for the violation of the laws of the empire." (*See Consular Manual, page 273, and regulations of the Treasury Department there referred to. Also U.S. treaty, Art. xiv.*)

A wise discretion should be exercised by the consuls in granting passports to travel into the interior. The right to grant these is derived from Art. ix of the British treaty through the favored nation clause (Art. xxx). And though I do not hold that we are bound to take the construction of a treaty from the power through which we derive a privilege, still a desire for uniformity would suggest that such construction should receive our respectful consideration. (*See my dispatch No. 26 approved by the government.*)

I therefore call your attention to Sir Frederick Bruce's circular of November 21st, 1860, to the British consuls, approved by his Government, and commend its several suggestions to you for your guidance. "When an application is made by a person, claiming to be a native citizen of the United States, for a passport, before it be granted, he should make a written declaration to that effect, stating also his age and place of birth, which paper should be filed. The consul may however require such other evidence as he may deem necessary to establish the fact of the applicant's citizenship. If the applicant claims to be a naturalized citizen, he should be required to produce either the original or a certified copy of his certificate of naturalization, or such other evidence as shall be fully satisfactory to the consul." (*Extract from Instructions to the Diplomatic Agents of the United States, page 17; and my letter to Acting Consul Pomeroy at Tientsin.*)

I have already written you in relation to the so-called concessions. There are no such things as concessions in the sense generally understood by that term. It is the right of our citizens to buy, sell, and live in any part of the treaty ports; and any claim by a treaty power of a concession of territory from the Chinese government, by virtue of which it can exercise jurisdiction over the persons or property of our citizens, would, if admitted, be an abridgement of our rights. (*See dispatch of Mr. Marshall to Mr. Marcy, July 26th, 1853, with history of efforts of Consuls Griswold and Cunningham against concession claims, and disavowed by the British government of concession views through Consul Alcock. Letter of Sir Frederick Bruce to Consul Medhurst approved by British government; and my dispatch (42) approved by U.S. government in Mr. Seward's dispatch (40), and that in relation to municipal affairs at Shanghai (37), approved by government.*)

We have no right for municipal or other purposes, to take jurisdiction of Chinese, or of the subjects of non-treaty powers, even though requested to do so by the Chinese authorities. We should seek to strengthen the Chinese administration in the direction of order, to see to it that they should not shirk their treaty obligations. (*See my letter to Consul-general Seward, and Sir F. Bruce to Consul Sir Henry Parkes at Shanghai.*)

With reference to the entrance of American citizens into the Chinese service, I can only say that there can be no objection to their entrance into the civil service; but there are strong objections to their active participation in the strife in which this people is unhappily engaged.² The penalty for entering the rebel service is well known; and there is a decree of my predecessor Mr. McLane, of December 5th, 1854, still unrepealed, against taking military or naval service under the government against the insurgents. In the peril of our interests at Shanghai from the rebels, this decree was not enforced; but subsequent events, leading to the death of General [John E.] Ward and the Burgevine imbroglio, convinced me that the taking of such service not only endangered our relations with China, but might lead to complications with other treaty powers. I accordingly, in my despatch No. 44, expressed myself in this sense, and my views were "specially commended" by the government.

I therefore reiterate them to the end that such service may be discouraged. The British government has already withdrawn its permission to the officers to take military service; and every effort has been, and is being made, by the British minister at Peking, to induce the Chinese to strengthen themselves so as to relieve the British government, not only from the expense of keeping troops in China, but from the common danger of a Chinese force headed by adventurers. Major [Charles G.] Gordon, who has done so well, earnestly wishes to be relieved, but is retained by a common sense of danger until he can weed the force of its dangerous elements, and hand it over safely to the entire control of the comparatively well-drilled and patriotic Chinese officers.

Mr. Berthemy, the enlightened representative of France, is equally desirous with the British minister of removing all cause of expense and anxiety to his country, and looks forward with hope to the day when the Chinese will triumph over their difficulties, and be able to maintain order without external aid. I am happy also to inform you that Mr. Vlangaly, the able minister of Russia, is deeply impressed with the importance of repressing that adventurous element, which, if fostered, can only lead to disaster in China.

At an early period of my mission, I was instructed by the Government to co-operate with the other treaty powers in China. In my dispatch No. 42, you will find a history of my efforts in that direction, and of the policy agreed upon; that policy has been fully approved by our government, and I believe that of every other treaty power. It is briefly this: to consult and co-operate in China upon all material questions; to defend the treaty ports so far as shall be necessary to maintain our treaty rights; to support the foreign customs' service in a pure administration and upon a cosmopolitan basis; to encourage the Chinese government in its efforts to maintain order; to neither ask for nor take concessions of territory in the treaty ports, nor in any manner to interfere with the jurisdiction of the Chinese government over its own people, nor ever menace the territorial integrity of the Chinese empire.

I call your attention to this policy in order that you may know the commitments of our own government and ourselves with the other treaty powers. You will perceive that we are making an effort to substitute fair diplomatic action in China for force; that we seek to do justice that we may have justice, and thus co-operation becomes the rule in carrying out these relations. It should be sincere; and to be effective requires, in the first place, a predisposition to get on well with one's colleagues; and, in the second, that just moderation which cannot fail to win the respect and confidence of one's associates.

While such are our obligations with respect to the foreign representatives in China, they are equally strong towards the Chinese officials, whether native or foreign, for it is through these that we maintain our relations with China, and any want of courtesy or consideration for them at once reacts upon ourselves, and destroys our power for usefulness. (*See my dispatch approving the conduct of Consul Clark at Fuchau* [Foochow].)

Hoping for your continued support, together with that of the other consuls and my countrymen generally, of the views I have expressed, and the generous policy I have stated, I am, Sir, etc., etc.

P.S. I have submitted the above letter to the British, French, and Russian ministers, and they authorize me to inform you that they entirely approve of its views and policy.

NOTES

[1] This diplomatic dispatch, dated June 15, 1864, was addressed by the United States minister at Peking to the United States consul-general at Shanghai. Source: *The International Relations of the Chinese Empire*, vol. II, appendix A, pp. 419–424.
[2] This refers to the Taiping Rebellion.

34 • CHIANG KAI-SHEK: *The Unequal Treaties*[1]

The Sino-British Treaty of Nanking of 1842 was the first of the unequal treaties that China concluded. It came about as a result of China's defeat in the Opium War, which was the first of her many national humiliations. From then on and until 1911 China's relations with foreign countries may be divided into three periods.

The first period began with the Opium War and ended in the War of 1894–1895[2] during which the conclusion of the Treaty of Tientsin[3] proved to be the most important event. During this period the various powers secured from China ports for trade and used these ports as bases to advance their special interests. At the beginning there were only five treaty ports—Canton, Foochow, Amoy, Ningpo, and Shanghai—where the nationals of the treaty powers, under the protection of extraterritoriality, refused to obey the Chinese law and constituted themselves a special, privileged class. Moreover, by invoking the agreement on the regulated tariff, they paid less customs duties than otherwise would have been the case, thus enabling them to gain undue advantages at the expense of China in the Chinese market. Later, Great Britain, France, and other powers secured additional ports for trade so as to enlarge their sphere of commercial activities; in each of these treaty ports they further strengthened their special rights and privileges by unjustifiably taking advantage of the Ch'ing officials' ignorance and stupidity. Whenever one power acquired a new privilege in its treaty with China, all other powers, by invoking the detestable most-favored-nation clause, claimed and received the enjoyment of the same. Moreover, all the special rights and privileges in the treaties were subject to interpretations as provided only in the foreign texts of the treaties concerned,[4] and the treaty powers, by playing with words, increasingly enlarged the existing concessions. At other times they forced the Ch'ing government to recognize the legality of one and another *fait accompli* and thus strengthened further their special privileges. Take the so-called concessions as an example. There were no such things as concessions in any of the treaties that China had concluded with foreign powers; they came about as a result of the extension of consular jurisdiction. By constantly enlarging their special privileges, the guests had indeed usurped the position of the host in the latter's own house. . . .

The unequal treaties of the first period may be divided into two groups, those concluded before and those concluded after the Arrow War of 1858.[5] The treaties that belonged to the former group were the Sino-British Treaty of Nanking of 1842, the Treaty of The Bogue that governed the trade in the five treaty ports (1843), the Sino-American Treaty of Wanghia of 1844,[6] the Sino-French Treaty of Whampoa of 1844, the Sino-Swedish-Norwegian Treaty of 1847, and the Sino-Russian Treaty of Kaldja of 1851. Under these treaties the various powers acquired the following special rights and privileges:

I. *Consular Jurisdiction*

1. Chinese officials would refrain from participating in any trial of cases involving foreigners only.

2. In civil cases that involved both Chinese and foreigners, the consular officials of the country concerned were to seek a settlement by mediation. If this attempt failed, they were to hold a joint trial with local Chinese authorities so as to reach an equitable settlement.

3. In criminal cases that involved both Chinese and foreigners, local Chinese authorities were to try the defendants in accordance with the Chinese law if the defendants were Chinese. If the defendants were foreigners, they were to be tried by their consular officials in accordance with the laws of their own country.

The consular jurisdiction of foreign powers in China not only undermined the judicial power of China in her own territory but also constituted a serious impairment of her sovereign rights as a nation. Under these circumstances it was senseless to speak of equality in commercial transactions between foreigners and Chinese. Our economy, on the national as well as the personal level, suffered a fatal blow as a result.

II. *The Regulated Tariff*

1. The duties on imported and exported foreign goods were to be 5 percent *ad valorem,* with the exception of those on tea, lumber, metals, and spices, which were to be 10 percent *ad valorem.*

2. The tonnage dues for foreign ships entering Chinese ports were to be 0.5 taels per ton for those over 150 tons and 0.1 taels per ton for those less than 150 tons.

The presence of the regulated tariff enabled the treaty powers to control, directly or indirectly, China's economy and finance. Was it really surprising that the livelihood of our people continued to deteriorate and that our very fate as a nation may have been sealed as a result?

The unequal treaties that belonged to the second group during the period under discussion were the Sino-British, Sino-French, Sino-American, and Sino-Russian Treaties of Tientsin of 1858, the Sino-Russian Supplementary Treaty of 1860, the Sino-German Treaty of Tientsin of 1861, the Sino-Portuguese Treaty of Tientsin of 1862, the Sino-Danish and Sino-Dutch Treaties of Tientsin of 1863, the

Sino-Spanish Treaty of Tientsin of 1864, the Sino-Belgian Treaty of Peking of 1865, the Sino-Italian Treaty of Peking of 1866, the Sino-Austrian Treaty of Peking of 1869, the Sino-Peruvian Treaty of Tientsin of 1874, the Sino-British Treaty of Chefoo of 1876, the Sino-American Supplementary Treaty of 1880, and the Sino-Brazilian Treaty of Tientsin of 1881. By virtue of these treaties, the various powers acquired for themselves many coastal and river ports for trade and special rights and privileges therein. These rights and privileges may be summarized as follows:

I. *Consular Jurisdiction*

From the treaties mentioned above, the various powers obtained two special rights in connection with consular jurisdiction, in addition to those that had been accrued to them before. These two special rights were:

1. THE RIGHT TO OBSERVE COURT PROCEEDINGS. In the treaties concluded after the Treaty of Nanking there was the phrase "to hold joint trials" (*hui-tung shen-hsün*) which was meant to be applicable to civil cases only. Through a mistranslation on the part of the Ch'ing officials, this phrase became equally applicable to criminal cases. Taking advantage of this mistranslation, the various powers established their right to observe court proceedings. In other words, in both civil and criminal cases that involve foreigners, foreign consulates had the right to send representatives to watch court proceedings.

2. THE RIGHT TO JOINT TRIALS. In 1869 the local authorities in Shanghai concluded with the British and American consulates the "Yangchingpin Regulations for Joint Trials." From then on, not only civil or criminal cases involving foreigners were to be subject to the trial by a Mixed Court but also those involving Chinese nationals only, if the cases in question occurred in the International Settlement. Once the precedent was established, other powers demanded and acquired the same right. Consequently there was the establishment of a Mixed Court in the French Concession in Shanghai, of the Bureau of Foreign Affairs[7] in Hankow, of the Department of Diplomatic and Railroad Affairs in Harbin, and of a Mixed Court in Kulangyü, all of which needless to say, were abnormal, extralegal institutions.

After the consulates of the various powers had acquired the right to observe and participate in trials, their nationals not only exempted themselves from the legal jurisdiction of China but also interfered positively with the judicial proceedings of China. In other words, not only did they place themselves above the reach of the Chinese law but they also tried Chinese in the territory of China.

II. *Concessions*

With the exception of the International Settlement and the French Concession in Shanghai, the boundaries of which are delimited in 1845 and 1849 respectively, the various foreign concessions the boundaries of which were delimited during this period include the British and French Concessions in Tientsin, the British and French Concessions in Shamen of Canton, and the British Concessions in Hankow, Kiukiang, Chinkiang, Amoy, and Shamen of Canton. The boundaries of all these concessions were determined in 1861.[8]

Originally, consular jurisdiction was intended to be applicable only to persons. However, after the establishment of concessions and the delimitation of their boundaries, it was extended to apply to geographical areas. This amounts to saying that many sovereign states were created within the territory of China.

III. *The Right of Foreign Warships to Navigate and to be Stationed in Chinese Waters*

This right of foreign warships to navigate and to be stationed in China's inland waters as well as along her coast was provided in the Treaty of The Bogue, the Sino-American Treaty of Wanghia, and the American-French Treaty of Whampoa. It was further detailed in the Treaty of Tientsin.

As foreign warships could freely navigate and be stationed in China's inland waters as well as along her coast, China no longer had any coastal defense. In fact, all of her major cities were from then on subject to the menace of the imperialists' "gunboat policy."

IV. *The Administration of Chinese Customs Offices*

There was some degree of foreign control of the Shanghai Customs Office even before the conclusion of the Treaty of Tientsin. In the Sino-British Commercial Agreement of 1858 it was stipulated that the Chinese Customs Administration might invite British nationals to assist in the discharge of its duties. Thereafter, the Inspector-General of the Chinese Customs was always a British subject. In 1864 the Office of General Management [Tsung-li ya-men] of the Ch'ing government promulgated the "Regulations Governing the Employment of Foreign Nationals to Assist in the Customs Administration," which specially authorized the Inspector-General to employ foreigners. From then on, all the Customs Commissioners in the treaty ports were foreigners.

Now that foreign powers had secured direct administration of our Customs Office, they not only regulated our tariffs but also controlled our customs revenues.

V. *The Regulated Tariff*

As for the revision of tariff rates provided in the Treaty of Tientsin and subsequent treaties, its main points were as follows:

1. The tariff rate was revised at 5 percent *ad valorem*.
2. Transit dues were one-half as much as the regulated tariff, *i.e.,* 2.5 percent *ad valorem*.
3. Tonnage dues were reduced to 0.4 taels per ton.
4. The agreement on tariff matters was to be revised once every ten years.

It seems clear that the purpose of this revision was to reduce the tariff on the imported foreign goods and, by fixing in advance the transit dues, to enable foreign goods to move freely between different cities of China without assuming additional charges. In short, whenever revisions of tariff agreements occurred, their basic purpose was always to provide additional protection for foreign goods to be sold in China.

VI. *The Rights of Coastwise Trade and Inland Water Navigation*

Since the ports opened for trade in the Treaty of Nanking and subsequent treaties were all located along the seacoast of China, the right of foreign powers to coastal navigation became a matter that had been taken for granted. However, it was not until the Treaty of Tientsin that this right began to be specified in great detail. Since the Treaty of Tientsin and subsequent treaties also opened ports along the Yangtze River for trade, the various powers acquired an additional right to navigate China's inland waters.

The enjoyment by foreign powers of the right to coastwise trade and inland water navigation enabled them not only to market their goods in all parts of China but also to acquire for themselves the privilege of shipping and transporting goods on the inland waters of China. Eventually native as well as foreign goods began to depend upon foreign steamships for transportation.

The second period of China's foreign relations began with the Sino-Japanese War of 1894–1895 and ended with the Joint Expedition of the Eight Powers in 1900. . . . Looking at the unequal treaties concluded during this period, we may say that the conclusion of the Treaty of Shimonoseki[9] marked the turning point in Sino-Japanese relations. Prior to the conclusion of this treaty, the relationship between China and Japan had been on a footing of equality; now it was a relationship of inequality at the expense of China. The special features that characterized China's foreign relations during this period included the lease of Chinese territories to foreign powers, agreements to contract loans so as to build railroads, the unilateral declarations of foreign powers regarding the so-called "spheres of influence," and lastly, treaties concluded between the powers in connection with these so-called "spheres of influence." The main points in some of the treaties concluded during this period were as follows:

I. *"Spheres of Influence," Leased Territories, Railroad Construction, Railroad Zones, and Opening of Mines.*

1. ENGLAND. Even before the Sino-Japanese War of 1894–1895, precedents had been established to divide China into some kind of spheres of influence. After England had taken over Hong Kong, for instance, she specified in the Sino-British Convention of 1846 that China "shall not cede the Chusan Islands to any other foreign power" after the said islands had been returned to her by Great Britain. In the Sino-British Convention of 1894 for the delimitation of boundaries and the regulation of trade along the Yunnan-Burma border, again it was specifically expressed that the Ch'ing government "shall not cede Menglien and Chianghung, or any portion thereof, to any other foreign power." After the Sino-Japanese War of 1894–1895, Great Britain secured from China Weihaiwei and Kowloon as leased territories in two separate agreements concluded in 1898. In the following year Russia conceded to Great Britain that the Yangtze Valley was to be a British sphere in the construction of railroads. Meanwhile the British interests had obtained the right to work mines in the provinces of Shansi and Honan.

2. FRANCE. Upon her conquest of Vietnam, France secured from the Ch'ing government the assurance in 1897 that the Hainan Island "shall not be ceded to any other foreign power." The very next year she obtained the same kind of assurance in connection with the three provinces of Kwangtung, Kwangsi, and Yunnan. Meanwhile she also acquired the right to extend the Lungchow Railroad, construct the Yunnan-Vietnam Railroad, and work the mines in Kwangtung, Kwangsi, and Yunnan provinces. In 1899 she secured the Kwangchow Bay as a leased territory in a treaty concluded with the Ch'ing government.

3. GERMANY. In 1898 Germany concluded with the Ch'ing government the Treaty of Kiaochow whereby she acquired Kiaochow Bay as a leased territory, the permission to construct the Kiaochow-Tsinan Railroad, and the right to work mines located within 30 *li* along the railroad.

4. CZARIST RUSSIA. In 1896 Czarist Russia concluded two agreements with

the Ch'ing government, the Sino-Russian Bank Agreement and the Chinese Eastern Railroad Agreement, whereby the Three Eastern Provinces were recognized as her sphere of influence. In 1898 she obtained from the Ch'ing government, through a treaty, the lease of Port Arthur and Dairen. In a supplementary treaty she further acquired the right to construct railroads, work mines, and develop industry and commerce in the said leased territory. In the following year England and Russia reached an agreement whereby the area north of the Great Wall would be recognized as a Russian sphere insofar as the construction of railroads was concerned.

5. JAPAN. After her occupation of the Pescadores and Taiwan, Japan in 1898 secured assurance from the Ch'ing government that the latter "shall not cede Fukien and the areas along its coast to any other foreign power."

The division of China into "spheres of influence" was merely a preparatory stage for the partition of China among the various powers. Though the tragedy of partition was never actually performed, we had in the meantime lost our rights in connection with railroads, mines, industry, and commerce to the various foreign powers in these so-called "spheres of influence."

II. *Concessions*

During this period the concessions granted to foreign powers were as follows: the German Concessions in Tientsin and Hankow in 1895; the Russian and French Concessions in Hankow and the Japanese Concession in Hangchow in 1896; the Japanese Concession in Soochow in 1897; the Japanese Concession in Tientsin, Shashih, and Hankow in 1898; and the Japanese Concessions in Amoy and Foochow in 1899.

III. *The Right of Foreign Powers to Station Troops in China*

It was in this period that Russia forcibly stationed the so-called "Railroad Protection Guards" along the Chinese Eastern Railroad. From then on, foreign powers began to enjoy the privilege of stationing troops in China.

IV. *The Employment of Foreigners in the Chinese Postal System and the Establishment of Foreign Post Offices in China*

In 1898 France forced the Ch'ing government to employ foreigners in its postal system. Meanwhile the various powers had established their own post offices in China. Thus China's communication system had also fallen into the hands of foreign powers.

V. *The Right of Foreigners to Establish Factories and Manufacture Goods in China*

In the Treaty of Shimonoseki it was stipulated that in all the treaty ports of China Japanese nationals "may freely engage in all kinds of industrial and manufacturing enterprises and may also import all kinds of machinery subject only to the payment of duties according to the fixed tariff." Furthermore, all the Japanese goods produced in China were to be treated as imported goods with regard to exemption from or reduction of taxes. By invoking the most-favored-nation clause, all other powers also enjoyed the same special privileges.

The third period of China's foreign relations began with the signing of the Boxer Protocol of 1901[10] and ended with the Wuchang Uprising of 1911. The unequal treaties concluded during this period included, in addition to the Boxer Protocol, the Sino-British Treaty of Mackay of 1902, the Sino-American Treaty of Commerce and the Sino-Japanese Treaty of Navigation of 1903, the Sino-Japanese Treaty on Manchurian Problems of 1905, and the Sino-Swedish Treaty of 1908. Through these treaties the various powers secured from China additional special privileges as follows:

I. *The Legation Quarter*

In accordance with the Boxer Protocol of 1901, a special area in Peking, then the capital of China, was to be set aside as the site for the legations of the various powers. This area, known as the "Tungchiaomin Hsiang Legation Quarter," was to be administered and defended by the legations themselves. Within the Quarter foreign troops were permanently stationed, as well as special police. To all intents and purposes a sovereign state was created within the territory of another sovereign state.

II. *The Right of Foreign Powers to Station Troops in China*

According to the Boxer Protocol of 1901, foreign powers had the right to station troops not only in the Legation Quarter but also along the railroad that extended from Peking to Shanhaikuan via Tientsin for the ostensible purpose of protecting their line of communication between Peking and the sea.[11] Moreover, they destroyed all the Chinese forts along the aforesaid line of communication in addition to those at Taku. By taking these measures, they in fact deprived us of the right to set up our own coastal defense.

III. *Japan's "Sphere of Influence"*

After the Russo-Japanese War of 1904–1905, Japan occupied Port Arthur and Dairen in addition to the southern section of the Chinese Eastern Railroad and its branch lines. In the so-called Sino-Japanese Treaty on Manchurian Problems, the Ch'ing government recognized the legality of this *fait accompli*. As a result, the southern section of the Three Eastern Provinces, namely, the Liaotung peninsula, was converted into a Japanese sphere of influence. Meanwhile Port Arthur and Dairen had become Japan's leased territories.

IV. *Concessions*

The concessions conceded to foreign powers during this period included the Russian and Belgian Concessions in Tientsin and the Japanese Concession in Chungking in 1901, the Italian Concession in Tientsin and the International Settlement in Kulangyü in 1902, and finally, the Austrian Concession in Tientsin in 1903.

V. *The Administration of Chinese Customs Office*

In 1907 Japan obtained administrative control of the Customs Office in Dairen.

VI. *The Regulated Tariff*

In this connection the major changes as provided in the Boxer Protocol of 1901 and the Sino-British Treaty of Mackay of 1902 were as follows:

1. Duties on imported goods were fixed at 5 percent *ad valorem*. In some cases duties were levied in accordance with the quantity principle.
2. Tariff revenues collected by native customs at different ports were to be brought under the control of the Chinese Customs Administration.

3. Provisions were provided for the increase of tariff duties to 12.5 percent *ad valorem* for imported goods and 7.5 percent *ad valorem* for exported goods if and when *likin* were abolished.[12]

The underlying principle for all these regulations was to reduce tariff duties and transit dues on imported foreign goods so that foreign merchants would not have to pay so much to the Chinese government as they otherwise would have. Since foreign powers had exacted a large indemnity from China in accordance with the Boxer Protocol, China had to increase her duties and dues in order to fulfill her obligation to pay the indemnity. In view of the fact that foreign goods were either exempt from taxation or subject to only light taxation, the burden of paying the indemnity had to be shouldered by the taxation of native products. Consequently Chinese goods were unable to compete with foreign goods even in the territory of China.

VII. *The Right of Foreign Powers to Control Customs Revenue as well as Customs Surplus*

Having been set aside as security for the payment of the Boxer Indemnity, customs revenue had thus come under the control of the Inspector-General of Customs who was always a foreigner. Even the yearly surplus—the remaining revenue after the annual quota of the Boxer Indemnity had been paid—was deposited in foreign banks in the name of the Inspector-General. Thus the imperialists not only took over the most reliable of China's financial resources but also made sure that China could not have even the leftovers.

VIII. *The Improvement of Inland Waters, Employment of Foreigners as Pilots, and Construction of Lighthouses, Beacons, and Buoys*

As prescribed in the Boxer Protocol of 1901, foreign powers were given the right to improve the Pai River (which enters the sea at Taku) and the Whampoa River (which joins the Yangtze River at Wusung). In addition, they were given the right to employ foreigners as pilots and to construct buoys, signal ships, beacons, and lighthouses in all the treaty ports. From then on, the imperialists acquired not only complete knowledge but also full control of the most important of China's inland waters as well as her seaports. How in the world could China still maintain her coastal defense? . . .

NOTES

[1] Translated from Chapter II of the author's *China's Destiny* (*Chung-kuo chih ming-yün*), published in Chungking in 1943, shortly after the unequal treaties were officially abolished.

[2] The First Sino-Japanese War, 1894–1895.

[3] See Selection 31.

[4] As contrary to the Chinese texts.

[5] The Anglo-French War against China in 1858.

[6] See Selection 29.

[7] *Yang-wu kung-so.*

[8] This statement is not exactly correct since not all of these boundaries were determined in 1861.

[9] See Selection 70.

[10] See Selection 84.

[11] Gulf of Pohai.

[12] For *likin,* see p. 244, Footnote 13.

CHAPTER FIVE

The Taiping Rebellion

The easy but decisive victory which Great Britain won against China during the Opium War (Chapter III) was as much indicative of China's weakness as of Great Britain's strength; otherwise it would be difficult to explain the convincing effectiveness with which a small contingent of foreign forces, coming from a country several thousand miles away, was able to impose its will upon the largest nation on earth. The fact is that by the first half of the nineteenth century China had entered the declining stage of what historians call the dynastic cycle, characterized by such phenomena as increasing poverty among the people, famine, domestic disturbances, military ineptitude, and the government's inability to cope with them. In the 1840's organized banditry occurred in practically all the provinces; even in the capital area of Peking travelers were often robbed in broad daylight. This widespread banditry, together with economic hardship and bureaucratic incompetence, made the plight of the people all the more deplorable (Selection 35). The Manchu regime had lost the mandate of Heaven, according to a popular saying; and the nation was in a rebellious mood. Only a capable leader was required to organize a successful rebellion.

The rebel who almost succeeded was a man named Hung Hsiu-ch'üan (1814–1864). Having failed repeatedly to pass the civil service examination, he turned his attention, in due course, to religion and founded a secret society called the Society of God Worshippers (*Pai Shang-ti hui*). To enhance his popular appeal, he claimed (rather immodestly) that he was the younger son of God and the brother of Jesus and that he had been sent by his father the Almighty God to deliver the Chinese people from their sufferings. In time he gathered a large following, most of whom were the poorest peasants in the countryside, including some of his closest associates (Selection 36). From 1847 to 1849 natural disasters struck China repeatedly, and one of the regions most adversely affected was the border area between Kwangtung and Kwangsi where most of the Society's members lived. Believing that the opportune moment had finally arrived, Hung Hsiu-ch'üan raised the standard of revolt in the winter of 1850–1851 and called upon all the people in China to overthrow the Manchu regime.

The rebels met little or ineffective resistance from the armies that the government sent to oppose them. City after city fell before the rebel onslaught, and in March 1853 they captured the greatest prize of them all, the city of Nanking. The battle of Nanking was a blood bath, which was not altogether unexpected; stranger, however, were the events that followed, such as the forced separation of husbands from wives and children from parents, which, had it not been reported by eyewitnesses, might be dismissed as a nightmare (Selection 37). The capture of Nanking was followed by the proclamation of the establishment of a new kingdom called *T'ai-p'ing T'ien-kuo,* the Heavenly Kingdom of Great Peace, headed by Hung Hsiu-ch'üan who called himself T'ien Wang, or Prince of Heaven. The rebels meant to establish a heavenly kingdom on earth, in the way the Almighty would have wished.

Of the Taiping documents that have survived, one of the most important is that dealing with basic social, economic, and governmental reforms, here translated as *A Law of the Regime* (Selection 38). Quoting the Bible copiously, the leaders of the new regime proposed to carry out a radical policy, so radical in fact that it goes beyond even the wildest dreams of today's Communists. "We are all members of one family, headed by God the Father, the Supreme Lord," they declared. "No one should have private property of his own because everything on earth belongs to the Supreme Lord. Only when the Supreme Lord owns everything will all people on earth receive the goods they need and will no man suffer from cold or hunger." Everyone's life was to be carefully and strictly regulated from cradle to grave, and no one was allowed to deviate from the common norm as proclaimed by the Younger Son of God. The government to be established was not merely a theocratic dictatorship, but the society itself was to be highly organized and monolithically oriented. On each level of the social structure, all the duties and responsibilities in connection with the running of an orderly society were to be invested in the authority of one person, who was simultaneously a military commander, a civil bureaucrat, a high priest, and an educator in the normal sense of that term. The whole social structure was to be as simplistic as it was hierarchical.

So regimented a society as the Taipings attempted to establish had never met with success before, and it was certainly unrealistic for them to believe that they could somehow do better. Besides the sheer size of China's territory and population, which in themselves posed insurmountable obstacles for this kind of society to materialize, there were also the lack of modern means of communication and transportation, the landed interests, and the ancient Confucian ideology, the total weight of which made chances of success even slimmer. On top of all these difficulties was the lack of good leadership; one may say that seldom in history had so much been attempted so seriously by so mediocre a group. Until 1853 the military and political success which the Taipings were able to score could be attributed to the Ch'ing regime's weakness rather than any inherent strength of their own. No sooner was the new regime established in Nanking than internecine strife developed among the Taiping leaders. Even if contemporary descriptions of these leaders were only partially true (Selection 39), evidently the regime's collapse had been long a foregone conclusion. That the Taiping regime managed to last more than ten years was largely due to the military genius of one man, Li Hsiu-ch'eng (author of Selection 36), who was not one of the original leaders of the rebellion.

Complacency and internecine struggle on the part of the Taiping leaders provided the Ch'ing regime with much-needed time to launch a counteroffensive. The regular army of this period—the banner men and the "green battalions"—had become so inept and ineffective that the government relied more and more on regional or local forces for its anti-Taiping effort. The regional leader who eventually emerged as the most successful of all the commanders who confronted the Taiping forces was Tseng Kuo-fan (1811–1872, author of Selection 35), one of the most gifted Confucian statesmen of the nineteenth century. Slowly and gradually his men won the upper hand, and beginning in 1862 they lay siege to Nanking. In the summer of 1864 Tseng Kuo-ch'üan, a younger brother of Tseng Kuo-fan, finally succeeded in capturing the city after a bloody battle that lasted fifteen days (Selection 40). Hung Hsiu-ch'üan had committed suicide one month before, and his son and successor escaped from the city, only to be captured afterwards. The Taiping regime came to an end, and the Ch'ing Dynasty was destined to last another forty-five years.

35 • TSENG KUO-FAN: *The Plight of the Chinese People*[1]

To comply with Your Majesty's instruction to show compassion and love for all the people in the empire, your humble servant wishes to take this opportunity to describe their plight as follows.

The danger to a nation is not so much the paucity of material wealth as the lack of coherence among its people. In the course of our history rarely was a time so prosperous as the Sui Dynasty during Wen-ti's reign.[2] Yet the country was soon plunged into chaos, and the Sui regime eventually came to an end. Why? Because the people had lost faith in their government despite the country's material wealth. Conversely, seldom was the nation so poor as she was during the reign of Han Chao-ti.[3] Yet the country was peaceful and her people secure. Why? Because the people had faith and confidence in their own government. For a period of fifteen years, from the first to the sixteenth year of K'ang-hsi[4] during the present dynasty, the Yellow River broke its dikes every year with the exception of one, and flood damage was extremely heavy over a large region, especially in the Hsin-chuang and Kaoyen areas. As if this were not enough, the Three Viceroys' Rebellion erupted[5] and ravaged nine provinces; it took the government seven years to suppress it. By then the treasury was almost empty, emptier than it is today. Yet the dynasty remained secure and the country undisturbed. Why? Because the Saintly Progenitor[6] loved the people more than he did himself, and the people, in response, continued to pledge to him their unswerving allegiance and rallied for his support. Though Your Majesty undeniably loves your subjects to the same extent as the Saintly Progenitor loved his, local officials, being indifferent to the plight of their charges, have failed in conveying your compassionate sentiments to the people and bringing to your attention their grievances. Because of this lack of communication, your humble servant wishes to take this opportunity to describe in some detail the ills from which our people suffer most.

The first ill concerns the high price of silver which affects adversely the people's ability to fulfill their tax obligations. The tax load in Soochow, Sungkiang, Changchow, and Chinkiang[7] is the heaviest in the nation, and the people in these districts also suffer most. The yield for each *mou* of land is anywhere from 15 to 20 pecks of polished rice, and the landowner, after dividing it with his tenant on a fifty-fifty basis, receives approximately 8 pecks as his rent. Though his regular tax is only 2 pecks per *mou,* he has to pay another 2 pecks as rice tribute[8] and 2 pecks more for miscellaneous requisitions, totaling 6 pecks altogether. Thus, for each *mou* of land he owns, his net income is only 2 pecks of polished rice per year. If all these taxes could be paid in rice, the situation would not be so serious. But most of them have to be paid in silver. Rice tribute is sometimes paid in rice, but the regular tax and the miscellaneous requisitions have to be paid in silver. Since a farmer reaps only rice, he has to sell his harvest for standard coins in order to obtain the necessary cash; since the price of standard coins is high in terms of rice, he has understandable grievances. Moreover, in order to pay his taxes, he has to convert his standard coins into silver. Since the price of silver is high in terms of standard coins, his grievances become even greater. In the Southeast the price of rice has been 3,000 standard coins per picul for a long time. Formerly one tael of silver was worth 1,000 standard coins, and by selling one picul of rice, a farmer could obtain three taels of silver. Today one tael of silver is worth as much as 2,000 standard coins, and consequently one picul of rice can only bring 1.5 taels of silver. Formerly, selling 3 pecks of rice would bring enough silver to pay taxes for one *mou* of land; now, selling 6 pecks will not be enough to achieve the same purpose. While the return to the government remains the same, the burden to the people has been doubled. Besides, there are additional taxes on houses and family cemeteries, all of which have been doubled in terms of rice because they, like most of other taxes, have also to be paid in silver.

Under the circumstances it is not surprising that a large number of taxpayers have become delinquent, despite local governments' effort to enforce payment. Often special officials are assigned to help tax collections, and day and night soldiers are sent out to harass taxpayers. Sometimes corporal punishments are imposed upon tax delinquents; some of them are so badly beaten to exact the last penny that blood and flesh fly in all directions. Cruel though it is, this practice does not necessarily reflect the evil nature of local officials who, more often than not, do not believe that they have a better choice. If they fail to collect 70 percent of the amount due, not only will they be impeached and punished as a matter of routine, they may also have to pay the balance with their own money, that sometimes amounts to thousands of taels, and ruin their families in the process. In short, they are forced to do what they loathe.

Before the fifteenth year of Tao-kuang [1835] the province of Kiangsu had been able to collect and ship to the capital its annual quota of tribute rice. Since the sixteenth year [1836], however, the collection has been deficient each and every year, and the imperial government has been forced to order a moratorium in each case. It is not true that the officials of the former years were more conscientious in performing their duties than their contemporary counterparts; the real culprit is the continuous rise in silver price. The high price of silver brings not only difficulties to taxpayers and tax collectors alike but also damages to the nation as a whole. In this regard the situation in Chekiang is similar to that in Kiangsu because both provinces have approximately the same tax rates. As taxpayers continue to dodge payment, the officials-in-charge become more hard pressed to perform their collection duties. As a result, a new device, called "interception,"[9] has been invented. This device calls for the payment of annual taxes after the spring rather than the autumn harvest as has been hitherto the case, and also the payment of taxes one year in advance. When taxpayers refuse to go along with this device, the officials-in-charge reduce the amount to be levied so as to provide them with some incentive to pay their taxes in advance. As "interception" continues year after year, an official in a later period will find that the taxes which he is supposed to collect have been paid a long time ago, and there is no more for him to collect. Being unable to collect taxes, he cannot hope to preserve his position, however honest he is. Meanwhile, his more corrupt and less principled colleagues will use the alleged tax delinquency as a pretext to demonstrate their extortion skills: they will employ every trick they can think of to exact money, minus any moral scruples.

Though tax rates for Kiangsi and Hukuang are comparatively lower, the people have nevertheless great difficulties in fulfilling their tax obligations. The culprit, once again, is the high price of silver. The greater the difficulty in collecting taxes becomes, the harsher will be the means with which the officials-in-charge press for payment. Whenever a man is found to be unable to pay, one of his clan members, if he happens to be well-to-do, may be arrested and then forced to pay all the taxes on his behalf. At other times his relatives or even neighbors are locked up for the same purpose. Under the circumstances it is not surprising that the people are complaining and angry, and often the resistance to tax payment bursts forth and mushrooms into full-fledged riot. The popular riots in Leiyang and Ch'ungyang of Hukuang and Kueihsi and Fuchou of Kiangsi are only the most serious examples. While the knavish nature of the rioters does play an important role in these riots, it cannot be denied that the 100 percent increase in the price of silver, the heavy, extralegal levy that exceeds what is normally due, the excessive punishments that are imposed upon the alleged tax evaders, and the almost insurmountable difficulties of earning a livelihood among the poor have all contributed to make these riots possible. In the judgment of your humble servant, the high price of silver in terms of produce is the first ill from which our people suffer most.

The second ill of our nation is the great number of bandits which threaten the security of our law-abiding citizens. The area that comprises the districts of Lüchou, Fengyang, Yingchou, and Po[10] has been notorious as a bandits' gathering ground since ancient times. To its north are Feng, P'ei, Hsiao, and T'angchou,[11] and to its west are Nanyang, Junan, Kuangchou, and Kushih.[12] These areas constitute the central or most strategic region in China; and once the bandits begin to gather, nobody knows what the ultimate danger will be.[13] Lately your humble servant has heard that the bandits in this region have become bolder and more numerous, robbed and raped in broad daylight, and kidnaped people for ransom. Whenever an act of banditry is reported to the government, the local official announces in advance his intention to send troops against the bandits and advertises it in public proclamations, so as to make sure that the bandits know the soldiers are coming. Upon arriving at the village where the banditry took place, the official-in-charge expects to learn from the village chiefs, who are afraid of the bandits, that the offenders have already fled. Without anything worthwhile to do, he orders the burning of some of the houses in the village before his departure, so as to impress the villagers with the power of his office. Meanwhile his soldiers use a variety of excuses to exact payment from the bandits' victim, who by then is only too regretful that he reported the banditry to the government in the first place. While the soldiers are busy taking away from his house whatever they can carry, the bandits are still at large, hiding somewhere in the village. Sometimes the official announces that the responsible bandit has in fact been killed and that the case is therefore closed; then he proceeds to show off the bandit's body, after killing some prisoner in his jail who has nothing to do with this particular crime. Not only does the bandits' victim fail to get his grievances redressed and his stolen properties restored; he may also lose everything he has and go bankrupt. After all this, he will probably swallow his tears in silence and make no more complaint, since by then he is no longer financially able to make any appeals.

Suppose he does appeal and that the government responds by mobilizing a large force in its attempt to arrest the bandits. Since these soldiers have always been in collusion with the bandits, they will release the offenders soon after their capture, in return for a handsome bribe, and the offenders will quickly disappear without leaving a trace. Sometimes the soldiers use the reported presence of bandits as an excuse to blackmail the villagers; if the latter refuse to pay the bribes they demand, they will accuse them as the bandits' accomplices, burn their houses, and bring them to the city in chains. At other times they order the villagers to look for and arrest the bandits. If the villagers follow this order and bring the bandits in, they will find to their great surprise when they reach the city that they have to pay all the expenses not only for transporting the prisoners to be tried in a high court but also for maintaining the captured in prison before the trial takes place. Thus, whenever banditry occurs, not only will its victim suffer great damages; even his remote relatives and distant neighbors may be also adversely affected: they either become bankrupt or wind up in jail themselves, and often both. During the Ch'uan-Shan[14] rebellion that occurred in the Chia-ch'ing period (1796–1820), the rebel chieftain Liu Chih-k'uei was actually captured at one time. Yet the constables of the T'aiho district,[15] having received heavy bribes, set the prisoner free. The result was predictable: the rebellion snowballed until it covered a wide area. Today corrupt constables and vicious soldiers can be found everywhere in the empire. They cultivate banditry and then let the bandits do whatever they please. My blood runs cold whenever they are mentioned.

Serving Your Majesty at the Ministry of Justice, your humble servant reads dozens of cases involving banditry each day. From travelers who come to Peking, he has also learned that numerous cases of banditry have never been reported or have been reported without being followed by official action. In either case the banditry involved never receives the attention of the imperial government which it deserves. In South China there are numerous secret societies that practice banditry.[16] Of every ten households three might choose to submit themselves to the bandits, not because they have lost their sense of right and wrong, but because, by temporarily providing these bandits with money, food, and wine, they hope to buy a moment of peace and security for themselves. Your humble servant has questioned many local officials about why they do not choose to report banditry when they know that it has taken place within their jurisdiction. They inform me that there are in fact several reasons. First, when they send their troops to arraign the bandits, the latter might resist arrest and fight back. Second, even after the bandits have been arrested, there is the danger that they will be intercepted by their friends when they are transported to the provincial capital for trial. Third, the procedure involving the transfer of prisoners is so laden with red tape and the distance so long—several hundred *li* in many cases—that the officials-in-charge simply do not wish to be bothered with it. Fourth, during each transfer procedure, the man-in-charge always demands payment to facilitate the process, and the total amount can reach as high as several hundred taels of silver for each prisoner. Since the amount of expenses officially allowed is far from adequate to meet the need, the official-in-charge is forced to make up the difference with his own money. Moreover, if he reports banditry and fails to come up with the bandits, he will be ordered by his superior to arraign them in a specified period; failing that, he himself may be impeached. Sometimes a high official might wish to conceal unfortunate happenings and pretend that everything is well within his jurisdiction; in that case, an official who reports banditry to him may be reprimanded as a troublemaker. In view of all these considerations, it is not surprising that a local official will choose to drift along by concealing what is unpleasant; in fact, only in this way can he hope to keep his position. However, the more he tries to conceal banditry, the faster it grows, until the moment eventually arrives when robbers and thieves rage through the countryside without encountering any resistance, and all the law-abiding citizens within his jurisdiction cannot have a single night of good sleep. The widespread banditry, in the judgment of your humble servant, is another serious ill from which the nation now suffers.

    The third ill which your humble servant wishes to stress is the great number of cases in which innocent men are condemned and the inability on the part of the people to have a wrong redressed. Since his appointment at the Ministry of Justice, your humble servant has reviewed several hundred cases of appeal. In the case of Huang Ch'ing-an of Honan and Ah Hsiang of Miyüan,[17] the plaintiffs, having presented undisputable evidence, were finally able to win their respective litigations. In most of the other cases, however, it was the plaintiffs who received punishment in the end, on the ground that they had made false accusations, while the defendants went through the whole litigation unscathed and free. Generally speaking, the officials-in-charge invoke the following rules in the law as legitimate ground to impose heavy penalties upon the plaintiffs. First, the plaintiff has failed to present the truth in his petition, and for such failure he is to receive one hundred blows by a striking rod. Second, the case he presents is not serious enough for him to bypass the local courts and to go straight to the nation's capital, and for such offense he is to be punished by banishment to the frontier as a soldier. Third, he intimidates the government under the pretense of offering constructive suggestions, and for such offense he is to be punished by banishment to a nearby area as a soldier. Fourth, he harbors personal grudges against the official under whose jurisdiction he lives and falsely accuses him of wrongdoing before the latter's superior. For this offense he is to be punished by banishment to the malarious regions[18] as a soldier. Sometimes the official-in-charge may not wish to go so far as to impose such heavy penalties as those described above; he may instead issue an ambiguous verdict to make sure that the plaintiff does not know where he stands. The verdict might be: "It seems likely that the plaintiff has made a false accusation," or "It does not seem that the plaintiff is completely without any ground to make such an accusation." What should a plaintiff do after he has received a verdict like this? Should he press his charge or withdraw it? While he may congratulate himself for having escaped severe punishment, the official-in-charge, by rendering an ambiguous decision like this, has in fact cleared the defendant of all charges and consequently he will not be punished at all.

    Though it is definitely wrong to encourage ordinary citizens to sue their jurisdictional superiors, such a lawsuit is clearly justified if these officials are admittedly corrupt or if their constables are actually engaging in blackmail. Who can believe that all lawsuits brought against government officials are without an exception based upon false accusations? Who can believe that when an ordinary citizen is a plaintiff and a government official a defendant, the defendant is always right and the plaintiff always wrong? The answer to both questions would have to be a clear "No one" if we had conscientious, enlightened officials sitting on the bench as judges.

As your humble servant checks with trial procedures, he finds that whenever litigation reaches as far as the nation's capital, it can be settled in a variety of ways. The Ministry of Justice can order the transfer of all pertinent files to the capital, where the final hearings, in the presence of both plaintiffs and defendants, will be conducted. As an alternative, it can authorize the governor-general, under whose jurisdiction the lawsuit began, to conduct the aforesaid hearings. It can also send an inspector-general, with full authority from the imperial government, to proceed to the province where the lawsuit originally began and conduct the hearings. Lately, whenever a case reaches the nation's capital, it is always the second procedure that is followed; namely, the governor-general is authorized to conduct the final hearings. Without an exception the governor-general will transfer such an authority to the governor, and there has never been a case in recent years that he conducts the hearings himself. The governor is more interested in protecting his fellow officials than in serving justice whenever these officials are accused of wrongdoing by those who live under their jurisdiction. He uses a variety of tactics—intentional delay in starting the hearings, harassment, and even intimidation—to achieve his ultimate goal, i.e., the admission on the part of the plaintiff that he has made false accusations. As this practice has become the fashion of the day, it is followed in all the provinces without exception. When one household becomes unfortunately involved in a long, protracted lawsuit, ten households will become bankrupt as a result. When one man's grievances are not redressed, a hundred others share the pain with him. Sometimes a lawsuit involving only small stakes can drag on for many years until black has become white and right has become wrong. The dispute is eventually settled by itself after the parties involved have finally died in jail. An honest man cannot but feel angry whenever he hears a situation like this. The condemnation of the innocent and the inability on the part of the people to have a wrong redressed are, in the judgment of your humble servant, the third ill from which our nation presently suffers most.

These three ills are the most serious the nation faces today, and the search for their cure is our most urgent task. Insofar as the second and the third ills—the widespread banditry and the condemnation of innocent men—are concerned, Your Majesty is hereby requested to issue a strict order to all the governors-general and governors to think carefully about them and to devise ways for their cure. As for the first ill or the increasingly higher price of silver, we should find remedies in terms of stabilizing the existing price. Your humble servant is at present drafting a proposal aimed at the attainment of this goal, which, when completed, will be presented to Your Majesty for reference purposes.[19]

The people are the very foundation of a nation, and it is certainly the fault of us ministers that their sufferings, however small, are not made known to Your Majesty. Insignificant though his opinion is, your humble servant begs for Your Majesty's indulgence to let it be submitted.

NOTES

[1] This is a memorial presented to Emperor Hsien-feng on February 7, 1852, shortly after the Taipings had raised their standard of revolt in Kwangtung and Kwangsi

provinces. Source: *The Complete Works of Tseng Kuo-fan* (*Tseng Wen-cheng kung ch'üan-chi*), vol. 2, pp. 15–17.

2 Sui Wen-ti (r. 589–604), founder of the Sui Dynasty.
3 Han Chao-ti (r. 86–74 B.C.).
4 1662–1677.
5 The three viceroys were Wu San-kuei, Keng Chung-ming, and Shang K'o-hsi. The rebellion was suppressed in 1678.
6 Emperor K'ang-hsi (r. 1662–1772).
7 All of these districts are located in the Lower Yangtze Valley, Kiangsu province.
8 *Ts'ao-hu.*
9 *Chieh-ch'uan.*
10 All these districts are located in the northern section of Anhwei province. Lüchou and Yingchou are also known as Hofei and Fuyang, respectively.
11 All these districts are located in the northern section of Kiangsu province.
12 All these districts are located in the southern section of Honan province. Kuangchou is also known as Huangch'uan.
13 The author was adequately guided by historical experience. Liu Pang, founder of the Han Dynasty, was born in P'ei, and Chu Yüan-chang, founder of the Ming Dynasty, was born in Fengyang. Each started his career as a "bandit-hero," eventually succeeded in toppling the existing regime, and established a new dynasty.
14 Szechuan and Shensi provinces.
15 Located in the northern section of Anhwei province.
16 One of them was the Society of God Worshippers, the religious organization of the Taipings. See Selection 36.
17 Located in the northern section of modern Hopeh province.
18 Yunnan, Kweichow, and Kwangsi provinces.
19 The proposal, dated February 8, 1852, was presented later.

36 • LI HSIU-CH'ENG: *The Beginnings of the Rebellion*[1]

The Prince of Heaven was born in the district of Hua, Kwangtung Province. His real name was Hung Hsiu-ch'üan. He had two stepbrothers, Hung Jen-fa and Hung Jen-ta, both of whom were born to his father's first wife and were older than he was. While the two stepbrothers tilled the field as farmers, Hung was allowed to study at home. His best friend and study companion was a man named Feng Yün-shan.

One day in 1837 the Prince of Heaven suddenly became ill. He was in a coma for seven consecutive days; when he finally regained his consciousness, he spoke in mysterious terms. He exhorted people to worship God and to be good and pious. Those who worshipped God, said he, would not suffer from illness or hardship; those who did not would on the other hand be bitten by snakes and tigers. He also said that a God worshipper could not worship any other deity except God. Because of his preachings, whenever a person followed his advice by worshipping the true God, he did not dare to worship other gods or spirits any more. Since most of the people in the world are afraid of death, who would not follow the Prince of Heaven's leadership, once they were convinced that the unbelievers would be bitten by snakes and tigers?

To the west of Hua and for an area measuring several thousand square *li* are such districts as Hsin, Kueip'ing, Wuhsüan, Hsiang, T'eng, Luch'uan, and Popai, all of Kwangsi Province. The Prince of Heaven often hid himself deep in the mountains, where he exhorted people to worship God. Sometimes four or five of every ten households were converted to the new faith; other times as many as eight

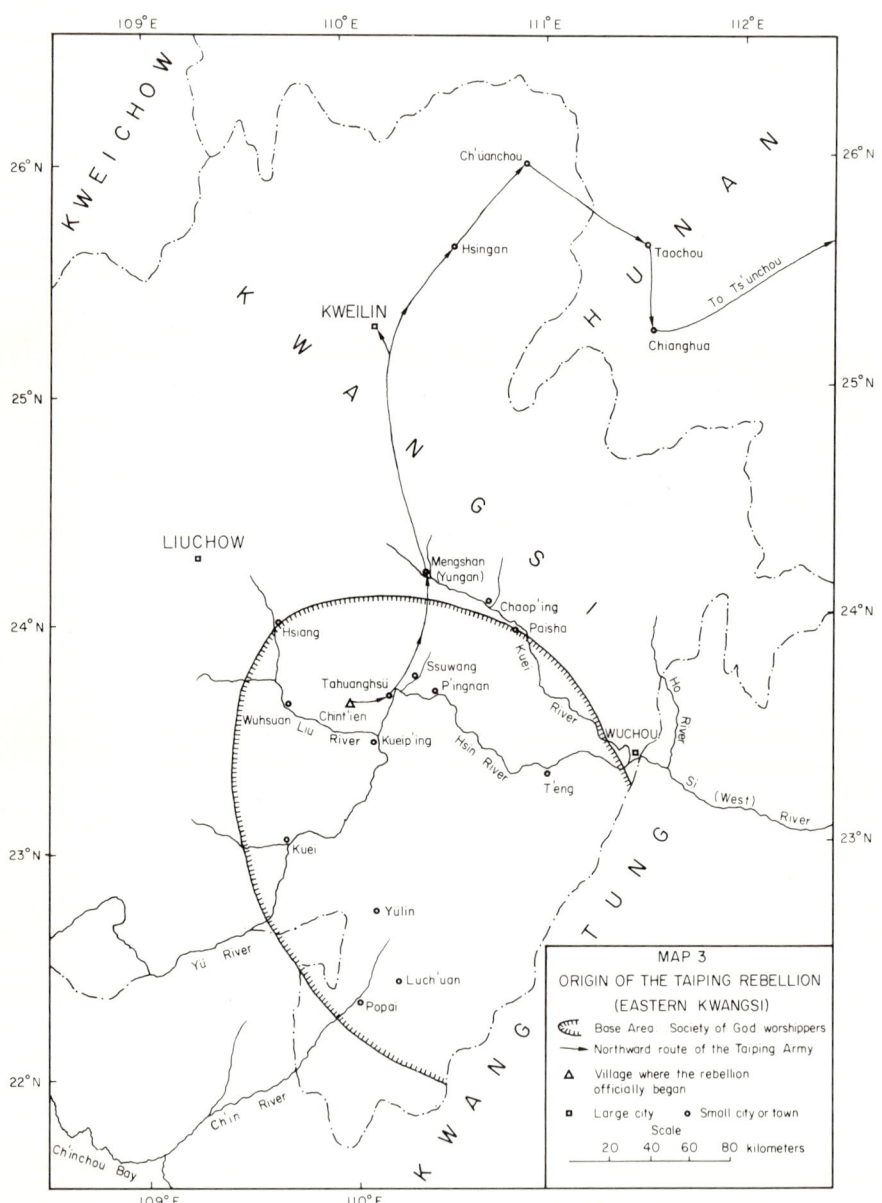

joined the new organization.² Practically all the converts were poor peasants; generally speaking, scholars and intellectuals did not wish to have anything to do with this new faith. Nevertheless, the organization's membership continued to increase and became larger and larger with the passage of time.

The ultimate goal of the Society of God Worshippers, i.e., the establishment of a new kingdom on earth, was known only to a few, such as the King of the East Yang Hsiu-ch'ing, the King of the West Hsiao Ch'ao-kuei, the King of the South Feng Yün-shan, the King of the North Wei Ch'ang-hui, the King of Yi Shih Ta-k'ai, and Prime Minister Ch'in Jih-ch'ang. In fact, outside of these six persons nobody knew what the Prince of Heaven's true intention was in founding this new organization.

Yang Hsiu-ch'ing, the King of the East, was born in the village of P'ingyishan, Kueip'ing District. He earned a livelihood by cutting wood and making charcoal and was not particularly brilliant or ingenious. Once he joined the Society of God Worshippers, however, he suddenly knew everything that was to be known—even today I still do not understand how Heaven could transform this man in such a drastic manner in such a short time. He enjoyed the confidence of the Prince of Heaven, who entrusted him with all important matters in connection with the state. He was strict in enforcing military orders and rewarded and punished with absolute impartiality. Hsiao Ch'ao-kuei, the King of the West, was born in the village of Lulut'ung, Wuhsüan District. He earned a livelihood by cutting wood and tilling the field. He was married to the Prince of Heaven's younger sister and was entrusted with great responsibilities. A strong, courageous man, he was famous for his audacity on the battlefield. Feng Yün-shan, the King of the South, was a student then studying at home. Able and wise, he was the man who had helped the Prince of Heaven most in planning the establishment of a new kingdom. He provided the intellect during the initial stage of the rebellion.

Wei Ch'ang-hui, the King of the North, was a native of the village of Chint'ien, Kueip'ing District. He was a scholar duly recognized by the government and often visited the district office. He was so intelligent that he could change his strategy quickly whenever facing a new situation. Shih Ta-k'ai, the King of Yi, was born to a wealthy family in the village of Paisha, Kueip'ing District. Though well known as a learned man, he was equally proficient as a man of valor on the battlefield. Ch'in Jih-ch'ang, the Prime Minister, was born in the same village; but unlike Shih, he was a manual worker employed by others and had no ability or talent to speak of. The Prince of Heaven trusted him on account of his unswerving loyalty and also his bravery on the battlefield.

These six men were the proselytizers for the Society of God Worshippers. But at that time Hung Hsiu-ch'üan had not acquired the title of the Prince of Heaven. The villagers referred to him as Mr. Hung.

For several years there were no overtly rebellious activities on the part of the Society of God Worshippers. In the years 1847 and 1848, bandit groups mushroomed all over Kwangsi Province, ravaging towns and cities. For self-defense, people organized their own militias. The militiamen and the God Worshippers were separate, rival groups, each trying to show that it was stronger than the other. The rivalry between the two groups was in fact the immediate cause of the uprising staged by the God Worshippers. At the time of the uprising, militiamen and God Worshippers resided in the same village in most cases. In other cases, however, each group inhabited its own village to the exclusion of the other group.

One day in the sixth month of 1850[3] the standard of revolt was raised simultaneously in the following places: Chint'ien, Huachou, Luch'uan, Popai, and Paishashih. The Prince of Heaven was then hiding in the house of Hu Yi-huang, in the Shanjen village of Huachou, a hiding place nobody then knew. The Kings of the East, the North, and Yi, together with the Prime Minister, were at Chint'ien, however. Shanjen was a village adjacent to the T'eng District, though under the jurisdiction of the Nanp'ing [sic, P'ingnan] District. Chint'ien, where the first standard of revolt was raised, was about 70 or 80 li from my home. The roads in this area were all mountainous and extremely difficult to traverse. While at home, I heard that the moment the uprising was officially announced, the King of the East immediately sent troops to Huachou, whence they escorted the Prince of Heaven to Chint'ien for a conference on strategy.

Among those who came to Chint'ien for the purpose of joining the rebellion were three bandit leaders who had been active in the mouth of the Tahuang River for a long time. The three were Ta-t'ou-yang, Ta-li-yü,[4] and Lo Ta-kang. Taking a look at the God Worshippers, who did not seem to be strong and rugged enough, Ta-t'ou-yang decided not to join them and later joined forces with General Hsiang[5] of the Ch'ing army[6] instead. Since Ta-t'ou-yang and Lo Ta-kang had been rivals and hated each other, the latter decided to put his forces under the command of the Prince of Heaven. Upon his arrival at Chint'ien, Lo stationed his troops in the three villages east of Wuhsüan where he called upon the God Worshippers to become his soldiers....

At the time of the uprising, I was still at home. I knew, however, that the rebels, taking the land route from Wuchou and T'eng to Yungan, would have to pass through our village Tali. My family was very poor, and my father had a difficult time to support me and my younger brother Li Ming-ch'eng. To help the family's finance, I chopped wood in the mountains and sometimes worked as a hired hand. Between the age of seven and nine, however, I did learn to read a little from my uncle.[7] After that I helped my parents in search of food. This continued until I was twenty-five or twenty-six, when for the first time I heard a man named Mr. Hung who taught people to worship God.

The Prince of Heaven led his troops from Ssuwang to Tahuanghsü, whence they were to move to Yungan, by both land and water routes. The troops that were to take the land route would pass through our village Tali, located in a level area of several hundred square li which was surrounded by high mountains on all sides. These troops were led by the King of the West, the King of the North, the Prime Minister, and Lo Ta-kang, while those traveling by the water route were under the command of the King of the East and the King of the South.

In Tali, where they stayed for five days, the rebels took food and clothing from the villagers with little or no scruple. The King of the West, who was then stationed in a neighboring village, gave the order that all the God Worshippers should share food together like members of one family and that the villagers should have no fear for his army and should not try to run away from it. Before the rebels left the village, they ordered the burning of all houses that belonged to the God Worshippers. With their houses destroyed and their food and clothing taken away from them, the God Worshippers had no choice but to follow the rebel army. People in the countryside seldom travel very far, and they would not know how to return home after they had traveled a hundred li. Meanwhile the enemy[8] was chasing them from the rear. From Tali to Yungan we attacked and captured many towns and cities. After Yungan was captured, we were stationed in Hoch'ih for several months....

NOTES

¹ This selection comprises the opening passages of a written testimony of considerable length. The author wrote this testimony in a prisoner's cage after his capture by government troops in the summer of 1864. Shortly after it was written, he was executed. See also Selection 40. A copy of the Chinese original can be found in Tso Shun-sheng (ed.), *Source Materials on China for the Past One Hundred Years* (Chung-kuo chin-pai-nien shih tzu-liao), vol. 2, pp. 1–4.
² The Society of God Worshippers.
³ The sixth lunar month of 1850 covers the period from July 9 to August 7 inclusive.
⁴ Ta-t'ou-yang and Ta-li-yü, literally, meant "the Big-headed Goat" and "the Big Carp." In Chinese villages some of the poorest peasants never acquired regular names throughout their lives and were known to their friends or acquaintances by their nicknames only. Here the peasant background of the Taiping Rebellion was clearly shown.
⁵ General Hsiang Yung.
⁶ The government's army.
⁷ A brother of his mother.
⁸ This refers to the Ch'ing (the government's) army.

37 • CHANG JU-NAN: *The Days When the Taipings Arrived at Nanking*[1]

The moment they entered the city [Nanking], the bandits [the Taiping rebels] went up and down the streets, shouting aloud that all residents must close their front doors and that anyone who dared to venture into the streets would be immediately killed. They also issued an order that a piece of paper with the word OBEDIENCE on it must be pasted on each front door, that an altar with three cups of tea on it must be set up inside each house,[2] and that all residents, men or women, must not wear any hats.[3] Full of apprehension, all the people in the city obeyed the order without asking any questions.

Moments later, the bandits gathered their forces and surrounded the Manchu City.[4] The roaring of cannons and the firing of rifles, intermingled with cries of "Kill," could be heard several *li* away. The Manchu City, called the Inner City during the Ming Dynasty, was high and well-fortified. All of its residents rallied to defend the city wall, including the Manchu women who, like their men, were proficient in the handling of weapons. The bandits attacked the city in large numbers and suffered heavy casualties. As dead bodies were piled up higher and higher outside the wall, the attackers were also able to climb higher and higher to assault the city. The moment eventually arrived when the defenders were simply overwhelmed by heavy waves of attack from all sides. Upon the fall of the Manchu City it was learned that all Manchu generals and commanders, including Ku-shan, had died in action. The Manchu soldiers who managed to escape by fighting their way through layer after layer of besiegers number no more than four hundred. Even women and children fought as best as they could; though they killed many of their enemies, their own casualties were also extremely heavy. The Manchu women who survived the battle numbered no more than a few thousand; later, after being chased out from the Ch'ao-yang Gate,[5] they were completely surrounded and then slaughtered one by one. Between 8 and 12 A.M., when the Manchu City fell, even the sun looked melancholy and dispirited, and the spirit of death could be felt miles away. As the battle raged on, all the people outside the city were tormented by agony and frozen with fear: how helpless they must have felt! After the fall of the Manchu City and for the rest of the day, Nanking was as still and motionless as in the middle of the night.

The next day, the twelfth of the second month [March 21, 1853], the bandits in small groups of three or four each once again emerged in the streets. They knocked at people's doors, announcing that they were searching for "devils," by which they meant government officials, soldiers, or Manchus. If they found inside a house such things as official hats, boots, or clothing, or governmental seals and documents that had been carefully hidden, the head of the household would be immediately put under arrest and sped away. Before entering a house, they parked their rifles outside the door and carried with them only short knives. "Are you a devil?" they would ask. Upon receiving a negative answer, they would ask again: "Do you hide any devils inside your house?" If the response was again negative, they would not ask any more questions. Then they would order the residents to open their chests and drawers and, whenever they saw something particularly valuable, such as silk, velvet, gold, or curios, they would take it away as if it had always belonged to them. It may be added, however, that some of the bandits never asked people to open their chests or drawers. On a given day, a household might encounter this kind of search three or four times; in each case, the searchers would not allow its residents to go through the ritual of welcoming them or escorting them out of the house. A certain banker named Yang, a native of Shaohsing [in Chekiang Province], who resided at the Shui-hsi Gate,[6] had amassed a large fortune as a result of his shrewd business dealings. He was so wealthy that he even purchased an official title from the government. Expecting the bandits to arrive, he put on his ceremonial robe, set up an altar on which he burned incense, and proceeded to perform the ritual of kowtow before them. Hardly had he knelt down, however, when they chopped his head off.[2]

The bandits had a variety of titles for their officials. Those who were attached to the so-called Inner Court resided in governmental buildings; those who belonged to the so-called Military Command took residence among the local inhabitants. They would not live inside any kind of temples, saying that all the gods in these temples were merely "dead devils."

On the thirteenth day of the month [March 22, 1853], the people in Nanking saw proclamations posted all over the city. Each was written on a piece of yellow paper fringed with paintings of dragons and phoenixes and was issued under the name of "Yang,[8] King of the East and Military Chancellor of the Heavenly Kingdom of Great Peace." It said, among other things, that because of man's failure to worship Heaven, the Heavenly Father in anger had not only caused a great flood but also sent to earth such evil animals as dogs and snakes. Its contents were so absurd that they need not be repeated here in detail. In a red poster issued under the same name, the author said that the Prince of Heaven [Hung Hsiu-ch'üan], having been authorized by the Heavenly Father and the Heavenly Elder Brother [Jesus] to govern this world, wanted all men to recognize the Heavenly Father as the true God and the Prince of Heaven as their sovereign ruler, and that they should assist the Prince of Heaven to unify China so they themselves could enjoy heavenly bliss. On the front door of each house where a bandit resided, the following words were written: "Everyone should worship God so he can go to paradise. Come, let us all worship God!" Should a man show surprise or astonishment when reading these words, very likely he would not return home alive.

Shortly after it took over Nanking, the bandit government issued an order saying that men and women should be segregated and should in fact live in separate dormitories. Understandably the people did not take kindly to this order, and force was therefore used to carry it out. (Whenever a bandit saw a child he liked, he would compel its parents to let him adopt it. The child would be from then on called a *tai-tsai*.[9]) This order for sexual segregation separated husband from wife, parents from children, and brothers from sisters, and in short, broke up the whole family. Sometimes a family would request the bandit authorities to postpone the enforcement of their segregation order for one day. Then, in the middle of the night, all of its members would commit suicide: they either hanged themselves, jumped into a nearby river, or set their own house on fire and burned themselves to death. Previously the bandits had forced local residents to serve as night watchmen the moment they entered the city. Now, seeing houses catching fire at night, they sent these watchmen to fight the fire. They were afraid that some of the government's soldiers, who still hid inside the city, might use the fire as a smokescreen to launch a counterattack.

The next day [March 23, 1853] the order to segregate the sexes was even more strictly enforced. Among those who had been living in segregated quarters some managed to sneak out at night and committed suicide at home. As this situation continued, strong measures were introduced to prevent its repetition. Each female dormitory housed approximately twenty residents, all of whom were required to address each other as "new sisters," regardless of their age differences. At the head of the twenty "new sisters" was an "old sister," their "squad leader" who, more often than not, was a Kwangsi woman.[10] Most of the female dormitories were located near the Hsi-hua Gate; collectively, they were called the "women's battalion." The women's battalion was divided into five armies—the front, the rear, the left, the right, and the center—and each army was jointly commanded by a female commander, usually a Kwangsi woman, and a male inspector. Husbands were not allowed to go inside a female dormitory to visit their wives; nor were sons allowed to go inside to see their mothers. Whenever a visit took place, the visitor and the visited could only speak to each other across a fence and at a considerable distance. The bandits were very strict with adultery; once an act of adultery was discovered, both the adulterer and the adulteress would be immediately put to death on the ground that they had violated a heavenly commandment. Even the old bandits from Kwangsi were not exempted from this rule.

Whenever the bandit government issued an order, it was the duty of the inspector to transmit it to the military commander, who in turn would transmit it to the squad leader. The duty of the squad leader was to carry out the order, whether it be the digging of trenches or the transportation of bricks. Those who were slow in performing their assigned tasks would be whipped without mercy. "Since you are eating the food provided by the Heavenly Father," the bandits would say, "you should of course work for Him. Why should you think about your husbands all the time? When the Prince of Heaven conquers China and unifies the country, you can have as many husbands as you want." Such were the comforting remarks they offered to any woman when she complained. Each day they searched all the back alleys to locate women who had not been rounded up. These women would be chased out of the Southern Gate if they were found in the southern section of the city, and the Shen-ts'e Gate if they were found in the northern section. Knowing how ferocious the bandits were, many women jumped into the city moats and committed suicide rather than let themselves be captured alive. Having heard about the fate of the Manchu women, they simply did not wish to see the same thing happen to them. Only later did the bandit chieftain, the King of the North [Wei Ch'ang-hui], learn about this evil practice. He immediately put a stop to it. The women who had been rounded up were brought to the female dormitories, and thus six or seven new "armies" were added to the "women's battalion." The total number of female soldiers reached several hundred thousand in Nanking alone.

In the "men's battalion," all men addressed each other as "new brothers." Twenty men resided in each male dormitory and were headed by a *liang-ssu-ma,* or teacher-priest. All the teacher-priests were natives of Hupeh or Hunan; they were not addressed as "old brothers," however, as this title was reserved exclusively for those whose hair had grown unusually long.[11] Above every four teacher-priests was a platoon leader; four platoons made a brigade, headed by a brigade commander; five brigades formed a division, commanded by a divisional commander; and finally, five divisions made an army, commanded by an army superintendent. A general director had within his jurisdiction two army superintendents, each of whom divided his forces into five units—the front, the rear, the left, the right, and the center. More than ten armies were created in Nanking alone. Young and able-bodied soldiers were called "squad fronts"; those above the age of fifty or below the age of twenty were called "squad tails." The aged were addressed as "old fellows," and the very young were referred to as "babies." The duty of the aged and the very young was to cook food, clean the dormitories, cut grass, or serve as horsegrooms, while the able-bodied performed more arduous tasks such as the transportation of grain.

After the bandit chieftain, the King of the North, arrived at the city on the seventeenth [March 26, 1853], he issued an order that all the able-bodied should be stationed in barracks outside of the city. When another bandit chieftain, the King of the East, entered the city on the nineteenth [March 28] the rumor began to spread that the "new brothers" would be mobilized to attack Chinkiang and Yangchow.[12] All the "new brothers" were frightened, but there was not much they could do.

The bandit regime had a variety of official ranks and titles. Besides its regular officials, it also hired outsiders to perform various duties. These hired men were called "servicemen at large" and resided in civilian houses which they had forcibly taken over. They called this forcible occupation of private housing "temporary inhabitation." The number of "servicemen at large" varied in accordance with the amount or urgency of the tasks to be performed. They were not the first-line soldiers; only when the bandits were face to face with a formidable enemy would they be called upon to fight. All these "new brothers" were required not only to wear turbans made of red cloth but also to have two pieces of yellow cloth sewed to their clothes, one on the chest and the other on the back. On the front piece were the characters "T'ai P'ing"[13] and on the back piece were such words as "Servicemen at Large for This or That Office." In the case of a regular soldier, the front piece would bear the words "The First (or Second, Third, etc.) Army of the Heavenly Dynasty," while the back piece would be marked "Saintly Soldier." These markings were called "identifications." Without them a man would be questioned by the bandits whenever he appeared in public; he might be mistaken for a "devil"[14] and be immediately killed. Each dormitory chose its most learned men and titled them "scribes," and their position was higher than that of either the "servicemen at large" or the "saintly soldiers." To differentiate themselves from others, they had the word "Scribe" written on their backs. They had many duties to perform, one of which was to assist the head of a dormitory to make registers.

Once every ten days each dormitory sent a man to the "saintly granary" to receive its share of rice. Before each meal, a gong was sounded to summon all residents of the dormitory to a room. In the center of the room was a table on which were placed three cups of tea, three bowls of rice, and well-lit lamps; there were no incense burners. The meal-takers were then seated on both sides of the table, closed their eyes, and began to chant, much as a Buddhist monk chants in the presence of Buddha. The hymn was composed by the bandit chieftain Hung Hsiu-ch'üan and read as follows:

Glory to God who is our Heavenly Father;
Glory to Jesus who is the Savior of the World;
Glory to the Holy Ghost who is the Divine Spirit;
Glory to all the Three who are unified as
One—the true, only God.
The Way of Heaven is the same as the Way of Man;
Those who save man will enjoy eternal bliss.
Wise man, come quickly and receive Him—
That thou mayst share His blessing.
Ignorant man, wake up—
That to thee the road to Heaven may also be open.
God's grace is unlimited and abounding.
He sent to earth His only begotten Son
Who sacrificed His life to redeem us from our sins.
Repent, lest thou go not to Paradise!

After the chanting was over, all knelt down, facing outside. The scribe of the dormitory would then pray, in a barely audible voice, as follows: "This humble son (in the female dormitory, "daughter") of Yours entreats You, Heavenly Father, to bestow upon us all Your infinite blessing," etc. Towards the end of the prayer and before he stood up, he would suddenly raise his voice and shout aloud: "Kill off all the devils and demons!" Only after all these rituals were over could the diners sit down and take their meal. The same rituals were observed in the Inner Court as well as among the military ranks.

NOTES

[1] This selection is part of an eyewitness report on the situation of Nanking shortly after it had been captured by the Taiping rebels. The author was in Nanking when it fell to the rebels early in 1853 and did not leave the city until the autumn of 1854. The report, in the form of an article, was completed in 1856. Source: *Chung-kuo chin-pai-nien shih tzu-liao*, vol. 2, pp. 73-93.

[2] The three cups of tea symbolized the Trinity.

[3] See note 11 below.

[4] A city inside Nanking, then inhabited by the Manchu residents.

[5] A gate leading to the eastern suburb of Nanking. It is called Chung-shan Gate today.

[6] A gate that leads to the southwestern suburb of Nanking.

[7] Presumably he had violated the First Commandment by worshipping idols.

[8] Yang Hsiu-ch'ing.

[9] A Cantonese term for "adopted child."

¹⁰ A woman from Kwangsi Province, where the rebellion began.
¹¹ Once a man joined the rebels, he was not allowed to shave his hair, so as to distinguish him from the Ch'ing loyalists. The latter often referred to the Taipings as *ch'ang-mao tze,* or "long-haired bandits."
¹² Both are located in Kiangsu Province, east of Nanking.
¹³ Often romanized as Taiping, which means Great Peace.
¹⁴ A Manchu or any person who had served the Ch'ing government.

38 • T'AI-P'ING T'IEN-KUO: *A Law of the Regime*¹

Within each army there are to be two men in charge of each of the following departments: land distribution, law enforcement, money and grain, income, and expenditure. Of the two men, one is the head and the other his deputy; the two offices are concurrently held by a divisional commander and a brigade commander, respectively. Those who are assigned to a task should of course be responsible for its performance; even those who are not assigned to it should nevertheless render assistance to advance its progress. Within each army any important matter, such as the imposition of a death sentence or the demotion or dismissal of an offending officer, should be reported in detail by the army commander to the army superintendent, who will in turn report it to the royal chief of staff. The royal chief of staff will report it to the general, the general to the captain of the palace guards, the captain of the palace guards to the director, the director to the marshal, the marshal to the prime minister, and the prime minister to the military chancellor.² The military chancellor will in turn report it to the Prince of Heaven [Hung Hsiu-ch'üan], who alone can make the decision. The decision will be then carried out by the military chancellor.

Ministers of the state who have achieved great deeds will enjoy rank and salary throughout their lives, and their descendants will do likewise. As for households that have voluntarily submitted themselves to the new regime, each of them must contribute one man to the army unit within whose jurisdiction it resides. This man will be a soldier and led to combat by his leader during the time of war; he will be supervised in his agricultural activities by the same leader in time of peace. People like him till the field so as to support the government.

All the land in China is to be divided into nine classes in accordance with its productivity. The nine classes are: high-high, high-middle, high-low, middle-high, middle-middle, middle-low, low-high, low-middle, and finally, low-low; their annual yields per *mou* are 1,200, 1,100, 1,000, 900, 800, 700, 600, 500, and 400 catties, respectively. For purposes of distribution, a *mou* of high-high land is regarded as equivalent to 1.1 *mou* of the high-middle land, 1.2 *mou* of high-low land, 1.35 *mou* of the middle-high land, 1.5 *mou* of the middle-middle land, 1.75 *mou* of the middle-low land, 2 *mou* of the low-high land, 2.4 *mou* of low-middle land, or 3 *mou* of the low-low land.

The amount of land each household receives depends upon its size: the more members it has the more land it will receive. A female member receives exactly the same amount as her male counterpart. When land is distributed, the government should see to it that a household receives high-quality as well as low-quality land. For instance, in a household of six, if three of its members receive low-quality land, the other three should receive high-quality land. In other words,

THE TAIPING REBELLION

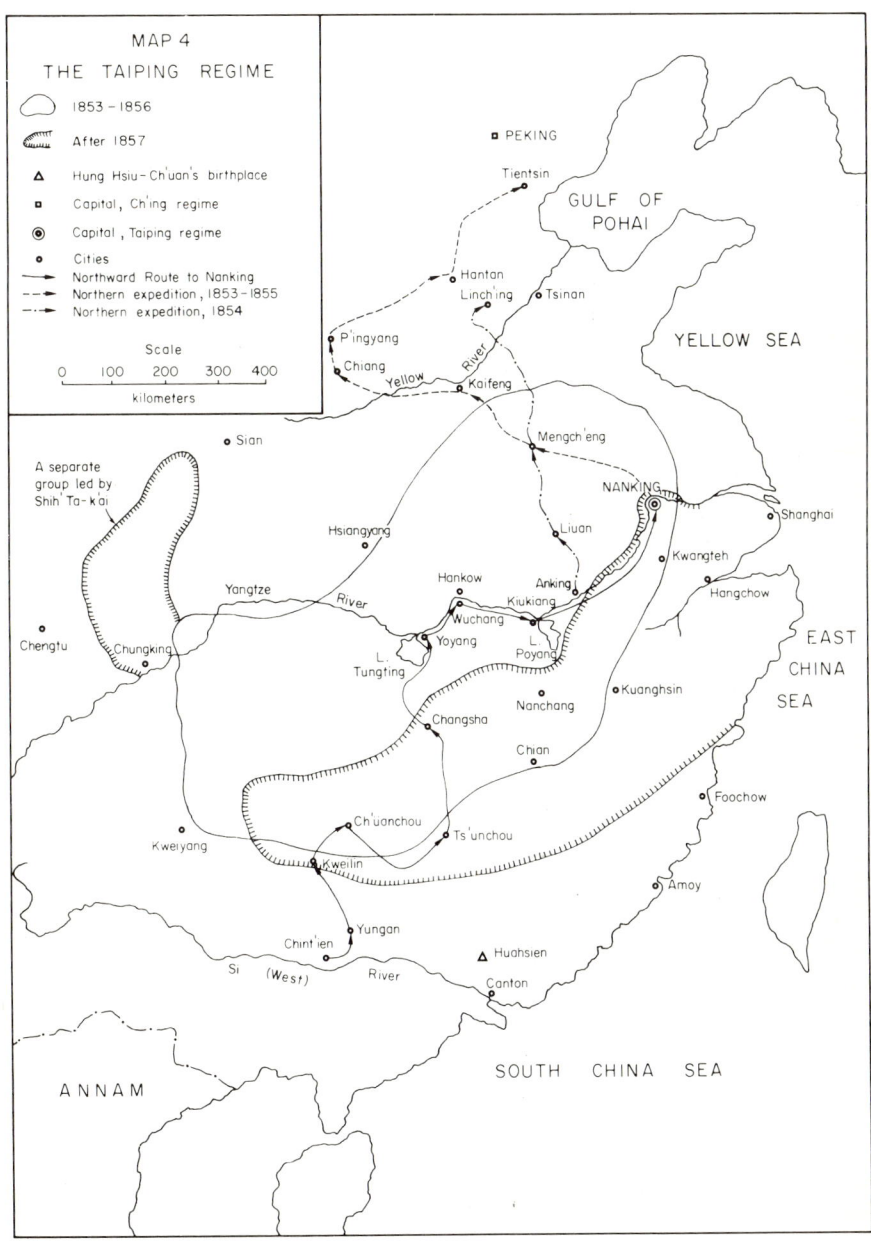

the difference between high-quality and low-quality land for each household should be maintained at a ratio of 50 percent for each.

All the land in China is to be tilled by all the people in China. If the amount of arable land in one area is inadequate to support all the people in that area, some of its people should be moved to places where arable land is more than sufficient. All the people share the land's yield in common: if one area suffers from famine, the areas that have reaped bumper crops are obligated to make their surplus grain available for relief. This is done so that everyone in China can enjoy the blessings of God the Father, the Supreme Lord. Land is shared; so are food, clothing, and money. The principle of egalitarianism is to be followed throughout the country; no man, from now on, is to suffer from hunger or cold.

A person sixteen years old or older will receive twice as much land as a person below that age. If he or she receives 1 *mou* of the high-high land, a person below that age will receive one half as much, namely, 0.5 *mou* of the same quality of land. Likewise, if he or she receives 3 *mou* of the low-low land, a person below that age will receive one half as much, namely, 1.5 *mou* of the same quality of land. Open spaces around a house should be planted with mulberry trees, and every woman in the nation must apply herself to productive work, whether it be sericulture, weaving, or the making of clothes. Each household should raise at least five chickens and two pigs, so as to take advantage of the benefit each season brings.

At the time of harvest, the teacher-priest [*liang-ssu-ma*] of each comradeship [*wu*] is to direct the comrade leader [*wu chang*] to collect all the grain from each household outside of what it needs for its maintenance and to return the collected grain to the common treasury of the comradeship. This rule is applicable not only to the regular crops like rice but also to wheat, beans, hemp, cloth, silk, chickens, silver, copper coins, and all other items. We are all members of one family, headed by God the Father, the Supreme Lord. No one should have private property of his own because everything on earth belongs to the Supreme Lord. Only when the Supreme Lord owns everything will all people on earth receive the amount of goods they need and will no man suffer from cold or hunger. This is the meaning underlying a special instruction given by the Supreme Lord to the Prince of Peace [Hung Hsiu-ch'üan], an instruction that is aimed at the salvation of this world.

The teacher-priest of each comradeship must keep a record of income and expenditures, including all the money and grain he has received or given out.

Each comradeship of twenty-five households should have a common treasury, in addition to a church of worship in which the teacher-priest resides. All expenses occasioned by weddings, childbirth, and other festivities are drawn from the common treasury, but they should not exceed by even one penny the regulated amount for each of these occasions. If we say that the expenses for a wedding or childbirth are regulated at 1,000 standard coins and 100 catties of grain, the same rate should be applied to all the households in China. In short, thrift should be practiced so that a surplus will be available in time of famine or war. As for marriage, money should never be a consideration on the part of either of the contracting parties. All the work traditionally done by potters, blacksmiths, carpenters, and stoneworkers should from now on be done by the comrade leader and his soldiers and be done only at times when farmers are not busy in the field. During a wedding or any other festivity the teacher-priest only needs to lead his congregation in praying to God the Father, the Supreme Lord; the pagan ritual of the past should be eliminated altogether.

Every weekday all children in a comradeship's twenty-five households are required to go to the comradeship church, where the teacher-priest will teach them the Old and New Testaments and also the decrees issued by the Prince of Heaven. On Sunday the comrade leader will lead all people of the comradeship to worship in the church, where men and women are seated in separate sections and where they listen to sermons and sing hymns to the glory of God the Father, the Supreme Lord.

Rewards will be given to those who have worked diligently in the field, and penalties will be imposed upon those who have not. Whenever a dispute develops between two families, both sides should proceed to the teacher-priest, who hears their presentation and renders a judgment. If they do not consent to his judgment, the teacher-priest will take them to the platoon leader who will hear their presentation and will render a judgment of his own. If they do not consent to the platoon leader's judgment, the latter will take them to the brigade commander, who in turn will take them to the divisional commander, if the parties to the dispute continue to disagree with the judgment in each of the ascending steps. If the divisional commander fails to settle the dispute, he will present it to the head of the department of law enforcement and the army commander, who will conduct a joint hearing and render a final decision. The proceedings of this hearing will be presented by the army commander to the army superintendent, who in turn presents them to the royal chief of staff. This process continues through each of the succeeding stages—the general, the captain of the palace guards, the director, and the marshal—until the proceedings reach the office of the prime minister. The prime minister will present them to the military chancellor, who in turn presents them to the Prince of Heaven. The Prince of Heaven will then issue a decree ordering the military chancellor, the prime minister, the marshal, and the head of the department of law enforcement to review the case in detail and find for themselves whether the facts as presented in the proceedings are correct. If, after the review, the above-mentioned officials are satisfied with the facts as presented, they will submit their view to the Prince of Heaven for a final decision. The Prince of Heaven can either sentence the accused to death or spare his life; he can take or give as he pleases. His decision will be carried out by the military chancellor.

A loyal official is one who observes the Ten Commandments and the orders of the regime and who devotes all of his energy and effort to the service of his country. He will be promoted to a higher rank and will retain his post throughout his life. An official who violates the Ten Commandments, disobeys the orders of the government, accepts bribes, or practices fraud is in fact a scoundrel; he will be either demoted or reclassified as a farmer. A citizen who obeys the Ten Commandments and the government's orders and who works diligently in the field is a virtuous or good man; he will be either given material reward or recommended to the government for possible appointment as an official. A citizen who violates the Ten Commandments and the government's orders and who neglects his duty as a farmer is an evil or bad man; he will be either sentenced to death or punished in accordance with his offense.

Recommendations for filling governmental posts are held once a year. The official who has recommended a good man will be rewarded; the official who has recommended a bad man will be punished. If a teacher-priest discovers in his comradeship a man who has observed the Ten Commandments and the orders of the government and who has worked diligently as a farmer, he should report this man's name and deeds, together with his own name, to the platoon leader. The platoon leader will then examine the recommendee and compare him with all the people in the hundred households within his jurisdiction. If the facts about this man are found to be correct as reported after the examination, the platoon leader will describe him in detail and recommend him to the brigade commander. The brigade commander will examine the recommendee and compare him with all the people in the five hundred households within his jurisdiction. If the facts about the man are found to be correct as reported after the examination, the brigade commander will indicate his approval by recommending him to the divisional commander. The divisional commander will then examine the recommendee and compare him with all the people in the 2,500 households within his jurisdiction. If the facts about the man are found to be correct as reported after the examination, the divisional commander will indicate his approval by recommending him to the army commander. The army commander will then examine the man and compare him with all the people within his jurisdiction. If he is satisfied with the result, he will indicate his approval by recommending him to the army superintendent. The procedure of examination and recommendation continues through the succeeding stages—the royal chief of staff, the general, the captain of the palace guards, the director, and the marshal—until it reaches the prime minister. The prime minister will make a report on the recommendee to the military chancellor, who in turn will report him to the Prince of Heaven. From those who have been recommended to him the Prince of Heaven will select an appropriate number of candidates to be appointed as army commanders, divisional commanders, brigade commanders, platoon leaders, teacher-priests, and comrade leaders. Those who recommend unfit or unqualified persons will be dismissed from their official posts and be reclassified as farmers.

In order to show the impartiality of the Heavenly Regime, the evaluation of all officials will be conducted once every three years; they can be either promoted or demoted as a result of this evaluation. Those who recommend unqualified men for promotion or petition for the demotion of worthy personnel will be dismissed from their official posts and be reclassified as farmers. During the year of evaluation, each official is required to recommend the promotion or suggest the demotion of his subordinates. The platoon leader will examine in detail all the teacher-priests and comrade leaders within his jurisdiction, record their good as well as their bad deeds, indicate his own judgment whether a particular official should be promoted or demoted, and then present his findings to his immediate superior, the brigade commander. If an official is not good enough to be promoted or bad enough to be demoted, his name need not be mentioned in the presentation. The brigade commander will do likewise with regard to all the platoon leaders, teacher-priests, and comrade leaders within his jurisdiction and present his findings to the divisional commander. The divisional commander will do the same thing as the brigade commander has done with regard to all of his subordinates and report his findings to the army commander. This process continues through each of the succeeding stages—the army superintendent, the royal chief of staff, and the general and the chief general. The general and the chief general will present their recommendations to the six ministeries, who in turn present them to the military chancellor. The military chancellor reports directly to the Prince of Heaven, who alone can make the necessary decisions.

After all the recommendations are in, the Prince of Heaven will issue a decree authorizing promotions or demotions. He can promote the army superintendents, whose promotions have been recommended by their royal chief of staff, to either royal chiefs of staff or captains of the palace guards. He can demote the army superintendents, whose demotions have been advised by their royal chief of staff, to either army commanders or divisional commanders. He can promote the army commanders, whose promotions have been recommended by their army superintendent, to either army superintendents or captains of the palace guards. He can demote the army commanders, whose demotions have been advised by their army superintendent, to either divisional commander, brigade commander, or platoon leader. An official recommended by an army commander for promotion can be promoted by either one or two ranks, or to the rank of an army commander. An official whose demotion has been advised by an army commander can be demoted by either one or two ranks, or be reclassified as a farmer.

Once a decision regarding promotion or demotion is made, the Prince of Heaven will make it known to the military chancellor, who in turn makes it known to the various kings.[3] The various kings will then order their subordinates to obey it without fail. All officials below the rank of army superintendent are promoted or demoted upon the advice of their superiors. In the case of a royal chief of staff, however, the Prince of Heaven allows his subordinates, namely, the army superintendents, to make suggestions for his promotion or demotion, in addition to his superiors who of course can do likewise. As for such high officials as the prime minister, the marshal, the director, the general, and the captain of the palace guards, they can make suggestions for each other's promotion or demotion irrespective of their relative ranks. This rule is necessary in order to eliminate reciprocal favoritism between superiors and inferiors. If an official has achieved great or unusual deeds for the government or, on the other hand, has committed treason or a crime of unforgivable nature, all other officials, regardless of their ranks and titles, can at any time make a proposal for his promotion in the former case and his demotion in the latter case, and they do not have to wait for the year when the evaluation of all officials is due. An official who has fraudulently recommended a subordinate for promotion or petitioned for his demotion will be reclassified as a farmer upon the revelation of the fraud. An official who has fraudulently recommended his superior for promotion or petitioned for his demotion will be punished as a criminal upon the revelation of the fraud. When making a recommendation for promotion, the petitioner must list the virtuous deeds of the recommendee; when making a proposal for demotion, he likewise must describe in detail the evil conduct of the offending official. In either case, the availability of concrete facts is essential to the rendering of a decision.

An army, headed by an army commander, has within its jurisdiction 13,156 households, and is divided into five divisions, each of which is headed by a divisional commander. A division has within its jurisdiction five brigades, each of which is composed of five platoons, each platoon being headed by a platoon leader. Each platoon has within its jurisdiction four teacher-priests, each of whom commands five comrade leaders. Each comrade leader in turn commands four comrade soldiers. In short, an army has 1 army commander, 5 divisional commanders, 25 brigade commanders, 125 platoon leaders, 500 teacher-priests, 2,500 comrade leaders, and 10,000 comrade soldiers, totaling 13,156 men. With the increase of households within an army, a corresponding number of new organizational units will be added. For the increase of every five households, a new comrade leader will be installed; for the increase of every twenty-six households, a new teacher-priest will be added. Likewise a new platoon, brigade, or division will be created within the army if the number of households has been increased by 105 or 526 or 2,631, respectively. If the increase reaches a total of 13,156 households, a new army will be established. Before its establishment, however, the army commander of the parent unit continues to command all the officials in the new units, including the divisional commanders. Upon his appointment, a new army commander will take over the command of this newly created army.

All officials and common people are required to attend church on Sundays, where they listen to the reading of the Holy Bible, worship and pray, and sing hymns to the glory of God the Father, the Supreme Lord. Once every seven weeks a divisional commander, brigade commander, or platoon leader should take turns in lecturing on the Bible in each of the churches within his jurisdiction, not only to teach goodness and virtuous conduct but also to find out for himself whether the people under his jurisdiction have been diligent as farmers and have consistently observed the Ten Commandments and the orders of the government. If a divisional commander lectures in teacher-priest A's church on the first Sunday, he should do likewise on teacher-priest B's church on the second Sunday, and so on until he has preached in all the churches within his jurisdiction. Then he will return to teacher-priest A's church, and the cycle starts over again. Like his divisional superior, a brigade commander or a platoon leader should do the same thing with regard to all the churches within his jurisdiction.

A household with a husband and a wife and a total membership of no fewer than three and no more than nine must contribute one man as a soldier. The widower, the widow, the orphaned, the lonely or sole member of a household, the crippled, and the chronically ill—all these people are exempt from military service. They are to be supported by the common treasury in each of the communities where they live.

On Sundays all officials should prepare various sacrifices with the utmost piety in accordance with their rank and title and then offer these sacrifices to the church which they attend. Inside the church they worship God the Father, the Supreme Lord, sing to His glory, and listen to the reading of the Holy Bible. Those who show negligence in this matter will be dismissed from their official posts and be reclassified as farmers.

Let all the people abide by this decree without fail.

NOTES

[1] This is one of the most important documents for Taiping institutions. Its Chinese original can be found in most collections of source materials dealing with the Taiping Rebellion.

[2] The post of military chancellor (*chün-shih*) was held by Yang Hsiu-ch'ing (King of the East) before he was killed in 1856.

[3] For the names of these various kings, see p. 119.

39 • LO TUN-YUNG: *Internecine Strife Among the Taiping Leaders*[1]

As Yang Hsiu-ch'ing's power and influence became greater and greater, people only knew that there was a King of the East, completely forgetting the fact that the Prince of Heaven still existed. All officials went to Hsiu-ch'ing's office for instructions, while the Prince of Heaven, residing deep in his palace, only occasionally granted an audience. All memorials had first to be submitted to Hsiu-ch'ing before they could be presented to the Prince, and Hsiu-ch'ing would not present any that dealt with military matters. The orders issued by Hsiu-ch'ing were called Golden Edicts and had to be received with elaborate rituals. Ten *li* from the city gate the receiver must set up an altar, on which he burned incense and before which he knelt; only then would the herald begin to read aloud Hsiu-ch'ing's Golden Edict. An official who failed to observe these rituals would be severely punished, whether he was as high as a governor or as lowly as a magistrate. Wherever Hsiu-ch'ing happened to live, security guards were posted around his apartment.

Hsiu-ch'ing liked Shih Ta-k'ai but detested Wei Ch'ang-hui. The latter's unsparing effort to please him only succeeded in making him even more arrogant. To curry favor, Ch'ang-hui led him into a variety of sensual dissipations, all of which he indulged in in the most ostentatious manner. Inside the palace there were several hundred courtesans with whom Hsiu-ch'ing satisfied his lusts night and day. Even his personal servants were young maidens of great beauty. To amuse himself, he built a dragon-shaped vehicle on the palace's upper floor and ordered naked women to pull it for fun. Indulgence of this nature was bound to ruin him, and eventually made him impotent. To cure the impotence, Ch'ang-hui searched for the best physicians in China, who were promised high rank and title if somehow they could make Hsiu-ch'ing a virile man again. To show his sympathy and sorrow, he often wept whenever Hsiu-ch'ing complained to him about his illness. Being a good actor, he eventually succeeded in winning Hsiu-ch'ing's gratitude.

Whenever he went out, Hsiu-ch'ing's insignia and entourage were as ostentatious as those that accompanied the Prince of Heaven. Inside his sedan chair were one bed and four thrones; it was so large that two servants could go in and out to wait on him. It took thirty-two bearers to carry this chair, all of whom were uniformed in the most luxurious embroideries. Wherever he went, two sculptured dragons, one blue and one white, would clear the way as vanguards. Addressed as "Nine Thousand Years,"[2] he loved to amuse himself with theatrical entertainment. . . .

For a long time Hsiu-ch'ing wished to usurp the throne by forcing Hsiu-ch'üan to abdicate in his favor. Hsiu-ch'üan, of course, had heard about this, though indirectly. One day Hsiu-ch'ing pretended that he was seriously ill and then hinted that the Prince of Heaven should pay him a visit. Before his visitor's arrival, however, he deployed a large number of guards around his bedroom. When Hsiu-ch'üan arrived, he found his host lying on his back, waited upon by four girls. He seated himself on a small couch next to the bed and then expressed his concern about his host's illness. The latter only murmured as if he were talking in a dream. "People say that there can never be two suns in the sky," said Hsiu-ch'ing. "Why is it that at one time during the Ch'in Dynasty two suns were actually fighting in the sky?" Knowing what he meant, Hsiu-ch'üan immediately ordered his officials-in-attendance to kneel down and kowtow nine times.[3] "Ten thousand years for the King of the East!" these officials shouted consecutively for three times.

Hsiu-ch'ing was astonished since he had not been prepared for this kind of response. He had in fact hoped for a wrong answer from Hsiu-ch'üan in connection with the two suns. In such a case, he could either force him to abdicate or kill him if he refused to comply with the demand. Now that Hsiu-ch'üan had unexpectedly ordered his officials-in-attendance to address him as "Ten Thousand Years," he simply did not know how to respond. He closed his eyes as if he were about to go to sleep again. Pretending that he had to go to the bathroom,

Hsiu-ch'üan lost no time in sneaking out. "Where is the Prince of Heaven?" Hsiu-ch'ing yelled after he opened his eyes. Upon hearing from his servants that the visitor had gone, he sighed and buried his scheme for the time being.

Knowing that he was in serious danger, Hsiu-ch'üan cut one of his own fingers and with the blood wrote an order that summoned Wei Ch'ang-hui to his defense. Upon receiving this order, Wei Ch'ang-hui and Ch'in Jih-ch'ang led 500 of their elite troops and galloped towards the city late at night. They knocked at the Shui-hsi Gate, but the guards refused to let them in. "We cannot open this gate as long as you do not have the King of the East's commanding arrow,"[4] said the guards. "I rushed here in response to the King of the East's secret order," Ch'ang-hui retorted in anger; "I will kill you if you refuse to let us in." Frightened, the guards opened the gate.

Arriving at Hsiu-ch'ing's residence, Ch'ang-hui was blocked by the guards. When he and his elite troops tried to force themselves through the gate, they quickly found themselves engaged in heavy fighting with the defenders. "I have been authorized by the Prince of Heaven to arrest the traitor," Ch'ang-hui shouted aloud to the defenders; "those who stop their resistance immediately will not be punished." Having heard these words, the defenders gradually dispersed.

Inside his bedroom, Hsiu-ch'ing hid himself underneath a water fountain when his enemy arrived. Ch'ang-hui immediately tied him up, with the intended purpose of presenting him to the Prince of Heaven. Meanwhile all members of the Yang family had been slaughtered on the spot.

Learning about the sudden turn of events, Hsiu-ch'üan ordered the palace gates to be closed. Shortly afterwards, Ch'ang-hui arrived and knocked at the palace door, announcing that the traitor Yang had indeed been arrested and that he, Ch'ang-hui, was waiting for further orders. Fearful that Ch'ang-hui would become more dictatorial after he had eliminated all members of the Yang family, Hsiu-ch'üan intimated that Hsiu-ch'ing's life should be spared. Ch'ang-hui was furious when he heard this order; instead of sparing his captive's life as he had been ordered, he immediately put him to death. Hsiu-ch'üan then decreed that no more bloodletting would be allowed from then on, while saying nothing about Ch'ang-hui's "accomplishment." This, of course, made Ch'ang-hui even more furious. Obsessed with the fact that Hsiu-ch'ing's followers would be difficult for him in the future if left alone, he forged an imperial decree, saying that all those who surrendered themselves voluntarily would be forgiven, while those who did not would be killed without mercy. More than 3,000 of Hsiu-ch'ing's followers surrendered themselves, all of whom were subsequently put to death by Ch'ang-hui's order. Then he closed all the city gates and for a period of ten days continued to search for Hsiu-ch'ing's followers.

Shih Ta-k'ai was then stationed at Hupeh; he quickly went to Nanking upon hearing this sudden change of events. "It is enough to execute Hsiu-ch'ing the traitor, who certainly deserved this punishment," he admonished Ch'ang-hui. "However, if all of his followers are punished as severely as he was, nobody will feel safe, and endless anarchy will prevail. This state of affairs cannot possibly please anybody except our common enemy."[5] Thinking that Ta-k'ai was defending Hsiu-ch'ing and jealous of the fact that he was very popular with the people, Ch'ang-hui decided to kill him too. Fortunately for Ta-k'ai, he heard about this plot before it could be carried out. He left Nanking in a hurry by sliding down a rope over the city wall. Unable to find him, Ch'ang-hui killed all members of his family, the old as well as the young.

Ta-k'ai escaped to Anking[6] and then called upon all the Taiping forces to eliminate the evil influence behind the throne. The army under his command moved to Ningkuo[7] where it defeated a detachment that was then besieging the city. Having heard that Ta-k'ai was about to arrive at Nanking, Ch'ang-hui became more sadistic than ever; each day he tried to get rid of his frustration by killing a few of Hsiu-ch'üan's personal guards. The guards pleaded with their master in the most sorrowful terms, saying that they could not protect the Prince's life if their own lives were in constant danger. "When the right moment arrives," Hsiu-ch'üan replied, "I will let you people do whatever you please." Thinking that they had obtained the necessary permission, dozens of these guards armed themselves and proposed to attack Ch'ang-hui before dawn. The time being so early, their intended victim was still soundly asleep in the East Barrack when the attackers arrived; moreover, all his personal guards, being weary, had become careless. The attackers moved in quickly, found their victim, and killed him on the spot. Hsiu-ch'üan ordered Ch'ang-hui's head to be shown to Ta-k'ai's army at Ningkuo, saying that since the real culprit of this sad state of affairs was dead, the army need not advance on Nanking.

Leaving his army behind at Ningkuo, Ta-k'ai went to Nanking to see Hsiu-ch'üan with approximately 100 retainers. Some official presented the Prince with a petition, maintaining that it would be difficult from then on to satisfy all of Ta-k'ai's ambitions in view of the fact that not only had he accomplished great deeds for the government, he was also at the head of a powerful army. "He should be kept in the capital while efforts be made to take over his military command," the petitioner suggested; "otherwise he will become another Yang Hsiu-ch'ing." Impressed with the wisdom of this advice, Hsiu-ch'üan decreed that Ta-k'ai would remain in the capital to serve as his adviser in view of the great deeds he had accomplished and that his military command would be taken over by Li Hsiu-ch'eng. But Ta-k'ai was an adviser in name only, since the Prince had delegated all authority of a political nature to Jen-ta and Jen-fa, his two older brothers.

Living in Nanking without much to do, Ta-k'ai was unhappy with the idleness that had been imposed upon him. "Since you, sir, enjoy the confidence of the army," said Chang Sui-mou, one of his lieutenants, "why should you allow yourself to be controlled by others and then be unhappy about your own fate? It is of course very difficult to conquer North China.[8] It is not difficult, however, to follow the example of Liu Hsüan-teh[9] by taking over Szechuan so as to create a situation similar to that prevailing during the period of the Three Kingdoms."[10] Accepting Chang's advice, Ta-k'ai requested Hsiu-ch'üan's permission to leave. Meanwhile he pasted posters all over the city indicating his intention to leave, a subtle way to instigate other people to follow his leadership. More than 100,000 of the city's population did leave Nanking with him.

Arriving at Anking, he invited Ch'en Yü-ch'eng and Li Hsiu-ch'eng to join their forces with his. Yü-ch'eng accepted the invitation. Before his army was about to leave, however, he journeyed to Hsiu-ch'eng to inform the latter of his decision. "We left our home and risked our lives to accomplish great deeds," Hsiu-ch'eng protested. "How will posterity judge us if we change our original goal in the midst of our effort? You make your own decision about this matter; but as far as I am concerned, I will not go." "I am almost led astray by this man but for your advice," Yü-ch'eng replied.

Ta-k'ai was certain that the two generals would follow him when they were invited. He was very disappointed when they refused. Since he could no longer return to Nanking, he led his army, numbering several hundred thousand, to Anhwei. Hearing about this, Hsiu-ch'üan began to regret the mistake he had made....

NOTES

[1] This selection is taken from an article entitled *T'ai-p'ing T'ien-kuo: A Record of Warfare* (*T'ai-p'ing T'ien-kuo chan-chi*), written in 1913. The author claims that the materials contained in this article were derived from a personal memoir (entitled *Hsin-shih*) written by Wei Yi-ch'eng, a son of Wei Ch'ang-hui ("King of the North") who is a central figure in this selection. A copy of the Chinese original can be found in *Chung-kuo chin-pai-nien shih tzu-liao*, vol. 2, pp. 81–85.
[2] An emperor was addressed as "Ten Thousand Years."
[3] A ritual performed before an emperor.
[4] A commanding arrow (*ling chien*) identified the authority of the person who issued it. It was often used in situations of great emergency, especially on the battlefield.
[5] By the common enemy was meant the Manchus or the Ch'ing government.
[6] Capital of Anhwei Province.
[7] Located in south Anhwei.
[8] Then under the control of the Ch'ing government.
[9] Liu Pei (d. 223 A.D.), founder of the kingdom of Shu during the period of the Three Kingdoms (220–265).
[10] The adviser apparently had in mind a situation in which Shih Ta-k'ai controlled the Southwest, Hung Hsiu-ch'üan the Southeast, and the Manchu government the North.

40 • TSENG KUO-CH'ÜAN: *The Capture of Nanking*[1]

About midnight Li Hsiu-ch'eng issued an order to his bandit followers that the Prince of Heaven's palace, together with all other palaces occupied by the various kings of the puppet regime, was to be set on fire. When the order was carried out, heavy smoke rose high towards the clouds and seemed to spread over the whole city. Suddenly, from the southern gate of the bandit chieftain's palace emerged a thousand or so bandits of the most ferocious type who, armed with rifles and other military equipment, dashed towards the residential areas. Thinking that the bandit chieftain Hung Hsiu-ch'üan must be among them, Yüan Ta-sheng, Chou Heng-li, and Shen Hung-pin quickly led their troops to intercept them. They killed more than 700 and obtained, among other things, two jade seals and one golden seal. The golden seal has a width of approximately 7 inches and was once used as a royal stamp by the bandit chieftain Hung. Inside the palace ground several hundred servant girls hanged themselves in the front park, and those who were drowned in the moat were approximately 2,000. The fire was so intense and widespread that it was impossible to come close to it. The bandits set fire in every lane and every street so as to create a barrier of fire and smoke between themselves and our pursuing soldiers. Owing to the darkness of the night and the unfamiliar street pattern, our soldiers were unable to fight as effectively as they otherwise could have. They were given the order to forgo battle for the time being and to return to their units, which were stationed in many strategic positions inside the city.

This was the situation on the night of the sixteenth [July 19, 1864] after the Inner City[2] of the puppet regime had been captured. Before the night was over, a large number of the bandits had been killed.

About two o'clock the next morning, a detachment of 1,000 bandits, dressed in government uniforms and equipped with rifles and ammunitions, dashed towards the opening above the tunnel of the T'ai-p'ing Gate and attempted to escape from the city. Two battalions of government troops went quickly to intercept them, and using blazing barrels and flaming missiles, burned and killed a large number of the enemy's men and horses. More than 600 of them, however, managed to escape through the opening; once outside of the city, they galloped as fast as they could in the direction of Hsiaolingwei and Tinglinchen.[3] Wu Wei-shou, Yang Chia-nan, and T'ao Li-chung quickly led their cavalry in hot pursuit. The moment I heard about this escape, I dispatched 700 more horsemen, headed by Chang Ting-k'uei, Li T'ai-shan, Huang Wan-p'eng, and Huang Ting-chüeh, to push the pursuit. Meanwhile I sent an urgent message to the garrison commanders in Lishui, Tungpa, and Chüyung[4] to intercept the fleeing bandits.

It was not until 6 P.M. on the nineteenth [July 22, 1864] that Wu Wei-shou, Huang Wan-p'eng, and others returned to Nanking and reported their experiences to me in person. At Shunhuachen they captured Li Wan-ts'ai, the former King of Lieh in the puppet regime. Bringing their prisoner with them, they continued their pursuit and caught up with the fleeing bandits in the Hushu area. There our cavalrymen quickly surrounded them, and not a single bandit was able to escape alive. After this engagement our troops moved to Liyang,[5] where, according to the local population, no bandits had ever passed through. This, in essence, is what my lieutenants have reported.

When Li Wan-ts'ai was brought in, I personally questioned him about the whereabouts of the bandit leaders. "After the fall of the city," Li replied, "King Chü (an elder brother of King Chung [Li Hsiu-ch'eng]), King Yu-hsi, King Yu-nan, King Ting, King Ch'ung, and King Chung—all of them escaped from the city under the darkness of the night. However, they were soon caught up by the pursuers near a bridge in Hushu, where they all died in action. So far as I know, none of them has survived." Other bandits captured inside the city testified that Hung Hsiu-ch'üan, the bandit chieftain, had committed suicide by taking poison sometime during the fifth month [between June 4 and July 3, 1864] when Nanking was under heavy attack by government troops, and that he was buried somewhere within the palace ground. After his death, his son Hung Fu-chen inherited the throne. Upon the fall of the city, the prisoners continued, the young prince piled firewood inside his palace, which he set on fire, and burned himself to death. Once the fire is extinguished, I intend to dig up Hung Hsiu-ch'üan's corpse and also to check the assertion that his son has indeed been burned to death. I shall make a follow-up report on this and other related matters.

As for King Chung or Li Hsiu-ch'eng, he was wounded at the time that the city fell and subsequently hid himself in a civilian household in a mountain village. Captain Hsiao Fu-ssu personally led the search and captured him on the evening of the nineteenth [July 22]. Hung Jen-ta, an elder brother of Hung Hsiu-ch'üan, was also taken prisoner. On the twentieth [July 23] I personally questioned both of them, and they identified themselves without much hesitation. I request to know whether they should be sent to the capital in a cage or be executed here in Nanking.

For three days, from the seventeenth to the nineteenth, more than 100,000 ferocious bandits—the same bandits who had ravaged Liangkwang [Kwangtung and Kwangsi] Lianghu [Hupeh and Hunan] and Kiangpeh[6] for many years—were slaughtered. . . . So many people were killed that the Ch'inhuai River[7] was full of dead bodies. Half of the approximately three thousand rebel leaders, such as kings and generals, were killed in combat, while the other half either were drowned in rivers (including the city moat) or burned themselves to death. The fire in the city has raged on continuously for the past three days, and as late as the nineteenth there were still snipers perching on tall buildings and shooting government troops with foreign-made rifles.

The above narrative is a brief account of the ways whereby our cavalrymen pursued and captured the fleeing bandits and of the circumstances under which the bandits and their leaders were killed or captured.

At this moment I am sending soldiers to fight the fire, bury the bandits' dead bodies, and take care of the refugees. I shall be busy with the reconstruction work for some time. Many thoughts come to my mind, and as I look back, I cannot but feel a sense of sadness. The army assigned to the siege and capture of Nanking has been fighting for more than two years. More than 10,000 of its rank and file have died of diseases of one kind or another, and more than 8,000 have perished in combat. Thanks to His Majesty's authority and prestige, we have been able, finally, to achieve the goal which we set out to achieve.

NOTES

[1] Tseng Kuo-ch'üan, a younger brother of Tseng Kuo-fan, was given the overall responsibility for capturing Nanking, capital of the Taiping regime. He succeeded in his assigned task in the summer of 1864. This selection is the last part of a long report which he submitted to Tseng Kuo-fan, his immediate superior. Later Tseng Kuo-fan presented this report, together with his own comment, to the imperial government. Source: *Tseng Wen-cheng kung ch'üan-chi,* vol. 4, pp. 657–658.

[2] See Footnote 4, p. 125.
[3] Located in the eastern suburb of Nanking.
[4] Cities located to the south of Nanking.
[5] A city located to the south of Nanking, modern Kiangsu Province.
[6] Areas north of the Yangtze River.
[7] A river that passes through the city of Nanking.

CHAPTER SIX

The Imitation of the West: The Technological Phase

For three decades after 1839 the Ch'ing Dynasty was plagued by not only a mighty rebellion (Chapter V) but also repeated foreign invasions (Chapters III and IV). Pressed from within and without, it seemed that the dynasty could end at any moment. In the summer of 1864 the Taiping Rebellion was finally crushed, and for the first time in a long period a ray of hope began to glimmer. Though domestic problems were enormous, many of China's statesmen nevertheless believed that the danger to the country was more likely to be foreign than domestic in origin. For one thing, they were quite confident that China would be able to cope with a domestic rebellion such as that launched by the Taipings, but were altogether uncertain what might happen if China were invaded again by one or more Western powers. Since China had been defeated by Western powers through military might, it was not surprising that her initial response should be expressed in strong nationalistic terms. Chinese nationalism in its modern form was then born and has remained a most dynamic force in shaping the nation's history. How could China become strong enough to resist future foreign encroachments? She must make the necessary changes, the new nationalists replied. From this determination to make changes emerged the much-discussed self-strengthening movement.

The three major leaders of the self-strengthening movement, Tseng Kuo-fan (1811–1872), Li Hung-chang (1823–1901), and Chang Chih-tung (1837–1909), all conceded the superiority of Western technology, to which they attributed the West's easy success against China. They were convinced that in order to be strong, China must learn Western technology, especially that related to the military: "the construction of fast ships and the making of powerful cannons" (Selection 41). Some beginnings along this line were made in the 1860's, such as the construction of two modern shipyards (one in Shanghai and the other in Foochow) and the renovation of a Tientsin factory for manufacturing modern weapons. To learn about Western technology, the Chinese, of course, had to read Western books. In 1862 the first foreign language school was established in Peking; this was followed by the establishment of two others, one in Shanghai and one in Canton (Selection 42). Some suggested that the entire civil service examination system should be renovated, and renovated in such a way as to place Western or technological knowledge on the same footing as Chinese philosophy or Confucian classics (Selection 43). Other reform measures included the establishment of Westernized schools in China and a program for study abroad in which boys in their teens were sent to Western countries to learn about such subjects as "mathematics, manufacturing, shipbuilding and navigation, and military science" (Selection 44). Despite criticisms, a new crusade was on its way, and China's very survival, as the crusaders contended, might well depend upon it.

It should be reminded, however, that by promoting the new programs, the crusaders had no intention of "transforming Chinese into barbarians," as their critics contended they would. What they wished to learn from the West was science and technology, and nothing else. They believed in the superiority of Chinese political and social structure, the Confucian ideology behind it, and the Chinese moral values that governed the relationships among men. All reforms, they maintained, should be carried out within China's own traditional framework. This attitude was well summarized in Chang Chih-tung's famous remark: "Chinese values should govern the basic matters, while the Western learning should be confined to the technical or utilitarian sphere" (*Chung hsüeh wei t'i; Hsi hsüeh wei yung*). The ultimate purpose was to acquire enough technological knowledge and military capacity to defend China as a nation and Confucianism as her ideological foundation.

It was not until late in the nineteenth century that many well-educated Chinese, having gained first-hand knowledge about the West, began to raise doubts about China's alleged superiority on "basic matters." They believed that the strength of the Western countries lay in the rationality of their political, social, economic, or even ethical systems, and that their technological superiority was merely one of the outward manifestations of the basic soundness of their society. If China were to become as strong as her Western counterparts, they maintained, she had to make more than technological reforms; she needed reforms that involved not only the establishment of a more responsible government but also new orientations in social values. As long as Chinese men continued to smoke opium and Chinese women continued to bind their feet, China did not deserve to survive, let alone to become strong (Selection 45). This kind of argument doubtless shocked many complacent Chinese who had always been convinced of China's moral superiority, but seen from the vantage of hindsight, it did contain a great deal of truth.

In the eyes of conservative intellectuals, however, the very idea of learning from the West was absurd, if not blasphemous. Remembering fondly that foreigners (Japanese, Koreans, and the rest) had always come to China to learn and never the other way around, and conveniently forgetting that Chinese monks and scholars had indeed once gone to India to study Buddhism, they were indignant at the thought that China was no longer the center of a great civilization as she used to be. Whatever the facts were, the humiliation was simply too great to take. In this regard we may brush aside the remarks of such a man as Wo-jen (author of Selection 46) by saying that he was merely an ignorant, bigoted Manchu; but we cannot so easily dismiss Yü Yüeh (author of Selection 47), who was considered one of the greatest men of letters of his time. The simple fact is that never having been exposed to any culture except their own, these Chinese simply could not conceive that an equally great or greater civilization actually existed. Mentally they dismissed all the evidence to the contrary, even though this evidence was there for all to see. Looking at the Chinese problems during this particular period, we may say that China's worst enemy was always her own complacency and ignorance, or perhaps more correctly, her seeming inability to acknowledge them as such.

41 • Li Hung-chang: *The Necessity of Learning about Western Technology*[1]

I believe that changes must be made when the old ways are no longer adequate to serve our purpose and that only through changes can we find new alternatives to meet our present need. Today our intellectuals continue to busy themselves with rhetoric and calligraphy, while our military men, being uncouth and ill-educated, are too ignorant to be regarded as being proficient in their trade. There is a wide gap between what we learn and what we need to learn; learning has in fact been completely separated from utility. In time of peace we look down upon Western technology, which we characterize as clever but insignificant, and comfort ourselves by saying that there is no real need to learn about it. When war comes, however, we are astonished at what Western technology can do, but nevertheless refuse to learn about it on the ground that it is too advanced for us to try to master it. We do not stop to think that it has taken the Westerners several hundred years to develop their present advanced technology, and their mastery of it certainly did not come about overnight. While a Western soldier may not know the principle underlying the construction of a weapon which he uses, the engineer who builds this weapon knows all its intricacies. Unlike our craftsmen, he is held in high esteem by his countrymen because of his knowledge.

Why is it that we are so far behind the Western countries in technology even though our civil and military institutions are much superior to theirs? In China the scholars who understand the principle of making equipment have no communication whatsoever with the artisans who make it; consequently the knowledge of one group cannot be coordinated with the skill of another to bring about the best possible result. Moreover, being looked down upon, a technician cannot hope to acquire a better position than that of a foreman in charge of a group of artisans. The situation is entirely different in Western countries. If a Westerner invents a piece of machinery acknowledged to be beneficial to the society, he will be installed as a high official. After his death, his descendants will inherit his position and continue to receive salaries. Thus, if for some reason he is unable to improve upon a particular piece of machinery, his descendants will continue to work on it until the improvement is made. Whoever they are, people will gather wherever fame or profit is. Since a Western government promotes technology by providing expert technicians with fame and material reward, it is no wonder that its people do their utmost to improve their mastery of technology.

Formerly, such Western countries as England and France regarded Japan as merely one of their prospective colonies and made all kinds of unreasonable demands. Aroused to action, the Japanese government selected the most talented young men from the royal household and high-ranking ministerial families and sent them to study technology in Western countries. Meanwhile it purchased machinery from these Western countries so that other Japanese could study it at home. Today the Japanese not only operate steamships but also manufacture their own weaponry. Last year the British attempted to blackmail them by threatening an invasion, but the Japanese, having mastered the Western skills, refused to be blackmailed. The British, consequently, did not dare make a move.

Today's Japanese are the same people whom we referred to as "dwarfish bandits"[2] during the Ming Dynasty. Being geographically near us and far away from Europe, they will look to us for leadership as long as we remain strong. Now that they have seen with their own eyes how weak we are and how strong the Western countries are, they naturally wish to imitate the West so as to master Western skills, knowing fully where the advantage lies. If a small island kingdom like Japan can make timely changes and know what it should or should not adopt, it is even more necessary for a country like China to do likewise, once we come to the conclusion that only through changes can we find new alternatives to meet our need, at a time when the old ways are no longer adequate....

I firmly believe that to strengthen herself as a nation, China must learn Western technology. To learn Western technology and thus to be able to make Western machinery, we must first acquire mother machines so as to make other machines. This does not mean, however, that we have to employ Westerners for this purpose. One of the measures we can take is to introduce a new category in the civil service examination system, namely, the category of technology, so as to provide scholars with the necessary incentive to perfect their skills in this field. Once this measure is taken, not only will our technology continue to improve, but a new profession will be created, a profession that in due course will attract many talented men from the nation as a whole.

NOTES

[1] This selection is part of a letter written sometime in 1864 and addressed to the Office of General Management (Tsung-li ya-men). Source: *Ch'ou-pan yi-wu shih-mo*, the Reign of T'ung-chih, roll 25, pp. 9–10.
[2] *Wo k'ou*.

42 • LI HUNG-CHANG: *A Proposal to Establish a Language School in Shanghai*[1]

This is to petition for the establishment of a foreign-language and literature school in response to a memorandum from the Office of General Management[2] concerning the establishment of the same.

In our contacts with foreigners, it is important to know their real intentions and true desires before a relationship of equality can be established between them and ourselves. Twenty years have elapsed since the opening of our ports for foreign trade, and during this period many foreigners have learned our language and familiarized themselves with our literature. The most outstanding of them are even able to read our classics and history and discuss our laws and institutions, customs and traditions like experts. On the other hand, few of our gentry and scholar-officials know anything about foreign languages or literature; worse still, they do not even wish to bother themselves to learn about them. Nowadays each of the foreign trading nations has stationed in Shanghai one or two translators, and whenever there are negotiations between foreign and Chinese ministers, these translators are called on to transmit messages from each side to the other. Since the translators are foreigners, it is inevitable that in the performance of their translation duties they should from time to time prejudice our position on behalf of their own respective governments. The only Chinese who know something about foreign languages are the interpreters[3] who are employed to facilitate conversation whenever negotiations are being conducted between a Chinese bureau, customs office, or military unit and its Western counterpart.

These interpreters, in the judgment of your humble servant, are most harmful to the management of foreign affairs. The wealth they acquire is tremendous, so large that in Shanghai, for instance, they constitute a special class, outside of the regular professions such as scholars, farmers, artisans, and merchants. Almost without exception, they come from two sources. First, there are the youngsters in the merchant families of Kwangtung or Ningpo who, being vagrant and frivolous by nature, cannot hope to acquire a managerial position on their own merit and pursue an interpreter's career only as a way to escape from their normal duties. Second, there are in England, France, and some other countries charity schools which, having recruited Chinese children from poor families, take upon themselves the duty of feeding, clothing, and educating them; these children, when grown, provide another source of today's interpreters. We do not know the background of these interpreters; we have no idea, for instance, whether they were brought up in the cities or in the countryside. However, practically all of them have acquired the repugnant, uncouth mannerisms of the Westerners; without exception they preach and try to convert others to Western religions. The interpreters of both of these categories are low in intelligence and vile in personal character, and they have nothing more in mind than material gain and sensual pleasure.

Moreover, more than 80 percent of these interpreters do not know how to read a foreign language, even though they do know how to converse in it. Even among those who do know how to read, their vocabulary is by and large confined to the names of the wares they help to buy or sell and their prices. Their command of foreign languages is as superficial as their delivery is vulgar. Not only are they completely ignorant of such important subjects as Western economics, military science, law, and government; when performing their duties as interpreters, they often misinterpret the original meaning on account of their unfamiliarity with the language's cadence. All they know is how to use foreign power and influence to engage in scheming and intrigue so as to satisfy their own selfish desire for material gain. They look down upon government officials and bully ordinary citizens; there is nothing in the world they seem to be afraid of.

Let your humble servant cite one instance to illustrate the case in point. After we concluded a mutual defense agreement with the foreigners,[4] I often had the opportunity of conversing with foreign commanders who spoke Chinese. In my contact with them, I was impressed with their reasonableness and good common sense. However, since we obviously could not discuss everything in person, we were forced to employ interpreters. This gave these interpreters an opportunity to create difficulties between the parties involved. They conspired with foreign soldiers for profit, provoked unnecessarily, and reported nonexistent expenses. In short, there was no limit to their avarice. Taking advantage of the fact that we do not know any foreign languages, they treated us as if we were deaf and dumb. They created mischief by spreading unfounded rumors, and small differences, whenever handled by them, eventually became large disputes.

The management of Western affairs is one of the most important functions of our government at the present time, and yet the crucial link in this management is controlled by people of this sort. Because of this sad state of affairs, foreigners and Chinese are ignorant of each other, and we have no way of knowing whether foreigners are sincere or otherwise whenever an issue arises. We lose the initiative as a result and are at a loss to know whether we should retreat or advance at a given moment. This is not a small matter by any means.

We certainly did the right thing when we established the T'ung-wen Kuan[5] in Peking. With the passage of time this institution is bound to produce statesmen of impeccable character and scholars of unusual merit. They will certainly master the Western technique which will enable them to deal more effectively with the Westerners. In short, the maintenance of peaceful relations with Western powers depends very much upon our success or failure in producing men of talent proficient in Western affairs.

Shanghai and Canton are the two cities in which a large number of foreigners live and where one can find all kinds of books not easily available in other parts of China. For those who wish to learn about Western affairs, there are no better places than these two cities. If a person wishes to learn only the rudiments of a foreign language, all he needs is a teacher. If on the other hand he wishes to be really proficient in it, he needs to read extensively over a large range of topics. For this there is no place in China more conducive to the fulfillment of his ambitions than Shanghai or Canton. One's knowledge of Western affairs, or the lack of it, is severely tested in these two cities.

Ignorant though your humble servant is, he would like to propose the establishment of a foreign-language and literature school in Shanghai, organized in the same fashion as the T'ung-wen Kuan in Peking. Let the prospective students be selected from nearby districts, students who are fourteen years old or younger, highly intelligent, and sound in moral character. Let Westerners be employed to teach them. As far as Chinese subjects (classics, history, and literature) are concerned, their teachers should be those who are not only morally sound and intellectually superior but have also passed the provincial examinations. After a student has completed his studies in the language school, he will be returned to his native province as an extra candidate in the civil service examination system and be allowed to take the examinations. Candidates for minor and miscellaneous positions in the government should also be allowed to apply for enrollment in the language school if they are young, intelligent, and willing to learn. Their applications will not be considered, however, if they have failed to obtain a certificate from an official in their native district that attests to their good character. Upon graduation they would be considered for promotion to a higher governmental position as a reward.

The prospective school, if established, will be operated on a provisional basis under the overall supervision of the Superintendent of Maritime Customs, who is to make a detailed report on its operation from time to time. In a period of three to five years intelligent and well-trained language experts might be expected to graduate from this institution. Whenever a governmental agency, whether a commercial office or the Maritime Customs, needs a translator to handle its relations with foreigners, it can select and then employ a graduate from this school. Only when these language experts are employed to manage Western affairs can we be reasonably sure that all reports on tariff duties and military supplies[6] are reliable and accurate. Meanwhile the unprincipled interpreters already described will gradually fade from the scene.

Though the general policy on foreign trade is formulated and decided upon by the Office of General Management in Peking, actual negotiations are conducted locally in the two ports of Shanghai and Canton. Since these two ports are too far away from Peking, we cannot rely on the Manchu students in the capital to serve as translators. It seems to your humble servant that we should widen the recruiting avenue and search for local talent in meeting this pressing demand. When the recruiting avenue is widened, there will be many, many young men who wish to study foreign languages, and some of them, by the operation of the law of averages, are bound to be talented or even outstanding.

The Westerners are most proficient in such subjects as mathematics, physics, chemistry, and mechanical engineering. They constantly search for more specialized and more accurate knowledge; and whenever new findings are made, they record these findings in books. Of these books less than twenty percent have been translated into Chinese. Only when we read all the hitherto untranslated books and familiarize ourselves with all the hidden secrets they contain can we graduate from the rudimentary and the superficial to the profound and the specialized. In terms of intellectual capacity, we Chinese are certainly not inferior to the Westerners. Once proficient in the Western languages, we will, in due course, master all the Western technology involving the building of ships, the manufacturing of firearms, and other endeavors of similar importance. Proficiency in foreign languages thus has an indirect bearing on strengthening the nation as a whole.

If the above proposal meets Your Majesty's approval, your humble servant will consult related agencies in formulating a school charter and in making a provisional budget. The required funds can conceivably be derived from port and tonnage dues. Your Majesty may also wish to instruct the governor-general and governor in Kwangtung to see whether a school of the same nature should be established in Canton.[7]

Ignorant as your humble servant is, he does not know whether the above proposal is really proper. He respectfully submits it for Your Majesty's consideration and will abide by whatever instruction Your Majesty chooses to give.

NOTES

[1] This petition, dated March 11, 1863, resulted in the establishment of Kuang-fang Yen-kuan, one of the first schools in China teaching foreign language and literature. A copy of the Chinese original appears in *The Complete Works of Li Hung-chang* (*Li Wen-chung kung ch'uan-chi*), roll 3.

[2] Tsung-li ya-men.

[3] *T'ung-shih.*

[4] This apparently refers to the cooperation between Li Hung-chang's Huai Army and the Ever-Victorious Army led by the Englishman Charles G. Gordon ("Chinese Gordon") during the time of the Taiping Rebellion.

[5] The first foreign-language school in China, established in 1862.

[6] China was then purchasing a large amount of military supplies from the West.

[7] The language school at Canton, called Kwangtung T'ung-wen Kuan, was later established.

43 • CHANG CHIH-TUNG: *A Proposed Reform for the Examination System*[1]

"If this country is to be regenerated," Chu Hsi[2] once quoted a commentator of contemporary affairs, "one of the best measures we can take is to stop giving civil service examinations for thirty years." How forceful and yet pathetic this remark is in view of the fact that the civil service examination system is the normal course through which the government recruits its officials! To be sure, other ways do exist whereby one can become a government official, but practically all good positions with great power and prestige are filled by those who have successfully passed the examination. The examination system in its present form began in the Ming Dynasty[3] and has been in force for more than 500 years. Like all systems, it generates abuse after a long period of usage; though still impressive in appearance, it has actually declined. Today the administrators of the examination system are merely interested in hiding their own inadequacies by passing those who are the least controversial; the candidates, meanwhile, rely heavily on good luck for their own success, realizing that they do not really deserve to pass. In theory there are three tests in each examination, but actually only one test really matters. Speaking pretentiously about the lofty ideals of the [Confucian] classics, the examination candidates are actually reading essays of questionable merit, easily obtainable in the market.[4] They do not know much about the teachings of our great scholars in the past, let alone the classics.

During the past few decades, the situation has deteriorated even further. As the writing style has become more frivolous, the candidates themselves are even less familiar with history and subjects of practical value. They do not even know how to write properly the so-called "contemporary essays." Now that a new situation has developed,[5] they are as defensive as they have been confused. They speak proudly of what they have learned—"the best that Confucius and Mencius have ever taught and the eternal law of government advocated by Yao and Shun"[6]—and attack and look down upon those who have applied themselves to subjects of a more contemporary and practical nature in order to cover their own inadequacies. Because of this situation, talented men have become less and less numerous, and few people are informed and able enough to avenge the nation's humiliation and protect her from further encroachment by foreign powers.

Realizing the danger the nation is in, the government has decreed the establishment of schools to cultivate talents who, upon graduation, are expected to be more familiar with subjects of practical or contemporary value. It also gives special examinations to recruit men particularly proficient in these subjects. Though schools have been established, few people bother to enroll in them because they are not sure that graduation from these schools will be followed by entry into officialdom. Students who have enrolled in them are mostly those from a humble background with an intelligence far below average, while young men of talent from well-established families continue to pursue a career through the civil service examinations. As far as special examinations are concerned, the law says that they will be given only once every twenty years. How can we expect candidates to wait patiently for such a long interval before another special examination will take place? In their impatience they are very likely to return to their old routine: practicing calligraphy, writing poetry, and attempting to improve upon their eight-legged essays. How can men of talent ever be cultivated to meet the challenge of our time? . . .

The people inevitably follow what the government favors. Because the Han government emphasized knowledge of the classics as a sure road to officialdom, the study of the Confucian classics prospered. Today the ability to write "contemporary essays" is still regarded as the most important factor in passing or failing a metropolitan or provincial examination; sadder still, if a man wishes to secure a position with the central government, he is well advised to strive to improve his calligraphy rather than anything else. As long as a situation like this exists, it is useless for us to speak of the serious danger the nation is in, because our warning will be met only with apathy and indifference. Nor will the response be better if we insist that our intellectuals should learn about practical subjects and that the government should actively seek men of versatility and then employ them. However loudly we cry about the nation's impending peril, we encounter only passivity and inaction. Our intellectuals, both inside and outside the government, remain blind and deaf to the fast-moving events in the contemporary world.

To meet the challenge of our time, we have to make reforms, and the first important reform, in my judgment, is the rectification of the civil service examination system. Some people might ask: Will not the rectification of the examination system, with abolition of "contemporary essays" in the examinations, reduce incentives to study the *Four Books* and the *Five Classics* on the part of our students? In reply, those of us who have favored the establishment of schools as a means to cultivate talents would say that the rectification of the examination system does not imply, even in the remotest sense, that our students should not study the *Four Books* and the *Five Classics*; it merely means that "contemporary essays," calligraphy, poetry, and the like will not be so heavily emphasized as they have been in the past. I firmly believe that the basic structure of our examination system is sound and should therefore be preserved, and that it needs only renovations to make it better.

While serving in the censorate, Ou-yang Hsiu[7] was extremely unhappy with the poor quality of the examination candidates at that time—with their ignorance, bad behavior, and plagiarism. He proposed a remedy which, if adopted, would authorize the examiners to evaluate the three tests in an examination separately. In other words, only candidates who had passed the first test were allowed to take the second test, and only the successful candidates of the second test would be allowed to take the third test. "In this way," he said, "the vile and the eccentric will be gradually eliminated from consideration during the examination process. As the number of candidates becomes smaller, not only would it be easier to evaluate them; the examiners, having more time to read the papers, would also be less subject to error. A careful procedure like this will assure that the totally ignorant are no longer able to pass the examination."

The suggestion made by Ou-yang Hsiu can be adopted with profit today. The replacement of poetry by essays, suggested by him, can be compared to the replacement of "contemporary essays" by Chinese and Western subjects of practical value when and if the present examination system is rectified. We should further adopt his idea of "step-by-step elimination" and merely reverse the sequence of the three tests, so the whole procedure may look more like that followed in the reexamination of candidates on the prefectural or subprefectural level. The first test is that on Chinese subjects of practical value, which consist of Chinese history and contemporary government, and the candidates are to be required to write five essays on the latter topic. If a province has been assigned a quota of, say, 80 successful candidates in the metropolitan examination, 800 candidates should be allowed to pass this first test; if the quota is 40, then 400 candidates should be allowed to pass. In other words, a ratio of 10 to 1 should be maintained between those who pass the first test and those who eventually pass the metropolitan examination. The names of the successful candidates in the first test will be immediately made public once they are known, while those who have failed will be asked to return home. Only those who have succeeded in the first test are allowed to take the second.

The second test is that on Western subjects, including comparative governments and physical sciences and technology. The candidates are to write five essays on world affairs, with emphasis on the various institutions of foreign countries in each of the five continents. In addition, their knowledge of foreign geography, governmental institutions, education system, finance, armed forces, commerce, and industry should be also tested. As far as physical sciences and technology are concerned, they should be tested on their knowledge of physics, chemistry, manufacturing, acoustics, optics, electrical engineering, and other related subjects. If they interpret Western learning in an eccentric or irrational manner, an interpretation which clearly violates the basic tenets of Confucianism, they are not allowed to pass, of course. If a province has been assigned a quota of, say, 80 successful candidates in the metropolitan examination, 240 candidates should be allowed to pass this second test; if the quota is 40, then 120 candidates should be allowed to pass. In other words, a ratio of 3 to 1 should be maintained between those who pass the second test and those who eventually pass the metropolitan examination. The names of the successful candidates in the second test will be made public once they are known, while those who have failed will be sent home. Only the successful candidates in the second test are allowed to take the third or final test.

In the third or final test the candidates will be examined on their knowledge of the *Four Books* and the *Five Classics*. They are required to write two essays on the former and one on the latter. Under no circumstances, however, should the questions on the *Four Books* be those of a fine, minute type. A successful candidate of all the three tests will be regarded as having passed the metropolitan examination, and his name will be made public. The number of successful candidates allowed to pass for each province is to be exactly the same as the quota assigned to that province.

It is easy to see that the candidates who have passed the first test and are therefore eligible for the second test must be those who have had a broad background on things Chinese: history, government, and domestic policies. Fearful that they might know little about Western learning despite their great knowledge about their own country, we test them on their understanding of Western institutions and Western technology in the second test. The candidates who have passed the second test must be those who, having devoted themselves to the Western learning, are familiar with world affairs and contemporary subjects. Fearful that their minds are less than orthodox and their life goals less than pure, we examine them on their knowledge of the *Four Books* and the *Five Classics* in the third test. The candidates who have passed this test must be those who, having studied the teachings of our ancient sages, keep their minds pure and their ideas orthodox.

Thus the first test stresses the importance of extensiveness in learning, while the second test emphasizes the necessity of versatility in knowledge. The third test, on the other hand, is concerned with orthodoxy in ideas and purity in thought. The process is one that begins with extensiveness and ends in specialization, from general knowledge of all subjects to expertness in one field. If the examination system is renovated in the way as described above, one will not find among the successful candidates those who are mediocre or eccentric. Since each test has a special emphasis and carries with it a special meaning, the renovated system, if adopted, would be a great improvement over the one now in use, which unduly and unjustifiably emphasizes one test and one test alone. Moreover, as the unsuccessful candidates are successively dismissed from consideration, the number of papers to be read by the examiners would become smaller and smaller after each test. Their number being small, it would be much easier to read them. There are other advantages, too. First, candidates who are financially poor do not have to wait too long in the capital for the result; second, examination copiers have a smaller number of papers to duplicate and are thus less subject to error;[8] third, the examiners, having more time to evaluate each paper, will be less in a hurry and can perform a more satisfactory task. Thus we reap three advantages by changing a single procedure. The new procedure will definitely yield better results.

Some people who disagree with me might ask this question: How can one say that "contemporary essays" are useless in view of the fact that a large number of our famous ministers are products of the examination system which requires the composition of these essays? The answer is that as long as the advance to prominence is limited to one road and one road only, men of talent will have no choice but to travel on that road. In other words, our famous ministers, being unusually talented, also happen to know how to write "contemporary essays." This is different from saying that "contemporary essays" are a reliable standard for measuring a man's talent. Furthermore, most of the knowledge, wisdom, and experience which we ascribe to these ministers is acquired after they have passed the civil service examinations.[9] Let us not forget that before reaching their middle age, they have spent a great deal of time and energy in preparing for these examinations. It is reasonable to assume that had the government not used exclusively eight-legged essays and poetry to judge a person's worth, there would have been more famous ministers and great scholars who could shoulder the burden of national affairs today.

NOTES

[1] This selection is translated from the author's famous essay, *Exhortation to Learning* (*Ch'uan-hsüeh p'ien*).

[2] Chu Hsi (1130–1200) was a famous philosopher of the Sung Dynasty.

[3] This refers to the writing of eight-legged essays in the examinations.

[4] By this the author apparently means the so-called "contemporary essays" (*shih wen*), essays written in the eight-legged style that could be memorized to good effect when taking the civil service examinations.

[5] This refers to the necessity of conducting educational reform as a result of China's humiliation at the hands of Western powers.

[6] Yao and Shun were two legendary emperors of China's remote past, hailed by Confucians as model rulers.

[7] Ou-yang Hsiu (1007–1072) was a writer and statesman of the Sung Dynasty.

[8] During the Ch'ing Dynasty all papers in the metropolitan examination were required by law to be duplicated by professional copiers; only the duplicates rather than the originals were presented to the examiners to be evaluated. This step was taken so as to make sure that the examiners would not show favor for or be prejudiced against a particular candidate as a result of recognizing his handwriting.

[9] By "famous ministers" (*ming ch'en*) the author had apparently in mind such men as Tseng Kuo-fan and Li Hung-chang.

44 • TSENG KUO-FAN AND LI HUNG-CHANG: *The Selection of Intelligent Boys to Study in Foreign Countries*[1]

Tseng Kuo-fan, Grand Chancellor and Governor-General of Liangkiang, and Li Hung-chang, Grand Chancellor and Governor-General of Chihli, petition His Majesty the Emperor as follows:

Last year, while your humble servant Kuo-fan was managing Western affairs at Tientsin, he had an opportunity to speak with Ting Jih-ch'ang, the former governor of Kiangsu, who in compliance with Your Majesty's command often came to Tientsin to assist him in the performance of his duties. Time and again we discussed the possibility of sending boys of high intelligence to Western countries to study such subjects as mathematics, manufacturing, shipbuilding and navigation, and military science. If this proposal is adopted, these boys will be able to complete their studies in a period of ten or more years and will then be proficient in the skills for which the Westerners are deservedly famous. Both of us felt strongly that China cannot hope to become self-reliant unless she has enough experts versed in Western technology. Ting also stated that either Ch'en Lan-pin of the Ministry of Justice or Yung Hung of Kiangsu Province could be entrusted with the responsibility of accompanying these boys to foreign countries. Since your humble servant Kuo-fan was in complete agreement with Ting's suggestion, he has presented this proposal for Your Majesty's consideration twice in the past—first in the ninth month of last year and again in the first month of this year.

Meanwhile your humble servant Hung-chang has also discussed this matter with various persons by correspondence. He feels that since people like Pin-ch'un, Chih-kang, and Sun Chia-ku have twice visited foreign countries in compliance with Your Majesty's command, we have indirectly acquired some background knowledge about these countries. We know, for instance, that cartography, mathematics, astronomy, oceanography, shipbuilding, and manufacturing are all closely related to the development of a strong military force. As soon as a Chinese student has completed his studies abroad and has thus acquired special skills in his field of learning, he will be invited to teach in a school once he returns home, so that these skills, whatever they are, will be transmitted to the younger generation and be improved further from then on. Western countries regard military science and shipbuilding as two of the most important fields of learning for a nation that wishes to remain strong. Your humble servant Hung-chang believes that we should follow their example in this regard until we too are proficient in these skills. Since China is still to be enlightened as far as Western learning is concerned, to send young men of high intelligence to study abroad at the earliest moment seems to be a logical step to take. As they diligently learn about Western skills, Your Majesty's fervent wish to make China strong will be eventually fulfilled.

According to Article 7 in the treaty recently concluded with the United States,[2] any Chinese who wishes to study in American schools will be treated with great consideration in accordance with the most-favored-nation clause. The treaty also stipulates that the United States and China can establish schools in each other's territories on a reciprocal basis. When the American minister passed through Tientsin this spring, your humble servant Hung-chang had an opportunity to speak with him about this matter; he gave a very favorable response, saying that he would be happy to transmit our request to his home government the moment he received a formal notification from us. In the third month of this year the British minister came to see Hung-chang; he wished to know about our intention to send students to study in the United States. He seemed to be pleased when informed of our intention to do so. He further stated that since there were many universities and colleges in England, other groups of Chinese students might be sent to England at some future time. It seems that all the Western countries are anxious to cooperate with us in this undertaking, an undertaking that is more likely to improve rather than harm the friendly relations between China and Western countries.

As your humble servants see it, all conditions are favorable for a successful completion of this project. First, Western countries are willing to let us learn their special skills. Second, we have among us people like Chih-kang and Sun Chia-ku who have already paved the way by visiting foreign countries and who can now serve as advisers for this new project. Third, it would take only a month or so to sail by boat from China to the United States. All things considered, it does not seem to be too difficult to carry out this project. Some people might say that this project is really superfluous in view of the fact that we have already erected plants in Tientsin, Shanghai, and Foochow to build ships and manufacture military equipment in the Western style, and have also established foreign-language schools in China such as T'ung-wen Kuan in Peking and Kuang-fang Yen-kuan[3] in Shanghai where Westerners are employed to teach Chinese students of high intelligence. Why should we have to send students to study abroad, they may ask, when a solid foundation has already been laid for our Westernization programs? These critics, in the judgment of your humble servants, do not realize the difference in purpose of each of these projects. The erection of plants and the establishment of language schools are important in the sense that they help the nation to build itself; they are by no means in conflict with the study-abroad program, which is to enlarge our intellectual horizons and may bring about greater benefit in the long run.

In the matter of learning, the Westerners emphasize utility and practicality. Whether a person is a scholar, artisan, or soldier, he goes to school to learn about his profession. Not only does he study theories, he also works with equipment, the equipment which he will have to use after his graduation. He does his best to improve upon what he has learned from others and then transmit his findings to people in his own field of specialization. As people like him continue to improve themselves, new knowledge is added every year.

If we attempted to do in China what the Westerners are doing in their own countries, we would have to buy all of their equipment at once. This is of course financially impossible. Even if it were possible, we would still be unable to understand the principle underlying the equipment we had bought and how to operate it, since such an understanding can be acquired only through careful observation and repeated experimentation. An ancient proverb says: "To learn about the Ch'i language, you have to live among the Ch'i people."[4] Another proverb says: "To see it once is more important than to hear about it a thousand times." There is a great deal of truth in these proverbs. Once we learn the Western way of doing things, we can bring it home and apply it to all possible fields. For expanding our knowledge, would this approach not be infinitely better than working diligently by ourselves and reaping only ineffective results?

As this is the first time we plan to send students to study abroad, we may encounter two difficulties. One is to select talented students, and the other is to provide adequate funds. Besides the fact that boys of unusual intelligence are difficult to find, the students we have in mind must be ambitious in pursuing their life goals and honest and sincere in their personal character. They should not be the gaudy or ostentatious type, and they should not have any family worries at home. Only when these conditions are successfully met can the prospective students concentrate on their studies abroad. Unfortunately, not very many can meet these conditions. As for funds to be used for this project, they have to be raised outside the regular budget, since the revenue the government can collect each year remains constant. Thus the raising of funds is another difficulty we will have to face. While your humble servants do not in any way belittle the seriousness of these two difficulties, they feel strongly that "the building of a mountain begins with the first shovelful of earth" and that "it takes three years for an artemisia to yield fruit." Only if we plant our tree today can we hope to see it grow tomorrow. Once it starts to grow, it will become bigger and taller each day without great further effort.

Your humble servants have instructed Ch'en Lan-pin, Yung Hung, and others to study this project carefully before they submit their report to us. It is hereby suggested that a new office should be established in Shanghai, to be staffed by officials whose duty it is to recruit and select boys of high intelligence in the coastal provinces as prospective candidates. The number of selected candidates should be limited to thirty per year, and the total number in a four-year period should be one hundred twenty. Each year they would sail to foreign countries to pursue their studies and would return home at the end of a fifteen-year period. By the time they return home, these boys would be about thirty years old, and being in their prime, could serve most effectively their country, to which they owe their gratitude.

We have heard that many young men in Kwangtung, Fukien, and Ningpo have gone to foreign countries to study in the past, but their purpose was merely to learn the rudiments of a foreign language so that when they returned home they would be able to trade more effectively with foreigners and thus make a better living. The purpose of the proposed project is entirely different. We should of course be extremely careful in selecting our candidates; once in a foreign country, they should also be carefully guided by officials sent by our government. Each of them is to study a specialized field in which he is expected to be proficient. Moreover, they will be taught Chinese and related subjects by qualified personnel while abroad, so that they will know how to establish themselves as ethical beings[5] despite their residence abroad. Though it is too much to expect all of them to become great men, it is reasonable to assume that they will become useful personnel. Since so many students are to be sent abroad, some of them are bound to be outstanding. This expectation conforms to the old saying that by the operation of the law of averages, one can be wrong only half the time.

As for expenses, the amount for a twenty-year period is about one million twenty thousand taels, a very large sum indeed. However, this amount does not have to be raised all at once. The average is about sixty thousand taels per year and does not seem to be too difficult to raise at the moment. Except for traveling expenses that are to be entrusted with officials who accompany and supervise these students abroad, other expenses will be appropriated and remitted via banks on a yearly basis. No difficulties should arise on this score. In short, we cannot expect to reap great rewards in the long run if we are parsimonious at the very beginning. Moreover, once the students are far away in a foreign country, we cannot very

Since China emphasizes the "investigation of objects and things" as the method for acquiring knowledge,[7] the Chinese approach to knowledge does not seem to be very different from that in the Western world. Why is it that China has lagged far behind Western Europe intellectually? Some people answer this question by saying that Chinese intellectuals have traditionally applied themselves to speculative science while their Western counterparts pay more attention to physical or technological knowledge. Nothing can be further from the truth. It can be even argued that the Western knowledge is more "speculative," or less "practical," than its Chinese counterpart. In short, the fact that China is intellectually behind has nothing to do with the difference in emphasis on either speculative or practical knowledge.

Before the Ming Dynasty the intellectual level of the Western world was about the same as that of China. It is only in the modern period that the Western world emphasizes the importance of content rather than rhetoric, the practical or utilitarian rather than the pedantic or superfluous. In education, it teaches its youngsters how to observe things with their eyes and ears and how to think through what they have observed. It stresses the importance of originality rather than tradition, credibility rather than credulity. In the field of logic and mathematics, for instance, the students are taught the process of rational thinking, the method of tracing an idea from the very beginning to its ultimate conclusion. Likewise, they are taught in natural sciences to observe the ever-changing physical phenomena in the universe and to draw their own conclusions with regard to these changes. It matters not whether the conclusions are utilitarian in nature; it is all-important, however, that they should be real and true. To acquire knowledge by reading books is only secondary in the learning process, says Thomas H. Huxley; the correct attitude towards learning is to regard the whole universe as one's book and all things in it as means to express one's findings. This, in summary, is the way the Western world teaches its students.

Now let us look at the situation in China. Chu Hsi[8] is correct when he says that the "reason" for an object exists in the object itself and that only by investigating the outward objects and things can we acquire knowledge. He is not at his best, however, when he says that we have to search out "reasons" in written works. In China we place great importance on the teachings of the ancients. Not only do we fail to point out ancient people's errors when they are wrong; we also do not know why they are right when they are right. We mistake rhetoric for knowledge, and having confined ourselves to the classics and their variety of interpretations, we seem never to have been able to escape their strenuous hold. Today we have the so-called eight-legged essays that, more than anything else, are responsible for destroying whatever talent there is. Under the circumstances, how is it possible for the Chinese people to broaden their minds and to accept new ideas?

Nowadays when a child of five or six enters school, he is immediately exposed to the most philosophical language ever known, even though, young as he is, he is far from ready for it. He memorizes but does not understand his lessons. How can this memorized work open up his intellect? The only means which his teacher relies on to open up his intellect is word-matching,[9] which is far from adequate. In our curriculum there is not a single subject that teaches students how to observe and examine the physical world around us or to differentiate truth from falsehood from a logical rather than a doctrinaire point of view. Such being the case, is it really surprising that nine out of every ten successful candidates in the civil service examinations are sometimes inferior to farmers, artisans, and merchants in the application of common sense to the solution of our daily problems? Those who are concerned with China's decline as a nation of power and wealth often sigh with regret that she has not produced as many educated people as she should have. However, if education can produce only the kind of intellectuals described above, China will be better off in having fewer, rather than more, people with education.

The general state of affairs in education is so bad today that it has to change. Some people say that we should not only establish more schools and revise the old curriculum but should also introduce and teach Western subjects. All these are highly commendable suggestions, but to say that we are bound to reap good results in ten years if these suggestions were followed seems to me to be too optimistic a statement. Our main difficulty is the obstacle posed by the old institutions that still exist, while the inducements to open a new road are totally lacking. An intellectual who pursues the new studies[10] would have to be a person who truly loves and enjoys what he does, since he cannot expect any encouragement or reward from the society for his labor or effort. If he is less than totally devoted, the difficulties he is confronted with are simply tremendous: endless work without any hope of being financially rewarded, jealousy and resentment on the part of his fellow intellectuals, and false accusations from those who do not understand what he is doing. He would be a rare man indeed if he did not change his mind and abandon his pursuit. In short, to broaden people's minds and to enhance their intellect, we know that we must promote Western learning and utilitarian studies. To provide enough incentive for people to advance along this road, we have to revise the old ways whereby government officials are selected. The present civil service examination system that emphasizes the eight-legged essays should be abolished forthwith.

Of the three essentials for building a new nation, the refinement of moral character is definitely the most difficult. Here let me say a few words about the role which the Western religion plays in this matter. Once every seven days a priest or minister preaches before his congregation. Generally speaking, his sermon contains two basic themes: the omnipotence of God and the importance of life. Whatever a person's station in society is, be he king, duke, or helpless pauper, he is God's child and is therefore entitled to the same consideration by the society as anybody else. As this principle of egalitarianism is made clear and understood by all, people acquire a sense of self-respect and encourage one another towards goodness. Since God is everywhere, a person should be morally upright even though nobody is near to watch him. This, incidentally, is exactly what a Chinese gentleman strives for but sometimes fails to achieve. Yet an ordinary Westerner, because of the religious training he has received and the faith he has in his religion, conducts his daily life according to the highest principles and, morally speaking, stands on the same level as a Chinese gentleman. As long as his conscience is clear and his motive pure and honest, he does not surrender himself to power or influence, however great it is; nor will he be tempted to do evil for the simple purpose of acquiring material wealth. This is what his religion normally expects from him—he is not regarded as a superior or extraordinary person simply because he has followed his religious precepts. The net result is as beneficial to the society as it is to the individuals who compose it. People are also happier because they have in their minds a moral principle which they can steadfastly hold, a principle that will not change with the change of time.

As for China, schools in the ancient sense have long ceased to exist. Even when they did exist in ancient times, their primary function was to select unusually bright and talented students and then educate them. As for ordinary people, they went from cradle to grave without receiving any formal education at all. Mencius says, "A man is no different from an animal if he is only interested in good food, fine clothing, and a pleasurable life, without in the meantime striving to have an education." If a man of adequate means shows little interest in receiving an education, the interest is understandably less among poor people who work hard all year round to stay alive and sometimes fail to do so. Being poor and uneducated, do they really surprise us if they choose to place material gain above moral principles and sometimes resort to deception and treachery to obtain their ends?

During the Sino-Japanese War of 1894, it is reported, some of our torpedoes and shells failed to explode after they had reached enemy targets because many of our navy men, in order to line their own pockets, had substituted iron dust, sand, and mud for gunpowder when making the explosives. Foreign newspapers were correct when they criticized us for being so selfish as to exchange humiliating defeat and territorial losses for personal, material gains. When a nation has sunk so low in morality it is only proper that she should be defeated or be exterminated altogether. I know that all of us were furious when we heard about this incident. But have we studied it more carefully and traced its real causes? Beginning with the Ch'in Dynasty, practically all of the Chinese regimes have treated their people as if they were slaves, though some of these regimes were more lenient and less harsh than others. When a government treats its people as slaves, the people also regard themselves as such. But this does not mean that they really love their government or rulers and wish to preserve or protect them; it merely means that being intimidated or controlled by the power which only their masters possess, they have no choice but to adopt the attitude of a humble slave. As long as the government can maintain its power of control and its laws are effectively enforced, the people will go on praising the wisdom or superiority of their mighty rulers and endlessly repeating how inferior and insignificant they themselves are, without any sense of shame, for which they really care very little. Once the government loses its power of control and when its laws can no longer be effectively enforced, however, they will pursue a course in accordance with their own self-interest; by then we should not be surprised at all if they should decide to raise the standard of revolt.

In China, whenever we wish to curse somebody, we call him a dog or a pig. For a Westerner, to compare a man to an animal does not carry any meaning of abuse at all. If on the other hand you call him a liar or a coward, very likely he will challenge you to a duel even before you finish your words, because for him, to be characterized as a liar or a coward is much more humiliating than to be compared to an animal. He prefers to die rather than to endure the presence of a man who has so little respect for him. In China, on the other hand, lying and cowardice are merely dismissed as the unavoidable attributes of a small or mean man whom a gentleman would simply keep at arm's length. One can readily see the vast difference between Western and Chinese customs.

Why is there such a vast difference? The West preaches the principle of equality and consequently emphasizes the importance of popular will as the ideological foundation of its government. It places high priority on the virtues of freedom, honesty, and faithfulness. We in China make filial piety the cardinal principle of governing the nation and the world; the honoring of parents is often given such priority that it outweighs any other virtues, including honesty. The corollary of this overemphasis is hypocrisy and mutual deception—each person merely wishes to shift the burden of his own responsibility to the shoulders of somebody else. To me at least, "loyalty" and "filial piety" which we cherish seem much slighter virtues than "sincerity" and "truthfulness" emphasized by the Westerners.

It is not a mere coincidence that a Western government commands the absolute loyalty of its people; that its people, loving their country, are truly patriotic; and that during the time of war they fight heroically on the battlefield as if they were avenging a personal grievance. Its laws are those enacted by the representatives of the people; they are not edicts or decrees issued by an omnipotent emperor. From the prime minister downward, all important officials are elected by the people, who create official posts for the sole purpose of serving their own interests. Unlike their Chinese counterparts, these officials are not meant to be worshiped or even looked up to; they neither oppress nor provide comfort for those who put them in office. The people gladly pay taxes to support their government or protect their industry as if they were merely investing money in their own farms or homesteads. When they march to the battlefield to combat their enemy, they have in mind the defense of their own home or family. We Chinese are often surprised at the love or affection with which an Englishman speaks of England, a Frenchman speaks of France, or any Westerner speaks of the country from which he originates—the kind of love or affection which we Chinese reserve exclusively for our parents. But we should not be surprised. A Westerner has the same regard for his country as we Chinese have for our own family.

To refine our moral character, which in turn will enable us to be united to resist foreign aggression, there is only one road that we can follow, namely, to regard China—all of China—as our private possession and to strive for the advancement of her welfare. Mr. Ku[11] once said: "All people are selfish; it is the sage's task to harness individual selfishness and transform it into public good." What should we do if we wish every Chinese to regard the national welfare as the proper end of his private efforts? We should first establish a popular parliament in the nation's capital and should in the meantime allow the people to choose their own officials in each of the districts or provinces where they live. Once this step is taken, the people will love and be loyal to the government which serves their interest; educational and cultural activities will advance; natural resources will be opened up; roads and bridges will be built; and commerce and industry will prosper. Then the people will rise above their selfishness and work diligently for the common good.

I believe that if our ancient sages were living today, they would not disagree with me on what I have said above. In my judgment, the three essentials—the strengthening of physical prowess, the enlargement of intellectual capacity, and the refinement of moral character—are the true basis for the nation's self-strengthening movement. Without them, even a statesman like Yi Yin[12] or Lü Shang[13] could not carry out his policies and a general like Wu Ch'i[14] or Li Mu[15] would suffer defeat on the battlefield. In short, without them China can never be strong and self-reliant. To be sure, there are things less basic which we can do, such as the training of troops, the raising of funds for public projects, the opening of mines, the construction of railroads, and the promotion of industry and commerce. We should not belittle their importance, of course. However, without the three essentials previously described, they will come to nought in the end, however successful they may look on the surface. Since 1895 when China was defeated by Japan, all of these projects have been undertaken in various parts of China. Are they really effective? In what ways have they made this country stronger? Anyone who has followed current events can answer these questions himself.

Among the less basic measures that have to be adopted, the most urgent, in my judgment, is the replacement of old with new personnel in the central government. If some extraordinary measure like this were adopted, not only would all the Chinese be given a new hope for the future, foreign powers might be also hesitant to carry out their conspiracies by imposing humiliation upon us again. Without these extraordinary measures, all the new projects that have been introduced to strengthen the country will remain ineffective, as they have been. My friend Liang Ch'i-ch'ao of Hsinhui[16] once said: "As foreign powers continue to exercise pressure upon us, we have to make the necessary changes, even though we may not like these changes." When we make changes because we want to, the initiative is ours. If on the other hand we are forced to make changes, the initiative has been taken over by others. *The Commentaries of Tso* [17] says: "Do not render assistance to those who are intent on bringing you harm." This statement was made under extraordinary circumstances which characterize the situation of China today. All of us who are genuinely concerned with the present state of national affairs should repeat this statement three times a day. The future of this country remains bright if we make changes when there is still time.

NOTES

[1] Though speaking strongly for Westernized reforms in this selection, the author had reservations later in his life. A copy of the Chinese original can be found in Su Yüan-lei (ed.), *A Collection of Essays (Ching-shih wen-tsung)* [Chungking: Huang-chung Press, 1943], pp. 488–501.

[2] The secondary goals the author apparently has in mind are the strengthening of the army and the navy, the adoption of Western methods in industry and communications, and all other things that are technical in nature. The primary goal is of course the attainment of the three essentials.

[3] A Turkish-speaking non-Chinese tribe.

[4] Northern Chinese are generally taller and bigger than their southern counterparts.

[5] A game in which arrows were thrown into a vase placed at some distance.

[6] *Shen Pao*; one of the largest dailies in Shanghai.

[7] *Chih-chih tsai ke-wu*; this is a paraphrased quotation from the *Great Learning (Ta hsüeh)*, a Confucian classic.

[8] Chu Hsi (1130–1200) was a philosopher of the Sung Dynasty.

[9] *Tui-ou*; matching "fire" with "water," "good" with "bad," and the like.

[10] Western subjects such as science and technology.

[11] Ku Yen-wu (1613–1682), a scholar of the late Ming and early Ch'ing Dynasty.

[12] Yi Yin (eighteenth century B.C.) is reported to have served as prime minister to T'ang, founder of the Shang Dynasty.

[13] Lü Shang, also known as Chiang Tzu-ya (twelfth century B.C.), served as minister-adviser to King Wen and King Wu, founders of the Chou Dynasty.

[14] A famous military strategist of the fourth century B.C.

[15] Serving in the feudal state of Chao, Li Mu (fourth century B.C.) earned his reputation as a brilliant general by repeatedly defeating the Hsiung-nu and the state of Ch'in.

[16] Hsinhui is located in Kwangtung Province. For Liang Ch'i-ch'ao, see pp. 227–228.

[17] *Tso chuan*; an ancient classic written perhaps in the fourth century B.C.

46 • WO-JEN: *No Need for Western Learning*[1]

In his petition Censor Chang Shang-tsao maintains that the government has no need whatever to recruit successful candidates in the civil service examinations to learn about mathematics and astronomy. However, in a decree issued by Your

Majesty it is stated that the government-operated T'ung-wen Kuan[2] should in fact recruit these candidates to study these two subjects on the grounds that the subjects are more than technical in nature and are thus not entirely beneath a gentleman's serious concern and that in the pursuit of knowledge a Confucian scholar should not concentrate on one field to the exclusion of all others.

Your Majesty is certainly correct when you say that mathematics, being one of the Six Arts,[3] is a legitimate field of study and should by no means be confused with heretical or unorthodox learning. However, as your humble servant sees it, whatever small advantage can be derived from studying mathematics and astronomy is more than offset by the great harm that would certainly come about when we have to employ Westerners to teach them. In the opinion of your humble servant, we should certainly study this project more carefully before carrying it out. Let me elaborate on this point.

Your humble servant has heard that the foundation of a nation lies in the virtues (such as righteousness and propriety) she possesses rather than in transient advantages she may have or fanciful expedients she can devise. Her true strength is derived from the collective mind of her citizens rather than some unusual skills she happens to possess. Now we are asked not only to pursue a small and insignificant skill but also to honor foreigners as teachers. Since foreigners are known for their treachery, it is extremely doubtful if they will reveal to us all of their secrets. Even if they did, their contribution would amount to no more than the training of technicians. Throughout history no country has ever become strong by relying on achievement in technology.

Being so large, China has many talented men within her national boundaries. If, say, such subjects as mathematics and astronomy are really important enough to be taught, we can certainly find, if our search is wide and intense enough, Chinese experts to teach them. Why do we have to employ foreigners? Why do we have to honor them as our teachers?

Moreover, foreigners have always been our enemies. In the tenth year of Hsien-feng (1860), they launched a vicious attack against China without any provocation. They ravaged our capital, thus shaking the nation to its very foundation. They not only set fire to the Summer Palace and destroyed it but also indiscriminately murdered civilians and officials alike.[4] This humiliation was unprecedented in the 200-year history of our dynasty and has been deeply resented by both scholars and officials. Though the government was then forced to negotiate peace with these foreigners, how can it ever forget the unavenged shame? Since the conclusion of the peace treaty, Christianity has spread far and wide and with great cunning has beguiled and entrapped many innocent but ignorant citizens. In these critical times the only thing the nation can rely on for its survival is the rectitude of its intelligentsia, who, we hope, can continue to maintain people's integrity by pointing out to them the correct path to follow. Now that we are asked to transform our most talented young men, upon whom the future of our nation relies, into the followers of foreign ways, not only will the best of our tradition suffer regression, but the unorthodox, alien spirit will continue to spread. If this situation continues, I am afraid that in a few years all of us will become foreigners instead of remaining Chinese.

Your humble servant has had the occasion of reading the collected works of the late Emperor Shen-tsu Jen.[5] In a decree issued to the Grand Chancellor and the Nine Ministers. he said that China would suffer at the hands of Western powers for several hundred years. How farsighted he was! Though he adopted foreign ways for his own purpose, deep in his heart he never trusted foreigners. In view of the fact that China has suffered greatly at the hands of foreigners for such a long time, why should we insist on spreading their evil ideas? I have heard that foreign missionaries often resent the fact that Chinese intellectuals do not wish to learn about their religion. If we allow successful examination candidates to learn from these people, they will be deluded and led astray by this alien religion before they can learn anything really useful. This is a trap the foreigners have carefully set up: by no means should we fall into it!

It is the hope of your humble servant that Your Majesty, by invoking the power you alone possess, will immediately put an end to the proposal in question, so that the hidden danger contained in it will be eliminated before it can emerge and the future of the nation will remain orthodox and safe. This action on your part will bring great benefit to the nation as a whole.

NOTES

[1] This memorial was dated March 20, 1867 (the 15th day of the second month in the sixth year of T'ung-chih). Source: *Ch'ou-pan yi-wu shih-mo*, the Reign of T'ung-chih, roll 47, pp. 24–25.
[2] A foreign-language school in Peking.
[3] The Six Arts are rites, music, archery, chariot-riding, calligraphy, and mathematics.
[4] In 1860, after the allies (England and France) captured Peking, the British commander ordered the burning of the Yüan Ming Yüan, the Emperor's Summer Palace. By then Emperor Hsien-feng had already fled to Jehol. The hostilities ended with the signing of the Peking Convention (1860).
[5] Emperor K'ang-hsi (r. 1662–1722).

47 • YÜ YÜEH: *My Three Fears*[1]

As I look at the situation of China today, there are three things I am most fearful about. One is that the name of China or "Central Nation" will be changed. The ancients say that nine continents existed prior to the Shen-nung[2] period. Beginning with the Huang-ti[3] period, however, our ancestors could no longer extend their influence over all of these continents; they had to be satisfied with the occupation of only one continent, which they divided into nine provinces for administrative purposes. This continent was China or "Central Nation."

China can remain China or "Central Nation" as long as she does not communicate with any of the other eight continents. Since the time of Huang-ti, Yao, and Shun[4] and until recently, this has indeed been the case. During the reign of King Ch'eng of Chou,[5] the kingdom of Yüeh-shang[6] sent an envoy to China to pay its homage and tribute. "A gentleman will not accept tribute from a country which has not felt the good influence of his virtue," said Duke Chou;[7] "he, in fact, refuses to take any people as his subjects over whom he does not exercise administrative control." This was the way our sages maintained the dignity of China! If Huang-ti could not even transform people outside of China into Chinese subjects, how can we hope to do so? If we cannot transform them into Chinese subjects and yet communicate with them, we would have to treat them as equals. In such a case, the dignity of China as the "Central Nation" could no longer be preserved.

Suppose there is a married couple who own one *mou* of land where they build their house. They construct a wall around their property and erect a gate to make sure that no stranger can come in if uninvited. Within the wall and inside the gate are the members of one family where the parents, through teaching and discipline, raise their children in the most proper manner. If neighbors or strangers can come into the house at any time they want to and make noise and cause disturbances whenever they please, the family is no longer a family in the truest sense of that word. Who would believe this couple if they brazenly declared that theirs is an old, respectable family when in fact it has become a family for all people on earth? Unfortunately, China today is like this family. If the situation continues, it will not be long before she loses her identity as the "Central Nation."

My second fear is that Confucianism will be undermined and eventually destroyed. During the period of Warring States (403–221 B.C.) when Confucianism was still in its infancy, the Ch'in state adopted the philosophy of Shen Pu-hai and Shang Yang[8] and forced its people to be diligent in farming and brave in warfare. Those who wished to become rich had to work hard in the fields, and those who wanted to be honored by the government had to distinguish themselves on the battlefield. Diligence in farming increased the nation's wealth, while bravery in warfare enhanced the nation's military strength. Following this policy, the Ch'in state was able to conquer the six rival states and eventually unify China. Had the Ch'in Dynasty lasted as long as the Han, Confucianism would have disappeared; fortunately, it lasted only two reigns. After the establishment of the Han Dynasty, the government searched for the Confucian works that had not been destroyed, thus making it manifest that it intended to elevate the *Six Classics*[9] above all other works. From then on and for more than 2,000 years, all people in China have honored the teachings of Confucius, though different groups may emphasize different aspects of his teachings and thus maintain separate schools.

Today the situation is entirely different. Though still studying Confucian works, our scholars today also busy themselves with Western learning, which in fact has absorbed all of their attention. In the capital, which is by far the most important place in the nation, these Western-oriented scholars establish schools and recruit students to learn about alien ideas. The most radical of them even suggest the selection of talented young men to be sent abroad to study Western subjects. Can we infer from their action that the Confucian classics are no longer good enough as topics of learning? The number of translated works has increased each day; all of them, as far as I can see, deal with petty, abstruse subjects and are full of strange, unorthodox ideas. Overwhelmed with joy when reading these books, many of our scholars begin to look down upon the Confucian classics, which to them have become prosaic and commonplace. Some of them even criticize Confucius for being a conservative who could not generate new ideas. This kind of criticism has never existed since the beginning of the Han Dynasty! If the present trend continues, I do not know what the end will be. It will not be long before Confucianism disappears completely from the face of the earth.

My third fear is that the universe as we know it may end soon. According to one theory, the beginning of our universe was preceded by a period of chaos and confusion, a theory that does not seem to be incompatible with good reasoning. During this long period of chaos and confusion, the universe as it then existed was totally inanimate—no form of life existed, to say nothing of human beings. It was a period of rest and inactivity in preparation for the emergence of an animate universe. Millions of years must have elapsed before the animate universe began when all living things, including human beings, made their first appearance. This universe, living and organic, has to pass through the same cycle as all organisms on earth. As a man grows, matures, and eventually dies, so the universe will proceed from life to its eventual death. Cosmic in his outlook and concern, a sage is as much devoted to the conservation of the vitality of the universe as he is to the preservation of his own health.

The *Book of Rites* says: "A fisherman can find fish in lakes and rivers only because the otter, as a matter of habit, eats only a small fraction of its catch. A hunter can find game in the forest only because the jackal, as a matter of habit, kills only a small portion of its booty. No man should trap a pigeon until it has transformed itself into an eagle,[10] and only in wintertime should a man be allowed to collect firewood in the forest." Mencius, on his part, also advises us to refrain from fishing without restraint and to fell trees only at the right time. The meaning of all this advice is clear: man should conserve not only the useful objects in the world but also the vitality of the universe.

The Westerners, doing their best to exhaust all the natural resources to meet temporary needs, have acted in direct opposition to this principle. As one of our ancient proverbs says, "To dry a lake to fish is to end fishing forever." I have learned that the Westerners consume coal in a ruthless manner and consequently their coal reserves have become smaller and smaller each day. As for this matter called coal, it has a form visible to man, but its vitality, which cannot be expressed in concrete terms, remains unknown. If the supply of coal can be exhausted when consumed in a ruthless manner, all the natural resources in the universe will become extinct if they are to be destroyed in the same manner. Then the universe will become barren and unproductive, and all living things, including human beings, will disappear from the face of the earth. This is what I mean when I say that the universe may come to an end soon.

NOTES

[1] Source: *The Complete Works of Yü Yüeh* (*Ch'un-tsai-t'ang ch'üan-chi*), vol. 6.
[2] A sage ruler of the legendary period.
[3] Huang-ti or the Yellow Emperor was a legendary ruler of China's remote past.
[4] Legendary rulers of the remote past.
[5] Chou Ch'eng-wang (r. c. 1115–c. 1079 B.C.).
[6] Located in either modern Cambodia or South Vietnam.
[7] Duke Chou or Chou Kung then served as prime minister to King Ch'eng, who was actually his nephew.
[8] Both were Legalist philosophers of the fourth century B.C.
[9] The *Six Classics* are the *Book of Odes,* the *Book of History,* the *Book of Changes,* the *Book of Rites,* the *Spring and Autumn Annals,* and the *Book of Music.* The last-mentioned has been lost since the third century B.C.
[10] A misinterpretation of the origin of the eagle.

CHAPTER SEVEN

Sino-Russian Relations, 1689-1896

With Russia's emergence as a powerful state in the sixteenth century, the direction of territorial expansion over the Eurasian continent was reversed. Previously the Tartars, starting from their home base in Mongolia, had moved westward to occupy all of West Asia and part of Eastern Europe; now Europe found its agent of expansion across the same continent in Russia. During the sixteenth and seventeenth centuries when the Western Europeans were spreading eastward along the southern sea routes, the Russians pushed steadily in the same direction overland in the north. In 1639 they finally reached the eastern end of the Eurasian continent and "discovered" the Sea of Okhotsk. Unlike the Western Europeans, whose purpose of expansion along the southern sea routes was primarily commercial, the Russians had in mind territorial aggrandizement as well as commercial advantages. By the middle of the seventeenth century the vast area south of the Arctic Circle and north of the ancient silk route had been brought under Russian influence. This area being sparsely populated, its tint on the world map was irrevocably dyed a Russian color.

As Russia continued to expand eastward, she was bound sooner or later to clash with the rising power of the Ch'ing empire. Before conquering China in 1644, the Manchu regime had been content to let the Russians do whatever they pleased in pursuing their territorial conquests. Now that China was firmly brought under its control, the regime began for the first time to turn its attention to the security of its northeastern frontier. Intermittent clashes between Russian and Chinese forces continued throughout the 1650's and 1660's; it was not until the 1680's, however, that the Manchu rulers decided to take more forcible action. Emperor K'ang-hsi warned the Russians against their "turbulent" behavior in the Amur River area and vowed to exterminate them if it continued (Selection 48). Later, when it became clear that neither side could impose its will upon the other, a compromise was reached in the Treaty of Nerchinsk in 1689 (Selection 49), the first treaty that China ever concluded with a Western power. The treaty delimited the Russo-Chinese boundary in the Amur region and was later supplemented by another treaty (the Treaty of Kiakhta, 1727) that regulated the boundary line in the Mongolian area.

After 1689 and for more than a century and a half, peace prevailed on the northern frontier, and trade prospered to the benefit of both sides. From time to time Russia sent envoys to China, and China, on her part, responded in her own fashion (Selection 50). However, when Russian merchants arrived over the sea routes and attempted to trade at Canton, the Chinese refused, on the grounds that different foreign countries could trade only at different, predesignated markets and that no exception would be made to this rule (Selection 51). For her own reasons China insisted that trade with Russia should be confined to the northern frontier.

The generally amiable relations between the two countries came to an end in 1847 when Russia seized upon China's weakness, as revealed in the Opium War, as a golden opportunity for expanding territorially at China's expense. In that year the tsar appointed Count Nikolai Muraviev as governor-general of eastern Siberia with special instructions to investigate and explore the Amur region. Seven years later Muraviev and his agents succeeded in occupying the entire region, which according to the Treaty of Nerchinsk was clearly Chinese (Selection 52). In 1858 when England and France were invading China from the sea and the Taiping rebels were ravaging the Yangtze Valley on land, Muraviev presented to the local Chinese officials a set of territorial demands. The officials, knowing that they could not count on the central government to send reinforcements against any military action the Russians might take, consented to the demands (Selection 53). In the Treaty of Aigun (Selection 54), the Chinese agreed not only to the cession to Russia of all territories north of the Amur River but also to joint control of the land lying between the Ussuri River and the sea. Two years later, when the allied troops of England and France were on a rampage in Peking (Chapter IV), the Russians saw another opportunity. General Ignatief, the Russian minister to China, successfully "persuaded" the Chinese to sign another document, the Treaty of Peking, whereby China agreed to cede to Russia the territories between the Ussuri and the sea (Selection 55).

After the Treaty of Peking, no major issue developed between Russia and China until 1871, when Russia sent her troops to occupy Ili, an enclave on the northwestern corner of Sinkiang (Selection 56). When the news arrived at Peking, counsel among the Chinese officials was divided as to what China should do: some advocated an all-out offensive to recover the lost territory, while others were in favor of its abandonment. Eventually a middle course was followed, which called for negotiations with Russia to regain the lost territory in return for China's willingness to make some commercial and pecuniary concessions (Selection 57). In the final settlement, as incorporated in the Treaty of Ili (Selection 58), China conceded to Russia the western portion of Ili, in addition to the payment of 9,000,000 rubles to compensate Russia for "the expenses occasioned by her occupation of Ili since 1871" and the opening of two more Chinese cities for Russian trade; Russia, on her part, agreed to surrender to China the eastern or larger portion of the contested territory. After the treaty was signed, each country hailed it as a victory for itself.

Ironically, the last major concession to the Russians during the period under discussion was made by China of her own accord. In 1895 China was defeated by Japan in the Sino-Japanese War and was forced to conclude the most humiliating treaty that she had ever had to sign with a foreign power (Selection 70). To prevent further Japanese encroachment and perhaps also to seek revenge, she turned to Russia for help. A secret treaty of alliance was finally concluded which called for mutual assistance against future Japanese aggression, for the use of Chinese ports by Russia in case of war, and for China's agreement to Russia's construction of a railroad (later known as the Chinese Eastern Railroad) across Manchuria to reach Vladivostok (Selection 59). Though the treaty said explicitly that Russia should not use the construction of the railroad as an excuse to occupy Chinese territories, she was nevertheless formally invited into Manchuria. The future of Manchuria was to be determined by the Russo-Japanese struggle, while the Chinese were forced to the sidelines.

48 • K'ANG-HSI: *On the Repulsion of the Russians*[1]

War is never a good policy to follow and should be employed only as the last resort. Some time ago the Russians invaded our border regions without any provocation on our part; they passed across our national boundaries and slowly and gradually infiltrated into areas within our jurisdiction. Our people at Solun, Heichen, Feiyak'e, and Ch'ileherh became the victims of their rampages and were not given a moment's peace. Their villages were looted, their relatives were kidnaped, and their property such as animal hides and furs was forcibly taken away from them. The invaders also shielded Chinese criminals who had escaped to the Russian side but were wanted by the law in China.

Because of the great damage the Russians inflicted over a number of years, I once gave them this warning: "I want you to know that there has never been any lack of reason for us to send an expeditionary force to exterminate you, since you have repeatedly invaded our territories without provocation and robbed our border people without restraint. But I have been reluctant to take this step without warning you in advance. Consequently I have time and again ordered you to withdraw your looters from our territories and to return to us all the Chinese criminals who have escaped to your side and are now under your protection. Only in this way can the citizens of both countries live in peace, each in its own territory, and trade with each other to the benefit of both." Time and again I sent men and letters to the other side to explain clearly my intentions, but Russia, unfortunately, did not choose to reply. Instead, she and her men continued to rob and steal in Haichen, Feiyak'e, and other border areas. Reluctantly I sent troops to Aigun so as to intercept their lines of transportation, but they maintained their occupation of our territories as before and refused to extradite to us criminals who had escaped from our jurisdiction.

Though I am now forced to employ military means to redress an outstanding wrong, I keep reminding myself that war is never a good policy. Whatever I do, I want all of you to know that I am merely following the wishes of Heaven. The moment the expeditionary force reaches Albazin [Ya-k'e-sa] it should send to the Russians a messenger bearing the following message from me:

"For several years I have repeatedly sent to you envoys and messages, ordering you to withdraw from our territories and to return to us the absconders who are now under your protection. So far I have received no word of reply. Not only have you failed to return our absconders, you have also invaded our territories, ravaged local communities, and kidnaped our men, women, and children. It seems that you propose no limit to your outrages. Though I am now forced by your action to send an expeditionary force to intercept your lines of transportation, I have nevertheless issued an order that the Russians living in the Hengkun and its neighboring areas should be allowed to be naturalized as Chinese citizens. The Russians who choose to surrender themselves voluntarily will not only have their lives spared but also be given a means of livelihood. Since you have refused to leave Albazin, I have no choice but to dislodge you with military might. I wish to warn you that once the expeditionary force arrives, your city will be destroyed and all of its defenders will be reduced to ashes.

"I, as Emperor of China, extend my love and compassion to all people on earth, including the Russians. It is my hope that all people on earth will live in peace and security and earn a satisfactory livelihood for themselves and their families. Time and again I have warned you about your outrages precisely because I cannot bear to see all of you exterminated. If you wish to live in peace and enjoy your occupation, you should immediately withdraw to the Ya-k'u [Yakutsk] area, which will be used as a point of demarcation between your country and ours. You can do whatever you wish on your side of the boundary line, but you will not be allowed to cross the boundary line into our territories to engage in improper activities. If you choose to extradite to us our absconders, we shall return to you those Russians who have surrendered to us. Only in this way can the peace of the frontier be secured, trade be conducted to the benefit of both sides, and people in the border regions be spared from looting and disorder. If you refuse to listen to reason, however, the expeditionary force will march toward Albazin, destroy the city, and exterminate all of its defenders."

We should send a man to the Russians to bring to them this message, telling them what we intend to do. If they comply with our demand, we, on our part, would agree to use Ya-k'u as a point of demarcation between our two countries. The garrison troops stationed at Aigun should be ordered to post sentries in the Albazin region to secure peace and order in this general area. If the Russians continue to resist and refuse to cooperate, the expeditionary force should be given the authority to do what it considers most appropriate under the circumstances. If we did not have a plan like that outlined above, there would be no end to the war even if we captured Albazin. When we advanced, the Russians would retreat; when we withdrew, the Russians would advance. Thus the people in the border areas would never know a moment of peace.

Whether my plan is proper, let all counselors, princes, and ministers deliberate carefully and report their findings to me.

NOTES

[1] This decree was issued on January 20, 1685, shortly before an expeditionary force was sent to attack the Russian stronghold Albazin. Source: *Personal Writings of Emperor K'ang-hsi* (*K'ang-hsi yü-chih wen*), vol. 2.

49 • *Treaty of Nerchinsk (1689): A Summary*[1]

1. The boundary line between China and Russia shall be the Gorbitsa, the river that is the closest to Chorna, also named Ourouan,[2] which flows northward into the Amur River. From the mouth of this river the boundary line follows the watershed of the Outer Hsingan Mountains[3] all the way towards the sea.[4] All the rivers south of this watershed belong to China; all the rivers north of the watershed belong to Russia. The only exception is a group of local rivers that lie south of the Oudi[5] and north of the Outer Hsingan Mountains, whose ownership will not be decided upon at this time. A decision will be made after the plenipotentiaries of the contracting powers return to their respective countries and have an opportunity to study this matter more carefully. The matter shall be then settled via diplomatic dispatches or ambassadorial conferences.

2. The Argun River, which flows into the Amur River, shall be the boundary line between China and Russia. The territories south of this river belong to China; the territories north of the river belong to Russia. The Russian settlements presently located at the mouth of the Meritken River, which drains an area south of the Argun River, shall be evacuated and moved to the northern bank of the Argun River.

3. All the fortifications built by the Russians at Albazin[6] shall be completely demolished. The subjects of Russia who presently inhabit Albazin shall be moved to an area or areas under the jurisdiction of the Russian Czar.

4. The hunters of China and Russia shall not be allowed to pass over the delimited boundaries. If one or two unprincipled persons secretly and without authorization cross the boundary lines to steal cattle or engage in other predatory activities, they shall be arrested and returned to the officials under whose jurisdiction they have lived. They shall be punished in accordance with their offense. In the event of an armed gathering of ten or fifteen persons that is found to have been engaged in robbery, murder, or both, a report shall and must be made to the Emperors of both of the contracting powers, and the offenders shall be put to death on the spot. Under no circumstances, however, shall China or Russia resort to the use of military forces against the other side on account of some unauthorized offensive acts committed by subjects of either of the contracting powers.

5. The events that have occurred in the past shall not be the subject of discussion between the two contracting powers. The Russians who now live under Chinese jurisdiction and the Chinese who presently live under Russian jurisdiction shall be allowed to stay where they are. Neither China nor Russia shall demand their return to their respective countries.

6. Having pledged eternal peace for each other, the two contracting powers agree that all the traders and travelers, as long as they possess valid passports, shall be allowed to trade on each other's territories.

7. Beginning with the date on which this treaty is signed, neither of the contracting powers shall take into her protection fugitives or deserters who come from the other side. The said fugitives or deserters shall be arrested and returned to the side wherefrom they come.

NOTES

[1] This is a summarized version translated by this author from the Chinese, with references from the French version. A copy of the Chinese original can be found in *A*

SINO-RUSSIAN RELATIONS, 1689-1896

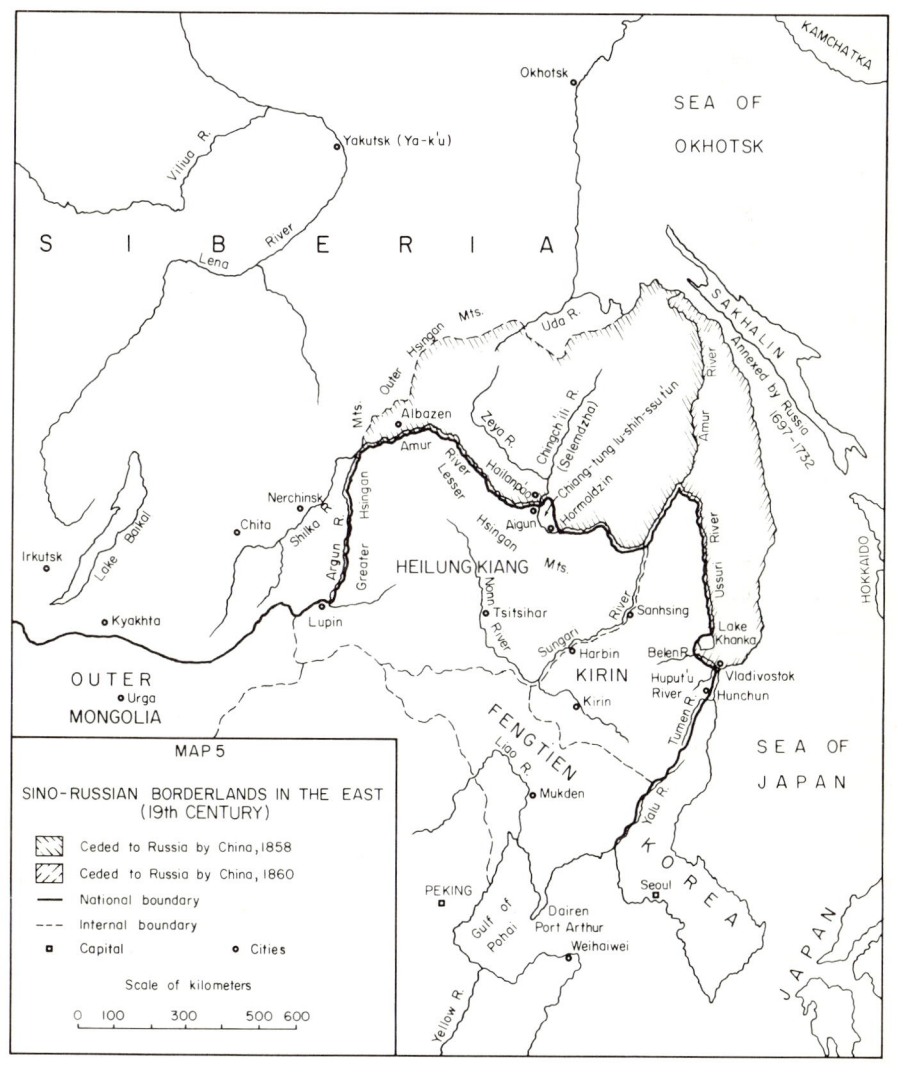

Description of the Northern Countries (*Shuo-fang pei-ch'eng*), roll 8. A French version can be found in Edward Hertslet, *Treaties, &c., between Great Britain and China and Between China and Foreign Powers,* vol. I, pp. 292–294.

[2] Sometimes spelled Ourouon.

[3] In the French version these mountains are referred to as "cette longue chaîne de montagnes" without naming them.

[4] Sea of Okhotsk. It is referred to as "la mer Orientale" in the French version.

[5] Sometimes spelled as Oud or Uda.

[6] In the French version it is spelled Yacsa, which is closer to the Chinese pronunciation (*Ya-k'e-sa*).

50 • K'ANG-HSI: *Instructions to a Chinese Envoy*[1]

The Russian tsar may wish to meet you when you are traveling in Russian territories on your way to or from the Torguts. If he does, you can either pay him a visit immediately or send a man to confirm the invitation before you proceed to see him, all depending upon the circumstances. In any event, both of you, T'u-li-tseng and Hsin-man-chu, should make the trip in person, when and if you are invited. If the tsar does not wish to meet you, do not insist that you have to see him. Upon meeting with him, you should perform the ritual according to the Russian custom. You may also remark something like this to his ministers: "When your envoy Ni-kuo-lai[2] came to China, his behavior was outrageous. We, as envoys from China, do not wish to follow his bad example."

If the tsar questions you about the faith the Chinese believe in, you should answer him as follows: "All people in our country believe in loyalty, filial piety, love, righteousness, and trustfulness, and they attach great importance to proper conduct. They rely on these virtues not only to cultivate themselves as ethical beings but to govern their country as well. They uphold these virtues with great perseverance and will not deviate from them even when confronted with the most serious danger or facing the worst temptation. . . . As a result, all people in China live in peace and harmony with one another, and the threat of disturbance or war is altogether absent. Few ever commit crimes, and consequently there is no need for severe punishment. We, in fact, have enjoyed peace for a long time." If he questions you about the way our people earn their livelihood, you may say that there are all kinds of occupation in China and that there are poor as well as rich people.

Several years ago, I heard that there was a war between Russia and some neighboring country of hers [Sweden]. Russia would like to move her troops from her border with China to Europe, where they would be employed to combat her enemy. She hesitated, however, because she was afraid that we might take advantage of her weakened position in the East to expand Chinese territories. Bearing in mind that Russia and China had lived in peace for many years, I specially instructed the General of Heilungkiang to send a message to the Russian garrison at Ni-pu-ch'u [Nerchinsk] expressing unmistakably my peaceful intentions. I assured the Russians that they need have no fear of us and that they were free to move their troops from the East to Europe.

If the tsar questions you about the aged people in China, you should say, "Each year our emperor takes a census of the aged population in China and finds that there are twenty or thirty 100 years old or older and more than 10,000 between 90 and 100 years old in each of the provinces." You should also mention that aged citizens, when certified, receive generous rewards from the emperor.

It is perhaps inevitable that the Russians will mention cannons and other firearms. If they request these things from China, you should say that it is extremely difficult to transport them from China to Russia in view of the great distance between these two countries. Furthermore, according to the Chinese law, no man in China can export firearms to foreign countries without the government's special permission.

The Russians are a proud people and love to show off. It is almost certain that they will display their products to impress you. If they do, you should by no means show amazement or astonishment. Nor should you show contempt or condescension either. You should instead remark as follows: "It is difficult for me to say whether we have these products in China or not. Each of us in China has his own assigned duties. I may have seen things other Chinese have never seen. On the other hand, there are things which I may not have seen myself but which are nevertheless familiar to others. In short, it is very difficult for me to answer your question."

During your journey in Russia, all of you should consult among yourselves and reach a consensus before you act together. You should never drink to excess. You should of course enforce strict discipline among your retainers. The customs in the areas where you have to travel, including Russia, are extremely bad, and women of loose morals can be found everywhere. Strict discipline must be maintained among your retainers, who are not allowed to engage in improper conduct under any circumstances. When you see a Russian woman or witness something really funny, you should not let yourselves go; i.e., you should not laugh or make casual remarks. Remember that you must conduct yourselves in a serious manner at all times.

If the Russians present you with gifts, you should not accept them immediately. You should return them with thanks, saying: "Since we do not have anything special to present to the tsar, how dare we accept such generous gifts from him?" If they insist, in that case you should accept only one or two items. In return you should present to the tsar the silk and velvet that you have brought with you. You should say to him: "In view of the great distance between Russia and China, we have not been able to bring with us any fine items. This is only a small token showing the pleasure we take in meeting you." If the tsar, not wishing to meet you in person, sends an envoy to speak with you instead, you should give the gifts to his envoy, saying: "We have nothing special to present to the tsar as gifts, and these small items are merely tokens of the affection which we have always felt toward him."

Since Russian law is extremely harsh, you should not mention to Russian officials minor offenses that your retainers may have committed inadvertently. You should be generous, proper, and serious at all times.

If the Russians question you about the kind of posts you hold in China, you should say that you are merely officials in the Outer Court and are not close to the emperor by any means.

During your journey you should pay attention to the way the Russians make their livelihood and also Russian geography.³

NOTES

¹ In 1712 Emperor K'ang-hsi sent T'u-li-tseng (Tulisen), an official then associated with the Bureau of Foreign Affairs (*Chih-fang ssu*), to serve as personal envoy to the Torguts with whom the emperor wished to form an alliance against Dzungaria, a country

then located in modern Turkestan. Originally situated in the T'ach'eng area (northern section of modern Sinkiang province), the Torguts, a nomadic tribe, were forced by the Dzungars to move westward, and finally settled in the lower valley of the Volga. Since the Chinese envoy had to pass through Russian territories before he could reach his destination, Emperor K'ang-hsi went to great detail telling him how he should behave when meeting with the Russians. The "Instruction" was dated May 26, 1712. Source: Ho Ch'iu-t'ao, *A Description of the Northern Countries (Shuo-fang pei-ch'eng)*, roll 43.

[2] Nicholas Gavrilovitch Spathar-Milescu came to China as a Russian envoy in 1675. Upon his arrival, he insisted on presenting his credentials to Emperor K'ang-hsi in person, without these credentials being examined in advance by Chinese officials in accordance with the Chinese custom; he also refused to perform the ritual of kowtow when introduced to the Chinese emperor. Though he performed the kowtow during a later audience, he refused to repeat it when he received presents from K'ang-hsi on behalf of the Russian tsar. That is why K'ang-hsi regarded his behavior as outrageous.

[3] K'ang-hsi's envoy never did see Peter the Great, who was then engaged in a life-and-death struggle against Charles XII of Sweden.

51 • YEN-FENG ET AL.: *Russian Ships at Canton*[1]

On the twenty-ninth day of the tenth year of Chia-ch'ing [December 19, 1805] Yen-feng, Superintendent of Customs at Canton, memorialized the government as follows:

"On the eighth day of this month [November 28, 1805] our commissioner at Macao reported that a Lu-ch'en merchant named Lu-ch'en-tun [Krusenstern] arrived at Macao in a commercial ship. On the seventeenth day [December 7] he again reported that a commercial ship, loaded with animal hides and silver and owned by a Lu-ch'en merchant named Li-tsan-shih [Lisiansky], came to Canton to trade. According to the Co-hong merchants who have made an investigation, Lu-ch'en is actually Russia [O-lo-ssu], since these two names, in transliteration, really sound similar. Your humble servant has read the petitions of these Lu-ch'en traders rendered into Chinese by the Co-hong merchants.

"According to these petitions, the home port of these ships for their eastward voyage is in Russia. Traditionally the trade between Russia and China has been conducted in the markets north of the capital [Peking]. Since the routes from Russia to these markets are by land, they are extremely difficult to traverse. The sea routes from Russia to Canton are somewhat longer, but the expenses involved are much smaller than by the land routes. That is why some Russian traders prefer to come to China by the sea route. The two Russian ships mentioned above had animal hides for sale; they were not warships by any means. Their owners asked us as a special favor to allow them to unload their cargoes.

"Russia, being located in the extreme north, has not until now come to Canton to trade by the sea route. Now these two Russian traders, having undergone all kinds of danger on the high seas, have finally arrived at Canton to request the same privilege that traders of other countries have long enjoyed. Your humble servant realized that this privilege had never been granted to Russians before and that it was difficult to establish a precedent. However, their words were humble and sincere, and to turn them back empty-handed would seem to be incompatible with Your Majesty's desire of maintaining friendly relations with all countries. Therefore, having ordered responsible officials to make the necessary inspection, in accordance with the established rules, of both ships and the cargoes therein, your humble servant instructed the Co-hong merchants to go ahead and trade with these

Russian merchants. He insisted, however, that the trade must be conducted fairly and on a mutually beneficial basis.

"Russia has traded in Ch'ia-k'e-t'u [Kyakhta] for years, and there have never been any clashes between her merchants and ours. Now suddenly her merchants come to Canton by sea. Their action in this regard is doubtless motivated by their desire to save expenses and thus realize a larger profit. If we allow them to trade at Canton, the trade volume in our northern market will be gradually but inevitably reduced, and the revenue hitherto collected at Kalgan will suffer as a result. Your humble servant cannot make any comment on the trading situation in Ch'ia-k'e-t'u, since he is altogether unfamiliar with it. As for Russian trade at Canton, he is requesting Your Majesty's instruction with regard to future course to follow...."

On the ninth day of the twelfth month [January 28, 1806] the imperial government issued a decree which read as follows:

"What Yen-feng did in connection with the Russian traders at Canton was rash and careless in the extreme. Different foreign countries are allowed to trade at different, predesignated markets, and no exception should be made to this rule. We have never heard of a country called Lu-ch'en before, and the arrival of her merchants at Canton for the purpose of trade was certainly unprecedented. The superintendent of customs at Canton should have followed the established rule, either ordering the ships to return wherever they came from or allowing them to anchor at the port temporarily while petitioning the imperial government for instructions. But he chose to act at the behest of the Co-hong merchants and allowed the ships to unload their cargoes.

"Yen-feng, Na-yen-ch'eng,[2] and Sun Yü-t'ing[3] should all be reprimanded for their rash action. Since Yen-feng was primarily responsible. he should also be handed over to the Ministry of Justice for trial and punishment. As for Na-yen-ch'eng and Sun Yü-t'ing, the Ministry of Justice should investigate their cases individually and see whether there is ground for indictment.

"The moment Wu Hsiang-kuang[4] arrives at his post, he should immediately make inquiry to ascertain whether the so-called Lu'ch'en is really Russia. . . . If at some future time a ship arrives in Canton from a country that has never traded there before, the responsible officials should petition the imperial government for instructions, and under no circumstances are they allowed to make decisions on their own."

NOTES

[1] *Ch'ing-tai wai-chiao shih-liao*, vol. 1, p. 37 and p. 45.
[2] Governor-general of Kwangtung and Kwangsi Provinces.
[3] Governor of Kwangtung.
[4] The new governor-general.

52 • CHING-CH'UN: *Russian Ships on the Amur*[1]

In the fifth month of this year a memorandum was received from the General of Heilungkiang in connection with the sailing of Russian ships toward the Eastern Seas for the alleged purpose of setting up defenses against the British.[2] In a memorandum to the General, we inquired about the number of people in these ships as well as their destination and requested a speedy reply to our questions. The reply, which has just arrived, quotes a report made by Hu Sun-pu, the deputy military commander of Heilungkiang, saying that upon boarding the Russian ships and inquiring about the purpose of their trip, he was informed by the Russians that they intended to reach the Eastern Seas by way of the Amur and the Sungari for the purpose of setting up defenses against the British who, they contended, had occupied some Russian islands on the eastern fringe of the Russian territory. "Since we have already notified the Chinese authorities in Peking of the trip," they continued, "we request your permission to let us pass."

Since Hu Sun-pu had not received any instructions from the Bureau of Foreign Affairs[3] in connection with this trip, he decided to stop the Russians from advancing any further. The Russians replied that they must wait for the arrival of their governor-general before discussion could be resumed. About noon a large ship with bronze chimneys, flanked on both sides by a number of small ships, arrived and was subsequently anchored north of the city. Together with his assistant Hsi-li-pu, Hu Sun-pu boarded this ship and met with a Russian official named [Nikolai] Muraviev. The Russian stated that some of the Russian islands on the eastern fringe of the Russian territory had been occupied by the British, that he was ordered by his government to take a short route down the Amur and the Sungari to reach the Eastern Seas, that he and his men would not disturb local Chinese communities on their way to the east, and that to deny him passage would be a violation of the friendly relations between our two countries. When Hu Sun-pu questioned him about his failure to notify Chinese authorities in advance of his proposed trip, the Russian replied that none of the Chinese frontier stations along the route had tried to stop him. Questioned again whether there would be other ships following him, he replied that he had only 1,000 men with him, with no reinforcements whatever. An official of ours was then dispatched to the other side of the river to make an investigation. Upon his return, he reported that the Russians had 83 ships and about 2,000 men, and that these ships were more provisioned with food than with firearms. Besides these, there were 4 barges, approximately 100 horses, and more than 80 head of cattle, in addition to 2 boats loaded with women.

Since their entry into Chinese territory, the Russians have not caused any damage or disturbance in the areas where they traveled. As we do not have enough men and arms in the Eastern Provinces [Manchuria], it does not seem wise to provoke an argument. One day, while Hu Sun-pu was speaking with the Russians in the most friendly terms, the latter's small boats suddenly hoisted their sails and began to move. Had Hu been determined to prevent them from sailing, the friendly atmosphere which had prevailed would have been immediately destroyed. Instead, he dispatched a reliable official to follow the Russians wherever they went.

Enclosed please find the original copy of Muraviev's memorandum to the Bureau of Foreign Affairs, plus a letter addressed by him to the city of Eh-erh-k'ou. I have written to Me-erh-ken, Pu-t'e-ha, and other areas, informing them of his voyage. We cannot of course take the Russian words at their face value; we should watch very carefully what these Russians intend to do. Sanhsing, being strategically located, should take special precautionary measures to counteract any move the Russians may make. The province of Kirin has never had any navy or battleships, and we have only fifty ships, primarily for shipping food. We are now taking emergency steps to strengthen our defense with whatever we have. We intend to instruct Superintendent Ta-sheng-wu-la to recruit sailors among expert swimmers who, once chosen, will be put on the reserve list for possible action. Sanhsing is 1,300 *li* from the provincial capital, and the fort of Heiho is another 1,000 *li* from Sanhsing. Of all the upper valleys in this remote region, only that of the Sungari is navigable. I intend to instruct all officials in the areas near Sanhsing, such as K'o-leh-ch'u-k'e and Pai-tu-na, to strengthen their river patrol.

NOTES

[1] This memorial, written by the General (Governor) of Kirin, is dated June 24, 1854. Source: *Ch'ou-pan yi-wu shih-mo*, roll 8, pp. 5–6.
[2] This was the time of the Crimean War.
[3] Li-fan Yüan.

53 • YI-SHAN: *Negotiations with Muraviev*[1]

On the fifth day of the fourth month [May 17, 1858] your humble servant arrived at the city of Heilungkiang [Aigun] from the provincial capital. Shortly after his arrival, he received a report from one of our frontier officials, saying that Muraviev[2] was sailing downstream on the Amur River and would arrive at Hailanp'ao[3] on or about the sixth [May 18]. Your humble servant immediately sent Lieutenant Colonel Chi-la-ming-oh to meet him. Upon his return, Chi-la-ming-oh reported that Muraviev would not stay at Hailanp'ao for long, since he was very busy and had to leave for K'uot'un shortly to take care of urgent business. Only after repeated requests did the Russian finally agree to meet with me on the tenth [May 22]. On that day, accompanied by a translator named Shishmarev and scores of other Russian officials, he left the boat and entered the city. Muraviev's words, as interpreted by Shishmarev, went something like this: Owing to the necessity of taking preventive measures against the British,[4] his country found it necessary to navigate the Amur River and to build houses on its left [northern] bank. In addition to its present strength, Russia would dispatch several hundred more ships to this area for garrison duties during the current year. Moreover, the Amur area was actually Russian territory, and all the Chinese households located on the left bank of the river should be moved to the right [southern] bank. If moving expenses were needed, said Muraviev, Russia would be happy to defray them. As for the boundary line between Russia and China, all the rivers between the Chabigai Mountains and the sea, such as the Argun that flows into the Amur, the Ussuri, and the Sungari, were jointly owned by Russia and China, and only these two countries could navigate these rivers, to the exclusion of all others. The Russian further stated that he had sent a memorandum to the Bureau of Foreign Affairs in Peking on this important point: that from then on all ports along the above-mentioned rivers would be open to trade and that both Russia and China should send officials to the trading ports for supervisory duties. The province of Heilungkiang, he added, should not be an exception. "Since we are governors of our respective countries with authority duly entrusted to us by our respective sovereigns," he continued, "we should immediately ratify what I have stated and exchange pertinent documents, so that each side can defend its own territories and peace between our two countries can be maintained."

In reply, your humble servant stated that the boundary line between Russia and China had always been the Gorbitsa River and the [Outer] Hsingan Mountains, that no changes had been made since its delimitation was agreed upon by both sides, and that I, as a border official, could not agree to the suggestions which he had just made. As far as trade was concerned, your humble servant continued, Heilungkiang was cold, barren, and unproductive and did not produce anything worthy of trade. Even the food we produced—rice, wheat, and vegetables—was barely adequate for our own sustenance and certainly could not be used as trade items. Moreover, the people in this area were truculent and violent by nature and were extremely difficult to administer, and the opening of ports for trade might create dissensions and feuds between Russians and Chinese which would affect adversely the good relations between our two countries. "I earnestly hope," your humble servant concluded, "that you will withdraw your men and ships at the earliest moment so that the good relations between our two countries can continue."

Muraviev was treacherous and cunning in his arguments. He resorted to defensive language whenever he ran short of rationalizations. Sometimes he pretended ignorance. The arguments continued until the sunset, but nothing was resolved. About ten o'clock the next morning, Muraviev, accompanied by the same retinue, arrived and was received with courtesy as usual. He presented two copies of his proposals, one in Chinese and the other in Russian. The language in his written proposals was even more absurd than it had been in oral form, and your humble servant reminded him, time and again, of his mistakes. But he continued to argue in the most irrational manner. Finally, knowing that he had no more arguments to advance, he left and returned to his ship. Meanwhile your humble servant sent Lieutenant Ai-shen-t'ai to return to him the Russian copy of his proposals. Later, Muraviev ordered his translator to submit his proposals to us again, one copy in Russian and the other in Chinese. The proposals said in effect that to maintain the friendly relations between our two countries, the Chinese households on the left bank of the Amur River and also those between River Chingch'ili in the north and the village of Huolehmuerhchin in the south could stay in their present sites permanently, but the vast, unoccupied expanse bordering the Russian territories should be used for stationing Russian troops against possible attacks by the British. As for trade, the proposals called for the implementation of the same rules that governed China's sea ports, i.e., trade to be supervised by appointed officials from both sides. The proposals further stated that the entire lengths, from their origins to the sea, of such rivers as the Argan, Amur, Sungari, and Ussuri, together with their adjacent territories, were to be jointly owned by Russia and China, and only these two countries were to navigate them, to the exclusion of all others.

Being determined to delete or change the clause that said in effect that certain rivers were to serve as boundary lines between Russia and China, your humble servant sent Lieutenant Ai-shen-t'ai to Muraviev's boat, carrying my counterproposals. Upon his return, Ai-shen-t'ai reported that the Russian, while accepting the document, nevertheless maintained that the clause governing the delimitation of boundaries by rivers could not be either changed or deleted. All other matters, said the Russian, would be discussed the next day when he entered the city to confer with me. For two days your humble servant waited for him in vain; allegedly he was ill. It was not until the noon of the fourteenth [May 26, 1858] that he suddenly arrived at my residence with several of his lieutenants. Taking notice of his failure to make any deletions or changes in his proposals, your humble servant began to reason with him. Moreover, as the Ussuri River areas were within the territorial jurisdiction of Kirin and since, under pressure from Muraviev, the issue could not be postponed, I consulted San-lung, the commissioner from Kirin, with regard to the situation in these areas. San-lung replied that he would have to make an inquiry before he could provide a definite answer. As the discussion went on, Muraviev suddenly lost his temper and acted in a violent, lunatic manner. He shouted to his interpreter in a language which nobody could understand, picked up the Russian copy of his proposals, and then left without a departing word. San-lung asked Shishmarev why Muraviev had suddenly become angry, but the Russian interpreter did not reply, only saying that they would deliver to us another proposal the next day. Hurriedly Muraviev and his lieutenants returned to their ships, which were anchored on the other side of the river.

Already before Muraviev's arrival, five Russian ships loaded with several hundred well-equipped soldiers had sailed downstream and were finally anchored less than 100 *li* from this place. When Muraviev arrived, he was accompanied by two large ships with two or three hundred men, all of them equipped with rifles, cannons, and other military hardware. So far these ships had been peaceful and quiet. The evening after Muraviev had angrily returned to his ship, however, the situation completely changed. Across the river we saw all the Russian ships brightly lighted, and the sound of rifles and cannons continued throughout the night. On the next morning Lieutenant Colonel Chi-la-oh-p'eng, together with many other officials, came to see me; they reported that Muraviev seemed to be determined to provoke a conflict by firing rifles and cannons at night, because we had not granted him the boundary concessions he requested during the day. If hostilities began, said Chi-la-oh-p'eng, there was no telling when they would end, since Muraviev had in his rear military reserves upon which he could rely for reinforcement. Moreover, the Chinese who lived on the eastern bank of the river had already panicked; they entered the city and pleaded with the government for protection. If hostilities did begin, Chi-la-oh-p'eng continued, we could rely on Hsi-tan and his militiamen for the defense of the city, but it was extremely doubtful whether we could protect the villages on the banks of the river. The lieutenant colonel concluded by saying that he and other officials would be less than candid if they did not report to me the facts as they saw them and asked me to send officials to calm and assure the villagers.

Upon hearing this report, your humble servant dispatched several officials to the left bank of the river, secretly assuring the villagers that they should carry on life as usual and should not be alarmed. Meanwhile he sent another official to the Russian ship, ostensibly to inquire after Muraviev's health but actually to find out for ourselves what the situation really was. But Muraviev was as arrogant and unreasonable as ever. Through his interpreter he remarked to my envoy as follows: "It was your superior, His Excellency the Governor, who requested a conference with me in connection with the delimitation of boundaries between our two countries. I did not wish to attend this conference; I finally agreed only after his persistent and repeated requests. Yet, when the conference was held, he refused most of the proposals I made, saying that he had no authority to agree to them and that he had to petition the imperial government, which alone could make the decisions. Since Russians have lived in such areas as K'uot'un and Ch'ichi within the jurisdiction of Kirin Province for many years, how is it possible that your government does not know this fact? Now Russian troops are stationed in these areas, to make sure that the British will not dare to come there to make trouble. I myself have given assurance that the Chinese households in the Amur River region do not have to move. Since your governor has been authorized by your government to come here to discuss the delimitation of boundaries, how can he say that he does not have any authority to make boundary changes? Moreover, prior to my arrival, my government conveyed our proposals to the Bureau of Foreign Affairs in Peking, and these proposals have not been turned down as far as we know. Since your governor is the emperor's trusted minister, his refusal to honor our request is obviously a deliberate evasion of responsibilities. Though you have been ordered by your governor to come here to express goodwill, it does not seem to us that your governor is sincerely interested in maintaining peaceful relations between our two countries. Tomorrow I shall send my translator to see your governor, and he will bring with him the pertinent documents. We shall sign and exchange these documents as a testimony to our agreement. If he refuses to sign, I will not allow the Chinese households to live on the left bank of the Amur River and will in fact destroy them."

About 10 A.M. of the fifteenth [May 27] the Russian translator arrived and presented both the Russian and the Chinese copies of the proposed agreement. Though the language in the proposed agreement remains tricky and confused, it seems to be simpler and clearer than the one advanced before. In this agreement it is specified that the Chinese villages will remain where they are.[5] Outside this settlement there is nothing but a vast, empty expanse where few people have so far settled. Since the Sungari and the Ussuri areas are within the jurisdiction of Kirin, your humble servant could not, of course, grant any concessions with regard to them. But the Russians have already occupied such places as K'out'un and Ch'ichi. The proposed agreement also says that the area between the Ussuri River and the sea is jointly owned by Russia and China and that trade between our two countries will be regulated in the same manner as it has been in the coastal ports of China.

Your humble servant realizes that the delimitation of national boundaries is a serious matter and should not be dealt with in a casual manner. In fact, he would have followed the old treaties to settle this dispute, had his situation not been so difficult and untenable. If he had not been flexible enough to sign and exchange the documents, Muraviev would have been very angry and would have opened hostilities. If that occurred, it would be too late to pacify him, and the security of our frontier would in that case be seriously jeopardized. Therefore, risking blame for being rash and ignorant, your humble servant granted the Russians' request and signed the documents, hoping that their greed would be at least temporarily satisfied and the danger we faced would be over. After the exchange of documents,[6] Muraviev withdrew his men and ships. On the sixteenth [May 28] he returned to Hailanp'ao, where he said he would stay for a few days before proceeding to K'out'un and other areas to take care of his urgent business. The Russian residents in Hailanp'ao are now peaceful and quiet.

NOTES

[1] This is a memorial written by Yi-shan, General (Governor) of Heilungkiang, on June 14, 1858. Source: *Ch'ou-pan yi-wu shih-mo*, roll 25, pp. 11–15.

[2] Throughout this translation, "Muraviev," instead of its Chinese version "Mu-li-fei-yo-fu," will be used.

[3] Located on the northern bank of the Amur, across the river from Aigun.

[4] Actually the Crimean War ended before the date of this encounter.

[5] In some maps these villages are called "Sixty-four Villages East of the River" (Chiang-tung lu-shih-ssu t'un), a fraction of an area that was ceded to Russia under the Treaty of Aigun.

[6] This refers to the Treaty of Aigun.

54 • Treaty of Aigun (1858): A Summary[1]

1. The left [northern] bank of the Amur River, from its junction with the Argun River to the point where it pours into the sea [the Gulf of Tatary] shall belong to Russia. Its right [southern] bank, from its junction with the Argun River to its intersection with the Ussuri River, shall belong to China. All areas between the Ussuri River and the Sea [of Japan] that border on both Chinese and Russian territories, shall be held in common by the two contracting powers. No vessels except those of China and Russia shall be allowed to navigate the Amur, the Sungari, and the Ussuri Rivers. The Manchurian inhabitants now settled on the left bank of the Amur, from the Zéia River[2] to the village of Hormoldzin,[3] shall be allowed to live there as usual under the Chinese jurisdiction. Russians shall not be allowed to disturb, harass, or harm them.

2. To secure peace and harmony between the subjects of the two contracting powers, the Chinese and Russian inhabitants on the Ussuri, the Amur, and the Sungari River shall be allowed to trade with each other and among themselves. Chinese and Russian officials have the duty and the obligation to protect these traders on a reciprocal basis.[4]

NOTES

[1] This is a summarized version translated by this author from the Chinese, with references from the French version. A copy of the Chinese original can be found in *Ch'ou-pan yi-wu shih-mo*, the Reign of Hsien-feng, roll 25, p. 16. The French version can be found in Edward Hertslet, *Treaties, &c., Between Great Britain and China and Between China and Foreign Powers*, vol. I, pp. 310-311.

[2] Zéia River in the French text and Chingch'ili River in the Chinese text.

[3] Hormoldzin in the French text and Huoerhmolehchin in the Chinese text.

[4] This treaty was signed by Yi-shan for China and Nikolai Muraviev for Russia on May 6, 1858, at the city of Aigun.

55 • Treaty of Peking (1860): A Summary[1]

1. From the date on which this treaty is signed, the eastern boundary between the two contracting powers [Russia and China] shall begin at the junction of the Ussuri and the Amur Rivers and shall then move upstream along the Ussuri River until it reaches the point where it meets the Sunggali River.[2] Thence it shall move upstream along the Sunggali River until it meets Lake Khanka, across which it passes to reach the mouth of the Belen River. From the mouth of the Belen River it shall follow the crest of the mountains to the mouth of the Huput'u River.[3] Thence it shall move along the mountains between the Hunchun River[4] and the sea to reach the Tumen River. It shall then follow the middle stream of the Tumen River until the latter pours into the Sea [of Japan]. The territories east of this boundary line shall belong to Russia, and the territories west of it shall belong to China.

2. As for the boundary line in the west hitherto undelimited, it shall from now on follow the ridge of the mountains, the course of the great rivers, and the line along which the Chinese government has maintained permanent watchtowers. Beginning with the last watchtower, the boundary line shall move westward to Lake Zaysan[5] and then southwestward along the Tien Shan Mountains to Lake Issyk-Kul'.[6] Thence it shall move southward to the border of Kokand.

3. The Russians shall continue to have the right to trade in Urga, Kalgan, and Peking by the route of Kyakhta. The Chinese shall likewise have the right to trade in Russia. The contracting parties agree to protect each other's merchants along the trade routes on a reciprocal basis and shall do their utmost to prevent cheating and exactions. The Russian merchants can buy and sell as much as they please and stay as long as they choose.

4. To supervise its merchants and to prevent misunderstanding between them and the Chinese inhabitants, the Russian government shall have the right to establish consulates in Kashgar and Urga, in addition to Ili and Tarbagatai. Litigation and complaints over commercial matters shall be settled by arbitration, and the arbiters shall be chosen by the merchants among themselves. The consul and the local authorities shall render assistance for an amiable settlement but shall not assume responsibility for the claims that are advanced by either or both sides to the dispute. Litigation and complaints not related to commercial matters shall be judged by mutual agreement between the consul and the local authorities. The accused, when found guilty, shall be punished in accordance with the laws of his own country. In the event of serious crimes such as murder, robbery, or arson, the culprit shall be sent to Russia to be punished in accordance with the Russian law if he is a Russian and shall be punished by the local Chinese authorities in accordance with the Chinese law if he is a Chinese.

NOTES

[1] This selection consists of some of the major provisions of this Sino-Russian treaty, paraphrased from the Chinese original, a copy of which can be found in *Ch'ou-pan yi-wu shih-mo*, the Reign of Hsien-feng, roll 39, pp. 27–29. A copy of the French version can be found in *Treaties, &c., Between Great Britain and China and Between China and Foreign Powers*, Vol. I, pp. 318–328. The treaty was signed in Peking by Prince Kung for China and Nikolai Ignatiev for Russia on November 14, 1860.

[2] It is Son'gatcha River in the French text.
[3] It is Houpitou River in the French text.
[4] It is Khoun-tchoun River in the French text.
[5] It is Lake Dsai-sang in the French text.
[6] It is Lake Issyk-koul in the French text.

56 • PRINCE KUNG: *Russian Occupation of Ili*[1]

On the thirteenth of this month [August 28, 1871], translator Lenzy of the Russian Embassy arrived at this office and personally presented to me a translated copy of a Russian telegram which was addressed by the Russian official at Hsi-hsi-pi-erh to George Vlangaly,[2] Russian minister to China at Peking. It is stated in this telegram that Governor Kaufmann of Ch'i-ho province, after sending a contingent of troops to Ili, captured that city on the seventeenth of the fifth month [July 4]. The governor was requesting further instructions, the telegram said.

Ili was occupied by a gang of bandits for a long time. Since it was located not far from the Russian border, the Russian minister in Peking repeatedly requested our government to send an expeditionary force to recapture the city and even offered troops to help, on the ground that as long as the bandits stayed in Ili, Russia could not withdraw her troops from the frontier. Each time the Office of

SINO-RUSSIAN RELATIONS, 1689-1896

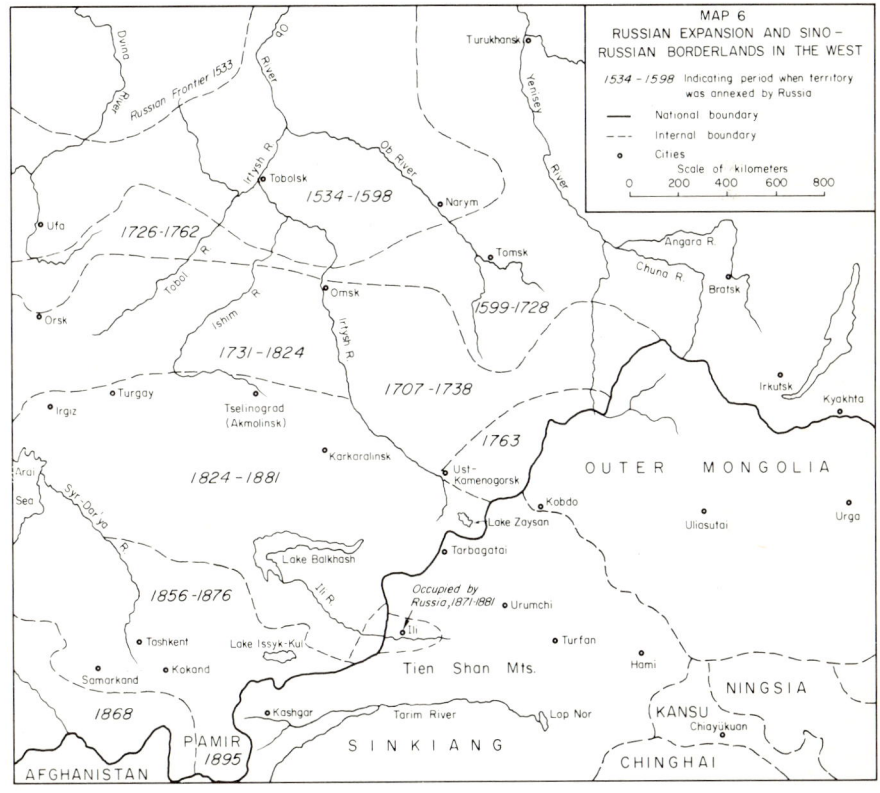

General Management turned down the Russian offer of assistance with thanks, saying that China could not send any expeditionary force to Ili at the moment because of the unsettled situation in Kansu.³ The telegram in question is short and does not describe in detail the Russian occupation. We have no idea at this moment what Russia's next move will be: whether she intends to invade other Chinese territories or whether she has some kind of demand in mind. In either case we should prepare ourselves.

Since Ili is far away from the capital [Peking], we have had great difficulty finding out what the situation really is. Since Uliasutai and Kobdo are close to Ili, it is hereby suggested that the generals and ministers in these areas should be instructed to answer the following questions: Is it true that the Russians have captured Ili? How far is Ili from Uliasutai and Kobdo? To reach there, does one have to take the route of Tarbagatai? Are there any bandits on the road? How are troops to be dispatched to Ili? How are food and military supplies to be transported? We hope for a reply to these questions at the earliest possible moment. Meanwhile your humble servants in this office will send an urgent, secret dispatch to generals and ministers in these areas and ask them to make a thorough investigation of the latest Russian move. A decision will be made based upon their report. The Russian minister to China is now at Yentai [in Shantung Province] and has not returned to the capital yet. Any message from him will be reported in a later memorial.

NOTES

¹ This memorial, dated September 1, 1871, was written by the chief minister in the Office of General Management (Tsung-li ya-men). Source: *Ch'ou-pan yi-wu shih-mo*, Reign of T'ung-chih, roll 82, pp. 6–7.
² Wo-liang-chia-li in transliteration.
³ To reach Sinkiang, Chinese troops had to pass through Kansu Province.

57 • TSENG CHI-TS'E: *The Ili Issue*¹

There are three problems involved in the Ili issue—delimitation of boundaries, trade, and payment of indemnities. There are also three ways to resolve each and all of these problems—offensive warfare, passive defense, and negotiations.

Those who advocate the launching of an offensive warfare contend that with the heavy concentration of forces led by such men as Tso Tsung-t'ang, Chin Shun, and Liu Chin-t'ang in the border areas, it will be easy for us to attack and recapture Ili. On the surface this contention looks plausible. However, the rugged terrain of the Ili area is difficult for the attackers to cross, but easy to defend. Moreover, since they are well equipped with offensive and defensive weapons, the Russians are superior to the Muslim rioters whose rebellion we have recently suppressed. To march an army into dangerous areas to challenge a strong opponent is a risky undertaking, to say the least, and there is no guarantee that we will win. Even if we recover Ili through the use of military force, we merely recapture what we have lost, since Ili has always been our territory in the first place. In other words, its recovery causes no loss to the Russians. However, once hostilities begin, there is no telling when they will end, and there could be serious consequences. The recovery of Ili, even if realized, merely marks the beginning of a long war which we cannot end unilaterally after we have achieved our own purpose.

Relying on her treachery and deceit as well as her material strength, Russia is competing with other Western powers in the attainment of world supremacy, and her naval power extends all the way from Europe to the Orient. In the judgment of your humble servant, she merely wishes to use the Ili issue as an excuse to open hostilities against us; and if war breaks out, she will attack us from the east by sea rather than from the west over land. We have only recently recovered from the suppression of a devastating rebellion, the scars of which are still very much in evidence. We are only beginning to build a navy for coastal defense, and it is by no means complete. While the future of our naval strength is perhaps promising, it is not good enough at this moment, either as an effective bulwark against foreign aggression or as a bargaining asset in negotiations. Moreover, the Three Eastern Provinces [Manchuria], a most important strategic area for the nation as a whole, have a long, winding boundary with Russia. Being so far from the center of the nation, they cannot be defended easily along this long boundary line once hostilities begin. Some people say that Russia is suffering from internal chaos at the moment and will not choose to create difficulty with us. But this chaos, as far as your humble servant knows, is confined to the poor, the unemployed, and the fugitives in the least productive areas. Russia may have deliberately created border incidents to start a war which would enable her to conscript rioters or potential rioters into the army and to divert her people from their domestic difficulties. Her devious, contemptible strategy of using foreign wars to restore internal peace is well-known to all the Western countries that have a common boundary with her, and these countries have been careful not to fall into her vicious trap. For this reason, none of the Western countries ever enjoys the prospect of Russia in difficulties with her own people.

Some people say that we should actively seek an alliance with some European countries so as to improve our posture vis-à-vis Russia. In effect, they wish to repeat the strategy prevalent during the Warring States period.[2] They do not realize that the countries in Western Europe are entirely different from the Chinese principalities of the Warring States period, not only in governmental structure but also in the way of making policy decisions. Though they practice democracy in various degrees, the political body that has the greatest influence in the shaping of policies is the parliament, and such important decisions as the conclusion of a military alliance and the declaration of war will not be made until a consensus has been reached among the members of the parliament. Even if our envoy had the eloquence of Su Ch'in and Chang Yi and the wisdom of Sui Ho and Lu Chia,[3] he could not possibly speak with every member of the parliament in each of the Western countries. Even if he succeeded in persuading these countries to help us by arousing their sense of righteous anger or by tempting them with material gain, how would we satisfy their greedy demands for a reward for having assisted us after the Ili issue was settled? During the Russo-Turkish war, England came to the assistance of Turkey to resist Russian aggression, and upon the conclusion of the war, won great plaudits at the Conference of Berlin as a nation that had helped a small country in its hour of peril. However, what England had in mind when entering the war was not chivalry at all, but the enhancement of her own interest. Hardly had the Russian troops left Turkish territory when England annexed the Turkish island of Cyprus. The Western powers may be jealous of each other and quarrel among themselves, but they will cooperate instantly and without fail in the exaction of concessions from China. Why? This is because of the existence of the most-favored-nation clause, which entitles all of them to enjoy any privilege that any one of them, through coercion, has been able to exact from China. They are so busy looking after their own interest that it is inconceivable that they would violate international law to send a military detachment to assist us. For the reasons stated above, your humble servant does not believe that the launching of an offensive war is the proper method to settle this Ili problem.

Those who advocate the policy of passive defense say that Ili is merely an area in the border region; that to recover it by granting Russia trade concessions or bribing her with cash payments is to regain a border area at the expense of the rest of China, which is far more important; and that the best policy to follow is to abandon it so that we will be able to preserve not only peace but also the territories we now have. Your humble servant, however, does not agree to this kind of reasoning. Since the beginning of our dynasty, we have devoted much of our resources to the development of the Western Regions. During the K'ang-hsi and Yung-cheng periods [1662–1735] we shipped food and military supplies for thousands of *li* to maintain our position in these regions. Sometimes we took offensive actions and sometimes we merely defended ourselves. Because of this intermittent warfare, not only did our people in the Western Regions fail to enjoy peace, but China herself was subject to tremendous financial strains. Yet Emperors K'ang-hsi and Yung-cheng did not hesitate to mobilize the total resources of the nation to subjugate these regions because, as long as they were not pacified, China herself would remain insecure and our people could not really enjoy peace. It was not until the twenty-second year of Ch'ien-lung [1757] when Ili was pacified that our western border became secure and that the rest of China was free from the heavy financial burden. Though located in a corner of China, Ili is a doorway to the Western Regions and a strategic point for all of the nation. The British and the French are certainly correct when they say that the Ili area is like a fortress for Sinkiang and that to defend Sinkiang, the Chinese have to defend this area. It is not difficult to predict what would happen to Sinkiang if we abandoned Ili, and it would be naive to assume that this abandonment would not have a serious impact upon the political situation as a whole.

Some say that the abandonment of Ili will provide us with a moment of reprieve during which we shall prepare ourselves for the eventual recovery of the lost territory in some future time. If a policy following this line of thinking is adopted, what shall we do with the army now commanded by Tso Tsung-t'ang and others? If we call it back, we will have no forces in the border regions to cope with an emergency that may suddenly arise. As long as the boundary is not clearly delimited, there is no guarantee that there will not be border incidents. Moreover, once an army is demobilized, it will be extremely difficult to put it back in operational form. If on the other hand this army is ordered to remain in the border regions, the period of its stay will be indefinite and the expenses involved will be tremendous. These expenses may be justified if the army is eventually used in combat, but will be wasted if no occasion ever arises which calls for its employment. While the nation centers its attention on the western frontier in a continuous state of military stalemate, great changes could take place within our own ranks. The present generals may be replaced by new ones whose military strategy could be entirely different. Meanwhile the quality of our fighting men may not necessarily remain the same. While we are wasting the nation's resources in anticipation of a land warfare that may never occur, we forfeit the opportunity to develop a strong navy for coastal defense by diverting our energy and financial resources. In the judgment of your humble servant, the abandonment of Ili, if carried out, would be a serious mistake. It is hoped that the responsible ministers in the court as well as those in the frontier will view the situation as a whole and act accordingly, and that they will not be so occupied with a present need that they ignore the evil consequences that may arise in the future.

Feeling compassionate for millions of your subjects whom you do not wish to see suffer the horrors of war once again, Your Highness the Empress Dowager [Tz'u Hsi] and Your Majesty the Emperor [Kuang-hsü] have conferred upon your humble servant the greatest honor by asking him to deliberate carefully on the ways and means to preserve a peace that has existed between China and Russia for the past two hundred years. At the moment there are three issues involved: delimitation of boundaries, trade, and payment of indemnities. Of the three, the payment of indemnities is the least important. Between the delimitation of boundaries and the agreement on trade, the latter issue is of lesser consequence. According to the Western custom, there are two kinds of treaties: permanent and transitional. The treaty to delimit national boundaries belongs to the former group in which the interests of the contracting parties cannot be simultaneously satisfied because the gain of one side is bound to be the loss of the other. Special caution and great prudence have to be exercised when negotiating a treaty of this kind. The treaty to regulate trade, on the other hand, belongs to the transitional group. At the time of the treaty negotiations, neither side can foresee the many eventualities that will not come about until the treaty has been put into practice. In some cases the advantages or disadvantages to one side or the other will not emerge in a clear form until a long period of time has elapsed. The advantages or disadvantages could be completely one-sided; they could be also mutual. For this reason there is always the provision in a commercial treaty which says that the treaty will be revised after a certain length of time mutually agreed upon. At the time of revision the disadvantages to one or the other side will be eliminated, while those provisions that have brought benefits to the contracting parties will be maintained. Since the beginning of our treaty relations with the Western powers, their ministers to China have often exercised great pressure upon us to revise the existing treaties whenever revisions are due, having in mind that the revisions will be made in such a way as to enhance their interest at our expense. But there is no reason why we cannot revise a treaty to our advantage as well. Once the advantages or disadvantages in a treaty provision are clearly seen, we can and must invoke the principle of equity to eliminate the disadvantages that were not foreseen at the time of the treaty negotiations but have become clear with the passage of time. In other words, treaty revisions are not necessarily one-sided, to benefit only one side at the expense of the other.

The treaty which Ch'ung-hou has signed with the Russians carries with it great disadvantages to our side.[4] However, if we are to abolish it unilaterally, we are bound to encounter resistance from the Russians. Such an action will be resented by even the smallest, weakest power in Europe, let alone Russia, a country that is notorious for her treachery and ruthlessness. She would create difficulties for us even without provocation; the unilateral abolition of a treaty on our part will provide her with the needed excuse. If we were in her position, we would perhaps resent it too. In short, we should conduct our diplomacy in such a way as to provide her with an honorable way of reversing herself.

Ignorant though your humble servant is, he nevertheless feels that we should insist on the preservation of our territorial integrity and should in fact never yield one inch as far as the delimitation of boundary is concerned, because boundaries are meant to be permanent. On the other hand, we should be flexible in the matter of trade. While we must insist upon the revision of certain treaty provisions that have proved much too one-sided, we can nevertheless agree to other provisions the harm of which, if any, is not so clear-cut. Whatever harm there is, we can effectively modify it by applying Li Hung-chang's[5] maxim that a good man, when called upon to enforce a bad policy, can reduce its badness. If abuse continues to accumulate despite our effort to make remedies, we are entitled to request its elimination when time arrives for treaty revisions. In other words, gains or losses of this nature are temporary, and we should do our very best to avoid a break with Russia so as to preserve peace between our two countries. But this goal of peace cannot be achieved unless we are able to present our case in the most rational, convincing manner. The negotiations must be expected to go on for a considerable time. . . .

NOTES

[1] This memorial, dated May 27, 1880, was written after Tseng had been designated as a special envoy to Russia to settle the Ili issue. The author was a son of Tseng Kuo-fan, the man primarily responsible for the suppression of the Taiping Rebellion. Source: *Tseng Chi-ts'e's Memorials* (*Tseng Hui-min kung tsou-su*), roll 2, p. 3.

[2] The period of Warring States (403–221 B.C.).

[3] Su Ch'in and Chang Yi were the chief ministers of the states of Chao and Ch'in, respectively, during the fourth century B.C.; both were famous for their talent of debate. Sui Ho and Lu Chia served Han Kao-tsu, founder of the Han Dynasty, in the third century B.C.; both were famous for their diplomatic skills.

[4] In a treaty signed with Russia in the spring of 1879, Ch'ung-hou, the Chinese envoy to Russia, had made sizable territorial concessions to the Russians.

[5] For Li Hung-chang, see Selection 42.

58 • *Treaty of Ili* (1881): *A Summary*[1]

1. Russia agrees to the reestablishment of Chinese authority in Ili, temporarily occupied by Russian troops since 1871, with the exception of its western section, which shall be incorporated with Russia.

2. The Chinese Government shall pay Russia a sum of 9,000,000 rubles to compensate her for the expenses occasioned by her occupation of Ili since 1871.

3. The boundary line between Russia and China in the Ili area shall be the Pichentao Mountains,[2] the Huoerhkuoshih River,[3] and then, passing across the Ili River, the Wutsungtao Mountains.[4]

4. Russia shall have the right to establish consulates in Chiayükuan[5] and Turfan in addition to Ili, Tarbagatai, Kashgar, and Urga.

5. Russian merchants shall be exempt from the payment of duties when they trade in Ili, Tarbagatai, Kashgar, Urumchi, and other cities north and south of the Tien Shan Mountains, as well as in Mongolia. The payment of duties shall be introduced, however, when trade becomes more prosperous. The amount of duties to be paid shall be negotiated and mutually agreed upon before they are imposed. Russian trade on the seacoast of China shall be governed by the same general regulations that presently govern the trade relations between China and other powers.[6]

6. Whenever they arise, disputes between Russian merchants and Chinese subjects, that occur in the territory of China, shall be settled jointly by the Russian consul and local Chinese authorities.

NOTES

¹ This selection consists of some of the major provisions of the Treaty of Ili, officially entitled "Treaty between Russia and China respecting the Reestablishment of Chinese Authority in the Country of Ili; Boundary; Consuls, Commerce; and Frontier Trade," signed at St. Petersburg on February 24, 1881. A copy of the Chinese original can be found in *Ch'ing-tai wai-chiao shih-liao*, roll 23. A copy of the French version can be found in *Treaties, &c., Between Great Britain and China and Between China and Foreign Powers*, vol. I, pp. 340–348.
² Bédjin-Taou Mountains in the French text.
³ Khorgos River in the French text.
⁴ Ouzontaou Mountains in the French text.
⁵ Sou-Tcheou (Tsia-yu-kouan) in the French text.
⁶ England, France, the United States, etc.

59 • *The Sino-Russian Secret Treaty of 1896*[1]

ARTICLE I

This treaty shall be regarded as having been involved and all the provisions prescribed in it become immediately operative in the event of a Japanese invasion of the territory of Russia in East Asia, the territory of China, or the territory of Korea.

In such an event, both of the contracting powers shall dispatch all the military and naval forces that can be mobilized at the moment to assist each other. They shall also assist each other in the supply of military equipment and provisions to the best of their ability.

ARTICLE II

Since China and Russia have agreed [by virtue of the existence of this treaty] to assist each other to resist the enemy, neither China nor Russia can enter negotiations with the enemy, with the intended purpose of concluding a separate peace agreement with him, without prior consultation with the other contracting power.

ARTICLE III

Should an emergency arise in the course of the war, Russian warships shall be allowed to enter any of the ports on the Chinese coast. If aid is needed, local authorities [in these ports] shall provide it to the best of their ability.

ARTICLE IV

For the purpose of securing safe transportation of Russian troops, together with military supplies and provisions, in the future, the Chinese Government agrees to let Russia build a railroad through the Chinese territory of Heilungkiang and Kirin to reach Vladivostok. However, the construction of this railroad shall not be used as a pretext for the unlawful occupation of Chinese territories or the encroachment upon the rights and privileges that rightfully belong to His Majesty the Emperor of China. The Chinese Government will entrust the Sino-Russian Bank in this matter [of constructing the aforesaid railroad]. As for the contracting terms, the Chinese Minister to Russia will discuss them with the above-named bank on the spot.

ARTICLE V

When and if Russia invokes Article I to transport troops, she may use the railroad as prescribed in Article IV; she may also use it for the shipment of provisions and military supplies. Moreover, she may use it for the transportation of troops and provisions, in transit, in time of peace. [In the latter case], the train may make temporary stops for loading and unloading purposes and shall not stop for any other reason.

ARTICLE VI

This treaty shall be effective for a period of fifteen years, beginning with the date on which the contract, as prescribed in Article IV, is approved and becomes operative. Six months prior to the expiration of this treaty, the two contracting powers shall consult each other for its extension.

Done at Moscow on the 22nd day of the fourth month of the 22nd year of Kuang-hsü, corresponding to the 22nd day of the fifth month, 1896, in the Russian calendar.[2]

NOTES

[1] Translated by this author from the Chinese. A copy of the Chinese original can be found in Chang Hsiao-ch'ien, *A Political History of Modern China* (*Chung-kuo chin-tai cheng-chih shih*) (Taipei: The China Cultural Press, 1959), pp. 67–68.

[2] June 3, 1896. This treaty was signed by Li Hung-chang for China and Prince Lobanov for Russia. It was not made public until 1922.

CHAPTER EIGHT

Sino-Japanese Relations, 1871-1895

During the initial stage of the Western impact, Japan reacted the same as China, having been fully convinced of the superiority of her own culture and of the undesirability of subjecting herself to the "barbarian" influence of the West. However, once the advantages of Westernization had become too clear for her to ignore, she introduced and implemented her modernization programs with vigor. The modernization of Japan began with the Meiji Restoration (1867), and in one generation that country was transformed from a feudal agricultural society into the most industrialized society in all of Asia. No one who studies the history of modern Japan can fail to admire the great success she was able to score.

Unfortunately for her neighbors, however, the modernization of Japan was closely tied up with her ambition to become an imperialist power: to play the same role as England and France were then playing in East Asia. The only difference was that she happened to be more aggressive than any of the Western powers. Like Russia, she was more interested in territorial than commercial advantages; but unlike Russia, she directed her energy towards the heavily populated rather than sparsely inhabited areas.

The first conflict between China and Japan involved Liu-ch'iu (Ryukyu) and Taiwan. In 1871 some fifty-four Liu-ch'iu islanders, shipwrecked at Taiwan, were murdered by the aborigines. Japan claimed that Liu-ch'iu was its vassal state and asked China to punish the aborigines. Receiving no satisfaction from the Chinese, Japan sent a military expedition to Taiwan and occupied a strip of territory on the northern coast. When China responded by proposing to send a larger force to counteract the Japanese move, Japan requested England's good offices. The result was the treaty of 1874 which not only entitled Japan to seek financial compensation from China, but also, by implication, recognized Japan's claim as protector of the Liu-ch'iu islands (Selection 60). Japan, however, was more interested in conquering than protecting these islands. Many Chinese officials, knowing her intention, advocated the adoption of a firm stand so as to prevent Liu-ch'iu from being absorbed by the Japanese, but the official policy of China was to avoid a clash with Japan over "some insignificant islands" (Selection 61). Time and again Liu-ch'iu appealed to China for assistance, only to be ignored by the Chinese (Selection 62). In 1879 Liu-ch'iu was formally annexed by Japan without a murmur of protest from any of the concerned powers, including China.

Hardly had the Liu-ch'iu issue been resolved before Japan directed her expansionist moves towards Korea. In 1876, as a result of a series of successful diplomatic maneuvers, a demonstration of force, and the outright occupation of some Korean islands, the Japanese secured a treaty with Korea which opened two Korean ports for Japanese trade and recognized Korea as an independent state. China, knowing her own military weakness, did not bother to protest. Instead, she persuaded Korea to open her ports to all Western countries, including England, France, the United States, and Russia, to counteract the increasing Japanese influence (Selection 63).

Meanwhile in Korea two political factions had developed, the Progressive group that relied on Japan for support and the Conservative group that leaned heavily upon the Chinese. In 1884 the Progressives, aided by the Japanese, staged a *coup d'etat,* only to be suppressed by the Chinese and their Korean allies (Selection 64). The following year a treaty was concluded between China and Japan in which each party pledged in the case of future disturbances in Korea to notify the other party before sending troops (Selection 65). By then it was clear that China was as determined to keep Korea a dependent state as Japan was determined to detach her from China.

In 1894 a semireligious, ultraconservative group called the Eastern Learning Society staged a revolt against the Korean government, vowing not only to eliminate "all the aristocrats" in Seoul but also to expel and exterminate "all the Japanese invaders" (Selection 66). Unable to cope with this revolt, Korea requested China's help. China responded by sending a military expedition to Korea, after notifying Japan of her intention. Japan moved quickly to counteract the Chinese move and succeeded in capturing Seoul. After the rebellion of the Eastern Learning Society was suppressed, China proposed the withdrawal of both Chinese and Japanese forces from Korea, a proposal which Japan rejected (Selection 67). Meanwhile the Japanese had deposed the Korean king and placed his natural father (known as Tai-wun-kun) on the throne. The new king concluded a treaty of alliance with Japan and requested his new ally to drive the Chinese troops from Korea. When China sent more reinforcements to Korea, her ships were fired upon by the Japanese navy and one of them, with more than 900 men aboard, was sunk off the Korean coast. The Chinese declared war (Selection 68), and the First Sino-Japanese War (1894–1895) officially began.

Nowhere was the difference between a modernized Japan and a backward China better demonstrated than it was during the First Sino-Japanese War. A small Japan, superior in modern technology and adept in Westernized efficiency, quickly overwhelmed the best armed forces the largest nation in the world could then muster and won decisive victories against China on both land and sea. Once again China was brought to her knees, this time by Japan, a country which the Chinese had viewed with a sense of paternization, if not condescension, in all of their recorded history. Li Hung-chang, who had worked hard against great opposition to modernize China, was now compelled to play a humiliating role: to go personally to Japan to ask the victors to moderate their demands (Selection 69). Li's pleadings notwithstanding, the resultant treaty, the Treaty of Shimonoseki (Selection 70), was one of the harshest that a foreign power had ever been able to impose upon China. It called for not only the payment of a huge indemnity but also the cession of large chunks of Chinese territories (Taiwan, Pescadores, and Liaotung Peninsula), in addition to the enjoyment by Japan of all rights and privileges that the Western powers had been able to exact from China in the past. To the Chinese there was no question about Japan's ultimate objective: the eventual conquest of all of China. The seeds of deep hatred were sown when, from hindsight, there should have been nothing but brotherhood and goodwill between these two close neighbors in East Asia.

60 • *The Okubo-Kung Understanding* (1874) [1]

In the matter of the savages of Formosa, reference being had to an understanding arrived at with the two Governments [of China and Japan] by British Minister, Mr. Wade,[2] and to the Instrument this day signed recording the action to be taken respectively by the two parties thereto, the Chinese Government will at once give the sum of 100,000 taels to compensate the shipwrecked Japanese who were killed. In addition to this, the Chinese Government will not fail to pay a farther sum of 400,000 taels on account of the expense occasioned by the construction of roads and erection of buildings, which, when the Japanese troops are withdrawn, the Chinese Government will retain for its own use. It is further agreed that on [or by] the 20th day of the 12th month of the 7th year of the reign of Ming Chih[3] [Japanese style], and on the 12th day of the 11th moon of the 13th year of the reign of T'ung Chi[4] [20th December, 1874], the Government of Japan shall withdraw the whole of its troops, and the Government of China shall pay the whole of the money; neither party being behind the time now fixed. The payment of the sum guaranteed will not be completed by the Chinese Government so long as any part of the troops of the Government of Japan be not withdrawn.

This Instrument is drawn up in guarantee of the Agreement.[5] [It is in two parts, whereof] each party to it retains one.

NOTES

[1] This document is a supplement to the "Agreement between the High Commissioner of Japan and the Chinese Ministers of Foreign Affairs with reference to the Island of Formosa," signed at Peking, October 31, 1874. Okubo Toshimichi was the Japanese High Commissioner, and Prince Kung was the President of the Chinese Foreign Office (Office of General Management). Source: *Treaties, &c., between Great Britain and China*, vol. I, pp. 254–255.

[2] Sir Thomas Wade.
[3] Meiji.
[4] T'ung-chih.
[5] See Footnote 1.

61 • HO JU-CHANG: *The Annexation of Liu-ch'iu by Japan*[1]

While I was in Kobe, a Liu-ch'iu official came to visit me in connection with Japan's effort to prevent Liu-ch'iu from sending a tribute mission to China. Having heard what he had to say, I am in complete agreement with my government's evaluation that Liu-ch'iu had been forced to do what it really loathed. I instructed him to make duplicate copies of all the correspondence between his government and Japan beginning with the time when the latter successfully prevented Liu-ch'iu from sending a tribute mission to China. After my arrival at Tokyo, Mao Feng-lai, the Liu-ch'iu envoy to Japan, repeatedly requested to see me. I agreed to accept his petitions which I have studied with great care.

Because Liu-ch'iu had also sent tribute missions to the feudal domain of Satsuma, Japan, after the abolition of feudalism, was anxious to annex this tributary state and converted it into a Japanese province. However, since Liu-ch'iu was simultaneously a tributary state to China, obviously Japan had to force it to renounce its fealty towards China before she could fulfill her own ambition. This was the reason she was so determined to prevent it from sending a tribute mission to China. Being weak and small and having to face a powerful enemy, Liu-ch'iu found itself in the most precarious situation; it had no choice except to seek protection from us to maintain its very existence. It is not surprising that it should repeatedly send envoys to China to plead for assistance. It made a mistake, however, by stressing Japan's effort to prevent it from sending a tribute mission to China without saying anything about what had happened in Japan in the meantime, such as the abolition of feudalism and the establishment of a new regime.

When Liu-ch'iu submitted itself to the Tokyo overlordship, the Japanese government agreed to its request of following the old tradition by being the vassal state to both China and Japan at the same time. Later Japan changed her mind. Not only did she refuse to allow Liu-ch'iu to send tribute missions to China, she also dispatched officials to reside in Liu-ch'iu and threatened to stage a blockade if Liu-ch'iu failed to meet all of her demands. Realizing the dangerous situation they were in, the Liu-ch'iu people decided to resist; they almost resorted to rioting to kidnap Japanese officials who were to be held as hostages. Each time they presented a petition, the Japanese officials said that "the request is unreasonable and completely without any merit"; this amounted to saying that they could not grant the request regardless of its merit. In refusing to grant the Liu-ch'iu people's legitimate requests, the Japanese knew that they were wrong, but they could not do otherwise since their government had been committed to annex these islands. The reason Japan had not annexed these islands outright was her fear of possible reaction from China. She would certainly go ahead with her annexation plan if she could be assured of China's noninterference.

That the Liu-ch'iu officials sought our assistance to maintain their independence was well-known to the Japanese. Since we had not chosen to utter one word to help them for a long time, the Japanese obviously thought that either we had decided to abandon them or we were simply too cowardly to do anything. Now that Japan has annexed Liu-ch'iu and converted it into a province, it is doubtless more difficult to protest. But protest we must, and for good reasons.

Some people might say that our protest might precipitate a war between our two countries. They do not realize that being a small, poor country, Japan has a difficult time even to defend herself, let alone attempt aggression against others. Her national debt is estimated to be more than 200 million yen at the moment. Last year the Satsuma clan revolted, and even today the Japanese people are far from being pacified. The government did not help the situation by suggesting a tax reduction which further weakened the nation's financial structure. Recently it ordered the people to buy 12 million yen worth of its bonds, but few have responded. In fact, it relies almost exclusively on the issuance of paper currency to keep itself going. Once a war begins, it would need hard cash to purchase all the necessary military equipment from foreign countries, but it does not have much hard cash. Its standing army numbers only 32,000 men; its navy consists of 4,000 men and 15 ships, and most of the ships are old and useless. Recently there was some discussion of purchasing ships from England; however, due to the lack of funds, only one ship has arrived. This ship is called an ironclad, but it is only iron-surfaced. Lately the government has followed the example of Germany by adopting a universal conscription system; it conscripts and trains ordinary civilians as soldiers in the hope that a strong army will emerge at the end of three years. The Japanese know very well that their position of being surrounded by the sea is a precarious one and that they need to build an army to defend themselves.

Moreover, if Japan launches an all-out war, the regular army will certainly not be adequate, and the government will have to impose conscription upon the old feudal domains. These feudal lords have never really reconciled themselves to the abolition of the feudal system, and they might decide to take advantage of the government's preoccupation with a foreign war to reassert themselves and thus precipitate a civil war. Those presently in charge of the Japanese government such as Iwakura Tomomi and Okubo Toshimichi are not the reckless and adventurous type, because they know the weaknesses of their country only too well. The Taiwan campaign was practically the work of one man, namely, Saigo Takamori. The government wished to call him back after he and his fleet had left Nagasaki, but finally decided to take a chance with him when it was unable to stop him. Later, it sent Okubo to China to negotiate peace; when he returned, the Japanese congratulated themselves because they had not only won a diplomatic victory but also avoided a prolonged war. Dissatisfied with the government's policy of caution, Saigo advocated a military campaign against Korea, an advocacy which was vigorously denounced by the responsible officials in the government. He left the government and staged a rebellion, only to bring death to himself. Today the Japanese elite are extremely reluctant to talk about this event as if it were a taboo; it is not difficult to imagine how they feel about this man. In China the reports on Japan's financial strength are often exaggerated, and many Chinese have been wrongly impressed with the Japanese might after the Taiwan campaign. I have been here for several months, and from what I have observed, I know that Japan is not as strong as China believes. I expressed this view to Your Excellency in my previous dispatch; today I am even more convinced that Japan will not dare to start a war over the Liu-ch'iu issue.

If one assumes, as some do, that the Japanese are unreasonable and irrational by nature and that they will act like wild dogs or unprincipled hooligans, then there could never be any peace between our two countries. In that case Japan would annex Liu-ch'iu after they had prevented the latter from sending a tribute mission to China; once Liu-ch'iu is annexed, they would certainly try to conquer Korea. As long as we give in whenever Japan demands something, they will of course raise new demands; how, in that case, can we maintain ourselves as a nation? Even if we give Liu-ch'iu to them, hostilities will still be inevitable at some future time, because once the decision is made to start a war, it is always easy to find excuses. Moreover, if the Japanese are as unprincipled as some of us assume, they will perhaps not even bother with excuses once they have decided on a warpath.

Besides, there are other things to consider. Since Liu-ch'iu is close to Taiwan, its abandonment to Japan will pose a direct threat to the latter island. After its annexation by Japan and its conversion into a Japanese province, the Japanese will doubtless conscript its people into their armed forces. The Liu-ch'ius would resent us for abandoning them and would be happy to cooperate with the Japanese. The Liu-ch'ius are a group of hardy, persistent, and pugnacious people; once equipped with Japanese ships and guns at some future time when Japan is strong, they will doubtless be used by the Japanese to raid our coastal areas. By then there will not be a moment of peace as far as Taiwan and P'eng-hu[2] are concerned. Thus, if we value the security of Taiwan as we must, it is preferable to dispute with Japan over the Liu-ch'iu issue today than to abandon the islands which in my judgment will create great difficulties for us in the future. In short, we are obligated to contest the Japanese demand even if such a contest results in war. The chance is good that there will be no war even if we press our legitimate demand.

I know that our government does not wish to engage in war at this time. The Japanese are fully aware that being generous and lenient in nature, we will not send an expedition to punish the aggressors on behalf of a small group of islands such as Liu-ch'iu; moreover, they also know that we, as a people, do not like long and endless arguments. Whatever course we may eventually decide to take, it will certainly be better than the self-imposed silence we are maintaining today. Suppose we decide to negotiate with Japan. Even if the negotiation lasts for a long time, it will at least give the Japanese something to worry about and will in the meantime prolong Liu-ch'iu's independent existence. The gains resulting from the pursuance of this course are by no means inconsequential. If on the other hand we continue to maintain silence, Japan, after annexing Liu-ch'iu, will doubtless train its people as soldiers and will eventually use them to raid our coastal areas. In such a case there will never be an end to the danger of our frontier. As I look at the situation and study it carefully, I cannot but express candidly how I feel. The letters from Fukien indicate that the authorities in that province are very fearful about the opening of hostilities; they wish the government to drop this Liu-ch'iu issue without contesting it. I, of course, view the situation differently and have taken the liberty to present my views to the Office of General Management.[3] The issue that confronts us is indeed very serious. Though knowing only too well my own inadequacies, I nevertheless wish to present my observations to Your Excellency for consideration.

NOTES

[1] This letter, dated May 8, 1878, was addressed to Li Hung-chang by the Chinese minister to Japan who was then in Tokyo. Source: *The Complete Works of Li Hung-chang* (*Li Wen-chung kung ch'üan-shu*), roll 8, pp. 2-4.

[2] Pescadores.

[3] Tsung-li ya-men.

62 • Hsiang Teh-hung: *A Refutation of Japanese Claims*[1]

On this day, the twenty-first day of the sixth month [August 8, 1879], Hsiang Teh-hung, a hereditary official from Liu-ch'iu, respectfully complies with Your Excellency's [Li Hung-chang] command to reply to a letter from the Japanese Foreign Minister Terashima as follows:

1. It is wrong for Japan to say that my country, being part of the Inan Islands, has long been under Japanese political and cultural influence; nor is it correct for her to assert that according to Japanese history, my country paid tribute to Japan as early as the Sui-T'ang period [590–906] of China. The truth is that while my country did maintain some kind of relationship with China during the Sui-T'ang period, her intercourse with such countries as Japan, Korea, Siam, Java, and Burma was purely commercial. During the Wan-li period [1573–1619] of the Ming Dynasty a Japanese named Mago Shichiro, well-learned in geography, frequently came to our country to trade. Knowing the martial reputation of General Toyotomi Hideyoshi, he suggested, through the intermediary of some of the general's close associates, that if Japan intimated to Liu-ch'iu her intention of making war on China, Liu-ch'iu would be compelled to send a mission to pay her tribute. Acting upon this suggestion, Hideyoshi wrote a letter to my country which read, in brief, as follows: "For more than a hundred years many heroes in my country had competed for hegemony until I appeared on the scene. Knowing that I was destined by Heaven to rule, many countries, even in the most remote areas, have sent envoys here to pay their tribute. It is Heaven's wish that I should conquer China; it has nothing to do with any personal ambition of mine. You, the people of Liu-ch'iu, should mobilize your troops and should, in the spring of next year, send them to the Gate of Hizen. If they are tardy in their arrival, I shall send my navy to exterminate all of you islanders." Fearful for what Hideyoshi might do, my country did send a tribute mission to Japan at that time.

Had Liu-ch'iu belonged to Japan as early as the Sui-T'ang period, why is it that as late as the Wan-li period of the Ming Dynasty she had not yet sent a tribute mission to that country? It does not require great intelligence to refute the Japanese assertion on this score. As for the official history of Japan, it is so full of distortions that any reference from that source does not in the least make the argument any more convincing. . . .

2. Between my country and Fukien is a chain of islands that stretches a distance of 4,000 *li*. The islands of the Pach'ungshan group are only 400 *li* from Taiwan. The assertion in the ancient record that "From Fukien to Liu-ch'iu and over a distance of 10,000 *li* there is not a single piece of land where one can stay overnight" is erroneous. Between Liu-ch'iu and Satsuma is another chain of islands that stretches a distance of 3,000 more *li*. My country has within its jurisdiction thirty-six islands, seven or eight of which are part of this group. The five islands that were annexed by Japan in the thirty-seventh year of Wan-li [1609] also belong to this group. The assertion in the ancient record that "A small boat can sail from Liu-ch'iu straight to Satsuma" is of course erroneous. There is no justification whatsoever for Japan to regard my country as part of Satsuma or the Inan Islands. In fact, she deliberately maintains this falsehood for the sole purpose of deceiving others.

3. It is true that at one time King Shang-ning was captured by the Japanese.

Then Hideyoshi was preparing himself for the conquest of China after he had sent an expeditionary force against Korea. Since my country was a neighbor of Japan, the Japanese requested our assistance in the supply of troops and provisions. We declined the request despite the great pressure they exercised upon us. Later Yoshihisa summoned many Liu-ch'iu monks then stationed at Satsuma for a conference. He informed them about the situation in Japan, saying that they must return to Liu-ch'iu and request King Shang-ning to send a tribute mission to Satsuma as early as possible. King Shang-ning refused to comply with this demand and was subsequently captured by an expeditionary force sent by Japan. In accordance with an agreement forced upon us by the invaders, we were to ship 8,000 piculs of grain to Satsuma every year. This is how Liu-ch'iu came to pay tribute to Satsuma, dictated by the compelling circumstance that by then King Shang-ning and his ministers had been imprisoned by the Japanese for three years. . . .

At the time when the above event took place, namely, the thirty-seventh year of Wan-li [1609], my country had sent tribute missions to China for a long time. Even in the agreement we concluded with Satsuma, there is not a single word that says we cannot continue these tribute missions. When the present dynasty[2] was established, we once again expressed our utmost sincerity to be loyal and obedient. In observance of the Chinese law, we sent tribute missions to China once every other year and requested a new investiture whenever a new king of Liu-ch'iu was installed on the throne. Even the Japanese agreed that our country had always been respectful and obedient. Beginning in the tenth year of T'ung-chih [1871], however, Japan's attitude changed completely. It unjustifiably changed the name of our country from "Kingdom of Liu-ch'iu" to "Feudatory of Liu-ch'iu" and addressed our ruler as "a feudal prince" instead of "a king." Subsequently they sent administrative officials, supported by soldiers, to take over our government.

4. The people of Liu-ch'iu worshiped gods and goddesses at the very beginning of the nation's history. Though the worship of the Goddess of Ise may have originated from Japan, it should be reminded that we, as a people, also worship Kuan Yü,[3] Kuan-yin,[4] and earth gods, all of which did not originate from Japan.

5. As far as customs are concerned, we follow the Chinese way in such matters as dress, wedding and funeral ceremonies, and worshiping and offering sacrifices. It is true that we sit on the floor instead of chairs and that we take our meals from separate instead of common utensils. But these habits were clearly those of ancient China as recorded in the Chinese classics. Is it not more likely that the Japanese borrowed these habits from Liu-ch'iu which in turn had borrowed them from China? If cultural borrowings justify jurisdictional relationship, the whole nation of Japan should have belonged to China in the first place. There is no evidence whatsoever that we borrowed our cooking method from the Japanese clan of Ogasahara. There is more evidence that the clan of Ogasahara borrowed it from China. Where will Japan be if this kind of argument is accepted for establishing jurisdictional relationship?

6. It is true that we use an alphabet of forty-eight letters as do the Japanese. But we also use Chinese characters. If Japan can claim jurisdiction over Liu-ch'iu on a specious argument like this, China can certainly do likewise with regard to the whole country of Japan since the Japanese have always used Chinese characters in addition to this alphabet of forty-eight letters.

7. As for the spoken language, we have our own and the Japanese have theirs. It is true that some of my countrymen can speak and understand Japanese, but this comes about because of commercial relationships between the two countries. Had there been no such relationships, the Japanese would not be able to understand our language; nor would we be able to understand theirs. . . . If the ability of speaking a foreign language entitled one to lay claim on the territory of another country where the language is spoken, Liu-ch'iu is as much entitled to annex Japan as Japan is entitled to annex Liu-ch'iu. Will Japan accept Liu-ch'iu's claim on the same ground?

8. The Japanese say that they have always been protective towards the people of Liu-ch'iu, providing relief in time of famine and dispatching troops for their defense whenever the necessity arose. The truth is that every kernel of grain we borrowed from Japan during time of famine was always paid back in time of bumper crops. To provide a country with famine relief does not entitle one to claim the territory of that country. If it does, the Western countries could have claimed China as theirs and China could have claimed Austria as hers since the Western countries have at one time provided famine relief for China's Shansi province and Chinese merchants have at one time done the same thing for Austria. But we know that claims of this kind are too absurd to be raised, let alone to be entertained.

9. The Japanese say that the very body politic of Liu-ch'iu originated with Japan and that Liu-ch'iu has no right of self-government. Speaking of Liu-ch'iu's body politic, there is nothing more important than those relating to the granting of an investiture, naming of the country as well as of the royal household, observance of a certain calendar, and adoption of laws and institutions from a foreign country. In all these respects Liu-ch'iu's legal and political orientation is definitely Chinese. In the fifth year of Hung-wu [1372] my country sent a tribute mission to China to pay her homage. In response, China named her "Kingdom of Liu-ch'iu" and invested her ruler as "King of Chung-shan" who, later during the Yung-lo period [1403–1424], was granted the surname "Shang." We adopted the Chinese calendar and observed Chinese laws and institutions. We have not made any changes since then. During this long period we appointed and dismissed our own officials, with no interference from Japan whatsoever. Now suddenly she claims that my country belongs to her! Not long ago when we conducted negotiations with France, the United States, and Holland, we used the Chinese calendar in all of our diplomatic dispatches which bore the names of our own officials. We made clear that we had the authority to manage our own affairs, a fact with which all the foreign countries were thoroughly familiar.

In short, my country does not belong to Japan. This is so valid a statement that no specious arguments can make it less so.

NOTES

[1] This is one of several petitions that Hsiang Teh-hung, an envoy from Liu-ch'iu, presented to the Chinese government from which he sought assistance to restore to Liu-ch'iu her former independent status. The document was dated August 8, 1879, two months after Japan had annexed the island kingdom. Source: *Chung-kuo chin-pai-nien shih tzu-liao,* vol. I, pp. 399–405.

[2] The Ch'ing or Manchu Dynasty.

[3] A Chinese civil war hero during the period of the Three Kingdoms (220–265).

[4] Goddess of Mercy in Buddhist religion.

63 • LI HUNG-CHANG: *The Opening of Korea to the Trade of All Countries*[1]

For the past decade Japan, by placing a high priority on Westernization, has introduced and carried out many Westernized programs. She believes that she has mastered the secrets of making herself wealthy and strong. However, the implementation of these programs is so expensive that not only is her treasury empty, but her national debt also continues to grow. To recoup the huge expenses, she feels that she must engage in conquest. As she looks around and examines her neighbors, she finds two territories most attractive for her purpose, namely, Korea in the north and Chinese Taiwan in the south. Liu-ch'iu was an old country of several hundred years and had never offended Japan. Yet, in the spring of this year Japan suddenly dispatched her warships to depose and kidnap its king and annex its territory. It is almost inevitable that following her present course, Japan will in some future time try to annex some part of your country or ours when and if the opportunity presents itself. Being ten times stronger than Japan in both military strength and economic resources, we in China believe that we should be able to cope with any attempt she makes against us. It is a different matter, however, with Korea. I have often thought about what I would do if I were in your position. First, I would try to strengthen my armed forces for defense and open up financial resources to support them. Meanwhile I would not let the Japanese know how I really feel about them and would in fact continue to maintain friendly relations. I would observe punctiliously every provision in the treaty so as not to give them an excuse to open hostilities. If they invaded my country despite the fact that I have been scrupulously correct, they would be wrong and I would be right, and the side that is right will always prevail over the side that is wrong.

Your honorable country is called a land of cultural refinement, though it is not particularly rich in financial resources. Even if you begin to carry out the self-strengthening programs this very day, it will take a long time before they yield noticeable results. I have heard that the Japanese have stationed two warships outside of the Fu-shan[2] Bay for a long time and that these ships, with their huge cannons, have been conducting military maneuvers. I do not know with certainty what the Japanese intention is. Should Japan start something against Korea, we in China will of course immediately come to her rescue. It should be quickly added, however, that there is a long distance between Chinese naval bases and the area of action, and we may not be able to come in time to be truly useful. What worries me most is that Japan, having employed Westerners to teach them the art of war, possesses ships and cannons that are perhaps far superior to any that Korea has at the moment, though admittedly they are still inferior to those owned by the Western powers.

Now Japan imitates the West like a sycophant. On their part, the Western powers may wish to use her as an instrument to humiliate or intimidate all her neighbors. Formerly, when they requested the opening of Korean ports for trade, your honorable country refused; I should not be surprised if they still resent this refusal. The danger doubtless will be greater if Japan chooses to conspire with England, France, and the United States and forces Korea to open her ports for Western trade or if she forms an unholy alliance with Russia for the sole purpose of annexing Korean territories. In either case Korea would be completely isolated. Would it not be better to avoid an unfortunate situation before it occurs than to correct it after it has already happened? How much better off the world would be if we could all live in isolation without all the worries and cares that accompany contact with the West! But the Westerners, relying on their superior strength and roaming all over the world, simply will not leave us alone. This is unprecedented since the beginning of mankind, a destiny of man which no effort of ours, however great, can control or change.

Since your honorable country has already signed a treaty with Japan to open ports for trade, inevitably other countries will wish to follow suit. Since Japan will want to monopolize Korean trade, she will not take kindly to this. However, from Korea's point of view, I think the best policy is to use one poison to fight another and to neutralize all her enemies by setting them against each other. In other words, Korea should conclude treaties with all the Western powers so as to counterbalance the influence of Japan. Aggressive and treacherous, Japan will definitely continue her present policy of conquest and expansion, either by outright annexation or by slow, gradual infiltration. Her annexation of Liu-ch'iu indicates clearly her true intention toward all her neighbors. Under the circumstances, how can Korea not be alert enough to prepare for any eventuality?

The countries Japan fears most are the Western powers. Though Korea is not strong enough to resist Japan, she will be able to maintain her independent existence if somehow she can secure cooperation from the Western countries in her effort. According to the Western custom, one country cannot conquer or annex another country without a justifiable cause, and international law governs relations between nations. Last year Russia invaded Turkey and placed it in a most dangerous position; however, England, Austria, and other countries quickly intervened, and Russia was forced to withdraw her troops. Had Turkey been isolated without allies, Russia would have certainly conquered her. In Europe such countries as Belgium and Denmark are very small. Yet, because they have treaty relations with all the countries, none of the great powers dares to invade them and exterminate their independent status. This is a good example of how weak countries can preserve themselves by maintaining relations with all the great powers.

To conquer and annex a distant country is a task which even the great conquerors of ancient times found extremely difficult. Such Western countries as England, Germany, France, and the United States only desire to trade with Korea and to protect their ships in transit. Russia's intentions are entirely different, however. Having occupied the areas drained by the Suifen and Tumen Rivers in addition to the Sakhalin Island, she has now a common boundary with Korea and thus poses a constant threat. Once Korea establishes diplomatic relations with England, Germany, France, and the United States, not only will she acquire a counterbalance against the increasing influence of Japan but may also forestall any overtly evil act on the part of the Russians. Once she knows that she cannot fulfill her ambitions, Russia may decide to maintain friendly relations with Korea.

This does not mean that Korea should make a sudden, complete reversal of her present policy. The new policy, if adopted, does not call for the opening of more ports for trade; it merely allows the Western countries to trade in ports that Korea has already opened for Japan. The Western countries will in this case share with Japan what has been hitherto a Japanese monopoly; certainly Korea will not suffer the slightest from this sharing. Meanwhile the increasingly higher revenue from tariff duties will help to strengthen Korea's finances and may also be profitably employed for the purchase of Western arms once Korea becomes familiar with the trade situation in the Western countries. From time to time envoys should be sent to these treaty powers to strengthen the bond of friendship—as you maintain friendly relations with them during the time of peace, you may request their assistance to serve justice when and if a country is so unprincipled as to commit aggression against you. Only in this way can Korea forestall any ruthless action on the part of Japan. For her own benefit, Korea should study carefully the way of making friends and conducting relations. She should be neither too proud nor too servile; she should instead follow a middle path. This is the way to cope with Japan; this is also the way to forestall any overt act on the part of the Russians.

Lately the consuls of various countries have come to the Office of General Management and requested my assistance in persuading your honorable country to open her ports for foreign trade. I told them that since Korea has complete freedom in determining her own policies, I could not in any way intervene in such an important matter. However, considering that China and Korea are like two members of one family, that Korea, being the bulwark of the Three Eastern Provinces,[3] is extremely important to our own security, and that the worries of Korea are indeed our own, I cannot but express what I really feel, even though I may be imprudent in doing so. It is my hope that you will submit my proposal to your king who, I trust, will in turn discuss this matter with his ministers in secret. After careful study, if you feel that my proposal is not too absurd to be accepted, please notify me at your earliest convenience. Then, when the foreign consuls mention this trade matter again, we shall convey to them the good offices we intend to offer. The Office of General Management has had this thought for a long time but has not been able to present it to you until today.

Formerly, the Western powers, taking advantage of the difficulties China then faced, combined their military forces to impose their will upon us. They obtained the treaties they wanted through coercion rather than peaceful negotiations. These treaties have been in force for many years, and they are full of all kinds of abuse. Even foreigners do not deny the harm these treaties have brought to us. When the Western countries learn that Korea is willing to enter into treaty relations with them without them having to exercise pressure upon her, they would be so pleased that it is unlikely that they would put forward unreasonable demands. For instance, they might not object to your proposal that trade in opium is absolutely forbidden and that missionaries are not allowed to proselytize in the interior regions—the two cardinal evils from which China has suffered for many years. If I have anything further to suggest, I shall communicate with you from time to time, so as to fulfill my own obligation as a loyal friend. All of us in China sincerely hope that nothing harmful will ever visit your honorable country.

NOTES

[1] This letter, dated August 26, 1879, was addressed to Yi Ha-ŭng, the former regent to the reigning Korean king. Source: *Documents: Diplomacy towards the End of the Ch'ing Dynasty* (*Ch'ing-chi wai-chiao shih-liao*), roll 16, pp. 14–17.

[2] Pushan.

[3] Manchuria.

64 • YÜAN SHIH-K'AI: *Suppression of a Pro-Japanese Rebellion*[1]

I presume that Your Excellency has received my report on the battle with the Japanese and the subsequent return of the Korean king to his palace under our protection.

After France had opened hostilities against us this fall, the Korean Progressives became more and more violent and seditious each day. They wished to rely on Russian and Japanese support to attack our garrison troops, and such an attack, if successful, would be followed by a call to all provinces to revolt against China and to place Korea under Western auspices. My repeated admonitions to these Progressives against their proposed course yielded no constructive result. I have reported this to you in my previous letters. Thanks to Your Excellency's leadership and guidance, the outcome of events was not as these Progressives had hoped. Today I am happy to report that this unfortunate incident is largely over and has not in any way affected the body politic of this nation [Korea], extraordinary though it was. For the past few days I have visited many important Korean ministers and inquired about what they know; I have also interrogated captured cadets, such as Sŏ Chae-ch'ang, to obtain more information. Because of these inquiries, the origin of this incident and the dangerous path it followed have become very clear. I was unable to enunciate them in detail in my last report since it was written in a great hurry. I shall do so in this one.

Hong Yŏng-sik, Kim Ok-kyun, Pak Yŏng-hyo, Sŏ Kwang-bŏm, and Sŏ Chae-p'il were all members of the Progressive Party and pro-Japanese. The year before last I was instructed by Your Excellency to train three battalions of troops for the Korean government. Later, one battalion, called Pacification, was stationed at Chiang-hua [Kang-hwa], while the other two battalions, the First and the Second Royal, were posted inside the capital [Seoul]. While I was training troops for the Korean government, such Progressives as Pak Yŏng-hyo, Han Kyu-jik, and Min Ŭng-sik commissioned the Japanese to train one thousand of their own soldiers, divided into two battalions, the Front and the Rear, and placed them face to face with my units. They selected and sent to Japan twelve energetic young men to learn about military science. These young man, called cadets, served as Hong Yŏng-sik's personal guards upon their return; the captured Sŏ Chae-ch'ang was one of them. During the time when the Japanese minister Takezoe was in the capital, Hong Yŏng-sik proposed to invite Colonels Wu and Chang and myself to an evening party so as to stage a *coup d'etat*. His plan called for the beginning of the banquet at 10 P.M. and the assassination of his invited guests at 2 A.M.; the assassination was to be carried out by the cadets who, according to the plan, would hide themselves in a yard near the banquet hall. Once the assassination was successfully carried out, Hong Yŏng-sik would send his two battalions of troops, the Front and the Rear, to attack Colonel Chang's barracks, while the Japanese would launch a simultaneous attack upon Colonel Wu's units. If these attacks were successful, two contingents of fresh reserves would make an all-out assault against the battalion under my personal command.

Before it could be carried out, however, the whole plan was vetoed by the Japanese adviser Shimamura Hisami. The Japanese were dubious about its chance of success because first, the three battalions under my command were all war veterans and probably could not be easily defeated; second, there would be many armed retainers accompanying us in the banquet who might just possibly foil the assassination plot; and third, had the plan miscarried, the result would be disastrous. But Hong Yŏng-sik was not a man to be easily dissuaded. The very next morning he planned a surprise attack to take place in the middle of the night, only to call it off when his spies informed him that my men were ready and alert and that my barracks were heavily guarded. Though the danger of a massive revolt loomed larger and larger each day, the Korean king continued to vacillate; he simply could not decide what he wanted to do. This inaction on his part alienated many of his loyal ministers who had regular contact with me.

On the evening of the seventeenth of the tenth month [December 4, 1884], Hong Yŏng-sik gave a banquet in the Post Office. Among the invited guests were the Korean ministers Min Yŏng-ik, Kim Ok-kyun, Pak Yŏng-hyo, and Sŏ Kwang-bŏm, a German named P. G. von Möllendorf,[2] Governor Ch'en Shu-t'ang, and English, German, and American ministers. The Japanese minister Takezoe declined the invitation on the ground that he was "ill." During the banquet Kim Ok-kyun often left his seat and whispered to others. At midnight somebody shouted "Fire." Min Yŏng-ik stood up immediately, with the intended purpose of going outside to take a look himself. Hardly had he reached the door, however, before he was cut down by Hong Yŏng-sik's five cadets, including Sŏ Chae-ch'ang. Yŏng-ik's bodyguards fought back, but were all slaughtered. The foreign ministers fled in a hurry.

Later, Governor Ch'en Shu-t'ang came to see me and told me what had happened. I immediately took my men to the Post Office which by then had been completely deserted. I learned that Min Yŏng-ik had not died yet and that he was lying in Möllendorf's house. I found him in a coma; all he could say was that he had been stabbed by the Progressives. Then I made an inspection tour around the palace ground and noticed that the palace gates were closed as usual and that everything was peaceful and quiet. Colonels Wu and Chang led their troops in patrolling the streets and around the palace, though there was not a single soul in sight. It was not until dawn that they called off the patrol and their men returned to the barracks.

Immediately after Min Yŏng-ik was slain, Hong Yŏng-sik hurried to the royal palace. He told the king that the Chinese army had rioted outside the palace, that the king should leave the palace immediately, and that he should invite the Japanese to protect him. The king was hesitant and could not make up his mind. Then Pak Yŏng-hyo grabbed his hand and forced him to write on a piece of paper the following words: "Let the Japanese minister come to the palace for guarding duties."[3] Before a messenger could be sent to the Japanese embassy, however, the Japanese troops had already arrived. With the Japanese troops at their disposal, Takezoe and Hong-Yŏng-sik quickly arrested the king and all his close relatives: the queen, the royal concubine, the crown prince, and the crown prince's wife. They locked the royal captives inside a small room and ordered the cadets to watch them. Even the king's personal servants were not allowed to come close; consequently the king and his family had nothing to eat or drink during their captivity. Japanese soldiers guarded the palace gates, and no one could enter or leave the palace without their permission.

Later Hong Yŏng-sik forged a decree which called upon Min T'ae-ho, Cho Yŏng-ha, Min Yŏng-mok, and Yun T'ae-jun to come to the palace to wait upon the king. Let it be recalled that all these gentlemen had been on friendly terms with me and were pro-Chinese. Once they arrived at the palace, however, they were immediately put to death. Han Kyu-jik, though a member of the Progressive Party, did not agree with his party's plan to kill me; he, too, was put to death. The Progressives also killed Yi Cho-yŏn of the Left Battalion on account of his inability to persuade his command to join the coup, even though he himself was in favor of it. Court official Yu Chae-hyŏn and his son suffered the same fate simply because they had defended me in front of their colleagues. Outside of the palace, emotions were greatly aroused because of these senseless killings.

On the eighteenth [December 5, 1884] Hong Yŏng-sik and his friends forced the king to leave the palace and move to Yi Chae-won's residence. There they appointed themselves Korea's highest officials: Hong Yŏng-sik as the prime minister, Pak Yŏng-hyo as the minister of war, and Sŏ Kwang-bŏm as the minister of foreign affairs. I sent a petition to the king, requesting permission to bring my troops to the palace to protect him. Pak Yŏng-hyo lied to me by saying that the king would not allow me to do so. It was not until 2 P.M. that these conspirators finally brought the king back to his palace. Korean ministers like Kim Yun-sik and Nam Chŏng-ch'ŏl pleaded with me in tears for assistance, and their pleadings were followed by an official message from the Korean government requesting me to come to the king's rescue. I hesitated because of the fear that any action on my part might precipitate a Sino-Japanese war since many Japanese were also inside the palace.

On the nineteenth [December 6, 1884] the Korean people became more agitated than ever, and hundreds of thousands gathered in the streets and vowed to stor the palace and kill all the Japanese. One report from the palace said that the queen had already been killed and that there was no knowledge whether the king was still living. Another report said that Hong Yŏng-sik had brought into the palace a nine-year-old son of the king's concubine and that he intended to depose the king and replace him with this young prince, while he himself would serve as the regent with full power of the state. Once in power, the report continued, he would betray China and make Korea an ally of Japan. By this time the situation had definitely reached the most dangerous point. If the Japanese succeeded in kidnapping the king, shipping him to Japan, and installing a new ruler in his place, we would lose not only a king but a kingdom as well. In such a case I would have committed a very serious offense indeed. Having made up my mind about what I had to do, I sent a letter to the Japanese minister Takezoe at 10 A.M., informing him of the situation outside the palace and also of my intention of taking over the palace so as to protect the king as well as the Japanese. When there was no reply as late as 4 P.M., I led my troops in storming the palace.

Before the attack, I spoke to the soldiers of the First and Second Royal Battalions on the importance of loyalty and righteousness and asked them to join in our efforts to save the king. Their duty, I told them, was to enter the palace by scaling its rear wall, while I and my men were to attack the palace from the front. When the attack began, I personally led my contingent in storming the front gate, so as to give Colonel Wu and his men the opportunity to enter the palace via the left gate. Colonel Chang and his men were in the meantime held in reserve. The buildings inside the palace ground were many-storied, and the roads separating them were narrow and crooked. We found maneuvering extremely difficult under the circumstances. Seeing that our troops had already entered the palace, the Japanese climbed to the upper stories of the tallest buildings and started to shoot: the shooting was so heavy that bullets came down like raindrops. I sent officer Ch'en Ch'ang-ch'ing, who had negotiated with the Japanese minister before, as my envoy to speak to the Japanese; I wished to explain to them why we had to enter the palace. But the Japanese minister refused to see him. While Officer Ch'en waited for a reply, bullets buzzed all around him.

In the meantime the Front and Rear Battalions led by Pak Yŏng-hyo had arrived to strengthen the Japanese defense. Meeting even greater resistance, my men and I had no choice but to continue fighting. We were soon joined by the First and Second

Royal Battalions that I had trained; they provided me with great help in winning a decisive victory. I was very proud of these men who fought as bravely as good soldiers should. The enemy suffered heavy casualties: only fifty of Pak Yŏng-hyo's Front Battalion and one hundred and ten of his Rear Battalion survived the battle and all of them subsequently surrendered. Pak Yŏng-hyo himself fled from the battlefield without a trace. Seeing their allies defeated and themselves isolated, the Japanese also decided to flee. My men followed in hot pursuit, and at a park in the rear of the palace the Japanese suddenly turned around to battle with us. In this battle my men and I charged from the front, while the two battalions led by Colonels Wu and Chang attacked from the left and the right respectively. In the midst of the battle, a mine which had been placed in advance by the Japanese suddenly exploded and killed six and wounded fourteen. Since my battalion was closest to the place where the mine exploded, most of those killed and wounded were my personal guards. In desperation the Japanese retreated to a mountain which was again surrounded. As the evening drew near, I was afraid that we might accidentally kill the king if we continued firing; then we thought that the Japanese might have taken him to the mountain. I called off the siege and returned my troops to the barracks. After we left, the Japanese sneaked back to their embassy under the cover of darkness.

We waited and waited, but there was no news about the king. By then I was greatly alarmed. I promised a reward of 2,000 taels of silver to anyone who reported to us the king's whereabouts; the reward would be increased to 20,000 if he could bring the king to our headquarters. At midnight a secret report came in, saying that the king was detained by Hong Yŏng-sik in the Temple of Kuan-ti[4] inside the Northern Gate. Upon hearing this report, I sent Deputy Mao, together with Colonels Wu and Chang, to the temple at the head of a contingent of troops. Since the road to the temple was hilly and most difficult to traverse and since I was greatly concerned that the enemy might attempt an ambush, I ordered intense patrol all along the road. Colonel Wu entered the temple and requested the king to come to the headquarters of the First Battalion to rest himself. Hong Yŏng-sik, who was standing beside the king, said that the king should not go unless Yüan Shih-k'ai came to make the request himself. The king agreed. However, as Colonel Wu continued his persuasion, the king stood up and was ready to leave, only to sit down again when Hong Yŏng-sik looked at him with disapproving eyes. Hong said that since Yüan Shih-k'ai did not choose to come himself, he would like to send a man to the palace to see whether it was safe. Actually he was proposing to send a messenger to call upon the Japanese to come to his rescue.

Previously, before Colonel Wu's arrival, Korean troops had already made their way into the temple. On their way they captured eight Japanese spies. Other Japanese changed into Korean clothes and were actually waiting upon the king when Colonel Wu arrived. A moment later, a stranger came in and acted in a peculiar manner. The king's guards grabbed him and exposed him as a Japanese soldier—they noticed how short his hair was when his hat fell off. They immediately put him to death. Suddenly Hong Yŏng-sik became tense and his facial expression changed. Under the candlelight and beside the king's seat, Colonel Chang spotted two men hidden inside a casket. Fearful for the king's life, he decided to take drastic measures. He and Colonel Wu brought a sedan chair to the terrace, while Deputy Mao tried to lead the king to the door. Disregarding Hong Yŏng-sik's strong admonition not to leave, the king stood up and walked out, while holding onto Deputy Mao's clothes. He stepped into the sedan chair and was immediately carried away. Seeing that the king was gone, Hong Yŏng-sik tried to escape by disappearing into the crowd. He did not succeed, however.

Deputy Mao held him by his hand and engaged him in small talk while they walked towards the outside together. Hong responded by holding Mao's hand as protection from the soldiers. However, hardly had he reached the door before a group of Korean soldiers cut him down. He slumped to the floor while still holding Mao's pigtail tightly. Pak Yŏng-hyo and his cadets—nine of them altogether—were killed in the temple yard.

The soldiers escorted the king to Colonel Wu's battalion headquarters where he summoned his ministers for a conference and announced the change of policies. Lest he again be bewitched by the Progressives and change his mind, the next day I requested he move his residence to my headquarters where I could observe him more closely. Once he began to live with me, I thought, the people would be pacified and their minds set at ease, while the intrigues of foreigners [Japanese] would also be put to an end. The king stayed in my headquarters for a period of four days, at the end of which peace and order once again returned to the people. Meanwhile he was even more determined as to what policy he was going to follow. Thinking that a longer stay at my headquarters would generate criticism, I requested the king's return to his palace on the twenty-third [December 10, 1884]. Before his return, however, the deputy battalion commander and I made the necessary arrangements inside and around the palace to assure that a similar incident would not happen again. Even if the members of the Progressive Party once more tried to confuse him, they would not dare to plot another coup with our troops stationed all around the palace.

Previously, when the king arrived at Colonel Wu's headquarters, I went inside to pay my respect. The king, holding my hand, was in tears. "I did not even dare to dream that I could see you again," he said; "you almost lost your life while trying to save mine." Then he told me what had happened to him during the recent crisis. On the day of the crisis Hong Yŏng-sik ordered him to change into ordinary civilian clothes in preparation for a journey to Inch'ŏn where a Japanese warship would take him to Japan. The king, however, refused to cooperate. Having failed in their persuasion, Hong Yŏng-sik and Pak Yŏng-hyo began to use a variety of ways to coerce him. All five members of the king's family pleaded in tears, but their captors simply would not listen to them. Without requesting the king's permission, Hong Yŏng-sik sent a man to look for civilian clothes; when they arrived, he put them on the king against the latter's wishes. Hardly had the king finished the change of clothes before he heard gun shots outside. Hong Yŏng-sik knew that our troops had by then entered the palace. He forced the king to leave and eventually settled him in the Temple of Kuan-ti. On that eventful evening when he heard that my troops were about to arrive, he stationed men inside the temple to kill Colonel Wu, Colonel Chang, and myself if and when we came into sight. Fortunately we discovered his plot before he could carry it out. At the time the king was kidnapped and brought to the temple, the queen and the crown prince managed to escape. Korean Captain Yu Tong-kŭn of the First Battalion hired two sedan chairs for their transportation and personally escorted them to safety. They were settled in a small village 15 *li* outside of the Eastern Gate and disguised themselves as Yu's relatives to avoid detection. Their whereabouts were not made known until the king, having been brought to my headquarters, was safe.

On the twenty-third [December 10, 1884] the troops of my battalion escorted the king back to his palace. The next day I sent Colonel Liu Ch'ao-kuei and Captain Yu Tong-kŭn to the eastern suburb to bring back the queen and the crown prince. At present the king is residing in a side palace. Our troops are now patrolling the compound day and night and will not relax their effort in protecting the king.

On the twentieth [December 7, 1884] Takezoe burned his embassy before he and his men left the city for Inch'ŏn. All along the road they met resistance from Korean citizens who attempted to bar their exit with force. Many of these Koreans were wounded by the fleeing Japanese, though the Japanese also suffered heavy casualties. In their flight the Japanese left behind their women and children. I ordered my men to escort these dependents to Inch'ŏn where they were received by their minister Takezoe. I did this in order to show our kindness and generosity.

On the twenty-first [December 8, 1884] the king received ministers from various countries in my headquarters. He related to them the conspiratorial alliance between his disloyal ministers and Japanese troops to stage a rebellion, the murdering by them of many of his loyal ministers, and finally, the threat and coercion which they had used against him. He said that he knew with certainty that some of these rebellious ministers, such as Pak Yŏng-hyo, Kim Ok-kyun, Sŏ Kwang-bŏm, and Sŏ Chae-p'il, were still hiding inside foreign embassies and that he was willing to reestablish diplomatic relations with all foreign countries and in fact to accept their good offices if they would surrender these fugitives to him. Instigated by the English consul Aston[5] who was pro-Japanese, all the foreign ministers refused the king's request. Governor Ch'en, Möllendorf, and I presented our case in the most convincing manner, and the American and German ministers finally changed their minds. But the English consul persisted in his pro-Japanese and anti-Chinese prejudice; he proposed that all the foreign ministers should proceed to Inch'ŏn to persuade Takezoe to remain in Korea so he could serve as a mediator in this dispute. The ministers accepted this proposal and acted accordingly. However, having found Takezoe in an irrational mood, the American and German ministers soon returned to the capital, though Aston is still staying at Inch'on at this moment. Lately I have noticed that the English consul is trying hard not to make his pro-Japanese sentiment too obvious, especially in this case when the difference between right and wrong has become too clear-cut even for him to ignore. We held a conference with the foreign ministers today during which Governor Ch'en and I suggested that a petition be presented to the king requesting the authorization of Hsü Hsiang-yü and Möllendorf to journey to Japan to reason with the Japanese government. The American minister also volunteered for this trip. There are no ships sailing for Japan at this moment, and I have no idea when this journey will take place.

The basic cause of this incident was the desire of people like Kim Ok-kyun and Hong Yŏng-sik to betray China and to make Korea an ally of a stronger country [Japan]. They promised to make the king an emperor if he went along with their scheme. Being a man of weak character, the king was taken in and subsequently brought them into his government as his favorite ministers. They in turn placed their henchmen in strategic government positions. Before the seventeenth when the coup took place, the king had some inkling of what they intended to do, but he was too weak a person to make a speedy decision. To persuade him to make up his mind in their favor, Kim Ok-kyun and his friends brought in the Japanese army to coerce him. The Japanese army, regarding him as an extremely ignorant and stupid person, had a treacherous plot to depose him from the throne. The Japanese put to death some of the king's senior ministers and were about to install a new king when the incident occurred. By then the king deeply regretted his own folly and knew he had been betrayed by his evil ministers. Kim Ok-kyun and his fellow Progressives contended that the Chinese army would not intervene because it was too cautious and restrained to make such a move. They repeated this contention whenever the Japanese declined their request to cooperate with them. The Japanese were really surprised when the Chinese did intervene on the nineteenth. In this sense these Progressives may be said to have betrayed their Japanese allies as well as their own king. Confident that they had the king on their side, they went ahead with the coup. Even after the king had been brought under our protection on the evening of the nineteenth, Kim Yun-sik and Kim Kwang-jip continued to be in control of the government. But their government was doomed. There was such a public uproar on the part of the Korean people against it that the king was forced to punish these evil men. Finally the king was able to even the score by betraying his own ministers who had tried to betray him.

For the future of Korea, China must make a decision on this issue of peace and war, a decision which, under normal circumstances, would not have been difficult to make. But we happen to live in a time when the Western powers are at their prime. Inevitably they will plot again in a few years; by then it will be even more difficult to stop them. It is hereby suggested that at this moment, while the Korean people still feel a strong sense of loyalty and gratitude towards us, we should send to this country a high-ranking official to serve as the Supervisor of the State in command of large concentrations of troops and with full authority over its foreign and domestic affairs. This is an opportunity that we should not lose. In my previous report I stated that the Japanese had already mobilized their armed forces and would like to take advantage of our difficulties with France to open hostilities against us. It is unlikely that suffering one setback, they would graciously concede defeat. Moreover, the leaders of the Progressive Party such as Kim Ok-kyun, Pak Yŏng-hyo, Sŏ Kwang-bŏm, and Sŏ Chae-p'il, plus two cadets, are presently in Japan, having been shipped to that country in wooden boxes by the Japanese. It is common knowledge that Japan will use these six evil men as vanguards and will send a large number of troops to Korea to play the same trickery as she is accustomed to.

Owing deep gratitude to my country and knowing well my duty as a soldier, I know what I should do, whatever the circumstances. But Korea is not a Liu-ch'iu or an Annam. If Korea is lost to a foreign power, the security of China will be irreparably jeopardized. It is for this reason that I request Your Excellency to dispatch a dozen warships and several thousand men to be stationed in Korea at the earliest moment. Once they find out that they are not popular with the Koreans and that we have large concentrations of troops in this country, the Japanese may decide to change their policy and negotiate for peace. If the Japanese troops arrive before ours do, it will be even more difficult to cope with them. I have heard that Takezoe is an arrogant and aggressive man; it is my hope that Your Excellency will send to Korea such veteran diplomats as Governor Ma Chien-chung and missionary Lo Feng-lu to help conduct negotiations. There will be no war if our diplomats come in the wake of a strong army. In short, if we show the Japanese that we intend to fight, they will not fight and consequently there will be peace. If on the other hand we give the impression that we want to obtain peace at any price, war will inevitably come about. It goes without saying that Your Excellency is thoroughly familiar with Japanese treachery.

NOTES

[1] This letter, addressed to Li Hung-chang, was dated December 15, 1884. Source: *Documents: Sinco-Japanese Relations during the Ch'ing Dynasty* (*Chung Jih chiao-sheh shih-liao*), the Reign of Kuang-hsü, roll 6, pp. 16-20.

[2] Sinicized as Mu Lin-teh.

[3] *Jih shih yü wei* ("Japanese minister enter guard").

[4] Kuan-ti (or Kuan Yü) was a civil war hero in China during the period of the Three Kingdoms (220 265).

[5] William George Aston.

65 • *The Li-Ito Agreement* (1885)[1]

It is hereby agreed that China shall withdraw her troops now stationed in Corea [Korea], and that Japan shall withdraw hers stationed therein for the protection of her Legation. The specific term for effecting the same shall be four months commencing from the date of the signing and sealing of this Convention, within which term they shall respectively accomplish the withdrawal of the whole number of each of their troops, in order to avoid effectively any complications between the respective countries; the Chinese troops shall embark from Masan-Po, and the Japanese from the port of Ninsen.

The said respective Powers mutually agree to invite the King of Corea to instruct and drill a sufficient armed force, that she may herself assure her public security, and to invite him to engage in his service an officer or officers from among those of a third Power, who shall be entrusted with the instruction of the said force. The respective Powers also bind themselves, each to the other, henceforth not to send any of their own officers to Corea for the purpose of giving said instruction.

In case of any disturbance of a grave nature occurring in Corea which necessitates the respective countries or either of them to send troops to Corea, it is hereby understood that they shall give, each to the other, previous notice in writing of their intention to do so, and that after the matter is settled they shall withdraw their troops and not further station them there.

Signed and sealed this 18th day of the 4th month of the 18th year of Meiji (Japanese Calendar); the 4th day of the 3rd moon of the 11th year of Kocho[2] (Chinese Calendar).

NOTES

[1] This document, officially entitled "Convention between China and Japan for the Withdrawal of Chinese and Japanese Troops from Corea," as signed at Tientsin on April 18, 1885. Li and Ito are Li Hung-chang and Ito Hirobumi respectively. Source: *Treaties, &c., between Great Britain and China,* vol. I, pp. 256.

[2] Yi-yu; 11th year of Kuang-hsü or 1885.

66 • LI HUNG-CHANG: *The Eastern Learning Society*[1]

I have received a telegram from Yüan Shih-k'ai which reads as follows:

"The members of the heretical Eastern Learning [Tong-hak] Society has petitioned the Korean king to drive out all the Westerners from Korea. The same intention is also expressed in their posters and handbills. They go from one Westerner's house to another, stating in the most abusive language that if these Westerners do not leave Korea immediately, they will be killed in due course. All the Westerners in Han-ch'eng [Seoul] are greatly frightened. Most Japanese carry their knives with them when walking even in broad daylight and create worse disturbances than even the Eastern Learning Society. I have repeatedly urged the Korean government to crack down on these lawless elements, but it is too fearful to take any step.

"A moment ago an English officer named Walter C. Hillier came to see me, saying that he had informed his fellow Westerners that since China alone had the responsibility of restoring order in Korea, they should wait for the Chinese initiative, despite the fact that they had consulted among themselves regarding the possibility of sending for warships from their respective countries. He further urged me to dispatch several Chinese warships to Korea at the earliest moment so as to make sure that no tragic incidents will ensue and that foreigners in Korea can live in peace without worry or fear.

"It is a good thing that the Westerners are waiting for the Chinese initiative to restore order in Korea. Your Excellency is hereby urgently requested to send two warships to Jen-ch'uan [Inch'ŏn] at the earliest moment. Since the Korean government, being beset by rumors, is inert and inept, it is further requested that Your Excellency urge it to take speedy measures to suppress the lawless elements."

I have already dispatched two warships, Ch'ing-yüan and Lai-yüan, to sail speedily to Jen-ch'uan, and these two ships are to cooperate with Yüan Shih-k'ai in the performance of patrolling duties and in the restoration of peace and order in Korea. A telegram has been sent to Yüan Shih-k'ai ordering him, in the name of China, to address the Korean government with regard to the suppression and punishment of lawless elements.

NOTES

[1] This is a telegram sent to the Office of General Management on April 6, 1893. Source: *The Complete Works of Li Hung-chang* (*Li Wen-chung kung ch'üan-chi*), roll 14, pp. 28–29.

67 • ANONYMOUS: *A Conversation between Komura Jutaro and a Chinese Diplomat*[1]

Chinese Diplomat: I presume that you have received our letter.

Komura: Yes, I have. Thanks. The purpose of this visit is to discuss the matter that we went over last month. My government desires very much an early settlement. If your government wishes to enter into negotiations, my government has authorized me to represent it.

Chinese Diplomat: China and Japan have always maintained the closest relations, and we do not need a third party to offer its good offices. Some of these powers are sincere when they offer to mediate, but others only wish to take undue advantage. If both of our countries withdraw our troops from Korea in accordance with our previous agreement, other powers, seeing that we have peacefully settled our differences, will have no excuse to intervene.

Komura: There are still bandits[2] in Korea, and we cannot say that peace has been restored.

Chinese Diplomat: All the remaining bandits have surrendered themselves, together with their military equipment which is now in the hands of the governor of Ch'üan-lo [Chŏlla] province. Those who are still at large are few in number and can be easily handled by the Korean government. The Korean government has requested the earliest withdrawal of both Chinese and Japanese troops.

Komura: I have heard that some of these bandits have escaped to the areas south of the Ch'üan-lo province. I am afraid that once we withdraw our troops, they will reemerge. My government does agree, however, that sooner or later both of our two countries will have to withdraw our troops.

Chinese Diplomat: I believe that we should withdraw now in accordance with our agreement. If disturbances do develop after our withdrawal, we can send troops to Korea again in accordance with our agreement. I believe that we should at this time agree to a date of withdrawal and make our intention known throughout the world. Otherwise there could be unfortunate ramifications.

Komura: My government shares your government's view that we should negotiate with each other directly without the interference from a third power. The sooner we settle this matter, the better it will be for both of our countries. If your government agrees in advance to the several proposals we made during the previous conference, we will of course withdraw our troops.

Chinese Diplomat: I do not know whether we can agree to the many details listed in your proposals. In any case we should discuss them, but we cannot discuss them unless the troops are withdrawn. Other countries are waiting for an opportunity to interfere with Korean affairs. They are bound to intervene if we discuss troop withdrawal and your proposals at the same time. If they do, the issue would become more complicated and difficult to resolve.

Komura: Russia also mentioned to my government about troop withdrawal. My government replied that we would not withdraw unless the many issues regarding Korea were settled. If we promise China to withdraw our troops, how are we going to answer Russia?

Chinese Diplomat: It is stipulated in our agreement that we will send troops to Korea when disorder occurs and will withdraw our troops when order is restored. This agreement has nothing to do with other countries. Moreover, the situation changes every day. Since peace has been reestablished in Korea, what objection can Russia possibly have to the withdrawal of troops?

Komura: Is it true that your government has requested Russia's good offices in settling this dispute?

Chinese Diplomat: On his way to Russia, the Russian minister A.P. Cassini passed through Tientsin and heard about our differences. He told His Excellency Li [Li Hung-chang] that he had been authorized by his government to stay in Tientsin to help resolve the Korean problem. Russia has a common boundary with Korea and believes that her own interest is involved. When she says that she wishes to mediate, she is not really interested in bringing our two parties together; she merely wishes to exploit our differences for her own benefit. I have heard from the British minister Nicolas R. O'Conor that Russia has proposed to call a three-power conference. Is this true?

Komura: We have not heard anything of this sort. Though Russia has a common boundary with Korea, she is not so closely related to that country as China and Japan are. We will under no circumstances agree to this so-called three-power conference. If the Russians want a war over this issue, they can have it.

Chinese Diplomat: Not only does Russia wish to intervene, but several European powers as well. They want to intervene because Japan has refused to withdraw her troops.

Komura: Is it the wish of Your Excellency that China and Japan should first agree to the simultaneous withdrawal of troops before they can discuss the future of Korea? If it is, I shall convey it to our Foreign Office. But we will not withdraw our troops simply because the Russians insist that we should. I do not think that our Foreign Office will agree to the withdrawal of our troops until it knows what China intends to do about Korea.

Chinese Diplomat: We cannot specify at this moment what we intend to do about Korea. But we would say that we will do everything we can to advance the interest of the Korean people. The refusal by Japan to withdraw her troops is clearly a violation of our agreement. If other countries use Japan's refusal to withdraw as a pretext to send their troops to Korea and if meanwhile they insist on holding an international conference to determine the future of Korea, on what ground can Japan refuse them? The longer Japan postpones the withdrawal of her troops, the more complicated the situation will be and the more difficult it will be to solve existing problems.

Komura: If you can tell me what China intends to do about Korea, I shall telegraph my government and propose the withdrawal of our troops at the earliest moment. Will you put down in written words an outline of China's policy towards Korea so I can transmit it to my government?

Chinese Diplomat: I believe that I have stated to you very clearly our policy towards Korea. There is no need to put it down in written words. In short, we will not discuss any matter relating to Korea until the last Japanese soldier has left that country.

Komura left without a word.

NOTES

[1] This conversation was conducted on July 9, 1894 shortly before the outbreak of the Sino-Japanese War. This translator has not been able to identify either the Chinese diplomat who took part in this conversation or the secretary who transcribed it. Source: *Chung Jih chiao-sheh shih-liao*, roll 14, p. 19.

[2] This refers to the members of the Eastern Learning Society.

68 • KUANG-HSÜ: *A Declaration of War against Japan*[1]

It is common knowledge, here and abroad, that Korea has been a tributary state of the Great Ch'ing Dynasty for more than 200 years and has sent tribute missions to China, without fail, each and every year. During the past ten years, time and again civil disturbances raged the country and our government, feeling compassionate for the common and the innocent, repeatedly dispatched troops to restore order. A commissioner was sent to that country to reside in its capital and provide protection for all the Korean people whenever it was needed.

In the fourth month of this year[2] once again there were bandits[3] who staged a rebellion. Having received an urgent request from the king of Korea for assistance, I ordered Li Hung-chang to send a contingent of troops to Korea to restore order. The bandits were scattered as soon as our expeditionary force reached Ya-shan.[4] We did not expect Japan to take the unjustifiable course of sending troops to Korea too, and her troops, which had not been invited by the Korean government, nevertheless occupied its capital Han-ch'eng [Seoul]. Later, by increasing her military strength to more than 10,000 men, she forced the Korean government to change its policies, foreign as well as domestic, in addition to other unreasonable demands too numerous to mention. Our dynasty has always maintained the most cordial relationship with all of its tributary states and has followed a policy of noninterference in their domestic affairs. Since Korea has concluded a treaty with Japan, she is sovereign as far as Japan is concerned. On what ground can Japan be justified in the employment of military might to intimidate her, thus forcing her to change her existing policies? Regarding the Japanese expedition as unjustifiable and unwarranted, all of the foreign countries have advised Japan to withdraw her troops and to enter into peaceful negotiations with China. Japan ignored this advice in the most arrogant manner, and consequently nothing constructive has come about. Meanwhile she continued to increase her military strength in Korea.

As Korean citizens and Chinese traders in Korea continued to suffer from Japanese harassment, the Chinese government had no choice but to send more men to protect them. On their way towards Korea and on the open seas outside the port of Ya-shan, our transports were suddenly fired upon by Japanese warships. Because of our unpreparedness, we received heavy damages. This treachery on the part of Japan violates not only existing treaties but also international law as commonly recognized by all nations. Her ruthlessness in the conduct of her relations with other countries and her employment of duplicity and deceit to further her ends have thus become clear for all people to see. She opened hostilities against us without the slightest provocation.

It is hoped that through this proclamation all the people in the world will know that this government has done its utmost to avoid conflict and that Japan, by violating treaty obligations and opening hostilities, has committed an unjustifiable act of the greatest extreme which we can no longer tolerate. Let Li Hung-chang dispatch our armed forces to Korea in the speediest manner possible—they are to crush all resistance in order to save the Korean people from their unbearable sufferings. Meanwhile all the generals, governors, and military commanders who have been charged with the responsibility of coastal and river defense should maintain vigilance and diligently prepare themselves and their men for possible action. If Japanese ships ever sail into the ports under their jurisdiction, they should immediately launch an attack to exterminate them. They will be severely punished if they show cowardliness.

Let this decree be made known to all of our citizens!

NOTES

[1] This declaration of war was dated August 1, 1894, in the form of a decree issued by Emperor Kuang-hsü to the government (*nei-ko*). Source: *Chung Jih chiao-she shih-liao*, roll 16, p. 2.

[2] The fourth lunar month of 1894 covers the period between May 5 and June 3 inclusive.

[3] Members of the Eastern Learning Society.

[4] Asan in Korean.

69 • ANONYMOUS: *Minutes: The Fifth Conference between Li Hung-chang and Ito Hirobumi*[1]

(The conference began at 2:30 P.M., March 21, 1895. Location: Shumpanro[2])

Li: How is His Excellency Mutsu?[3] How does he feel today?

Ito: He is feeling better now. He wanted to come to this conference, but Dr. Sato would not let him.

Li: Dr. Sato told me this morning that Mr. Mutsu has not completely recovered and should not go outside. Yesterday I sent Ching-fang to speak with Your Excellency; he told me that you, sir, were very harsh and that you would not give even one inch.

Ito: I have said many times before that I have given as much as I can. As far as I am concerned, the decision has already been made, and there will not be any change. I am sorry that there is not much I can do.

Li: I was ordered by my government to come here to negotiate; now I find how difficult it is to negotiate. Please put yourself in my place. There is no more ground where I can retreat.

Ito: My situation is the same as yours.

Li: Nobody in your country dares to criticize you.

Ito: Sometimes they do.

Li: But they would not criticize you so severely as my countrymen have criticized me in China.

Ito: On the contrary, my situation in Japan is much more difficult than yours in China. Your position in China is high and your prestige enormous; nobody can downgrade you from your present position. In my country, however, the Diet has tremendous power. If I make a single mistake, I will be criticized.

Li: Last year I was repeatedly criticized by officials for being too friendly with Prime Minister Ito of Japan. They were correct, of course. The very fact that I am now negotiating a treaty with you can be cited as evidence.

Ito: These officials did not understand the true situation; that is why they criticized you. Now that they know it, they must regret what they did and admit their own errors.

Li: The terms of this treaty are so harsh that I will be severely criticized if I put my name on it. What can I do?

Ito: Let them give vent to their irresponsible criticism if they like. They know very well that they cannot shoulder this great responsibility. In China only you, sir, can shoulder this responsibility.

Li: But, once I sign this treaty, they will attack me as one man.

Ito: Wherever a person is, he will always find irresponsible men making irresponsible remarks. In this respect, my situation is no different from yours.

Li: Let us not proceed with this matter any further. When I came here to negotiate for peace, I was ordered by His Majesty the Emperor to make some changes with regard to the draft treaty. I feel strongly that unless some changes are made, I simply cannot assume the grave responsibility of putting my name on it. I hope that you, sir, will give this matter your careful thought and decide on which items you can give a little. In this matter of ceding territories and paying indemnities, for instance, I would like to request some concessions from you before we make it final.

Ito: I have stated at the beginning that there is no more we can give. I told

Envoy Pai-hsing yesterday that we have done our very best as far as making concession is concerned. In fact, we did not retreat as far as our present position until we had held four or five conferences. Even from China's point of view, the concessions we have made should be regarded as the best we can do. Moreover, we are negotiating for peace; it is rather improper that we should haggle like merchants who buy or sell a piece of merchandise.

Li: When I saw you last, you seemed to have agreed that the indemnity could be reduced by 50 million taels. I will sign the treaty this very moment if the indemnity is reduced by such an amount.

Ito: If there is any concession I could make, I would have made it a long time ago without you ever having to mention it.

Li: If you cannot reduce the indemnity by 50 million, will it be possible for you to reduce it by 20 million? I have a newspaper item here which says that Japan's total expenditure for this war does not exceed 80 million. I am not saying that this news item is completely reliable, but it must have its source.

(Ito took the newspaper from Li and read it.)

Ito: This is only the opinion of one newspaper. It is anti-government throughout; you should by no means take it seriously.

Li: Let us not talk about this newspaper any more. As far as the indemnity is concerned, I still hope that you will reduce it somewhat.

Ito: Japan's expenditure in this war is much larger than the amount cited by this newspaper.

Li: If you are kind enough to reduce the indemnity somewhat, the whole matter will be immediately settled. In such a case, I will telegraph the settlement to my government which in turn will express its gratitude to Japan.

Ito: If I could reduce the indemnity somewhat, I would have done it a long time ago.

Li: Through this treaty your country will obtain from us many new territories that are rich in natural resources. Please look at this matter from a broad perspective; you should not be solely concerned with immediate gains.

Ito: These natural resources belong to the future; they cannot be viewed as part of the indemnity which concerns us at this very moment.

Li: When natural resources are rich, the profit realized from them must also be very large.

Ito: Whatever profit we realize from the exploitation of these resources will be reinvested. There cannot be any surplus.

Li: With these natural resources, economic prosperity is assured.

Ito: It requires a large amount of capital to open up natural resources.

Li: Take Taiwan as an example. It is rich in coal, petroleum, and gold deposits. But the Chinese on the island did not know how to utilize them. These natural resources would have been exploited had I been the governor.

Ito: Once these deposits are opened up, we would be happy to sell them to the Chinese at a low price.

Li: Certainly the Chinese businessmen cannot obtain them free of charge.

Ito: It takes a large amount of capital to open up virgin fields.

Li: The larger the expenditure is, the larger the profit will be. Why is it that you cannot reduce the indemnity by a small amount since you will be more than adequately compensated by the natural resources you are going to acquire from us? Once you acquire these natural resources, you will be in a good position to negotiate loans with foreigners. When I was in Peking, some foreigners proposed to lend us 20 million pounds if we would agree to mortgage Taiwan to them. Later, after I had arrived at Japan, they learned that the Japanese were forcing us to cede to them this island; consequently the offer was withdrawn. If Taiwan can be mortgaged for 20 million pounds, its selling price must be much higher.

Ito: With her rich natural resources, China should have no difficulty obtaining loans from foreigners.

Li: Whatever you say, I am still asking you to reduce the indemnity by 20 or 30 million taels. How can you possibly be so tight?

Ito: As I have said time and again, there is absolutely no further concession I can make.

Li: You want us to pay you indemnity; you also want us to cede you territories. You are holding a gun with two barrels. Do you not think that you are a little too harsh? You are embarrassing me.

Ito: This is not an ordinary conference; this is a conference to negotiate a treaty to end a war.

Li: Nevertheless we are negotiating for peace. Both sides should give a little. You are too harsh; you certainly have the ability to get what you want.

Ito: This has nothing to do with ability. This is a normal situation after the conclusion of a war. As far as ability is concerned, I am far inferior to you.

Li: Since you cannot reduce the indemnity, will you consider the reduction of territories you want to take away from us? Do you mean to tell me that you cannot spare even one hair from your body?

Ito: I am afraid to say that we cannot reduce our territorial demands either. As I have said many times before, we have absolutely reached the limit. There cannot be any change, however small it is.

Li: I do not mean that I do not intend to sign this treaty; I only request that you modify some of the harshest terms. I will sign the treaty the moment you make some concessions. I wish you to consider these small concessions as a farewell present from you to me. When I return to my own country, I will kindly remember them.

Ito: The concessions I have already made are my farewell present. I told Envoy Pai-hsing yesterday that originally I was determined not to change one word of the draft treaty and that it was out of consideration of my long-time friendship with you that I reduced the indemnity by a large amount.

Li: Your mouth is as tight as your hands are clenched. I promise you that I will never forget this.[4]

Ito: I have already made great concessions because of my long-time friendship with you. My countrymen will criticize, of course; but I think I can shoulder this responsibility. I request you to sign this treaty speedily before an armistice can be arranged. If you delay further, the amount of indemnity we will ask will be much larger. This, I can assure you, is the unanimous opinion of all of us Japanese.

Li: If the amount of indemnity cannot be reduced, will you consider the cancellation of interest payment?

Ito: We have stated in the conference held the other day that within one year after the ratification of the treaty there should be two payments of 50 million taels each and that the balance, or 100 million, should be paid before the end of the second year. If these payments are made when they are due, we will be willing to forgo the interest payment.

Li: Suppose that we cannot obtain a loan for a scheduled payment when payment is due, will you be satisfied, for the time being, with the payment of interest only?

Ito: No, I will not. What I am saying is the same as I have said before. If we accept only interest payment without in the meantime demanding the payment of capital, we should be only like a creditor to you. Japan is not wealthy enough to be a creditor to China.

Li: China's financial situation is much worse off than that of Japan. Since the beginning of the present hostilities, Japan has never borrowed any money from the Western countries, while China has done it several times. This is a good indication that Japan is wealthier than China.

Ito: It is not true that Japan is wealthier than China. Japan knows a little better about financial management.

Li: We are going to learn from Japan about financial management. At the moment, however, we are so poor that it is very difficult for us to contract more loans.

Ito: I do not see why it should be so difficult.

Li: I have no idea at the moment. After my return home, I shall discuss this matter with others. If we pay off the total amount within a three-year period, will you agree not to charge any interest?

Ito: If the total amount is really paid within a three-year period, there will be no interest charge.

Li: I would like to suggest that a clause be inserted in the treaty which reads something like this: "If the last payment is made after the three-year period, etc." This clause will not only make the term more flexible but will also enable China to look more respectable in the eyes of the world. Whatever advantage we might derive from this clause will not be too great.

Ito: The draft treaty says that after the first scheduled payment, interest will be charged on the balance, etc. If total payment is not made within a three-year period, interest will be retroactive for the entire period.

Li: May I suggest that if total payment is made within a three-year period, there will be no interest charge and that a compound interest will be charged on the unpaid balance if total payment is not made within a three-year period?

Ito: Your suggestion makes the terms even more confusing.

Li: We can simplify the matter by deducting 20 million from the total of 200 million as compensation for our interest payment, making 180 million as the total payment. The rest will follow the draft treaty.

Ito: This cannot be done. It should be specified in the treaty that only when total payment is made within a three-year period will there be no interest charge. These terms should be made specific so that there will not be any misunderstanding.

Li: Since this indemnity is so large, how can I say for certainty that total payment will be made in three years?

Ito: I was afraid that you might not be able to pay the entire indemnity in two years. That is why I made the payment period three years.

Li: If you are kind enough to reduce the total amount by 20 million, China would borrow 20 million less from foreign countries.

Ito: This is an impossible proposition. . . .

Li: Formerly when China paid indemnities to England and France, it was stipulated in our agreement that only when China failed to pay when payment was due would interest be charged. Do you not think that you are extremely harsh in wanting interest to be paid at the very beginning?[5]

Ito: England and France are wealthy countries; that is why they could afford to forgo interest payment.

Li: You love money too much. The amount you have demanded is enormous; the interest is huge.

Ito: When England and France waged war against you, they did not put on the battlefield so many men as we have been doing in this war.

Li: At that time England sent to China large contingents of Indian sepoys.

Ito: The number was not very large.

Li: Can we insert a clause saying that all interest paid during the first two years will be considered as capital deductions?

Ito thought carefully for a long time and then said: If you wish to forgo interest payment, there is only one way you can do it. First, you will agree to the payment of interest during the three-year period as stipulated; second, if you have paid the total indemnity in full at the end of the three-year period, the interest so far paid will be regarded as capital deductions.

Li: Do I understand correctly that we will have to pay interest during the three-year period and that the paid interest will be computed as capital payment if the total amount of indemnity is paid within the said period?

Ito: What I mean is this: In the first six months after the ratification of the treaty, you will pay 50 million; you will pay another 50 million in the second six-month period. In other words, in one year you will have to pay 100 million, all of which will be regarded as interest payment. The same thing can be said about the third and the fourth payments. If, at the end of the three-year period, you are able to pay the unpaid balance and have thus paid in full the entire indemnity, the interest so far paid during the previous two and one-half years will be regarded as capital deductions. The three-year period begins with the ratification of the treaty.

Li: A clause should be added to Article 4. The clause reads: "If the total indemnity is paid within a three-year period, etc." Please take a look at it and see whether it meets your approval.

After consulting with his assistants, Ito replied: Let it be added to Article 4.

Li: There are several other things which I would like to discuss with you. I want you to understand that I do not mean to suggest substantial changes in the draft treaty; I merely wish to make the treaty terms clearer so there will not be any misunderstanding in the future. For instance, there is this matter of the boundary line at the mouth of the Liao River.[6] In my judgment, this boundary line, once reaching the Liao River of Yingk'ou,[7] should follow the middle of the current all the way until the river reaches the sea. This is the usage under international law, commonly recognized by all nations that use rivers as boundary lines.

Ito: This matter will be taken care of when the boundary line is actually delimited.

Li: Why do you not add this provision to Section 2, Article 2?

Ito: You are right; let it be done.

Li: Section 5 should say that those Chinese who choose not to move out from the ceded territory at the end of a two-year period should be regarded as Japanese subjects, that those Chinese who are not residents of the ceded territory but who have properties in the aforesaid territory can, at the end of the two-year period, request Japanese authorities to protect their property rights, and that these property rights should enjoy the same protection as those of Japanese subjects.

Ito: I am afraid that I cannot agree to this proposition. In the treaties which she has signed with the Western powers, Japan does not allow foreigners to establish property rights within Japanese territory.

Li: I am not talking about property rights newly established by foreigners; I am talking about properties owned by the Chinese prior to the cession of territories.

Ito: We cannot accept your proposal because it is contrary to the Japanese law. If we do, other foreigners will use this as a pretext to demand the same right.

Li: These properties owned by the Chinese are inherited properties from their ancestors. I do not see any difficulty in this matter since these Chinese will pay taxes in accordance with your law. A Chinese of one county, for instance, can buy and establish property rights in another county.

Ito: What you have proposed is entirely different from the establishment of property rights by a Chinese in a neighboring Chinese county. If Japan allows the Chinese to establish property rights in a territory which China has ceded to Japan, other powers will invoke the most-favored-nation clause for their nationals.

Li: The Chinese in Taiwan do not wish to move out; nor do they want to sell out their property. Once the Japanese government makes known what it intends to do with them and their property, I am afraid that there will be unfortunate incidents. I hope that you will not blame the Chinese government when these incidents occur.

Ito: Once we take over Taiwan, the responsibility is ours.

Li: I have received a telegram from the governor of Taiwan which says that the Taiwanese were in an uproar when they heard that their government had ceded the island to Japan; they swore that they would never become Japanese subjects.

Ito: Let them make as much noise as they like; I can cope with them.

Li: I did not mean to threaten you. Mine are honest remarks with good intentions.

Ito: I have also heard about their uproars.

Li: The Taiwanese often form clandestine groups to attack their officials. When similar incidents occur in the future, please do not blame us.

Ito: Once the Chinese government relinquishes sovereign rights over Taiwan to us, the responsibility is ours.

Li: But I feel obligated to warn you beforehand.

Ito: All the Chinese government needs to do is to withdraw its soldiers as well as its officials.

Li: We cannot withdraw the "green battalions"[8] that are composed of the native population, but we will withdraw the garrison troops.

(At this moment Ito began to read the English version of the clause that deals with the cancellation of interest payment, checked it with the Chinese version, and found them in agreement.)

Ito: This clause should be added to the treaty in its present form.

Li: There will be difficulties and complications in trying to persuade Taiwanese officials and gentry to accept the decisions we have made here. I suggest that after the treaty's ratification a period of six months be allowed to elapse before the transfer of sovereignty takes place. I further suggest that this provision be inserted as part of the treaty.

Ito: In a few weeks after the treaty's ratification, I intend to send soldiers and officials to take over Taiwan.

Li: You should send a man beforehand to discuss the transfer with the governor of Taiwan.

Ito: I am requesting that after the treaty's ratification, the Chinese officials proclaim to the Taiwanese people that the Japanese government is sending soldiers and officials to take over the island. These officials should take under their temporary custody all the military equipment in the island.

Li: Will you also send civilian officials?

Ito: Yes, we will.

Li: The transfer of territory is a serious matter. We should establish a simple but clear procedure to follow, so there will not be any confusion or disagreement when the transfer takes place sometime in the future.

Ito: I cannot wait six months and then discuss the transfer. Once the treaty is ratified, I will send my men to take over that island. . . .

NOTES

[1] A copy of the Chinese original can be found in *Chung-kuo chin-pai-nien shih tzu-liao,* edited by Tso Shun-sheng, vol. 2, pp. 275–285.

[2] Located in Shimonoseki, Japan.

[3] Mutsu Munemitsu.

[4] One year later, Li signed a treaty of alliance with Russia in which Japan was specified as a potential enemy.

[5] This refers to the retroactive interest if China failed to pay in full in a three-year period.

[6] According to the draft treaty, China should cede to Japan the Liaotung Peninsula. Later, Russia, France, and Germany intervened, and Japan was forced by these three powers to return the peninsula to China.

[7] Located at the mouth of the Liao River.

[8] Militia-like organizations.

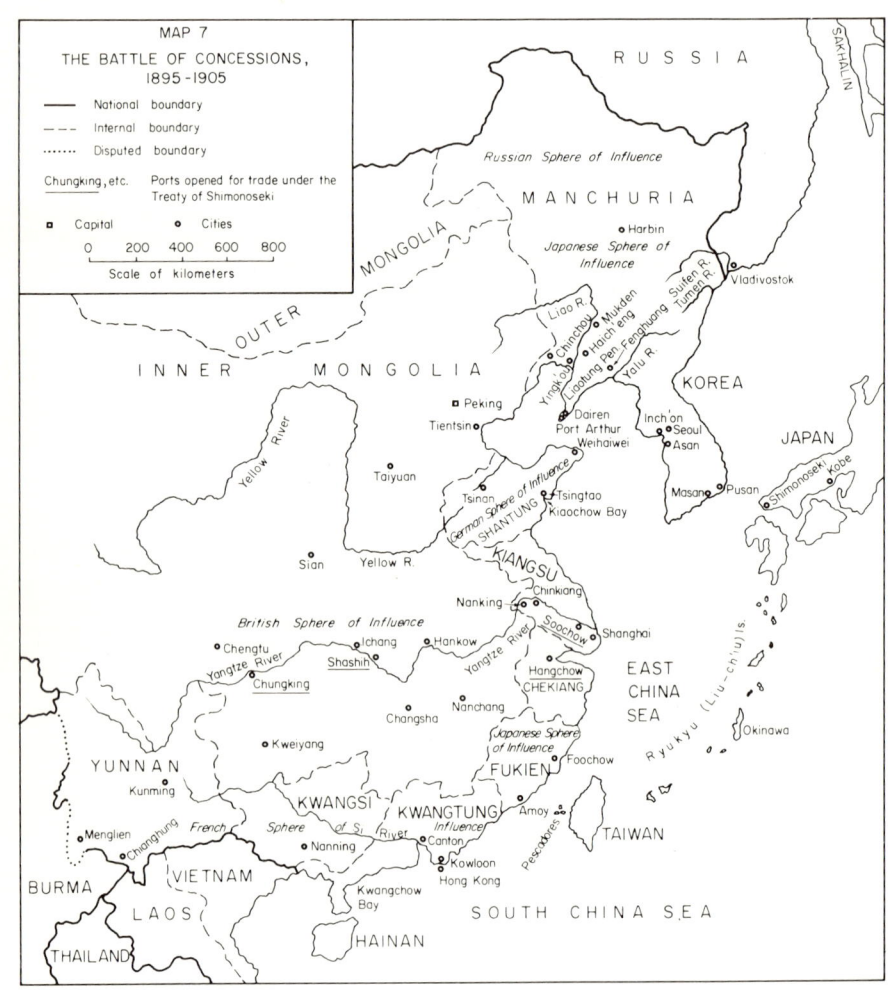

70 • *The Treaty of Shimonoseki* (1895)[1]

ARTICLE I

China recognizes definitely the full and complete independence and autonomy of Corea, and in consequence the payment of tribute and the performance of ceremonies and formalities by Corea to China, in derogation of such independence and autonomy, shall wholly cease for the future.

ARTICLE II

China cedes to Japan in perpetuity and full sovereignty the following territories, together with all fortifications thereon:

a. The southern portion of the province of Feng Tien[2] within the following boundaries:

The line of demarcation begins at the mouth of the River Yalu and ascends that stream to the mouth of the River An-ping; from thence the line runs to Feng Huang; from thence to Haicheng; from thence to Ying Kow, forming a line which describes the southern portion of the territory. The places above named are included in the ceded territory. When the line reaches the River Liao at Feng Kow, it follows the course of that stream to its mouth, where it terminates. The mid-channel of the River Liao shall be taken as the line of demarcation.

The cession also includes all islands appertaining or belonging to the province of Feng Tien, situated in the eastern portion of the Bay of Liao Tung and in the northern part of the Yellow Sea.

b. The island of Formosa, together with all the islands appertaining or belonging to said island of Formosa.

c. The Pescardores Group—that is to say, all islands lying between the 119 and 120th degrees of longitude east of Greenwich and the 23rd and 24th degrees of north latitude.

ARTICLE III

The alignments of portions described in the preceding article and shown on the annexed map shall be subject to verification and demarcation on the spot, by a joint commission of delimitation consisting of two or more Chinese and two or more Japanese delegates to be appointed immediately after the exchange of the ratifications of this act. In case the boundaries laid down in this act are found to be defective at any point, either on account of topography or in consideration of good administration, it shall also be the duty of the delimitation commission to rectify the same.

The delimitation commission will enter upon its duties as soon as possible and will bring its labors to a conclusion within the period of one year after appointment.

The alignments laid down in this act shall, however, be maintained until the rectifications of the delimitation commission, if any are made, shall have received the approval of the Governments of China and Japan.

ARTICLE IV

China agrees to pay to Japan as a war indemnity the sum of 200,000,000 Kuping taels.[3] The said sum is to be paid in eight installments; the first installment of 50,000,000 taels to be paid within six months and the second installment of 50,000,000 taels to be paid within twelve months after the exchange of the ratifications of this act; the remaining sum to be paid in six equal annual installments, as follows:

The first of such equal annual installments to be paid within two years; the second, within three years; the third, within four years; the fourth, within five years; the fifth, within six years; and the sixth, within seven years; after the exchange of the ratifications of this act. Interest at the rate of 5 per centum per annum shall begin to run on all unpaid portions of the said indemnity from the date the first installment falls due.

China shall, however, have the right to pay by anticipation at any time any or all of said installments. In case the whole amount of the said indemnity is paid within three years after the exchange of the ratifications of the present act, all interest shall be waived, and the interest for two years and a half or for any less period, if then already paid, shall be included as part of the principal amount of the indemnity.

ARTICLE V

The inhabitants of the territory ceded to Japan, who wish to take up their residence outside the ceded districts, shall be at liberty to sell their real property and retire.

For this purpose a period of two years from the date of the exchange of the ratifications of the present act shall be granted. At the expiration of that period those of the inhabitants who shall not have left said territories shall, at the option of Japan, be deemed Japanese subjects.

Each of the two Governments shall immediately upon the exchange of the ratifications of the present act send one or more commissioners to Formosa to effect a final transfer of that province, and within the space of two months after the exchange of the ratifications of this act such transfer shall be completed.

ARTICLE VI

All treaties between China and Japan having come to an end, in consequence of war, China engages immediately upon the exchange of the ratifications of this act to appoint plenipotentiaries to conclude with the Japanese plenipotentiaries a treaty of commerce and navigation and a convention to regulate frontier intercourse and trade.

The treaties, conventions, and regulations now subsisting between China and European powers shall serve as a basis for the said treaty and convention between China and Japan. From the date of the exchange of the ratifications of this act until the said treaty and convention are brought into actual operation, the Japanese Government, its officials, commerce, navigation, frontier intercourse and trade, industries, ships, and subjects, shall, in every respect, be accorded, by China, most-favored-nation treatment.

China makes, in addition, the following concessions, to take effect six months after the date of the present act:

First. The following cities, towns, and ports, in addition to those already opened, shall be opened to the trade, residence, industries, and manufactures of Japanese subjects, under the same conditions and with the same privileges and facilities as exist at the present open cities, towns, and ports of China.

1. Shashih, in the province of Hupeh.
2. Chungking, in the province of Szechan.
3. Suchow, in the province of Kian Su.[4]
4. Hang Chow, in the province of Chekiang.

The Japanese Government shall have the right to station consuls at any or all of the above-named places.

Second. Steam navigation for vessels under the Japanese flag for the conveyance of passengers and cargo shall be extended to the following places:
1. On the upper Yangtze River, from Ichang to Chungking.
2. On the Woosung River and the canal,[5] from Shanghai to Suchow and Hangchow.

The rules and regulations which now govern the navigation of the inland waters of China by foreign vessels shall, so far as applicable, be enforced in respect of the above-named routes until new rules and regulations are conjointly agreed to.

Third. Japanese subjects purchasing goods or produce in the interior of China or transporting imported merchandise into the interior of China shall have the right temporarily to rent or hire warehouses for the storage of the articles so purchased or transported without the payment of any taxes or exactions whatever.

Fourth. Japanese subjects shall be free to engage in all kinds of manufacturing industries in all the open cities, towns, and ports of China, and shall be at liberty to import into China all kinds of machinery, paying only the stipulated duties thereon.

All articles manufactured by Japanese subjects in China shall, in respect of inland transit and internal taxes, duties, charges, and exaction of all kinds, and also in respect of warehousing and storage facilities in the interior of China, stand upon the same footing and enjoy the same privileges and exemptions as merchandise imported by Japanese subjects into China.

In the event additional rules and regulations are necessary in connection with these concessions, they shall be embodied in the treaty of commerce and navigation provided by this article.

ARTICLE VII

Subject to the provisions of the next succeeding article, the evacuation of China by the armies of Japan shall be completely effected within three months after the exchange of the ratifications of the present act.

ARTICLE VIII

As a guarantee of the faithful performance of the stipulations of this act, China consents to the temporary occupation by the military forces of Japan of Wei-hai-wei in the province of Shantung.

Upon the payment of the first two installments of the war indemnity herein stipulated and the exchange of the ratifications of the treaty of commerce and navigation the said place shall be evacuated by the Japanese forces, provided the Chinese Government consent to pledge, under suitable and sufficient arrangements, the customs revenue of China as a security for the payment of the principal and interest of the remaining installments of said indemnity.

It is, however, expressly understood, that no such evacuation shall take place until after the exchange of the ratifications of the treaty of commerce and navigation.

ARTICLE IX

Immediately upon the exchange of the ratifications of this act all prisoners of war then held shall be restored, and China undertakes not to ill-treat or punish prisoners of war so restored to her by Japan. China also engages to at once release all Japanese subjects accused of being military spies or charged with any other military offenses. China further engages not to punish in any manner nor to allow to be punished those Chinese subjects who have in any manner been compromised in their relations with the Japanese army during the war.

ARTICLE X

All offensive military operations shall cease upon the exchange of the ratifications of this act.

ARTICLE XI

The present act shall be ratified by their majesties the Emperor of China and the Emperor of Japan, and the ratifications shall be exchanged at Chefoo, on the 14th day of the 4th month of the 21st year of Kwang Hsü,[6] corresponding to the 8th day of the 5th month of the 28th year of Meiji.

In witness whereof the respective plenipotentiaries[7] have signed the same and have affixed thereto the seal of their arms.

Done at Shimonoseki, in duplicate, this 23rd day of the 3rd month of the 21st year of Kwang Hsü, corresponding to the 17th day of the 4th month of the 28th year of Meiji.

NOTES

[1] This treaty was signed on April 17, 1895. Source: U.S. Department of State, *Papers Relating to the Foreign Relations of the United States,* Part I (Washington D.C.: Government Printing Office, 1896), pp. 200–203.

[2] Fengtien or modern Liaoning Province.

[3] One Kuping tael equals 1.3158 ozs.

[4] Kiangsu.

[5] The Grand Canal.

[6] Kuang-hsü.

[7] Li Hung-chang for China and Ito Hirobumi for Japan.

CHAPTER NINE

China's Response to the West: The Reform Movement

The weakness of China as revealed during the Sino-Japanese War triggered a series of demands for Chinese territories by the Western powers and Japan. Before the year 1898 ended, the eastern one-third of China that constituted the country's most productive and heavily populated regions was divided into spheres of influence among the contending foreign powers: Russia in Manchuria, Germany in Shantung, Great Britain in the Yangtze Valley, Japan in Fukien, and France in Kwangtung, Kwangsi, and Yunnan provinces. This was the way that Africa had been partitioned, and many Chinese believed that if nothing drastic were done, the same fate would doubtless fall upon them.

Out of this desperation emerged numerous patriotic societies headed by prominent leaders. The most outstanding among these leaders was K'ang Yu-wei (1858–1927) who sponsored the National Protection Society (Pao-kuo hui), besides several other similarly oriented organizations. Through his writings and public speeches he emphasized one important point: China was in serious danger of being exterminated as a nation; therefore immediate reforms should be carried out to assure her continual survival (Selection 71). Fortunately for him, Emperor Kuang-hsü, who had taken over the reins of government in 1889 when he reached his majority, was in a receptive mood. He felt deeply the humiliation China had suffered at foreign hands, and he wished to become, to quote court sources, another George Washington or Peter the Great. He ordered K'ang to submit a concrete proposal incorporating his reform ideas. K'ang responded by suggesting that China follow the Japanese model as the most practical way to become "wealthy and strong" (Selection 72). The emperor was pleased with his presentation and soon appointed him and some of his close associates such as Liang Ch'i-ch'ao (1873–1929) and T'an Ssu-t'ung (1865–1898) as imperial officials. Their duty was to conduct speedy reforms so that China could become "as strong as Japan."

With imperial authority behind them, K'ang and his associates lost no time going into action. From June 11 to September 16, 1898, a series of imperial decrees were handed down, which, if carried out, would mean, among other things: (1) the abolition of the eight-legged essays and the introduction of tests on current affairs in all civil service examinations; (2) the establishment of Westernized schools; (3) the organization and training of armed forces according to Western methods and the increased use of modern weapons; (4) the establishment of modern banks, the opening of mines, and the construction of railroads; and (5) the establishment of an economic bureau coordinating all industrial and commercial activities across the nation. For one hundred days (hence the name: Hundred Days' Reform) the reformers reigned supreme since they had the emperor on their side.

Mild though these reforms were, they ran immediately into opposition from the Conservatives. For one thing, the Conservatives, who constituted by far the largest and strongest group of the scholar-official class, feared that if this reform trend were allowed to continue its course, they would lose their power and influence (Selection 73). They rallied behind the emperor's foster mother Tz'u Hsi (1835-1908) and urged her to take over the government and force the emperor to abdicate. The empress dowager, being ultraconservative, did not need much prompting, and soon tension between her and the emperor began to build to a climax. Surrounded in his palace by the empress dowager's allies and isolated from contact with his loyal supporters outside, the emperor felt that he could be deposed at any moment (Selection 74). The capital was full of rumors, including the rumor that the emperor's very life was in serious danger.

It was under these circumstances that one of the most curious events in the history of modern China took place. To preserve the emperor's throne and therefore the reforms, T'an Ssu-t'ung, a sincere but headstrong, tactless reformer, approached Yüan Shih-k'ai (1859-1916), a powerful military commander then stationed in Tientsin. He requested Yüan's assistance in staging a coup to put an end to "that old rotten thing" (Tz'u Hsi). Yüan, of course, had his own interest to protect. He reported the proposed plot to Jung-lu, the governor-general of Chihli, who in turn lost no time reporting it to the empress dowager (Selection 75). Whatever reservation she might have had about the resumption of power before, Tz'u Hsi did not have it any more. She issued a decree saying that the emperor was ill and that it was necessary for her to attend to state affairs. The emperor was ordered to live in confinement and the reform was finished. K'ang and Liang managed to escape to foreign countries, but other reform leaders were captured and sentenced to death or long imprisonment.

What kind of person was Tz'u Hsi who could install and dismiss emperors at will even though Chinese emperors, as Sons of Heaven, were supposedly omnipotent and responsible to no one on earth? To learn about this woman was to study some of the startling weaknesses ingrained in the Chinese political, social, and familial systems (Selection 76). While on the one hand China's repeated humiliations can be rightfully attributed to the aggressiveness of foreign powers, there was something more basic, namely, the degeneration of the Chinese society as a whole which rendered impotent any move to make it more rational and dynamic, thus enabling it to resist foreign encroachment. As long as this degeneration continued, as some of the reformers correctly pointed out, China would remain a weak country, to survive only by leave of her more powerful neighbors.

71 • K'ANG YU-WEI: *The Nation Is in Danger*[1]

It matters little whether we are rich or poor; we 400 million Chinese are today in serious difficulties. We live in a house which is about to collapse, a boat which, leaking badly, is about to topple over. We are on a pile of firewood which has already caught fire; indeed, our position is no better than that of a bird in a cage, a fish in a frying pan, or a prisoner in a cell. We are treated like slaves; no, we are treated worse than slaves. We are treated like horses and cattle or dogs and sheep that are to be pushed around as our masters please, or cut into pieces whenever they choose. This tragedy of enormous proportion is unprecedented in our history, a history that has lasted twenty dynasties or 4,000 years. The decline of our sage's teachings[2] and the impending extermination of the very life of the nation—how can any tragedy be more painful than this one? It is so painful that words are inadequate to describe it.

Since ancient times we Chinese have been proud of the fact that ours is a nation of great achievement. Around us are such small countries as Burma, Korea, Annam, and Liu-ch'iu that we once dominated. We have in fact maintained a sense of superiority for a long time. Because of this sense of superiority, we, at the beginning of the present dynasty [the Ch'ing or Manchu Dynasty], viewed England and France as small island kingdoms in the South China Sea. Even our most informed men of letters, such as Chi Wen-ta[3] (editor of the *Four Treasuries*[4]), Chao Ou-pai[5] (author of *Random Notes on the Twenty-two Dynastic Histories*[6]), and Yüan Wen-ta,[7] did not know much outside the cultural confines of China. Chi Wen-ta, commenting on Julius Aleni's *Foreign Nations*[8] and Ferdinandus Verbiest's *World Atlas Illustrated*,[9] said that these two foreign authors compared China to an Elysium or paradise, a comparison which cannot be taken too seriously today. Chao Ou-pai maintained that north of Russia was a great country named Chun-ko-erh and that the wall of its capital was made of bronze and encompassed an area of 200 square *li*. In his book, *Mathematicians and Astronomers*,[10] Yüan Wen-ta ridiculed the idea that the world was round. Yet today many people have traveled around the world, including some of you in this audience. The learned scholars of the eighteenth century did not have even the most rudimentary knowledge which the merchants of our Kwangtung province have long taken for granted.

By 1832 the British had perfected their steamships; as a result, they met little or no resistance wherever they went. In that year they sent two of their warships to attack Canton. The imperial government ordered Lu Min-su, the governor-general of Liangkwang,[11] to head 3,000 sailors and 20,000 soldiers in defense. Yet Lu, the same man who had once suppressed the Yao[12] rebellion led by the bandit chieftain Chao Chin-lung, was defeated. Having heard about his defeat, Emperor Tao-kuang, in an edict, expressed surprise at Lu's lack of ability in view of his previous success in suppressing the Yao rebellion. Lu replied that he was defeated because of the enormous size and power of the enemy's warships, but he could not make himself understood since photography had not yet been invented and the emperor had no comprehension of the capacity of these foreign ships.

It was not until 1840 that Lin Wen-chung[13] first sponsored the translation of foreign newspapers to familiarize the reading public with the situation outside of China. But most Chinese were as ignorant of Western countries as their ancestors had been. During the Opium War, our armed forces were easily defeated at Tinghai and Chushan.[14] This defeat was followed by others; none of our commanders such as Yü-shan, Niu Chien, and Liu Yün-k'o were able to stop the enemy's advance. The enemy's warships entered the Yangtze, and his cannons could be heard as far as Tientsin. Having been defeated, China was forced to open five ports for Western trade. For the first time Emperor Tao-kuang became convinced of the Westerners' strength: the durability of their warships and the efficacy of their cannons. He gave the order that from then on the Chinese should learn to manufacture and use Western weaponry. However, despite his enthusiasm for Western technology, he knew very little about Western countries.

Our defeat during the Opium War was followed by similar defeats in 1849, 1856, 1858, and 1860. We paid an indemnity totaling tens of millions, opened eleven ports for trade, and allowed foreign ministers to reside in Peking. In one instance, foreign troops captured the nation's capital and Emperor Hsien-feng was forced to flee to Jehol. All these were extraordinary occurrences, and our intellectuals should have been awakened by then. But they were not. They continued to look down upon foreigners and shut themselves from foreign contact.

In 1866 Pin-ch'un was ordered to travel around the world; but, being the kind of man he was, he was only interested in amusing himself and did not study foreign countries in a serious or profound manner. Of all the statesmen at that time, only Tseng Wen-cheng,[15] who had done business with Westerners, knew something about Western countries. He established translation bureaus, language schools, and steamship companies. He employed Anson Burlingame, an American, who was accompanied by Chih-kang and Sun Chia-ku, as China's roving ambassador to foreign countries. This was the first time in modern history that a foreigner was employed in this capacity, a situation preceded by the employment of such men as An Shih-na and Chin Jih-shan[16] in ancient times. In any case, this appointment was regarded as unusual and extraordinary by Tseng's contemporaries. Of all of Tseng's recommendations, the most farsighted was perhaps the enrollment in the T'ung-wen Kuan[17] of Hanlin scholars with the fifth rank or below who then served in the central government. However, due to the obstruction of such men as Wo Wen-tuan,[18] this recommendation was never carried out. From then on, even though the government had time and again solicited opinions for reforms, our intellectuals continued to resist new ideas because they were so resentful of foreigners.

During the war of 1884, Chang Nan-kuan scored some small success against the French;[19] as a result, he was as much conceited as he was complacent. But, having studied the situation of the world at that time, I was far from being optimistic. Then Russia was coveting the Three Eastern Provinces [Manchuria], and Japan, who had suddenly become strong because of successful reforms, only waited for an opportunity to demonstrate her newly acquired strength by forcibly taking over Korea. Knowing the impending peril, I petitioned our government to adopt reform measures to strengthen ourselves. Many people responded to my recommendation by saying that I was insane.

In 1892 Fu Lan-ya stated in his book *A Brief Account of Translated Books*[20] that the total sale of translated books published by the Shanghai Manufacturing Company amounted to only 10,300 copies. The nation had a population of 400 million; yet only 10,000 people cared to learn about Western affairs through reading translated books, indicating clearly that few of our intellectuals were really interested in knowing anything outside the sphere of China. It took defeat in the war of 1894[21] to wake up our intellectuals once more; after the defeat, one recalls, we had to cede Taiwan to Japan and pay a huge indemnity besides. The pain was great as the wound was deep; it was only then that the more determined intellectuals began to study seriously the causes of our weakness. The mushrooming of patriotic organizations was soon followed by the establishment of a government-operated publishing house and by the publication of numerous newspapers. For the first time in modern history many people began to speak enthusiastically about the "New Learning."

However, no basic reforms were ever carried out after 1894. Here and there some suggestions were made, but these suggestions never went beyond the oratorial stage. Even reforms that were supposedly implemented were only partially effective; this was clearly the case in connection with the building of a strong navy, the construction of telegraphy and railroads, the strengthening of our merchant marine, and shipbuilding. The problem with reform is that one cannot change A without in the meantime changing B because A and B are closely related. In other words, the reform on A will come to nought if B remains unchanged. Even after our defeat in the Sino-Japanese War, we have not purchased one single warship; nor have we doubled our efforts to strengthen our armed forces training program. In 1894, we had 600,000 men in the "green battalions," plus 300,000 under the jurisdiction of the "eight banners." All of these soldiers were either too old or too weak; many of them were actually engaged in their own respective occupations even though their names appeared in the military roster. The Western countries make soldiers out of civilians; we, on the other hand, make civilians out of soldiers. How is it possible for us to fight a successful war against them?

Moreover, the Western countries make a clear distinction between the essential and the less significant, and it is to the former that they attach the greatest importance. They stress the importance of schools where students are taught the best ways to preserve and strengthen their own nation. They have parliaments where the voice of the people can be heard; the king is not all-important, nor are the people all-insignificant. Goods produced by the society are not to be one man's monopoly; they are to be enjoyed by all members of the society. In short, the Western practice is in full accord with our Confucian doctrine, and it should not surprise us that these Western countries have become wealthy and strong. We, on the other hand, have consistently neglected our industry, agriculture, and education, as well as our national defense. No workable system has been devised to protect, nourish, and educate the people, and a wide gap exists between the government above and the people below and between the rich and the poor who cannot communicate with each other. Since we have acted in contrary to our own Confucian principles, it is no wonder that we remain as weak as we are.

Our weakness prompted foreign powers to use coercive methods to press their unreasonable demands. In a period of forty days these powers engineered twenty national disasters at our expense. First, Germany demanded the lease of Kiaochow, an event which has become widely known. Second, England wished to impose upon us a loan at an interest of 3 percent, a loan that was viewed with disfavor by the Russians. Third, Germany wanted to open Kiaochow Bay for trade; this, again, was opposed by the Russians. Fourth, France wanted us to open

Nanning[22] for trade, and to this the Russians also objected. Fifth, although unable to impose a loan upon us, the British nevertheless succeeded in opening all of our internal rivers to foreign traffic. Sixth, after the Vietnamese had burned some Catholic churches in Saigon, the French forced us to pay an indemnity of 100,000 taels. Seventh, after Yao Hsi-tsan's appointment as governor of Shantung, Germany objected and demanded our government to withdraw the appointment in twenty-four hours; our government, of course, had no choice but to comply with the German demand. Eighth, we proposed to build the Chin-Chen Railroad[23] across the Shantung province, and wired the German government for approval three times. But the German government refused. Ninth, when we redesigned the route so the proposed railroad would pass through Honan instead of Shantung, Germany again raised objections. Approval was finally secured after the British and American ministers had offered their good offices.

Tenth, in the contract whereby Russian advisers were to be employed to train the Nieh Army,[24] it was specifically stipulated that the Russian advisers, instead of the Chinese officers, were the true commanding personnel. Eleventh, these advisers could be retained or dismissed at the pleasure of the Russian czar instead of the Chinese government. Twelfth, Russia succeeded in compelling our government to dismiss four German advisers. Thirteenth, our government was forced to hire Russian advisers in the training of troops in Chihli, Shansi, and the Three Eastern Provinces. Fourteenth, the revenue derived from surtax charges on all commercial traffic along both banks of the Yangtze River was to be assigned to the Shanghai Maritime Customs, a foreign-controlled organization headed by the British interest. Fifteenth, having acquired the territory around Kiaochow, Germany made intensive efforts to acquire more. Sixteenth, having acquired more, she demanded the right to build railroads on it. Seventeenth, having built railroads on it, she complained that the territory was not really large enough and demanded the whole Shantung province as her sphere of influence. Eighteenth, having acquired the whole province, she proceeded to monopolize all industry and commerce in it. Nineteenth, the Russians demanded the cession to them of Dairen, Port Arthur, and Chinchou.[25] Lastly, the French not only demanded the cession of Kwangchow Bay but also insisted that we must not cede Kwangsi, Yunnan, or Kweichow to any other countries.

All the aforesaid events occurred before the second month of this year [1898]. Since then Great Britain has demanded the cession of Weihaiwei, and Japan has imposed upon us another treaty whereby we would not be allowed to cede Fukien to any other power except, of course, Japan.

What has happened to the authority of the Chinese emperor when he has to obtain approval from the German court before he can build a railroad through his own territory and when he in fact cannot even appoint or dismiss his own officials? This is exactly what Chia Yi[26] meant when he said that it was a pity indeed that the emperor of China had become a vassal of the barbarians. In a period of two months, more than twenty national disasters have occurred that involve either loss of territories or encroachment upon our national sovereignty. There are days and years ahead; who knows what the future will bring? If the present situation continues, sooner or later we would have to follow the path of Burma, Annam, India, and Poland and cease to exist as an independent nation. Look at the situation in Poland. When it was partitioned, the foreign powers intimidated its king, insulted its high officials, and oppressed and abused its gentry members. Is Poland the road for us to follow? If it is not, what will enable us to escape the fate that has been destined for all weak nations?

After India was conquered by Great Britain, no Indian could become a government official with the sixth rank or above. From 1771 to 1876, in a period of more than 100 years, only two Indians had served as members of parliament. Hong Kong has been British for a long time, and yet no civil service examination has taken place. Shamelessly the Chinese in that colony think of honor or glory in terms of becoming a comprador; meanwhile even the humblest British can look forward to becoming a manager or even a president. There is, say, a Chinese millionaire who formerly occupied the position of a prefectural governor and, for his meritorious service, was once awarded a red or blue button for his hat. Now he is a broker for a foreign firm, standing humbly beside his foreign superior whom he must learn to please at all times. What a pity! How pathetic this situation really is! If our country continues to be as weak as she presently is, I am afraid that sometime in the future the best kind of honor we 400 million Chinese can hope for will be no better than that "enjoyed" by this particular Chinese we have described.

During the Yüan Dynasty the Mongols abolished the civil service examination system;[27] under the Mongol rule Chinese intellectuals were treated no better than their modern counterparts in Annam who peddle cloth or silk for a meager livelihood. Thinking about the future, how can we intellectuals not be concerned? Once our country is conquered, are we going to follow the shameless path of serving our new masters, a path that has been viewed with disgust by all the patriots since ancient times? Moreover, once foreigners take over our country, it is unlikely that they would employ us Chinese. To become an official in the Western sense requires specialization in a certain field, since only men with special skills can perform the duties assigned to them. Had Wu Mei-tsun[28] lived under foreign rule, he could not have even found a position as an ordinary teacher; how could he possibly hope to become the head of the Department of Cultural Affairs? Someone might say that if foreigners ever conquer our country, a man like Wu Mei-tsun would follow the example of Hsiung K'ai-yüan by joining the monastic ranks. He does not realize that the Westerners, believing a religion called Christianity, would destroy Buddhism once they take over. After all Buddhist temples in the nation are reduced to ashes, to which temple can a man like Wu Mei-tsun attach himself as a Buddhist monk? Another man might say that if China is conquered, he would jump into the East China Sea and commit suicide. Since we do not have a navy of our own, the East China Sea is not even ours. The man, in fact, would die in an alien, unpurified place. What can we do? We have 400 million people and tens of thousands of scholars. Is there any road open to us?

Like an army that has recently suffered a decisive defeat, each of us is fighting for his own survival. There is no way to salvation except to exert ourselves and work doubly hard. Hard pressed on a lonely road, we have no choice but to march forward. There cannot be any retreat; nor is there any short cut. Like Han Hsin who was pushed towards the edge of a river and like Hsiang Yü who sank his own ships after passing across the Yangtze,[29] we have no more ground where we can retreat. Only when every Chinese feels this way is there any hope for China's survival.

Yet the government today refuses to speak candidly on the cession of territories and the loss of national sovereignty; it hides them as if they were taboo. Moreover, there are no public media to enable the people to know how dangerous our position really is. In the Paris Museum there are paintings that depict the tragedy of defeat; their purpose is to arouse every Frenchman's patriotism and inspire him to a better effort. Our countrymen, not knowing what has happened to their

234   CHAPTER NINE

country, remain complacent. They dance and sing as if the world were still an Elysium. They seek fame and fortune in the usual manner, and many of them do not mind violating moral or legal principles as long as they can achieve their goal. Mencius once said: "A country cannot be defeated unless it has already defeated itself." In this sense, we may say that the loss of our territories and the deprivation of our national sovereignty are not a result of foreign coercion or aggression; nor should the whole blame be placed upon our government. We ourselves are the truly guilty ones. If we absolutely refuse to give away our territories, how can we possibly lose any? If we are determined to preserve our national sovereignty, how does any country dare to encroach upon it? In short, if we 400 million Chinese really exert ourselves, how dare any foreigners look down upon us? Yet, instead of exerting ourselves, we are complacent and enjoy ourselves as usual. Who, would you say, are responsible for ceding territories to foreign countries? I, for one, will not blame either our government or the common people. I blame you and me, the intellectuals who have not expressed righteous anger and who in fact have remained undisturbed. If the nation is destroyed, the blame should be squarely placed upon the shoulders of each and everyone of us. If the nation is to be saved, every Chinese has both the right and the obligation to save it.

Once Japan was as weak as China is today. She was pushed around by such countries as England and the United States. Today she is strong enough to conquer Liu-ch'iu, control Korea, and snatch Taiwan from China; she has gone as far as to impose upon us an indemnity payment totaling 200 million taels. Is the strength of the Japanese army responsible for this feat? The answer is no. Should the credit go to the Japanese premier Ito or the Japanese general Oyama? Again the answer is no. It is my considered opinion that the credit for this tremendous achievement should really go to a commoner named Takayama Masashiba. Grieved because Japan, a weak nation, could not carry out reforms and resentful of the monopoly of power by the shogunate, he cried for reforms in the streets of Tokyo until finally he died of exhaustion. It was his example that inspired people like Saigo, Yoshida, Fujita, Gamou, and Hidesane to speak of "reverence for the emperor and resistance to the barbarians." It was his example that inspired such men as Okubo Toshimichi, Iwakura Tomomi, Kido Koin, Itagaki Taisuke, Sanjo Sanemitsu, and Okuma Shigenobu to advocate reforms. Because of these men's efforts, Japan has become strong. In rewarding outstanding men who had made substantial contributions to the Meiji Restoration, the Japanese government awarded Takayama Masashiba posthumously with a ministerial portfolio of the fourth rank and a feudal title of the fifth rank. The remarkable example of this man shows clearly that an achievement, however great, begins with small simple deeds. How many of us know that the success of modern Japan began with the patriotism of a humble, tactless intellectual named Takayama Masashiba?

Everything's growth requires thermogenetic energy. This energy created heaven as well as the sun. Though the sun is millions of *li* away from the earth, every square foot of the earth receives as much energy as ninety horsepower. Because of the energy it receives, the earth can grow a multitude of things; in fact, wherever there is energy, there is growth. The earth contains magma of extremely high temperature which provides the motive force that makes it rotate all year round without cessation. Before a doctor can forecast a man's life span, he has to first examine the amount of "fire" within the man's body. If the amount of fire has been reduced substantially, the man is going to die. From the above observation we know definitely that heat alone generates growth, luxuriance, expansion, and mobility, while coldness causes shrinkage, weathering, decay, and finally, extinction.

Today we Chinese, by stressing the importance of inactivity, have not completed one worthwhile project. Our soldiers are weak and our scholars are ignorant. We speak approvingly of peace and tranquility and detest any kind of innovations. Meanwhile our territory is snatched away from us piece by piece, and our national sovereignty is rendered less and less effective with the passing of each day. The "fire" within us is flickering out, and we become cold, dry, and decadent. We, in short, are in serious danger.

How can we rescue our nation from its impending extinction? The only way is to increase the thermogenetic energy within ourselves. This energy is essential to those who wish to avenge wrongs and perform great deeds; a man who has lost his will power is a man whose "fire" within himself has been flickering out. Hu Wen-chung[30] once said that China lacked but needed red-blooded, selfless patriots. That the Han Dynasty did not fall during the 100 years of the Huan-Ling period[31] despite its precarious position, said Fan Wei-tsung,[32] was due to the combined efforts of many righteous, selfless men who refused to give up the struggle. In ancient literature we often encounter such terms as "martyrs," "men of will," "men of righteousness," and "men of love." One thing that characterizes them is that they are all hot-blooded. The amount of heat one can generate is in direct proportion to the size of achievement one can make. It might be as small as that generated by a firefly—if a man cannot generate even that much, he is as good as dead. A great man, on the other hand, generates as much heat as a huge fireball. This heat can make water boil and can scorch anything in sight. Like the heat from the sun, it illuminates as well as burns. The more intensive it is, the more its power of expansion will be. Not only do all things grow under it, but they also grow taller, larger, and more luxuriantly.

In short, there is no way of serving our country except to arouse and enhance our will power. Let not a single moment pass without thinking about our own duties. A prairie fire begins with the striking of a match, and every river originates from a trickle. If we 400 million Chinese bother to arouse ourselves, we can generate enough heat to do whatever we please, and succeed as well. Who, then, can say that our nation cannot be saved?

NOTES

[1] This speech was made on April 17, 1898, before an audience gathered at the National Protection Society (Pao-kuo hui) in Peking. Source: *Chung-kuo chin-pai-nien shih-liao*, vol. 1, pp. 501–508.
[2] Confucianism.
[3] Wen-ta was the courtesy name of Chi Yün, eighteenth century.
[4] *The Complete Library of the Four Treasuries (Ssu-k'u ch'üan-shu)*.
[5] Ou-pai was the courtesy name of Chao Yi, eighteenth century.
[6] *Erh-shih-erh shih cha-chi*.
[7] Wen-ta was the courtesy name of Yüan Yüan, eighteenth century.
[8] *Chih-fang wai-chi*.
[9] *K'un-yü t'u-shuo*.
[10] *Ch'ou-jen chuan*.
[11] Kwangtung and Kwangsi Provinces.
[12] An ethnic minority who lived in Yunnan and Kweichow Provinces.
[13] Lin Tse-hsü (1785–1850).
[14] Tinghai is a subprefecture located on Chushan Island, off the eastern coast of Chekiang Province.

¹⁵ Tseng Kuo-fan (1811–1872).
¹⁶ Chin Jih-shan was a Hsiung-nu prince who, after surrendering himself to the Han government, rose to become a cavalry general during the time of Han Wu-ti (r. 140–87 B.C.). An Shih-na cannot be easily identified. The author perhaps had in mind An Lu-shan and Shih Ssu-ming who served the T'ang Dynasty during the eighth century A.D. An was of Tartar origin; Shih, however, was Turkish.
¹⁷ A foreign language school in Peking.
¹⁸ Wen-tuan was the courtesy name of Wo-jen, an ultraconservative and the author of Selection 46.
¹⁹ Nan-kuan was the courtesy name of Chang Shu-sheng, the governor-general of Liangkwang in 1884. In that year one of his generals named Liu Yung-fu defeated the French in Annam.
²⁰ *Yi-shu shih-lioh.*
²¹ The First Sino-Japanese War (1894–1895).
²² Located in Kwangsi Province.
²³ A railroad that linked Tientsin and Chinkiang.
²⁴ An army headed by General Nieh Shih-ch'eng.
²⁵ Located in Liaoning Province, Manchuria.
²⁶ Chia Yi (201–168 B.C.), a famous scholar and essayist of the Han Dynasty.
²⁷ During the Yüan Dynasty the civil service examination was not revived until 1315.
²⁸ Mei-tsun was the courtesy name of Wu Wei-yeh, a famous poet and painter of the seventeenth century.
²⁹ Han Hsin (third century B.C.) was a famous general under Liu Pang, founder of the Han Dynasty. Hsiang Yü (third century 2.3.), a civil war hero, competed with Liu Pang for the vacated Ch'in throne. Later defeated, he committed suicide.
³⁰ Wen-chung was the courtesy name of Hu Lin-yi (nineteenth century), a general and statesman who assisted Tseng Kuo-fan in suppressing the Taiping Rebellion.
³¹ The reigns of Han Huan-ti (r. 147–167 A.D.) and Han Ling-ti (r. 168–188 A.D.). The Later Han Dynasty did not come to an end until 220 A.D.
³² Wei-tsung was the courtesy name of Fan Yeh (fifth century A.D.), author of the *History of the Later Han* (*Hou Han shu*).

72 • K'ANG YU-WEI: *The Need for Reform* [1]

K'ang Yu-wei, your humble servant presently serving in the Ministry of Public Works, prostrates before Your Majesty and reports as follows:

Subject: The necessity of conducting speedy reforms and of planning ahead for the future of our nation in view of the extreme danger she is presently in and of the possibility of her extinction as a result of being partitioned among the various powers.

The Germans have taken over Kiaochow, and the Russians are threatening to annex Port Arthur and Dairen.[2] All the countries around China are waiting to lend a helping hand for the final extinction of China as a nation. After the conclusion of the Sino-Japanese War (1894), your humble servant repeatedly sent petitions to Your Majesty's Government, warning about the impending danger and urging strongly for reforms. Since my presentations were not favorably received, I had no choice but to return home. For three years I bowed to circumstances by shutting myself behind my humble homestead, and helplessly I shed tears for the fate of our nation which I could not help to change or reverse. Now there is the present crisis.[3] Once again I sailed across the sea and, after a distance of 10,000 *li*,[4] reached the capital. Not considering me ignorant, Your Majesty has ordered the Office of General Management to seek my opinions on state affairs. In addition to my two books, *A Study of the Japanese Reform*[5] and *A Study of the Reform* by *Peter the Great of Russia*,⁶ which have been presented to you in compliance with your command, Your Majesty has instructed me to express my ideas in a memorial. This is unprecedented in the history of our dynasty, and demonstrates clearly the great virtue in a true sage who does not mind seeking advice from even the most lowly and the least significant. Ignorant though I am, how can I not but feel a strong sense of gratitude? The nation being in great danger, how can I not express fully what I have on my mind?

In recent history many countries have suffered the tragic fate of being divided and exterminated because of their stubborn refusal to make the necessary changes in order to survive. Poland's land and population were repeatedly divided until she ceased to exist. Burma's conqueror took away all of her sovereign rights and then exterminated her outright. Annam's enemy annexed one piece of territory after another until she had nothing left except an empty name. India's conqueror deprived her of every right and privilege she had as a nation before ending her existence altogether. There were also countries like Turkey and Egypt that underwent a slow process of depletion of sovereign rights before their territories were partitioned among the great powers. As for China, let us ask ourselves this question: Do we have the necessary military strength and adequate financial resources to forestall a fate similar to those described above? While in name we still exist as a nation, all our national resources, such as land, railroads, steamships, banks, and commerce and trade, are effectively controlled by foreigners who, in fact, can take everything from us anytime they please. We possess the form of an independent nation, but we have long lost the reality of one. I cannot bear to think what the future holds for us.

As we look at the world situation today, it seems abundantly clear that those countries that have introduced and carried out reforms will survive while those who insist on continuing their old ways will inevitably perish. The relative merit between progressivism and conservativism is so clear-cut that, if we keep our eyes open, we really do not have to hesitate too long to make a choice. Being so wise as Your Majesty is, there is no need for me to mention the fact that a country willing and able to make changes will survive, otherwise she will perish. Small changes will not necessarily guarantee a nation's survival, but complete changes will. The moment Your Majesty and his ministers realize the causes of China's illness, the prescription for its cure is already there. In short, the basic illness of China is her insistence on continuing the old ways and her inability to make the necessary reforms. Living in a world of intense competition while maintaining a policy of inactivity is like wearing heavy furs during a hot summer or attempting to cross a deep river by riding a fancy vehicle—how can a man who does either hope to avoid attack by fever or drowning in the water?

The *Great Learning*⁷ speaks of the necessity of changes as time changes, and Mencius praises highly a nation of new citizens. In the *Analects* Confucius says that a filial son does not change the way of his parents for a period of three years after the latter's demise; this clearly indicates that he *can* change his parents' way of doing things after the prescribed period. A thing that is new is fresh, alive, and flexible; it grows strong. A thing that is old is inert, sluggish, and inflexible; it is destined to die. An institution, long in usage, is bound to generate abuse; in all history there has never been such a thing as an unchangeable system. Moreover, the institutions we have today are those of the worst kind handed down to us from the Han, T'ang, Yüan, and Ming dynasties. How can they be characterized as the enlightened institutions of our venerable ancestors?⁸ They have in fact become hotbeds of corruption, incompetence, and intrigue that are far from what our venerable ancestors intended. To say that they are institutions of enlightenment and should therefore not be changed is an insult to the men whom we allegedly honor and respect. Moreover, to preserve an institution requires a piece of territory where it can be preserved. How can we preserve the enlightened institutions of our venerable ancestors if the territory we have inherited from them is lost to our enemy? Between the preservation of our ancestors' institutions at the expense of losing China and the modification of these institutions to preserve her existence, which should one choose? Does one have to be really intelligent to know which choice is wiser and more advantageous?

However, reforms cannot be conducted unless we know what kind of government we wish to have. As long as the basic issues involving the national polity are not decided, there is no way we can discard the old and adopt the new. Polity to a nation is like helm to a ship; it determines the direction towards which the nation moves as well as the center of emphasis around which her citizens can rally. If the helm, being vacillating and unsteady, has lost its sense of direction, the voyagers in the ship will know neither where they are nor where they are heading. Pity on this ship if it is placed in a river's middle stream! If it is used to sail across a stormy sea where it has to brave strong wind, high waves, and dense fog, it would be a miracle if it does not sink. Our government has in the past introduced some modest reforms. However, whenever Your Majesty takes steps to carry them out, they are obstructed by powerful ministers, criticized by renowned scholars, and attacked by officials from all levels. The critics do not mind using the most dubious means to achieve their purpose, including the worst kind of deception and slanders; they say, for instance, that these reforms are aimed at the barbarization of China and that they are a violation of the saintly system of our ancestors. To wish reform measures to yield fruitful results under these kinds of circumstances is to wish to advance while standing still—it simply cannot be done.

Your Majesty is hereby requested to decide once and for all the kind of polity we should have. This decision in itself, however, does not mean that the reforms, once introduced, will be carried out with dispatch and without errors. Their success requires not only a sense of priority and emphasis but also detailed planning with regard to rules and regulations. Ignorant though your humble servant is, he has studied the institutions of ancient and modern times, both here and abroad. The institutions prevalent during the time of Yao, Shun, and Three Dynasties[9] are too antiquated to be used today, perfect though they once were. Instead, I would like Your Majesty to read Mencius so as to share with him the profound love for the people. There were institutions during the Han, T'ang, Sung, and Ming dynasties which can be profitably adopted, but we must keep in mind the difference between the institutions at the time when China was divided and those when China was unified. I would also like Your Majesty to study Kuan-tzu[10] to learn how to run a government. As for the democratic institutions of England, France, Germany, and the United States, they flourish in remote lands and are derived from different cultures; moreover, they have changed too greatly from their beginnings for us to follow. Instead, I would like Your Majesty to have the same spirit as Peter the Great of Russia and to regard the Meiji policies of Japan as the model to follow. The reason we should adopt the Japanese model is twofold: its time and geographical proximity and the similarity between Chinese and Japanese culture. Since Japan has successfully carried out her reforms, all we need to do is to transplant her successful experience to our own soil. A new piece of calligraphy or painting is easy to trace, and a ready-made dress is easy to copy; to reap speedy results, we cannot do better than to follow the Japanese reformation of the Meiji period.

At the beginning Japan was as conservative as China; she adopted the policy of "repelling barbarians" in the same manner as China has. Her feudal structure and shogunate system, which reduced the role of monarch to that of a figurehead, made the conduct of reforms even more difficult. Yet she succeeded in a short period. Why? Because at the very beginning of her reforms she knew exactly the direction towards which she wanted to move and took correct measures to implement what she wished to achieve. There were many things she did during this early period, but three of them stand out as the most prominent. First, the announcement by the emperor to all his ministers of the basic policy of the nation; second, the encouragement of petition writing to recruit talented personnel; and third, the establishment of the Bureau of Institutions to draft a constitution. In the *Charter Oath* the Meiji emperor stated that all public policies should be deliberated upon and decided by the people as a whole; that Japan was to adopt and put into practice the most advanced institutions in the world; that all citizens, regardless of their clan affiliations, should be united as one man; that all officials, regardless of their positions, should discuss the national goal and reach a consensus; and that all ministers should make a pledge that they would follow any new policy without reservation or doubt once it was adopted. The basic policy of the nation to carry out reforms was thus decided, as a consensus of opinion had been reached among all the Japanese people. The Meiji emperor called upon men of talent to submit their ideas in written form and received them for personal interviews once every five days; those who responded well to the imperial wish would be given governmental posts. In this way not only was the popular will made known to the government, but men of talent could also be recruited to serve the nation in accordance with their specializations. The Bureau of Institutions was established within the palace, and twenty eminent men, including commoners as well as nobility, were selected as directors. These men were to plan and deliberate upon the proposed reforms and to draft a constitution. The establishment of this bureau enabled the deliberations to be thorough and exhaustive and the rules and regulations that came about as a result of these deliberations were consumate and conclusive. This is the reason why Japan has become wealthy and strong.

If Your Majesty has firmly determined to carry out reforms, I suggest that the three measures previously described be adopted. Your Majesty may wish to summon all your ministers in the Imperial Temple of the Heavenly Altar or in front of the Ch'ien-ch'ing Gate where you would announce to them the new policy of the nation and personally lead them in taking a solemn oath that from then on they would abandon the old and adopt the new and start afresh with all the people in the nation. All ministers should be ordered to pledge to support the new reforms; if they cannot conscientiously do so, they should be asked to tender their resignation. Only in this way can the people be aroused to undertake the new task with vigor and can a consensus of opinion be reached to carry out the much-needed reforms. Meanwhile, let a petition-receiving desk be set up in the imperial palace, and every day two censors be assigned to this desk to receive all the petitions from the nation. If the petitioners happen to be officials, they should be allowed to present their petitions directly to the throne, bypassing their immediate superiors who in the past have made a habit of pigeonholing any presentation not to their liking. If the ideas expressed in these petitions are worthy and proper, the petitioners should be summoned for an interview and given posts to hold in accordance with their talent and ability. By this device the people would be able to convey their thoughts to the government, and the government, in turn, would be able to utilize all the talents of the nation.

As for the establishment of the Bureau of Institutions within the palace, it is hereby suggested that it should consist of a dozen or so directors, chosen from men of talent and versatility, who, regardless of their origins, common or noble, would have equal rights and privileges as members of the bureau. Its structure should be similar to that of the Southern Study[11] during the K'ang-hsi period [1662–1722] or Privy Council[12] during the Yung-cheng period [1723–1735]. Personally supervised by Your Majesty on a daily basis, the Bureau of Institutions, when and if established, would have complete authority over the introduction, modification, or discontinuance of all reform measures to be adopted, and would also draft rules and regulations to carry them out. There should be careful deliberations before a measure is proclaimed in public; only then can it be successfully implemented without being accompanied by too many errors.

The political scientists in the Western countries often speak of the three branches of government, namely, the legislative, the executive, and the judiciary. They also say that only when a government has all these branches can it be considered complete. Insofar as our dynasty is concerned, the emperor is the head of the state and commands obedience from all of his subjects. The power of the government is vested in the Privy Council which sees to it that imperial wishes are carried out. Before the imperial presence its deliberation on each issue is generally brief. For all practical purposes, it merely serves as the emperor's mouthpiece, since it has never been regarded as a body of deliberation in the truest sense. As for ministers and directors in the imperial government and governors-general and governors on the local level, they are merely administrative officials; like hands and feet to be directed by the brain, they do not participate in making policy decisions. To make the situation worse, governmental ministers take it for granted that they should always follow precedents and traditions. Since any reform is by definition a violation of precedents or traditions, they will intuitively reject it without pausing for a moment to consider its merit. When and if we decide upon a policy of reforms, these ministers should be told in the clearest language possible that, as administrative officials, their duty is not to judge which reform measures should or should not be carried out; on the contrary, their sole duty is to carry them out successfully.

In recent years the new programs which we have so far introduced are entrusted to the Office of General Management for implementation. How can this organization be charged with so many additional responsibilities when its primary function is in the field of foreign relations? Moreover, most of the officials in this organization are either too old or are holding several posts simultaneously. It is physically impossible for them to be thorough and consumate in the deliberation of the new programs brought before them. Today we have censors who serve as eyes and ears of the government; we have judges and magistrates who preside at trials and administer justice. In short, we have all kinds of officials except one, namely, the decision-makers whose sole duty is to deliberate and then decide. The decision of whether a new program should be adopted concerns the very security of the nation. Yet we lack not only a body of men to deliberate its merit but also a written constitution to measure its legality. People clamor for its implementation without thinking carefully about it, and responsible officials, whenever confronted with difficulties, are not provided with possible alternatives. Hurriedly it is handed over to the government to be carried out, only to suffer all kinds of vicissitudes which it does not deserve. Those who dislike it boycott its implementation under a variety of cunning excuses, and even those who are convinced of its merit cannot successfully carry it out because they are too anxious for quick results. The doubters hesitate to make a move, while the doers are handicapped by the lack of detailed plans that are necessary for real success. Our present system is like a man who possesses all the physical attributes of a human being—head, torso, limbs, and so on—except one, namely, a brain that directs the movement of his body. Without a central organ in control, the body moves blindly and without a specific purpose—it will eventually collapse. Under a situation like this, how can we carry out the needed reforms?

The establishment of the Bureau of Institutions is a prerequisite to the conduct of reforms, since it is unlikely that we can either change or modify the existing institutions, all of which are staffed by conservative officials, for this purpose. Once a reform measure is adopted by the Bureau of Institutions, it should be carried out by one or more of the twelve offices under its jurisdiction. The twelve offices are as follows:

The Office of Law. The fact that foreigners enjoy extraterritorial rights in China which set them above the reach of our law is most humiliating from the Chinese point of view. Foreigners contend that the enjoyment of these rights is necessary because of the difference between Chinese and Western legal codes and the extreme harshness with which the Chinese government enforces its law. It is hereby suggested that our legal code be revised to take as references not only the Roman law but also the legal practices prevalent in such modern countries as England, France, the United States, Germany, and Japan. At the moment it may not be practical to adopt this new code for interior regions; it should nevertheless be put into practice in the treaty ports. For a long time the Western countries have had legal statutes governing civil disputes, commerce, shipping, court procedure, and international relations. Since we cannot close China to foreign trade or cut off diplomatic relations with foreign countries, we obviously have no choice but to continue them. Yet we have no law that governs either foreign trade or foreign relations. In doing business with foreigners, the people simply do not know what course to follow and this results in all kinds of abuse. To correct the situation described above, the Office of Law should be authorized to enact laws in all fields of important activities so that whenever a problem arises, the people would know what is legal or proper.

The Office of Finance. The size of China is comparable to that of Europe, and we have a population twice as large. Yet we suffer from extreme poverty, and our tax revenue is as small as that of Chile or Greece. Why? Because we do not know how to manage finance. We should learn from the Western countries about such matters as paper currency, banks and credit agencies, stamp tax, stocks and bonds, litigation fees, taxes on tobacco and liquor, mining, forest products, public debt, and many others. We have not yet introduced some of these revenue-raising devices, and a special office should be established for this purpose.

The Office of Education. We should establish universities and colleges in the nation's capital, middle schools in the provincial capitals, and elementary schools in all the districts. Besides, there should be institutions of a technical nature such as army and navy academies, schools of medicine or law, normal colleges, and finally, Western language schools for the training of translators. An Office of Education should be created to supervise the establishment and operation of these schools, since the Ministry of Rites is unable to perform this task successfully by itself.

The Office of Agriculture. This office, once established, will be responsible for all matters in connection with farms, forests, fishery, and livestock. It should strive to improve both the quantity and the quality of our agricultural products.

The Office of Industry. This office, when created, is to provide promotion as well as assistance for the designing and manufacturing of new machinery or mechanical devices. It will also have jurisdiction over the construction of ships, bridges, dykes and dams, and highways.

The Office of Commerce. This office will be responsible for the promotion of trade and commerce, plus all matters in connection with them, such as trade research, trade associations, market information, and the enactment of laws in regulation of trade.

The Office of Railroads. This office will be in charge of the planning, construction, and supervision of all railroads in the nation. It will also formulate rules to regulate the rights and obligations of each of the railroads.

Post Office. Post offices should be established all over China, including the countryside. This office should also have jurisdiction over telegraphy.

The Office of Mines. This office, when created, will have jurisdiction over all matters in connection with mining, such as the extraction of minerals, taxation on mines, and research in mineralogy.

The Office of Travel. This office will serve as a governing body for all travel by Chinese abroad, including travels by members of political organizations, learning societies, and churches, as well as by students and tourists. It should do its utmost to promote such travels.

The Office of the Army. This office will be responsible for the recruitment and training of the nation's armed forces.

The Office of the Navy. This office will be responsible for the development and operation of a strong navy.

In the judgment of your humble servant, the establishment of these twelve offices is a prerequisite to the conduct of political reforms.

The purpose of organizing a government is to bring benefit to the governed. A government is no longer worthwhile if it fails to achieve this purpose. In this sense we may say that our government is far short of what a government should be. Under the jurisdiction of a magistrate on the subprefectural level there are a few clerks of miscellaneous orientations who are neither qualified nor held responsible for the operation of a government, while the magistrate himself feels he has no other functions except to collect taxes and sit occasionally as a judge. His rank is low and his salary small; more often than not he is chosen for the magistral post in the most casual or arbitrary manner, though his responsibilities are acknowledgedly great. Between him and the governor of his province there are four layers of officials (provincial treasurer, circuit judge, intendant, and prefectural magistrate), and all of them can be correctly characterized as supernumeraries who contribute nothing except more red tape and larger expenditures. The real power in a province is in the hands of its governor. To reach this position, he has to accumulate many years of service in the bureaucracy; by the time he finally succeeds, he is old and has already lost his drive and vitality. Yet the territory he governs is very large, and the businesses that demand his attention are numerous and varied. Mentally as well as physically he is too weak even to enforce existing laws; how can he possibly be relied upon to carry out reforms? During the past years time and again the imperial government has ordered reforms in the fields of education, agriculture, and commerce, but most of the provinces regard these orders merely as formalities and ignore them.

To remedy the situation described above, we have to revise our governmental structure. In Japan the national government has direct jurisdiction over the prefectures, a situation similar to that prevalent during the Han Dynasty when the magistrate of each of the 100 districts could report directly to the Son of Heaven. Since the territory of China is much larger than that of Japan, we cannot of course adopt the Japanese system, but we may be able to profitably implement a modified Han system. Let a civil bureau headed by a superintendent, chosen from versatile men of great talent, be established in each circuit of the nation. He could be chosen from officials of the first to the seventh rank presently serving in the central government, a procedure that has its precedents in the composition of the Southern Study and in the appointment of examination superintendents. He should have the same rights and privileges as the governor-general and the governor and could report directly to the emperor. Besides, he should be given the authority to recruit his own assistants. If men of good qualifications were found within his circuit, he could appoint them as his assistants and allow them to take their posts immediately. If not, the positions should remain open until qualified personnel are found.

As for the funds necessary for the implementation of the new programs, I would like to suggest that they be apportioned from the revenue derived from the *likin* tax.[13] Besides the civil bureau in each of the circuits, there should also be branch bureaus on the subprefectural level. Except for the enforcement of law and the collection of taxes which, for the time being, should remain in the hands of the magistrate, all the new programs in connection with land survey, census taking, road construction, forestation, the establishment and operation of schools, the promotion of industry and commerce, education in sanitation and hygiene, and the building of an effective police force should be carried out by officials serving in the branch bureau. Though appointed by and responsible to the circuit superintendent, these officials should seek full cooperation from the local gentry in order to make their work more effective. It is hoped that the groundwork of these programs will be completed in a period of three months and that there will be some constructive results in a period of one year. While these programs are carried out in and outside the government, a constitution will be drafted and then adopted to serve as the guideline for all our efforts. Only in this way can our political reform become effective and our new programs successful. . . .

NOTES

[1] This memorial, dated January 29, 1898, was written at the special request of Emperor Kuang-hsü. Source: Liang Ch'i-ch'ao, *The Political Crisis of* 1898 (*Wu-hsi cheng-pien chi*), Chapter I.
[2] Two weeks later, the two ports were taken over by the Russians.
[3] This refers to the impending division of China into spheres of influence among the Western powers and Japan.
[4] Before the construction of the Peking-Canton Railroad it was much more convenient and timesaving to take the sea route when traveling between Canton and Peking.
[5] *Jih-pen pien-cheng k'ao.*
[6] *Wo ta pi-teh pien-cheng k'ao.*
[7] *Ta hsüeh*; one of the *Four Books of Confucianism.*
[8] By "venerable ancestors" is meant the founders or first emperors of the Ch'ing Dynasty.
[9] Yao and Shun were two of the "good emperors" of the legendary past; the Three Dynasties were Hsia (c.2205–c.1766 B.C.), Shang (c.1766–c.1122 B.C.), and Chou (c.1122–249 B.C.).
[10] Kuan-tzu or Kuan Chung who lived in the seventh century B.C.

¹¹ *Nan shu-fang.*
¹² *Chün-chi ch'u*; sometimes translated as Office of Strategic Affairs.
¹³ The *likin* tax was originally collected as a surcharge on all sales to make up the deficiency in the land tax caused by the Taiping Rebellion, but continued long after the rebellion had been suppressed.

73 • YÜN YÜ-TING: *The Hundred Days' Reform*¹

After China's defeat by Japan in the year of chia-wu [1894], Emperor Kuang-hsü [r. 1875–1908], facing increasing pressures from foreign powers and realizing the danger China was in, made a firm determination to initiate reforms to make China wealthy and strong. He surveyed his chief minister-advisers, but none of them seemed able or enlightened enough to assist him in the implementation of his ideas, since all of them were either weak, uninformed, and obstinate or too entrapped in their own inertia to make a new, important move. In the year of chia-wu, K'ang Yu-wei of Nanhai had presented him with the Examination Candidates' Petition and followed it with several other memorials. These memorials greatly impressed the emperor. After the dismissal of Weng T'ung-ho in the fourth month of wu-hsi,² there was a slow, gradual change in the orientation of the court. Chang Pai-hsü and Hsü Chih-ching, at one time or another, recommended K'ang Yu-wei to the emperor in their petitions. During the audiences that followed, K'ang spoke of the reforms that had taken place in Japan, and the emperor, listening to his presentation, was overjoyed. At that time the appointment of any official above the second rank³ had to be approved by the empress dowager [Tz'u Hsi] and the emperor, despite his appreciation of K'ang's wisdom and ability, could only appoint him as an assistant⁴ in the Ministry of Public Works, to be temporarily assigned to the Office of General Management as an official-at-large.⁵ For the same reason, K'ang's disciple Liang Ch'i-ch'ao did not receive a better position than that of an editor in the Translation Bureau. The powerful ministers in the cabinet did not like these two men, but they could not invalidate the appointments.

During the period immediately following the Sino-Japanese War, the government encouraged people to speak frankly on public affairs, and even an ordinary citizen could petition the government on what he considered important. Wang Chao, an assistant in the Ministry of Rites, made four proposals in a petition to the emperor, one of which was that the emperor should make a grand tour throughout the world. Ministers Huai-t'a-pu and Hsü Ying-k'uei suppressed this petition by not forwarding it to the emperor, and this suppression, subsequently revealed, caused a great uproar among all the government officials. The emperor had long been looking for an opportunity to dismiss one or two of these conservative ministers and to use such dismissals as an instrument to bring into line all those officials who had refused to go along with his proposed reforms. Upon hearing of the suppression of Wang's petition, the emperor was furious and issued a special decree to dismiss the six deputy ministers in the Ministry of Rites. Then he broke the seniority rule by promoting Wang Hsi-fan, a junior official in the Bureau of Instruction, and Hsü Chih-ching, a reader in the Hanlin Academy, to the posts of first and second deputy ministers of the Ministry of Rites respectively. After this incident, all the officials began to realize what the emperor intended to do and followed his instructions without resistance.

Huai-t'a-pu's wife often served as a lady-in-waiting in the Yi-ho Yüan;[6] one day she spoke in tears to the empress dowager about the dismissal of Manchu officials. "Pretty soon all the Manchu officials will lose their governmental posts," she added. Needless to say, the empress dowager was not pleased with what the emperor had done.

Shortly afterwards the emperor elevated T'an Ssu-t'ung, Yang Jui, Liu Kuang-ti, and Lin Hsü to the position of advisers in the Privy Council with the special responsibility of supervising the conduct of reforms. These four were then called the "Four Honorable Men" whom even the powerful ministers in the cabinet viewed with envy. T'an Ssu-t'ung and Yang Jui resented the fact that the emperor was controlled by the empress dowager and often spoke openly about their resentment. In reply, the emperor issued them a personal order which contained the following remarks: "There is not much I can do about those ignorant, obstinate, and reactionary ministers. You gentlemen should be reminded that it is your duty to do your utmost to carry out the reforms without antagonizing them. Though our purpose is to make the country wealthy and strong, we should nevertheless proceed with caution and care so that the powerful ministers in the government will not offer stubborn resistance, and I will not lose the affection of my beloved mother.[7] Otherwise I cannot even keep my throne, let alone bring benefit to my people." From then on rumors began to multiply until eventually they reached the ears of the empress dowager. Guessing well what the empress dowager intended to do, censors Yang Ch'ung-yi and P'ang Hung-shu, in a secret meeting with Yi-k'uang [Prince Ch'ing], presented him with a petition in which they reported a possible coup and requested the empress dowager to assume the power of the state. Yi-k'uang took this petition and presented it in person to the empress dowager.

Early in the morning on the fourth of the eighth month [September 19, 1898], the emperor went to the empress dowager's residence to pay his respect as usual. Before he reached his destination, however, he heard that the empress dowager had taken a short cut to his palace and had in fact entered the Hsi-chih Gate. Surprised at this sudden turn of events, he quickly returned to his own residence. The empress dowager went straight to his bedroom and took away all the memorials that had been presented to him. Summoning the emperor to her presence, she let him know how angry she was. "I have been feeding you and taking care of you for more than twenty years and yet you listen to the words of those churls to plot against me," she scolded. The emperor, trembling visibly, did not utter a word. "I had no such intentions," he finally murmured after a long silence. "Stupid son," the empress dowager scolded and spit in his face; "if I died today, there would not be you tomorrow." Then she issued a decree that the emperor was ill and could no longer attend state affairs and that from then on she, the empress dowager, would serve as the regent. All the reforms that had been introduced by the emperor were declared invalid and were abolished forthwith.

The man who first advocated a summary death sentence for all the reformers— T'an Ssu-t'ung, Yang Jui, Liu Kuang-ti, Lin Hsü, and K'ang Kuang-jen—was censor Huang Kuei-chün who maintained in a petition that since the crime of the accused was so obvious and clear-cut, there was no need for a trial. Some people say that the reason behind his suggestion was the fear that if a trial were conducted, the emperor would be inevitably implicated.

From then on the scholar-officials viewed the reform as if it were a deadly disease. However, the men who had been recommended for governmental posts before the eighth month[8] were still obligated under the law to proceed to the capital. They were received after their arrival, but none of them received an appointment.

NOTES

[1] *The Ch'ung-ling Records (Ch'ung-ling ch'uan-hsin lu)*, from which this selection is made, was written in 1910 by Yün Yü-ting who served as Emperor Kuang-hsü's secretary-adviser for more than nineteen years.
[2] The fourth month of wu-hsi covers the period between May 20 and June 18, 1898 inclusive.
[3] Under the Ch'ing system there were nine ranks of officials altogether.
[4] *Chu-shih.*
[5] *Hsing-tsou.*
[6] The official residence of Tz'u Hsi, the empress dowager.
[7] Tz'u Hsi who adopted the emperor as her son when the latter was a child. She was actually his aunt, the sister of his mother.
[8] That is, during the period of the Hundred Days' Reform.

74 • Lo Tun-yung: *Kuang-hsü's Three Secret Decrees*[1]

On the twenty-eighth day of the seventh month in the year of wu-hsi [September 13, 1898], Emperor Kuang-hsü (r. 1875–1907) issued a decree to Yang Jui[2] which read as follows:

"Lately, as I respectfully gauge the wishes of Her Ladyship the Empress Dowager [Tz'u Hsi], I feel that she does not wish to change all the laws at once; nor is she willing to dismiss all the old, reactionary ministers and to bring into the government young men of vigor and knowledge. Her reason is that if we do any of these things, we will lose the confidence of the people. Though time and again I have issued decrees to clarify the issues involved and have often remonstrated with Her Ladyship on this important matter, she remains unconvinced. Since Her Ladyship has already made up her mind, there is little more I can do. Her Ladyship regards the decree of the nineteenth as too excessive in content and too wide in scope; I am afraid to say that we have no choice but to go slow on our proposed reforms. This, in short, is the difficult situation we are in.

"It is incorrect to say that I do not realize the culpability of these old, reactionary ministers who are primarily responsible for China's accumulated weakness and her inability to arouse herself, which in turn invite the danger she is presently in. You gentlemen insist that I should change all of the old laws and dismiss all of those old, reactionary ministers at once; but let me say that I do not have the power to do it. If I did all the things that you gentlemen have suggested, I would not even be able to preserve my own throne, let alone any other considerations.

"I am hereby asking you to present to me proposals whereby the old laws can be slowly changed and all of those old, reactionary ministers gradually dismissed, so that young men of vigor and knowledge can be brought into the government to deliberate on policies and China can be transformed from a weak country of precarious position to a strong nation with security. At the same time you should not suggest anything that could be interpreted as contrary to Her Ladyship's wishes. You should discuss this matter at the earliest moment with Lin Hsü, T'an

Ssu-t'ung, Liu Kuang-ti,³ and others, and, after deliberation, put your proposals in written form. These proposals should be put in a sealed envelope and transmitted to me via the Grand Minister of the Privy Council.⁴ I shall study them carefully before putting them into practice. I am looking forward to receiving them."

On the same day the following decree was issued to K'ang Yu-wei:

"Knowing the extremely difficult situation China is in, I am convinced that our country cannot be saved unless we conduct reforms and that we cannot conduct reforms unless the self-centered, ultraconservative ministers are dismissed and men of vigor and knowledge are brought into the government. But Her Ladyship the Empress Dowager does not agree with me. Time and again I remonstrated with Her Ladyship, but my remonstration only makes her more angry. Now that my position as the emperor is in danger, you should speedily and secretly discuss with Yang Jui, Lin Hsü, T'an Ssu-t'ung, and Liu Kuang-ti a plan to rescue me. I am extremely worried; I am anxious for your answer."

The above decree was taken from the palace by Yang Jui.

On the second day of the eighth month [September 17, 1898] another decree was issued to K'ang Yu-wei which read as follows:

"I want you to understand that it is with reluctance and sorrow that I can do no better than to appoint you as the publisher of our government newspaper, an agony which words are inadequate to describe. Leave the country immediately; you should not delay even for a brief moment. I know very well your loyalty and love towards me. Please take care of yourself so that sometime in the future we can accomplish great deeds together. Good luck and my best wishes."

The above decree was taken from the palace by Lin Hsü. It is what K'ang Yu-wei refers to as the "pocket edict."⁵

NOTES

¹ According to the author, a famous historian and a friend of K'ang Yu-wei's chief disciple Liang Ch'i-ch'ao, the Chinese original of the "Three Secret Decrees" in the emperor's handwriting was preserved in the Palace Museum of Peking as late as 1911. A copy can be found in *Chung-kuo chin-pai-nien shih tzu-liao*, vol. 2, pp. 421–422.

² A reformer and one of K'ang Yu-wei's political disciples. He was put to death after the failure of K'ang's reform.

³ All of these men were executed after the failure of the Hundred Days' Reform.

⁴ *Chün-chi ta-ch'en.*

⁵ *Yi-tai chao*; literally, "garment-belt edict," an edict that was hidden between the garment and the belt when taken from the palace in order to avoid detection.

75 • YÜAN SHIH-K'AI: *The Day When I Was Invited to Commit Treason*¹

While drafting a memorial by candlelight in the inner room, I suddenly heard footsteps outside. My valet came in with a personal card in his hand, saying that His Excellency T'an² of the Privy Council wished to see me on a matter of great urgency and that he had walked straight to the guest room without waiting to be announced. I quickly took the personal card and noticed that the uninvited guest was none other than T'an Ssu-t'ung.

Knowing that T'an had been recently elevated to an important position and was close to the emperor, I sensed that he must have important matters to discuss with me, especially since he chose to make this unannounced visit at night. I dropped my writing brush immediately and went out to receive him. He congratulated me on my recent promotion and then added that he would like to speak with me alone in the inner room where the servants would not be able to overhear our conversation. I was surprised at his request for secrecy, but nevertheless agreed. Inside the inner room we expressed our long admiration for each other and the regret that we had not been able to get acquainted earlier. T'an said that as an amateur physiognomist he could tell that someday I would become a great general and play a very important role in national affairs. "Do you have an appointment with the emperor on the fifth?"[3] he asked me suddenly. In reply I said that in view of the activities of the British fleet off our coast I intended to make my report to His Majesty the very next day.[4] I would return to Tientsin immediately after the audience, I added.

"In my judgment," said T'an, "the danger to the nation is internal rather than external."

"What do you mean?"

"Since His Majesty has bestowed upon you a great honor,[5] I know that you will seek an opportunity to show your gratitude. His Majesty is in serious danger. No one but you can save him."

I was astonished by these remarks. "Throughout my life I have been indebted to my country, and I certainly will do my very best to show my gratitude," I replied. "Now that I have been granted an honor which I do not feel that I really deserve, how can I not repay His Majesty with everything I have, including my own life? But pray, what is the danger you have spoken of?"

"Do you know that Jung-lu[6] has recently proposed to depose and then kill the emperor?"

"While at Tientsin I had the opportunity of speaking with Jung-lu often, and it is my impression that he is a loyal and righteous person," I replied. "He never indicated to me that he had this idea in mind. What you have heard cannot be anything except hearsay to which you should not attach any significance."

"You are a straightforward and honest man," said T'an; "that is why you do not know how treacherous this man Jung-lu really is. He is suspicious and jealous of you; yet outwardly he pretends to be your friend. You, sir, have had a distinguished career for many years, and all people, both here and abroad, have praised your achievements highly. Do you know why you were promoted by only one rank last year? Because Jung-lu used his influence to hinder your advancement. Once when Mr. K'ang [K'ang Yu-wei] recommended you to His Majesty for a high position, the latter said that, according to what he had heard from the empress dowager, time and again Jung-lu intimated to her that you were too supercilious to be entrusted with a sensitive post. What I am telling you is the truth, and not a few know about it. I personally also recommended you to His Majesty, but I failed in each of my attempts because of Jung-lu's opposition. 'Yüan Shih-k'ai seems to be a talented man,' commented the emperor, 'but there are people who say that he is too independent to be reliable.' It was certainly not an easy task to obtain this latest promotion for you. If you really wish to help the Emperor, I have a plan which I would like very much to discuss with you."

Upon finishing these remarks, T'an presented a draft proposal to me which was written on stationary shaped like a personal card.[7] In this proposal was the statement that since Jung-lu was presently plotting for the deposition and murder of the reigning emperor, he was in fact committing high treason and, if he were not exterminated immediately, not only would the emperor be unable to keep his throne, but his life would be in danger. It was hereby suggested, continued the proposal, that when Yüan Shih-k'ai paid his respect to the emperor on the fifth day of the month, he would be given a written order by His Majesty in person. This written order was to authorize Yüan to lead his troops back to Tientsin where, upon seeing Jung-lu, he would first read the order aloud in the latter's presence and then immediately put him to death. Yüan would then replace Jung-lu as governor-general of Chihli. Upon the assumption of the governor-general's office, the proposal continued, Yüan would make public the treasonable acts of the executed among his subordinates and then, by means of public proclamation, make them known to all the people in the nation. Meanwhile he should cut off all means of communication and transportation such as telegraph and railroad and lead his troops back to Peking. Upon arriving at the capital, he would dispatch one half of his soldiers to surround the Yi-ho Yüan[8] and the other half to protect the imperial palace.[9] Success would be assured, said T'an, if I would follow this proposal closely. If I refused to go along with his plan, he continued, he would commit suicide immediately.

Upon hearing these remarks, I was so startled that I felt my spirit had already left my body. "What is the purpose of surrounding the Yi-ho Yüan?" I asked.

"The nation cannot be preserved as long as that old rotten thing [Tz'u Hsi] remains alive," he replied. "I take full responsibility for this, and I beg you not to ask any more questions."

"During her regency of more than thirty years," I said, "the Empress Dowager has time and again overcome great difficulties and is in fact very popular with the people. I have always taught my subordinates to be loyal and righteous toward their imperial superiors; how can I now order them to commit an act of rebellion? I cannot possibly follow your advice."

"I have already hired dozens of strong men for this purpose," said T'an. "Besides, I have sent a telegram to Hunan[10] to recruit more, and they will arrive in a few days. In short, I do not need your help to eliminate this old rotten thing; I can do it myself. There are only two things for which I need your assistance: to execute Jung-lu and to surround Yi-ho Yüan with your troops. If you do not grant my request, I will die before you at this moment. At this moment your life is in my hand and mine in yours. We should settle the whole matter this very evening; and, upon reaching an agreement, I shall immediately repair to the palace to secure His Majesty's approval."

"This is an extremely serious matter," I said, "and I certainly cannot make a decision without thinking carefully about it. I cannot make up my mind quickly even if you threaten to kill me. I doubt very much that you can secure the approval of your plan by His Majesty when you see him tonight."

"I have a way to persuade him," said T'an. "In fact, I can give you the guarantee that by the fifth of this month you will receive an imperial order to carry out my proposal."

T'an spoke and acted in such an arrogant and irrational manner that he seemed to be almost insane. However, since he was the emperor's trusted minister and since I did not know whether he had been authorized to make this proposal, I decided not to refuse him outright. I feared that had I done so, he might be angry enough to take drastic and harmful measures. I, consequently, adopted a delaying technique. "In Tientsin there are nationals of a variety of countries," I said. "If the governor-general were suddenly killed, great disturbances would be created in the foreign community as well as among the Chinese. The nation would be placed in such a precarious position that foreigners might decide to partition it. Moreover, there are from forty to fifty thousand soldiers stationed in North China under the commandership of Generals Sung, Tung, and Nieh, in addition to the Huai Army which has within its jurisdiction more than seventy battalions of troops. Even within the capital there are tens of thousands of banner men.[11] I have only 7,000 men under my command, and the total number I can put on the battlefield cannot exceed 6,000. How can I possibly carry out the plan that you have suggested? Moreover, the moment our troops are mobilized the capital will take immediate measures for defense. We would put His Majesty's life in jeopardy long before we could arrive in time to save it."

"None of these worries amounts to much if you move fast enough," said T'an. "As soon as your troops are mobilized, you should send to each of the armies the emperor's personal order. Meanwhile a diplomatic note explaining this move should be delivered to all of the foreign countries. If you do all these things, no one in the world would dare to give you any trouble."

"All of the military equipment we have such as guns and ammunitions is presently stored in the Tientsin barracks, and I can assure you that it is far from adequate to launch an operation such as you suggest. We should wait until we are ready."

"Since that is the way you want it, I shall give you the imperial order for you to keep. When you are ready to move, notify me secretly of the date."

"I am not so cowardly that I fear death," I said. "I am worried, however, that if the plan ever leaks out, His Majesty would be inevitably implicated, and in such a case, even my death would not be good enough to redeem my guilt. To put anything down in black and white is in fact to invite disclosure, and I insist that you should not hand me the imperial order at this moment. Now you should proceed home; I, on my part, will think carefully about this matter. It will take anywhere between fifteen and twenty days before I can reveal to you my plan."

"His Majesty is anxious to see results at the earliest possible moment," said T'an. "In fact, I have in my hand the imperial order we have spoken of. I cannot report to His Majesty unless a plan is agreed upon between you and me at this very moment."

T'an then showed me the imperial order which was written in black ink and in excellent calligraphy. The writing style seemed to be that of His Majesty the Emperor. The order said in effect that he, the emperor, had been determined to initiate reforms, but unfortunately his old ministers at the court did not see eye to eye with him. If he were to carry out the reforms regardless of opposition, he was afraid that he might displease the empress dowager. The order concluded by saying that he, the emperor, had ordered Yang Jui, Liu Kuang-ti, Lin Hsü, and T'an Ssu-t'ung to devise new plans to carry out the needed reforms.[12]

Judging from the tune of the writing, it seemed that the emperor had politely turned down the request of the four men who had insisted upon the implementation of speedy reforms. "This is not the handwriting of His Majesty the Emperor," I retorted. "Moreover, there is no mention of either executing governor-general Jung-lu or surrounding the Yi-ho Yüan."

"The original copy of the imperial order is in the hand of Lin Hsü; the one you have seen is the exact duplicate of the original made for me by Yang Jui," said T'an. "I can assure you that the order which was issued three days ago does exist. I resent the fact that Lin Hsü refused to give me the original; his failure almost ruined our plan. When the emperor says that we should devise new plans to carry out the reforms, he implies the two measures that I have spoken of."

Knowing that the document was forged and resenting the highhanded method which T'an was using against me, I decided not to argue with him any more and said: "Let Heaven be my witness, I, Yüan Shih-k'ai, will never repay Heavenly favor with ingratitude. My only concern is that I might inadvertently implicate His Majesty the Emperor. We cannot proceed with the implementation of your proposal until we have made it foolproof. I am not a bullheaded person; I will never do anything hasty that makes me look like a criminal in the eyes of the world."

However, T'an insisted that an agreement be made that very moment so he could report to the emperor. His facial expression suddenly changed; he raised his voice even higher. The garment above his belt bulged like a small mound; it seemed that a weapon had been hidden inside. I knew that he would not leave the room empty-handed.

"His Majesty will make an inspection tour of Tientsin in the ninth month, and a large number of troops will be concentrated in that city," I said. "All we need then is a note from him; nobody will dare to disobey his order. Your proposal will be easily carried out then."

"How can we wait until the ninth month?" said T'an. "The emperor would be deposed and killed by that time."

"I do not think that this will happen since the Emperor has already issued the order of making this inspection tour. We have to wait until the next month to decide for ourselves when your plan can be safely carried out."

"Suppose that the Emperor does not make an inspection tour in the ninth month?"

"He will, since hundreds of thousands of dollars have already been spent in preparation for it," I replied. "Moreover, I shall request Governor-general Jung-lu to plead with the empress dowager to grant His Majesty permission to make this trip. I guarantee that there will be no change of plans. You can rest assured."

"The whole thing is now in your hands, and it is up to you to decide what you wish to do," said T'an. "You can come to the rescue of the emperor who is presently in danger, establish a great deed for yourself, and become one of the most powerful men in the nation. Or, if you wish to covet rank and wealth, you can reveal our plan before it can be carried out and thus endanger the very life of His Majesty the Emperor."

"Who do you think I am?" I said. "Our family has been deeply indebted to the dynasty for three generations. Unless I am insane, I cannot possibly indulge in my selfish desire at the expense of my country. If there is anything I can do to bring benefit to my country and my sovereign king, I will risk my life to do it."

T'an seemed to be convinced. He stood up, saluted, and called me "an extraordinary man."[13] "You and I have been strangers to each other," I added. "My retainers and guards must be wondering about the purpose of this late visit. If they reveal your visit to others, people will become suspect and will perhaps conclude that there is some kind of political plot being formed between you and me. This kind of suspicion is perhaps inevitable since you are a minister close to the emperor and I have in my hand the authority of a military command. If I were you, I would pretend to be ill for the coming month. I would not come here again; nor would I visit the imperial palace." T'an nodded in agreement.

Then I asked him the causes of disagreement between the empress dowager and the emperor. "The disagreement stems from the dismissal of six officials in the

Ministry of Rites under the reform program,"[14] T'an replied. "Saddened by this dismissal, the ministers in the Inner Court pleaded and cried before the empress dowager, vilifying the intent of the reform and exaggerating its evil consequences. Meanwhile such officials as Huai-t'a-pu, Li-san, and Yang Ch'ung-yi[15] went secretly to Tientsin to plot with Governor-general Jung-lu. As this went on, the disagreement between the empress dowager and the emperor went from bad to worse."

"If His Majesty really believes that reforms are necessary, why does he not present in detail the reasons for these reforms to the empress dowager and seek her advice on each of the reforms he intends to carry out?" I asked. "It will help a great deal should he decide to reinstate the six officials whom he has dismissed so they, too, can present their side of the case. Moreover, reforms should be introduced in conformity with public opinion and should never be rushed through in a hasty manner. They should be either slowed down or stopped altogether in accordance with the circumstances. What is the hurry when rashness can bring about harmful results unrelated to the reforms?"

"From ancient to modern times no reforms have been carried out successfully without shedding blood," T'an replied. "We cannot succeed in our effort without killing off all those old, rotten reactionaries."

By then I realized he was only interested in killing people. I made the decision that I would not have anything to do with him any more. Under the pretext that the night was deep and that I had the memorial to write, I requested his departure. After he left, I thought about this matter for a long time and felt numb and sick. I never did complete the memorial which I had intended to write. I said to myself that if people like T'an were allowed to do whatever they pleased, not only would they bring about a chain of events of catastrophic proportions, they would also endanger the very existence of the nation. It was then that I decided to present to the emperor my own ideas in a very subtle manner, in the hope that the march towards disaster could be somehow arrested.

On the fifth day of the month when I was granted an audience, I spoke to His Majesty as follows: "From ancient to modern times no country has been able to carry out reforms with complete ease. Reforms that are implemented without being carefully thought out might cause domestic disturbances or even bring about foreign incursions. Even if these reforms are necessary, I humbly request Your Majesty to be patient in your approach, introduce them only at the most propitious moment, and carry them out gradually, one at a time. Rashness may in fact bring about the greatest harm. Moreover, successful implementation of these reforms requires good judgment on the part of mature, knowledgeable, intelligent men, men like Governor-general Chang Chih-tung.[16] Only when people of this description are in charge can Your Majesty's wish of bringing about reforms be fulfilled. It is true that some of the recently promoted ministers[17] are knowledgeable and courageous, but unfortunately they lack experience in government and are not careful and thorough enough in handling administrative details. The consequence will be very grave indeed if, through their own carelessness, they implicate Your Majesty in some unbecoming manner. I earnestly request Your Majesty to pay close attention to this matter; if you do, the whole country will benefit. Since your humble servant is deeply indebted to you, he is duty-bound to risk his life to speak to you in the most frank manner."

His Majesty did not reply, but he was visibly moved. I saluted and then withdrew.

Having left the palace, I went straight to the railroad station where I waited for Inspector Ta Yu-wen to accompany me to Tientsin. By the time we arrived at our destination, it was already dark; nevertheless I went immediately to the governor-general's residence and reported to him what I had heard in Peking. I emphasized the fact that His Majesty was as pious towards the empress dowager as he had always been and that, wherever there were difficulties, the fault lay with a group of small men who tried to confuse and mislead him and conspired to bring great harm to this nation without realizing it themselves. It was our duty, I added, to come to the emperor's rescue so as to bring peace and calm to our beloved country. Before I had the opportunity to reveal the whole story, Yeh Tsu-kuei arrived and was followed by Ta Yu-wen. Soon it was nine o'clock, and I decided to excuse myself for supper. Before I left, however, I told the governor-general that I would be back the next morning to continue our conversation.

The next morning the governor-general came to see me instead. When I told him the details of my conversation with T'an Ssu-t'ung, his facial expression completely changed. "Let Heaven put me to death if I, Jung-lu, have ever harbored any intention to harm His Majesty the Emperor," he cried aloud in bitterness. "Lately there have been people coming to Tientsin who inform me about events in the capital, but no one has told me the details."

"I want you to know that the emperor had nothing to do with the plot," once more I emphasized this important point. "If His Majesty's position as the emperor is adversely affected by it, the only course open to me is to take poison and commit suicide."

We discussed this matter for a long time and were at a loss to find a good course to follow. After the governor-general's departure, I called upon Ta Yu-wen to continue the discussion. In the evening I received a note from Jung-lu requesting my presence at his residence. Yang Hsin-pai was already there when I arrived. He showed me a telegram which he said had come from the imperial palace.[18] Upon hearing this, Jung-lu gently touched my tea cup and smiled. "This tea does not contain poison," he said; "you can drink it." What worried me most then was that the march of events might adversely affect His Majesty's position as the emperor.

Four days later the governor-general was summoned to Peking. Before his departure, he and I made a pledge that we would risk our very life, if necessary, to protect the life and the throne of His Majesty the Emperor. "Even though the historians record 'Chao Tun murdered the king,' we know that Chao Tun did not do it," I said.[19] "Your Excellency is noted for your honesty, integrity, and unswerving loyalty to the emperor and is currently occupying one of the most important positions in the government. If anything happens to His Majesty, posterity will place blame on you, regardless of whether you deserve it. I and my family have likewise received great favors from the royal house for generations. If anything happens to His Majesty, I will commit suicide to avenge it."

"This matter will be settled between Prince Ch'ing[20] and me, and I can assure you that the throne of His Majesty will not be adversely affected," said the governor-general. "Please do not worry. I revere the empress dowager as if she were my own grandmother.[21] As for His Majesty the Emperor, I respect him as if he were my own father. Whenever there is a quarrel between a man's grandmother and his own father, he should do his very best to effect a reconciliation between them. He does not wish to say or hear anything that might be construed as a violation of the correct relationship between familial superiors and inferiors."

While I respectfully write down the above event, my heart is burned with agony. I write it at the governor-general's office, Tientsin, on the fourteenth day of the eighth month [September 29, 1898].

NOTES

[1] The author wrote this memorandum on September 29, 1898, shortly after the collapse of the Hundred Days' Reform. Source: *Chung-kuo chin-pai-nien shih tzu-liao,* vol. I, pp. 493–500.

[2] T'an Ssu-t'ung (1865–1898), a disciple of K'ang Yu-wei and a member of the reform party.

[3] The fifth day of the eighth month, or September 20, 1898.

[4] The fourth day of the eighth month, or September 19, 1898.

[5] This refers to Yüan's latest promotion.

[6] Tz'u Hsi's cousin and confidant.

[7] The Chinese personal or visiting card was several times larger in size than its Western counterpart.

[8] The palace ground where Tz'u Hsi resided.

[9] The palace where the emperor lived.

[10] T'an Ssu-t'ung was a Hunanese.

[11] Manchu troops.

[12] This imperial order could be the first of the "Three Secret Decrees" that appear in this book as Selection 74.

[13] *Ch'i nan-tzu.*

[14] See Selection 73, p. 244.

[15] Members of the conservative group and allies of Tz'u Hsi.

[16] Governor-general of Hupeh Province and author of Selection 43 of this book.

[17] K'ang Yu-wei, Liang Ch'i-ch'ao, T'an Ssu-t'ung, and others.

[18] This was the telegram which announced that the emperor was ill and that Tz'u Hsi, the empress dowager, had assumed the power of the state. The conservatives had won a decisive victory, and the Hundred Days' Reform was over. See also Selection 73.

[19] What Yüan referred to was an incident that occurred in the feudal state of Tsin during the seventh century B.C. Chao Tun, the prime minister, left the capital and was in hiding after the king had demanded his death sentence on an alleged offense. During his absence, the unpopular king was assassinated. Having returned to the capital upon the death of the king, the prime minister, for his own reasons, chose not to bring the assassin to justice. Displeased with his inactivity, the official historian recorded: "Chao Tun murdered the king." Asked why he recorded what he did when obviously this was not the truth, the historian replied: "As the prime minister, you have the duty to bring the assassin to justice. When you do not, you are as guilty as the assassin."

[20] Yi-k'uang.

[21] Tz'u Hsi was actually Jung-lu's cousin.

76 • YÜN YÜ-TING: *The Emperor and the Empress Dowager*[1]

Emperor Kuang-hsü was a grandson of Emperor Tao-kuang and the eldest son of Prince Ch'un and his wife, Na-la of Yeh-heh. He was born on the twenty-eighth day of the sixth month in the tenth year of T'ung-chih [August 14, 1871].

On the fifth day of the twelfth month in the thirteenth year of T'ung-chih [January 12, 1874], Emperor T'ung-chih died. Empressess Dowager Tz'u An and Tz'u Hsi decided that the eldest son of Prince Ch'un should be the sucessor. At midnight on the sixth [January 13, 1874] the imperial carriage was sent out to take the young prince to the palace to be installed as the new emperor. He was then four years old.[2] It was not until the next day or the seventh [January 14, 1874] that the palace made the official announcement that Emperor T'ung-chih had died. ...

In the first month of the fifteenth year of his reign,[3] Emperor Kuang-hsü was married to Na-la of Yeh-heh,[4] the eldest daughter of Kuei-hsiang of Manchu and the niece of Empress Dowager Tz'u Hsi. Two daughters of Deputy Minister Ch'ang-hsi, Chen[5] and Chin, were made imperial concubines. Only after the royal marriage did the emperor take over the supervision of state affairs.

During his boyhood the emperor studied at the Yü-ch'ing Palace. Weng T'ung-ho of Ch'angshu, Sun Chia-nai of Shouchou, Hsia T'ung-shan of Jenho, and Sun Yi-ching all served as tutors at one time or another. Sung-kuei was his instructor of Manchu. According to a court custom, a teacher of Manchu could not be called a "tutor,"[6] and the courtesy accorded to him was also not as great as that normally reserved for a tutor. Later Mr. Hsia left his tutorial position to become a superintendent of education and died while holding that post. Both Mr. Sun Yi-ching and Mr. Weng T'ung-ho lost their respective positions through dismissal; in the latter's case, he had somehow managed to offend the emperor. Of the four tutors only Mr. Sun Chia-nai was favorably regarded throughout his life.

The cause of Emperor T'ung-chih's death was smallpox; the widespread rumor that he died of veneral disease was without factual basis. On the fourth day of the twelfth month [January 11, 1875], his illness had changed for the better, and the sores on his body had formed scabs. The people in the palace, following an ancient custom, proceeded to offer thanks to the Goddess of the Smallpox who, accompanied by banners and protected by an umbrella, was escorted outside the Ta-ch'ing Gate amid music and flowers. On the same day the royal physician Li Teh-li came in to feel the emperor's pulse, and reported that the patient had completely recovered. Upon hearing this good news, the two empresses dowager[7] promised the physician that he would be abundantly rewarded. Suddenly, in the middle of the night, Li was summoned to the palace on an emergency call. He hurried to the Ch'ien-ch'ing Palace where he found that the emperor's countenance had completely changed and that the scabs, which had broken, emitted an extremely unpleasant odor. Li was startled by this sudden change for the worse and could not understand it. He knew, however, that there was nothing more he could do. Shortly afterwards, the sad news came from the palace that the emperor had died.

A considerable time elapsed before the events that led to the emperor's sudden death became known to the outside world. Empress Che-yi was a daughter of Ch'ung-ch'i, a ministrial vice president. Being a woman of high intelligence, she was much loved by the emperor. But for some unknown reasons, she was never able to please her mother-in-law, Empress Dowager Tz'u Hsi, who did not treat her as well as a mother-in-law should. On the fourth day of the twelfth month [January 11, 1875], the empress dowager scolded her again for some alleged offense, and the empress, when she visited her husband to inquire about his illness, tearfully complained to him about the harsh treatment she suffered at the hands of her mother-in-law. The emperor was then lying in the "warm apartment"[8] which was rectangular and unusually large. Because of the extreme cold weather, the room was divided into two sections by a hanging curtain. Seeing that the empress was proceeding towards the emperor's room, Tz'u Hsi tailed her without her knowledge. She waved the palace attendants aside when they were about to enter the room to announce her presence. She took off her shoes and walked gingerly towards the curtain. She leaned her ear against it and heard the empress's complaints which were followed by the emperor's words of comfort. "Please be patient," she heard him say, "someday we will become masters in our own house." Infuriated by this remark, Tz'u Hsi pushed aside the curtain and quickly entered. She grabbed the empress' hair, hit her with all her might, and dragged her out of the emperor's presence. She then ordered the palace guards to get striking rods ready to punish the empress for her impudence.

Caught by this unexpected event, the emperor was as much grieved as he was frightened; he fell on the floor and fainted. When he regained consciousness, his illness took a sudden turn for the worse. Only after Tz'u Hsi learned about the seriousness of her son's illness did she agree to release the empress. However, she announced that the emperor's illness had suddenly become serious largely because of the empress' attempt to conduct sexual relations with him—a naked lie, of course. After Kuang-hsü's accession to the throne, the empress was given a new title, Chia-chun; but, grieved by the death of her husband, she had long lost the desire to live. On the twentieth day of the second month in the next year [March 27, 1875], she committed suicide by swallowing gold. Ch'ung-ch'i, her father, also lost favor with Empress Dowager Tz'u Hsi on account of his daughter. For more than twenty years he was not given a governmental post to hold.

Empress Dowager Tz'u An died on the eleventh day of the third month in the year of hsin-ssu [April 9, 1881]. Previously it had been reported that Tz'u Hsi was seriously ill while Tz'u An was enjoying her best health. When the sad news arrived, all officials in the court thought that the Western Dowager had died; they were astonished beyond belief when they learned that it was the Eastern Dowager who had ascended to Heaven. (As Tz'u An and Tz'u Hsi lived in two separate palaces, East and West, they were referred to as Eastern Dowager and Western Dowager respectively. The people inside the palaces, however, addressed Tz'u An as Eastern Buddha and Tz'u Hsi as Western Buddha.) According to a story circulated in the palace, one day during a recession from their attendance to state affairs, the two dowagers casually reminisced about the old days at the end of Emperor Hsien-feng's reign. Suddenly Tz'u An said to Tz'u Hsi: "There is something I have wished to relate to you for a long time. I have an important document which I believe you should read." Opening a trunk, she took out a roll of paper that was penned in the late emperor's [Emperor Hsien-feng] handwriting. The royal decree said in effect that according to an old custom of the royal house, no woman of the Yeh-heh clan[9] should ever serve as a spouse to the reigning emperor. Since Tz'u Hsi had borne to the emperor the crown prince, she would be honored someday on account of her son and would inevitably occupy the high position of empress dowager. "But I do not trust her," the royal decree continued. "If she behaves, that would be fine. If she does not, you should make public this decree and order the responsible ministers to follow my instruction to put her to death." Tz'u An handed this document to Tz'u Hsi and asked her to read it for herself. "We have been friends for a long time and no differences have existed between us," Tz'u An smiled. "Why should we wish to preserve this decree?" Upon finishing this remark, she immediately burned the document herself. With a reddened face, Tz'u Hsi expressed her gratitude. Obviously she was not pleased with what she had read; she left shortly afterwards.

On the eleventh day of the third month [April 9, 1881], while standing in her own yard and leaning against a water pool to watch golden fish, Tz'u An saw a eunuch from the Western Palace walk towards her with a box which he held with both hands. The eunuch knelt down and said: "This is the cake which people outside the palace presented to the Western Buddha as a tribute. Having tasted it and found it delicious, the Western Buddha wishes to share it with Your Ladyship." Tz'u An was extremely pleased, and to show her appreciation, she opened the box, picked up one of the cakes, and ate it right in front of the eunuch. A moment later, the Eastern Palace sent for the royal physician on an emergency call, saying that the Eastern Dowager had suffered a sudden attack of asthma. She died even before the royal physician could be brought to her presence.

Tz'u An was quiet, serious, and seldom indulged herself in impulsive laughter or small talks. She followed the rules of the royal household scrupulously and attached great importance to matters of principle. With the assistance of such men as Prince Kung and Tseng Kuo-fan, she, as a regent, was responsible for adopting new policies that brought about the regeneration of China during the early years of the T'ung-chih period. Because of her uprightness, even Tz'u Hsi had always been fearful of her. Only after Tz'u An's death in the year of hsin-ssu [1881] did the construction of luxurious buildings and the pursuit of pleasure become fashionable in the royal household....

As a child, Emperor Kuang-hsü was fearful of thunderstorms. Whenever thunder struck, he would rush towards his tutor Weng T'ung-ho and hide himself between the latter's arms. After the royal marriage, the empress, unfortunately, was unable to bear him an heir. Rumor had it that he had some kind of hidden disease, but nobody outside the palace really knew much about it. However, he looked healthy and strong and never had a day of illness during a period of thirty-four years. He never failed to appear before the court and grant audiences; he personally offered scarifices during every religious ritual he was scheduled to attend. Even during the days of strong wind and heavy snow, he did not show any semblance of being tired. His walk was steady and fast; his ministers-in-attendance often had a difficult time keeping pace with him. By nature he was a generous and lenient person; he would simply ignore a minister's occasional backsliding in the performance of proper rituals when meeting with him.

According to the court custom, after each metropolitan examination, the examiners would present the ten best papers to the emperor for personal reviews. Only after the emperor had read them would the seals on the papers be opened and the names of the candidates made known. Normally Emperor Kuang-hsü would not change the order of the ten successful candidates that had been decided upon by the examiners. He made one exception, however, during the palace examination in the year of yi-wei.[10] Realizing the great danger China was then in, the emperor was anxious to locate the most patriotic among the scholars to be appointed to governmental posts. Lo Ch'eng-hsiang of Szechuan was ranked number ten, but was immediately promoted to number one when the emperor read in his paper the statement that "The minister should feel insulted whenever the emperor is grieved and should volunteer to die whenever the emperor is insulted." Needless to say, the emperor was very pleased with this statement.

After the emperor had taken over the power of the state, Yi-ho Yüan was designated as the place where Tz'u Hsi, the empress dowager, was to live in retirement. The emperor went to Yi-ho Yüan to pay his respect every other day, and all memorials, after he had read them, were resealed and presented to the empress dowager for examination. One day in the year of ting-yu [1897], I, the emperor's secretary, attached a note to the memorial I wrote in which I impeached a eunuch named Niu for accepting bribes and peddling influence and requested the emperor to punish him severely in accordance with the ancestral system. Niu, however, was very close to the empress dowager, whose confidant he was. The emperor said to tutor Weng: "If this note ever reaches the empress dowager, the petitioner will surely be put to death. I shall try to save his life." He detached the note from the memorial before presenting it to the empress dowager. Later, when tutor Weng told me about this, I was so grateful to His Majesty that I could not hold back my tears. . . .

After the eighth month of wu-hsi[11] there were rumors in and outside the palace that the emperor was about to be deposed. . . . Ching Yüan-shan, a candidate for a magistral post, took the lead in obtaining signatures of many oversea Chinese for a telegram to the Western Dowager, requesting her to protect the emperor. Though an order was subsequently issued for Ching's arrest, the rumor about the emperor's deposition nevertheless began to calm down. The year after the above incident [1899], the emperor reached the age of thirty-nine.[12] Then Ch'ung-ch'i had been without a governmental post for a long time, and Hsü T'ung, a grand chancellor, also wished to obtain an important post for himself. Hsü was a friend of Ch'i-hsiu, and all three of them—Ch'ung-ch'i, Hsü, and Ch'i-hsiu—secretly plotted to establish "unusual deeds" to achieve their own selfish ends. But the man whom Tz'u Hsi really trusted and listened to was Jung-lu[13] who had real power in his hands, even though he was ranked below the princes. The three plotted day and night, and finally agreed to repair to Jung-lu's residence, one at a time, to persuade him to follow the example of Yi Yin and Huo Kuang.[14] Ch'ung-ch'i and Hsü T'ung secretly prepared a memorial which they wanted Jung-lu to endorse before presenting it to the empress dowager. On the twenty-eighth day of the eleventh month [December 30, 1899], Ch'i-hsiu went to see Jung-lu soon after the morning audience and reported to him what Ch'ung-ch'i and Hsü T'ung intended to do. Astonished beyond belief, Jung-lu asked Ch'i-hsiu to leave his house immediately without committing himself one way or another. After the visitor left, he instructed the gatekeeper not to announce any more visitors. When Ch'ung-ch'i and Hsü T'ung arrived later, the gatekeeper declined to announce their presence as he had been instructed to do.

The next day Jung-lu requested a private conversation with the empress dowager shortly after the morning audience. "Is it true that the emperor will be deposed?" he asked.

"It is not true," the empress dowager replied. "However, can this be done according to your judgment?"

"If Your Ladyship has decided that it should be done," said Jung-lu, "who dare say that it cannot be done? However, the emperor has not committed any notorious crimes. If he is deposed, the foreign ministers in China might decide to intervene. We should be very careful about this matter."

"But the news about his impending deposition is about to come out at any moment. What should I do?"

"There is not much to worry about," Jung-lu replied. "The emperor has already reached middle age, and he still does not have a son. In my judgment, Your Ladyship should at this time choose a close relative to be installed as the crown prince. The young man, whoever he is, would be regarded as the heir to both the late Emperor Mu-tsung [T'ung-chih] and the present emperor. He would be raised inside the palace and, when the right moment arrives, would be installed on the throne to replace the present emperor. Whichever way we look at it, a measure like this cannot but be regarded as proper and certainly will not meet many objections."

Tz'u Hsi thought about this suggestion for a long time and finally commented: "You are right."

On the twenty-fourth day [January 24, 1900] all princes, ministers, and high-ranking officials were summoned to the Yi-luan Palace for an audience with the empress dowager. The rumor spread fast that the emperor would be deposed. Su-la, an official in the Inner Court, did not help the matter by announcing publicly: "There will be a change of emperors today!" Only after a decree had been issued during the audience did the officials know that the purpose of this audience was to announce the installation of P'u-yi as the crown prince....[15]

On the twentieth day of the seventh month [August 14, 1900], the British captured Peking. The very next day the troops of other allies entered the city. Early in the morning the empress dowager and the emperor rode civilian carriages and hurriedly left the city through the Teh-sheng Gate. Hardly had they left the city before white flags appeared all over the city wall. The empress dowager wore summer clothes, and her hair was tied into a bun in the most casual manner. The emperor had on a long gown of blue silk. The only members of the royal family who joined the exodus were the empress and the crown prince, and few of the royal concubines chose to follow. Before she left the palace ground, however, the empress dowager instructed an eunuch named Ts'ui to bring her the Pearl Concubine from San-so where the latter had been hitherto confined. Once she was brought in, the empress dowager ordered her to be pushed into a deep well where she perished.

Prior to her imprisonment, the Pearl Concubine, being highly intelligent, had been the emperor's true favorite. As a child, she studied at home and had as her tutor one of the most learned men at that time, Wen T'ing-shih of Kiangsi. Because of her training she was well versed in history and literature. After Wen passed the metropolitan examination in the year of keng-yin [1890] with the third highest score, she repeatedly recommended him to her spouse, the emperor. In the grand examination of chia-wu [1894] when the Hanlin scholars were chosen, the emperor personally handed Wen's papers to the examiners and Wen, consequently, was ranked number one. He was promoted to the post of a Hanlin reader and simultaneously served as an instructor. Deeply grateful for the royal patronage, Wen repeatedly commented on current affairs in his memorials to the emperor. When the news of China's defeat at Liaotung[16] arrived, he, together with many other ministers, petitioned the emperor to reappoint Prince Kung to a high post in charge of the nation's civilian and military affairs. The empress dowager had always disliked Prince Kung and everything he did; it was due to the emperor's insistence that Prince Kung finally received the appointment. In the year of ping-shen [1896] someone accused Pearl Concubine of having meddled in political affairs. The empress dowager was so angry that she ordered the accused to be caned before she was sent to prison in San-so. The prisoner was fed food and water, but she was not allowed to communicate with the outside world. Her brother, Chih-jui, who had until then served as a vice-president in the Ministry of Rites, was exiled to Uliasutai.[17] After this incident, the emperor was a sad, depressed man. During the allies' occupation of Peking, the Japanese were assigned to guard the Forbidden City which had become deadly quiet. They dug out Pearl Concubine's body from the well and buried her in a shallow grave in T'ien, a village to the west of the capital....

Tz'u Hsi came from the Na-la clan of the Yeh-heh tribe. When the tribe was conquered during the early period of the dynastic establishment, a large number of its members were slaughtered, and few of its adult males were able to escape.

Before he died, Pu-yang-ku, the head of the tribe, said angrily: "Even if only one woman of our tribe managed to survive, she would certainly seek revenge and overthrow the Manchus." Because of this remark, the founder of the Manchu Dynasty made it a rule that no women from the Yeh-heh tribe should ever be imperial consorts, a rule that was to bind all of his descendants.

Tz'u Hsi's father died while serving as a lieutenant commander in Hunan. He left behind him two daughters, Tz'u Hsi and her younger sister. The family was so poor that the two sisters did not even have enough money to ship their father's body to the north for burial. But somehow they managed to proceed with their journey. When the boat reached Ch'ingchiangp'u,[18] another funeral boat was anchored nearby, and the dead man in this boat also had been a former lieutenant commander. Wu Ch'in-hui, the magistrate of Ch'ingchiangp'u, had been a friend of the dead man in the second boat, and learning about the latter's arrival, dispatched a servant bearing 300 taels of silver to be given to the bereaved family as a gift. (Some people have maintained, incorrectly, that the amount was 2,000 taels.) The servant, however, delivered the silver to the wrong boat. Wu was very angry; he was about to dispatch the servant to demand the return of his silver when he was stopped by one of his secretary-advisers. "I have heard that the people in the boat were Manchu maidens who are journeying to the capital to be selected as the emperor's spouses," said the secretary-adviser. "They may be powerful and influential someday. Maybe it is to your advantage to be friendly with them." Accepting this advice, Wu, instead of demanding the return of his silver, personally went to the boat to pay his respect to the dead man. Tz'u Hsi was greatly moved. Carefully storing Wu's personal card away in one of her dressers, she said to her younger sister: "If someday you and I achieve what we wish to achieve, we shall not forget this man."

Once entering the palace, Tz'u Hsi soon became the emperor's favorite and in due course gave birth to a son, later known as Emperor T'ung-chih. Meanwhile her younger sister married Prince Ch'un and also gave birth to a son, later known as Emperor Kuang-hsü. By the time Tz'u Hsi became a regent, Wu Ch'in-hui had already been promoted to the position of a district governor. In a period of a few years, he was promoted to the governor-general of Szechuan. Wu had no special ability to speak of; although he had been repeatedly impeached by the censors, the empress dowager chose not to pay any attention. After he died in his post, he was given the posthumous title "Hui,"[19] an indication that even then the empress dowager had not forgotten the favor that she had once received from him. According to another story, when Wu was jailed on a criminal charge, Tz'u Hsi impersonated one of his close relatives so as to visit him in the prison. She summoned the late Shen Chia-pen, then a vice-president in charge of criminal affairs, and questioned him in great detail about the condition of prisons throughout the nation.

Long after she had passed seventy, Tz'u Hsi still looked like a woman of about forty. For one thing, not a single strand of her hair had turned white. The rumor had it that early during the T'ung-chih period the eunuch Li Lien-ying obtained for her a large *ho-shou-wu*[20] which, being prepared in an improper manner, melted into a bowl of gruel. Nevertheless, Tz'u Hsi continued to take it. According to tradition, a thousand-year-old *ho-shou-wu*, when prepared by the proper method (boiling and drying alternatively for nine times), is the best rejuvenation drug. A person who takes it can live a long time. . . .

Emperor Kuang-hsü had a quiet, dignified countenance. His forehead was broad, and his chin was fleshy and wide. He should have enjoyed a long life according to the physiognomists. He not only was intelligent but also loved learning.

However, whenever someone asked tutor Weng about the intellectual capacity of his royal charge, Weng always replied that the emperor was not particularly bright. He deliberately lied so that the empress dowager would not become jealous. The emperor was a thrifty man; he wore clothes that had been repeatedly washed or mended. He did not care for sensual pleasures. The empress dowager, on the other hand, loved theaters, and the emperor, out of deference to her, attended them. Rumor had it that he was an expert drummer, but there are no known facts to substantiate it. Throughout his life he was afraid of the empress dowager. He suffered from stuttering and could not utter a single word and his whole body shook with fear whenever the empress dowager reprimanded or scolded him. After his return from Sian,[21] he lived in retirement and no longer participated in state affairs; he was in fact a figurehead. His eunuch attendants had been completely changed; all the new ones were those sent by the empress dowager to watch him. All day all year round he sat inside his room, a bored, lonely man without much to do.

In the fall of wu-shen [1908] it was suddenly reported that the emperor was indisposed, and famous physicians in and outside the capital were invited to diagnose his illness. When he met with the physicians, the emperor placed both of his hands on a table for them to feel his pulse, but he would not utter a single word. Instead, he wrote down what he thought his trouble was on a piece of paper which was then placed on the table. He became angry if the physicians asked him any questions. He became angrier if they ventured the opinion that he suffered from a weakened constitution. All the physicians agreed, however, that all of his six pulses functioned normally and that he did not suffer from any illness to the best of their knowledge....

On the morning of the tenth day of the tenth month [November 3, 1908], the emperor led all the ministers to the empress dowager's residence to congratulate the latter on her birthday and to pay her their respect.... He walked all the way from Nanhai to the Teh-ch'ang Gate, only to find the door to the empress dowager's residence closed. One official-in-attendance noticed that the emperor, placing one hand on the shoulder of a eunuch, was alternatively bending and stretching his knees; he was relaxing his muscles to prepare himself for the kowtow ritual that would be expected when he saw the empress dowager. Shortly afterwards an order from the empress dowager arrived, saying that the emperor was ill and lying in bed and that he should not bother to lead the officials to her residence to pay their respect.[22] Upon receiving this order, the emperor was overwhelmed with grief, because he knew that the empress dowager had suffered from diarrhea for a period of several days. Someone slandered the emperor by saying that he seemed to be pleased when he heard that the empress dowager was ill. "I cannot die before he does," she commented in anger....

On the eighteenth day [November 11, 1908], Prince Ch'ing (Yi-k'uang) was ordered by the empress dowager to proceed to P'ut'oyü to make an inspection tour of the prepared tomb; he did not return until the twenty-first [November 14, 1908]. It was said that the empress dowager sent him away on purpose.

On the nineteenth day [November 12, 1908] additional sentries were posted on all gates leading to the Forbidden City. They intensified their vigilance by checking everyone who passed through the gates with great thoroughness. Shortly afterwards some eunuchs emerged from the Tung-hua Gate and announced that the emperor had died. There was no news from the palace the next day; not until the afternoon was an order issued from the palace that Prince Ch'un had been designated as the provisional regent. According to palace sources, it was not until the twenty-first day

[November 14, 1908] that the empress had the opportunity to visit the emperor, only to see his dead body on the bed when she arrived. She, in fact, had no idea when her husband had died. She cried and rushed to report what she had seen to the empress dowager. The latter only sighed. . . .

The very next day after the emperor's demise, the empress dowager also died.[23]

NOTES

[1] Translated from *Ch'ung-ling ch'uan-hsin lu*. As for the author, see footnote 00, p. 000.

[2] Three years old according to the Western custom.

[3] This corresponds to the period between January 31 and March 1, inclusive, 1889.

[4] Na-la was actually the name of a clan; a female member of that clan was usually addressed as Na-la Shih, regardless of generations.

[5] This was the famous Pearl Concubine.

[6] *Shih-fu.*

[7] Tz'u An and Tz'u Hsi.

[8] *Nuan-ko.*

[9] Tz'u Hsi came from the Na-la clan of the Yeh-heh tribe.

[10] Yi-wei or 1895 was the year after China had been defeated by Japan.

[11] That is, after the collapse of the Hundred Days' Reform.

[12] Thirty-eight according to the Western custom.

[13] See Selection 75.

[14] Yi Yin, a minister during the Shang Dynasty, deposed King T'ai-chia (eighteenth century B.C.); Huo Kuang, a minister during the Han Dynasty, deposed King Ch'ang-yi and installed on the throne a prince who was later known as Han Chao-ti (r. 86–74 B.C.). Since in each case the deposed ruler was regarded as morally unfit to rule, Yi Yin and Huo Kuang were praised highly by traditional historians for the courageous action they took.

[15] P'u-yi, the last emperor of the Ch'ing Dynasty, abdicated on behalf of the Republic in 1912 and died in 1967.

[16] Sino-Japanese War, 1894–1895.

[17] Located in Outer Mongolia.

[18] Located in the northern section of Kiangsu, near Huaiyin.

[19] *Hui*, literally, means "favor."

[20] *Polygonum multiflorum.*

[21] The emperor and the empress dowager had fled to Sian during the allied occupation of Peking. They returned to Peking after the signing of the Boxer Protocol in 1901.

[22] Obviously the empress dowager did not know that the emperor had already arrived.

[23] We know with certainty that Tz'u Hsi died on November 15, 1908. Historians still debate as to the exact date when Kuang-hsü died.

CHAPTER TEN

Missionaries, Boxers, and the Open Door

When two different cultures are brought face to face with each other, there are bound to be tensions and conflicts. In terms of relations on a national basis, the differences are often settled by force, with the victors dictating terms which the vanquished are compelled to abide by. The relationship between individuals of different cultural orientations is much more complicated if, by necessity or design, they have to live together. What is regarded as proper and correct by one group may be denounced as strange or even immoral by another. Each looks down upon the other until slights degenerate into resentment and resentment consolidates to become hatred. A minor incident may trigger long-suppressed feelings and precipitate open conflicts. When individuals resort to the use of force to settle their differences, they can be as barbaric as nations.

During the past 500 years an exuberant, dynamic Europe not only sent its merchants and soldiers all over the world but also its missionaries whose duty it was to press upon the "natives" that Europe was as superior in religion as it was mighty on the battlefield. Regardless of the comparative merits of different religions which were highly partisan and perhaps impossible to determine, the very fact that missionary work was thought necessary presupposed the superiority of one set of spiritual values to another, a supposition that was deeply resented by those among whom the missionaries worked. Understandably there were tensions even under the best of circumstances, but the circumstances, at least in the case of China, were far from ideal. In China, the missionaries encountered one of the oldest civilizations in the world, with all its biases and prejudices about its own superiority and its undisguised contempt for anything "barbarian." The superiority of Western technology was easy to see; but who in the world could convince the Chinese that St. Augustine or St. Thomas was infinitely wiser than Mencius or Chu Hsi?

The moderate Jesuit success in China during the seventeenth and early eighteenth centuries was due in no small measure to the tact and understanding of a small group of truly remarkable men whose knowledge of China has never been equaled despite our modern means of instant communication. Even then the end result was far from satisfactory, as we have noted in an earlier chapter. With the imposition of unequal treaties upon China during the middle decades of the nineteenth century (Chapter Four), the situation took a turn for the worse insofar as missionary work was concerned. Behind the missionaries was the mighty power of Western Europe which, by the use or the threat of use of force, would see to it that the wishes of its nationals in China were always fulfilled. By relying on force as the ultimate arbiter of differences, the missionaries lost their power of persuasion. The way Christianity was imposed upon China and the privileged position it enjoyed made its failure almost a foregone conclusion. Ironically, its sponsors, by insisting on a privileged position for their religion, did not give it a chance to compete fairly and equally with other religions in China. It could have succeeded, but it did not. To many Chinese the missionaries were an aggressive arm of Western imperialism, despite the many utilitarian things (such as schools and hospitals) they brought to the Chinese people.

To compound the difficulties, the early missionaries were not always well trained. They were certainly not the best the West could have sent to China. Practically all of them were illiterate in the Chinese language, and some of them were barely literate in their own. Yet they were all determined to "lead the heathen Chinese out of the darkness." This attitude was, of course, not the best way of making friends and influencing people. Enjoying extraterritoriality, not only did they place themselves above the reach of the Chinese law, they also assisted their converts to sidetrack the normal functioning of Chinese justice (Selection 78). Not surprisingly, many lawless, unscrupulous elements swelled the Christian ranks because of the protection the missionaries could provide in case they ran into difficulties with the law enforcement officials. Thus the Christian community, which had historically set an example in humility and virtue in many hostile lands, fell far short of being the ideal society in China which a good Christian would have wished.

It would be wrong, of course, to place the entire burden of blame upon the shoulders of the missionaries. If the missionaries knew less than they should about China, the Chinese were even more pathetic insofar as their knowledge of Western Europe or Christianity was concerned. Even the best informed of them tended to regard the missionaries as black magicians who knew not only how to transform ordinary metals into gold or silver but also, dreadfully, how to make direful drugs by using eyes and hearts extracted from infants as raw materials (Selection 77). If the educated were so credulous as to believe such nonsense, the uneducated were of course much worse. Throughout the second half of the nineteenth century, anti-missionary riots repeatedly occurred in all the provinces where the missionaries were active, and some of these riots had behind them the organized support of local gentry and Confucian scholars (Selection 79). Of all the enemies of mankind, the worst has always been ignorance.

Prior to 1900 when the Boxer movement developed, the most serious riot involving the missionaries was the Tientsin Incident (1870) when more than twenty foreign lives were lost (Selection 80). Because such knowledgeable men as Tseng Kuo-fan were still in power, the incident was eventually settled

MISSIONARIES, BOXERS AND THE OPEN DOOR 265

to the satisfaction of both sides (Selection 81). With the Boxer movement, however, the situation was entirely different. Enchanted with the Boxers' slogan: "Support the Manchus and Exterminate the Foreigners" (*Fu Ch'ing mieh yang*), Tz'u Hsi, then the ultimate power in China, plunged the country into one of the most disastrous, unnecessary wars ever fought in modern history (Selection 82). As one may have expected, China was defeated and the allied troops of eight countries marched into Peking without encountering too much opposition. The occupation of Peking was followed by large-scale massacre, rape, and looting, such as had not been seen since the days of the Mongols (Selection 83). The existence of China could have ended then; it was saved by the disagreement among the powers as to how China should be divided among themselves. As they could not agree, they postponed their division of China by concluding a peace treaty with their vanquished foe (Selection 84). Besides such familiar terms as the payment of indemnities and the granting of commercial concessions, the treaty also called for the punishment of "war criminals."

One of the products of the scramble for Chinese territories and the subsequent Boxer episode was the famous Open Door policy. In September, 1899, the American Secretary of State John Hay sent a diplomatic note to Great Britain, Germany, and Russia requesting that equal commercial opportunity be maintained in all parts of China. This note was followed by another one in July, 1900, in which the Secretary of State stated that the United States aimed "to seek a solution which may bring about permanent safety and peace to China, preserve Chinese territorial and administrative entity, protect all rights guaranteed to friendly Powers by treaty and international law, and safeguard for the world the principle of equal and impartial trade with all parts of the Chinese empire" (Selection 85). Once proclaimed, the Open Door remained the basic policy of the United States towards China until the Communists closed China's door in 1949.

77 • CHANG TEH-CHIEN: *Christianity and the Taiping Rebels*[1]

From the beginning of history, whenever a bandit leader decided to start a rebellion, he most likely used a heterodox religion as a rally point. This was certainly true of Chang Chüeh toward the end of the Han Dynasty, Wang Tse of the Sung Dynasty, and T'ang Sai-erh of the Ming Dynasty. During recent years the White Lotus Society and the Eight Diagram Society all invoked gods and spirits to deceive the ignorant, while their real purpose was to organize large followings so as to achieve their own selfish ends. Once they succeeded in gathering a large following and thus acquired organizational strength, they might decide not to rely on their so-called religion; instead, they increasingly attached greater importance to physical might for their eventual success. In any event, the spread of a heterodox religion usually marked the beginning of political anarchy accompanied by social chaos.

The Christian religion had persisted in Kwangtung, Kwangsi, and Fukien for a long time. Later, due to strict suppression on the part of local officials and the arrest of many of its followers, it changed its name from that of a religion to that of a society. Consequently a number of Christian societies emerged, such as the Society of God Worshippers, the Society of Added Brethren, and the Society of Small Swords. During the years immediately following the establishment of peace between Great Britain and China,[2] some of the worst elements in Kwangtung and Fukien were as arrogant as they were unruly, and the followers of the above-mentioned societies became even more numerous. The society organized by the rebel Hung Hsiu-ch'üan was called the Society of God Worshippers[3] at the beginning, but was renamed the Society of Heavenly King[4] in a later period. It was also known as the Society of Added Brethren[5] because it regarded all the new converts, regardless of their age, as younger brothers to those who had been converted earlier. Though the name varied, it was the same Christianity.

In his book *Conversations of a Wanderer*,[6] Liang Ts'ai-lin related to us some of the major points contained in Wu Teh-chih's essay *On Christianity*.[7] According to Wu, China had never heard about the Christianity of the Western world before the Ming Dynasty; not until the last decades of the Ming Dynasty, said he, did many Chinese begin to be converted to it, largely on account of the missionary work conducted by such men as Matteo Ricci, Joannes Adam Schall von Bell, and Ferdinandus Verbiest. These missionaries were expert mathematicians and were uncannily effective whenever they were asked to revise the Chinese calendar. Besides, they were proficient in making mechanical devices and clever in useful skills. They knew, for instance, how to transform ordinary metals into gold or silver. Consequently, despite the fact that they did not till one *mou* of land or weave one yard of cloth, they always lived in comfort.

As their influence continued to spread, the missionaries and their converts built churches in cities and towns in all of the provinces of China. They called their churches the Halls of the Heavenly Lord,[8] each of which was as spacious as it was beautifully decorated. In each community a Christian church was usually headed by a Westerner and operated in total secrecy; it did not allow outsiders to take a look at its activities. Whenever a Chinese wished to be converted to this religion, he had first to destroy not only his ancestral tablets but also the tablets or scrolls that honored the "Five Immortals."[9] Once accepted as a convert, he would then be known as a religion-eater.[10] Each religion-eater received four taels of silver from his church and pasted a piece of yellow paper on his front door. On the paper was drawn an oval-shaped circle inside of which were painted a cross, a knife, an awl, a hook, a lance, and similar items. People said that the deity whom the Christians worshipped was a victim of public execution, and they painted instruments of execution on their front doors as a memorial to him. On the first and the fifteenth days of each lunar month the Christians, men and women, gathered inside their church, closed the door behind them, and recited their holy book; they would not disperse until sunset.

The Christians refused to take medicine when they were sick; instead, they invited some of their religious compatriots to their house to practice acupuncture and cauterization upon them. Even women were stripped naked to receive this kind of treatment. Whenever a man died, the head of the church would send a representative to examine the dead body. The representative would first chase out all the relatives of the dead man from the death room and then close the door behind him before proceeding to dress the body for burial purposes. During the dressing process he covered each of the dead man's eyes with a plaster and then wrapped his head with a bag made of red cloth; the bag, called a "clothed womb,"[11] was stitched at its upper end. Only after this procedure was completed could the dead man be put inside his coffin. Some people said that the dead man's eyes were actually carved out during the dressing procedure and that these eyes were used by the missionaries as a magic catalyst to transform ordinary metals into gold or silver. This was the reason, they said, that a convert was given four taels of silver at the time of his conversion, to be repaid with his own eyes at the time of his death, a payment that was carefully hidden from his knowledge as long as he lived. If the dead man's relatives refused to follow the dressing procedure previously described, the church called them traitors and sent its henchmen to their house to scold and insult them. It also demanded the return of the four taels of silver, plus interest, which the dead man had received from the church upon his conversion to Christianity. A man might feel that he had been deceived from the very beginning; but how could he, being so poor, escape this kind of entrapment?

There were those among the intellectuals who, being avaricious and shameless, honored these missionaries in the hope that they might also be able to master the secrets whereby ordinary metals could be transformed into high-priced gold or silver. They in fact called these missionaries Western scholars. Wherever a missionary went, he presented expensive gifts to local officials to cultivate their friendship, and these officials, to show their gratitude, protected him whenever he got into trouble. Not surprisingly, Christianity became more and more widespread.

A catechism published by the Christian church asserts that the Lord, sometimes called the Heavenly Lord, created all the things in the universe, that all worship performed before Heaven, Earth, and ancestors should be rightfully condemned and dispensed with, and that everyone on earth must worship the Heavenly Lord alone, with undivided loyalty and total devotion. It also says that had it not been for the fact that the Heavenly Lord has consistently upheld the universe since its creation by him, Heaven would have collapsed and the Earth would have turned over a long time ago. Yet, it also maintains that this so-called Heavenly Lord was actually born in the fourteenth year of Han Ai-ti.[12] How contradictory and absurd these remarks are!

The Christian missionaries are expert painters; even the printed copies of the original are very realistic. They paint clouds, mists, people, and objects, of different shapes and of a variety of moods; yet the theme behind all these paintings is what an ordinary person would characterize as pornographic. They also use ordinary materials to make a naked woman whose flesh, skin, bones, ears, eyes, teeth, tongue, and even vagina are exactly the same as those of a living woman. Once made, she can be folded and carried away like a piece of clothing. When air is blown into her by one's mouth, she is immediately transformed into a soft, warm, lively beauty whom one could embrace and with whom one could conduct sexual intercourse. The immorality of these missionaries is as great as their skill to produce it.

In the Keng-tzu year of Tao-kuang [1840 A.D.], Yi Hsin-nung, an army commander, captured thirty-six English soldiers at Yüyao[13] and, while searching their luggage, found two books, entitled *Jesus' Descent on Earth* and *The Salvation of the World*.[14] Since both books are written in Chinese rather than English, many of Yi's secretary-advisers have read them and can even today remember their contents. The author of *Jesus' Descent on Earth* says that Jesus was the son of God, born in the kingdom of Judea during the reign of Han Ai-ti, that he taught people the virtue of goodness, and performed a variety of miracles. A king named Herod[15] became very jealous, entrapped and captured him, and finally crucified him on a cross. Seven days after he had been buried, Jesus succeeded in gathering his dissipated spirit, came to life again, broke his tomb, and emerged once again on earth. For three days he preached; when the preaching was over, he left the earth and ascended to Heaven. He is still in Heaven, according to this book, and will remain the Heavenly Lord forever. *The Salvation of the World* teaches people to worship the Heavenly Lord only, saying that we should under no circumstances worship any false gods. It lists the Heavenly commands which forbid people to murder, scheme, commit adultery, theft or robbery, deception, and irreverence towards one's parents. All marriages are to be arranged by a priest, and no person can conduct sexual intercourse without his permission. If a man can abide by all of these Heavenly commands, says this book, his soul will go to paradise after he dies; otherwise he will go to hell.

This theory of Jesus' descent on earth is too absurd to be elaborated here. This religion has some good points however in that it teaches people to refrain from such evil practices as murder and adultery. The oversea barbarians, cut off from any communication with China and living a life of the most primitive nature, could not be expected to know the right rules that governed human relationships, and the tragedy of aggression and mutual slaughter must have been a recurrent phenomenon in their part of the world. It is conceivable that the Heavenly Lord, being compassionate towards them as he certainly must have been, sent a man to earth to teach them the proper way of conducting their lives. It is futile for us to speculate whether a man named Jesus ever lived; but some of the teachings attributed to him do have their telling point. Fearful that men might indulge in superstitious practices and thus be bewitched by heretical ideas, he asked them to worship Heaven and Heaven only. Fearful that they might relish deception, robbery, and murder and that they might desert their parents for their own selfish ends, he promulgated the Heavenly commands to forbid them to do these evil things. Fearful that men and women might be subject to animal impulse and conduct their relationships in the same manner as birds and beasts, he prohibited them to marry each other without his permission. From the Chinese point of view, this religion of Jesus is of course unorthodox or heretical, even though it has nothing to do with Moism or the philosophy of Yang Chu.[16] However, by guiding these ignorant barbarians towards goodness in accordance with their own peculiar customs, Jesus might be said to have been a farsighted, enlightened man, and it is perhaps proper that they should regard him as the Heavenly Lord.

What Jesus could not foresee is that 2,000 years after his death, his alleged followers would invoke his name to engage in the most abominable activities. They mix men and women together to teach them illicit sexual relations; they give people a few taels of silver to appropriate for themselves the right to carve out their eyes upon their death and to use these eyes as a catalyst to make gold or silver; and they paint pornographic pictures and make sexual instruments so as to enhance their own lascivious pleasure. All this is not what Jesus once taught, and certainly we cannot blame him for his alleged followers' immoral behavior. However treacherous and unprincipled these missionaries are, even they realize that their obnoxious ideas could not possibly spread all over China. So far they have only succeeded in satisfying a temporary desire of their own by sowing the seeds of hatred and distrust among the Chinese people and by searching for money and beautiful women in the coastal areas.

In this respect the Kwangtung bandits[17] are definitely much worse. At the beginning they used this heretical religion as a rallying point to prepare for their rebellion and hid the real intention of their evil schemes. Using trickery peculiar only to men of their kind, they succeeded in catching us in our weakest moment when our generals were negligent, our soldiers unprepared, and our people in a confused state of affairs. As their evil influence increased, their followers became more addicted to this so-called religion of theirs. Not only did they attempt to destroy the teachings of our ancient sage kings, they also wished to abolish all the deities that were in charge of our mountains and rivers. They wanted everybody to worship no other god except Jesus; they were in fact trying to transform the saintly ways of China into the customs of the barbarians. The poison they emitted was of the worst kind and of the greatest intensity, a corruption of religion which Jesus could not have anticipated.

The strange thing about this Christianity is that when you read the books the Kwangtung bandits have published and the Heavenly commands they have promulgated, and when you attend their services and listen to their sermons, it seems that they have advocated nothing except Jesus' teachings and have forbidden nothing except Jesus' prohibitions. Yet, once you look at their actions, suddenly you realize that they are the direct opposite of what they profess to be. They slaughter people without the slightest provocation; they rape the innocent and loot the helpless without showing any self-restraint. They teach people to be dutiful sons; yet they kidnap law-abiding citizens whom they forbid to see their parents. They warn people against deception; yet they themselves are the true masters of deceptive schemes. Since their actions have become the direct opposite of their preachings, they themselves are the real violators of their own teachings. What has happened to the principle of marriage only by the consent of a priest when in fact they impose the harshest punishment upon married couples who choose to share one bed? What has happened to the principle of worshiping the true god only, when their leaders call themselves gods of rain, clouds, or divine wind,[18] even though they are as mortal as anybody else?

In short, one might say that these Kwangtung bandits are the craziest, wildest rebels since the beginning of mankind. Not only will they not be tolerated by the law; they will also be condemned by history as the mortal enemy of all of mankind. They in fact are traitors to their own professed religion. If Jesus in Heaven knew what his alleged followers were doing in China, he would certainly help all other deities to exterminate these cruel, brutal, and treacherous bandits.

NOTES

[1] Source: *Information on the Kwangtung Bandits* (*Tse-ch'ing hui-tsuan*), roll 9. The author, a scholar-official then serving the Ch'ing regime, wrote this book late in the 1850's or early in the 1860's.
[2] This refers to the Treaty of Nanking (1842) concluded after the Opium War.
[3] Shang-ti hui.
[4] T'ien-ti hui.
[5] T'ieh ("added")-ti ("younger brother") hui ("society" or "association").
[6] *Lang-yi ts'ung-t'an.*
[7] *T'ien-chu-chiao shu shih.*
[8] T'ien-chu t'ang.
[9] The Chinese original is *wu ssu* ("Five Immortals") which is subject to different interpretations. According to one interpretation, the "Five Immortals" are "Heaven, Earth, Kings, Ancestors, and Teachers" (*t'ien, ti, chün, ch'in, shih*). Scrolls or tablets that bore the five Chinese characters corresponding to Heaven, Earth, etc. could be found in the family altars of many Chinese households throughout the nineteenth century and in fact had remained there until the Communists conquered China in 1949.

¹⁰ *Ch'ih-chiao.*
¹¹ *Yi-pao.*
¹² This could have been the "fourth," instead of the "fourteenth," year of Han Ai-ti, namely, 3 B.C. Han Ai-ti's reign lasted only six years. The error in the Chinese original may have been typographical.
¹³ Loacated in Chekiang Province.
¹⁴ *Yeh-su chiang-shih shu* and *Chiu-shih shu,* respectively.
¹⁵ Hsi-lo-teh in Chinese.
¹⁶ Moism, founded by Mo Ti, advocated universal love, while Yang Chu preached an extreme form of selfishness. The two schools were often cited by Confucian scholars as typical of what they regarded as heretical ideas.
¹⁷ The Taiping rebels. See Chapter Five.
¹⁸ All these divine titles were at one time assumed by Yang Hsiu-ch'ing, the second (second only to Hung Hsiu-ch'üan) most important leader of the Taiping rebels.

78 ● PRINCE KUNG: *On the Treatment of Christian Converts*¹

Christian missionaries were permitted to preach in China during the K'ang-hsi period (1662–1722). Later, this permission was revoked on the ground that Christianity was an alien religion which the Chinese should not attempt to embrace. As a result of the treaties of 1858,² however, the missionaries were once again allowed to preach in China. Though this religion does possess some merit since its basic purpose is to teach people to be good, it has always been feared that with the passage of time abuse is bound to arise and incidents to multiply. This is the reason why in my discussions with the former French minister to China I strongly urged him to instruct all the French missionaries not to interfere with Chinese affairs, foreign or domestic. It is our good fortune that during the past years we have not heard of any criminal act committed by the Christian converts.

Recently, in a letter addressed to me, the French minister Klekowski³ spoke on behalf of a Shensi convert named Tuan Chen-hui who refused to pay a larger amount of rent to his landlord even though he had opened up new fields that belonged to the same landlord. The French minister, acting upon Tuan's request, urged the Office of General Management to instruct the governor of Shensi to prohibit the landlord to increase Tuan's rent and to allow Tuan, the tenant, to determine for himself the amount of rent he should pay to his landlord. Since the amount of rent is predetermined in a contract, how can any tenant change it unilaterally without securing his landlord's approval in advance? Obviously this man Tuan was counting on the fact that being a Christian, he could do whatever he pleased. If we allow him to have his way, eventually a situation may develop in which the Christian converts not only can forcibly take over other people's land but may also refuse to pay taxes as well.

According to a report I received from the governor of Shensi, such missionaries as Liang To-ming and Fu An-tang,⁴ having repeatedly interferred with other people's affairs, are the major cause of many endless lawsuits between the Christian converts and the non-Christians. They, for instance, prompt the Christian converts to pledge not to make any contributions to the staging of theatrical shows in honor of local gods, saying that those who do will cease to be Christians and will in fact backslide as pagans.⁵ The staging of theatrical shows to honor local gods has been a regular custom in the rural community since time immemorial, and there has never been any law to prohibit it. Now these foreign missionaries not only order their converts not to contribute funds to make it a success but also insult all other Chinese by calling them pagans. Thus by one stroke they succeed in dividing people into two groups, the Christians and the non-Christians. The Christians, relying on the missionaries' support, insult and bully the law-abiding citizens, while the latter, in retaliation, look down upon what they regard as their oppressors. Animosity thus aroused, each group refuses to make any concession to the other.

The situation described above creates great difficulties for local officials. Lest incidents occur that might provide foreign powers with the pretext to intervene in China's domestic affairs, they tend to yield and make compromises whenever the missionaries put pressure upon them. This weak stand not only whips the appetite of the Christians who become more aggressive as a result but also causes great resentment on the part of the non-Christians. If the government does not promulgate specific rules to govern disputes of this kind, local officials will not know what to follow and will not be able to act properly whenever a dispute involving Christians occurs. Meanwhile, as tensions continue to build up, sooner or later there will be serious incidents.

It is hereby suggested that a decree be issued to all governors-general and governors who in turn should instruct all their subordinates as follows: In each dispute involving Christians, the local officials should examine carefully its causes and, taking into consideration the circumstances under which the dispute arises and in observation of the principle of equity and justice, render the necessary decision. If a Christian convert is law-abiding and has no other interest except to practice his religion, he should be protected to the same extent as a non-Christian because, despite his religion, he is still a Chinese citizen and is therefore entitled to protection by Chinese law. If, on the other hand, he thinks that he should enjoy preferential treatment because he is a Christian, commits criminal acts in violation of the law, forcibly takes over other people's land and refuses to pay rent, oppresses or bullies law-abiding citizens, and, in short, does things that are not to be tolerated by the law, he should be prosecuted to the same extent as other citizens. In other words, he should not receive extralegal privileges simply because he happens to be a Christian. Only in this way will the Christians know that there is something to be fearful about and will the non-Christians stop their suspicions. Only in this way can we hope that both groups will live harmoniously together until eternity to come.

NOTES

[1] This memorial, dated December 1, 1861, represented the official attitude towards Christian converts in China. The author was then the President of the Office of General Management (Tsung-li ya-men) in charge of foreign affairs. Source: *Ch'ou-pan yi-wu shih-mo,* the Reign of T'ung-chih, roll 2, pp. 45–46.

[2] This refers to the Treaties of Tientsin between China on the one hand and France and Great Britain on the other. One article in these treaties guaranteed the protection of missionaries by Chinese authorities since "The Christian religion, as professed by Protestants and Roman Catholics, inculcates the practice of virtue, and teaches man to do as he would be done by." See Selection 31, pp. 89–90.

[3] Ko-shih-ch'i in Chinese transliteration.

[4] Presumably French missionaries who had adopted Chinese names.

[5] *Yi-tuan* which literally means "strange extremes." There is no exact Chinese equivalent for the word "pagan."

79 • ANONYMOUS: *Public Denunciation of Christian Missionaries*[1]

After consultations among themselves, the scholars, elders, and common people of Kiangsi province have agreed to issue the following proclamation:

Taking into consideration the fact that foreigners had come from remote countries, the Emperor of the Celestial Empire granted their request to conclude commercial treaties so they could continue to trade in China and make profits for themselves. He did so in order to show his love and generosity for people of distant lands.[2]

However, there were among foreigners such devious men as Lo An-tang and Fang An-tzu[3] who, by prompting their heretical religion, attempted to confuse the ignorant and deceive the credulous. Moreover, they murdered innocent people so as to use their victims' vital parts to make rejuvenation drugs, raped or indulged sexually with our women, and kidnapped and imprisoned our children. As a group, their conduct was as mysterious as their movement was secretive. How much we resented what they had done to us!

In the second month of this year the righteous people in our province were determined to destroy all the Roman Catholic churches to vent the common anger. Before we had a chance to exterminate these two thieves, Lo and Fang, they heard our intentions and fled. Recently we learned that they not only have gone as far as the nation's capital with the intended purpose of suing us but have also instigated their consul to write a letter to His Excellency the Governor to condemn us. In this letter they demand an indemnity payment amounting to 70,000 taels of silver and the building of a new Catholic church in the site where the public orphanage is presently located. This kind of demand is nothing but a bandit's blackmail! During a time when funds are urgently needed for national defense, how can we throw money away into this bottomless hole?

Through this proclamation we hope that all of you will express your righteous anger as vigorously as we have. If these missionaries dare to return to Kiangsi to continue their devilish task of bewitching innocent people, millions of us will rise as one man and use whatever weapons we have, including farm implements, to chase them out. Motivated by the nobility of our cause, even our white-haired men and yellow-breeched children will become first-rate warriors. We will not cease our efforts until the last vestige of this heretical religion is wiped out from this territory of ours. If we kill one of them, we shall surrender one of us to them to be killed; if we kill ten of them, we shall surrender ten of us to them to be killed. We, in short, want to be fair!

However, there will be absolutely no mercy for those Chinese who have chosen to be converted to this alien religion. Once they are located by their community elders, they should be immediately put to death in accordance with the community will without having their presence reported to government officials. Their death will serve as a warning to all those who, by voluntarily surrendering themselves to this heretical religion, have failed to honor their ancestors.[4]

NOTES

[1] This anonymous poster was found in Kiangsi in 1862. Source: *Ch'ou-pan yi-wu shih-mo,* the Reign of T'ung-chih, roll 12, p. 34.

² Actually the treaties were imposed upon China by force of arms.
³ Sinicized names for two French missionaries.
⁴ Despite the jingoistic nature of this proclamation, not one of the things it vowed to do was ever carried out.

80 • CH'UNG-HOU: *The Tientsin Incident*[1]

Since the beginning of summer, Tientsin and its neighboring areas suffered a serious drought. People were disturbed, and rumors multiplied everywhere. According to one rumor, a large number of small children were drugged and kidnapped; skeletons of small children were found in public cemeteries; and finally, these children were none other than those abandoned by the Roman Catholic churches. Another rumor went even further, saying that the Catholic missionaries, being sadistic in nature, were practicing black art in China: they scooped out people's eyes and carved out their hearts. Yet none of these rumors could be substantiated. Not long ago, the prefecture of Tientsin arrested two bandits, Chang Shuan and Kuo Kuai, who confessed that they had used drugs to kidnap small children. Upon this confession, both of them were subsequently executed. But the rumors about the drugging and kidnapping of small children did not die with this execution; in fact, they multiplied. People in the city were greatly disturbed and as tensions continued to build up, some of them began to take the law into their own hands. They, for instance, arrested a man named Shen Hsi-hsien, a teacher in the French mission, whom they beat up before reporting him to the authorities. After an inquiry conducted by Judge Liu Chieh of the Tientsin subprefecture, it was learned that the accused had merely escorted some of his students to their respective homes and that he had done nothing improper, let alone kidnapping small children. The accused was cleared of all charges and was immediately sent home.

On the twentieth of this month [June 18, 1870], the residents in the T'aohuak'ou village arrested a man named Wu Lan-chen on a drugging-and-kidnapping charge. During the trial conducted by the Tientsin subprefecture, a Wang San of the local Catholic church was somehow implicated. Emotions were aroused and some of the local residents were ready to take drastic actions. To investigate Wang San's alleged role in this kidnapping case, Chou Chia-shun, the prefect of Tientsin, went to see the French consul Henry-Victor Fontanier[2] who, upon Chou's request, agreed to cooperate in the investigation. Knowing how emotionally explosive the people of Tientsin were at this moment and fearful of the occurrence of incidents, your humble servant went to see the French consul himself, and informed him of the rash actions the city people might take and of the necessity of conducting a thorough investigation so as to avoid incidents. Both the French consul and the missionary Claude-Marie Chevrier[3] said that they would cooperate in this investigation, and we agreed that at 10 A.M. of the twenty-third [June 21, 1870], the prefect of Tientsin would bring the accused to the French mission to identify the person whom he had implicated. On the scheduled date Chou Chia-shun, the prefect, together with magistrates Chang Kuang-tsao and Liu Chieh, personally brought the accused Wu Lan-chen to the French mission where they met Chevrier who was very cooperative. The accused was ordered to identify the places in the French mission which he claimed he had visited, but his identification was far from satisfactory. For instance, he said in his confession that there were straw canopies and wooden railings inside the French mission, but none of these actually existed. Nor could he recognize any person in the mission, let alone identify the man whom he had implicated. Unable to substantiate any of his own accusations, he was subsequently brought back to the city prison.

Later Chevrier came to my office to discuss ways whereby the Christian converts and the rest of the Chinese population could continue to live in peace. I made it clear to him that whenever a person died in his mission, he should report to the government for an autopsy and that the dead person should not be buried unless the burial was witnessed by a government official. Moreover, he should provide us with a list of those Chinese who studied in his mission and also the children whom the mission had adopted, so we could make periodical checks on its accuracy. Only in this way, I told him, could the general suspicion in connection with the French mission be dispelled for good. The French missionary agreed to follow my suggestions without reservation.

I was about to issue a proclamation to pacify the people after the missionary's departure when suddenly I heard, at about 2 P.M., that the Christian converts and the spectators in the streets had been engaging in brawls and physical violence, throwing bricks and tiles at one another. I immediately dispatched troops to restore order. At this moment Fontanier arrived at my office and requested to see me, a request to which I readily agreed. I was surprised to see that he wore two pistols on his waist belt and that his expression was harsh. Another foreigner, brandishing a sharp knife, followed him in quick succession. Hardly had Fontanier entered my room before he spouted words of abuse. I told him to calm down and to speak quietly whatever he had on his mind. Pretending that he did not hear me, he took out his pistols and started to shoot. Fortunately nobody was hurt. Seeing his irrational and unreasonable mood, I decided to leave him for awhile. After I left, he shifted his anger to the objects in my room and smashed them one by one, while roaring and blustering like a man possessed. When I reappeared, I told him that the anger of the people had been aroused and that several thousand people had been gathering in the streets. I tried to persuade him not to leave my office so as to avoid incidents. "I am not afraid of the Chinese," he shouted and left in great anger. To prevent any incident, I ordered my guards to escort and protect him wherever he went.

On his way home the French consul unexpectedly encountered Magistrate Liu Chieh of the Tientsin subprefecture who had just returned from suppressing a mob outside of the French mission. Seeing Liu, the French consul immediately fired at him, only to hit one of Liu's servants. Infuriated at what they had seen, the people in the streets rushed towards the Frenchman and beat him to death. Then they beat gongs to gather even larger crowds who burned not only the French mission but also the House of Mercy[4] outside of the Eastern Gate. Meanwhile a missionary school was also reported to have been destroyed. Many Christians, missionaries as well as converts, were killed or wounded as a result. Though your humble servant had taken speedy measures to lead all officials, civilian and military, to restore order and to dispatch troops to suppress the mob, unfortunately the crowds were too large to be controlled. In a short time all the burning and killing had become *fait accompli*. Meanwhile the Christian converts in the French mission had fled in a hurry. Subsequently I sent officials and soldiers to all the groups concerned to calm them down, while personally leading my men to fight the fire to make sure that it would not spread to private residences. I have already instructed the prefecture and the subprefecture of Tientsin to make a detailed report on the number of foreign and Chinese Christians who had been killed or wounded and also the number of churches that had been either burned or destroyed. I have further instructed them to present this report to me as early as possible.

The real cause of this incident lies with the rumor that the missionaries, to practice black magic, scooped out children's eyes and carved out their hearts before committing them to burial. When a convicted kidnapper implicated a man of the French mission as his accomplice, the accumulated suspicion and anger that had been suppressed so far suddenly exploded. Now that we have successfully enlightened the people, the mob, at this time of writing, has already dispersed. However, since this incident is extremely serious in nature, your humble servant begs Your Majesty to order Tseng Kuo-fan, the governor-general of Chihli, to come to Tientsin to make a thorough investigation.

NOTES

[1] This memorial, dated June 23, 1870, was presented by Ch'ung-hou, Superintendent of Trade for Three Treaty Ports and concurrently First Vice-President of the Ministry of Defense. Source: *Ch'ou-pan yi-wu shih-mo,* the Reign of T'ung-chih, roll 72, pp. 22–24.
[2] Feng Ta-yeh in Chinese transliteration.
[3] Hsieh Fu-yin in Chinese transliteration.
[4] Jen-tz'u t'ang.

81 • TSENG KUO-FAN AND CH'UNG-HOU: *The Background of the Tientsin Incident*[1]

On the ninth of the sixth month [July 7, 1870], while staying at Chinghai[2] during my latest trip, I, your humble servant Kuo-fan, received Your Majesty's order of the eighth of the sixth month [July 6, 1870] that had been forwarded to me via the President of the Privy Council. The imperial order reads as follows:

"In the memorial submitted by Tseng Kuo-fan in connection with his impending journey to Tientsin for the purpose of settling the Tientsin Incident, it is stated that some clues have been found in connection with the French mission's alleged implication in the drugging and kidnapping of small children, though the investigators have not been able to locate any concrete evidence, etc., etc. Since the cause of this incident had to do with the drugging and kidnapping of small children, the most important thing to be constantly kept in mind is to establish, without the slightest doubt, whether there is or is not any concrete evidence to substantiate the allegations. No effort should be spared to search the causes of each and every event in the hope that the alleged rights and wrongs will in the end be made clear for all to see. Only then can we speak of the settlement of this incident. As for the killing and wounding of foreigners, it is of course a much more serious matter. If we do not punish the leaders who instigated it, there is little likelihood that we can resolve this dispute in an amicable manner. Tseng Kuo-fan and Ch'ung-hou are hereby instructed to consult with each other and carefully study this matter, so an equitable settlement can be reached at the earliest moment and similar incidents will not again occur in the future. Tseng Kuo-fan has suggested that the disputes involving the accidental killing of some Russians and the burning of English and American churches through mistaken identity should be resolved first, apart from any proposed settlement that is to be negotiated with the French at a later date. He is correct in his suggestions. Let him consult immediately with Ch'ung-hou to find a proper way to settle this incident and everything in connection with it, so the disputes involved will not last indefinitely and thus create more confusion. This order is to be transmitted to each of the receivers in secret."

As your humble servant Kuo-fan sees it, this incident began with a drugging-and-kidnapping case which eventually involved the French mission. Besides the drugging-and-kidnapping charge, there was also the rumor that the missionaries extracted people's eyes and hearts to make direful drugs. The accumulated suspicion coalesced to become anger which, when intensified, precipitated this serious incident. It is my firm belief that only after all the allegations are carefully investigated can truth be differentiated from falsehood and can justice be served.

After my arrival at Tientsin, I studied very carefully the case of Wang San which, as one recalls, has to do with the alleged drugging and kidnapping of small children. Though Wang San did confess at one time that he had given drugs to Wu Lan-chen, he has since then changed his testimony several times; sometimes he admits his guilt and other times he absolutely denies it. Wang was born in Tientsin, and yet Wu Lan-chen, in his testimony, stated that he was really a native of Ningchin. Even if drugs had changed hands between the two accused, there is no evidence that the authorities in the French mission had any knowledge of this transaction. In the House of Mercy operated by the French mission, there were approximately 150 men and women prior to this incident. I have interrogated each of them in person, and all of them stated categorically that they had been sent by their families to be "fed and clothed" in this foreign institution and that they had not been kidnapped by the French in any sense of that word. As for the missionaries' alleged activity of extracting people's eyes and hearts, it is no more than hearsay and completely unsubstantiated.

The day when your humble servant Kuo-fan arrived at Tientsin, several hundred citizens, at one time or another, blocked his sedan chair and presented their petitions. When I asked them what evidence they had that could prove beyond any doubt that the missionaries had indeed engaged in the activity of extracting people's eyes and hearts, none of them could give me a satisfactory answer. I also inquired, in and outside the Tientsin city, about the alleged missing children; the result of my inquiry shows that none of the families had lost any children or had reported to the government the loss of any children. This kind of rumor about foreigners kidnapping Chinese children is not new; similar rumors have also existed in Hunan and Kiangsi in the past. In recent years anonymous posters were found in Yangchow and T'ienmen and also in Tamin and Kuangp'ing of Chihli province, accusing the missionaries of having committed a variety of crimes, such as kidnapping, extracting people's eyes and hearts, and seducing and raping innocent women. Though each of the cases involving foreign missionaries was eventually settled, there has never been any effort to explain to the public the fallacy of each of these groundless charges. Take the present case as an example. Our thorough investigation indicates that there has never been the slightest evidence that the missionaries engaged in any of these activities for which they have been accused, and the widespread rumor that they have in their compound large earthen jars full of human eyes is nothing but sheer fantasy. The killing of small children and the slicing of their bodies so as to find the right elements to make rejuvenation drugs are too outrageous even for the wildest savages; how can one possibly believe that such great, civilized countries as England and France would indulge in them? Their alleged wrongdoings in this regard are so much against common sense that they could not have possibly existed.

Since the purpose of the Roman Catholic Church was to teach people to be good, Emperor K'ang-hsi had specifically allowed its missionaries to preach in China. Had it been engaged in such atrocities as killing innocent people, the Saintly Emperor [Emperor K'ang-hsi] would not have allowed it to function in China in the first place. As for the Houses of Mercy, their functions are similar to those of our own orphanages and houses of relief: to take in the helpless and the poor who cannot otherwise support themselves. It costs foreigners large sums each year to maintain these charitable organizations; yet they receive no other reward except our slanderings when we say that they engage in inhuman, atrocious activities. How can we blame them if they complain (as they do) that they have been treated unfairly?

This does not mean, however, that there are no valid reasons whatsoever for the inhabitants in Tientsin to entertain suspicion or even anger against these foreigners. In the first place, these foreigners place a high priority on secrecy and close and bolt their church doors all year round; nobody outside the church knows what is going on inside. In each of the churches or houses of mercy they maintain there is a cellar, constructed by workers who came from areas outside of Tientsin. I have personally inspected the cellars of the burned churches; I learned that the purpose of these cellars was to insulate the buildings against dampness and also to provide storage areas for such items as coal. They were not used for any other purposes. However, the people in Tientsin had never seen those cellars; they only heard that these cellars, being large and deep, were used to imprison small, innocent children. Their suspicion was further intensified when it was pointed out to them that these foreigners only hired outside laborers to build these cellars.

Secondly, whenever a Chinese went to the House of Mercy as a patient, he often wished to stay there on a permanent basis instead of returning home after he had recovered from his illness. A case in point was the stubborn refusal by Mrs. Ho, a daughter of Wei Hsi-chen (Wei, incidentally, was the former magistrate of Chinhsien, Kiangsi province), to return to her own home after a long stay in the House of Mercy where her father had taken her for the treatment of a certain illness. This refusal caused many to speculate that she must have been drugged by the missionaries and consequently lost all the natural affections which she had previously had for her parents.

Thirdly, the House of Mercy accepted not only orphans and beggars but also patients on the verge of death. According to the Western custom, a man is not really a good man if he has not undergone a ritual called baptism. Whenever he dies, his priest sprinkles water over his forehead and closes his eyes, saying that the dead man would go to paradise since he has undergone this ritual of baptism. The people in Tientsin could not understand why these foreigners wanted to take dying men into their compound and why they had to wash people's eyes after they had already died. Their suspicion was further enhanced when they saw people from other areas enter the mission compound, never to emerge.

Fourthly, there were numerous yards and rooms inside the mission compound, each of which was specified for a particular purpose: chanting of scriptures, studying books, manual work, or caring for patients. A mother might be assigned to reside in one of the back yards while her son lived in the front quarters; or, the mother might live in the House of Mercy while her son was ordered to work in the faraway Holou church. It is not unusual that mother and son were not allowed to see each other for years.

Finally, in the fourth and fifth months of this year there was the widespread rumor that many innocent people had been drugged and kidnapped. Unfortunately for the mission, this rumor occurred at a time when there was a large number of deaths within the mission compound. The fact that the missionaries chose to bury their dead at night and sometimes put two or three bodies into one coffin did not help the matter either. On the sixth day of the fifth month [June 4, 1870] a dog, in search for food in a desolate cemetery east of the river, found a coffin with two bodies in it. Lieutenant Tso Pao-kuei of the Second Battalion of the Tientsin Garrison personally toured the cemetery and confirmed the report. Under normal circumstances the decomposition of a dead body begins from within and then slowly works its way towards the outside. In this particular case, however, not only did the decomposition work in the opposite direction, but the bowels and intestines of the dead men were also exposed. Rumors about the causes of their deaths began to multiply overnight.

Since the people in Tientsin had read or heard about the anonymous posters previously described and had been thus thoroughly familiar with the charges against the missionaries, the discovery of these two bodies seemed to have convinced them that all these charges had been indeed based upon undeniable facts. Suspicion was suddenly transformed into resentment and anger. The anger became irrepressible when it was reported that the church had been implicated in the kidnapping of small children. When the French consul Fontanier fired his pistols at public officials at a time that Wang San, the alleged accomplice in this kidnapping case, was brought to trial, the people in Tientsin simply could not control their anger any longer. While thousands shouted for revenge, the mob, simultaneously and of their own accord, ran wild in the streets, thus precipitating this grave, tragic incident. While their rash action can in no way be condoned, it should be pointed out that the accumulated suspicion and resentment did not come about overnight.

Now that the causes of the Tientsin Incident have been thoroughly investigated and thus made clear, it is hereby suggested that a decree be issued by Your Majesty to all the people in the provinces, informing them that the missionaries' alleged atrocities of murdering innocent people by extracting their eyes and hearts, that have been widely publicized in anonymous posters and handbills, are nothing but falsehoods. The decree should be made public throughout the nation so everyone can be thoroughly familiar with it. In this way not only will the foreigners' innocence be vindicated; our people's suspicions with regard to these foreigners will also be dispelled. It is further suggested that this decree also explain why the people in Tientsin had entertained such suspicions.

The inhabitants in this city are a group of resolute people, well-known for their strong sense of righteousness. They will go a long distance to perform what they regard as a noble act. In this particular case, the majority merely followed the crowd, however misguided they really were. They should of course be ignored. However, the leaders who actually resorted to violence and killed or wounded people and the hooligans who took advantage of the confused situation to engage in looting should be prosecuted to the fullest extent of the law and severely punished, as a warning to all those who might choose to follow their example in the future. Any man who kills another man has to pay with his own life; the killing of foreigners is definitely much more serious because it just might precipitate an international war. In short, we should take all the necessary measures to make sure that a similar incident will not happen again. The difficulty with the present case is that there were no known leaders who had planned ahead in gathering the crowds, the crowds that subsequently committed this most serious crime. Abominable though it certainly was, the crime resulted from spontaneous explosion and did not have any leaders.

The Tientsin area has not enjoyed unmarred peace for a long time. There is a group called "Confused Stars"[3] who, as organized hooligans, love anarchy and relish disaster. To cope with them, your humble servants, Kuo-fan and Ch'ung-hou, have transferred 3,000 troops from Paoting to Chinhai. These troops are under the command of Ting Shou-ch'ang, presently serving as the Prefect of Tientsin. Their duty is to search for the responsible criminals once the people in this city begin to calm down. It may also be added that when your humble servant Ch'ung-hou ordered local officials to make an investigation of the French mission in connection with the Wu Lan-chen case, he merely followed the precedent set in coping with similar situations in the Yangtze area; the purpose of making such an investigation was to dispel the suspicions that the public had long entertained with regard to the French establishment. Later Fontanier was killed and foreign churches were burned to the ground. All of this occurred so suddenly that no man, however wise he was, could have prevented it.

However, in a great tragedy like this the ultimate responsibility has to be placed upon local officials who failed not only to teach the people proper conduct but also to take preventive measures. We have already dismissed the prefect, the intendant, and the magistrate of Tientsin from their respective posts, and their responsibility in connection with this incident will be investigated pending prosecution. Meanwhile your humble servant Kuo-fan will search for proper candidates to replace them. The names of these candidates, once chosen, will be reported to Your Majesty for approval. With the exception of five missing women whose bodies have not yet been found in the House of Mercy, all the dead persons have been identified and dressed for burial. The three dead Russians were handed over to the Russian consul K'ang-ch'i, while the rest of the foreign dead were placed under the custody of the English consul William Hyde Lay.[4] A list of their names is submitted herewith. Comte de Rochechouart,[5] the French consul, has already arrived at Tientsin to discuss the reconstruction of the burned churches at our expense; we shall soon appoint officials to negotiate with him. Reports on this negotiation will be presented to Your Majesty once it is in progress. We shall also report to Your Majesty on the killing of innocent Russians through mistaken identity and the burning of English and American churches, once more is known. The present memorial is to provide a background of this unfortunate incident based upon the investigation we have conducted so far. It is respectfully submitted to Your Ladyship the Empress Dowager and Your Majesty the Emperor for examination. Your humble servants are looking forward to further instructions.

NOTES

[1] This memorial was dated July 21, 1870. Source: *The Memorials of Tseng Kuo-fan* (*Tseng Wen-cheng kung tsou-kao*), roll 35, pp. 29–33.

[2] Located in modern Hopeh Province, southwest of Tientsin.

[3] *Hun hsin-tzu.*

[4] Li Wei-hai in Chinese transliteration.

[5] Lo Shu-ya in Chinese transliteration.

82 • YÜN YÜ-TING: *The Empress Dowager Goes to War*[1]

In less than a month after the Boxers had arrived at the Peking area, their influence began to spread. At Laishui[2] they were so bold as to shoot Lieutenant Yang Fu-t'ung. Though the imperial government ordered the arrest and trial of the offenders, the order was not followed through. Subsequently the government sent Minister Chao Shu-ch'iao to Chochou,[3] ostensibly to order their dissolution but actually to observe their capacities. Having noticed that the so-called Boxers consisted almost entirely of hoodlums, beggars, and poverty-stricken peasants, Chao concluded that they would not be of any use to the government. Nevertheless, upon his return to the capital, he did not tell the Empress Dowager Tz'u Hsi what he had observed and what he really thought, guessing correctly that the empress dowager was sympathetic towards these Boxers.

On the fifteenth day of the fifth month [June 11, 1900], the Boxers killed Sugiyama, a secretary of the Japanese Legation, at Machiapu. From then on they were on a rampage, burning churches and killing converts, most of whom had never done anything wrong but merely happened to be Christians. On the twentieth of the month [June 16, 1900], they set fire to the houses west of the Cheng-yang Gate; the fire eventually spread to the gate tower and destroyed it. All the structures in this area—the finest structures and more than 200 years old—were reduced to ashes in a moment's time. Meanwhile in the Legation Quarter the Western soldiers had been fully mobilized; they guarded both entries, eastern and western, day and night. They acted as if they were facing the most formidable enemy in the world.

Suddenly at noon, the imperial palace issued an order to summon all the princes, high-ranking officials, and heads of the Six Ministries and Nine Bureaus to meet at the East Room of the Yi-luan Palace. More than 100 officials arrived; the room was so packed with kneelers that those who arrived late had to kneel outside of the gate. Inside the room, the emperor and the empress dowager, with their backs against a window and their eyes looking northward, were sitting in their respective thrones. High officials like Prince Li, Shih-to, Jung-lu, Wang Wen-shao, and Chao Shu-ch'iao knelt next to the royal desk in a single file stretching from the north to the south; so neatly did they arrange their kneelings that they looked like a group of wild geese in flight. Among the important ministers only Kang-yi was absent. He had left the capital to inspect a group of Boxers in training and had not yet returned by the time of the imperial conference.

After the ritual of kowtow was performed, the emperor assumed a serious countenance and severely scolded those ministers who had not been able to supress the Boxer rioters. Liu Yung-heng, a reader in the Hanlin Academy, was then kneeling behind me; he whispered in my ear that he had seen Commander Tung Fu-hsiang recently and that Tung had volunteered to drive the Boxers out of the city. Prompted by me to report to the emperor what he knew, he crawled forward and said: "Your humble servant has just seen Tung Fu-hsiang who begs Your Majesty to issue him an order so as to drive the rioters out of the city." Hardly had he finished this remark before he was interrupted by Prince Tuan (Tsai-yi) who raised one of his thumbs and began to shout: "What a remarkable proposal you have made! It will surely make the people lose confidence in their government."

Liu was so frightened that he did not dare to utter one more word. During all this exchange the empress dowager remained silent.

Suddenly, outside of the palace gate someone broke the silence with a loud voice. "Your humble servant Yüan Ch'ang wishes to speak," the man yelled as loudly as he could. The emperor gave the order that Yüan, a minister in charge of sacrifice and worship, be allowed to come in. Yüan spoke in detail about the unreliability of the Boxers who, said he, were no more than a hodgepodge of hoodlums. Even if they did possess supernatural power, he continued, no men, since history began, had achieved true success through the use of magic. It was then that the empress dowager interrupted. "If magic cannot be relied on for success," said she, "would you say that the will of the people cannot be relied on for success either? Now that China's accumulated weakness has reached its highest point, the only thing we have is the will of our people. How can the nation be saved if the will of the people is no longer on our side? The capital is now in a state of chaos; there is even a rumor that foreign powers are mobilizing their troops to attack us. How do you view this situation? If any of you has an idea, he should report it to me at once."

Upon hearing the empress dowager's remarks, the ministers, one after another, responded with a variety of suggestions. Some said that the Boxers should be suppressed; others said that they should be brought under the government's control in a friendly manner. Some proposed that the movement of foreign troops should be stopped at once, while others suggested that Chinese soldiers should be sent to the Legation Quarter to protect foreigners. Having heard one minister after another, the empress dowager personally ordered two deputy ministers, Na-t'ung and Hsü Ching-teng, to leave the capital to carry out two missions: to admonish foreign troops not to advance further and to pacify and dissolve the rioters. Then she dismissed all the ministers in attendance.

After the meeting was adjourned, several of us—Tseng Kuang-han of the Bureau of Imperial Palace, Chang Heng-chia of the Supreme Court, Chu Tsu-mou of the Hanlin Academy, and I—did not leave immediately, knowing that the empress dowager was still bent on protecting the Boxer bandits. These bandits would continue their lawless activities, we believed, as long as the government was not determined to deal decisively with them. Once more we knelt down, announcing that we had some ideas we wished to express. Heng-chia spoke first, in a rather vigorous manner, emphasizing time and again that the Boxers should be suppressed. Once a few of their leaders were executed, he said, all of their followers would disperse by themselves. Being a Fukienese[4] and speaking rapidly, he had a difficult time making himself understood. When it was Tsu-mou's turn to speak, he cautioned the empress dowager not to count on these Boxer rioters to fight against the Westerners. "On whom does Your Ladyship rely to cope with the current crisis?" he finally ventured this important question.

"I rely on Tung Fu-hsiang," the empress dowager replied.

"Tung Fu-hsiang is the least reliable," said Tsu-mou.

The empress dowager was furious when she heard this remark. "What is your name?" she shouted with a harsh voice.

"The name of your humble servant is Chu Tsu-mou, a reader in the Hanlin Academy."

The empress dowager remained angry. "You say that Tung Fu-hsiang is not reliable. Will you recommend someone who is reliable?"

In a hurry Tsu-mou did not know how to respond. It was then that I decided to reply for him. "Yüan Shih-k'ai, Governor of Shantung, is farsighted, loyal, and courageous," I said. "He should be called to Peking to suppress the rioters."

"Liu Kun-yi, Governor-general of Liangchiang, can do equally well," added Tseng Kuang-han.

Jung-lu, the President of the Privy Council, was also present at this moment. "Liu Kun-yi is too far away," he commented. "We will call Yüan Shih-k'ai right away."

"It is rumored that the court will move westward, and I hope that this rumor is unfounded," I said. "The capital is the center of the nation; even if it were moved by merely one inch, the whole nation will be disturbed."

The empress dowager denied vigorously the validity of this rumor. All four of us then stood up from our kneeling position and proceeded to leave. As Tsu-mou left, the empress dowager continued to stare angrily at him.

At 2 P.M. of the twenty-first [June 17, 1900], the royal palace issued an urgent order, calling upon all important ministers to meet in the Yi-luan Palace at 4 P.M. When the meeting was held, the emperor first questioned Hsü Yung-yi, a minister then serving in the Office of General Management. Hsü's voice was so low that few of us knew what he was talking about. Then we heard the emperor pounding his desk. "Do you think that you can get away with this by simply beating around the bush?" he scolded in a sharp voice.

Shortly afterwards the empress dowager made the following announcement. "We have just received a diplomatic note from foreign countries that consists of four demands," she said. "They want first, the designation of a specific palace for the Chinese emperor to live; second, the right to collect all taxes in China on our behalf; and third, the authority over all our armed forces. It was they who started the hostilities; now they want to destroy our nation. If we ever decide to present our nation to them on a silver plate, I, for one, cannot face our deceased emperors when I die. It is better to die while fighting than to die without raising one finger to resist. How do you people feel about this?" "We will fight to the finish," all the ministers kowtowed and replied simultaneously. Some of them even had tears in their eyes.

The empress dowager spoke of four demands, but mentioned only three. After the meeting, I asked Jung-lu what the unmentioned demand was. He said that the foreigners wanted to force the empress dowager to hand over the power of the state to the emperor. Only then did I realize why the empress dowager did not choose to mention it.

Among the high officials, Tsai-yi and P'u-liang (a deputy minister) were the most enthusiastic about the impending war and defended their position in the strongest language. Doubtless influenced by them, the empress dowager finally announced her intention to go to war. "All of you high officials have heard with your own ears how serious the present situation is," she said. "For the survival of our nation, I am inclined to declare war, a course which I would not have taken had I been given a better choice. But war is by definition a risky undertaking. If we still cannot preserve our nation at the end of this war despite our best effort, you gentlemen who are here today should know that the blame cannot be placed upon my shoulders alone, knowing the tremendous difficulties that I have been subject to. At that time let nobody say that the empress dowager has put an end to a dynasty of 300 years." All the ministers kowtowed again. "We, as one man, will do our very best to serve the nation's cause," they announced unanimously. They were deeply moved because the empress dowager, for the first time anyone could recall, had referred to them as "you high officials"[5] or "you gentlemen."[6]

Subsequently the empress dowager ordered the dispatching of Hsü Yung-yi, Li-san, and Lien-yüan to inform the foreigners in the Legation Quarter of the grave consequences if they insisted upon opening hostilities. These foreigners were to be told that if they persisted in the pursuance of such a course, they should take down their flags and proceed home. Under the pretext that he did not work with the Office of General Management, Li-san declined to go. "Was it not you who served as the protocol officer last year when the foreign embassy personnel paid a visit to the Yi-ho Yüan?" asked the emperor in an angry voice. "Are you too cowardly to make this trip now?" The empress dowager was even angrier. "It does not make any difference whether you are cowardly or brave," she said; "you have to make this trip, period." After the three ministers left, she ordered Jung-lu to put his troops on alert. "The three ministers are proceeding towards the area of danger," she added; "a detachment of soldiers should be assigned to escort them at a distance."

After the meeting was adjourned, some of the ministers, gathering outside the Ying-hsia Gate, questioned the men in the Translation Bureau about the diplomatic note which the empress dowager had mentioned. Looking at each other, the men in the Translation Bureau simply did not know what we were talking about. Someone suggested that this particular diplomatic note might have been transmitted through Yü-lu, Superintendent of the Peiyang Army, instead of the Translation Bureau. But this speculation proved to be as false as many others. Only later did I know the truth about this matter. At midnight on the twentieth day [June 16, 1900], a man named Lo, who was a grain superintendent in Kiangsu, dispatched his son to Jung-lu's residence, saying that he had a confidential matter of the most urgent nature to report. Upon seeing Jung-lu, the man's son showed his host the so-called four demands that were supposed to have been originated from the foreign countries. For the rest of the evening Jung-lu paced up and down inside his house and could not go to sleep. As soon as the day broke, he went to see the empress dowager and reported what he had heard. Grieved and embittered, the empress dowager decided on war. The truth was that none of the foreign countries had made the so-called four demands—this man Lo must have taken an unfounded rumor too seriously. Since this rumor was never substantiated, the so-called four demands were not mentioned in the declaration of war on the twenty-fifth [June 21, 1900].

At 8 A.M. of the twenty-second [June 18, 1900], another meeting was called to deliberate on the issue of peace and war. It lasted for only a brief moment before it was adjourned. On the next day at 2 P.M., the ministers were again summoned to the Yi-luan Palace where the empress dowager made known her final and unequivocal decision to go to war. She ordered Hsü Ching-ch'eng to inform the ministers of all nations to leave the capital within a twenty-four-hour period, saying that troops would be provided to escort them to safeguard their departure. The emperor, not wishing to start a war on flimsy grounds, grabbed Hsü Ching-ch'eng's hand as if not to let him leave. "We must discuss this matter more thoroughly," he pleaded. "Hands off, emperor," scolded the empress dowager; "do not hinder serious business!" At this moment, Deputy Minister Lien-yüan also pleaded: "Since only France was interested in missionary activities and since it was she who first opened hostilities, we should declare war on her and her alone, if we have to declare any war at all. There is no reason to make all eleven countries our enemies. If we do, the nation will be put under serious jeopardy indeed." He wept while he was speaking; perspiration came down from his forehead so profusely that they looked like shining beads from a broken string. However, hardly had he finished his presentation before other officials began to argue with him.

The empress dowager ordered Tsai-yün to be more diligent in defending the palace walls and to also be prepared for whatever emergencies that might arise. All ministers attending the imperial conference would be fed from the royal kitchen, said she, so the meeting would not have to be adjourned for lunch. Finally, after the meeting had been adjourned, the attending ministers received another order, saying that another conference would be held at 8 A.M. the next day.

Early the next morning [the twenty-fourth (June 20, 1900)], the ministers gathered outside of the Ying-hsiu Gate as they had been ordered. It was then reported that the government had received word from the foreign legations requesting the presence of Prince Ch'ing and Prince Tuan at the Legation Quarter for a conference. In view of this request, the empress dowager ordered the two princes, together with other important ministers, to come in for an audience. Kang-yi, who had only recently returned to the capital, was one of those invited. Upon leaving the imperial presence, the two princes ordered the Office of General Management to send the foreign legations a note bearing the following words: "If you foreigners have anything to say, say it in a written document. The two princes will not be able to make a trip to the Legation Quarter." A moment later, other important ministers also emerged from the conference. They transmitted the order that since the decision to declare war had already been made, it would not be necessary to have any more discussion and that all ministers present were therefore dismissed.

In brief, these were the four imperial conferences prior to the declaration of war in the year of keng-tzu [1900].

NOTES

[1] Translated from *Ch'ung-ling ch'uan-hsin lu.* As for the author, see footnote 1, p. 246. The reader is advised to read this selection in conjunction with Selection 76, pp. 254–262.

[2] A subprefecture southwest of Peking.

[3] Located southwest of Peking.

[4] Most Fukienese (natives of Fukien Province) speak Mandarin with a Fukienese accent.

[5] *Chu ta-ch'en.*

[6] *Chu kung.*

83 • ALFRED VON WALDERSEE: *The Pillage of Peking*[1]

After the allied troops occupied Peking, their deployment was the same as when they first entered the city. In other words, each ally deployed its troops in areas which it had taken over and physically occupied. The Winter Palace fell into the hands of the Russians who, on the previous day, had also captured the Summer Palace[2] which is located 15 kilometers to the north of the city.

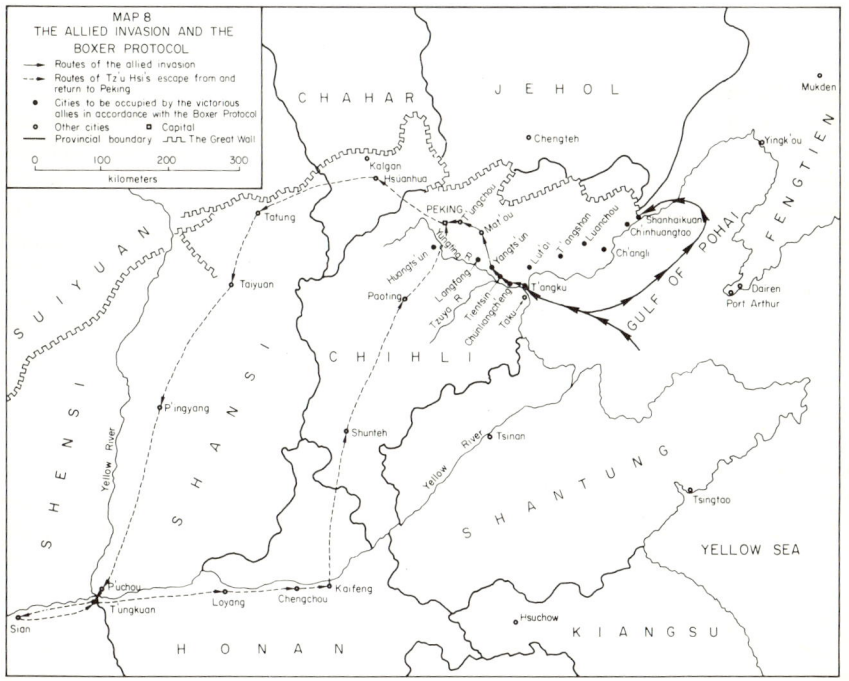

In the center of the imperial capital is the so-called Forbidden City. It is rectangular in shape and is surrounded by high walls. Until very recently it was the residence of the Chinese emperor. In accordance with the agreement between foreign ministers in China and the senior commanders of the allied forces, the Forbidden City was declared an area outside of the allied occupation. Nevertheless, the allied troops were accorded the privilege of transit through the city. All of its four gates are guarded by allied troops; at this moment three of these gates are guarded by the Japanese and the remaining one by the Americans. Arranged perhaps by Mr. Giers,[3] this agreement is, in my judgment, most unfortunate. It merely creates an impression of allied weakness. I will find some way to change it.

As a result of continuous fighting for days in the city, most of the business districts have been destroyed. Only the Forbidden City has been mostly preserved. Unlike other Chinese cities and towns that were constructed without any planning or foresight and where streets are narrow, crooked, and mazy, Peking has streets that are well designed and constructed. Within the city are several wide avenues, though none of them is paved with stones. In the other Chinese cities and towns I have visited, the houses are made mostly of hardened earth; the so-called city is really a cluster of earthen dwellings. Most houses in Peking, on the other hand, are constructed with stone, though the overwhelming majority of them are only one-storied.

After the capture of Peking by the allied forces, the victorious soldiers were given permission to conduct open looting for three days.[4] This official looting was followed by private looting on an individual basis. The material losses suffered by the Peking residents were enormous, though the exact amount cannot be ascertained at this time. Nowadays the allied powers try to pass the responsibility for authorizing this looting from one to another, but the fact remains that all of them participated in it in an all-out manner.

The British seem to be particularly sophisticated in this matter of looting and dispose of their spoils according to a special rule. All the loots are required to be handed over to the British authorities who in turn pile them up within their embassy compound. Then the British stage an official auction which lasts for several days; the proceeds of this auction are later distributed among the rank and file who receive an amount in proportion to their positions. Since the British view the loots in the nature of a war booty, none of the Englishmen I know regards this looting as illegal. A British officer once told me that it is beyond the comprehension of an Indian soldier—practically all the members of the British expeditionary force here are Indians—that victory should not be immediately followed by lootings. All the allied forces single out the Indian soldier as the most resourceful in locating hidden treasures.

As far as the Japanese are concerned, the spoils go to their government as a rule. The total amount is extremely large. According to a report made by a Japanese general, the loot collected at Tientsin alone is valued at more than 2 million taels. The American army has a rule prohibiting looting. But individual American soldiers, being so clever as they are, have violated this rule with impunity and have in fact done whatever they please without fearing any official sanction. Among the allied forces the Russians seem to be the most barbaric in this matter of looting. While engaging in it, they indiscriminately smash into pieces all the items which they either cannot or do not care to carry with them. As far as a French soldier is concerned, he makes sure that he is not behind others in collecting spoils.

In my previous report to Your Majesty I stated that the Russians had looted and carried away all the treasures in the Summer Palace. I also mentioned that they had shipped to Port Arthur the gifts which the German kings had previously presented to China. Now I wish to make a correction. Though it is true that the Russians did ship these gifts to Port Arthur as I have stated, they later returned these gifts to Major General Hoepfner who had sent them a vigorous protest. At present these gifts are carefully preserved in the German Embassy. After the Russians' withdrawal from Peking,[5] the British took over the occupation of the Summer Palace. Since then they have been carefully examining what remains in it.

The Winter Palace was guarded by two contingents of troops during the time it was occupied by the Russians. It is possible that in a period of several days after the empress dowager [Tz'u Hsi] had fled and before the Russians arrived to occupy it, many valuable items inside it were stolen and taken away by the servants. But the total amount could not be very large. It should be further noted that no other countries' troops had ever entered it. From time to time the Russians allowed the military officers of other countries to visit the palace, but in each case they were escorted and guided by a Russian officer. Some of the buildings inside the palace were sealed and locked; the seal was torn off and the door unlocked whenever a particular building was scheduled for the above-mentioned visits.

When Lieutenant General Linewitsch withdrew his two contingents of soldiers from Peking, he did not abide by the agreement between him and myself that the Winter Palace should be handed over directly to Major General Hoepfner. He violated this agreement on purpose, of course. Instead, he handed over the palace to Chinese officials. From the time when Major General Hoepfner heard about this to the time when he actually took over, there was an interval of at most one-half day. Some of the Russian officers were still there when he took over the palace.

By the time we entered the Winter Palace, all the valuable items that could be moved had been stolen and moved away with few exceptions. Only those that could not be easily transported were still inside the palace. The private residence of the imperial household—which is really too small to be characterized as a "palace"—did not suffer much damage. On the other hand, all other structures inside the palace ground such as theaters, temples, garrison quarters, and warehouses had been extensively pillaged; their doors were axed and destroyed if they happened to be sealed or locked. Those items that were considered worthless were thrown to the ground and scattered all over the yards.

To tidy up the buildings so they could be used as the Allied Headquarters, we employed ninety persons who worked for ten consecutive days. Though they are almost fit for occupancy at this moment, we have not yet cleaned them and put them in good order. The equipment used in the theater such as clothes, make-up, and cosmetics, all the broken porcelains and glasswares, and numerous household instruments and utensils are now piled up in those buildings that have not been assigned for use by the Allied Headquarters.

Within the Winter Palace ground was a building more beautiful and impressive than any of the others. I was told that this was the place where the Chinese emperor used to receive foreign envoys. Now broken articles are piled up in this building as well as the large yard adjacent to it. These articles were moved here when other buildings had to be cleaned for occupancy as the Allied Headquarters. Among these broken articles I saw dozens of clocks; apparently the faces of these clocks or some of their constituent parts had been inlaid with precious stones which tempted the greedy to break them so as to steal the stones. I want to assure Your Majesty that I will do my utmost to preserve the buildings and the articles in them while they remain in the custody of Germany. The bedrooms and the private apartments of the empress dowager and the emperor[6] are not occupied by me or any member of my staff. I wish particularly to mention that the moment I entered the Winter Palace, I ordered two German naval squadrons to gather in front of the empress dowager's residence for a prayer service as normally conducted on the battlefield.

It is impossible, now or anytime in the future, to assess the damages which China has suffered from pillage as well as from wartime destruction. But there is no question that the damages are enormous. The pity is that those who are responsible for this war have suffered very little. During the period of pillage, many women were raped, atrocities were committed everywhere, people were murdered without the slightest reason, and arson was practiced on a wide scale. All these have contributed to the sufferings of the local residents.

Lately order has been gradually restored. All I can say is that since my arrival, the illegal activities of the allied troops, with a few exceptions, have finally come to an end. I have asked the allied commanders of various countries to order their subordinates to pay close attention to military discipline so as to protect the peace-loving local residents, in the same manner as I myself have done with regard to my own men and officers. However, we shall continue to be strict with the Boxers for whom we will not show any mercy.

NOTES

[1] The Chinese version, from which this selection is translated, was translated from the German original by Wang Kuang-ch'i. Source: *Source Materials on the Fifty Years of the Republic of China* (*Chung-hua Min-kuo k'ai-kuo wu-shih-nien wen-hsien*), Series I, vol. 6, pp. 285–288. The original document was dated October 22, 1900.

[2] Yi-ho Yüan.

[3] The Russian minister to China.

[4] The allies entered Peking on August 14–16. The official looting was conducted on August 16, 17, and 18.

[5] The Russians began to withdraw from Peking on August 31, 1900.

[6] Tz'u Hsi and Kuang-hsü respectively.

84 • *The Boxer Protocol*[1]

ARTICLE Ia

By an imperial edict of the 9th of June last (Annex No. 2), Tsai Feng, Prince of Ch'ün, was appointed Ambassador of His Majesty the Emperor of China, and directed in that capacity to convey to His Majesty the German Emperor the expression of the regrets of His Majesty the Emperor of China and of the Chinese Government for the assassination of His Excellency the late Baron von Ketteler, German minister.

Prince Ch'ün left Peking the 12th of last July to carry out the orders which had been given him.

ARTICLE Ib

The Chinese Government has stated that it will erect on the spot of the assassination of His Excellency the late Baron von Ketteler a commemorative monument, worthy of the rank of the deceased, and bearing an inscription in the Latin, German, and Chinese languages, which shall express the regrets of His Majesty the Emperor of China for the murder committed.

Their Excellencies the Chinese Plenipotentiaries have informed His Excellency the German Plenipotentiary, in a letter dated the 22nd of July last (Annex No. 3) that an arch of the whole width of the street would be erected on the said spot, and that work on it was begun the 25th of June last.

ARTICLE IIa

Imperial edicts of the 13th and 21st of February, 1901 (Annexes Nos. 4, 5, and 6), inflicted the following punishments on the principal authors of the outrages and crimes committed against the foreign Governments and their nationals. . . .[2]

ARTICLE IIb

An Imperial Edict promulgated the 19th of August, 1901 (Annex No. 8), ordered the suspension of official examinations for five years in all cities where foreigners were massacred or submitted to cruel treatment.

ARTICLE III

So as to make honorable reparation for the assassination of Mr. Sugiyama, chancellor of the Japanese legation, His Majesty the Emperor of China by an Imperial Edict of the 18th of June, 1901 (Annex No. 9), appointed Na-Tung, Vice-President of the Board of Revenue, to be his Envoy Extraordinary, and specially directed him to convey to His Majesty the Emperor of Japan the expression of the regrets of His Majesty the Emperor of China and of his Government at the assassination of the late Mr. Sugiyama.

ARTICLE IV

The Chinese Government has agreed to erect an expiatory monument in each of the foreign or international cemeteries which were desecrated and in which the tombs were destroyed.

It has been agreed with the Representatives of the Powers that the legations interested shall settle the details for the erection of these monuments, China bearing all the expenses thereof, estimated at ten thousand taels for the cemeteries at Peking and within its neighborhood, and at five thousand taels for the cemeteries in the provinces. The amounts have been paid and the list of these cemeteries is enclosed herewith. (Annex No. 10.)

ARTICLE V

China has agreed to prohibit the importation into its territory of arms and ammunition, as well as of materials exclusively used for the manufacture of arms and ammunition.

An Imperial Edict has been issued on the 25th of August, 1901 (Annex No. 11), forbidding said importation for a term of two years. New Edicts may be issued subsequently extending this by other successive terms of two years in case of necessity recognized by the Powers.

ARTICLE VI

By an Imperial Edict dated the 29th of May, 1901 (Annex No. 12), His Majesty the Emperor of China agreed to pay the Powers an idemnity of four hundred and fifty millions of Haikwan Taels.[3] This sum represents the total amount of the indemnities for States, companies or societies, private individuals, and Chinese referred to in Article VI of the note of December 22nd, 1900. . . .[4]

ARTICLE VII

The Chinese Government has agreed that the quarter occupied by the legations shall be considered as one specially reserved for their use and placed under their exclusive control, in which Chinese shall not have the right to reside and which may be made defensible. . . .[5]

ARTICLE VIII

The Chinese Government has consented to raze the forts of Taku and those which might impede free communication between Peking and the sea; steps have been taken for carrying this out.

ARTICLE IX

The Chinese Government has conceded the right to the Powers in the protocol annexed to the letter of the 16th of January, 1901, to occupy certain points, to be determined by an agreement between them, for the maintenance of open communication between the capital and the sea. The points occupied by the powers are:

Huang-tsun, Lang-fang, Yang-tsun, Tientsin, Chun-liang, Ch'eng, Tang-ku, Lu-tai, Tang-shan, Lan-chou, Chang-li, Ch'in-wang tao, Shan-hai kuan.

ARTICLE X

The Chinese Government has agreed to post and to have published during two years in all district cities the following Imperial Edicts:

a. Edict of the 1st of February (Annex No. 15), prohibiting forever, under pain of death, membership in any antiforeign society.

b. Edicts of the 13th and 21st February, 29th April, and 19th August, enumerating the punishments inflicted on the guilty.

c. Edict of the 19th of August, 1901, prohibiting examinations in all cities where foreigners were massacred or subjected to cruel treatment.

d. Edict of the 1st of February, 1901 (Annex No. 16), declaring all governors-general, governors, and provincial or local officials responsible for order in their respective districts, and that in case of new antiforeign troubles or other infractions of the treaties which shall not be immediately repressed and the authors of which shall not have been punished, these officials shall be immediately dismissed, without possibility of being given new functions or new honors.

The posting of these edicts is being carried on throughout the Empire.

ARTICLE XI

The Chinese Government has agreed to negotiate the amendments deemed necessary by the foreign Governments to the treaties of commerce and navigation and other subjects concerning commercial relations, with the object of facilitating them.

At present, and as a result of the stipulation contained in Article VI concerning the indemnity, the Chinese Government agrees to assist in the improvement of the courses of the rivers Peiho and Whangpu. . . .[6]

ARTICLE XII

An Imperial Edict of the 24th of July, 1901 (Annex No. 18), reformed the Office of foreign affairs (Tsungli Yamen), on the lines indicated by the Powers, that is to say, transformed it into a Ministry of foreign affairs (Wai-wu Pu), which takes precedence over the six other Ministries of State. The same edict appointed the principal members of this Ministry.

An agreement has also been reached concerning the modification of Court ceremonial as regards the reception of foreign Representatives and has been the subject of several notes from the Chinese Plenipotentiaries, the substance of which is embodied in a memorandum herewith annexed (Annex No. 19).

Finally, it is expressly understood that as regards the declarations specified above and the annexed documents originating with the foreign Plenipotentiaries, the French text only is authoritative. . . .[7]

The present final Protocol has been drawn up in twelve identic copies and signed by all the Plenipotentiaries of the Contracting Countries. One copy shall be given to each of the foreign Plenipotentiaries, and one copy shall be given to the Chinese Plenipotentiaries.

Peking, 7th September, 1901

NOTES

[1] The complete text can be found in W.M. Malloy, ed., *Treaties, Conventions, International Acts, Protocols and Agreements between the United States of America and Other Powers, 1776-1909*, 2 vols. (Washington D.C.: Government Printing Office, 1910), vol. 2, pp. 2006-2012.

[2] This is followed by a list of high-ranking Chinese officials ("war criminals") to be condemned to death by execution, death by committing suicide, "posthumous degradation," etc.

[3] As defined by this Protocol, a Haikwan tael equals 3.055 marks, 3.595 Austro-Hungary crowns, 0.742 gold dollar, 3.750 francs, 3s 0d. pound sterling, 1.407 yens, 1.796 Netherlands florins, or 1.412 gold roubles (17.424 dolias fine).

[4] This is followed by detailed provisions whereby the indemnity will be paid.

[5] This is followed by the delimitation of the quarter's boundaries.

[6] This is followed by provisions whereby the courses of these two rivers can be improved.

[7] This is followed by provisions governing the withdrawal of allied troops from Peking and the province of Chihli "with the exception of the localities mentioned in Article IX."

85 • JOHN HAY: *The Open Door Notes*[1]

I. Secretary Hay to the Ambassador in Great Britain (Choate)

Washington, September 6, 1899

Sir: The Government of Her Britannic Majesty has declared that its policy and its very traditions precluded it from using any privileges which might be granted it in China as a weapon for excluding commercial rivals, and that freedom of trade for Great Britain in that Empire meant freedom of trade for all the world alike. While conceding by formal agreements, first with Germany and then with Russia, the possession of "spheres of influence or interest" in China in which they are to enjoy special rights and privileges, more especially in respect of railroads and mining enterprises, Her Britannic Majesty's Government has therefore sought to maintain at the same time what is called the "open-door" policy, to insure to the commerce of the world in China equality of treatment within said "spheres" for commerce and navigation. This latter policy is alike urgently demanded by the British mercantile communities and by those of the United States, as it is justly held by them to be the only one which will improve existing conditions, enable them to maintain their position in the markets of China, and extend their operations in the future. While the Government of the United States will in no way commit itself to a recognition of exclusive rights of any power within or control over any portion of the Chinese Empire under such agreements as have within the last year been made, it can not conceal its apprehension that under existing conditions there is a possibility, even a probability, of complications arising between the treaty powers which may imperil the rights insured to the United States under our treaties with China.

This Government is animated by a sincere desire that the interests of our citizens may not be prejudiced through exclusive treatment by any of the controlling powers within their so-called "spheres of interest" in China, and hopes also to retain there an open market for commerce of the world, remove dangerous sources of international irritation, and hasten thereby united or concerted action of the powers at Pekin in favor of the administrative reforms so urgently needed for strengthening the Imperial Government and maintaining the integrity of China in which the whole western world is alike concerned. It believes that such a result may be greatly assisted by a declaration by the various powers claiming "spheres of interest" in China of their intentions as regards treatment of foreign trade therein. The present moment seems a particularly opportune one for informing Her Britannic Majesty's Government of the desire of the United States to see it make a formal declaration and to lend its support in obtaining similar declarations from the various powers claiming "spheres of influence" in China, to the effect that each in its respective spheres of interest or influence—

First: Will in no wise interfere with any treaty port or any vested interest within any so-called "sphere of interest" or leased territory it may have in China.

Second: That the Chinese treaty tariff of the time being shall apply to all merchandise landed or shipped to all such ports as are within said "sphere of interest" (unless they be "free ports"), no matter to what nationality it may belong, and that duties so leviable shall be collected by the Chinese Government.

Third: That it will levy no higher harbor duties on vessels of another nationality frequenting any port in such "sphere" than shall be levied on vessels of its own nationality, and no higher railroad charges over lines built, controlled, or operated within its "sphere" on merchandise belonging to citizens or subjects of other nationalities transported through such "sphere" than shall be levied on similar merchandise belonging to its own nationals transported over equal distances.

The recent ukase of His Majesty the Emperor of Russia, declaring the port of Ta-lien-wan[2] open to the merchant ships of all nations during the whole of the lease under which it is to be held by Russia, removing as it does all uncertainty as to the liberal and conciliatory policy of that power, together with the assurances given this Government by Russia, justifies the expectation that His Majesty will cooperate in such an understanding as is here proposed, and our ambassador at the court of St. Petersburg has been instructed accordingly to submit the propositions above detailed to His Imperial Majesty, and ask their early consideration. A copy of my instruction to Mr. Tower is herewith inclosed for your confidential information.

The action of Germany in declaring the port of Kiaochao[3] a "free port," and the aid the Imperial Government has given China in the establishment there of a Chinese custom-house, coupled with the oral assurance conveyed the United States by Germany that our interests within its "sphere" would in no wise be affected by its occupation of this portion of the province of Shang-tung,[4] tend to show that little opposition may be anticipated from that power to the desired declaration.

The interests of Japan, the next most interested power in the trade of China, will be so clearly served by the proposed arrangement, and the declaration of its statesmen within the last year are so entirely in line with the views here expressed, that its hearty cooperation is confidently counted on.

You will, at as early date as practicable, submit the considerations to Her Britannic Majesty's principal secretary of state for foreign affairs and request their immediate consideration.

I inclose herewith a copy of the instruction sent to our ambassador at Berlin bearing on the above subject.

I have the honor to be [etc.] John Hay

II. Secretary Hay to American Diplomatic Representatives at Berlin, Paris, London, Rome, St. Petersburg, Vienna, Brussels, Madrid, Tokyo, The Hague, and Lisbon

Washington, July 3, 1900

In this critical posture of affairs in China it is deemed appropriate to define the attitude of the United States as far as present circumstances permit this to be done. We adhere to the policy initiated by us in 1857 of peace with the Chinese nation, of furtherance of lawful commerce, and of protection of lives and property of our citizens by all means guaranteed under extraterritorial treaty rights and by the law of nations. If wrong be done to our citizens we propose to hold the responsible authors to the uttermost accountability. We regard the condition at Peking as one of virtual anarchy, whereby power and responsibility are practically devolved upon the local provincial authorities. So long as they are not in overt collusion with rebellion and use their power to protect foreign life and property, we regard them as representing the Chinese people, with whom we seek to remain in peace and friendship. The purpose of the President is, as it has been heretofore, to act concurrently with the other powers; first, in opening up communication with Peking and rescuing the American officials, missionaries, and other Americans who are in danger; secondly, in affording all possible protection everywhere in China to American life and property; thirdly, in guarding and protecting all legitimate American interests; and fourthly, in aiding to prevent a spread of the disorders to the other provinces of the Empire and a recurrence of such disasters. It is of course too early to forecast the means of attaining this last result; but the policy of the Government of the United States is to seek a solution which may bring about permanent safety and peace to China, preserve Chinese territorial and administrative entity, protect all rights guaranteed to friendly powers by treaty and international law, and safeguard for the world the principle of equal and impartial trade with all parts of the Chinese Empire.

You will communicate the purport of this instruction to the minister for foreign affairs.

John Hay

NOTES

[1] Source: U. S. Department of State, *United States Relations with China: With Special Reference to the Period 1944-1949* (Washington, D.C.: Government Printing Office, 1949), p. 417.
[2] Dairen.
[3] Kiaochow.
[4] Shantung.

CHAPTER ELEVEN

The Downfall of the Manchu Regime

After she returned from Sian where she had fled during the allied occupation of Peking in 1900, Tz'u Hsi was more than convinced of Western superiority and was in a receptive mood for Westernized reforms. New schools were established where Western history, government, and science were taught side by side with Confucian classics and Chinese literature, and students who possessed the financial means were encouraged to go abroad to study. An attempt was also made to stamp out the opium traffic, though with negligible results. Shortly before she died in 1908, the empress dowager even authorized the proclamation of a draft constitution, to be operative in a period of eight years. Thus, fifty years after the British had demonstrated in the Opium War the backwardness of everything relating to China, the majority of the Chinese intellectual elite finally agreed that some fundamental changes had to be made.

However, to a small group of determined individuals all these changes made within the existing political framework were simply not fundamental enough. They wanted to establish a democratic republic instead of preserving a monarchy, constitutional or otherwise, which to them had become too anachronistic to meet the demands of a fast-changing modern world. They called themselves revolutionaries who vowed to overthrow the Manchu regime, no matter how long it would take or how much it would cost. Their leader was a man named Sun Yat-sen (1866–1925) who, born to a peasant family, was nevertheless able to rise to become a physician by profession. But to remain a wealthy, successful physician was the least of his intentions. He said that he decided to lead a revolution to overthrow the Manchu regime as early as 1885, and for the next twenty years (1885–1905) he and his small following tried to convince their countrymen of the danger China was in and of the necessity of establishing a new government to replace the old one. But the response he received was anything but enthusiastic; it was either nonexistent or outright hostile. He inspired or actively participated in several uprisings, but all of them met with dismal failure.

It was not until 1905 when The Alliance for Chinese Revolution was organized in Tokyo that for the first time in his revolutionary career Sun began to feel optimistic about the future. "Before this time I had never dared to hope that our revolutionary task of overthrowing the Manchu regime could succeed in my own lifetime, despite the fact that I had taken all the risks in pushing forward the revolutionary movement under the most difficult circumstances and amidst the worst kind of sarcasms and abuses that had been thrown at me as a person," he said many years later. "It was not until that day in the fall of 1905 when I gathered the best among my countrymen for the establishment of The Alliance for Chinese Revolution that I, finally, realized that our great revolutionary task could be completed in my own lifetime." About the same time the party organ, *The People* (*Min pao*), first appeared and soon turned out to be, again in Sun's words, "the most successful of all the revolutionary journals that had been published until then" (Selection 86). Its first editorial, written by Sun himself, emphasized the importance of the Three Principles of the People and the necessity of completing national, democratic, and social revolutions simultaneously (Selection 87). By then his revolution had taken on new dimensions; it was social and economic as well as political. The overthrow of the Manchu regime, whenever it occurred, was to be merely the beginning rather than the end of his revolution. It was clear to him even then that the establishment of social and economic justice was much more difficult to achieve than the overthrow of a discredited, corrupt regime.

However just or justifiable it was, a revolution was by definition a risky enterprise, totally defiant of any predictions. Shortly before the Wuchang Uprising in the fall of 1911 that eventually led to the establishment of the Chinese Republic, the prospect of a successful outcome for Sun's revolutionary cause was at one of its lowest points. Pessimism prevailed among the rank and file, and many of Sun's close associates openly voiced doubts about the future of their cause. Out of desperation some of the revolutionaries resorted to the assassination of "public enemies" as a way "to wake up the Chinese people from their slumber." One of them was Wang Ching-wei (1885-1944) who, after his arrest, wrote an ardent defense of the course which the revolutionaries intended to take (Selection 88).

No one expected the Wuchang Uprising to succeed, but succeed it did on account of a combination of unusual circumstances. Sun Yat-sen read about it in the newspapers while traveling in the United States and could not believe his own eyes. By the way of England and France he eventually returned to his beloved China where on January 1, 1912, he assumed the provisional presidency of the newly established Republic of China. In a written address to his countrymen, he called for the attainment of territorial and administrative unity (Selection 89); but, as he was later to sadly learn, there was not to be any unity. The establishment of the Republic was followed by a long period of civil war, with all the miseries and sufferings implied in that term. Yet, more than 4,000 years of autocratic rule finally came to an end, and for the first time in history the Chinese began to accept the idea that they, indeed, could govern themselves. For the acceptance of this idea, if for nothing else, no man in China was more responsible than Sun Yat-sen. It is no wonder that even today many Chinese still affectionately refer to him as "Father of the Nation."

86 • SUN YAT-SEN: *My Role in the Chinese Revolution*[1]

My determination to overthrow the Manchu regime and establish a republic began in 1885 when China was defeated by France. For more than ten years I used schools as a base for propaganda and medicine as a means to enter the world. When I was a student at the Pochi Medical School of Canton, I met among my schoolmates an unusually courageous and righteous man named Cheng Shih-liang (courtesy name: Pi-ch'en) who had among his friends many adventurers all over China. He stood so prominently above others that none of my other schoolmates could be compared with him. At our very first meeting I was impressed; and, after becoming better acquainted with him, I mentioned my ambition to start a revolution. No sooner did he hear of my ambition than he expressed pleasure and agreement. He told me that he was a member of a secret society and that whenever the necessity arose, he would be happy to gather his fellow members and put them at my disposal.

After studying medicine at Canton for one year, I heard that a British medical school had been established at Hong Kong. Thinking that this school was better than the one I then attended and that in Hong Kong I would enjoy more freedom in doing propaganda work as a revolutionary, I went to the British colony and enrolled in the new medical school as a student. For several years I devoted myself to revolutionary propaganda whenever my studies permitted me the time. I traveled frequently between Hong Kong and Macao; wherever I went, I spoke frankly and uninhibitedly about the revolution. However, only a few responded favorably to my ideas. Among them were Ch'en Shao-pai, Yu Shao-huan, and Yang Ho-ling of Hong Kong and Lu Hao-tung of Shanghai. My other acquaintances called me a traitor whenever they heard my revolutionary remarks and avoided me as if I were a plague, saying aloud that I must be insane. Since Ch'en, Yu, Yang, and I lived in Hong Kong, we visited each other often. Whenever we met, we spoke of nothing except the revolution, entertained no other ideas except those relating to the revolution, and studied only those problems that might arise as a result of the revolution. Though we four were very close, the only pleasure we shared was the discussion of the revolution which, in fact, continued on a more or less daily basis for several years. In Hong Kong and Macao all of our relatives, friends, and acquaintances called us the "Four Notorious Bandits." As far as my own career was concerned, these several years might be regarded as the period of promoting revolutionary ideas.

I practiced medicine between Macao and Canton after my graduation which, actually, marked the beginning of translating my revolutionary ideas into action. Then Cheng Shih-liang was making contacts with members of secret societies as well as with officers and soldiers of the Manchu garrisons. Once the roads to various organizations were open, we began to have some ideas as to what we wanted to do. Subsequently I sent Lu Hao-tung to Peking and Tientsin to assess the Ch'ing government's capacity; this was followed by his trip to the Wu-Han area to evaluate the political situation along the Yangtze Valley. In 1894 when the Sino-Japanese War began, I thought that the opportunity to do something more concrete had arrived. Consequently I went to Hawaii and hoped to also go to the United States for the purpose of establishing the China Rejuvenation Society.[2] My purpose was to rally the oversea Chinese for the revolutionary cause, but unfortunately these Chinese were too conservative to accept any new ideas. At Hawaii I spoke of the necessity of the revolution for several months, but only a few responded. Teng Yin-lan and my elder brother Teh-chang were the two persons who pledged all-out help, while two or three scores of my friends and relatives only agreed to the principle of the necessity of the revolution. Then, suffering successive defeats at the hands of Japan, the Ch'ing government first lost Korea and then Port Arthur and Weihaiwei; even Tientsin and Peking were threatened by the invaders. Since its corruption and incompetence had been thus exposed for all to see, anger and anguish began to occupy the heart of every Chinese. Sung Yo-ju, a comrade then stationed at Shanghai, sent me a letter asking me to speed home; my plan to visit the United States was consequently canceled. Accompanied by Teng Yin-lan and a few other comrades, I returned to China to plan our next step.

Our plan called for the seizure of Canton as the revolutionary base. To carry out this plan, we opened a store called Ch'ien-heng Hang at Hong Kong, which actually was a center for training cadres. At Canton we established an organization called the Association for the Study of Agriculture which became our revolutionary headquarters in disguise. The comrades who helped me in the cadre training program included Teng Yin-lan, Yang Ch'ü-yün, Huang Yung-shang, and Ch'en Shao-pai; meanwhile Lu Hao-tung, Cheng Shih-liang, and several European and American technicians and military officers were planning strategy at our Canton headquarters. I myself traveled frequently between Canton and Hong Kong, and carefully planned the forthcoming event. After a period of six months, we had acquired a large force and were ready to carry out the uprising that had been carefully thought out. We believed that by one stroke of violence we would be able to make our influence felt in the nation as a whole. Unfortunately, due to our own carelessness in transporting military supplies, the maritime customs discovered and seized more than 600 items of firearms. This discovery led to the revelation of the whole plot, and Lu Hao-tung, a powerful leader within our party, died as a martyr. He, in fact, was the first man in our history who died for the establishment of a republic. Two other men, Ch'iu Ssu and Chu Kuei-ch'üan, who were implicated with him, also died. More than seventy people were arrested, including Ch'eng K'uei-kuang who had been a navy captain in the Kwangtung province prior to his arrest and later died of illness in prison. The others arrested were either released or sentenced to imprisonment. The event described above occurred on October 26, 1895, and marked the first failure of my career as a revolutionary.

Three days after this failure I was still within the city wall of Canton. More than ten days elapsed before I could escape danger and reach Hong Kong by a tortuous route. Shortly afterwards I sailed for Japan with Cheng Shih-liang and Ch'en Shao-pai and took temporary residence at Yokohama. Knowing that it would be a long time before I could return to China, I cut off my hair[3] and began to wear Western clothes. I was to revisit Hawaii, while Shih-liang was to return to China and gather the remaining revolutionaries to prepare for another effort at some future time. Of us three, Shao-pai alone would stay in Japan to study and observe its national affairs. I introduced him to my Japanese friend Sugawara Den whom I had met at Hawaii. Later Sugawara introduced Shao-pai to Sone Toshitora who in turn introduced him to Miyazaki Yazo. I may add that the last-mentioned was an elder brother of Miyazaki Torazo. These introductions marked the beginning of contact between Chinese revolutionaries and members of the Japanese gentry.

After my arrival at Hawaii, once again I rallied my revolutionary friends to promote the activities of the China Rejuvenation Society. Some of the old

THE DOWNFALL OF THE MANCHU REGIME 299

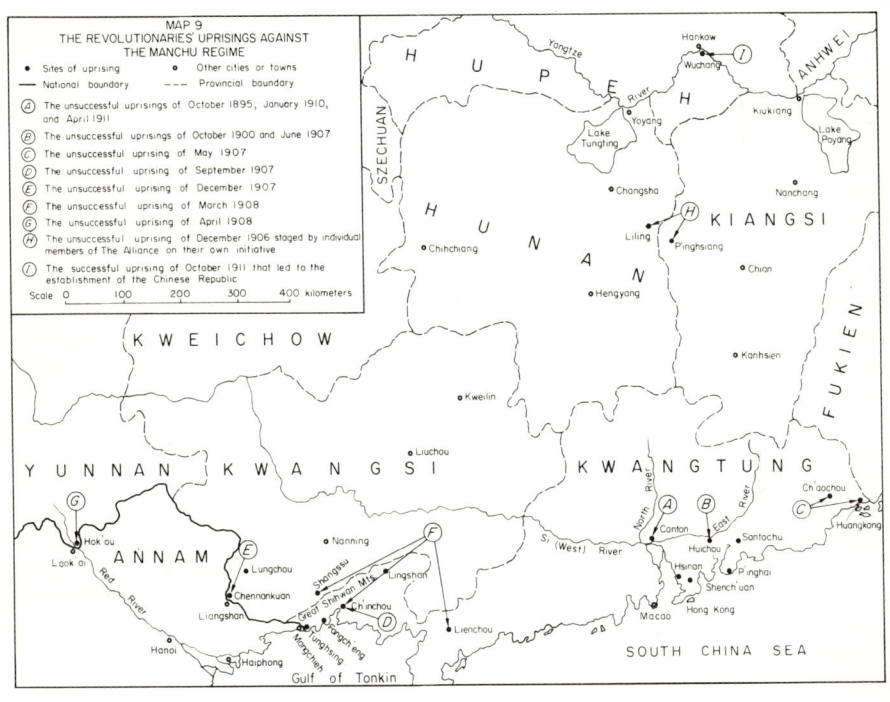

comrades had already lost interest because of the latest defeat, while others, who had only recently heard about our activities, joined our organization. Largely due to ignorance, the general atmosphere among the Chinese community in Hawaii was anything but propitious, and our progress was extremely slow. Knowing that there was not much I could do, I decided to sail for the United States where the Chinese community was several times larger and where I could, I thought, give a better account of myself.

One day before my scheduled sailing, I took a stroll outside of the city and suddenly encountered a carriage that moved directly towards me. Recognizing that the riders were my former teacher Cantlie[4] and his wife, I mounted their carriage with one broad jump. They were of course very surprised and suspected that I was a bandit, because by then I had changed to Western costume and they could not recognize me. I said, "I am Sun Yat-sen," and we laughed while shaking hands. I asked them how in the world they wound up in Hawaii; they replied that they were on their way home[5] and that they were merely sight-seeing while their ship was anchored in the harbor. Then I rode with them and volunteered to be a tourist guide. Finally, after seeing them on board, I mentioned that I was to travel around the world, would sail for the United States soon, and would repair to England after my American tour. It would not be too long, said I, before I would see them again. We shook hands and bid each other good-bye.

The Chinese community in the United States was even more conservative and uninformed than that in Hawaii. I landed at San Francisco on the eastern shore of the Pacific, crossed the American continent, and eventually reached New York on the western shore of the Atlantic. Along the route I stopped at several places and stayed anywhere between a few to more than ten days. Wherever I went, I spoke of the peril that our fatherland was in, the necessity of beginning a national revolution so as to save the country, and the responsibility of everyone to become a part of this revolution. Though I was as persuasive as I could be, the audience was generally apathetic or indifferent. In each of the cities I visited, the people who openly welcomed a revolution numbered no more than a few or at most a dozen.

In most of the Chinese communities in the United States one of the most influential organizations was the Hung-men Society. This society was first established in China by the Ming loyalists during the reign of Emperor K'ang-hsi [t. 1662–1722]. After the fall of the Ming Dynasty, the Ming loyalists refused to pledge allegiance to the Ch'ing regime; time and again they staged uprisings in the hope of restoring the fallen Chinese regime, only to be crushed in each and every attempt. By the reign of K'ang-hsi when the new dynasty had become too powerful to be dislodged, most of the Ming loyalists had already died. Knowing that there was nothing more they could do, a small group of the remaining loyalists decided to plant the seeds of nationalism upon the soil of posterity. With the principle of "overthrowing the Manchu regime and restoring the Ming Dynasty" as their ideological basis, they formed secret societies in the hope that Chinese of the succeeding generations would continue to fight for the cause which they had sponsored. This, in brief, was the original purpose of founding the Hung-men Society. The society had to be secret so that the government would not discover it. Since government officials were the existing regime's eyes and ears, the society felt it necessary to prohibit members of the intelligentsia from infiltrating its organization. Only by strictly enforcing this rule, it believed, could it maintain its continuance and, in fact, grow under the dictatorship of an alien rule.

Now that the society had been established upon the principle I have described, what were the methods it used to approach the people? To spread nationalistic ideas among the masses, it naturally chose to use methods that were psychologically more attractive to them. Thus, whenever it wished to hold a meeting, it staged a theatrical show. Whenever it wished to spread its ideas, it camouflaged them in tales and stories that portrayed the grievances of the oppressed and the revenges that they were eventually able to make. It employed these stories because they were the easiest way to stir up the emotions of ordinary people. As far as slogans and catchwords were concerned, it deliberately used vulgar or slangy words to keep away the intellectuals who loathed and looked down upon any person who used them. To consolidate its organization, it emphasized universal love and mutual help, thus satisfying an important need of the homeless and the adventurous. But its final or basic purpose was to spread nationalistic ideas so as to achieve its goal of overthrowing the Manchu regime and restoring the Ming Dynasty.

Due to the frequency of conflicts between them and government officials, the members of the Hung-men Society within China had not forgotten their opposite or antagonistic position vis-a-vis the Ch'ing government. However, even in China few of them fully understood the catchwords that camouflaged the society's message of overthrowing the Manchu regime and restoring the Ming Dynasty. Its oversea members, living in a free society, regarded its continuance as a mere necessity to render mutual help, and the political meaning of its existence was consequently lost. Many of them did not know the true meaning of the catchwords they used.

When I arrived in the United States to advocate revolution, the members of the Hung-men Society did not at first understand my purpose. Whenever I asked them what was meant by the phrase "overthrowing the Manchu regime and restoring the Ming dynasty," few of them could give me a satisfactory answer. It took several years of educational work on the part of our revolutionary comrades in the United States before they finally realized that they were in fact members of a nationalistic, revolutionary organization. While I was touring the United States, I merely sowed revolutionary seeds of the most rudimentary stage which had little or no effect on the future of the Chinese revolution. Yet somehow I had aroused the anger of the Ch'ing government. Hardly had I arrived at London before I was kidnapped by the Chinese embassy. I would have lost my life were it not for the valiant efforts of my former teacher Cantlie who rescued me. Thus the unplanned encounter at Hawaii seemed to have been heavenly ordained for the sake of my life. Otherwise Cantlie would not have known that I was going to visit London; nor would I have realized that he had returned to his native England.

After the London episode, I decided to stay in Europe for the time being to study European governments and to make friends with European gentlemen, in or outside of the government. In a period of two years I learned a great deal about Europe. It was my considered opinion that even though some of the European powers were economically prosperous, militarily strong, and politically democratic, their people were not happy with their lot. This was the reason that many farsighted Europeans advocated and promoted the socialist movement. Wishing to bring about a better society for China with one stroke, I decided to adopt the principle of people's livelihood so that the problem of economic security would be solved simultaneously with that of nationalism and democracy. The Three Principles of the People, nationalism, democracy, and people's livelihood, were thus conceived.

At that time there were no Chinese students in Europe; nor, for that matter, were there many oversea Chinese. In short, there was no way I could propagandize for the Chinese revolution in Europe. For a man who had dedicated his life to the cause of the revolution, to stay indefinitely in Europe would be a waste of time. Once my mind was made up, I sailed for Japan. Since Japan, being geographically proximate to China, was a place where information about China could be easily obtained, I could better plan my next move there. When I arrived at Japan, Inukai Tsuyoshi, then a political leader, sent Miyazaki Torazo and Hirayama Shu to Yokohama to welcome me. They accompanied me to Tokyo where I met Inukai for the first time. We talked about the world situation in a frank manner as if we had been friends for a long time. The Japanese political parties had only recently acquired power; Inukai was the assistant to Foreign Minister Okuma Shiegenobu, over whom he exercised a great deal of influence. Later, through Inukai I met Okuma, Oishi, Ozaki, and many others. This marked the beginning of my contact with Japanese political leaders. Shortly afterwards, I also met Soejima Taneomi, and such gentlemen as Toyama, Akiyama, Nakano, and Suzuki who did not have any positions with the government. Still later, I became acquainted with Yasukawa, Inuzuka, and Kuhara. Among the Japanese gentlemen who had provided financial help for the Chinese revolution, Kuhara and Inuzuka were the most prominent. The Japanese who had traveled tirelessly for our revolution included the Yamada brothers, the Miyazaki brothers, Kikuchi, and Kayano. Two other Japanese, Drs. Soejima and Terao, also did their best to advance our revolutionary cause. I had direct contact with all these Japanese gentlemen; I mention them, though briefly, because I do not want to forget the gratitude I owe them. There were many other Japanese who indirectly assisted our revolutionary cause, but their contributions cannot be described here in detail due to the limited space. Someday when the history of the Chinese revolution is written, their contributions will be doubtless acknowledged in a more appropriate fashion.

There were more than 10,000 Chinese in Japan; however, like oversea Chinese elsewhere, they were extremely conservative in outlook and were scared to death whenever the word "revolution" was mentioned. For several years our comrades traveled between Yokohama and Kobe to publicize our cause, but those Chinese who responded to our call numbered only a little more than 100, less than 1 percent of the total Chinese residents in Japan. If it was so difficult to spread revolutionary ideas among the oversea Chinese, it was doubtless more difficult to do so among the Chinese within China.

Among the Chinese within China, the only groups that were not surprised to hear about the revolution or the overthrow of the Manchu regime were the secret societies; but members of these societies were almost without exception poorly educated and their organizations lacked discipline. They could not be relied on to undertake major tasks—they knew how to respond, but they were unable to function as an active, generating force. The five years between 1895 (when my first coup failed) and 1900 were the most difficult insofar as our revolutionary task was concerned. After the 1895 failure, our revolutionary base within China was destroyed; my own career as a revolutionary, my ability to be continuously active, and the revolutionary foundation that I had built for the previous ten years seemed to have all evaporated. Even my efforts to spread revolutionary ideas among the oversea Chinese were met with failure. Besides, there was the Emperor Protection Society[6] which, as an accomplice of the Ch'ing regime, was more anti-revolutionary and anti-republican than the Ch'ing regime itself. At this moment the future of the revolution seemed to be as dark as it was hopeless. The only factor that prevented our comrades from giving up the struggle was the firm belief that a new regime, whatever difficulties it might encounter at the beginning, must and should be established.

Based upon this belief, I ordered Ch'en Shao-pai to return to Hong Kong to found the newspaper *China Journal*[7] in order to continue to advocate the revolution. I sent Shih Chien-ju to the Yangtze Valley to make contact with the secret societies, and Cheng Shih-liang to Hong Kong to establish a revolutionary headquarters to recruit members of the secret societies as vanguards of our revolutionary party. Because of these efforts, the secret societies of the Yangtze Valley and those in Kwangtung, Kwangsi, and Fukien provinces were subsequently merged with the China Rejuvenation Society.

Shortly afterwards, the Ch'ing government, relying on the support it had received from the Boxers, began to promote an anti-foreign movement.[8] A series of incidents such as the killing of foreigners and the attempt to seize the Legation Quarter at Peking eventually led to a military expedition launched by eight allied powers against China. Thinking that this was a good opportunity, I sent Cheng Shih-liang to Huichou[9] to mobilize our comrades to stage an uprising. Meanwhile I also sent Shih Chien-ju to Canton to rally our comrades there to respond to this uprising whenever it occurred. When our plan was about to be completed, I, accompanied by several military officers of foreign nationalities, went to Hong Kong by a circuitous route, in the hope that eventually I would be able to enter China and lead a well-disciplined revolutionary army to save China from her impending peril. Unfortunately my whereabouts was betrayed by some informers. The moment our ship arrived at Hong Kong, I was put under surveillance by the Hong Kong authority. Since I was not allowed to land, I had to abandon my original plan. I entrusted the responsibility of staging the uprising at Huichou to Cheng Shih-liang and ordered Yang Ch'ü-yün, Li Chi-t'ang, and Ch'en Shao-pai to provide him with supplies from Hong Kong. Meanwhile I was supposed to return to Japan.

Instead of returning to Japan, I went to Taiwan wherefrom I hoped to eventually sail across the strait [Taiwan Strait] to reach the Chinese mainland. Kodama, the Japanese governor of Taiwan, was very enthusiastic about the Chinese revolution, knowing that North China had been by then reduced to a status of anarchy. He ordered Goto, a senior official in his administration, to talk with me, and promised assistance once the uprising was under way. Having received this promise, I began to enlarge the original plan; I recruited many badly needed military officers since our revolutionary party did not have any with modern training. Meanwhile I ordered Cheng Shih-liang to start work immediately on the revised plan. Instead of making a front attack on the provincial capital [Canton], he should first occupy many points along the sea coast, rally as many of our comrades as possible, and wait for my return before launching any major attacks.

Having received my order, Shih-liang went to China immediately. He personally led the people whom he had mobilized in Sanchout'ien to attack the Ch'ing troops stationed at Hsinan and Shench'üan; he was so successful in his attacks that he captured all of his enemy's equipment. Then he fought in Lungkang, Tanshui, Yanghu, Lianghua, Paimanghua, Santochu, and many other places. Wherever he went, he won; the Ch'ing troops, frightened under his vigorous attacks, simply fled. As a result, he occupied all the points along the coast from Hsinan and Tap'eng to

Huichou and P'inghai. Then he waited for my arrival and the arrival of my cadres, together with the supply of guns and ammunition that I had promised him.

What he did not know was that ten days after the Huichou uprising, there was a sudden change of Japanese government. The China policy of Ito, the new premier, was completely different from that of his predecessor. The new premier prohibited the governor of Taiwan to have anything to do with the Chinese revolutionary party, imposed an embargo on the exportation of military equipment, and forbade Japanese military officers to join our revolutionary army. Consequently my plan of secretly sailing across the strait to reach China could no longer be carried out. I sent Yamada Yoshimasa and several other comrades to China to report to Shih-liang what had happened; the latter, from then on, was to do whatever he thought most appropriate or advantageous under the changed circumstances.

By the time that Yamada reached Cheng Shih-liang's headquarters, more than thirty days had elapsed since the uprising. After more than one month's fighting, Shih-liang's ammunition had been exhausted. He had under his command more than 10,000 men and was waiting impatiently for the arrival of cadres, officers, and military equipment. Then he heard the bad news which gave him no other choice except to disband the army which he had organized. He himself led several hundred men to Hong Kong, while Yamada, losing his way, was captured by the Ch'ing troops and subsequently executed. Yamada was in fact the first foreigner who had sacrificed his life for the establishment of a Chinese republic.

While Cheng Shih-liang was fighting a bitter battle at Huichou, time and again Shih Chien-ju tried to respond to his efforts at Canton, but each time he failed to succeed. Finally he decided to dynamite the official residence of Teh-shou, the governor-general of Liangkwang, so as to kill him. His dynamite missed its target, and he himself was captured and later executed. He was the second Chinese hero who had died for the establishment of the republic. Like his predecessor Lu Hao-tung, Chien-ju was intelligent, well-learned, honest, and sincere. Both were exceptionally talented, manly, and handsome. Both knew how to paint and compose poetry. Hao-tung concealed his extreme courage inside, while Chien-ju was more dashing and determined. Their premature deaths were not only a great loss to the nation but also cast a dark shadow on the future of the revolution. However, the heroic way they died inspired thousands of others who would eventually follow their example. Every time I think of them, my heart is filled with admiration and esteem. Die they did, but their spirit has never left me even for a moment, day or night.

The campaign of 1900 marked the second failure of my career as a revolutionary. After the first failure, practically everyone in China regarded us as rebellious elements who had committed high treason. There was no ending to the cursing and deriding we endured. Wherever we went, anybody who recognized us would avoid us as if we were poisonous snakes or carnivorous beasts. After the failure of 1900, however, the situation completely changed. Very few people cursed or derided us any more; in fact, the more enlightened intellectuals even expressed regret that we had not succeeded in our efforts. What a difference! Needless to say, we were delighted at this change of attitude. Slowly and gradually my countrymen were waking up from their long slumber.

Then the troops of the eight allied nations captured Peking, and both the empress dowager and the emperor [Tz'u Hsi and Kuang-hsü] were forced to flee. When peace was finally concluded, China had to pay an indemnity amounting to 900 million taels. The prestige of the Ch'ing regime had never been so low.

THE DOWNFALL OF THE MANCHU REGIME 305

Moreover, the livelihood of the people would become more difficult from then on; the nation was in such a precarious position that it could collapse and perish at any moment. As a strong sense of patriotism began to spread among the more determined individuals, the rising tide of a revolutionary movement was born.

This was the time when many Chinese provinces began to send students to be educated in Japan. These students were a proud lot; they also were open-minded and unprejudiced, thus susceptible to revolutionary ideals. In fact, these ideals spread so fast that soon they became a vogue; seldom did Chinese students meet in Tokyo without discussing the problems of the revolution. Liu Ch'eng-yü, for instance, spoke of the importance of overthrowing the Manchu regime by revolutionary methods before the Chinese students during a New Year celebration, only to be expelled from school at the insistence of the Ch'ing minister to Japan. Others like Chi Yüan-ch'eng, Shen Ch'iu-chai, and Chang Fu-ch'ien founded the *People's Journal*[10] to propagandize the revolution.

Promoted and sponsored by the Chinese students in Japan in the beginning, these revolutionary endeavors soon found their response among the students at home. Before long the revolutionary movement began to surge ahead in all the provinces of China. In Shanghai, Chang T'ai-yen, Wu Chih-hui, and Chou Yung wrote extensively in *Su Pao*[11] to advocate the necessity of revolution. The Ch'ing government sued these gentlemen; subsequently both Chang T'ai-yen and Chou Yung were thrown into jail in the Foreign Settlement, while Wu Chih-hui fled to Europe. This lawsuit implicated even the Manchu emperor, an unprecedented event in that for the first time in history a Chinese government had become a plaintiff in a lawsuit against its own citizens. Though the Ch'ing government did win this case, Chang T'ai-yen and Chou Yung were sentenced for only two years in prison. Ironically this lawsuit, started by the Ch'ing government, later provided inspiration and encouragement for all the revolutionaries against the Ch'ing government. Chou Yung wrote a book entitled *The Revolutionary Army*[12] in which he spoke most fervently of the necessity of overthrowing the Manchu regime. This book was very popular among the oversea Chinese and was greatly responsible for opening their eyes. The revolutionary movement, finally, had built up momentum.

Between 1902 and 1903, time and again I was informed by the French minister in Tokyo that T'ao-mei, the French viceroy of Annam, would like to invite me to that southern country for a visit. I was too busy to make the trip until sometime later when a state fair was scheduled to open in Hanoi. By the time I arrived, however, T'ao-mei had already left his post and returned home. Nevertheless I was well received since the French viceroy had instructed his secretary Ha-teh-an to serve as my host before his departure. In Hanoi I met many Chinese businessmen such as Huang Lung-sheng, Chen Chi-t'ing, Yang Shou-p'eng, and Tseng Ch'i, all of whom subsequently joined our revolutionary party and contributed generously to the Ch'in-Lien and˙Hok'ou campaigns.

After the conclusion of the Hanoi fair, I decided to make another world tour. My itinerary included Japan, Hawaii, the United States, and Europe. In Japan, Mr. and Mrs. Liao Chung-k'ai, Ma Chün-wu, Wu Yi-sheng, Li Chung-shih, and many others came to see me and expressed their approval of the revolution. I asked them to search for interested Chinese students in Japan who would then be invited to join our organization and be entrusted with organizational responsibilities. Later, when The Alliance for Chinese Revolution[13] was established, these gentlemen contributed greatly to its success.

Between the failure of the Huichou uprising and the establishment of The Alliance [between 1900 and 1905], there were several uprisings inspired by the revolutionary movement, including those led by Li Chi-t'ang and Hung Ch'üan-fu in Kwangtung and Huang K'e-ch'iang and Ma Fu-yi in Hunan. Though they failed to attain their declared goals, these gentlemen were nevertheless praised highly for their efforts. Slowly and gradually the oversea Chinese communities were affected by the revolutionary movement promoted by the Chinese students in Tokyo and by the uprisings within China itself. Wherever I went during my second world tour, the oversea Chinese welcomed me, giving me the kind of response that I had not encountered during my first world tour.

In the spring of 1905, once again I visited Europe. Most of the Chinese students I met were on the side of the revolution. Having been influenced by revolutionary ideas for one or two years prior to their recent arrival from China or Japan, they were now ready to move from the realm of ideas to the realm of action. I told them what I had thought about for a long time, namely, the Three Principles of the People and a constitution based upon a five-power concept.[14] With these ideas to rally them, I proceeded to organize a revolutionary party. The first meeting was held in Brussels, Belgium, and more than thirty people joined the new organization. This was followed by the second meeting in Berlin during which more than twenty people joined and the third meeting in Paris when approximately ten persons were added as new members. The most enthusiastic response, however, did not come about until the fourth meeting in Tokyo when several hundred persons joined the new organization. These new members represented all of the eighteen provinces in China except Kansu which had not yet sent any students to Japan. This was the founding of The Alliance for Chinese Revolution, then known simply as The Alliance[15] because most people still shunned the word "revolution."

The establishment of The Alliance for Chinese Revolution marked the beginning of a new era as far as my hope for the future was concerned. Before this time I had never dared to hope that our revolutionary task of overthrowing the Manchu regime could succeed in my own lifetime, even though I had taken great risks in pushing forward the revolutionary movement under the most difficult circumstances and amidst the worst kinds of abuses. The reason I did not give up despite repeated failures was twofold: to revive my fellow citizens' self-confidence that had been dead for a long time and to wake up the national spirit that was about to disappear for good. All I had dared to hope was that after my death other people would follow my path and eventually succeed. It was not until that day in the fall of 1905 when I gathered the best among my countrymen for the establishment of The Alliance for Chinese Revolution that I, finally, realized that our great revolutionary task could be completed in my lifetime.

Based upon such confidence, I made public to our party members the new name for our country; it would be called the Republic of China once the Manchu regime was overthrown. I asked the party members to return to their respective provinces to propagandize our revolutionary cause and to spread the idea of a new Republic of China. In less than a year more than 10,000 people joined The Alliance, and party branches were established in all the provinces of China. From then on the revolutionary movement built up its own momentum; the progress was so fast that it bettered even our most optimistic expectation.

Amidst this progress even foreign governments began to view our revolutionary party under a new light. One day while our ship was anchored at Wusung[16] during my journey from Southeast Asia to Japan, a military attaché from the French embassy named Pu-chia-pei came to visit me, saying that he had been instructed by the French Minister of War to express his government's willingness to assist the Chinese revolution. He asked me the size of our military forces, and I told him the situation as I knew it. He then asked me how the revolutionary armies in different provinces were coordinated, saying that his government was ready to provide immediate assistance if the coordination had been completed. I replied that the coordination was anything but complete and that I would appreciate his assistance in investigation and liaison work. He responded favorably to my request and assigned seven military officers from his Tientsin headquarters to my command.

Subsequently I sent Liao Chung-k'ai to establish a revolutionary headquarters in Tientsin. Meanwhile I ordered Li Chung-shih, together with a foreign officer, to repair to Kwangtung and Kwangsi. Hu Yi-sheng, accompanied by another foreign officer, was to go to Szechuan and Yunnan, while Ch'iao Yi-chai and another foreign officer were to work in Nanking and Wuchang. Their duty was to canvass and coordinate all the revolutionary forces in each of the areas to which they were assigned. In both Nanking and Wuchang the newly established battalions of the Ch'ing government gave our coordinators a great welcome. In Nanking, as a result of a successful negotiation conducted by Chao Pai-hsien, our coordinator secretly met all military officers with the rank of major or above, and jointly they planned the next move. Through the efforts of the liaison officer in Wuchang, Liu Chia-yün, a meeting was called in a Christian church, to be attended by the military officers who had joined the revolutionary party. A large number of people showed up; it was reported that Chang Piao, the commander of the new battalions, attended in the guise of an ordinary soldier. During the meeting several men, including a French officer, spoke eloquently for the revolution. Ironically, because of this successful meeting, our planning at Wuchang could no longer be kept secret.

After the meeting, Chang Chih-tung, the governor-general of Hupeh and Hunan, sent a Western employee of the customs office to tail the French officer who had spoken enthusiastically about the revolution. Approaching the French officer, this Western employee pretended that he, too, was in sympathy with the Chinese revolution. Since the pretender was a fellow Westerner, our French friend was not at all suspicious and revealed to him many secrets which he should have kept to himself. Based upon the information thus acquired, Chang Chih-tung made a detailed report to the Ch'ing government on the plans of a scheduled uprising, some of which were accurate while others were not. Having received this report, the Ch'ing government made a strong protest to the French minister at Peking. Not knowing what to do under the circumstances, the French minister requested instructions from his home government. The French government ordered him to ignore the Chinese protest, and the Ch'ing government could not do anything about this non-cooperation. Shortly afterwards there was a change of the French government. The new cabinet did not approve French cooperation with the Chinese revolutionaries and ordered Pu-chia-pei to return home. As this incident developed, Liu Chia-yün was eventually implicated; the Ch'ing government arrested him and later put him to death. This was the first time that our revolutionary movement became involved with an act of international diplomacy.

Shortly after the establishment of The Alliance, we published a newspaper called *The People*.[17] The purpose of this newspaper was to publicize the Three Principles of the People so that our revolutionary ideas would spread to all parts of China. Of all the revolutionary journals that had been published until then, *The People* turned out to be the most successful. Responding to our call, individual patriots raised their own standards of revolt and performed righteous and heroic deeds; so heroic were they that one man's unfortunate death only inspired others to follow his path. In this regard the most noted were Hsü Hsi-lin, Hsiung Ch'eng-chi, and Ch'iu Chin.[18]

In 1907 the members of The Alliance staged an armed revolt in the P'ing-Li area.[19] While the revolutionary army was fighting a ferocious battle against the Ch'ing forces in interior China, its comrades in Tokyo were greatly excited about the outcome, so excited that they almost wished they had wings with which they could fly across the ocean so that they, too, could participate in the battle. Each day many people came to our Tokyo headquarters to enlist for military service. If we were only a little hesitant in granting their wishes, many of them would weep, feeling doubtless disappointed that they might have been denied the privilege to die at a time when they believed they should. The uprising at P'inghsiang, however, was staged by individual members; it was not sponsored by the Tokyo headquarters which in fact had no advance knowledge whatsoever. We were completely surprised when it suddenly occurred. Once it did occur, however, a large number of our comrades left Japan for China to enlist in the revolutionary army. After the failure of the P'ing-Li campaign, many of them were captured, including Liu Tao-yi, Ning T'iao-yüan, and Hu Ying. Some of them were later put to death, while others were given jail terms. The P'inghsiang uprising marked the first time that members of The Alliance had died for the Chinese revolution.

From then on the revolutionary movement spread across the country with unprecedented speed, and our headquarters at Tokyo could no longer pretend that it was not involved. Fearful and worried, the Ch'ing government time and again protested to the Japanese government which subsequently ordered my deportation. I left Japan with Hu Han-min and Wang Ching-wei for Hanoi, Annam where a new headquarters was established to prepare for the next move. Shortly afterwards I started a military campaign at Ch'aochou and Huangkang, only to fail again. This was in fact the third failure in my career as a revolutionary. Later I ordered Teng Tzu-yü to stage an uprising in Huichou which also failed. As far as I was concerned, this was the fourth failure in my revolutionary career.

Not long afterwards a tax evasion movement developed among the people in Ch'inchou and Lienchou.[20] The Ch'ing government responded by sending Kuo Jen-chang and Chao Pai-hsien, each heading a contingent of three or four thousand men, to suppress them. Seeing that a new opportunity had developed, I ordered Huang K'e-ch'iang to contact the former and Hu Yi-sheng the latter, and to try to persuade the two Ch'ing commanders to switch to the side of the revolution. The two agreed, saying that if a respectable revolutionary force emerged, they would certainly switch sides. Having secured this promise, I sent my men to contact the gentry and the militia in the Ch'in-Lien area for joint action, while ordering Kayano Chochi to proceed to Japan to purchase firearms and other military equipment. Meanwhile efforts were made to recruit new comrades in Annam, to be trained by retired French officers who had been recently employed for this purpose. Our plan called for the occupation of the coastal areas from Fangch'eng to Tunghsing once the military equipment arrived and the employment of these areas as a base for the training of a revolutionary army. Nor would transportation pose any serious problems since Tunghsing was located across the Pailung River from Mangchieh which belonged to the French and could be easily reached via a bridge. The moment we had the military equipment, we thought, we could easily create a regular army of 2,000 men. This army, later joined by the six or seven thousand militiamen from Ch'inchou and the six thousand regular troops under the command of Kuo Jen-chang and Chao Pai-hsien, would become a sizable, powerful force. Given additional training to sharpen its striking ability, it would be used successfully to take over Kwangtung and Kwangsi provinces. Then it would move northward towards the Yangtze and eventually join forces with the new armies from Nanking and Wuchang. When this happened, it was unlikely that it would meet any effective resistance from then on. Our revolution would finally be crowned with success; at least that was what we thought.

What we could not foresee was the sudden emergence of dissensions among the party members in our Tokyo headquarters. Because of these dissensions, our original plan of purchasing and shipping military equipment could no longer be carried out. Though Fangch'eng was captured, the equipment did not arrive as had been promised. To the comrades who had been scheduled to receive this equipment and to the members of the gentry who had agreed to assist us with their militias, I could not do anything except to express my deepest regret. Although deprived of the promised equipment, the army responsible for the attack of Fangch'eng moved forward to put pressure on Ch'inchou in the hope that the contingent headed by Kuo Jen-chang would respond. Seeing how weak our army really was and being further immobilized by the presence of other troops in the nearby areas, Kuo did not choose to make a move. Under the circumstances, our army changed its plan again and proceeded to surround Lingshan, hoping that the contingent headed by Chao Pai-hsien would respond. Taking due notice that Kuo Jen-chang had not joined our forces, Chao thought it wise not to make a move either. Finally, not being able to advance any further, our army retreated to the Great Shihwan Mountains.[21] This campaign marked the fifth failure of my career as a revolutionary.

Since our strategy relating to Ch'inchou and Lienchou could no longer be carried out, I personally led Huang K'e-ch'iang and Hu Han-min, together with some French officers and more than a hundred Annamese comrades, to attack Chennankuan. We captured three important fortresses and took the surrendered soldiers under custody. Our plan was first, to join forces with the comrades in the Great Shihwan Mountains and second, to make a concerted attack on Lungchou. Unfortunately the comrades in the mountains were unable to rendezvous with us due to the long distance, and, as a result, our plan for a concerted attack failed. I and my 100 men held three cannon sites for seven days and seven nights against an attacking force of several thousand led by Lung Chi-kuang and Lu Yung-t'ing but finally had to pull out and retreat to Annam. While I was passing through Liangshan, my presence was discovered by a Ch'ing detective who, as expected, reported his findings to the Ch'ing government. The latter protested to the French government and I, as a result, was deported from Annam. This campaign marked the sixth failure of my career as a revolutionary.

Before I left Hanoi, I ordered Huang K'e-ch'iang to plan a second invasion of Ch'inchou and Lienchou in the hope of rallying the local comrades. Meanwhile I ordered Huang Ming-t'ang to seize Hok'ou and hopefully to occupy Yunnan which, when seized, would be used as a territorial basis for our revolutionary party. Later, K'e-ch'iang led 200 men from Annam and moved freely in the area of Ch'inchou, Lienchou, and Shangssu. He fought for several months and defeated all the forces the enemy sent to meet him. The enemy was frightened whenever his name was mentioned, and K'e-ch'iang's martial reputation became known throughout China. He retreated only after the supply of ammunition had been exhausted and at a time when there were no reinforcements in sight. His retreat marked the seventh failure of my career as a revolutionary.

Several months after my arrival at Singapore, Huang Ming-t'ang led more than 100 men to attack and then seize Hok'ou. The garrison commander was killed, and more than 1,000 enemy soldiers surrendered. After this victory, Huang Ming-t'ang waited for the arrival of cadres to take over the command of the surrendered soldiers. I was then faraway in Southeast Asia; moreover, I was no longer allowed to pass through any French territory. Unable to assume the over-all command in the frontier, I telegraphed Huang K'e-ch'iang to act in my stead. On his way to his assignment, K'e-ch'iang was unexpectedly detained by French authorities who suspected him of being Japanese; he was later sent back to Hanoi. When it learned about this episode, the Ch'ing government made a vigorous protest to the French who subsequently expelled K'e-ch'iang from the country [Annam]. Meanwhile in Hok'ou the troops had no one to command them, and the opportunity of making further advances was consequently lost. Otherwise we would have been able to take over Mengtzu and perhaps even Kunming where resistance, if any, was not expected to be too great. The telegrams which Hsi-liang, the governor-general of Yunnan and Kweichow, sent to plead for reinforcements, indicate how frightened he must have been and how helpless he must have felt. Huang Ming-t'ang waited for more than one month for the arrival of leadership, while each of his soldiers fought his own battle, with no discipline whatsoever. In the meantime the enemy troops gathered from all directions until they were ten times more numerous than we were. Hok'ou could no longer be defended, and Huang Ming-t'ang and his 600 men had to retreat to Annam. This campaign marked the eighth failure of my career as a revolutionary.

After this defeat, our party members were deported by the French government. Their destination was supposed to be Singapore which belonged to Great Britain. The day they arrived, the British authorities raised many questions and refused to let them land. The French consul went to speak with the governor of Singapore, maintaining that these 600 people were members of a revolutionary army who retreated to French territories after being defeated at Hok'ou and that they had voluntarily requested to be repatriated to Singapore. The governor of Singapore replied that these Chinese who had fought against their own government could not be regarded as political prisoners since they had not been recognized by any country as belligerants under the international law and that they, consequently, could only be viewed as common bandits whose entry into a British port would be a violation of the British law. For two days the negotiations went on while the French ship with our comrades in it was anchored in the harbor. Later the French consul stated that during the time of war at Hok'ou the French government took a position of neutrality towards both sides, and such a position amounted to the recognition of the revolutionary party as a belligerent. These revolutionaries could not in any way be viewed as common bandits, the French consul concluded. The British government accepted the French interpretation, and our comrades were finally allowed to land on Singapore. This was another episode when our revolutionary movement became involved with an act of international diplomacy.

The six campaigns, from Huangkang to Hok'ou, were conducted by members of The Alliance under my direct command. After six consecutive failures, Wang Ching-wei, understandably, was very much discouraged. Accompanied by several of his comrades, he proceeded to Peking with the intended purpose of exchanging his life for that of his enemy. His assassination attempt failed, and both he and Huang Fu-sheng were thrown into prison. It was not until the success of the Wuchang Uprising that they were finally released.[22]

Before the establishment of The Alliance, the people who contributed funds to our righteous cause were confined to a few of my friends and relatives. No other people either wished or dared to make any financial contributions. After the establishment of The Alliance, however, the situation completely changed. From then on we began to raise funds on a large scale. The most generous was Chang Ching-chiang who sold out his shop in Paris and gave us all the receipts that amounted to more than 60,000 dollars,[23] the largest contribution ever made by a single person. Another example of unusual generosity was provided by Huang Ching-nan of Annam, who gave all his lifetime savings of several thousand dollars to the revolutionary cause. Three wealthy merchants in Saigon, Annam[24]—Li Cho-feng, Tseng Hsi-chou, and Ma P'ei-sheng—each contributed tens of thousands of dollars, a rare example of generosity indeed.

After a succession of failures, all my operational bases within China were lost; nor could I remain active in those places that were geographically proximate to China, such as Annam, Japan, and Hong Kong. Therefore I entrusted all future operations within China to Huang K'e-ch'iang and Hu Han-min and traveled around the world, concentrating on raising funds so our revolutionary work could be continued. Later K'e-ch'iang and Han-min returned to Hong Kong where they established our southern headquarters. They were assisted by Chao Pai-hsien, Ni Ying-tien, Chu Chih-hsin, Ch'en Hsiung-ming, Yao Yü-p'ing, and many others.

Since the new army at Canton was ready for a revolt, our comrades at Hong Kong planned an uprising in the first month of 1910. However, one day before the scheduled uprising, some of the soldiers became nervous and rioted over some insignificant incident. Ni Ying-tien rushed to his battalion headquarters and personally led the soldiers from Shaho to attack Canton. At Hengchihkang his column was ambushed by the enemy; he himself was wounded by a bullet, captured, and later died. Without their commander, the soldiers were easily routed. This marked the ninth failure of my career as a revolutionary.

I was on my way to the United States when this campaign began. When I heard about the defeat upon my arrival at San Francisco, I immediately turned around by the way of Hawaii. I landed secretly in Japan, but unfortunately my presence was soon found out by the police. After the Japanese turned down my request to stay, I had no choice but to leave. Subsequently I sailed from Yokohama for Penang.[25]

Upon my arrival I called upon Chao Pai-hsien, Huang K'e-ch'iang, Hu Han-min, and many others to proceed to Penang for an important meeting during which we would discuss our future plans. This was a very bad time for our revolutionary cause in that our comrades had been recently defeated, our most efficient headquarters had been destroyed, and our most advantageous territorial positions had been lost to the enemy. Moreover, there were the new army comrades who had recently escaped to the south, and we were strained to the limit to find a livelihood for them. Even we ourselves were fearful that we might not be able to get enough funds that would enable us to continue to eat, live, and move around. When the meeting was finally held, all the attending comrades were in a pessimistic mood. Asked about their future plans, they whimpered, sighed, and looked at each other without a word.

"Why should we become so discouraged after this one defeat?" I asked. "I have been defeated many times before, and after each defeat the whole world looked down upon and despised me, confident that I would give up. The difficulties I had then were a hundred times more serious than those we have today. It is true that we are poor, but we should not forget that the revolutionary movement has already built up its own momentum. Moreover, the oversea Chinese are more informed and less conservative than they have been in the past. From now on all we need is good planning and unsuppressible courage. If you gentlemen can be united in your efforts, I shall see to it that our financial needs will be met." Seeing how poor our Penang comrades were and realizing the difficult situation we were then in as wanted fugitives, some of the people attending the meeting began to ask themselves where our next meal would come from, let alone new funds to continue our revolutionary work. I reiterated that ways could be found to solve this problem.

Chao Pai-hsien then remarked that if we really wished to continue our revolutionary activities, we should immediately send a man to China with several thousand dollars, to meet the urgent needs of certain comrades in an undisclosed area so that they would not disperse by themselves. "When this is done, we should be able to rally the scattered revolutionaries and plan the establishment of a new headquarters," he continued. "Meanwhile we should return to Hong Kong to make the necessary contacts. In short, we need $5,000 for traveling expenses in a few days and hundreds of thousands of dollars to finance another revolutionary effort."

After listening to Pai-hsien's remarks to which I readily agreed, I invited the leaders of the local Chinese community for a conference. I reminded them of their sacred duty to a righteous cause, and they responded generously by contributing more than $8,000 in one evening. Then I ordered our comrades to repair to other cities to raise funds, and in a few days they collected almost $60,000, excluding contributions in the more remote areas. Since this amount was large enough to implement the initial stage of our next move, each of us went on with his task as had been previously agreed.

Originally I had planned to visit all of the British and Dutch possessions in Southeast Asia. This plan had to be canceled when the Dutch authorities made it known that I was not welcome in their territories. I was equally unsuccessful when I tried to land on Siam and the British possessions. Large as the continent of Asia was and numerous as the islands in Southeast Asia were, there was not a single square foot where I could plant my two feet. Under the circumstances I had no choice but to go to such faraway places as Europe and the United States. Upon my arrival in the United States I traveled from one part of the country to another, admonishing the oversea Chinese to contribute funds to the cause of the revolution. Most of the Chinese I approached were happy to oblige.

Shortly afterwards an uprising was launched in Canton on the 27th of April, 1911. During this campaign the best among our comrades from all the provinces of China gathered together and attempted to deal a final blow to the enemy. Though they failed, the heroic deeds of the seventy-two martyrs at Huanghua-kang[26] truly shook the world. The favorable tendency towards revolution inside China was due in no small measure to the example which these martyrs had set for the nation.

Previously comrades like Ch'en Ying-shih, Sung Tun-ch'u, T'an Shih-p'ing, and Chü Chiao-sheng had been assigned to work under the overall supervision of our Hong Kong headquarters. Their duty was to provide the Canton comrades with needed assistance. After our Canton efforts had repeatedly failed, they began to turn their attention to the Wu-Han area.

THE DOWNFALL OF THE MANCHU REGIME   313

Since the time I sent French officers to make contact with them, the soldiers of the new army in the Wu-Han area had become more and more progressive until they were permeated with revolutionary ideas. Meanwhile the preventive measures taken by the Ch'ing government also became more strict. Previously, when Tuan-fang moved his troops to Szechuan, Shui-ch'eng, the governor-general of Hukuang, assigned to his command and thus sent away some of the most revolutionary-minded groups. He thought that by taking this measure, he could prevent any disturbances that might occur in the Wu-Han area. However, after the Canton campaign, rumors and fear spread in all the provinces. Wherever a Ch'ing official went, he stepped into an area of worry and fear; this was especially true in Wuchang. Anticipating an armed revolt, Shui-ch'eng made an agreement with a foreign consul in Hankow, according to which the latter would move warships to the Wu-Han area and fire upon the revolutionaries when and if an armed revolt did occur. The situation was so tense that few residents in the Wu-Han metropolis were able to sleep well at night.

Meanwhile Sun Wu and Liu Kung were working diligently in preparation for the forthcoming event. The soldiers in the new army were very enthusiastic about it. But somehow things do not always go so well as one wants them to. Suddenly and unexpectedly the enemy discovered our revolutionary headquarters and captured it; more than thirty of our comrades were arrested as a result. Having learned this bad news, Hu Ying, then still confined in the Wuchang prison, sent an urgent message to Ch'en Ying-shih, requesting him to cancel his scheduled trip. Meanwhile the soldiers in the artillery and engineering battalions, who had joined the revolutionary party, also heard about the sudden change of events. Realizing that the government had captured the roster of their membership in the revolutionary party and would certainly arrest them the very next day, they decided to take immediate action to save themselves. Hsiung Ping-k'un fired the first shot to signal the beginning of action, and soon Ts'ai Chi-min led his men to attack the governor-general's office with cannon fire. The moment he heard the cannons, Shui-ch'eng escaped to Hankow. Then he requested the consul previously mentioned to bombard the revolutionaries.

Under the treaty of 1900 none of the signatories could take unilaterial action with regard to China without consulting each other in advance. Because of this restriction, the aforesaid consul called other foreign consuls for a conference, hoping that once a majority vote was secured, he could go ahead with his bombardments and suppress the revolutionaries. Most consuls had no preconceived ideas on this matter; the only one who raised strong objections was the French consul, Mr. Lo. Lo, an old friend of mine, was thoroughly familiar with the purpose of our revolution, and on the very first day of the Wuchang Uprising, made my name widely known, saying that the uprising was indeed staged by my specific order. During the consular conference, he stressed the fact that the purpose of Sun Yat-sen's revolutionary party was to conduct political reforms, that this political party was not created to commit senseless violence, and that its activities should by no means be interferred with as if it were merely another group of Boxers.[27] The head of the consular group at that time was the Russian consul who happened to share the Frenchman's point of view. Their view eventually prevailed, and the consular group decided not to intervene. Once that decision was made, they publicized it through a proclamation of neutrality.

Seeing that the aforesaid consul could not keep his promise and that he had no one to rely upon from then on, Shui-ch'eng picked up his feet and fled to Shanghai. Once the governor-general was gone, Chang Piao decided to follow suit. The government's power of control suddenly evaporated without a trace, and complete chaos took over the rank and file. On the side of the revolutionaries, Sun Wu was still nursing the wounds he had received while making explosives. Liu Kung, on the other hand, was too modest to assume the high command. Meanwhile our comrades in Shanghai could not arrive in time. Under the circumstances the members of The Alliance such as Ts'ai Chi-min and Chang Chen-wu had no choice except to force Li Yüan-hung to accept the position as governor of Hupeh. It was only then that some kind of order was established in the metropolitan area. Later Huang K'e-ch'iang arrived. Dissension between the Hunan and Hupeh groups developed, and there was no longer a unified command.

The success of the Wuchang Uprising was completely unexpected. The major reason for this success was Shui-ch'eng's cowardly flight. Had he not chosen to flee, Chang Piao would have stayed; in such a case the government's power of control would not have suddenly evaporated and anarchy and chaos would not have taken place. Shortly before the uprising most soldiers sympathetic towards the revolution had been moved to Szechuan by Tuan-fang, and the remaining sympathizers constituted only a small group in the artillery and engineering battalions. As far as most soldiers in the new army were concerned, they did not care one way or another. It was this small group of soldiers who, fearing for their own lives after their party's secret headquarters had been discovered and captured, decided to take tremendous risks to achieve a great deed. They had not the slightest idea that they could succeed. Yet they succeeded by a single strike. Was it true that Heaven had finally decided to lend the Chinese people a helping hand in their efforts to overthrow an alien regime?

As long as the Wuchang comrades could maintain themselves for a reasonable length of time, the key to their continuous success and in fact to the success of the whole revolution lay in the willingness on the part of other provinces to respond to their call for nationwide endorsement. All of our comrades realized this need and, without either consultation or advance agreement, began to open new fronts of battle of their own accord. In a period of several months, fifteen provinces switched to the side of the revolution. The city that responded most vigorously to the call of our Wuchang comrades was Shanghai whose switch to the side of the revolution had the greatest impact on the nation as a whole. Ch'en Ying-shih, who had worked most diligently in this area, attacked and seized Shanghai the moment Hankow was lost to the enemy. From Shanghai it would be easy to attack Nanking. Because of this chain of events, the future of our revolutionary cause suddenly became very bright indeed. This is why I say that Ch'en Ying-shih's efforts in Shanghai were most responsible for our success.

The evening after the Wuchang Uprising, I happened to be in Denver, Colorado, U.S.A. Ten days earlier I had received a telegram sent by Huang K'e-ch'iang from Hong Kong. I was then traveling, and my luggage, including the code book, had been sent to Denver ahead of me. Without the code book I could not decipher the aforesaid telegram. It was not until I reached Denver that I was able to take out the code book and read the telegram. The telegram read: "Chü Cheng, who has arrived at Hong Kong from Wuchang, says that the new army is determined to make a move. Please remit funds to meet the emergency at the earliest moment." Since I was then in Denver and had no way of raising any funds, I thought that I should telegraph K'e-ch'iang and order him not to make a move. By then it was late at night, and, after a whole day's ride in the train, I was extremely tired. I decided not to send the telegram for the time being, being very confused as to what I should do. I thought that a good sleep would refresh me and I would be able to make a decision the next morning.

It was not until eleven o'clock that I finally woke up. I was hungry and decided to eat first. I bought a newspaper in the corridor on my way to the dining room. When I opened the newspaper I immediately noticed one news item from abroad: "Wuchang Has Been Occupied by the Revolutionaries." Whatever indecision I had about my telegram to Huang K'e-ch'iang was dispelled at that very moment. In the telegram I sent, I explained the reason for my delayed reply and also informed him of my forthcoming itinerary. Once the telegram was sent, I continued my journey to the eastern part of the United States. I could have secretly returned to China via the Pacific and have the pleasure of personally participating in the revolutionary war in a little more than twenty days. I did not do this because I felt that at this particular moment my contribution to the revolution would be more effective on the diplomatic front than on the battlefield. Once China's diplomatic problems were solved, I decided I would return to China.

The American government, adopting the policy of the Open Door and adhering to the principle of the equal opportunity of trade and the preservation of China's territorial integrity, did not have any fixed attitude towards the Chinese revolution. American public opinion, on the other hand, was overwhelmingly sympathetic towards our cause. The situation was even better in France where both the government and the people were sympathetic. As for England, though most of her people were sympathetic, her government chose to follow Japan's leadership as far as its policy towards China was concerned. Germany and Russia leaned towards the side of the Ch'ing government. Since our revolutionary party had little contact with either their governments or their people, it did not seem likely that we could exercise enough influence to enable them to change their policies. Japan was the country culturally and geographically closest to China. Not only were her more enlightened people sympathetic to our cause, some of them even sacrificed their lives to help the advance of our revolution. The policy of the Japanese government, however, was a different matter and totally incomprehensible to me. One time it deported me, and another time it refused to allow me to land. Its attitude towards the Chinese revolution could be easily judged from these two incidents. But fortunately for us, Japan could no longer take unilateral action in relation to China after she had signed the treaty of 1900.

In short, there were six countries in the world whose policies, in my judgment, would have the greatest impact on the future course of China. Of these six countries, the United States and France were sympathetic towards the revolution, while Germany and Russia were opposed to it. As for Japan, her people were sympathetic while her government was against it. In the case of England, her people were sympathetic, while her government had not yet made up its mind as to what it intended to do. In my judgment, to win British support for our revolution should be the center of our diplomatic effort; the success or failure of our revolution might well depend upon it. If England decided to be on our side, we would not have too much to fear from Japan. Following this reasoning, I left Denver for New York wherefrom I intended to sail for England as early as possible.

Upon arriving at St. Louis, I learned that the Wuchang Uprising was staged as a result of a specific order issued by Sun Yat-sen and that the revolutionary party intended to establish a republic of which Sun Yat-sen would become the first president. From then on I became more careful, avoiding all newspaper reporters so I could concentrate on practical matters. Moreover, I never did care much for publicity anyway. When I passed through Chicago, I decided to take comrade Chu Cho-wen with me to England. Upon arriving at New York, I heard that our comrades in Kwangtung were pressing hard on the city of Canton and it would fall into our hands at any moment. To avoid unnecessary bloodshed, I telegraphed Chang Ming-ch'i, the governor-general of Liangkwang, asking him to surrender the city in exchange for a safe conduct for himself. This was later achieved.

Once I arrived at England, I asked an American named Hsien-ma-li to contact the Director of the Banking Consortium of the Four Powers with a view to stop all the loans intended for the Ch'ing government. Previously the Ch'ing government had signed an agreement with the consortium to borrow $100 million for the construction of the Ch'uan-Han Railroad;[28] this loan was later augmented by a second or currency loan that amounted to another $100 million. The bonds that covered the first loan had already been sold; the money was then held in reserve, ready to be delivered. The agreement on the second loan had been signed, but the bonds had not yet been issued. My idea was that the consortium should stop delivering the money in connection with the first loan and should cancel any plan to float bonds for the second loan. The banker in charge informed me that in this matter of making loans to China he would abide by any decisions which the British foreign minister chose to make.

Upon hearing these words I requested the president of a British ammunition company as my representative to speak with the foreign minister. Through my representative I made three requests of the British government: first, stop any loans to the Ch'ing government; second, persuade Japan not to support the Ch'ing government; and third, rescind the deportation order in all of the British possessions so I could proceed to China. After the British government granted all of my requests, I opened negotiations with the Director of the Banking Consortium in the hope of securing a loan for the revolutionary government. The banker said: "Since our government has granted your request to stop making loans to the Ch'ing government, the Consortium will from now on only negotiate with the new government in the matter of making loans to China. However, this negotiation will not begin until your return to China and the formal establishment of a Chinese government. The Consortium will send a representative to go to China with you. The moment a government is formally established, he will discuss the negotiation of loans with you." Since I had accomplished all I could in England, I began my journey to China via France.

In Paris I met many leaders both in and out of the French government. They were all very friendly towards me, especially Clemenceau who was then the French premier. It took me more than thirty days to journey from France to Shanghai. At this time the negotiations for peace between the north and the south had already begun, and the fundamental form of the new government had not yet been decided. Before my arrival at Shanghai, both foreign and Chinese newspapers reported that I had brought a large amount of money with me to help the revolutionary army. This was what my comrades expected from me when I arrived; all the newspaper reporters, foreign as well as Chinese, all asked me the same question. I told them that I did not have a penny in my pocket and that the only thing I had brought home was the revolutionary spirit. I further stated that as long as the purpose of the revolution was not achieved, there would be no negotiations for peace.

THE DOWNFALL OF THE MANCHU REGIME   317

Subsequently the representatives of various provinces held a conference in Nanking and elected me the provisional president. I assumed the office of the presidency on January 1, 1912.²⁹ An order was issued to rename our country the Republic of China, to adopt the solar calendar, and to call the year 1912 the First Year of the Republic. Thus, after thirty years of relentless efforts, my goal of establishing a Chinese Republic was finally achieved.

NOTES

¹ With the exception of its introduction, this famous memoir is here translated in its entirety. A copy of the Chinese original can be found in *Chung-kuo chin-pai-nien shih tzu-liao*, vol. 1, pp. 623–649.
² *Hsing-Chung hui.*
³ The long pigtail.
⁴ James Cantlie, an English gentleman who later saved Sun's life in England.
⁵ England.
⁶ *Pao-huang tang*, headed by K'ang Yu-wei.
⁷ *Chung-kuo pao.*
⁸ See pp. 280–284.
⁹ Located in Kwangtung Province.
¹⁰ *Kuo-min pao.*
¹¹ A newspaper.
¹² *Ke-ming chün.*
¹³ *Chung-kuo ke-ming t'ung-meng hui.*
¹⁴ The five powers as visualized in Sun's constitution are those of the executive, legislative, judiciary, examination, and control (or censorship).
¹⁵ *T'ung-meng hui.*
¹⁶ Near Shanghai.
¹⁷ *Min pao*; see also Footnote 1, p. 319.
¹⁸ All three had attempted to assassinate the high-ranking Ch'ing officials. The last-mentioned was a woman.
¹⁹ P'inghsiang (Kiangsi Province) and Liling (Hunan Province).
²⁰ Both are located in Kwangtung Province.
²¹ Shihwan Ta Shan.
²² See Footnote 1, pp. 324–325.
²³ U.S. $20,000 approximately.
²⁴ The Chinese called all parts of today's Vietnam Annam during this period.
²⁵ A city on the west coast of the Malay Peninsula.
²⁶ Huanghuakang was the place where these martyrs were buried.
²⁷ As for the Boxers, see pp. 280–284.
²⁸ A proposed railroad that linked Hankow and the Szechuan Province.
²⁹ See also Footnote 1, p. 327.

87 • SUN YAT-SEN: *The Purpose of Our Revolution*¹

As I see it, the progress of the Euro-American society can be expressed in terms of three main ideas, namely, nationalism, democracy, and people's livelihood. Nationalism came about after the fall of the Roman Empire and in due course gave birth to the rise of national states. In each of the national states all power was concentrated in the hands of one man, namely, the king, whose autocratic conduct and abuse of power resulted in unbearable suffering by the people and, in time, paved the way for the rise of the principle of democracy. Towards the end of the eighteenth century and early in the nineteenth century, absolute monarchies fell one after another and were replaced by constitutional governments. As the Western world became more and more enlightened, intellectual achievement progressed side by side with material prosperity at such a pace that what once took one millennium to achieve was then attained in one century. Economic problems persisted, however, and the persistence of these problems gave birth to the principle of people's livelihood. One might even say that the twentieth century is the century of the principle of people's livelihood. These three principles—nationalism, democracy, and people's livelihood—formulated to serve the needs of the people, have taken turns to play a central role in the development of the Euro-American society and have in fact been primarily responsible for pushing its civilization ahead. All ideologies, whether on a personal or group basis, are merely elaborations or ramifications of these three basic principles.

While it is clear that there should be no delay in beginning our national and democratic revolution in view of the present circumstances, such as thousands of years of autocratic rule, oppression by an alien people,[2] and intensified encroachment of China by foreign powers, it should also be kept in mind that the causes of social revolution which have accumulated for a long time in Europe and the United States and which have not become serious in China should also be given adequate attention. As the disease is not serious, it is easy to cure. For other countries, the problems arising from economic development may have become a matter of the past, but they will pose great difficulties for us in the future. While we are concentrating on the principles of nationalism and democracy, we should by no means neglect the principle of people's livelihood. A man who walks on a low ground cannot see very far; it is indeed sad to see that people travel all around the world, buy the most beautiful clothes they can find simply because they happen to be fashionable, and never ask themselves whether they really fit. We do not deny that these people are seriously concerned with the welfare of China; yet they argue persistently that to build a strong China, we have to imitate Europe and the United States. They do not realize that strong as the Western powers are, their people remain poor. Labor strikes are frequent, and the anarchists and the socialists have become increasingly active. In the near future a social revolution is bound to take place. Even if we did succeed in imitating Europe and the United States by successfully completing our political revolution, there is no assurance that there will not be a second or social revolution sometime in the future. In short, there is serious doubt as to whether we can achieve our own goals by following a path which has been traveled by others. The seeds of evils in the Euro-American society were sown several decades ago, and such evils cannot be easily disposed of even after they have been discovered. If we can foresee these evils before they occur and prevent their occurrence by practicing the principle of people's livelihood, we can kill two birds with one stone and thus complete political and social revolution at the same time. The day will arrive when we will look over our shoulder and find Europe and America lagging behind.

China is the largest country in the world, and the Chinese can be compared favorably with any other people in intelligence and native ability. Yet this country has been in a long slumber and has refused to wake up. Meanwhile everything about and around her has gone from bad to worse. Fortunately, under the impact of the drastic change of events in recent years, she is now opening her eyes; in fact, she is fighting hard to rejuvenate herself so once more she can become strong. As long as she remains in a fighting mood, she may achieve in five years what normally takes a decade. To be sure, we need leaders. Since our country is so large, there is bound to be a small group of selfless people who are not only capable of assuming leadership but also know the most appropriate methods to push our progress ahead, methods that comform with the unique situation in China as well as with the general trend of the world. These are men of foresight and vision who believe that they have a great duty to perform. It is in this spirit that this publication, *The People,* is founded. It is hoped that revolutionary ideas, however strange or radical they may sound, will become commonplace after they have been made familiar. Once an idea becomes commonplace, it will not be long before it can be put into practice. The very appearance of this publication is witness to the soundness of this statement.

NOTES

[1] This is the editorial that appeared in the first issue of *The People* (*Min pao*), the organ of The Alliance for Chinese Revolution (*Chung-kuo ko-ming t'ung-meng hui*), on November 17, 1905. Translated from a photographed copy of the original that appears in *The Pictorial Biography of Dr. Sun Yat-sen* (*Kuo-fu hua-chuan*) (Taipei, 1954) by Lo Chia-lun, p. 43.

[2] The Manchus.

88 • WANG CHING-WEI: *We Want a Republic, Not a Constitutional Monarchy*[1]

Some people may ask: since China already has a constitution, why should we speak of revolution? Alas! People who ask this question must think that by having a constitution, China has laid the foundation of good government and everlasting peace and not realize that she is in serious danger at this very moment. From the point of view of us revolutionaries, the factors that contribute to our people's sufferings and insecurity have not been reduced by one iota during the past few years; in fact, they have become more numerous. The Constitutionists say that once the constitution takes effect, there will be equality between the Manchus and the Chinese and all the people in China will enjoy the same political rights. Our goal of nationalism and democracy will then be achieved. In short, the establishment of a constitutional monarchy will lead to the establishment of a good government. But we revolutionaries emphatically do not share this optimism. Not only do we doubt the validity of the assumption that the constitution will create equality between the Manchus and the Chinese; we also firmly believe that the establishment of a constitutional monarchy will not serve the best interest of the people and will instead bring the greatest harm to it.

The Constitutionists say that as long as the monarch is merely a symbol of the state whose power is clearly restricted by the constitution and as long as he does not have political responsibilities even though he is personally inviolable, constitutional monarchy will bring about good government. This statement, though it sounds like a legalist theory, does not, unfortunately, conform to the known facts. Without a single exception, the countries that have a constitutional government, whether it be a constitutional monarchy or a constitutional republic, acquired their constitution by revolutionary methods. This is so because monarchal power, through custom and usage that may have lasted for a long, long time, becomes in the end synonymous with the state power; and unless the monarchal power is destroyed, there is no way of eliminating the existing state system and replacing it with something new. A constitutional monarchy was almost established during the reign of Louis XVI, and yet France could not forego her experience of having a great revolution. The inevitability of revolution as a means of establishing a constitutional government is not only true in a republic like France but also true in monarchies like England, Germany, and Japan. While England is the oldest constitutional monarchy in the world, Germany and Japan are two of the strongest. People who speak of constitutional government often cite them as examples. Yet, have they taken time to trace the constitutional development of each of these three countries?

England does not have a written constitution. The Bill of Rights and the Magna Carta came into existence as a result of revolution. In the long history of England, there were many constitutional changes before she reached the position she has today. There is a great deal of truth in the statement that England is in fact a democracy though she still has a monarch. The constitutional government of Germany can be traced to the days of German Confederation when each of the confederated states enjoyed its own autonomy. That a constitutional monarchy can function in Germany without encountering too many difficulties results from this autonomy which flourished prior to the unification of Germany. As for Japan, her constitution gives the monarch the greatest power, greater than that enjoyed by the German emperor, let alone the English king.

Some of the Constitutionists in our country say that we should follow the Japanese model. Others take the opposite position, saying that the Japanese model is unworthy of our imitation in view of the fact that the great power enjoyed by the Japanese monarch is incompatible with the concept of a constitutional monarchy. The fallacy of the first group does not need much elaboration; the second group, unfortunately, only sees the literal or legal aspect of the Japanese constitution and fails to take into consideration how the constitution actually works. In theory the Japanese monarch enjoys great power, but actually the power he wields is more ritualistic than real. Before the Meiji Restoration the power of the state was vested in the shogunate, and the emperor was no more than a figurehead. The overthrow of the shogunate was not accomplished by peaceful methods; it came about as a result of staging a political revolution accompanied by bloodshed. Saigo Takamori led his troops eastward, and the Tokugawa shogunate surrendered shortly afterwards. From then on the political power in Japan was in the hands of the Reformers. In name the Tokugawa returned the government to the emperor who alone enjoyed all the power of the state. The reality was of course just the opposite. The emperor merely reigned, while all the important decisions on state affairs were made by the Reformers. Literally or legally, the power of the Japanese monarch has always been absolute. But he has never had any real power in terms of historical fact, either before or after the Meiji Restoration. The state power was transferred from one group of people to another, both of which were not monarchal in origin.

If we measure the situation in China against the constitutional development of these three countries, we will find that China has nothing in common with any of them. She does not share England's experience of a slow, gradual constitutional development; nor does she have a system of local autonomy that characterized Germany before her unification. She certainly has not had a great revolution which Japan experienced in overthrowing the shogunate. For several thousand years

China has practiced nothing but autocracy, an autocracy that reached the highest point or the most absolute stage during the past 260 years.[2] The state power is vested with the monarch, and officials on all levels, central or local, are merely his servants or slaves whom he can order to do whatever he pleases. Suddenly enchanted with the good name of constitution, this autocratic China decided to promulgate one.

At the very beginning, this so-called constitution states in unmistakable terms that its purpose is to strengthen autocracy, a goal which is in direct contrast with the spirit of constitutionism in other countries, namely, the limitation of the monarch's power. Since the strengthening of autocracy is clearly its declared goal, do we really exaggerate when we say that this constitution is merely designed as a protective shield for the status quo or a defensive gimmick for the existing government? A constitution like this cannot even solve our political problems, let alone attain our nationalist goals. The fact is that the principle of nationalism cannot and does not exist in isolation; it is closely related to the principle of democracy. The purpose of the former is to free one people from domination by another, while the latter is aimed at the emancipation of the majority of the people from political control by a minority government. Since the declared goal of the present constitution is to strengthen monarchy, autocracy will become all the more oppressive because of this constitutional existence. Is it not proper to say that this so-called constitution is really the enemy of the principles of nationalism and democracy?

Some people might say that the constitution's negative aspects only prevail during the transitional period; that is, before the parliament convenes, and that once the parliament opens its sessions, democracy will advance with the passage of time. Therefore, we should convene the parliament as early as possible in order to implement our goals of political revolution. I am afraid to say that those who entertain this optimistic hope have been greatly deceived. Since the purpose of this constitution is to strengthen absolute monarchy, the parliament as stipulated in the constitution is merely a child of this absolutism which depends upon its mother's milk for continual survival and will die instantly once its mother decides to cut off its milk supply. How can a parliament of this nature compete with the government for power? Does anyone really believe that it can represent the wishes of the people? I can state unequivocally that as long as the sovereignty of the state remains with the monarch, any parliament that can be devised will live or die at his pleasure. Under the circumstances the so-called parliament can take one of the following forms:

First, *Parliament as the Monarch's Puppet*. This kind of parliament is like that formerly in operation in Turkey. Though following closely the constitutions of other European countries in verbiage, the Turkish constitution bore no relations to reality whatsoever. Soon after it was proclaimed, the Turkish monarch ordered his personal friends to organize a cabinet, appointed provincial viceroys as members of the Upper House, and staffed the Lower House with his henchmen and sycophants. The so-called parliamentary procedure looked no better than a comedy of the poorest taste. Shortly afterwards the cabinet collapsed and the parliament was dissolved. Last year the Young Turks launched a revolution to overthrow the existing regime.

• Second, *Parliament as the Monarch's "Fish and Meat."*[3] This kind of parliament is like that in today's Russia. After Russia's defeat at the hand of Japan, there were popular uprisings all over the country, and the Russian government was forced to promulgate a constitution. Imperfect though it is, this constitution is still better than its Chinese counterpart, and the political parties in Russia are much stronger than those that might be able to emerge under the proposed parliamentary system in China. Moreover, unlike our so-called constitution, this Russian document came into existence only after a long period of bloody struggle waged by the popular parties against the absolute power of the monarch. Yet, despite its existence, the power of the state remains where it has always been, namely, with the government, and the parliament cannot compete with it in power or influence. Since its establishment, the parliament has been dissolved time and again for no other reason than that it continues to uphold the principles it believes in. Repeatedly the government arrests and imprisons parliamentary deputies against whom it holds grudges, for one reason or another. In this regard there has not been any change in Russia: the history of Russia is as bloody today as it has always been in the past. Meanwhile the revolutionary momentum has steadily become stronger with the passage of time.

Third, *Parliament as the Monarch's Vulture.* This kind of parliament is like that in today's Annam, a French colony. Fearful that its ruthless exploitation will incite the Annamese to riot or revolt, the French administration in Annam creates a parliament and staffs it with prominent Annamese as full or associate members. Whenever it wishes to increase taxes, it convenes the parliament and announces the tax increases by invoking the name of the Annamese parliament. In this case, the so-called parliament is merely a vulture or a dog in the employment of the French officials, with whom it cooperates wholeheartedly to attack or bite its own people.

A constitution that is granted by the government as a favor to the people cannot but be one of the three kinds described above. Do we really want a constitution of this sort? We would commit an unforgivable sin indeed were we interested only in a name that bears no relation to reality, while dismissing from our minds the danger that always goes side by side with false, unjustifiable pretensions.

Since no hope of establishing an honest constitutional government has existed or will exist, we revolutionaries believe that only by waging a life-and-death struggle can the goal of establishing a democracy be achieved in China. The Revolutionary Party made this decision a long time ago. It is our belief that only under a constitutional government established in the wake of a revolution can the principles of nationalism and democracy be carried out and can the disaster of a bloody war be avoided. Some people might say that this kind of constitutional government will not be advantageous to the Manchus. To refute this assertion, I would say that a constitution, monarchal or republican, must place all the citizens on a equal basis if it is to be true to its name. It is totally groundless to believe that the Manchus would be discriminated against under a republican form of government. Some people might say that this kind of constitution will not be advantageous to the monarch. This, of course, we will not deny. Yet, whatever disadvantage there is, it would still be better than the common fate prescribed for monarchs during the period of dynastic change; history is so full of details on this tragic topic that we should not try to elaborate. "I hope that you will never be again born to a royal family"; "why did you have to be born as a princess?" How tragic and pathetic these remarks were![4] If the Manchus do not lose their kingdom to the Chinese, they would certainly lose it to some foreign country or countries. Would they like to see a foreign country treat China the same way as France treats Annam or Japan treats Korea? Would they like to see this foreign country treat the Manchu monarch like a pair of worn-out, discarded shoes, or like a slave whose very life depends upon the whims of his masters? Would he not be better off if he chooses to follow the example of the Tokugawa shogunate in Japan by surrendering the government to his own people, so as to preserve not only his reputation but also his very life?

We have briefly described the domestic situation in China. Speaking of her relations with the outside world, we cannot but feel frightened and alarmed; she is so weak that her chance of survival, for all practical purposes, has become very slim indeed. Knowing her impending peril, how can any Chinese enjoy peace of mind even for the briefest moment? When China was invaded in 1900,[5] people realized how deadly our foreign enemies could be. Today they are indifferent— how much we should lament this indifference! The reason that China has not been partitioned by foreign powers since her defeat by Japan in 1894 has nothing to do with her ability to defend herself; she has survived because of the balance of power that has existed among these foreign powers themselves. During the war of 1900 Russia marched her troops into the Three Eastern Provinces, stayed, and refused to withdraw. She doubtless wished to annex that part of China. To maintain the balance of power, Japan declared war on Russia. With the conclusion of the Russo-Japanese War, the international situation completely changed. Before the war there were two major camps in the world: the Anglo-Japanese Alliance vis-a-vis the alliance between Russia, Germany, and France. After the war these two alliances were replaced by such international "understandings" as the Russo-Japanese Agreement, the Franco-Japanese Accord, and the Anglo-Russian Alliance. On what one point do all these powers agree? They agree to bring about the worst possible harm to China. Their attempt in this respect is of course not new. However, until very recently each of them had pursued her own goal without coordinating her efforts with those of others, and this unilateral action resulted in clashes and sometimes full-fledged wars among themselves. Knowing how disastrous war can be, they now resort to negotiations so as to maintain the balance of power. Now that this goal of the balance of power has been achieved, they can do two things insofar as China is concerned: either maintain the Chinese situation as it presently exists or divide China up among themselves.

The factor that prevents China from being partitioned at this moment is the fear on the part of England and France that Germany might not cooperate, and on the part of Japan that the United States might strike her from the rear. For several years there has been speculation about the inevitability of clashes between the United States and Japan, and several months ago there was even a rumor that these two countries would wage war against each other at any moment. Now suddenly there is talk about an alliance between England, Japan, and the United States. A Japanese newspaper recently commented that once this alliance is formed, it can quickly put an end to the old Chinese empire. How anxious the Japanese are to put an end to all of us!

The United States is wealthy, and Japan is strong. Though both countries harbor enmity towards each other, it is doubtful that they will follow the Russo-Japanese example by waging wars. In my judgment, they will in due course resolve their differences through negotiation. Once the major countries—England, Germany, France, Russia, Japan, and the United States—succeed in achieving a balance of power among themselves, the important factor upon which we have relied for the continuance of our precarious existence since 1894 will be lost. If they so choose, they can make China another Poland by dividing her up among themselves. Even if they decide to preserve China for the time being, we will nevertheless remain in serious danger. No nation can be properly called a nation if its very existence depends upon other people's whims. As long as this situation continues, we would remain "fish and meat," to be cut into pieces whenever foreign countries decide to play the role of a butcher. This is what I mean when I say that China is so weak that her chance of survival, for all practical purposes, has become very slim indeed.

There are people in this country who, recognizing the danger China is in, have advocated the conclusion of a Sino-American alliance. Since the purpose of negotiating an alliance is mutual help, genuine alliance can only exist between two equally powerful countries who can help each other whenever the necessity arises. There can never be a genuine alliance between a strong power and a weak country. Whenever an alliance of the latter kind exists, the stronger ally merely uses it as bait to annex the territories of its weaker partner. A good example is the former Sino-Russian Alliance.[6] Unless a country can become strong by its own efforts, it is worse than useless to make an alliance with a great power. And it is our belief that we cannot make China strong unless there is a basic change in the power structure of the state.

Yet, instead of worrying about China's basic weakness as they should have, some of our countrymen have been unduly pleased that lately foreign powers have treated us with some respect. One of the reasons for foreigners being unfriendly towards us in the past was our own contemptuous and anti-foreign attitude towards them. Yet this anti-foreign attitude did not prevent the Russians from being outwardly friendly towards us in order to reap advantages at our expense. Now this attitude of contempt and hostility towards foreigners has changed to that of servility or toadyism. Since other foreigners are no less shrewd than the Russians, they must know that we Chinese are more concerned with the maintenance of a respectable appearance than with such serious matters as the loss of territories and the deterioration of our sovereign rights as a nation. Knowing our weakness, they compete with one another to show their "friendship," and win one diplomatic victory after another without our realizing their strategy. Meanwhile we continue to congratulate ourselves by saying that they have treated us well. Whenever by chance we recover some of our lost rights, we become jubilant or even ecstatic, and close our eyes to their joint efforts to bring us the greatest harm. This is like a swallow that tries to make a nest underneath the main beam without knowing that the whole house is about to collapse. Why? The reason is that with a constitutional government scheduled to be established, everyone believes that all of China's problems, foreign and domestic, will be automatically resolved. Like a man who has taken hallucinatory drugs, we are fascinated with appearance at the expense of reality. It will be eight years before the constitution takes effect; I can easily visualize how intolerable the situation will be at the end of this long, long period.

Neither will the situation in China improve nor can she be rejuvenated unless there is a basic change in political structure. The time for making this change is very late, but by no means too late. I hope that all those who die after I do[7] will consider making this change their sacred responsibility.

NOTES

[1] In the spring of 1910 Wang Ching-wei was arrested on a charge of attempting to assassinate the Manchu regent Tsai-feng. He was released in the fall of 1911 after the revolutionaries had staged a successful uprising in Wuchang. This selection is his

testimony written while he was in prison. With the exception of the introduction which describes the circumstances under which he was arrested, the testimony is translated here in its entirety. Source: *Random Notes of Huang-hsi (Huang-hsi tsa-chi)*.

² This refers to the Ch'ing or Manchu Dynasty.

³ The term "fish and meat" (*yü ju*) denotes potential victims so helpless that they can be easily sacrificed whenever one chooses.

⁴ In 1643 the rebels led by Li Tzu-ch'eng captured Peking. Fearful that his beloved daughter, the First Princess, would be molested by the rebels if she fell into their hands, Ch'ung-chen, the last Ming emperor, proposed to kill her with a long sword. He only wounded her, however, because in the last minute he simply could not go through with killing his own daughter. Shortly afterwards, he himself committed suicide. These two remarks quoted by the author were addressed to the First Princess shortly before the emperor proposed to kill her.

⁵ This refers to the Boxer Rebellion and the invasion of China by allied powers that followed.

⁶ This refers to the Sino-Russian Alliance of 1896 which Russia used successfully to penetrate Manchuria. See also Selection 59.

⁷ At the time of writing this testimony, the author expected to be executed.

89 • Sun Yat-sen: *A Public Proclamation upon Assumption of Office as the Provisional President of the Chinese Republic*[1]

Untalented though I am, I have been bestowed the honor of appointment as the Provisional President of the Republic of China upon its very inception. Facing this great responsibility, I am fearful and apprehensive, not knowing whether I shall be able to justify the confidence that the nation has in me.

In China the abuse of autocracy reached its highest and most unbearable stage during the last 200 years. Thanks to the great and honest effort of our fellow citizens, this autocracy has been overthrown almost overnight. Less than three months have elapsed since the Wuchang Uprising; yet more than ten provinces have pledged their allegiance to the revolution and the republic. Throughout history never has a political deed of such enormous proportions been achieved in such a short period. Realizing that the establishment of a body politic is essential to the unification of China and to the representation of China as a sovereign state vis-a-vis foreign countries and that the task of reconstructing our country should not be delayed even for a moment, my fellow citizens have called upon me to organize a provisional government. I would not have responded to this call had I regarded ability or past performance as the only criterion governing my action. I did respond, however, because of a more important consideration: the obligation to serve my country to the best of my ability. Following the wishes of the people and in full cooperation with them, I shall do my very best to eliminate whatever despotism still remains and to lay a firm foundation for this new republic, so once again our people can live a happy, peaceful life. To attain the goal of our revolution and to fulfill the wishes of our people, we shall begin our work at this very moment. Facing the oncoming task, I cannot but express candidly to my fellow citizens the following:

The basis of a nation is its people. Insofar as China is concerned, national unity means not only the unification of Han, Manchu, Mongol, Muslim, and Tibetan territories as one country, but also the unification of all people in China as one man, regardless of their ethnic backgrounds. Since the Wuchang Uprising more than ten provinces have declared their independence. By independence is meant not only their separation from the Manchu regime but also the unification of all provinces, together with Mongolia and Tibet, to form one nation. The sovereign power of the nation rests with the central government which directs the local governments to the same extent as the brain directs the four limbs—one action is to be coordinated with another and no action is allowed to be divergent from the common purpose. This is what we mean by national or territorial unity.

Since the sounding of the bugle of revolt, the banners of revolution have been erected all over the nation: our gallant warriors are active in more than ten provinces. It is true that different fighting units are structured differently from one another and that they have not yet been brought under one command, but their purpose is nevertheless the same. Since they do wish to achieve a common purpose, I should not think that it would be too difficult to bring about common action, action which would be coordinated to make it more effective. This is the military unity that we should strive for.

Our country being so large, each province is bound to have its own characteristics. Formerly, the Manchu government proposed the implementation of centralism as a means to enforce its so-called constitution. Today we propose the alliance of all provinces to achieve the purpose of local autonomy, and the relationship between the central and local governments should and will be regulated in such a way as to make it rational as well as mutually beneficial. Once this broad principle is agreed upon by all the parties concerned, it should not be difficult to work upon the details. This is what we mean by administrative unity.

Formerly, the Manchu regime invoked the name of establishing a constitutional government to practice extortion—taxes were so heavy and numerous that our people had a difficult time maintaining their livelihood. From now on the nation's finance should be conducted in such a way as to conform to the most advanced theory and modern practice. Moreover, we should strive to make improvement upon our social organizations so that every man will know how enjoyable life can really be. This is what we mean by financial unity.

All these unities—national, territorial, military, administrative, and financial—are the objectives this government intends to achieve. Having them in mind at all times, we hope that we will not commit too many errors in the formation and implementation of our policies.

Though it is we who advocate it in China, the principle underlying our revolution is shared by all the people in the world. Time and again we stumbled and fell, only to stand up and fight again—our friends outside of China could not fail to understand our motive and appreciate our determination. Since the Wuchang Uprising in October and during the past months when the revolt has spread all over China, foreign countries have consistently taken a neutral attitude towards our revolution, entertaining the hope that peace will be restored to China at the earliest possible moment. We are particularly appreciative that newspapers and public opinion in these countries have been always sympathetic. Once the provisional government is established, we, as a civilized nation, intend to honor all our obligations, as well as to enjoy the privileges, as a member of the international community. The measures adopted by the Manchu government that have brought disgrace to this country, together with its anti-foreign attitude, will be abandoned forthwith. We shall uphold the principle of peace and strengthen friendly relations with foreign countries, in the hope that China will play an increasingly important role in the international community and that a world of brotherhood will eventually materialize. We intend to pursue our international goal in an orderly and peaceful fashion, and by no means shall we take an adventurous course. This in short is our foreign policy.

Since this republic has just begun, there are numerous problems, foreign and domestic, waiting to be resolved. Who am I to say that the provisional government will be able to shoulder this great responsibility? However, the provisional government is not an ordinary government; it is a government created to meet situations during a revolutionary period. For more than ten years we revolutionaries have overcome all obstacles with nothing more than a sincere and honest spirit. With the same revolutionary spirit, we shall continue to march forward and succeed, even though we realize that the difficulties ahead of us are much more serious than those we have encountered in the past. Only when the Republic of China is firmly established will the mission of the provisional government be completed. Then we can say that we have not betrayed the trust that our people have chosen to bestow upon us. As I present myself to the 400 million of my fellow citizens on this memorial day, I believe that I have an obligation to speak what I truly feel.

NOTES

[1] Sun Yat-sen was elected as the Provisional President of the Chinese Republic on December 29, 1911. He assumed office and issued this proclamation on January 1, 1912, the day when the founding of the republic was formally announced. A copy of the Chinese original can be found in *Kuo-fu hua-chuan,* p. 66.

Chronology

1368	Overthrow of the Mongol regime and establishment of the Ming Dynasty
1497–1498	Vasco da Gama's successful voyage around the Cape of Good Hope and his eventual arrival at Calicut in India
1505	Occupation of Goa by Portugal
1511	Conquest of Malacca by the Portuguese under Admiral d'Albuquerque
1514–1518	Arrival of Portuguese ships in the coast of Kwangtung, Fukien, and Chekiang provinces
1517	Arrival of Portuguese ships at Canton
1521–1522	Expulsion of Portuguese pirates
1523–1564	War against Japanese pirates
1557	Lease of Macao to the Portuguese on a permanent basis
1582	Arrival of the Jesuit missionary Matteo Ricci (1552–1610) at Macao
1587	Construction by Russia of the city of Tobolsk
1589	First known opium shipment to China by the Portuguese
1601	Arrival of Matteo Ricci at Peking where he received permission from the Chinese government to preach
Arrival of Dutch ships at Macao. The request for trade was refused
1604	Occupation of the Pescadores by the Dutch

1616	Nurhachi of the Manchus raised the standard of revolt against the Ming regime and proclaimed the establishment of the Later Chin regime
1618	Arrival of the first Russian diplomatic delegation at Peking
1623	Arrival at Peking of the first group of Portuguese artillery men, accompanied by the Jesuit Joannes B. Rodrigues
1624	Occupation of Taiwan (Formosa) by the Dutch
1627	Conquest of Korea by the Manchus
1630	Jesuit Johannes Adam Schall von Bell (1591–1666) was charged to reform the Chinese calendar
1632	Discovery by Russia of the Lena River; construction by Russia of the city of Yakutsk
1634	Conquest of Inner Mongolia by the Manchus
1635	Arrival at Macao of the first British ship "London." The request for trade was refused
1636	The Manchus changed their dynastic title from "Later Chin" to "Great Ch'ing"
1637	Arrival at Canton of four British ships. Sino-British trade began
1639	Russians reached the Sea of Okhotsk
1644	Surrender of the Ming general Wu San-kuei to the Manchus who subsequently occupied Peking. The last Ming emperor Ch'ung-chen committed suicide Russians reached the Amur River region
1652–1662	Intermittent warfare between the Russians and the Chinese in the Amur River region
1661–1662	The Dutch were expelled from Taiwan by Cheng Ch'eng-kung (Koxinga, 1624–1662)
1662	The K'ang-hsi reign began
1674–1681	Three Viceroys' rebellion
1676	Arrival at Peking of a Russian diplomatic mission headed by Nicholas Gavrilovitch Spathar-Milescu

CHRONOLOGY

1682	Appointment of the Jesuit Ferdinandus Verbiest as deputy minister in the Ministry of Public Works
1683	Conquest of Taiwan by the Ch'ing regime The Dutch received permission to trade in China
1685–1686	Occupation and destruction of the Russian city of Albazin by the Chinese
1689	Treaty of Nerchinsk
1712–1715	The diplomatic mission of Tulisen (T'u-li-tseng)
1723	The Yung-cheng reign began
1727	Treaty of Kiakhta
1729	Unsuccessful ban of opium traffic
1736	The Ch'ien-lung reign began
1751	Conquest of Tibet by the Ch'ing regime
1784	Arrival at Canton of the American ship "Empress of China"
1793	The Macartney Embassy
1796	The Chia-ch'ing reign began: end of a glorious era
1796–1804	Rebellion led by the White Lotus Society
1816	The Amherst Embassy
1821	The Tao-kuang reign began
1834	End of the East India Company's monopoly of British trade at Canton
1839–1842	The Opium War, ended with the conclusion of the Treaty of Nanking
1844	Treaty of Wanghia (American) and Treaty of Whampoa (French)
1850–1864	Taiping Rebellion
1851	The Hsien-feng reign began

1856–1858	The Arrow War: First Anglo-French Expedition
1858	Treaties of Tientsin; Treaty of Aigun
1860	Second Anglo-French Expedition; occupation of Peking. Peking Conventions (British and French); Treaty of Peking (Russian)
1861	Establishment of the Office of General Management (Tsung-li ya-men) in charge of foreign affairs
1862	The T'ung-chih reign began Establishment of T'ung-wen Kuan (first foreign language school)
1865	Construction of China's first modern shipyard at Shanghai
1868–1870	The Burlingame mission
1870	Modernization of the Tientsin Machine Factory for the manufacturing of modern weapons The Tientsin Incident
1871	Occupation of Ili by the Russians
1872	Establishment of China Merchants' Steam Navigation Company Arrival in the United States of the first group of Chinese students
1874	Construction of China's first railroad Occupation of part of Taiwan by a Japanese military expedition: The Obuko-Kung Understanding
1875	The Kuang-hsü reign began
1876	Korean-Japanese Treaty whereby Japan recognized Korea as "an independent state" The Chefoo Convention
1881	Treaty of Ili Japan annexed the Liu-ch'iu (Ryukyu) Islands
1882	Arrival of Yüan Shih-k'ai in Seoul as resident-general in Korea
1884–1885	Sino-French War, ended with the conclusion of the Treaty of Tientsin (June) whereby China recognized Annam as a French protectorate
1885	The Third Burmese War

1886	China recognized Burma a British protectorate
1894	Sun Yat-sen organized his first revolutionary party (Hsing-Chung hui, or Society to Rejuvenate China) in Hawaii
1894–1895	First Sino-Japanese War, ended with the conclusion of the Treaty of Shimonoseki
1895	Sun Yat-sen's first unsuccessful uprising in Canton
1896	Sino-Russian Secret Treaty
1897	German occupation of Tsingtao
1898	Lease of Kiaochow Bay to Germany, Dairen and Port Arthur to Russia, and Kwangchow Bay to France. Promise to Japan not to alienate any part of Fukien province The Hundred Days' Reform
1899	The first Open Door note
1900–1901	Boxer "Rebellion," concluded with the signing of the Boxer Protocol.
1900	The second Open Door note
1901	Sun Yat-sen's second unsuccessful uprising at Huichou
1904–1905	Russo-Japanese War, ended with the conclusion of the Treaty of Portsmouth
1905	Establishment of The Alliance for Chinese Revolution (Chung-kuo ke-ming t'ung-meng hui) in Tokyo; publication of *The People* (*Min pao*) as the party organ
1906	Unsuccessful uprising staged by members of The Alliance in P'ing-hsiang and Liling
1907	Sun Yat-sen's third, fourth, fifth, and sixth unsuccessful uprisings
1908	Sun Yat-sen's seventh and eighth unsuccessful uprisings Death of Emperor Kuang-hsü and Empress Dowager Tz'u Hsi Publication of a draft constitution
1909	The Hsüan-t'ung (Henry P'u-yi) reign began
1910	Sun Yat-sen's ninth unsuccessful uprising Japan formally annexed Korea

1911   Sun Yat-sen's tenth unsuccessful uprising (April 27); the successful Wuchang Uprising (October 10) that paved the way for the establishment of the Republic

1912   Sun Yat-sen was sworn in as the President of the Provisional Government of the Chinese Republic (January 1) in Nanking
Abdication of the last Manchu emperor Hsüan-t'ung (February 12) on behalf of the Republic

Index

Aberdeen, Lord, 74, 75
Act of Heretical Seduction Involving the Young and the Innocent, 56
Africa, 14, 49
Ah Hsiang, 115
Ai Ju-lioh, 17. *See also* Julius Aleni
Aigun, 69, 177, 180, 181
Ai-shen-t'ai, 78
Akiyama, 302
Albazin, 168, 169, 170
Albuquerque, Affonso de, 3
Aleni, Julius, 17, 229
Alexander VII, Pope, 24
Alliance for Chinese Revolution, The, 295, 296, 305 ff., 310, 311, 314
America, 14, 318. *See also* United States
American-French Treaty of Whampoa, 104
Americans, 36
Amherst, Lord, 28, 46 ff.
Amoy, 29, 79, 90, 101, 103, 106
Amur River, 166, 167, 170, 175 ff.
An Kuo-ning, 32. *See also* Andreas Rodriguez
An Lu-shan, 236
An Shih-na, 230, 236
An Wen-ssu, 21. *See also* Gabriel de Magalhaens
Analects of Confucius, 237
A-nan, 12
Andrade, Fernao Perez de, 3
Anglo-Japanese Alliance, 323
Anhwei, 25, 73, 117, 136
Anking, 135
Annam, 58, 229, 232, 236, 237, 305, 308 ff., 317, 322
Annamese, 58, 322
An-ping River, 223
Aomenk'o, 35
Arctic Circle, 166
Argun River, 170, 177, 181
Arrow War, 102
Asan, 214
Asia, 14, 49
Aston, William George, 208, 209
Atherton, William, 98
Atlantic Ocean, 39, 300
Atlas of the World, An, 19
Australia, 14
Austria, 199, 201

Bacon, Francis, 156
Batavians, 58

Bay of Liao Tung, 223
Bedjin-Taou Mountains, 189
Belen River, 181
Belgium, 201, 306
Bell, Johannes Adam Schall von, 16, 21, 266
Benedict XIV, Pope, 2, 26
Bengal, 40, 65
Berlin, 293, 306
Berthemy, 100
Bible, 110
Bill of Rights, 320
Board of Astronomy, 32, 33
Bombay, 58, 65
Book of Changes, 165
Book on Coastal Defense, A, 3
Book of History, 165
Book of Music, 165
Book of Odes, 165
Book of Rites, 165
Boxer Indemnity, 108
Boxer Protocol, 106 ff., 262, 288–291
Boxer Rebellion, 280 ff., 325
Boxers, 263, 280 ff., 317
Bowring, John, 88
Brief Account of the British Nation and Character, A, 29, 49–51
Brief Account of Translated Books, A, 230
British, 142, 175, 176, 178, 179, 259, 286, 295
British East India Company, 37, 51
British Empire, 51
Broad View of the Coastal Defense of Kwangtung, A, 7
Browne, Henry, 34
Bruce, Frederick, 98, 99
Brussels, 293, 306
Buddhism, 18, 19, 140, 233
Buglio, Ludovicus, 21
Bureau of Foreign Affairs, 173, 176, 177, 180
Burlingame, Anson, 78, 97, 153, 230
Burlingame Treaty (1781), 153
Burma, 48, 105, 197, 229, 232, 237

Cantlie, James, 300, 301, 317
Canton, 1, 3, 5, 6, 12, 14, 27 ff., 43, 49 ff., 53, 55, 56, 58, 61, 62, 67, 68, 73, 74, 79, 86, 90, 95, 96, 101, 103, 139, 144, 145, 167, 174, 175, 229, 297, 298, 303, 304, 311, 312, 316
Cassini, A.P., 212
Catholic Church, 24. *See also* Roman Catholic Church

337

INDEX

Catholicism, 25. *See also* Roman Catholicism
Celestial Empire, 9, 27, 41 ff., 46, 48, 61, 64 ff., 272
Central Asia, 38
Chabigai Mountains, 177
Chan Hsien-chung, 10
Chang Chen-wu, 314
Chang Chih-tung, 139, 146, 252, 307
Chang Ching-chiang, 311
Chang Ching-hsin, 13
Chang Chüeh, 265
Chang Fu-ch'ien, 305
Chang Heng-chia, 281
Chang Hsiao-ch'ien, 190
Chang Ju-nan, 121
Chang Kuang-tsao, 273
Chang Ming-ch'i, 316
Chang Nan-kuan, 230
Chang Pai-hsü, 244
Chang Piao, 307, 313, 314
Chang Shuan, 273
Chang Shu-sheng, 236
Chang Sui-mou, 135
Chang T'ai-yen, 305
Chang Teh-chien, 265
Chang Ting-k'uei, 137
Chang T'ing-yü, 5, 9, 14
Chang Yi, 185, 188
Changchou (Fukien province), 10
Changchow (Kiangsu province), 112
Ch'ang-hsi, 255
Ch'ang-hsien, 44
Chang-ku ts'ung-pien, 41, 43
Chang-li (Ch'angli), 290
Ch'ang-lin, 34
Ch'angshu, 255
Ch'ang-yi, King, 262
Chao, 161, 188
Chao Ch'ang, 21
Chao Chin-lung, 229
Chao Ou-pai, 229. *See also* Chao Yi
Chao Pai-hsien, 307 ff., 311, 312
Chao Shu-ch'iao, 280
Chao Tun, 253, 254
Chao Yi, 235
Ch'aochou, 94, 308
Charles XII, King, 174
Charter Oath, 239
Chau-chow, 90. *See also* Ch'aochou
Chefoo, 90, 226
Chekiang, 30, 32, 43, 55, 73, 74, 86, 97, 112, 122, 235, 270
Ch'en Ang, 26
Ch'en Ch'ang-ch'ing, 205
Ch'en Ch'ien, 13
Ch'en Chi-t'ing, 305
Ch'en Hsi-hsien, 3
Ch'en Hsiung-ming, 311
Ch'en Lan-pin, 150
Ch'en Shao-pai, 297, 298, 303
Ch'en Shih-ying, 12

Ch'en Shu-t'ang, 204, 208
Ch'en Ying-shih, 312 ff.
Ch'en Yü-ch'eng, 135
Ch'eng, 290
Ch'eng, King, 163
Cheng Ch'eng-kung, 13
Cheng Chih-lung, 12
Cheng Ho, 9
Ch'eng K'uei-kuang, 298
Cheng Shih-liang, 297 ff.
Chenhaikang, 12
Chennankuan, 309
Chevrier, Claude Marie, 273–274
Che-yi, Empress, 255
Ch'i, 151, 153
Chi Wen-ta, 229. *See also* Chi Yün
Chi Yüan-ch'eng, 305
Chi Yün, 235
Chia Yi, 232
Chia-ch'ing, 44, 47, 48, 55, 114
Ch'ia-k'e-t'u, 175. *See also* Kyakhta
Chiang Kai-shek, 101
Chiang Pin, 5
Chiang Tzu-ya, 161
Chiang Yu-hsien, 45
Chiang-hua, 203. *See also* Kang-hwa
Chianghung, 105
Ch'iao Yi-chai, 307
Chiao-liu-pa, 9, 12. *See also* Java
Chia-yüeh, 20–22. *See also* Patriarch Mezzabarba
Chiayükuan, 188
Chicago, 316
Ch'ichi, 179, 180, 291
Ch'ien-lung, 34, 37, 41, 43, 48, 186
Ch'ienshanchai, 8
Chih-fang wai-chi, 17, 235
Chih-jui, 259
Chih-kang, 150, 151, 230
Chihli, 73, 150, 232, 275, 276
Ch'i-ho, 182
Ch'i-hsiu, 258
Chi-la-ming-oh, 177
Chi-la-oh-p'eng, 179
Chile, 241
Ch'ileherh, 168
Ch'in, 161, 164, 188
Ch'in Dynasty, 19, 133, 159, 164
Ch'in Jih-ch'ang, 119, 134
Chin Jih-shan, 230, 236
Ch'in Shih-huang, 18, 19
Chin Shun, 184
China Journal, 303
China Rejuvenation Society, 297, 298, 303
China's Destiny, 108
China's Management of Barbarian Affairs, 60
Chin-Chen Railroad, 232
Chinchou (Liaoning province), 232
Ch'inchou (Kwangtung province), 308, 309
Chinese Eastern Railroad, 107, 168
Chinese Eastern Railroad Agreement, 105

INDEX 339

Ch'ing, Prince, 245, 253, 261, 284. *See also* Yi-k'uang
Ch'ing Dynasty, 60, 111, 139, 149, 161, 199, 213, 229, 243, 262, 325
Ching Yüan-shan, 258
Ch'ing-ch'ao ch'üan-shih, 26
Ch'ing-chi wai-chiao shih-liao, 202
Ch'ingchiangp'u, 260
Chingch'ili River, 178, 181
Ching-ch'un, 175
Ching-fang, 215
Chinghai, 275
Ching-shih wen-tsung, 161
Ch'ing-tai wai-chiao shih-liao, 46, 47, 49, 175, 189
Chinhai (Chenhai, Chekaing province), 82
Chinhai (Hopeh province), 279
Chinhsien, 277
Ch'inhuai River, 137
Chinkiang, 90, 98, 103, 112, 124, 236
Ch'in-Lien, 305, 308
Chin-tai chung-kuo shih, 9, 34, 37, 51, 61
Chint'ien, 120
Ch'in-wang tao (Ch'inhuangtao), 290
Ch'i-shan, 73
Ch'iu Chin, 308
Ch'iu Ssu, 298
Ch'iu Tao-lung, 5, 6
Chiu-shih shu, 270
Cho Yŏng-ha, 204
Chochou, 280
Chŏlla, 211
Chorna River, 170
Chou, Duke, 18, 19, 163, 165
Chou Ch'eng-wang, 165
Chou Chia-shun, 273
Chou Chih-fan, 11
Chou Dynasty, 19, 154, 243
Chou Heng-li, 136
Chou Kung, 165. *See also* Duke Chou
Chou Tzu-yü, 15
Chou Yung, 305
Ch'ou-hui t'u-p'ien, 3
Ch'ou-jen chuan, 235
Ch'ou-pan yi-wu shih-mo, 60, 74, 142, 153, 163, 177, 180, 181, 182, 184, 271, 272, 275
Christianity, 13, 25, 162, 233, 265 ff.
Chü Cheng, 314
Chü Chiao-sheng, 312
Chu Chih-hsin, 311
Chu Cho-wen, 316
Chu Hsi, 146, 149, 157, 161, 263
Chu Kuei-ch'üan, 298
Chu Tsu-mou, 281, 282
Chu Yüan-chang, 117
Ch'uan-Han Railroad, 316
Ch'uan-hsüeh p'ien, 149
Ch'üan-lo (Chŏlla), 211, 212
Ch'un, Prince, 254, 260, 261
Ch'ün, Prince, 288

Chün-chi ch'u, 244
Chung hsi chiao-t'ung shih, 18, 20
Chung Jih chiao-sheh shih-liao, 209, 213, 214
Ch'ung-chen, 325
Ch'ung-chen Calendar, 16
Ch'ung-ch'i, 255, 256, 258
Ch'ung-hou, 187, 188, 273, 275, 279
Chung-hua min-kuo k'ai-kuo wu-shih-nien wen-hsien, 288
Chungking, 107, 225
Chung-kuo chin-pai-nien shih tzu-liao, 121, 125, 136, 199, 221, 235, 247, 254, 317
Chung-kuo chin-tai cheng-chih shih, 190
Chung-kuo ke-ming t'ung-meng hui, 317, 319
Chung-kuo pao, 317
Ch'ung-ling ch'uan-hsin lu, 246, 262, 284
Ch'ung-ling Records, The, 246
Chungshan, 7
Chun-ko-erh, 229
Chun-liang (Chünliangch'eng), 290
Ch'un-tsai-t'ang ch'üan-chi, 165
Chushan Islands, 41, 43, 74, 96, 105, 230, 235
Chüyung, 137
Clarendon, Lord, 84, 87
Clemenceau, Georges, 316
Clement XI, Pope, 2, 20, 22, 24, 26
Co-hong, 30 ff., 62, 63, 72, 79, 174
Collection of Essays, A, 161
Collection of Old Documents, A, 41
Colombo, 49
Colorado, 314
Commentaries of Tso, The, 161
Communists, 265, 269
Complete History of the Ch'ing Dynasty, A, 26
Complete Library of the Four Treasuries, The, 235
Complete Works of Li Hung-chang, The, 145, 196, 211
Complete Works of Lin Tse-hsü, 63
Complete Works of Tseng Kuo-fan, The, 117
Complete Works of Yü Yüeh, The, 165
Conference of Berlin, 185
Confucianism, 19, 140, 164, 235
Confucians, 149, 155
Confucius, 18, 23, 24, 146, 164
Conversations of a Wanderer, 266
Cooke, G. Wingrove, 98
Corea, 210, 223 *See also* Korea
Council of Trent, 2
Cowloon, 96. *See also* Kowloon
Crimean War, 177, 180
Cyprus, 185
Czarist Russia, 105. *See also* Russia

Dairen, 106, 107, 232, 236, 294
Davis, John, 85
Denmark, 201
Denver, 314, 315
Department of Cultural Affairs, 233

Description of the Northern Countries, A, 172, 174
Diaz, Emmanuel, 16
Documents: Diplomacy Towards the End of the Ch'ing Dynasty, 202
Documents: Sino-Japanese Relations during the Ch'ing Dynasty, 209
D'Ollieres, J.F.M.D., 32
Dominicans, 2
Dsai-sang, Lake, 182
Dutch, 1–2, 9–13, 52, 58
Dzungaria, 173
Dzungars, 174

East Asia, 189, 191, 193
East China Sea, 233
East Indies, 6
Eastern Europe, 166
Eastern Learning Society, 192, 210–211, 214
Eastern Seas, 175, 176
Egypt, 237
Eh-erh-k'ou, 176
Eight Diagram Society, 265
Elliot, Charles, 64, 66, 67, 74
Elysium, 229, 234
Emperor Protection Society, 302
England, 27, 30, 39, 41, 46, 49, 51, 52, 58, 64 ff., 71, 82, 105, 106, 142, 143, 151, 160, 163, 167, 185, 189, 191, 192, 195, 200, 201, 218, 219, 229, 231, 234, 238, 241, 277, 296, 300, 301, 315ff., 320, 323
Erh-shih-erh shih cha-chi, 235
Europe, 2, 14, 29, 49, 52, 81, 166, 172, 201, 301, 302, 305, 306, 312, 318
Europeans, 1–3, 17
Ever-Victorious Army, 145
Ex illa die, 2, 22, 24
Ex quo singulari, 2
Examination Candidates' Petition, 244
Exhortation to Learning, 149

Fan Wei-tsung, 235. *See also* Fan Yeh
Fan Yeh, 235, 236
Fang An-tzu, 272
Fang Hao, 18
Fang Shou-yi, 32. *See also* J.F.M.D. d'Ollieres
Fangch'eng, 308, 309
Faraday, Michael, 156
Feiyak'e, 168
Feng, 113
Feng Huang (Fenghuang), 223
Feng Kow, 223
Feng Tien, 223. *See also* Fengtien
Feng Yün-shan, 117, 119
Fengkueitzu, 12
Fengtien, 73, 226
Fengyang, 113, 117
First Sino-Japanese War, 108, 192. *See also* Sino-Japanese War (1894–1895)
Five Classics, 147, 148
Flint, James, 29. *See also* Hung Jen-hui

Fontanier, Henry-Victor, 273–274, 279
Foochow, 61, 82, 86, 101, 106, 139, 151
Foochowfoo, 79, 86. *See also* Foochow
Forbidden City, 259, 261, 286
Foreign Countries, 14
Foreign Nations, 229
Formosa, 90, 93, 223. *See also* Taiwan
Four Books, 147, 148, 243
Four Treasuries, 229
France, 27, 52, 54, 77, 100, 101, 105, 106, 142, 143, 160, 163, 167, 189, 191, 192, 199 ff., 203, 218, 219, 221, 227, 229, 231, 238, 241, 277, 296, 297, 315, 316, 320, 322, 323
French, 286, 308
Franco-Chinese Treaty (1844), 77
Franco-Japanese Accord, 323
French Concession (Shanghai), 103
Fu An-tang, 270
Fu Lan-ya, 230
Fuchau, 101. *See also* Foochow
Fuchow, 90. *See also* Foochow
Fu-hsi, 18, 19
Fujita, 234
Fukien, 9, 12, 13, 52, 55, 61, 73, 106, 152, 196, 197, 227, 232, 265, 266, 284, 303
Fu-lang-chi, 3–7, 9, 11, 12, 15
Fu-shan, 200. *See also* Pushan
Fushank'o, 35
Fuyang, 117

Gamou, 234
Gate of Hizen, 197
George III, 39, 41, 43
German Confederation, 320
Germans, 155, 236
Germany, 105, 201, 221, 227, 231, 238, 241, 265, 292, 293, 315, 320, 323
Goa, 52
Goddess of Ise, 198
Goddess of Mercy, 199
Gorbitsa River, 170, 178
Gordon, Charles G., 100, 145
Goto, 303
Grand Canal, 82, 226
Great Britain, 27 ff., 39, 50, 53, 54, 71, 79, 88 ff., 94, 96, 101, 105, 109, 227, 232, 233, 265, 266, 292, 310. *See also* England
Great Learning, 161, 237
Great River, 90. *See also* Yangtze River
Great Shihwan Mountains, 309
Great Wall, 106
Great Western Ocean, 14, 17
Greece, 241
Greeks, 155
Grinaldi, Philippus, 22
Gulf of Pohai, 72, 108
Gulf of Tatary, 181
Gulph of Pechelee, 71. *See also* Gulf of Pohai

Hague, The, 293

INDEX 341

Haicheng (Haich'eng, Liaoning province), 223
Haich'eng (Fukien province), 10
Hailanp'ao, 177, 180
Hainan Island, 105
Hallerstein, Augustinus von, 32
Halls of the Heavenly Lord, 266
Hamilton-Gordon, George, 76
Hammond, E., 97
Han (Chinese), 325
Han Ai-ti, 14, 267, 270
Han Chao-ti, 111, 117, 262
Han Dynasty, 38, 117, 164, 188, 235 ff., 243, 262, 265
Han Hsin, 233, 236
Han Huan-ti, 236
Han Kao-tsu, 188. *See also* Liu Pang
Han Kyu-jik, 203, 204
Han Ling-ti, 236
Han Wu-ti, 236
Han Yü, 14, 17
Han-ch'eng, 213. *See also* Seoul
Hang Chow, 225. *See also* Hangchow
Hangchow, 106
Hankow, 90, 98, 103, 106, 313, 317
Hanlin Academy, 244, 280, 281
Hannen, James, 98
Hanoi, 305, 308, 309, 310
Harbin, 103
Harvey, William, 156
Ha-teh-an, 305
Hawaii, 297, 298, 300, 301, 305, 311
Hay, John, 265, 292–294
Heavenly Kingdom of Great Peace, 110
Heichen, 168
Heiho, 177
Heilungkiang, 172, 175 ff., 180, 189
Hengchihkang, 311
Hengkun, 169
Henriques, Christianus, 22
Herod, 267
Hertslet, Edward, 84, 94, 181
Hidesane, 234
Hien Fung, 94. *See also* Hsien-feng
Hillier, Walter C., 211
Hindustan, 40, 49
Hirayama Shu, 302
Historical Materials of Ch'ing Dynasty, 46
History of Intercourse Between China and the Non-Chinese World, A, 18
History of the Later Han, 236
History of the Ming, 6
History of Modern China, A, 9, 34
Ho Ao, 5, 6
Ho Ch'iu-t'ao, 174
Ho Ju-chang, 194
Ho Ya-pa, 7
Ho Yü-lin, 8
Hoch'ih, 120
Hofei, 117
Hok'ou, 305, 309, 310

Holland, 9, 11, 27, 199
Hollanders, 9–13
Holy Bible, 132
Honan, 105, 115, 117, 232
Hong Kong, 75, 95, 96, 105, 233, 297, 298, 303, 304, 311, 312, 314
Hong Yŏng-sik, 203 ff.
Hopeh, 74, 117, 279
Hormoldzin, 181
Hou Han shu, 236
Houpitou River, 182
Hsia Dynasty, 243
Hsia T'ung-shan, 255
Hsiamen, 11. *See also* Amoy
Hsiang (Kwangsi province), 117
Hsiang Teh-hung, 197, 199
Hsiang Yü, 233
Hsiang Yung, 121
Hsiangshan, 7, 8, 12, 13
Hsiao, 113
Hsiao Ch'ao-kuei, 119
Hsiao Fu-ssu, 137
Hsien-feng, 94, 116, 162, 230, 256
Hsien-ma-li, 316
Hsi-hsi-pi-erh, 182
Hsi-liang, 310
Hsi-li-pu, 176
Hsin, 117
Hsinan, 303
Hsing-Chung hui, 317
Hsinhui, 161
Hsin-man-chu, 172
Hsin-shih, 136
Hsint'ang, 33
Hsip'aot'ao, 35
Hsi-tan, 179
Hsiung Ch'eng-chi, 308
Hsiung K'ai-yüan, 233
Hsiung Ping-k'un, 313
Hsiung San-pa, 15. *See also* Debastianus de Ursis
Hsiung-nu, 236
Hsü Chih-ching, 244
Hsü Ching-ch'eng, 283
Hsü Ching-teng, 281
Hsü Hsiang-yü, 208
Hsü Hsi-lin, 308
Hsü Hsüeh-chü, 11
Hsü Jih-sheng, 21. *See also* Thomas Pereira
Hsü Ju-k'o, 15
Hsü Kuang-ch'i, 16, 17
Hsü T'ung, 258
Hsü Ying-k'uei, 244
Hsü Yung-yi, 282, 283
Hsüan-teh, 9
Hu Han-min, 308, 309, 311
Hu Hsia-mi, 28, 49, 60, 61. *See also* Hugh Hamilton Lindsay
Hu Lin-yi, 236
Hu Sun-pu, 176
Hu Tsung-hsien, 3

342 INDEX

Hu Wen-chung, 235. *See also* Hu Lin-yi
Hu Yi-huang, 120
Hu Ying, 308, 313
Hu Yi-sheng, 307, 308
Hua, 117
Huachou, 120
Huai Army, 145, 250
Huai-t'a-pu, 244, 245, 252
Huaiyin, 262
Huaiyüan Yi, 3, 5
Huang Ch'ing-an, 115
Huang Ching-nan, 311
Huang Chüeh-tz'u, 54
Huang Fu-sheng, 311
Huang K'e-ch'iang (Huang Hsing), 306, 308 ff., 314
Huang Kuei-chün, 245
Huang Lung-sheng, 305
Huang Ming-t'ang, 309, 310
Huang Ting-chüeh, 137
Huang Wan-p'eng, 137
Huang Yung-shang, 298
Huangch'uan, 117
Huang-hsi tsa-chi, 325
Huanghuakang, 312
Huangkang, 308, 310
Huangp'u, 33, 35. *See also* Whampoa
Huang-ti, 163, 165
Huang-tsun (Huangts'un), 290
Huashana, 97
Huichou, 303, 304, 306, 308
Hukuang, 113, 313
Humen, 73
Humen estuary, 55
Hunan, 73, 124, 137, 249, 260, 276, 306, 307, 314
Hunchen River, 181
Hundred Days' Reform, 228, 244–246, 247, 254, 262
Hung Ch'üan-fu, 306
Hung Fu-chen, 137
Hung Hsiu-ch'üan, 109 ff., 117 ff., 133 ff., 136, 137, 266, 270
Hung Jen-fa, 117, 135
Hung Jen-hui, 29, 31. *See also* James Flint
Hung Jen-ta, 117, 135, 137
Hung-men Society, 300, 301
Hung-wu, 199
Huo Ju-hsia, 6
Huo Kuang, 258, 262
Huo-che-ya-san, 5
Huoerhkuoshih River, 188
Huolehmuerhchin, 178
Hupeh, 73, 124, 134, 137, 307, 314
Huput'u River, 181
Hushu, 137
Hut'iaomen, 12
Huxley, Thomas H., 157
Hwashana, 95. *See also* Huashana

Ichang, 225

Ignatief, Nikolai, 167, 182
Ili, 38, 167, 182, 184, 186, 188
Ili River, 188
Imperial Temple of Heavenly Altar, 239
Inaba Kimiyama, 25, 26
Inan Islands, 197
Inch'ŏn, 208, 211
India, 27, 40, 81, 140, 232, 233, 237
Indian Ocean, 39
Indians, 286
Information on the Kwangtung Bandits, 269
Inner City, 136
Innocent XII, Pope, 22
Institutions of the Great Ming Dynasty, 3, 14
International Relations of the Chinese Empire, The, 72, 76, 88, 101
International Settlement (Shanghai), 103
Inukai Tsuyoshi, 302
Inuzuka, 302
Ireland, 65, 79, 94, 96
Issyk-koul, Lake, 182
Issyk-Kul', Lake, 181
Itagaki Taisuke, 234
Italians, 17
Italy, 14, 42
Ito Hirobumi, 210, 215–221, 226, 234, 304
Iwakura Tomomi, 195, 234

Japan, 78, 106, 107, 142, 191 ff., 227, 230, 232, 234, 241, 243, 244, 289, 293, 298, 302, 303, 305, 306, 308, 311, 315, 316, 320 ff.
Japanese, 140, 142, 155, 193 ff., 200 ff., 259, 286, 302, 311
Java, 9, 52, 197
Jehol, 230
Jen-ch'uan, 211. *See also* Inch'ŏn
Jenho, 255
Jesuits, 2–3, 14 ff., 43, 122, 263
Jesus, 14, 51, 109, 267 ff.
Jesus' Descent on Earth, 267
Je-wo-erh-jih Ti-san, 39. *See also* George III
Jih-pen pien-cheng k'ao, 243
Judea, 14, 267
Junan, 113
Jung-lu, 228, 248 ff., 258, 280, 282, 283

Kalgan, 175, 182
K'ang Kuang-jen, 245 ff.
K'ang Yu-wei, 227 ff., 244, 247, 248, 254, 317
K'ang-ch'i, 279
K'ang-hsi, 2, 20, 24, 26, 111, 117, 163, 166, 168, 172 ff., 186, 240, 270, 277, 300
K'ang-hsi yü-chih wen, 169
Kang-hwa, 203
Kang-yi, 280, 284
Kansu, 184, 306
Kao Ts'ai, 10, 11
Kao Wen-lü, 12
Kashgar, 182, 188
Kaufmann, Governor, 182

Kayano Chochi, 302, 308
Kelly, Fitzroy, 97
Ke-ming chün, 317
Keng Chung-ming, 117
Ketteler, Baron von, 288, 289
Keying, 85
Khanka, Lake, 181
Khorgos River, 189
Khoun-tchoun River, 182
Kian Su, 225. *See also* Kiangsu
Kiangnan, 25
Kiangsi, 15, 73, 113, 259, 272, 276, 277
Kiangsu, 25, 32, 112, 117, 126, 138, 150, 226, 262, 283
Kiaochao, 293. *See also* Kiaochow
Kiaochow, 231, 232, 236, 294
Kiaochow Bay, 105, 231
Kiaochow-Tsinan Railroad, 105
Kido Koin, 234
Kikuchi, 302
Kim Kwang-jip, 209
Kim Ok-kyun, 203, 204, 208, 209
Kim Yun-sik, 205, 209
Kingdom of Shu, 136
Kirin, 176, 177, 179, 180, 189
Kiukiang, 98, 103
Kiung-Chow (Kiungchow), 90
Klekowski, 270
Kobdo, 184
Kobe, 194, 302
Kodama, 303
Kokand, 181
K'o-leh-ch'u-k'e, 177
Komura Jutaro, 211–213
Koolungsoo, 82
Korea, 48, 189, 192, 195, 197, 200 ff., 229, 230, 234, 298, 322
Koreans, 140
Kowloon, 77, 96, 105
Koxinga, 13. *See also* Cheng Ch'eng-kung
Krusenstern, 174
Ku Yen-wu, 160, 161
Ku Yin-hsiang, 3
Kuan Ch'eng-fa, 44
Kuan Chung, 243
Kuan Hsiang, 44
Kuan Yü, 198, 209
Kuangchou, 113, 117
Kuang-fang Yen-kuan, 151, 153
Kuang-hsü, 187, 190, 210, 213, 214, 226, 227, 243, 244, 246, 254–262, 288, 304
Kuang-hui, 46, 47, 48
Kuangp'ing, 276
Kuang-tung hai-fang hui-lan, 7
Kuan-ti, 206, 207, 209. *See also* Kuan Yü
Kuan-tzu, 238, 243. *See also* Kuan Chung
Kuan-yin, 198. *See also* Goddess of Mercy
Kuei-hsiang, 255
Kueip'ing, 117, 119
Kuhara, 302
Kulangyü, 103, 107

Kung, Prince, 98, 99, 182, 193, 257, 259, 270
Kunming, 310
K'un-yü t'u-shuo, 235
Kuo Chen, 10
Kuo Jen-chang, 308, 309
Kuo Kuai, 273
Kuo Shou-ching, 18, 19
Kuo T'ing-yi, 9, 34, 61
Kuo-fu hua-chuan, 319, 327
Kuo-min pao, 317
K'uot'un, 177, 179, 180
Ku-shan, 121
Kushih, 113
Kwang Hsü, 226. *See also* Kuang-hsü
Kwangchow Bay, 105, 232
Kwangsi, 7, 9, 105, 109, 116, 117, 123, 126, 137, 175, 227, 232, 236, 265, 303, 307, 309
Kwangtung, 3, 5, 7 ff., 16, 25, 26, 30, 32, 37, 42, 48, 57, 63, 64, 73, 94, 96, 105, 109, 116, 117, 137, 143, 152, 161, 175, 227, 229, 235, 265, 266, 298, 303, 306, 307, 309, 316, 317
Kwang-tung T'ung-wen Kuan, 145
Kweichow, 9, 73, 117, 232, 235, 310
Kweiliang, 95
Kyakhta, 175, 182

Laishui, 280
Lan Tsung Kwang, 96. *See also* Lao Ch'ung-kuang
Lan-chou (Luanchou), 290
Land of the Red-Haired Barbarians, 9, 12
Lang-fang (Langfang), 290
Lang-yi ts'ung-t'an, 269
Lao Ch'ung-kuang, 97
Laos, 48
Lao-wan, 7
Laowanshan, 55
Later Han Dynasty, 236
Lay, William Hyde, 279
Legation Quarter, 107, 280, 281, 283, 284, 303
Lenzy, 182
Li, Prince, 280
Li (a minority group), 8
Li Chih-tsao, 17
Li Chih-ying, 37
Li Ching, 10, 11
Li Chi-t'ang, 303, 306
Li Cho-feng, 311
Li Chung-shih, 305, 307
Li Hsiu-ch'eng, 110, 117 ff., 135, 136
Li Hung-chang, 78, 139, 141, 145, 149, 150, 188, 190, 192, 196, 197, 200, 209 ff., 215–221, 226
Li Lei-ssu, 21. *See also* Ludovicus Buglio
Li Lien-ying, 260
Li Ma-tou, 14 ff., 19, 20. *See also* Matteo Ricci
Li Ming-ch'eng, 120
Li Mu, 160, 161
Li Shih-yao, 29, 36, 37

344   INDEX

Li T'ai-shan, 137
Li Tan, 12
Li Tao, 9
Li Teh-li, 255
Li Tzu-ch'eng, 325
Li Wan-ts'ai, 137
Li Wen-chung kung ch'üan-chi, 145, 196
Li Yeh-yung, 13
Li Yen-yü, 44
Li Yüan-hung, 314
Li Yung-hou, 17
Liang Ch'i-ch'ao, 161, 227, 243, 244, 247, 254
Liang To-ming, 270
Liang Ts'ai-lin, 266
Lianghu, 137
Lianghua, 303
Liangkiang, 150
Liangkwang, 7, 34, 37, 96, 137, 229, 236, 304, 316
Liangshan, 309
Liao Chung-k'ai, 305, 307
Liao River, 219, 221, 223
Liaoning, 74, 94, 226
Liaotung, 107, 193, 221, 259
Lienchou, 308, 309
Lien-yüan, 283
Li-fan Yüan, 177
Li-Ito Agreement, 210
Likin, 108, 243, 244
Liling, 317
Lin Hsü, 245 ff., 250
Lin Tse-hsü, 53 ff., 61, 64, 72, 235
Lin Wen-chung, 230. *See also* Lin Tse-hsü
Lin Wen-chung kung cheng-shu, 63, 67
Lin Yi-ch'ü, 13
Lindsay, Hugh Hamilton, 28–29, 49, 61
Lingshan, 309
Lintin, 68. *See also* Lingting
Lingting, 62
Li-san, 252, 283
Lisbon, 293
Lishui, 137
Lisiansky, 174
Liu Ch'ao-kuei, 207
Liu Ch'eng-yü, 305
Liu Chia-yün, 307
Liu Chieh, 273–274
Liu Chih-k'uei, 114
Liu Chin-t'ang, 184
Liu Hsüan-teh, 135. *See also* Liu Pei
Liu Kuang-ti, 245, 247, 250
Liu Kung, 313, 314
Liu Kun-yi, 282
Liu Pang, 117, 236
Liu Pei, 136
Liu Sung-ling, 32. *See also* Augustinus von Hallerstein
Liu Tao-yi, 308
Liu Ya-pien, 29, 31
Liu Yung-fu, 236
Liu Yung-heng, 280

Liu Yün-k'o, 230
Liu-ch'iu, 48, 191, 194 ff., 200, 201, 209, 229, 234
Liyang, 137
Lo An-tang, 272
Lo Ch'eng-hsiang, 257
Lo Chia-lun, 319
Lo Feng-lu, 209
Lo Li-shan, 21
Lo Ta-kang, 120
Lo Tun-yung, 132, 246
Lo Ya-hu, 16. *See also* Jacobus Rho
Lobanov, Prince, 190
Lo-erh A-mei-shih-teh, 48. *See also* Lord Amherst
London, 65, 293, 301
Longobardi, Nicolaus, 17
Louis XVI, 320
Lu Chia, 185, 188
Lu Hao-tung, 297, 298, 304
Lu K'un, 7
Lu Min-su, 229
Lü Shang, 160, 161
Lu Yo-han, 17. *See also* Joannes B. Rodrigues
Lu Yung-t'ing, 309
Lu-ch'en, 174, 175. *See also* Russia
Lu-ch'en-tun, 174. *See also* Krusenstern
Lüchou, 113, 117
Luch'uan, 117, 120
Lung Chi-kuang, 309
Lung Hua-min, 17. *See also* Nicolaus Longobardi
Lungchou, 309
Lungchow Railroad, 105
Lunghsi, 13
Lungkang, 303
Lü-sung, 9. *See also* Luzon
Lu-tai (Lut'ai), 290
Luzon, 9

Ma Chien-chung, 209
Ma Chün-wu, 305
Ma Fu-yi, 306
Ma Li-sun, 46. *See also* Robert Morrison
Ma P'ei-sheng, 311
Ma T'ang, 14
Macao, 1, 7 ff., 12 ff., 16, 26, 27, 30, 32 ff., 42, 48, 84, 174, 297
Macartney, George, 28, 34, 40
Machiapu, 280
Madras, 65
Madrid, 293
Magalhaens, Gabriel de, 21
Magna Carta, 320
Mago Shichiro, 197
Maigrot, 21
Malacca, 3, 5, 6, 49
Malay Peninsula, 317
Malloy, W.M., 291
Malwa, 65

INDEX

Manchu Dynasty, 199, 229, 260, 325. *See also* Ch'ing Dynasty
Manchuria, 17, 168, 176, 185, 202, 227, 230, 325
Manchus, 17, 122, 260, 319, 322
Mangchieh, 308
Mao Feng-lai, 194
Mao Tse-tung, 78
Martaban, 49
Masan-Po, 210
Mathematicians and Astronomers, 229
Ma-wei-lang, 10
Me-erh-ken, 176
Meiji, 210, 226, 239
Meiji Restoration, 191, 320
Memorials of Tseng Kuo-fan, The, 279
Mencius, 146, 155, 159, 165, 234, 237, 238, 263
Menglien, 105
Mengtzu, 310
Meritken River, 170
Mezzabarba, Patriarch, 20
Min pao, 296, 317, 319. *See also The People*
Min T'ae-ho, 204
Min Ŭng-sik, 203
Min Yŏng-sik, 204
Min Yŏng-mok, 204
Ming Cheng-teh, 3, 6. *See also* Ming Wu-tsung
Ming Chia-ching, 3
Ming Ch'ung-chen, 19. *See also* Ch'ung-chen
Ming Dynasty, 2, 8, 38, 117, 121, 142, 146, 157, 161, 197, 237, 238, 265, 266, 300, 301
Ming hui-tien, 17
Ming Institutions, 17
Ming shih, 6, 13, 17. *See also History of the Ming*
Ming Shih-tsung, 3
Ming Wu-tsung, 5, 6
Ministry of Interior, 26
Ministry of Justice, 37, 114, 115, 150, 175
Ministry of Public Works, 47, 236, 244
Ministry of Rites, 6, 14 ff., 241, 244, 252, 259
Ministry of War, 12
Miyazaki Torazo, 298, 302
Miyazaki Yazo, 298
Miyüan, 115
Mo Ti, 270
Moism, 268, 270
Möllendorf, P.G. von, 204, 208
Moluccas, 11
Mongolia, 166, 188, 326
Mongols, 233
Moor, Captain, 5
Morrison, Robert, 46
Morse, Hosea Ballou, 72, 76, 88
Mu Lin-teh, 209
Muraviev, Nikolai, 167, 176 ff.
Muslims, 3
Mutsu Munemitsu, 215, 221
Mu-tsung, 258. *See also* T'ung-chih

Nagasaki, 195
Nakano, 302
Nam Chŏng-ch'ŏl, 205
Nan Chü-yi, 12
Nan Huai-jen, 21. *See also* Ferdinandus Verbiest
Nan shu-fang, 244
Nanchang, 48. *See also* Laos
Nanhai, 244
Nanking, 14, 16, 54, 82, 86, 88, 94, 109, 110, 121 ff., 134, 135, 137, 138, 307, 309, 314, 317
Nanning, 232
Nanyang, 113
National Protection Society, 227, 235
Na-Tung, 289
Na-yen-ch'eng, 175
Nerchinsk, 172
New York, 300, 315, 316
New-Chwang, 90. *See also* Niuchuang
Newton, Isaac, 156
Ni Hung-wen, 37, 38
Ni Ying-tien, 311
Nieh Army, 232
Nieh Shih-ch'eng, 236
Ni-kuo-lai, 172. *See also* Nicholas Gvriloutch Spathar-Milescu
Ning T'iao-yüan, 308
Ningchin, 276
Ningkuo, 135
Ningpo, 29, 79, 90, 98, 101, 143, 152
Ninsen, 210
Ni-pu-ch'u, 172. *See also* Nerchinsk
Niu Chien, 230
Niuchuang, 94
North America, 14, 49
North China, 135, 155, 303

O'Conor, Nicolas R., 212
Office of General Management, 104, 142, 145, 153, 184, 193, 196, 202, 211, 236, 240, 244, 270, 271, 282 ff.
Office of Strategic Affairs, 244
Ogasahara, 198
Oishi, 302
Okubo Toshimichi, 193, 195, 234
Okuma Shigenobu, 234, 302
O-lo-ssu, 174. *See also* Russia
On Christianity, 266
Open Door, 265, 292–294, 315
Opium War, 26, 29, 52 ff., 101, 109, 167, 230, 269, 295
Orientals, 157
Oud, 172
Oudi, 170
Ourouan River, 170
Ourouon River, 172
Outer Hsingan Mountains, 170, 178
Outer Mongolia, 262
Ou-yang Hsiu, 147, 149
Ouzontaou Mountains, 189
Oyama, 234

346 INDEX

Ozaki, 302

Pach'ungshan, 197
Pacific Ocean, 300, 314
Pai River, 108
Pai Shang-ti hui, 109 ff.
Pai-hsing, 216, 217
Pai-ling, 44
Pailung River, 308
Paimanghua, 303
Paishashih, 120
Pai-tu-na, 177
Pak Yŏng-hyo, 203 ff.
Palace Museum of Peking, 247
Palmerston, Lord, 53, 67
P'an Hsiu, 10, 11
P'an Ssu-ch'ü, 7
P'ang Hung-shu, 245
P'ang Shang-p'eng, 8
P'ang Ti-o, 15, 16. *See also* Didacus de Pantoya
Pantoya, Didacus de, 15, 17
Pao-huang tang, 317
Pao-kuo hui, 227, 235
Paoting, 279
Papers Relating to the Foreign Relations of the United States, 226
Paris, 293, 306, 311, 316
Paris Museum, 233
Parkes, Harry Smith, 96, 99
Patna, 65
Pattani, 9
Pearl Concubine, 259, 262
P'ei, 113, 117
Peiho River, 71. *See also* Pai River
Peiyang Army, 283
Peking, 3, 5, 14, 15, 22, 26, 28, 32, 38, 40 ff., 50, 70, 71, 73, 77, 87, 88, 96, 100, 107, 139, 144, 151, 163, 167, 174, 176, 180, 182, 184, 217, 230, 235, 236, 249, 259, 262, 265, 280, 284 ff., 297, 298, 303, 304, 307, 310, 325
Peking Convention (1860), 77, 94–97, 163
Peking-Canton Railroad, 243
Penang, 311, 312
P'enghu Islands, 10, 11, 12, 196. *See also* Pescadores
People, The, 296, 307, 319
People's Journal, 305
Pereira, Thomas, 21
Personal Writings of Emperor K'ang-hsi, 169
Pescadores, 10, 106, 193, 223
Peter the Great, 174, 227
Pi Fang-chi, 17. *See also* Franciscus Sambiasi
Pichentao Mountains, 188
Pictorial Biography of Dr. Sun Yat-sen, The, 319
Pin-ch'un, 150, 230
P'inghai, 304
P'inghsiang, 308, 317
P'ing-Li, 308
P'ingnan, 120

Plato, 155
Po, 113
Pochi Medical School, 297
Poland, 232, 237
P'o-lang, 34. *See also* Henry Browne
Political Crisis of 1898, The, 243
Political History of Modern China, A, 190
Popai, 117, 120
Port Arthur, 106, 107, 232, 236, 287, 298
Portugal, 1, 3, 9, 27, 42
Portuguese, 1, 3, 52
Privy Council 240, 245, 247, 275
Protestant Reformation, 2
Protestants, 271
Pu-chia-pei, 307
P'u-liang, 282
Pushan, 202
Pu-t'e-ha, 176
P'ut'oyü, 261
Pu-yang-ku, 260
P'u-yi, 259, 262

Random Notes of Huang-hsi, 325
Random Notes on the Twenty-two Dynastic Histories, 229
Revolutionary Army, The, 305
Rho, Jacobus, 16
Ricci, Matteo, 2, 14 ff., 17, 19, 20, 266
Rochechouart, Comte de, 279
Rodrigues, Joannes B., 17
Rodriguez, Andreas, 32
Roman Catholic Church, 2, 26, 277
Roman Catholicism, 14 ff., 23
Roman Catholics, 271
Romans, 155
Rome, 24, 293
Russia, 40, 106, 166 ff., 191, 192, 200, 201, 212, 221, 227, 229, 232, 265, 292, 293, 315, 321 ff., 325
Russians, 166 ff., 201, 202, 236, 243, 276, 279, 284, 286, 287, 324
Russo-Japanese Agreement, 323
Russo-Japanese War, 323
Russo-Turkish War, 185
Ryukyu, 191

Saigo Takamori, 195, 234, 320
Saigon, 232, 311
St. Augustine, 263
St. Louis, 315
St. Petersburg, 293
St. Thomas, 263
Sajhalin Island, 201
Salvation of the World, The, 267, 268
Sambiasi, Franciscus, 17
San Francisco, 300, 311
Sanchout'ien, 303
San-chüeh, 12
Sanhsing, 176, 177
Sanjo Sanemitsu, 234
San-lung, 179

INDEX   347

San-so, 259
Santochu, 303
Sato, 215
Satsuma, 194, 195, 197
Scotland, 65
Sea of Japan, 181
Sea of Okhotsk, 166, 172
Seoul, 203, 213
Seven Years' War, 27
Shachiao, 73
Shaho, 311
Shameen, 95. *See also* Shamen
Shamen, 103
Shang Chou-tso, 11
Shang Dynasty, 161, 243, 262
Shang K'o-hsi, 117
Shang Yang, 164
Shanghai, 29, 79, 90, 92, 94, 99 ff., 103, 139, 143 ff., 151, 152, 225, 297, 298, 305, 313, 314, 316, 317
Shanghai Manufacturing Company, 230
Shanghai News, 155
Shang-ning, King, 197, 198
Shangssu, 309
Shang-tung, 293. *See also* Shantung
Shan-hai kuan, 290. *See also* Shanhaikuan
Shanhaikuan, 107
Shansi, 105, 199, 232
Shantung, 18, 55, 73, 94, 153, 184, 225, 227, 282, 293, 294
Shaohsing, 122
Shashih, 106, 225
Shen Chia-pen, 260
Shen Ch'iu-chai, 305
Shen Hsi-hsien, 273
Shen Huai, 15
Shen Hung-pin, 136
Shen Pao, 161
Shen Pu-hai, 164
Shen Yu-yung, 11
Shench'üan, 303
Shen-nung, 163
Shensi, 117, 270
Shen-tsu Jen, 162. *See also* K'ang-hsi
Shih Chien-ju, 303, 304
Shih Ssu-ming, 236
Shih Ta-k'ai, 119, 133 ff.
Shih Teh-cheng, 11
Shih-to, 280
Shihwan Ta Shan, 317
Shimamura Hisami, 203
Shimonoseki, 221
Shishmarev, 177, 179
Shouchou, 255
Shu-ch'eng,
Shui-ch'eng, 313, 314
Shumpanro, 215
Shun, 18, 19, 146, 149, 163, 239, 243
Shunteh, 6
Shuo-fang pei-ch'eng, 172
Siam, 48, 197

Sian, 262, 295
Siberia, 167
Singapore, 49, 310
Sinkiang, 167, 174, 184, 186
Sino-American Supplementary Treaty (1880), 103
Sino-American Treaty of Commerce (1903), 106
Sino-American Treaty of Tientsin (1858), 102
Sino-Austrian Treaty of Peking (1869), 103
Sino-Belgian Treaty of Peking (1865), 103
Sino-Brazilian Treaty of Tientsin (1881), 103
Sino-British Commercial Agreement (1858), 104
Sino-British Convention (1846), 105
Sino-British Convention (1894), 105
Sino-British Treaty of Chefoo (1876), 103
Sino-British Treaty of Mackay (1902), 106, 107
Sino-British Treaty of Tientsin (1858), 102
Sino-Danish Treaty of Tientsin (1863), 102
Sino-Dutch Treaty of Tientsin (1863), 102
Sino-French Treaty of Tientsin (1858), 102
Sino-French Treaty of Whampoa (1844), 102
Sino-German Treaty of Tientsin (1861), 102
Sino-Italian Treaty of Peking (1866), 103
Sino-Japanese Treaty on Manchurian Problems (1905), 107
Sino-Japanese Treaty of Navigation (1903), 107
Sino-Japanese War (1894–1895), 101, 105, 159, 169, 213, 227, 231, 236, 244, 262, 297
Sino-Peruvian Treaty of Tientsin (1874), 103
Sino-Portuguese Treaty of Tientsin (1862), 102
Sino-Russian Alliance, 324, 325
Sino-Russian Bank, 189
Sino-Russian Bank Agreement, 106
Sino-Russian Secret Treaty (1896), 189–190
Sino-Russian Supplementary Treaty (1860), 102
Sino-Russian Treaty of Kaldja (1851), 102
Sino-Russian Treaty of Tientsin (1858), 102
Sino-Spanish Treaty of Tientsin (1862), 103
Sino-Swedish Treaty (1908), 107
Sino-Swedish-Norwegian Treaty (1847), 102
Six Arts, 162, 163
Six Classics, 164, 165
Sixteen Sacred Injunctions, 24
Smith, Adam, 156
Sŏ Chae-ch'ang, 203, 204
Sŏ Chae-p'il, 203, 208, 209
Sŏ Kwang-bŏm, 203, 204, 208, 209
Society of Added Brethren, 266
Society of God Worshippers, 109 ff., 119 ff., 266
Society of Heavenly King, 266
Society of Jesus, 2
Society of Small Swords, 266
Soejima Taneomi, 302

Solun, 168
Sone Toshitora, 298
Son'gatcha River, 182
Source Material on China for the Past One Hundred Years, 121
Source Materials on the Fifty Years of the Republic of China, 288
Sou-Tcheou, 189
South America, 14
South China, 17
South China Sea, 229
South Pacific, 49
Southeast Asia, 306, 312
Southern Study, 240
Spaniards, 52
Spathar-Milescu, Nicholas Gavrilovitch, 174
Spring and Autumn Annals, 165
Ssu Tang-tung, 48. *See also* George T. Staunton
Ssu-k'u ch'üan-shu, 235
Ssuwang, 120
Staunton, George Leonard, 40
Staunton, George T., 49
Stephen, James, 97
Strait of Good Hope, 49
Study of the Japanese Reform, A, 236
Study of the Reform by Peter the Great of Russia, A, 236
Su Ch'in, 185, 188
Su Leng-eh, 46 ff.
Su Pao, 305
Su Yüan-lei, 161
Suchow, 225. *See also* Soochow
Sugawara Den, 298
Sugiyama, 280, 289
Sui Dynasty, 111, 117
Sui Ho, 185, 188
Sui Wen-ti, 111, 117
Suifen River, 201
Su-la, 259
Summer Palace, 162, 163, 284, 287
Sun Chia-ku, 150, 151, 230
Sun Chia-nai, 255
Sun Chung-shan, 7. *See also* Sun Yat-sen
Sun Teh-chang, 298
Sun Wu, 313, 314
Sun Yat-sen, 7, 78, 295–296, 297–317, 325, 327
Sun Yi-ching, 255
Sun Yü-t'ing, 175
Sung Dynasty, 38, 149, 161, 238, 265
Sung Tun-ch'u, 312
Sung Yo-ju, 298
Sungari River, 176, 177, 180, 181
Sunggali River, 181
Sungkiang, 112
Sung-kuei, 255
Supplementary Treaty of Humanchai, 85. *See also* Treaty of The Bogue
Suzuki, 302
Szechan, 225. *See also* Szechuan

Szechuan, 73, 117, 135, 257, 307, 313, 314, 317

Ta hsüeh, 161, 243
Ta Min hui-tien, 3
Ta Yu-wen, 253
Tachiao, 73
Tahuang River, 120
Tahuanghsü, 120
T'ai-chia, King, 262
T'aiho, 114
Taiping Rebellion, 88, 101, 109 ff., 139, 145, 188, 236, 244
Taipings, 109 ff., 139, 265, 270
T'ai-p'ing T'ien-kuo, 110, 126. *See also* Heavenly Kingdom of Great Peace
T'ai-p'ing T'ien-kuo: A Record of Warfare, 136
T'ai-p'ing T'ien-kuo chan-chi, 136
Taiwan, 11, 12, 13, 52, 106, 191, 193, 195 ff., 200, 217, 220, 231, 234, 303, 304
Tai-Wan, 90. *See also* Taiwan
Taiwan Gazette, 58
Taiwan Strait, 303
Taiwanese, 220
Tai-wun-kun, 192
Takayama Masashiba, 234
Takezoe, 203 ff., 207 ff.
Taku, 94, 96, 107, 108, 290
Takuan, 35
Tali, 120
Ta-lien-wan, 293. *See also* Dairen
Ta-li-yü, 120, 121
Tamin, 276
T'an Shih-p'ing, 312
T'an Ssu-t'ung, 227, 228, 245, 246, 247–254
T'ang, 161
T'ang Dynasty, 17, 19, 38, 155, 236 ff.
T'ang Jo-wang, 16, 21. *See also* Johannes Adam Schall von Bell
T'ang Sai-erh, 265
T'angchou, 113
Tang-Chow, 90. *See also* Tengchou
Tang-ku (T'angku), 290
Tang-shan (T'angshan), 290
Ta-ni, 9 ff. *See also* Pattani
Tanshui, 303
T'ao Kung-sheng, 10
T'ao Li-chung, 137
Taoism, 18, 19
Tao-kuang, 53, 55, 72, 82, 112, 229, 230, 267
T'ao-mei, 305
Taoukwang, 82. *See also* Tao-kuang
Tap'eng, 303
Tarbagatai, 182, 184, 188
Tartars, 166
Ta-sheng-wu-la, 177
Ta-t'ou-yang, 120, 121
Ta-t'ung Calendar, 16
Tayüshan, 55
Teh-ch'ing, 43

INDEX 349

Teh-shou, 304
T'eng, 117, 120
Teng Chao-hsiang, 44
Teng Tzu-yü, 308
Teng Yin,lan, 298
Teng Yü-han, 17. *See also* Johann Terrenz
Tengchou, 94
Terao, 302
Terashima, 197
Terrenz, Johann, 17
Three Dynasties, 238, 243
Three Eastern Provinces, 202, 230, 232, 323. *See also* Manchuria
Three Kingdoms, 135, 136, 199, 209
Three Principles of the People, 296, 301, 306, 307
Three Viceroys' Rebellion, 111
Tibet, 326
Tien Shan Mountains, 181, 188
T'ien Wang, 110
T'ien-chu-chiao shu shih, 269
T'ienmen, 276
Tientsin, 46, 47, 55, 77, 94 ff., 103, 106, 107, 139, 150, 151, 210, 230, 236, 248 ff., 253, 254, 273 ff., 286, 290, 297, 298, 307
Tientsin Incident, 264, 273–279
Ting Jih-ch'ang, 150
Ting Shou-ch'ang, 279
Tinghai, 72 ff., 230, 235
Tokugawa, 320, 323
Tokyo, 194, 196, 234, 293, 305, 306, 308, 309
Tong-hak, 210. *See also* Eastern Learning Society
Torguts, 172, 173–174
Tournon, Charles Mailland de, 26
Toyama, 302
Toyotomi Hideyoshi, 197, 198
Translation Bureau, 244, 283
Treaties, Conventions, etc., between China and Foreign States, 82
Treaties, &c., between Great Britain and China and between China and Foreign Powers, 84, 94, 96, 172, 181, 182, 189, 193, 210
Treaties, Conventions, International Acts, Protocols and Agreements between the United States of America and Other Powers, 291
Treaties of Tientsin, 77, 271
Treaty of Aigun, 167, 180, 181
Treaty of Humanchai, 85. *See also* Treaty of The Bogue
Treaty of Ili, 167, 188, 189
Treaty of Kiakhta, 166
Treaty of Kiaochow, 105
Treaty of Nanking, 26, 54, 77, 79–82, 90 ff., 94, 101 ff., 269
Treaty of Nerchinsk, 167, 170
Treaty of Peking, 167, 181–182
Treaty of Shimonoseki, 105, 106, 192, 223–226

Treaty of The Bogue, 77, 88, 102
Treaty of Tientsin, 77, 88–94, 97, 101, 104
Treaty of Wanghia, 77, 82–84, 102, 104
True Record of the Infinite Roman Catholicism, A, 20
Ts'ai Chi-min, 313, 314
Tsai Feng, 288. *See also* Tsai-feng
Tsai-feng, 324
Tsai-yi, 280, 282
Tsai-yün, 284
Tse-ch'ing hui-tsuan, 269
Tseng Ch'i, 305
Tseng Chi-ts'e, 184
Tseng Chi-ts'e's Memorials, 188
Tseng Hsi-chou, 311
Tseng Hui-min kung tsou-su, 188
Tseng Kuang-han, 281
Tseng Kuo-ch'üan, 111, 136, 138
Tseng Kuo-fan, 111, 138, 139, 149, 150, 236, 257, 264, 275 ff.
Tseng Wen-cheng, 230. *See also* Tseng Kuo-fan
Tseng Wen-cheng kung ch'üan-chi, 117, 138
Tseng Wen-cheng kung tsou-kao, 279
Tseng Yi-pen, 7
Tsin, 254
Tso chuan, 161
Tso Pao-kuei, 278
Tso Shun-sheng, 121, 221
Tso Tsung-t'ang, 184, 186
Tsunghsingk'ou, 35
Tsung-li ya-men, 104, 142, 145, 184, 196, 271. *See also* Office of General Management
Tuan, Prince, 280, 284. *See also* Tsai-yi
Tuan Chen-hui, 270
Tuan-fang, 313, 314
T'u-chüeh, 155
Tulisen, 173. *See also* T'u-li-tseng
T'u-li-tseng, 172, 173–174
Tumen River, 181
Tung Fu-hsiang, 280, 281
Tungchiaomin Hsiang Legation Quarter, 107
T'ung-chih, 193, 198, 254 ff.
Tunghsing, 308
Tung-hua lu, 38
Tung-hua Records, 38
T'ung-meng hui, 317
Tungmou, 17
Tungpa, 137
T'ung-wen Kuan, 144, 151, 162, 230
Turfan, 188
Turkestan, 174
Turkey, 185, 201, 237, 321
Two Kwang, 96. *See also* Liangkwang
Tz'u An, 254, 256–257
Tz'u Hsi, 187, 228, 244, 246, 249, 254, 265, 280 ff., 288, 295, 304
Tzunik'ou, 35

Uda, 172

Uliasutai, 184, 259
United States, 27, 52, 82 ff., 150, 151, 153, 189, 192, 199 ff., 234, 238, 241, 265, 292, 293, 296 ff., 300, 301, 305, 311, 312, 314, 315, 318, 323
United States Relations with China: With Special Reference to the Period 1944-1949, 294
Urga, 182, 188
Urumchi, 188
Ursis, Sebastianus de, 15
Ussuri River, 167, 177, 178, 180, 181

Van Waerwjik, Wijbrand, 13
Verbiest, Ferdinandus, 21, 229, 266
Victoria, Queen, 53, 64
Vienna, 293
Vietnam, 48, 105, 317
Vietnamese, 232
Villiers, George William Frederick, 88. *See also* Lord Clarendon
Virgin Mary, 17
Vladivostok, 168, 189
Vlangaly, George, 100, 182
Volga, 174

Wade, Thomas, 193
Waldersee, Alfred von, 284
Wang Chao, 244
Wang Ching-wei, 296, 308, 310, 319, 324
Wang Feng-su, 15, 16
Wang Hsi-fan, 244
Wang Kuang-ch'i, 288
Wang San, 273, 276, 278
Wang Sheng-yi, 31, 32
Wang Tse, 265
Wang Wen-shao, 280
Wanghia, 84. *See also* Wanghsia
Wanghsia, 84
Ward, John E., 100
Warring States, 164, 185, 188
Washington, George, 227
Watt, James, 156
Wealth of Nations, 156
Wei Ch'ang-hui, 119, 124, 133 ff.
Wei Hsi-chen, 277
Wei Yi-ch'eng, 136
Weihaiwei, 29, 105, 225, 232, 298
Wen, King, 18, 19, 161
Wen T'ing-shih, 259
Weng Cheng-ch'un, 15
Weng T'ung-ho, 244, 255, 257, 261
West Asia, 166
West Indies, 49
Western Europe, 157, 264
Western Ocean, 9, 13
Western Regions, 186
Westerners, 8, 15, 20 ff., 27, 33, 41, 141, 142, 144, 145, 150, 151, 165, 201, 230, 233
Whampoa, 33
Whampoa River, 108

Whangpu, 291. *See also* Whampoa or Huang-p'u River
White Lotus Society, 16, 265
Winter Palace, 284, 287, 288
Wo ta pi-teh pien-cheng kao, 243
Wo Wen-tuan, 230. *See also* Wo-jen
Wo-jen, 141, 161, 236
Wood, Francis, 37
Woosung River, 225
World Atlas Illustrated, 229
World War II, 78
Wu, King, 161
Wu Chao-p'ing, 42
Wu Ch'i, 160
Wu Chih-hui, 305
Wu Ch'in-hui, 260
Wu Hsiang-kuang, 175
Wu Lan-chen, 273, 276, 279
Wu Mei-tsun, 233. *See also* Wu Wei-yeh
Wu San-kuei, 117
Wu Shao-yung, 63
Wu Teh-chih, 266
Wu T'ing-chü, 5
Wu Wei-shou, 137
Wu Wei-yeh, 236
Wu Yi-sheng, 305
Wuchang, 307, 309, 313 ff., 325
Wuchang Uprising, 106, 296, 311, 313 ff., 325, 326
Wu-chi t'ien-chu cheng-chiao chen-ch'üan shih-lu, 20
Wuchou, 3
Wu-Han, 297, 312, 313
Wu-hsi cheng-pien chi, 243
Wuhsüan, 117, 119
Wusung, 108, 306
Wutsungtao Mountains, 188

Yacsa, 172. *See also* Albazin
Ya-k'e-sa, 168. *See also* Albazin
Ya-k'u, 169. *See also* Yakutsk
Yakutsk, 169
Yalu River, 223
Yamada Yoshimasa, 304
Yang Chia-nan, 137
Yang Chu, 268, 270
Yang Ch'ung-yi, 245, 252
Yang Ch'ü-yün, 298, 303
Yang Fu-t'ung, 280
Yang Ho-ling, 297
Yang Hsin-pai, 253
Yang Hsiu-ch'ing, 119 ff., 132 ff., 270
Yang Jui, 245 ff., 250
Yang Ma-no, 16. *See also* Emmanuel Diaz
Yang Shou-p'eng, 305
Yangchingpin Regulations for Joint Trials, 103
Yangchow, 124, 276
Yanghu, 303
Yang-tsu, 90. *See also* Yangtze River
Yang-tsun (Yangts'un), 290

INDEX

351

Yangtsze, 98. *See also* Yangtze River
Yangtze Kiang, 86. *See also* Yangtze River
Yangtze River, 98, 104, 108, 138, 225, 230, 232, 233, 309
Yangtze Valley, 105, 117, 167, 227, 297, 303
Yao (a minority group), 8, 229
Yao (a sage king), 18, 19, 146, 149, 163, 238, 243
Yao Hsi-tsan, 232
Yao Yü-p'ing, 311
Ya-shan, 213, 214. *See also* Asan
Yasukawa, 302
Yeh Tsu-kuei, 253
Yeh-su chiang-shih shu, 270
Yellow Emperor, 165. *See also* Huang-ti
Yellow River, 111
Yellow Sea, 223
Yen Fu, 153
Yen Tang, 21. *See also* Maigrot
Yen Wen-hui, 15
Yen-feng, 174, 175
Yentai, 184. *See also* Chefoo
Yi Chae-won, 205
Yi Cho-yŏn, 204
Yi Ha-ŭng, 202
Yi Hsin-nung, 267
Yi Tu-li, 21
Yi Yin, 160, 161, 258, 262
Yi-ho Yüan, 245, 249, 250, 257, 283, 288
Yi-k'uang, 245, 254, 261
Yi-li-pu, 73
Yi-luan Palace, 259, 280, 282, 283
Ying Kow, 223. *See also* Yingk'ou
Ying-chi-li kuo jen-p'in kuo-shih lioh-shuo, 29
Yingchou, 113, 117
Yingk'ou, 219, 223

Yi-shan, 177, 180
Yi-shu shih-lioh, 236
Yokohama, 298, 302, 311
Yoshida, 234
Yoshihisa, 198
Young Turks, 321
Yu Chae-hyŏn, 204
Yü Mo-tzu, 16
Yu Shao-huan, 297
Yu Tong-kŭn, 207
Yü Wen-yi, 58
Yü Yüeh, 141, 163
Yüan Ch'ang, 281
Yüan Ming Yüan, 163
Yüan Shih-k'ai, 203 ff., 206, 210, 211, 228, 247–254, 282
Yüan Ta-sheng, 136
Yüan Wen-ta, 229. *See also* Yüan Yüan
Yüan Yüan, 235
Yüeh-shang, 163
Yü-lu, 283
Yun T'ae-jun, 204
Yün Yü-ting, 244, 246, 254, 280
Yung Hung, 150, 152
Yungan, 120
Yung-cheng, 8, 186, 240
Yung-lo, 9, 199
Yunnan, 9, 51, 105, 117, 227, 232, 235, 307, 309, 310
Yunnan-Vietnam Railroad, 105
Yü-shan, 230
Yüyao, 267

Zaysan, Lake, 181
Zéia River, 181